The Editor

WILLIAM ROSSI is Professor of English at the University of Oregon, where he teaches American literature and environmental studies. He is author of essays on Thoreau, Ralph Waldo Emerson, and nineteenth-century natural science; editor of *"Wild Apples" and Other Natural History Essays* (Georgia, 2002); and co-editor of two volumes of Thoreau's journal for the Princeton University Press edition of *The Writings of Henry D. Thoreau: Journal 3: 1848–1851*, with Robert Sattelmeyer and Mark R. Patterson, and *Journal 6: 1853*, with Heather Kirk Thomas.

A NORTON CRITICAL EDITION

Henry D. Thoreau

WALDEN, CIVIL DISOBEDIENCE, AND OTHER WRITINGS

AUTHORITATIVE TEXTS
JOURNAL
REVIEWS AND POSTHUMOUS ASSESSMENTS
CRITICISM

THIRD EDITION

Edited by

WILLIAM ROSSI

UNIVERSITY OF OREGON

W. W. NORTON & COMPANY
New York • London

Copyright © 2008, 1992, 1966 by W. W. Norton & Company, Inc.

Every effort has been made to contact the copyright holders for each of the
selections. Rights holders of any selections not credited should contact
W. W. Norton & Company, Inc., 500 Fifth Avenue, New York, NY 10110,
for a correction to be made in the next reprinting of our work.

The text of this book is composed in Fairfield Medium
with the display set in Bernhard Modern.

Book design by Antonina Krass.
Composition by PennSet, Inc.
Manufacturing by RR Donnelley—Westford division.
Production manager: Benjamin Reynolds.

Library of Congress Cataloging-in-Publication Data

Thoreau, Henry David, 1817–1862.
    Walden, Civil disobedience, and other writings : authoritative texts,
journal, reviews and posthumous assessments, criticism / Henry D. Thoreau ;
edited by William Rossi. —3rd ed.
        p. cm.— (A Norton critical edition)
    Rev. and expanded ed. of: Walden and Resistance to civil government.
2nd ed. 1992.
    Includes bibliographical references.

ISBN 13: 978–0–393–93090–0 (pbk.)

    1. Thoreau, Henry David, 1817–1862—Homes and haunts—Massachusetts—
Walden Woods. 2. Walden Woods (Mass.)—Social life and customs. 3. Wilderness
areas—Massachusetts—Walden Woods. 4. Natural history—Massachusetts—
Walden Woods. 5. Authors, American—19th century—Biography. 6. Solitude.
7. Civil disobedience. I. Rossi, William John. II. Thoreau, Henry David,
1817–1862. Walden and Resistance to civil government. III. Thoreau, Henry
David, 1817–1862. Walden. IV. Thoreau, Henry David, 1817–1862. Civil
disobedience. V. Title.

PS3048.A1 2008b
818'.303—dc22

                                                              2007047542

W. W. Norton & Company, Inc., 500 Fifth Avenue, New York, NY 10110-0017
www.wwnorton.com

W. W. Norton & Company Ltd.
15 Carlisle Street, London W1D 3BS

2 3 4 5 6 7 8 9 0

Contents

Preface   ix
A Note on the Texts   xi
Map of Thoreau's Concord   xii

The Texts of *Walden*, Civil Disobedience, and Other Writings

WALDEN   5

Map of Walden Pond   193
Textual Appendix to *Walden*   225

OTHER WRITINGS

Civil Disobedience   227
Slavery in Massachusetts   247
Walking   260
Wild Apples   288

Journal

The Journal and *Walden*   313
Selections from the Journal, 1845–54   319

Reviews and Posthumous Assessments

[Review of *Walden*]   380
[Review of *Walden*]   381
[Gamaliel Bailey?] • [Review of *Walden*]   382
Elizabeth Barstow Stoddard • [Review of *Walden*]   383
Charles Frederick Briggs • A Yankee Diogenes   384
[Review of *Walden*]   387
[Lydia Maria Child?] • [Review of *A Week on the
   Concord and Merrimack Rivers* and *Walden*]   388
George Eliot • [Review of *Walden*]   390
[Review of *Excursions*]   391
[Review of *Excursions*]   392
[Review of *Excursions*]   393

[Review of *A Yankee in Canada, with Anti-Slavery and Reform Papers*]   393
Sidney H. Morse • [Review of *A Yankee in Canada, with Anti-Slavery and Reform Papers*]   394
Ralph Waldo Emerson • Thoreau   394
James Russell Lowell • Thoreau   410
John Burroughs • Another Word on Thoreau   418

Modern Criticism

WALDEN

F. O. Matthiessen • *Walden*: Craftsmanship vs. Technique   433
E. B. White • Walden—1954   442
Leo Marx • [*Walden*'s Transcendental Pastoral Design]   450
Stanley Cavell • [Captivity and Despair in *Walden* and "Civil Disobedience"]   465
Barbara Johnson • A Hound, a Bay Horse, and a Turtle Dove: Obscurity in *Walden*   482
Robert Sattelmeyer • The Remaking of *Walden*   489
H. Daniel Peck • The Worlding of Walden   507
Laura Dassow Walls • *Walden* as Feminist Manifesto   521
Lawrence Buell • Thoreau and the Natural Environment   527

"CIVIL DISOBEDIENCE" AND "SLAVERY IN MASSACHUSETTS"

Richard Drinnon • Thoreau's Politics of the Upright Man   544
Barry Wood • Thoreau's Narrative Art in "Civil Disobedience"   556
Evan Carton • The Price of Privilege: "Civil Disobedience" at 150   564
Robert A. Gross • Quiet War with the State: Henry Thoreau and Civil Disobedience   572
Albert J. von Frank • Fourth of July   586

"WALKING" AND "WILD APPLES"

William Rossi • "The Limits of an Afternoon Walk": Coleridgean Polarity in Thoreau's "Walking"   596
Neill Matheson • Thoreau's *Gramática Parda*: Conjugating Race and Nature   613
Steven Fink • The Language of Prophecy: Thoreau's "Wild Apples"   632

Lance Newman • [Capitalism and Community in
   Walden and *Wild Fruits*]   645

Henry D. Thoreau: A Chronology   661
Selected Bibliography   667

Preface

In the fifteen years since the second edition of this volume appeared, the influence and importance of *Walden* and "Civil Disobedience" have continued to grow both within and beyond the academy. If anything, these works have become even more timely. They speak to a present condition drenched with a daily awareness of the interdependence of all places and of the global consequences, for better and worse, of individual actions. In this, they confirm anew their author's faith that any universality his statement and actions might possess would arise out of an intimate, local knowledge, and a deep commitment to his chosen place.

To the texts of *Walden*, "Civil Disobedience," and the Journal (reprinted from Princeton Edition volumes that have since appeared), the third edition adds a contemporary map of mid-nineteenth-century Concord and three new Thoreau essays, considerably expanding this selection of his writings. Besides representing the full span of Thoreau's mature career, from 1845 to 1862, the volume now documents his greater political and proto-environmental activism after *Walden*. And, as several critical selections illustrate, these essays also open fruitful new approaches to Thoreau's masterpiece.

By adding new reviews of *Walden* as well as of the posthumous collections that contained "Walking," "Wild Apples," "Civil Disobedience," and "Slavery in Massachusetts," the third edition presents a fuller picture of Thoreau's contemporary reception. As an index of his late-nineteenth and early twentieth-century reputation as an environmental writer, I have also included John Burroughs's most comprehensive attempt to assess the work of his precursor. Both a non–New Englander and literary bioregionalist of comparable stature, Burroughs updates Thoreau for "modern" readers while answering the influential criticisms of Victorian sages Emerson and Lowell, who preceded him.

The "Criticism" section for the third edition has been revised and expanded to illuminate Thoreau's writings for a range of readers, including undergraduate and graduate students in any number of disciplines as well as interested general readers. Like the texts, the annotations, and the reviews, this criticism reflects both the revisionary and cumulative character of Thoreau scholarship, now almost seventy years' worth. These selections were chosen especially to highlight recent critical analyses of the complexity of Thoreau's engagements with questions of environment, race, political action, and gender. As curious readers who consult the updated bibliography will rapidly discover for themselves, but for limitations of space, any number of equally excellent studies might have been excerpted for inclusion here.

It is a pleasure to acknowledge the help of several people in preparing this new volume. This is a better book thanks to comments and helpful suggestions from Mike Berger, Mike Branch, Larry Buell, John Elder, Will Howarth, Bob Hudspeth, Dana Phillips, David Robinson, Laura Walls, and Leslie Perrin Wilson; for assistance that I received with texts from Brad Dean, Isabel Stirling, Andrew Wentink, and Beth Witherell; for new light on annotations from Jack Maddex, Matthew Watson, and previous annotators, including Brad Dean, Walter Harding, Lewis Hyde, Jeffrey Cramer, and Hershel Parker; for the kindness and patience of Carol Bemis, the curiosity and mischief of Rachel and Julia, and the love of Lynne Rossi.

William Rossi
Eugene, Oregon

A Note on the Texts

Thoreau's most famous essay began as a lecture on "The Relation of the Individual to the State," delivered before the Concord Lyceum on January 26, 1848. Solicited by Elizabeth P. Peabody, the essay first appeared in print as "Resistance to Civil Government" in Peabody's *Aesthetic Papers* in May 1849. After Thoreau's death in 1862, his sister Sophia and his friend William Ellery Channing reprinted it in *A Yankee in Canada, with Anti-Slavery and Reform Papers* (Boston: Ticknor and Fields, 1866). In addition to several alterations of wording and sentence structure, including the deletion of a clause seeming to anticipate civil war (n. 3, p. 227); the insertion of a quotation from George Peele's *Battle of Alcazar* (p. 243); and a paraphrase of Mencius (p. 246), the essay carried a new title: "Civil Disobedience."

No record exists of Thoreau's having discussed the posthumous publication of this essay, as he had the reprinting of *Walden* and three late essays; nor has the famous title phrase been found in his works. Consequently, in the early 1970s, when Wendell Glick edited *Reform Papers* for *The Writings of Henry D. Thoreau*, he conservatively chose as copy text the 1849 printing, "Resistance to Civil Government," judging the later printing non-authorial. Glick's edition spurred additional archival work and cogent arguments aimed at substantiating the authority of the second printing. The recent surfacing of Thoreau's copy of *Aesthetic Papers*, authenticated by the late Bradley P. Dean and showing several of the 1866 alterations in Thoreau's hand (unfortunately, not including the title), further increases the likelihood that the 1866 printing is indeed authoritative.[1] The present edition therefore restores all those changes as well as the more familiar title.

"Slavery in Massachusetts" was first published in a considerably shorter version in an anti-slavery periodical, *The Liberator*, for July 21, 1854. The revised address was then collected with "Civil Disobedience" and other reform essays in *A Yankee in Canada, with Anti-Slavery and Reform Papers* (Boston: Ticknor and Fields, 1866). The text of the essay used here is reprinted with permission from *Reform Papers*, ed-

---

1. See Wendell Glick, "Scholarly Editing and Dealing with Uncertainties: Thoreau's 'Resistance to Civil Government,' *Analytic and Enumerative Bibliography* 2 (1978): 103–15; Thomas Woodson, "The Title and Text of Thoreau's 'Civil Disobedience,' " *Bulletin of Research in the Humanities* 81 (1978): 103–12; Fritz Oehlschlaeger, "Another Look at the Text and Title of Thoreau's 'Civil Disobedience,' " *ESQ: A Journal of the American Renaissance* 36 (1990): 239–254; and James Dawson, "Recently Discovered Revisions Made by Thoreau to the First Edition Text of 'Civil Disobedience,' " forthcoming in *The Concord Saunterer: New Series* 15 (2007).

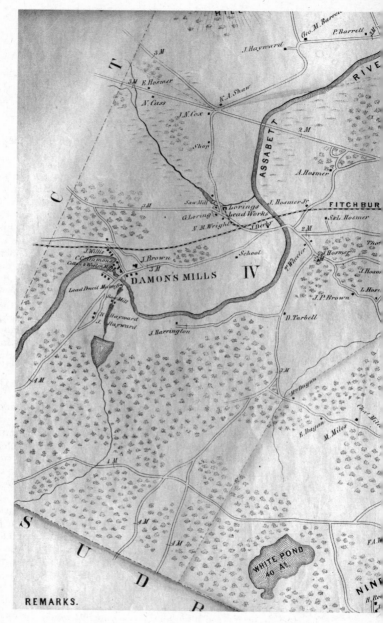

This map, completed in 1852 by Boston surveyor Henry F. Walling (1825–1888), depicts Concord village and environs at the time Thoreau was working on the *Walden* manuscript and writing "Walking" and the Journal. According to Walling's "Remarks," it incorporates "surveys of White Pond and Walden Pond by H. D. Thoreau, Civ. Engr." Notable features include the

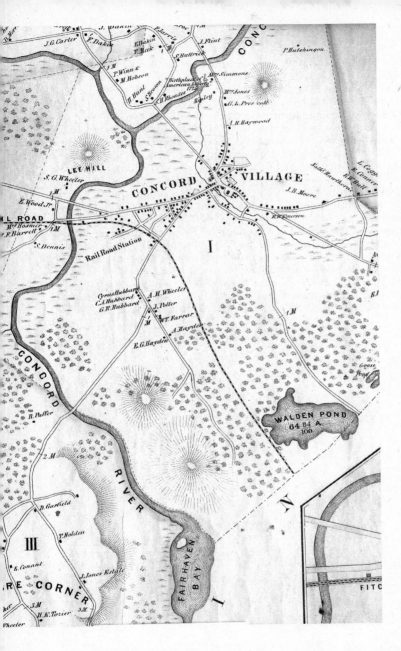

R. W. Emerson house, just east of the village center, and the Old Marlborough Road celebrated in "Walking," which runs southwest in the bottom left quadrant and exits at the Sudbury border, between "U" and "D." Reproduced courtesy of the Concord Free Public Library.

ited by Wendell Glick (Princeton: Princeton University Press, 1973), 91–109.

Parts of what became "Walking" were first presented before the Concord Lyceum as "Walking, or The Wild" on April 23, 1851. Delivered frequently on regional lecture circuits in the 1850s, by 1857 the manuscript had grown to more than one hundred pages and into two separate talks.[2] Thoreau rejoined them shortly before his death when he sold this and other essays to Boston publisher James T. Fields, junior partner of Ticknor and Fields, who had acquired the *Atlantic Monthly* in 1859. As Thoreau arranged, "Walking" and "Wild Apples" (as well as another natural history essay, "Autumnal Tints") appeared in the *Atlantic* during the months following. Along with earlier natural history and local travel writings, these essays were then collected by Sophia Thoreau and William Ellery Channing for *Excursions* (Boston: Ticknor and Fields, 1863). Because the first magazine printings were thus partially overseen by the author, they are reprinted in the present edition: "Walking," *Atlantic Monthly* 9, no. 56, (June 1862), 657–74; "Wild Apples," *Atlantic Monthly* 10, no. 61, (November 1862), 513–26.

For a textual description and editorial principles governing the present text of *Walden*, see the Textual Appendix to *Walden*, pp. 225–26.

2. For information on Thoreau's lectures, see Bradley P. Dean and Ronald Wesley Hoag, "Thoreau's Lectures before *Walden*: An Annotated Calendar" *Studies in the American Renaissance 1995*: 127–228 and "Thoreau's Lectures after *Walden*: An Annotated Calendar" *Studies in the American Renaissance 1996*: 241–362.

The Texts of
WALDEN,
CIVIL DISOBEDIENCE,
AND OTHER WRITINGS

The Contents of *Walden*

Economy	5
Where I Lived, and What I Lived For	58
Reading	71
Sounds	78
Solitude	90
Visitors	97
The Bean-Field	107
The Village	115
The Ponds	119
Baker Farm	137
Higher Laws	143
Brute Neighbors	151
House-Warming	161
Former Inhabitants; and Winter Visitors	172
Winter Animals	182
The Pond in Winter	189
Spring	201
Conclusion	214

Walden

I do not propose to write an ode to dejection, but to brag as lustily as chanticleer in the morning, standing on his roost, if only to wake my neighbors up.

Economy

When I wrote the following pages, or rather the bulk of them, I lived alone, in the woods, a mile from any neighbor, in a house which I had built myself, on the shore of Walden Pond, in Concord, Massachusetts, and earned my living by the labor of my hands only. I lived there two years and two months. At present I am a sojourner in civilized life again.

I should not obtrude my affairs so much on the notice of my readers if very particular inquiries had not been made by my townsmen concerning my mode of life, which some would call impertinent, though they do not appear to me at all impertinent, but, considering the circumstances, very natural and pertinent. Some have asked what I got to eat; if I did not feel lonesome; if I was not afraid; and the like. Others have been curious to learn what portion of my income I devoted to charitable purposes; and some, who have large families, how many poor children I maintained. I will therefore ask those of my readers who feel no particular interest in me to pardon me if I undertake to answer some of these questions in this book. In most books, the I, or first person, is omitted; in this it will be retained; that, in respect to egotism, is the main difference. We commonly do not remember that it is, after all, always the first person that is speaking. I should not talk so much about myself if there were any body else whom I knew as well. Unfortunately, I am confined to this theme by the narrowness of my experience. Moreover, I, on my side, require of every writer, first or last, a simple and sincere account of his own life, and not merely what he has heard of other men's lives; some such account as he would send to his kindred from a distant land; for if he has lived sincerely, it must have been in a distant land to me. Perhaps these pages are more particularly addressed to poor students. As for the rest of my read-

ers, they will accept such portions as apply to them. I trust that
none will stretch the seams in putting on the coat, for it may do
good service to him whom it fits.

I would fain say something, not so much concerning the Chinese
and Sandwich Islanders[1] as you who read these pages, who are said
to live in New England; something about your condition, especially
your outward condition or circumstances in this world, in this
town, what it is, whether it is necessary that it be as bad as it is,
whether it cannot be improved as well as not. I have travelled a
good deal in Concord; and every where, in shops, and offices, and
fields, the inhabitants have appeared to me to be doing penance in
a thousand remarkable ways. What I have heard of Bramins[2] sitting
exposed to four fires and looking in the face of the sun; or hanging
suspended, with their heads downward, over flames; or looking at
the heavens over their shoulders "until it becomes impossible for
them to resume their natural position, while from the twist of the
neck nothing but liquids can pass into the stomach;" or dwelling,
chained for life, at the foot of a tree; or measuring with their bodies, like caterpillars, the breadth of vast empires; or standing on one
leg on the tops of pillars,—even these forms of conscious penance
are hardly more incredible and astonishing than the scenes which I
daily witness. The twelve labors of Hercules[3] were trifling in comparison with those which my neighbors have undertaken; for they
were only twelve, and had an end; but I could never see that these
men slew or captured any monster or finished any labor. They have
no friend Iolas[4] to burn with a hot iron the root of the hydra's head,
but as soon as one head is crushed, two spring up.

I see young men, my townsmen, whose misfortune it is to have
inherited farms, houses, barns, cattle, and farming tools; for these
are more easily acquired than got rid of. Better if they had been
born in the open pasture and suckled by a wolf, that they might
have seen with clearer eyes what field they were called to labor in.[5]
Who made them serfs of the soil? Why should they eat their sixty
acres, when man is condemned to eat only his peck of dirt? Why
should they begin digging their graves as soon as they are born?
They have got to live a man's life, pushing all these things before
them, and get on as well as they can. How many a poor immortal
soul have I met well nigh crushed and smothered under its load,

1. Hawaiian islanders.
2. Generally spelled Brahmin or Brahman; a member of the highest caste of Hindus.
3. The son of Zeus, in Greek mythology, known for his great strength and for the performance of twelve seemingly impossible tasks.
4. A servant to Hercules who helped him to overcome the many-headed monster, Hydra, by
   singeing with fire the stumps that remained after Hercules chopped off its heads.
5. According to Roman legend, the founders of the Republic, Romulus and Remus, were
   adopted and suckled by a she-wolf.

creeping down the road of life, pushing before it a barn seventy-five feet by forty, its Augean stables[6] never cleansed, and one hundred acres of land, tillage, mowing, pasture, and woodlot! The portionless, who struggle with no such unnecessary inherited encumbrances, find it labor enough to subdue and cultivate a few cubic feet of flesh.

But men labor under a mistake. The better part of the man is soon ploughed into the soil for compost. By a seeming fate, commonly called necessity, they are employed, as it says in an old book, laying up treasures which moth and rust will corrupt and thieves break through and steal.[7] It is a fool's life, as they will find when they get to the end of it, if not before. It is said that Deucalion and Pyrrha[8] created men by throwing stones over their heads behind them:—

> Inde genus durum sumus, experiensque laborum,
> Et documenta damus quâ simus origine nati.

Or, as Raleigh rhymes it in his sonorous way,—

> "From thence our kind hard-hearted is, enduring pain
>   and care,
> Approving that our bodies of a stony nature are."

So much for a blind obedience to a blundering oracle, throwing the stones over their heads behind them, and not seeing where they fell.

Most men, even in this comparatively free country, through mere ignorance and mistake, are so occupied with the factitious cares and superfluously coarse labors of life that its finer fruits cannot be plucked by them. Their fingers, from excessive toil, are too clumsy and tremble too much for that. Actually, the laboring man has not leisure for a true integrity day by day; he cannot afford to sustain the manliest relations to men; his labor would be depreciated in the market. He has no time to be any thing but a machine. How can he remember well his ignorance—which his growth requires—who has so often to use his knowledge? We should feed and clothe him gratuitously sometimes, and recruit him with our cordials, before we judge of him. The finest qualities of our nature, like the bloom on fruits, can be preserved only by the most delicate handling. Yet we do not treat ourselves nor one another thus tenderly.

Some of you, we all know, are poor, find it hard to live, are some-

---

6. The home of thousands of cattle whose stalls had not been cleaned in years. As one of his tasks, Hercules was required to clean the stables in a single day.
7. Matthew 6.19.
8. The only human survivors when Jupiter destroyed mankind with a flood. Thoreau quotes from Ovid's *Metamorphoses* 1.414–15; the translation is from Sir Walter Raleigh's *History of the World* (1614).

times, as it were, gasping for breath. I have no doubt that some of you who read this book are unable to pay for all the dinners which you have actually eaten, or for the coats and shoes which are fast wearing or are already worn out, and have come to this page to spend borrowed or stolen time, robbing your creditors of an hour. It is very evident what mean and sneaking lives many of you live, for my sight has been whetted by experience; always on the limits, trying to get into business and trying to get out of debt, a very ancient slough, called by the Latins *æs alienum*,[9] another's brass, for some of their coins were made of brass; still living, and dying, and buried by this other's brass; always promising to pay, promising to pay, tomorrow, and dying to-day, insolvent; seeking to curry favor, to get custom, by how many modes, only not state-prison offences; lying, flattering, voting, contracting yourselves into a nutshell of civility, or dilating into an atmosphere of thin and vaporous generosity, that you may persuade your neighbor to let you make his shoes, or his hat, or his coat, or his carriage, or import his groceries for him; making yourselves sick, that you may lay up something against a sick day, something to be tucked away in an old chest, or in a stocking behind the plastering, or, more safely, in the brick bank; no matter where, no matter how much or how little.

I sometimes wonder that we can be so frivolous, I may almost say, as to attend to the gross but somewhat foreign form of servitude called Negro Slavery, there are so many keen and subtle masters that enslave both north and south. It is hard to have a southern overseer; it is worse to have a northern one; but worst of all when you are the slave-driver of yourself. Talk of a divinity in man! Look at the teamster on the highway, wending to market by day or night; does any divinity stir within him? His highest duty to fodder and water his horses! What is his destiny to him compared with the shipping interests? Does not he drive for Squire Make-a-stir? How godlike, how immortal, is he? See how he cowers and sneaks, how vaguely all the day he fears, not being immortal nor divine, but the slave and prisoner of his own opinion of himself, a fame won by his own deeds. Public opinion is a weak tyrant compared with our own private opinion. What a man thinks of himself, that it is which determines, or rather indicates, his fate. Self-emancipation even in the West Indian provinces of the fancy and imagination,—what Wilberforce[1] is there to bring that about? Think, also, of the ladies of the land weaving toilet cushions against the last day, not to betray too green an interest in their fates! As if you could kill time without injuring eternity.

The mass of men lead lives of quiet desperation. What is called

9. Literally, "another's brass"; metaphorically, "another person's money" or "debt."
1. William Wilberforce (1759–1833), leader of the anti-slavery forces in England.

resignation is confirmed desperation. From the desperate city you go into the desperate country, and have to console yourself with the bravery of minks and muskrats. A stereotyped but unconscious despair is concealed even under what are called the games and amusements of mankind. There is no play in them, for this comes after work. But it is a characteristic of wisdom not to do desperate things.

When we consider what, to use the words of the catechism, is the chief end of man,[2] and what are the true necessaries and means of life, it appears as if men had deliberately chosen the common mode of living because they preferred it to any other. Yet they honestly think there is no choice left. But alert and healthy natures remember that the sun rose clear. It is never too late to give up our prejudices. No way of thinking or doing, however ancient, can be trusted without proof. What every body echoes or in silence passes by as true to-day may turn out to be falsehood tomorrow, mere smoke of opinion, which some had trusted for a cloud that would sprinkle fertilizing rain on their fields. What old people say you cannot do you try and find that you can. Old deeds for old people, and new deeds for new. Old people did not know enough once, perchance, to fetch fresh fuel to keep the fire a-going; new people put a little dry wood under a pot, and are whirled round the globe with the speed of birds, in a way to kill old people, as the phrase is. Age is no better, hardly so well, qualified for an instructor as youth, for it has not profited so much as it has lost. One may almost doubt if the wisest man has learned any thing of absolute value by living. Practically, the old have no very important advice to give the young, their own experience has been so partial, and their lives have been such miserable failures, for private reasons, as they must believe; and it may be that they have some faith left which belies that experience, and they are only less young than they were. I have lived some thirty years on this planet, and I have yet to hear the first syllable of valuable or even earnest advice from my seniors. They have told me nothing, and probably cannot tell me any thing, to the purpose. Here is life, an experiment to a great extent untried by me; but it does not avail me that they have tried it. If I have any experience which I think valuable, I am sure to reflect that this my Mentors[3] said nothing about.

One farmer says to me, "You cannot live on vegetable food solely, for it furnishes nothing to make bones with;" and so he religiously devotes a part of his day to supplying his system with the raw mate-

---

2. According to the Shorter Catechism in the *New England Primer*, "the chief end of man" is "to glorify God and to enjoy him forever."
3. The wise protector of Telemachus, the son of Odysseus in Homer's *Odyssey*, metaphorically, any wise teacher.

rial of bones; walking all the while he talks behind his oxen, which, with vegetable-made bones, jerk him and his lumbering plough along in spite of every obstacle. Some things are really necessaries of life in some circles, the most helpless and diseased, which in others are luxuries merely, and in others still are entirely unknown.

The whole ground of human life seems to some to have been gone over by their predecessors, both the heights and the valleys, and all things to have been cared for. According to Evelyn, "the wise Solomon prescribed ordinances for the very distances of trees; and the Roman prætors have decided how often you may go into your neighbor's land to gather the acorns which fall on it without trespass, and what share belongs to that neighbor."[4] Hippocrates[5] has even left directions how we should cut our nails; that is, even with the ends of the fingers, neither shorter nor longer. Undoubtedly the very tedium and ennui which presume to have exhausted the variety and the joys of life are as old as Adam. But man's capacities have never been measured; nor are we to judge of what he can do by any precedents, so little has been tried. Whatever have been thy failures hitherto, "be not afflicted, my child, for who shall assign to thee what thou hast left undone?"[6]

We might try our lives by a thousand simple tests; as, for instance, that the same sun which ripens my beans illumines at once a system of earths like ours. If I had remembered this it would have prevented some mistakes. This was not the light in which I hoed them. The stars are the apexes of what wonderful triangles! What distant and different beings in the various mansions of the universe are contemplating the same one at the same moment! Nature and human life are as various as our several constitutions. Who shall say what prospect life offers to another? Could a greater miracle take place than for us to look through each other's eyes for an instant? We should live in all the ages of the world in an hour; ay, in all the worlds of the ages. History, Poetry, Mythology!—I know of no reading of another's experience so startling and informing as this would be.

The greater part of what my neighbors call good I believe in my soul to be bad, and if I repent of any thing, it is very likely to be my good behavior. What demon possessed me that I behaved so well? You may say the wisest thing you can old man,—you who have lived seventy years, not without honor of a kind,—I hear an irresistible voice which invites me away from all that. One generation abandons the enterprises of another like stranded vessels.

4. John Evelyn (1620–1706), English horticulturalist and author; from his *Sylva, or a Discourse of Forest-Trees* (1679).
5. An ancient Greek physician (fl. 300 B.C.E.), frequently called "the father of medicine."
6. From the *Vishnu Purana*, a Hindu scripture.

I think that we may safely trust a good deal more than we do. We may waive just so much care of ourselves as we honestly bestow elsewhere. Nature is as well adapted to our weakness as to our strength. The incessant anxiety and strain of some is a well nigh incurable form of disease. We are made to exaggerate the importance of what work we do; and yet how much is not done by us! or, what if we had been taken sick? How vigilant we are! determined not to live by faith if we can avoid it; all the day long on the alert, at night we unwillingly say our prayers and commit ourselves to uncertainties. So thoroughly and sincerely are we compelled to live, reverencing our life, and denying the possibility of change. This is the only way, we say; but there are as many ways as there can be drawn radii from one centre. All change is a miracle to contemplate; but it is a miracle which is taking place every instant. Confucius said, "To know that we know what we know, and that we do not know what we do not know, that is true knowledge."[7] When one man has reduced a fact of the imagination to be a fact to his understanding, I foresee that all men will at length establish their lives on that basis.

Let us consider for a moment what most of the trouble and anxiety which I have referred to is about, and how much it is necessary that we be troubled, or, at least, careful. It would be some advantage to live a primitive and frontier life, though in the midst of an outward civilization, if only to learn what are the gross necessaries of life and what methods have been taken to obtain them; or even to look over the old day-books of the merchants, to see what it was that men most commonly bought at the stores, what they stored, that is, what are the grossest groceries. For the improvements of ages have had but little influence on the essential laws of man's existence; as our skeletons, probably, are not to be distinguished from those of our ancestors.

By the words, *necessary of life,* I mean whatever, of all that man obtains by his own exertions, has been from the first, or from long use has become, so important to human life that few, if any, whether from savageness, or poverty, or philosophy, ever attempt to do without it. To many creatures there is in this sense but one necessary of life, Food. To the bison of the prairie it is a few inches of palatable grass, with water to drink; unless he seeks the Shelter of the forest or the mountain's shadow. None of the brute creation requires more than Food and Shelter. The necessaries of life for man in this climate may, accurately enough, be distributed under the several heads of Food, Shelter, Clothing, and Fuel; for not till we have secured these are we prepared to entertain the true problems

7. Chinese philosopher and teacher (551?–478? B.C.E.), from his *Analects* 2.17.

of life with freedom and a prospect of success. Man has invented, not only houses, but clothes and cooked food; and possibly from the accidental discovery of the warmth of fire, and the consequent use of it, at first a luxury, arose the present necessity to sit by it. We observe cats and dogs acquiring the same second nature. By proper Shelter and Clothing we legitimately retain our own internal heat; but with an excess of these, or of Fuel, that is, with an external heat greater than our own internal, may not cookery properly be said to begin? Darwin, the naturalist, says of the inhabitants of Tierra del Fuego, that while his own party, who were well clothed and sitting close to a fire, were far from too warm, these naked savages, who were farther off, were observed, to his great surprise, "to be streaming with perspiration at undergoing such a roasting."[8] So, we are told, the New Hollander[9] goes naked with impunity, while the European shivers in his clothes. Is it impossible to combine the hardiness of these savages with the intellectualness of the civilized man? According to Liebig,[1] man's body is a stove, and food the fuel which keeps up the internal combustion in the lungs. In cold weather we eat more, in warm less. The animal heat is the result of a slow combustion, and disease and death take place when this is too rapid; or for want of fuel, or from some defect in the draught, the fire goes out. Of course the vital heat is not to be confounded with fire; but so much for analogy. It appears, therefore, from the above list, that the expression, *animal life,* is nearly synonymous with the expression, *animal heat;* for while Food may be regarded as the Fuel which keeps up the fire within us,—and Fuel serves only to prepare that Food or to increase the warmth of our bodies by addition from without,—Shelter and Clothing also serve only to retain the *heat* thus generated and absorbed.

The grand necessity, then, for our bodies, is to keep warm, to keep the vital heat in us. What pains we accordingly take, not only with our Food, and Clothing, and Shelter, but with our beds, which are our night-clothes, robbing the nests and breasts of birds to prepare this shelter within a shelter, as the mole has its bed of grass and leaves at the end of its burrow! The poor man is wont to complain that this is a cold world; and to cold, no less physical than social, we refer directly a great part of our ails. The summer, in some climates, makes possible to man a sort of Elysian life.[2] Fuel, except

8. Charles Darwin (1809–1882), English naturalist; from his *Journal of Researches . . . during the Voyage of H.M.S. Beagle* (1839). Tierra del Fuego is an island off the southern tip of South America.
9. Aboriginal Australian.
1. Justus von Liebig (1803–1873), German organic chemist; from his *Animal Chemistry* (1842).
2. In Greek mythology, Elysium was the home of the blessed dead; also called the "Elysian fields."

to cook his Food, is then unnecessary; the sun is his fire, and many of the fruits are sufficiently cooked by its rays; while Food generally is more various, and more easily obtained, and Clothing and Shelter are wholly or half unnecessary. At the present day, and in this country, as I find by my own experience, a few implements, a knife, an axe, a spade, a wheelbarrow, &c., and for the studious, lamplight, stationery, and access to a few books, rank next to necessaries, and can all be obtained at a trifling cost. Yet some, not wise, go to the other side of the globe, to barbarous and unhealthy regions, and devote themselves to trade for ten or twenty years, in order that they may live,—that is, keep comfortably warm,—and die in New England at last. The luxuriously rich are not simply kept comfortably warm, but unnaturally hot; as I implied before, they are cooked, of course *à la mode*.[3]

Most of the luxuries, and many of the so called comforts of life, are not only not indispensable, but positive hinderances to the elevation of mankind. With respect to luxuries and comforts, the wisest have ever lived a more simple and meagre life than the poor. The ancient philosophers, Chinese, Hindoo, Persian, and Greek, were a class than which none has been poorer in outward riches, none so rich in inward. We know not much about them. It is remarkable that *we* know so much of them as we do. The same is true of the more modern reformers and benefactors of their race. None can be an impartial or wise observer of human life but from the vantage ground of what *we* should call voluntary poverty. Of a life of luxury the fruit is luxury, whether in agriculture, or commerce, or literature, or art. There are nowadays professors of philosophy, but not philosophers. Yet it is admirable to profess because it was once admirable to live. To be a philosopher is not merely to have subtle thoughts, nor even to found a school, but so to love wisdom as to live according to its dictates, a life of simplicity, independence, magnanimity, and trust. It is to solve some of the problems of life, not only theoretically, but practically. The success of great scholars and thinkers is commonly a courtier-like success, not kingly, not manly. They make shift to live merely by conformity, practically as their fathers did, and are in no sense the progenitors of a nobler race of men. But why do men degenerate ever? What makes families run out? What is the nature of the luxury which enervates and destroys nations? Are we sure that there is none of it in our own lives? The philosopher is in advance of his age even in the outward form of his life. He is not fed, sheltered, clothed, warmed, like his contemporaries. How can a man be a philosopher and not maintain his vital heat by better methods than other men?

3. In a fashionable style.

When a man is warmed by the several modes which I have described, what does he want next? Surely not more warmth of the same kind, as more and richer food, larger and more splendid houses, finer and more abundant clothing, more numerous incessant and hotter fires, and the like. When he has obtained those things which are necessary to life, there is another alternative than to obtain the superfluities; and that is, to adventure on life now, his vacation from humbler toil having commenced. The soil, it appears, is suited to the seed, for it has sent its radicle downward, and it may now send its shoot upward also with confidence. Why has man rooted himself thus firmly in the earth, but that he may rise in the same proportion into the heavens above?—for the nobler plants are valued for the fruit they bear at last in the air and light, far from the ground, and are not treated like the humbler esculents, which, though they may be biennials, are cultivated only till they have perfected their root, and often cut down at top for this purpose, so that most would not know them in their flowering season.

I do not mean to prescribe rules to strong and valiant natures, who will mind their own affairs whether in heaven or hell, and perchance build more magnificently and spend more lavishly than the richest, without ever impoverishing themselves, not knowing how they live,—if, indeed, there are any such, as has been dreamed; nor to those who find their encouragement and inspiration in precisely the present condition of things, and cherish it with the fondness and enthusiasm of lovers,—and, to some extent, I reckon myself in this number; I do not speak to those who are well employed, in whatever circumstances, and they know whether they are well employed or not;—but mainly to the mass of men who are discontented, and idly complaining of the hardness of their lot or of the times, when they might improve them. There are some who complain most energetically and inconsolably of any, because they are, as they say, doing their duty. I also have in my mind that seemingly wealthy, but most terribly impoverished class of all, who have accumulated dross, but know not how to use it, or get rid of it, and thus have forged their own golden or silver fetters.

If I should attempt to tell how I have desired to spend my life in years past, it would probably surprise those of my readers who are somewhat acquainted with its actual history; it would certainly astonish those who know nothing about it. I will only hint at some of the enterprises which I have cherished.

In any weather, at any hour of the day or night, I have been anxious to improve the nick of time, and notch it on my stick too; to stand on the meeting of two eternities, the past and future, which is precisely the present moment; to toe that line. You will pardon some obscurities, for there are more secrets in my trade than in most men's, and yet not voluntarily kept, but inseparable from its very nature. I would gladly tell all that I know about it, and never paint "No Admittance" on my gate.

I long ago lost a hound, a bay horse, and a turtle-dove,[4] and am still on their trail. Many are the travellers I have spoken concerning them, describing their tracks and what calls they answered to. I have met one or two who had heard the hound, and the tramp of the horse, and even seen the dove disappear behind a cloud, and they seemed as anxious to recover them as if they had lost them themselves.

To anticipate, not the sunrise and the dawn merely, but, if possible, Nature herself! How many mornings, summer and winter, before yet any neighbor was stirring about his business, have I been about mine! No doubt, many of my townsmen have met me returning from this enterprise, farmers starting for Boston in the twilight, or woodchoppers going to their work. It is true, I never assisted the sun materially in his rising, but, doubt not, it was of the last importance only to be present at it.

So many autumn, ay, and winter days, spent outside the town, trying to hear what was in the wind, to hear and carry it express! I well-nigh sunk all my capital in it, and lost my own breath into the bargain, running in the face of it. If it had concerned either of the political parties, depend upon it, it would have appeared in the Gazette[5] with the earliest intelligence. At other times watching from the observatory of some cliff or tree, to telegraph any new arrival; or waiting at evening on the hill-tops for the sky to fall, that I might catch something, though I never caught much, and that, manna-wise, would dissolve again in the sun.

For a long time I was reporter to a journal,[6] of no very wide circulation, whose editor has never yet seen fit to print the bulk of my contributions, and, as is too common with writers, I got only my labor for my pains. However, in this case my pains were their own reward.

For many years I was self-appointed inspector of snow storms and rain storms, and did my duty faithfully; surveyor, if not of highways, then of forest paths and all across-lot routes, keeping them open, and ravines bridged and passable at all seasons, where the public heel had testified to their utility.

---

4. Probably symbols for the unattainable things of life; critics differ over whether the symbols have specific references.
5. A common name for a newspaper, including the *Yeoman's Gazette* of Concord; by extension, any newspaper.
6. The *Dial*, a Transcendentalist magazine (1840–1844), published some of Thoreau's writing; he may refer as well to his own Journal, which remained unpublished during his lifetime.

I have looked after the wild stock of the town, which give a faithful herdsman a good deal of trouble by leaping fences; and I have
had an eye to the unfrequented nooks and corners of the farm;
though I did not always know whether Jonas or Solomon worked in
a particular field to-day; that was none of my business. I have watered the red huckleberry, the sand cherry and the nettle tree, the
red pine and the black ash, the white grape and the yellow violet,
which might have withered else in dry seasons.

In short, I went on thus for a long time, I may say it without
boasting, faithfully minding my business, till it became more and
more evident that my townsmen would not after all admit me into
the list of town officers, nor make my place a sinecure with a moderate allowance. My accounts, which I can swear to have kept
faithfully, I have, indeed, never got audited, still less accepted, still
less paid and settled. However, I have not set my heart on that.

Not long since, a strolling Indian went to sell baskets at the
house of a well-known lawyer in my neighborhood. "Do you wish to
buy any baskets?" he asked. "No, we do not want any," was the reply. "What!" exclaimed the Indian as he went out the gate, "do you
mean to starve us?" Having seen his industrious white neighbors so
well off,—that the lawyer had only to weave arguments, and by
some magic wealth and standing followed, he had said to himself; I
will go into business; I will weave baskets; it is a thing which I can
do. Thinking that when he had made the baskets he would have
done his part, and then it would be the white man's to buy them.
He had not discovered that it was necessary for him to make it
worth the other's while to buy them, or at least make him think that
it was so, or to make something else which it would be worth his
while to buy. I too had woven a kind of basket of a delicate texture,
but I had not made it worth any one's while to buy them.[7] Yet not
the less, in my case, did I think it worth my while to weave them,
and instead of studying how to make it worth men's while to buy
my baskets, I studied rather how to avoid the necessity of selling
them. The life which men praise and regard as successful is but
one kind. Why should we exaggerate any one kind at the expense of
the others?

Finding that my fellow-citizens were not likely to offer me any
room in the court house, or any curacy or living any where else, but
I must shift for myself, I turned my face more exclusively than ever
to the woods, where I was better known. I determined to go into
business at once, and not wait to acquire the usual capital, using
such slender means as I had already got. My purpose in going to

---

7. Thoreau's first book, *A Week on the Concord and Merrimack Rivers* (1849), sold poorly.
   It took him four years to repay the debt of $290 to his publisher.

Walden Pond was not to live cheaply nor to live dearly there, but to transact some private business with the fewest obstacles; to be hindered from accomplishing which for want of a little common sense, a little enterprise and business talent, appeared not so sad as foolish.

I have always endeavored to acquire strict business habits; they are indispensable to every man. If your trade is with the Celestial Empire,[8] then some small counting house on the coast, in some Salem[9] harbor, will be fixture enough. You will export such articles as the country affords, purely native products, much ice and pine timber and a little granite, always in native bottoms. These will be good ventures. To oversee all the details yourself in person; to be at once pilot and captain, and owner and underwriter; to buy and sell and keep the accounts; to read every letter received, and write or read every letter sent; to superintend the discharge of imports night and day; to be upon many parts of the coast almost at the same time;—often the richest freight will be discharged upon a Jersey shore;[1]—to be your own telegraph, unweariedly sweeping the horizon, speaking all passing vessels bound coastwise; to keep up a steady despatch of commodities, for the supply of such a distant and exorbitant market; to keep yourself informed of the state of the markets, prospects of war and peace every where, and anticipate the tendencies of trade and civilization,—taking advantage of the results of all exploring expeditions, using new passages and all improvements in navigation;—charts to be studied, the position of reefs and new lights and buoys to be ascertained, and ever, and ever, the logarithmic tables to be corrected, for by the error of some calculator the vessel often splits upon a rock that should have reached a friendly pier,—there is the untold fate of La Perouse;[2]—universal science to be kept pace with, studying the lives of all great discoverers and navigators, great adventurers and merchants, from Hanno[3] and the Phœnicians down to our day; in fine, account of stock to be taken from time to time, to know how you stand. It is a labor to task the faculties of a man,—such problems of profit and loss, of interest, of tare and tret,[4] and gauging of all kinds in it, as demand a universal knowledge.

I have thought that Walden Pond would be a good place for business, not solely on account of the railroad and the ice trade; it offers advantages which it may not be good policy to divulge; it is a

8. China.
9. An important port on the Massachusetts coast.
1. The coast of New Jersey, on which many ships were wrecked.
2. French explorer (1741–1788) whose ship was lost in the south Pacific.
3. Carthaginian explorer and navigator (ca. 500 B.C.E.)
4. In shipping, "tare" is a deduction for the weight of the container; "tret" is an allowance made to buyers for waste or damage.

good port and a good foundation. No Neva[5] marshes to be filled; though you must every where build on piles of your own driving. It is said that a flood-tide, with a westerly wind, and ice in the Neva, would sweep St. Petersburg from the face of the earth.

As this business was to be entered into without the usual capital, it may not be easy to conjecture where those means, that will still be indispensable to every such undertaking, were to be obtained. As for Clothing, to come at once to the practical part of the question, perhaps we are led oftener by the love of novelty, and a regard for the opinions of men, in procuring it, than by a true utility. Let him who has work to do recollect that the object of clothing is, first, to retain the vital heat, and secondly, in this state of society, to cover nakedness, and he may judge how much of any necessary or important work may be accomplished without adding to his wardrobe. Kings and queens who wear a suit but once, though made by some tailor or dressmaker to their majesties, cannot know the comfort of wearing a suit that fits. They are no better than wooden horses to hang the clean clothes on. Every day our garments become more assimilated to ourselves, receiving the impress of the wearer's character, until we hesitate to lay them aside, without such delay and medical appliances and some such solemnity even as our bodies. No man ever stood the lower in my estimation for having a patch in his clothes; yet I am sure that there is greater anxiety, commonly, to have fashionable, or at least clean and unpatched clothes, than to have a sound conscience. But even if the rent is not mended, perhaps the worst vice betrayed is improvidence. I sometimes try my acquaintances by such tests as this;—who could wear a patch, or two extra seams only, over the knee? Most behave as if they believed that their prospects for life would be ruined if they should do it. It would be easier for them to hobble to town with a broken leg than with a broken pantaloon. Often if an accident happens to a gentleman's legs, they can be mended; but if a similar accident happens to the legs of his pantaloons, there is no help for it; for he considers, not what is truly respectable, but what is respected. We know but few men, a great many coats and breeches. Dress a scarecrow in your last shift, you standing shiftless by, who would not soonest salute the scarecrow? Passing a cornfield the other day, close by a hat and coat on a stake, I recognized the owner of the farm. He was only a little more weather-beaten than when I saw him last. I have heard of a dog that barked at every stranger who approached his master's premises with clothes on, but was easily

5. St. Petersburg (from 1914 to 1924, Petrograd; from then to 1991, Leningrad) in Russia was built on the delta of the Neva River.

quieted by a naked thief. It is an interesting question how far men would retain their relative rank if they were divested of their clothes. Could you, in such a case, tell surely of any company of civilized men, which belonged to the most respected class? When Madam Pfeiffer, in her adventurous travels round the world, from east to west, had got so near home as Asiatic Russia, she says that she felt the necessity of wearing other than a travelling dress, when she went to meet the authorities, for she "was now in a civilized country, where—— —people are judged of by their clothes."[6] Even in our democratic New England towns the accidental possession of wealth, and its manifestation in dress and equipage alone, obtain for the possessor almost universal respect. But they who yield such respect, numerous as they are, are so far heathen, and need to have a missionary sent to them. Beside, clothes introduced sewing, a kind of work which you may call endless; a woman's dress, at least, is never done.

A man who has at length found something to do will not need to get a new suit to do it in; for him the old will do, that has lain dusty in the garret for an indeterminate period. Old shoes will serve a hero longer than they have served his valet,—if a hero ever has a valet,—bare feet are older than shoes, and he can make them do. Only they who go to soirées and legislative halls must have new coats, coats to change as often as the man changes in them. But if my jacket and trousers, my hat and shoes, are fit to worship God in, they will do; will they not? Who ever saw his old clothes,—his old coat, actually worn out, resolved into its primitive elements, so that it was not a deed of charity to bestow it on some poor boy, by him perchance to be bestowed on some poorer still, or shall we say richer, who could do with less? I say, beware of all enterprises that require new clothes, and not rather a new wearer of clothes. If there is not a new man, how can the new clothes be made to fit? If you have any enterprise before you, try it in your old clothes. All men want, not something to *do with*, but something to *do*, or rather something to *be*. Perhaps we should never procure a new suit, however ragged or dirty the old, until we have so conducted, so enterprised or sailed in some way, that we feel like new men in the old, and that to retain it would be like keeping new wine in old bottles.[7] Our moulting season, like that of the fowls, must be a crisis in our lives. The loon retires to solitary ponds to spend it. Thus also the snake casts its slough, and the caterpillar its wormy coat, by an in-

6. Ida Pfeiffer (1797–1858), Austrian traveler; from her *A Lady's Voyage Round the World* (1852).
7. An echo of Jesus' words to his disciples in Matthew 9.17: "Neither do men put new wine into old bottles, else the bottles break, and the wine runneth out, . . . ; but they put new wine into new bottles, and both are preserved."

ternal industry and expansion; for clothes are but our outmost cuticle and mortal coil. Otherwise we shall be found sailing under false colors, and be inevitably cashiered at last by our own opinion, as well as that of mankind.

We don garment after garment, as if we grew like exogenous plants by addition without. Our outside and often thin and fanciful clothes are our epidermis or false skin, which partakes not of our life, and may be stripped off here and there without fatal injury; our thicker garments, constantly worn, are our cellular integument, or cortex; but our shirts are our liber or true bark, which cannot be removed without girdling and so destroying the man. I believe that all races at some seasons wear something equivalent to the shirt. It is desirable that a man be clad so simply that he can lay his hands on himself in the dark, and that he live in all respects so compactly and preparedly, that, if an enemy take the town, he can, like the old philosopher, walk out the gate empty-handed without anxiety. While one thick garment is, for most purposes, as good as three thin ones, and cheap clothing can be obtained at prices really to suit customers; while a thick coat can be bought for five dollars, which will last as many years, thick pantaloons for two dollars, cowhide boots for a dollar and a half a pair, a summer hat for a quarter of a dollar, and a winter cap for sixty-two and a half cents, or a better be made at home at a nominal cost, where is he so poor that, clad in such a suit, *of his own earning*, there will not be found wise men to do him reverence?

When I ask for a garment of a particular form, my tailoress tells me gravely, "They do not make them so now," not emphasizing the "They" at all, as if she quoted an authority as impersonal as the Fates,[8] and I find it difficult to get made what I want, simply because she cannot believe that I mean what I say, that I am so rash. When I hear this oracular sentence, I am for a moment absorbed in thought, emphasizing to myself each word separately that I may come at the meaning of it, that I may find out by what degree of consanguinity *They* are related to *me*, and what authority they may have in an affair which affects me so nearly; and, finally, I am inclined to answer her with equal mystery, and without any more emphasis of the "they,"—"It is true, they did not make them so recently, but they do now." Of what use this measuring of me if she does not measure my character, but only the breadth of my shoulders, as it were a peg to hang the coat on? We worship not the Graces, nor the Parcæ,[9] but Fashion. She spins and weaves and

---

8. In classical mythology, the three goddesses who control human destiny.
9. The Fates in Roman mythology; the Graces were minor goddesses and personifications of grace and beauty in classical mythology.

cuts with full authority. The head monkey at Paris puts on a traveller's cap, and all the monkeys in America do the same. I sometimes despair of getting any thing quite simple and honest done in
this world by the help of men. They would have to be passed
through a powerful press first, to squeeze their old notions out of
them, so that they would not soon get upon their legs again, and
then there would be some one in the company with a maggot in his
head, hatched from an egg deposited there nobody knows when, for
not even fire kills these things, and you would have lost your labor.
Nevertheless, we will not forget that some Egyptian wheat is said to
have been handed down to us by a mummy.

On the whole, I think that it cannot be maintained that dressing
has in this or any country risen to the dignity of an art. At present
men make shift to wear what they can get. Like shipwrecked
sailors, they put on what they can find on the beach, and at a little
distance, whether of space or time, laugh at each other's masquerade. Every generation laughs at the old fashions, but follows religiously the new. We are amused at beholding the costume of
Henry VIII., or Queen Elizabeth, as much as if it was that of the
King and Queen of the Cannibal Islands. All costume off a man is
pitiful or grotesque. It is only the serious eye peering from and the
sincere life passed within it, which restrain laughter and consecrate the costume of any people. Let Harlequin[1] be taken with a fit
of the colic and his trappings will have to serve that mood too.
When the soldier is hit by a cannon ball rags are as becoming as
purple.

The childish and savage taste of men and women for new patterns keeps how many shaking and squinting through kaleido-
scopes that they may discover the particular figure which this
generation requires to-day. The manufacturers have learned that
this taste is merely whimsical. Of two patterns, which differ only by
a few threads more or less of a particular color, the one will be sold
readily, the other lie on the shelf, though it frequently happens that
after the lapse of a season the latter becomes the most fashionable.
Comparatively, tattooing is not the hideous custom which it is
called. It is not barbarous merely because the printing is skin-deep
and unalterable.

I cannot believe that our factory system is the best mode by
which men may get clothing. The condition of the operatives is becoming every day more like that of the English; and it cannot be
wondered at, since, as far as I have heard or observed, the principal
object is, not that mankind may be well and honestly clad, but, unquestionably, that the corporations may be enriched. In the long

1. A standard character in old Italian comedy, traditionally dressed in multicolored tights.

run men hit only what they aim at. Therefore, though they should fail immediately, they had better aim at something high.

As for a Shelter, I will not deny that this is now a necessary of life, though there are instances of men having done without it for long periods in colder countries than this. Samuel Laing says that "The Laplander in his skin dress, and in a skin bag which he puts over his head and shoulders, will sleep night after night on the snow—in a degree of cold which would extinguish the life of one exposed to it in any woollen clothing." He had seen them asleep thus. Yet he adds, "They are not hardier than other people."[2] But, probably, man did not live long on the earth without discovering the convenience which there is in a house, the domestic comforts, which phrase may have originally signified the satisfactions of the house more than of the family; though these must be extremely partial and occasional in those climates where the house is associated in our thoughts with winter or the rainy season chiefly, and two thirds of the year, except for a parasol, is unnecessary. In our climate, in the summer, it was formerly almost solely a covering at night. In the Indian gazettes a wigwam was the symbol of a day's march, and a row of them cut or painted on the bark of a tree signified that so many times they had camped. Man was not made so large limbed and robust but that he must seek to narrow his world, and wall in a space such as fitted him. He was at first bare and out of doors; but though this was pleasant enough in serene and warm weather, by daylight, the rainy season and the winter, to say nothing of the torrid sun, would perhaps have nipped his race in the bud if he had not made haste to clothe himself with the shelter of a house. Adam and Eve, according to the fable, wore the bower before other clothes. Man wanted a home, a place of warmth, or comfort, first of physical warmth, then the warmth of the affections.

We may imagine a time when, in the infancy of the human race, some enterprising mortal crept into a hollow in a rock for shelter. Every child begins the world again, to some extent, and loves to stay out doors, even in wet and cold. It plays house, as well as horse, having an instinct for it. Who does not remember the interest with which when young he looked at shelving rocks, or any approach to a cave? It was the natural yearning of that portion of our most primitive ancestor which still survived in us. From the cave we have advanced to roofs of palm leaves, of bark and boughs, of linen woven and stretched, of grass and straw, of boards and shingles, of stone and tiles. At last, we know not what it is to live in the

2. British traveler (1780–1868); from his *Journal of a Residence in Norway* (1837).

open air, and our lives are domestic in more senses than we think. From the hearth to the field is a great distance. It would be well perhaps if we were to spend more of our days and nights without any obstruction between us and the celestial bodies, if the poet did not speak so much from under a roof, or the saint dwell there so long. Birds do not sing in caves, nor do doves cherish their innocence in dovecots.

However, if one designs to construct a dwelling house, it behooves him to exercise a little Yankee shrewdness, lest after all he find himself in a workhouse, a labyrinth without a clew, a museum, an almshouse, a prison, or a splendid mausoleum instead. Consider first how slight a shelter is absolutely necessary. I have seen Penobscot Indians,[3] in this town, living in tents of thin cotton cloth, while the snow was nearly a foot deep around them, and I thought that they would be glad to have it deeper to keep out the wind. Formerly, when how to get my living honestly, with freedom left for my proper pursuits, was a question which vexed me even more than it does now, for unfortunately I am become somewhat callous, I used to see a large box by the railroad, six feet long by three wide, in which the laborers locked up their tools at night, and it suggested to me that every man who was hard pushed might get such a one for a dollar, and, having bored a few auger holes in it, to admit the air at least, get into it when it rained and at night, and hook down the lid, and so have freedom in his love, and in his soul be free. This did not appear the worst, nor by any means a despicable alternative. You could sit up as late as you pleased, and, whenever you got up, go abroad without any landlord or house-lord dogging you for rent. Many a man is harassed to death to pay the rent of a larger and more luxurious box who would not have frozen to death in such a box as this. I am far from jesting. Economy is a subject which admits of being treated with levity, but it cannot so be disposed of. A comfortable house for a rude and hardy race, that lived mostly out of doors, was once made here almost entirely of such materials as Nature furnished ready to their hands. Gookin, who was superintendent of the Indians subject to the Massachusetts Colony, writing in 1674, says, "The best of their houses are covered very neatly, tight and warm, with barks of trees, slipped from their bodies at those seasons when the sap is up, and made into great flakes, with pressure of weighty timber, when they are green . . . . The meaner sort are covered with mats which they make of a kind of bulrush, and are also indifferently tight and warm, but not so good as the former . . . . Some I have seen, sixty or a hundred feet long and thirty feet broad . . . . I have often lodged in their wigwams, and

3. A tribe originally from northern Maine.

found them as warm as the best English houses."[4] He adds, that they were commonly carpeted and lined within with well-wrought embroidered mats, and were furnished with various utensils. The Indians had advanced so far as to regulate the effect of the wind by a mat suspended over the hole in the roof and moved by a string. Such a lodge was in the first instance constructed in a day or two at most, and taken down and put up in a few hours; and every family owned one, or its apartment in one.

In the savage state every family owns a shelter as good as the best, and sufficient for its coarser and simpler wants; but I think that I speak within bounds when I say that, though the birds of the air have their nests, and the foxes their holes, and the savages their wigwams, in modern civilized society not more than one half the families own a shelter.[5] In the large towns and cities, where civilization especially prevails, the number of those who own a shelter is a very small fraction of the whole. The rest pay an annual tax for this outside garment of all, become indispensable summer and winter, which would buy a village of Indian wigwams, but now helps to keep them poor as long as they live. I do not mean to insist here on the disadvantage of hiring compared with owning, but it is evident that the savage owns his shelter because it costs so little, while the civilized man hires his commonly because he cannot afford to own it; nor can he, in the long run, any better afford to hire. But, answers one, by merely paying this tax the poor civilized man secures an abode which is a palace compared with the savage's. An annual rent of from twenty-five to a hundred dollars, these are the country rates, entitles him to the benefit of the improvements of centuries, spacious apartments, clean paint and paper, Rumford[6] fireplace, back plastering, Venetian blinds, copper pump, spring lock, a commodious cellar, and many other things. But how happens it that he who is said to enjoy these things is so commonly a *poor* civilized man, while the savage, who has them not, is rich as a savage? If it is asserted that civilization is a real advance in the condition of man,—and I think that it is, though only the wise improve their advantages,—it must be shown that it has produced better dwellings without making them more costly; and the cost of a thing is the amount of what I will call life which is required to be exchanged for it, immediately or in the long run. An average house in this neighborhood costs perhaps eight hundred dollars, and to lay up this sum will take from ten to fifteen years of the laborer's life, even if

4. Daniel Gookin (1612–1687), *Historical Collections of the Indians in New England* (1792).
5. Compare Matthew 8.20: "The foxes have holes, and the birds of the air have nests; but the Son of man hath not where to lay his head."
6. Benjamin Thompson, Count Rumford (1753–1814), designed a nonsmoking stove.

he is not encumbered with a family;—estimating the pecuniary value of every man's labor at one dollar a day, for if some receive more, others receive less;—so that he must have spent more than half his life commonly before *his* wigwam will be earned. If we suppose him to pay a rent instead, this is but a doubtful choice of evils. Would the savage have been wise to exchange his wigwam for a palace on these terms?

It may be guessed that I reduce almost the whole advantage of holding this superfluous property as a fund in store against the future, so far as the individual is concerned, mainly to the defraying of funeral expenses. But perhaps a man is not required to bury himself. Nevertheless this points to an important distinction between the civilized man and the savage; and, no doubt, they have designs on us for our benefit, in making the life of a civilized people an *institution*, in which the life of the individual is to a great extent absorbed, in order to preserve and perfect that of the race. But I wish to show at what a sacrifice this advantage is at present obtained, and to suggest that we may possibly so live as to secure all the advantage without suffering any of the disadvantage. What mean ye by saying that the poor ye have always with you, or that the fathers have eaten sour grapes, and the children's teeth are set on edge?

"As I live, saith the Lord God, ye shall not have occasion any more to use this proverb in Israel."

"Behold all souls are mine; as the soul of the father, so also the soul of the son is mine: the soul that sinneth it shall die."[7]

When I consider my neighbors, the farmers of Concord, who are at least as well off as the other classes, I find that for the most part they have been toiling twenty, thirty, or forty years, that they may become the real owners of their farms, which commonly they have inherited with encumbrances, or else bought with hired money,—and we may regard one third of that toil as the cost of their houses,—but commonly they have not paid for them yet. It is true, the encumbrances sometimes outweigh the value of the farm, so that the farm itself becomes one great encumbrance, and still a man is found to inherit it, being well acquainted with it, as he says. On applying to the assessors, I am surprised to learn that they cannot at once name a dozen in the town who own their farms free and clear. If you would know the history of these homesteads, inquire at the bank where they are mortgaged. The man who has actually paid for his farm with labor on it is so rare that every neighbor can point to him. I doubt if there are three such men in Concord. What has been said of the merchants, that a very large majority, even ninety-seven in a hundred, are sure to fail, is equally true of the farmers.

7. Matthew 26.11, Ezekiel 18.2–4.

With regard to the merchants, however, one of them says pertinently that a great part of their failures are not genuine pecuniary failures, but merely failures to fulfil their engagements, because it is inconvenient; that is, it is the moral character that breaks down. But this puts an infinitely worse face on the matter, and suggests, beside, that probably not even the other three succeed in saving their souls, but are perchance bankrupt in a worse sense than they who fail honestly. Bankruptcy and repudiation are the springboards from which much of our civilization vaults and turns its somersets, but the savage stands on the unelastic plank of famine. Yet the Middlesex Cattle Show[8] goes off here with *éclat*[9] annually, as if all the joints of the agricultural machine were suent.[1]

The farmer is endeavoring to solve the problem of a livelihood by a formula more complicated than the problem itself. To get his shoestrings he speculates in herds of cattle. With consummate skill he has set his trap with a hair springe to catch comfort and independence, and then, as he turned away, got his own leg into it. This is the reason he is poor; and for a similar reason we are all poor in respect to a thousand savage comforts, though surrounded by luxuries. As Chapman sings,—

> "The false society of men—
>   —for earthly greatness
> All heavenly comforts rarefies to air."[2]

And when the farmer has got his house, he may not be the richer but the poorer for it, and it be the house that has got him. As I understand it, that was a valid objection urged by Momus[3] against the house which Minerva made, that she "had not made it movable, by which means a bad neighborhood might be avoided;" and it may still be urged, for our houses are such unwieldy property that we are often imprisoned rather than housed in them; and the bad neighborhood to be avoided is our own scurvy selves. I know one or two families, at least, in this town, who, for nearly a generation, have been wishing to sell their houses in the outskirts and move into the village, but have not been able to accomplish it, and only death will set them free.

Granted that the *majority* are able at last either to own or hire the modern house with all its improvements. While civilization has been improving our houses, it has not equally improved the men who are to inhabit them. It has created palaces, but it was not so

---

8. Middlesex is the county of which Concord is a part; the Agricultural Fair was an annual event.
9. Conspicuous success.
1. Also spelled "suant"; a dialect term meaning "running smoothly."
2. George Chapman (1559?–1634), English dramatist, translator and poet; from his *The Tragedy of Caesar and Pompey* 5.2.
3. The Greek god of pleasure.

easy to create noblemen and kings. And *if the civilized man's pursuits are no worthier than the savage's, if he is employed the greater
part of his life in obtaining gross necessaries and comforts merely, why
should he have a better dwelling than the former?*

But how do the poor *minority* fare? Perhaps it will be found, that
just in proportion as some have been placed in outward circumstances above the savage, others have been degraded below him.
The luxury of one class is counterbalanced by the indigence of another. On the one side is the palace, on the other are the
almshouse and "silent poor."[4] The myriads who built the pyramids
to be the tombs of the Pharaohs were fed on garlic, and it may be
were not decently buried themselves. The mason who finishes the
cornice of the palace returns at night perchance to a hut not so
good as a wigwam. It is a mistake to suppose that, in a country
where the usual evidences of civilization exist, the condition of a
very large body of the inhabitants may not be as degraded as that of
savages. I refer to the degraded poor, not now to the degraded rich.
To know this I should not need to look farther than to the shanties
which every where border our railroads, that last improvement in
civilization; where I see in my daily walks human beings living in
sties, and all winter with an open door, for the sake of light, without
any visible, often imaginable, wood pile, and the forms of both old
and young are permanently contracted by the long habit of shrink-
ing from cold and misery, and the development of all their limbs
and faculties is checked. It certainly is fair to look at that class by
whose labor the works which distinguish this generation are accomplished. Such too, to a greater or less extent, is the condition of
the operatives of every denomination in England, which is the great
workhouse of the world. Or I could refer you to Ireland, which is
marked as one of the white or enlightened spots on the map. Contrast the physical condition of the Irish with that of the North
American Indian, or the South Sea Islander, or any other savage
race before it was degraded by contact with the civilized man. Yet I
have no doubt that that people's rulers are as wise as the average of
civilized rulers. Their condition only proves what squalidness may
consist with civilization. I hardly need refer now to the laborers in
our Southern States who produce the staple exports of this country,
and are themselves a staple production of the South. But to confine
myself to those who are said to be in *moderate* circumstances.

Most men appear never to have considered what a house is, and
are actually though needlessly poor all their lives because they
think that they must have such a one as their neighbors have. As if
one were to wear any sort of coat which the tailor might cut out for
him, or, gradually leaving off palmleaf hat or cap of woodchuck

4. Those who keep their debts secret to avoid being sent to the almshouse, or poorhouse.

skin, complain of hard times because he could not afford to buy
him a crown! It is possible to invent a house still more convenient
and luxurious than we have, which yet all would admit that man
could not afford to pay for. Shall we always study to obtain more of
these things, and not sometimes to be content with less? Shall the
respectable citizen thus gravely teach, by precept and example, the
necessity of the young man's providing a certain number of superfluous glowshoes,[5] and umbrellas, and empty guest chambers for
empty guests, before he dies? Why should not our furniture be as
simple as the Arab's or the Indian's? When I think of the benefactors of the race, whom we have apotheosized as messengers from
heaven, bearers of divine gifts to man, I do not see in my mind any
retinue at their heels, any car-load of fashionable furniture. Or
what if I were to allow—would it not be a singular allowance?—
that our furniture should be more complex than the Arab's, in proportion as we are morally and intellectually his superiors! At
present our houses are cluttered and defiled with it, and a good
housewife would sweep out the greater part into the dust hole, and
not leave her morning's work undone. Morning work! By the
blushes of Aurora and the music of Memnon,[6] what should be
man's *morning work* in this world? I had three pieces of limestone
on my desk, but I was terrified to find that they required to be
dusted daily, when the furniture of my mind was all undusted still,
and I threw them out the window in disgust. How, then, could I
have a furnished house? I would rather sit in the open air, for no
dust gathers on the grass, unless where man has broken ground.

It is the luxurious and dissipated who set the fashions which the
herd so diligently follow. The traveller who stops at the best houses,
so called, soon discovers this, for the publicans presume him to be
a Sardanapalus,[7] and if he resigned himself to their tender mercies
he would soon be completely emasculated. I think that in the railroad car we are inclined to spend more on luxury than on safety
and convenience, and it threatens without attaining these to become no better than a modern drawing room, with its divans, and
ottomans, and sunshades, and a hundred other oriental things,
which we are taking west with us, invented for the ladies of the
harem and the effeminate natives of the Celestial Empire, which
Jonathan[8] should be ashamed to know the names of. I would rather
sit on a pumpkin and have it all to myself, than be crowded on a

---

5. Galoshes, waterproof overshoes.
6. In Roman mythology, the goddess of dawn and her son. A statue of Memnon near
   Thebes supposedly emitted musical sounds at dawn.
7. A corrupt king of ancient Assyria (d. 880 B.C.E.).
8. A common nineteenth-century name for an inhabitant of the United States; also,
   "Brother Jonathan."

velvet cushion. I would rather ride on earth in an ox cart with a free circulation, than go to heaven in the fancy car of an excursion train and breathe a *malaria* all the way.

The very simplicity and nakedness of man's life in the primitive ages imply this advantage at least, that they left him still but a sojourner in nature. When he was refreshed with food and sleep he contemplated his journey again. He dwelt, as it were, in a tent in this world, and was either threading the valleys, or crossing the plains, or climbing the mountain tops. But lo! men have become the tools of their tools. The man who independently plucked the fruits when he was hungry is become a farmer; and he who stood under a tree for shelter, a housekeeper. We now no longer camp as for a night, but have settled down on earth and forgotten heaven. We have adopted Christianity merely as an improved method of *agri*-culture. We have built for this world a family mansion, and for the next a family tomb. The best works of art are the expression of man's struggle to free himself from this condition, but the effect of our art is merely to make this low state comfortable and that higher state to be forgotten. There is actually no place in this village for a work of *fine* art, if any had come down to us, to stand, for our lives, our houses and streets, furnish no proper pedestal for it. There is not a nail to hang a picture on, nor a shelf to receive the bust of a hero or a saint. When I consider how our houses are built and paid for, or not paid for, and their internal economy managed and sustained, I wonder that the floor does not give way under the visitor while he is admiring the gewgaws upon the mantel-piece, and let him through into the cellar, to some solid and honest though earthy foundation. I cannot but perceive that this so called rich and refined life is a thing jumped at, and I do not get on in the enjoyment of the *fine* arts which adorn it, my attention being wholly occupied with the jump; for I remember that the greatest genuine leap, due to human muscles alone, on record, is that of certain wandering Arabs, who are said to have cleared twenty-five feet on level ground. Without factitious support, man is sure to come to earth again beyond that distance. The first question which I am tempted to put to the proprietor of such great impropriety is, Who bolsters you? Are you one of the ninety-seven who fail, or the three who succeed? Answer me these questions, and then perhaps I may look at your bawbles and find them ornamental. The cart before the horse is neither beautiful nor useful. Before we can adorn our houses with beautiful objects the walls must be stripped, and our lives must be stripped, and beautiful housekeeping and beautiful living be laid for a foundation: now, a taste for the beautiful is most cultivated out of doors, where there is no house and no housekeeper.

Old Johnson, in his "Wonder-Working Providence," speaking of the first settlers of this town, with whom he was contemporary, tells us that "they burrow themselves in the earth for their first shelter under some hillside, and, casting the soil aloft upon timber, they make a smoky fire against the earth, at the highest side." They did not "provide them houses," says he, "till the earth, by the Lord's blessing, brought forth bread to feed them," and the first year's crop was so light that "they were forced to cut their bread very thin for a long season."[9] The secretary of the Province of New Netherland, writing in Dutch, in 1650, for the information of those who wished to take up land there, states more particularly, that "those in New Netherland, and especially in New England, who have no means to build farm houses at first according to their wishes, dig a square pit in the ground, cellar fashion, six or seven feet deep, as long and as broad as they think proper, case the earth inside with wood all round the wall, and line the wood with the bark of trees or something else to prevent the caving in of the earth; floor this cellar with plank, and wainscot it overhead for a ceiling, raise a roof of spars clear up, and cover the spars with bark or green sods, so that they can live dry and warm in these houses with their entire families for two, three, and four years, it being understood that partitions are run through those cellars which are adapted to the size of the family. The wealthy and principal men in New England, in the beginning of the colonies, commenced their first dwelling houses in this fashion for two reasons; firstly, in order not to waste time in building, and not to want food the next season; secondly, in order not to discourage poor laboring people whom they brought over in numbers from Fatherland. In the course of three or four years, when the country became adapted to agriculture, they built themselves handsome houses, spending on them several thousands."[1]

In this course which our ancestors took there was a show of prudence at least, as if their principle were to satisfy the more pressing wants first. But are the more pressing wants satisfied now? When I think of acquiring for myself one of our luxurious dwellings, I am deterred, for, so to speak, the country is not yet adapted to *human* culture, and we are still forced to cut our *spiritual* bread far thinner than our forefathers did their wheaten. Not that all architectural ornament is to be neglected even in the rudest periods; but let our houses first be lined with beauty, where they come in contact with our lives, like the tenement of the shellfish, and not overlaid with

9. Edward Johnson (1598–1672), *Wonder-working Providence of Sion's Saviour in New England* (1654).
1. Edmund Bailey O'Callaghan, *Documentary History of the State of New-York* (1851).

it. But, alas! I have been inside one or two of them, and know what they are lined with.

Though we are not so degenerate but that we might possibly live in a cave or a wigwam or wear skins to-day, it certainly is better to accept the advantages, though so dearly bought, which the invention and industry of mankind offer. In such a neighborhood as this, boards and shingles, lime and bricks, are cheaper and more easily obtained than suitable caves, or whole logs, or bark in sufficient quantities, or even well-tempered clay or flat stones. I speak understandingly on this subject, for I have made myself acquainted with it both theoretically and practically. With a little more wit we might use these materials so as to become richer than the richest now are, and make our civilization a blessing. The civilized man is a more experienced and wiser savage. But to make haste to my own experiment.

Near the end of March, 1845, I borrowed an axe and went down to the woods by Walden Pond, nearest to where I intended to build my house, and began to cut down some tall arrowy white pines, still in their youth, for timber. It is difficult to begin without borrowing, but perhaps it is the most generous course thus to permit your fellow-men to have an interest in your enterprise. The owner of the axe, as he released his hold on it, said that it was the apple of his eye; but I returned it sharper than I received it. It was a pleasant hillside where I worked, covered with pine woods, through which I looked out on the pond, and a small open field in the woods where pines and hickories were springing up. The ice in the pond was not yet dissolved, though there were some open spaces, and it was all dark colored and saturated with water. There were some slight flurries of snow during the days that I worked there; but for the most part when I came out on to the railroad, on my way home, its yellow sand heap stretched away gleaming in the hazy atmosphere, and the rails shone in the spring sun, and I heard the lark and pewee[2] and other birds already come to commence another year with us. They were pleasant spring days, in which the winter of man's discontent was thawing as well as the earth, and the life that had lain torpid began to stretch itself. One day, when my axe had come off and I had cut a green hickory for a wedge, driving it with a stone, and had placed the whole to soak in a pond hole in order to swell the wood, I saw a striped snake run into the water, and he lay on the bottom, apparently without inconvenience, as long as I staid there, or more than a quarter of an hour; perhaps because he had not yet fairly come out of the torpid state. It appeared to me that

2. The meadowlark and the phoebe.

for a like reason men remain in their present low and primitive condition; but if they should feel the influence of the spring of springs
arousing them, they would of necessity rise to a higher and more
ethereal life. I had previously seen the snakes in frosty mornings in
my path with portions of their bodies still numb and inflexible,
waiting for the sun to thaw them. On the 1st of April it rained and
melted the ice, and in the early part of the day, which was very
foggy, I heard a stray goose groping about over the pond and cackling as if lost, or like the spirit of the fog.

So I went on for some days cutting and hewing timber, and also
studs and rafters, all with my narrow axe, not having many commu-
nicable or scholar-like thoughts, singing to myself,—[3]

> Men say they know many things;
> But lo! they have taken wings,—
> The arts and sciences,
> And a thousand appliances;
> The wind that blows
> Is all that any body knows.

I hewed the main timbers six inches square, most of the studs on
two sides only, and the rafters and floor timbers on one side, leaving the rest of the bark on, so that they were just as straight and
much stronger than sawed ones. Each stick was carefully mortised
or tenoned by its stump, for I had borrowed other tools by this
time. My days in the woods were not very long ones; yet I usually
carried my dinner of bread and butter, and read the newspaper in
which it was wrapped, at noon, sitting amid the green pine boughs
which I had cut off, and to my bread was imparted some of their
fragrance, for my hands were covered with a thick coat of pitch.
Before I had done I was more the friend than the foe of the pine
tree, though I had cut down some of them, having become better
acquainted with it. Sometimes a rambler in the wood was attracted
by the sound of my axe, and we chatted pleasantly over the chips
which I had made.

By the middle of April, for I made no haste in my work, but
rather made the most of it, my house was framed and ready for the
raising. I had already bought the shanty of James Collins, an Irishman who worked on the Fitchburg Railroad,[4] for boards. James
Collins' shanty was considered an uncommonly fine one. When I
called to see it he was not at home. I walked about the outside, at
first unobserved from within, the window was so deep and high. It
was of small dimensions, with a peaked cottage roof, and not much

3. This poem, like all poems not enclosed within quotation marks, was written by Thoreau
   himself.
4. The Boston & Fitchburg Railroad, which ran near Walden Pond.

else to be seen, the dirt being raised five feet all around as if it were
a compost heap. The roof was the soundest part, though a good
deal warped and made brittle by the sun. Doorsill there was none,
but a perennial passage for the hens under the door board. Mrs. C.
came to the door and asked me to view it from the inside. The hens
were driven in by my approach. It was dark, and had a dirt floor for
the most part, dank, clammy, and aguish, only here a board and
there a board which would not bear removal. She lighted a lamp to
show me the inside of the roof and the walls, and also that the
board floor extended under the bed, warning me not to step into
the cellar, a sort of dust hole two feet deep. In her own words, they
were "good boards overhead, good boards all around, and a good
window,"—of two whole squares originally, only the cat had passed
out that way lately. There was a stove, a bed, and a place to sit, an
infant in the house where it was born, a silk parasol, gilt-framed
looking-glass, and a patent new coffee mill nailed to an oak sapling,
all told. The bargain was soon concluded, for James had in the
mean while returned. I to pay four dollars and twenty-five cents to-
night, he to vacate at five to-morrow morning, selling to nobody
else meanwhile: I to take possession at six. It were well, he said, to
be there early, and anticipate certain indistinct but wholly unjust
claims on the score of ground rent and fuel. This he assured me
was the only encumbrance. At six I passed him and his family on
the road. One large bundle held their all,—bed, coffee-mill, looking-glass, hens,—all but the cat, she took to the woods and became
a wild cat, and, as I learned afterward, trod in a trap set for woodchucks, and so became a dead cat at last.

I took down this dwelling the same morning, drawing the nails,
and removed it to the pond side by small cartloads, spreading the
boards on the grass there to bleach and warp back again in the sun.
One early thrush gave me a note or two as I drove along the woodland path. I was informed treacherously by a young Patrick[5] that
neighbor Seeley, an Irishman, in the intervals of the carting, transferred the still tolerable, straight, and drivable nails, staples, and
spikes to his pocket, and then stood when I came back to pass the
time of day, and look freshly up, unconcerned, with spring thoughts,
at the devastation; there being a dearth of work, as he said. He was
there to represent spectatordom, and help make this seemingly insignificant event one with the removal of the gods of Troy.[6]

I dug my cellar in the side of a hill sloping to the south, where a
woodchuck had formerly dug his burrow, down through sumach

5. A common name for any Irishman.
6. The removal of the images of gods from Troy precedes the defeat of the city in Virgil's
   Aeneid, Book 2.

and blackberry roots, and the lowest stain of vegetation, six feet square by seven deep, to a fine sand where potatoes would not freeze in any winter. The sides were left shelving, and not stoned; but the sun having never shone on them, the sand still keeps its place. It was but two hours' work. I took particular pleasure in this breaking of ground, for in almost all latitudes men dig into the earth for an equable temperature. Under the most splendid house in the city is still to be found the cellar where they store their roots as of old, and long after the superstructure has disappeared posterity remark its dent in the earth. The house is still but a sort of porch at the entrance of a burrow.

At length, in the beginning of May, with the help of some of my acquaintances, rather to improve so good an occasion for neighborliness than from any necessity, I set up the frame of my house. No man was ever more honored in the character of his raisers than I. They are destined, I trust, to assist at the raising of loftier structures one day. I began to occupy my house on the 4th of July, as soon as it was boarded and roofed, for the boards were carefully feather-edged and lapped, so that it was perfectly impervious to rain; but before boarding I laid the foundation of a chimney at one end, bringing two cartloads of stones up the hill from the pond in my arms. I built the chimney after my hoeing in the fall, before a fire became necessary for warmth, doing my cooking in the mean while out of doors on the ground, early in the morning: which mode I still think is in some respects more convenient and agreeable than the usual one. When it stormed before my bread was baked, I fixed a few boards over the fire, and sat under them to watch my loaf, and passed some pleasant hours in that way. In those days, when my hands were much employed, I read but little, but the least scraps of paper which lay on the ground, my holder, or tablecloth, afforded me as much entertainment, in fact answered the same purpose as the Iliad.[7]

It would be worth the while to build still more deliberately than I did, considering, for instance, what foundation a door, a window, a cellar, a garret, have in the nature of man, and perchance never raising any superstructure until we found a better reason for it than our temporal necessities even. There is some of the same fitness in a man's building his own house that there is in a bird's building its own nest. Who knows but if men constructed their dwellings with their own hands, and provided food for themselves and families simply and honestly enough, the poetic faculty would be universally

---

7. Epic poem by Homer that tells of the siege of Troy by the Greeks, and the tragic consequences of the wrath of Achilles, a great mythological Greek warrior.

developed, as birds universally sing when they are so engaged? But alas! we do like cowbirds and cuckoos, which lay their eggs in nests which other birds have built, and cheer no traveller with their chattering and unmusical notes. Shall we forever resign the pleasure of construction to the carpenter? What does architecture amount to in the experience of the mass of men? I never in all my walks came across a man engaged in so simple and natural an occupation as building his house. We belong to the community. It is not the tailor alone who is the ninth part of a man; it is as much the preacher, and the merchant, and the farmer. Where is this division of labor to end? and what object does it finally serve? No doubt another *may* also think for me; but it is not therefore desirable that he should do so to the exclusion of my thinking for myself.

True, there are architects so called in this country, and I have heard of one at least possessed with the idea of making architectural ornaments have a core of truth, a necessity, and hence a beauty, as if it were a revelation to him.[8] All very well perhaps from his point of view, but only a little better than the common dilettantism. A sentimental reformer in architecture, he began at the cornice, not at the foundation. It was only how to put a core of truth within the ornaments, that every sugar plum in fact might have an almond or caraway seed in it,—though I hold that almonds are most wholesome without the sugar,—and not how the inhabitant, the indweller, might build truly within and without, and let the ornaments take care of themselves. What reasonable man ever supposed that ornaments were something outward and in the skin merely,—that the tortoise got his spotted shell, or the shell-fish its mother-o'-pearl tints, by such a contract as the inhabitants of Broadway their Trinity Church?[9] But a man has no more to do with the style of architecture of his house than a tortoise with that of its shell: nor need the soldier be so idle as to try to paint the precise *color* of his virtue on his standard. The enemy will find it out. He may turn pale when the trial comes. This man seemed to me to lean over the cornice, and timidly whisper his half truth to the rude occupants who really knew it better than he. What of architectural beauty I now see, I know has gradually grown from within outward, out of the necessities and character of the indweller, who is the only builder,—out of some unconscious truthfulness, and nobleness, without ever a thought for the appearance; and whatever additional beauty of this kind is destined to be produced will be preceded by a like unconscious beauty of life. The most interesting

8. The sculptor Horatio Greenough (1805–1852), an early proponent of the idea that architectural decoration should be functional.
9. A famous church in New York City built by Richard Upjohn in the Gothic Revival style and completed in 1846.

dwellings in this country, as the painter knows, are the most unpretending, humble log huts and cottages of the poor commonly; it is the life of the inhabitants whose shells they are, and not any peculiarity in their surfaces merely, which makes them *picturesque*; and equally interesting will be the citizen's suburban box, when his life shall be as simple and as agreeable to the imagination, and there is as little straining after effect in the style of his dwelling. A great proportion of architectural ornaments are literally hollow, and a September gale would strip them off, like borrowed plumes, without injury to the substantials. They can do without *architecture* who have no olives nor wines in the cellar. What if an equal ado were made about the ornaments of style in literature, and the architects of our bibles spent as much time about their cornices as the architects of our churches do? So are made the *belles-lettres* and the *beaux-arts*[1] and their professors. Much it concerns a man, forsooth, how a few sticks are slanted over him or under him, and what colors are daubed upon his box. It would signify somewhat, if, in any earnest sense, *he* slanted them and daubed it; but the spirit having departed out of the tenant, it is of a piece with constructing his own coffin,—the architecture of the grave, and "carpenter," is but another name for "coffin-maker." One man says, in his despair or indifference to life, take up a handful of the earth at your feet, and paint your house that color. Is he thinking of his last and narrow house? Toss up a copper[2] for it as well. What an abundance of leisure he must have! Why do you take up a handful of dirt? Better paint your house your own complexion; let it turn pale or blush for you. An enterprise to improve the style of cottage architecture! When you have got my ornaments ready I will wear them.

Before winter I built a chimney, and shingled the sides of my house, which were already impervious to rain, with imperfect and sappy shingles made of the first slice of the log, whose edges I was obliged to straighten with a plane.

I have thus a tight shingled and plastered house, ten feet wide by fifteen long, and eight-feet posts, with a garret and a closet, a large window on each side, two trap doors, one door at the end, and a brick fireplace opposite. The exact cost of my house, paying the usual price for such materials as I used, but not counting the work, all of which was done by myself, was as follows; and I give the details because very few are able to tell exactly what their houses cost, and fewer still, if any, the separate cost of the various materials which compose them:—

1. Esthetic or polite literature and the fine arts.
2. A coin; perhaps a reference to the ancient Greek belief about giving a coin to the spirit who guides a corpse to the land of the dead.

Boards,	. . . .	$8 03½,	mostly shanty boards.
Refuse shingles for roof and sides,	.	4 00	
Laths,	. . . .	1 25	
Two second-hand windows with glass,		2 43	
One thousand old brick,	. . .	4 00	
Two casks of lime,	. . . . .	2 40	That was high.
Hair,	. . . .	0 31	More than I needed.
Mantle-tree iron,	. . . . .	0 15	
Nails,	. . . . . .	3 90	
Hinges and screws,	. . . .	0 14	
Latch,	. . . .	0 10	
Chalk,	. . . .	0 01	
Transportation,	. . . . .	1 40 }	I carried a good part on my back
In all,	. . . .	.$28 12½	

These are all the materials excepting the timber, stones and sand, which I claimed by squatter's right. I have also a small wood-shed adjoining, made chiefly of the stuff which was left after building the house.

I intend to build me a house which will surpass any on the main street in Concord in grandeur and luxury, as soon as it pleases me as much and will cost me no more than my present one.

I thus found that the student who wishes for a shelter can obtain one for a lifetime at an expense not greater than the rent which he now pays annually. If I seem to boast more than is becoming, my excuse is that I brag for humanity rather than for myself; and my shortcomings and inconsistencies do not affect the truth of my statement. Notwithstanding much cant and hypocrisy,—chaff which I find it difficult to separate from my wheat, but for which I am as sorry as any man,—I will breathe freely and stretch myself in this respect, it is such a relief to both the moral and physical system; and I am resolved that I will not through humility become the devil's attorney. I will endeavor to speak a good word for the truth. At Cambridge College[3] the mere rent of a student's room, which is only a little larger than my own, is thirty dollars each year, though the corporation had the advantage of building thirty-two side by side and under one roof, and the occupant suffers the inconvenience of many and noisy neighbors, and perhaps a residence in the fourth story. I cannot but think that if we had more true wisdom in these respects, not only less education would be needed, because, forsooth, more would already have been acquired, but the pecuniary expense of getting an education

3. Harvard College, Cambridge, Massachusetts; Thoreau's own college.

would in a great measure vanish. Those conveniences which the student requires at Cambridge or elsewhere cost him or somebody else ten times as great a sacrifice of life as they would with proper management on both sides. Those things for which the most money is demanded are never the things which the student most wants. Tuition, for instance, is an important item in the term bill, while for the far more valuable education which he gets by associating with the most cultivated of his contemporaries no charge is made. The mode of founding a college is, commonly, to get up a subscription of dollars and cents, and then following blindly the principles of a division of labor to its extreme,—a principle which should never be followed but with circumspection,—to call in a contractor who makes this a subject of speculation, and he employs Irishmen or other operatives actually to lay the foundations, while the students that are to be are said to be fitting themselves for it; and for these oversights successive generations have to pay. I think that it would be *better than this*, for the students, or those who desire to be benefited by it, even to lay the foundation themselves. The student who secures his coveted leisure and retirement by systematically shirking any labor necessary to man obtains but an ignoble and unprofitable leisure, defrauding himself of the experience which alone can make leisure fruitful. "But," says one, "you do not mean that the students should go to work with their hands instead of their heads?" I do not mean that exactly, but I mean something which he might think a good deal like that; I mean that they should not *play* life, or *study* it merely, while the community supports them at this expensive game, but earnestly *live* it from beginning to end. How could youths better learn to live than by at once trying the experiment of living? Methinks this would exercise their minds as much as mathematics. If I wished a boy to know something about the arts and sciences, for instance, I would not pursue the common course, which is merely to send him into the neighborhood of some professor, where any thing is professed and practised but the art of life;—to survey the world through a telescope or a microscope, and never with his natural eye; to study chemistry, and not learn how his bread is made, or mechanics, and not learn how it is earned; to discover new satellites to Neptune, and not detect the motes in his eyes, or to what vagabond he is a satellite himself; or to be devoured by the monsters that swarm all around him, while contemplating the monsters in a drop of vinegar. Which would have advanced the most at the end of a month,—the boy who had made his own jackknife from the ore which he had dug and smelted, reading as much as would be necessary for this,—or the boy who had attended the lectures on metallurgy at the Institute in the mean while, and had received a Rogers'[4] penknife from his father? Which would be most likely to cut his fingers? . . . To my astonishment I was informed on leaving college that I had studied navigation!—why, if I had taken one turn down the harbor I should have known more about it. Even the *poor* student studies and is taught only *political* economy, while that economy of living which is synonymous with philosophy is not even sincerely professed in our colleges. The consequence is, that while he is reading Adam Smith, Ricardo, and Say,[5] he runs his father in debt irretrievably.

As with our colleges, so with a hundred "modern improvements;" there is an illusion about them; there is not always a positive advance. The devil goes on exacting compound interest to the last for his early share and numerous succeeding investments in them. Our inventions are wont to be pretty toys, which distract our attention from serious things. They are but improved means to an unimproved end, an end which it was already but too easy to arrive at; as railroads lead to Boston or New York. We are in great haste to construct a magnetic telegraph from Maine to Texas; but Maine and Texas, it may be, have nothing important to communicate. Either is in such a predicament as the man who was earnest to be introduced to a distinguished deaf woman, but when he was presented, and one end of her ear trumpet was put into his hand, had nothing to say. As if the main object were to talk fast and not to talk sensibly. We are eager to tunnel under the Atlantic and bring the old world some weeks nearer to the new; but perchance the first news that will leak through into the broad, flapping American ear will be that the Princess Adelaide[6] has the whooping cough. After all, the man whose horse trots a mile in a minute does not carry the most important messages; he is not an evangelist, nor does he come round eating locusts and wild honey. I doubt if Flying Childers[7] ever carried a peck of corn to mill.

One says to me, "I wonder that you do not lay up money; you love to travel; you might take the cars and go to Fitchburg[8] today and see the country." But I am wiser than that. I have learned that the swiftest traveller is he that goes afoot. I say to my friend, Suppose we try who will get there first. The distance is thirty miles; the fare ninety cents. That is almost a day's wages. I remember when wages were sixty cents a day for laborers on this very road. Well, I start now on foot, and get there before night; I have travelled at

4. A relatively costly knife manufactured by Joseph Rodgers & Sons in Sheffield, England.
5. Three economists: Scottish Adam Smith (1723–1790), English David Ricardo (1772–1823), and French Jean Baptiste Say (1767–1823).
6. Perhaps the Princess of Orleans, the sister of King Louis Phillipe of France; figuratively, any famous but inconsequential person.
7. A famous English racehorse.
8. A town west of Concord.

that rate by the week together. You will in the mean while have earned your fare, and arrive there some time tomorrow, or possibly this evening, if you are lucky enough to get a job in season. Instead of going to Fitchburg, you will be working here the greater part of the day. And so, if the railroad reached round the world, I think that I should keep ahead of you; and as for seeing the country and getting experience of that kind, I should have to cut your acquaintance altogether.

Such is the universal law, which no man can ever outwit, and with regard to the railroad even we may say it is as broad as it is long. To make a railroad round the world available to all mankind is equivalent to grading the whole surface of the planet. Men have an indistinct notion that if they keep up this activity of joint stocks and spades long enough all will at length ride somewhere, in next to no time, and for nothing; but though a crowd rushes to the depot, and the conductor shouts "All aboard!" when the smoke is blown away and the vapor condensed, it will be perceived that a few are riding, but the rest are run over,—and it will be called, and will be, "A melancholy accident." No doubt they can ride at last who shall have earned their fare, that is, if they survive so long, but they will probably have lost their elasticity and desire to travel by that time. This spending of the best part of one's life earning money in order to enjoy a questionable liberty during the least valuable part of it, reminds me of the Englishman who went to India to make a fortune first, in order that he might return to England and live the life of a poet. He should have gone up garret at once. "What!" exclaim a million Irishmen starting up from all the shanties in the land, "is not this railroad which we have built a good thing?" Yes, I answer, *comparatively* good, that is, you might have done worse; but I wish, as you are brothers of mine, that you could have spent your time better than digging in this dirt.

Before I finished my house, wishing to earn ten or twelve dollars by some honest and agreeable method, in order to meet my unusual expenses, I planted about two acres and a half of light and sandy soil near it chiefly with beans, but also a small part with potatoes, corn, peas, and turnips. The whole lot contains eleven acres, mostly growing up to pines and hickories, and was sold the preceding season for eight dollars and eight cents an acre. One farmer said that it was "good for nothing but to raise cheeping squirrels on." I put no manure whatever on this land, not being the owner, but merely a squatter, and not expecting to cultivate so much again, and I did not quite hoe it all once. I got out several cords of stumps in ploughing, which supplied me with fuel for a long time, and left small circles of virgin mould, easily distinguish-

able through the summer by the greater luxuriance of the beans
there. The dead and for the most part unmerchantable wood behind my house, and the driftwood from the pond, have supplied the
remainder of my fuel. I was obliged to hire a team and a man for
the ploughing, though I held the plough myself. My farm outgoes for the first season were, for implements, seed, work, &c.,
$14 72½. The seed corn was given me. This never costs any thing
to speak of, unless you plant more than enough. I got twelve
bushels of beans, and eighteen bushels of potatoes, beside some
peas and sweet corn. The yellow corn and turnips were too late to
come to any thing. My whole income from the farm was

	$23 44.
Deducting the outgoes, . .	14 72½
there are left	$8 71½,

beside produce consumed and on hand at the time this estimate
was made of the value of $4 50,—the amount on hand much more
than balancing a little grass which I did not raise. All things considered, that is, considering the importance of a man's soul and of to-
day, notwithstanding the short time occupied by my experiment,
nay, partly even because of its transient character, I believe that
that was doing better than any farmer in Concord did that year.

The next year I did better still, for I spaded up all the land which
I required, about a third of an acre, and I learned from the experience of both years, not being in the least awed by many celebrated
works on husbandry, Arthur Young[9] among the rest, that if one
would live simply and eat only the crop which he raised, and raise
no more than he ate, and not exchange it for an insufficient quantity of more luxurious and expensive things, he would need to cultivate only a few rods of ground, and that it would be cheaper to
spade up that than to use oxen to plough it, and to select a fresh
spot from time to time than to manure the old, and he could do all
his necessary farm work as it were with his left hand at odd hours
in the summer; and thus he would not be tied to an ox, or horse, or
cow, or pig, as at present. I desire to speak impartially on this point,
and as one not interested in the success or failure of the present
economical and social arrangements. I was more independent than
any farmer in Concord, for I was not anchored to a house or farm,
but could follow the bent of my genius, which is a very crooked
one, every moment. Beside being better off than they already, if my
house had been burned or my crops had failed, I should have been
nearly as well off as before.

I am wont to think that men are not so much the keepers of

9. British agricultural author (1741–1820).

herds as herds are the keepers of men, the former are so much the freer. Men and oxen exchange work; but if we consider necessary work only, the oxen will be seen to have greatly the advantage, their farm is so much the larger. Man does some of his part of the exchange work in his six weeks of haying, and it is no boy's play. Certainly no nation that lived simply in all respects, that is, no nation of philosophers, would commit so great a blunder as to use the labor of animals. True, there never was and is not likely soon to be a nation of philosophers, nor am I certain it is desirable that there should be. However, I should never have broken a horse or bull and taken him to board for any work he might do for me, for fear I should become a horse-man or a herds-man merely; and if society seems to be the gainer by so doing, are we certain that what is one man's gain is not another's loss, and that the stable-boy has equal cause with his master to be satisfied? Granted that some public works would not have been constructed without this aid, and let man share the glory of such with the ox and horse; does it follow that he could not have accomplished works yet more worthy of himself in that case? When men begin to do, not merely unnecessary or artistic, but luxurious and idle work, with their assistance, it is inevitable that a few do all the exchange work with the oxen, or, in other words, become the slaves of the strongest. Man thus not only works for the animal within him, but, for a symbol of this, he works for the animal without him. Though we have many substantial houses of brick or stone, the prosperity of the farmer is still measured by the degree to which the barn overshadows the house. This town is said to have the largest houses for oxen, cows, and horses hereabouts, and it is not behindhand in its public buildings; but there are very few halls for free worship or free speech in this country. It should not be by their architecture, but why not even by their power of abstract thought, that nations should seek to commemorate themselves? How much more admirable the Bhagvat-Geeta[1] than all the ruins of the East! Towers and temples are the luxury of princes. A simple and independent mind does not toil at the bidding of any prince. Genius is not a retainer to any emperor, nor is its material silver, or gold, or marble, except to a trifling extent. To what end, pray, is so much stone hammered? In Arcadia,[2] when I was there, I did not see any hammering stone. Nations are possessed with an insane ambition to perpetuate the memory of themselves by the amount of hammered stone they leave. What if equal pains were taken to smooth and polish their manners? One piece of good sense would be more memorable than a monument as

---

1. A sacred Hindu text, frequently cited by Thoreau; also spelled "Bhagavad Gita."
2. Ancient Greek pastoral region; figuratively, any ideal land.

high as the moon. I love better to see stones in place. The grandeur of Thebes[3] was a vulgar grandeur. More sensible is a rod of stone wall that bounds an honest man's field than a hundred-gated Thebes that has wandered farther from the true end of life. The religion and civilization which are barbaric and heathenish build splendid temples; but what you might call Christianity does not. Most of the stone a nation hammers goes toward its tomb only. It buries itself alive. As for the Pyramids, there is nothing to wonder at in them so much as the fact that so many men could be found degraded enough to spend their lives constructing a tomb for some ambitious booby, whom it would have been wiser and manlier to have drowned in the Nile, and then given his body to the dogs. I might possibly invent some excuse for them and him, but I have no time for it. As for the religion and love of art of the builders, it is much the same all the world over, whether the building be an Egyptian temple or the United States Bank. It costs more than it comes to. The mainspring is vanity, assisted by the love of garlic and bread and butter. Mr. Balcom, a promising young architect, designs it on the back of his Vitruvius,[4] with hard pencil and ruler, and the job is let out to Dobson & Sons, stonecutters. When the thirty centuries begin to look down on it, mankind begin to look up at it. As for your high towers and monuments, there was a crazy fellow once in this town who undertook to dig through to China, and he got so far that, as he said, he heard the Chinese pots and kettles rattle; but I think that I shall not go out of my way to admire the hole which he made. Many are concerned about the monuments of the West and the East,—to know who built them. For my part, I should like to know who in those days did not build them,—who were above such trifling. But to proceed with my statistics.

By surveying, carpentry, and day-labor of various other kinds in the village in the mean while, for I have as many trades as fingers, I had earned $13 34. The expense of food for eight months, namely, from July 4th to March 1st, the time when these estimates were made, though I lived there more than two years,—not counting potatoes, a little green corn, and some peas, which I had raised, nor considering the value of what was on hand at the last date, was

Rice	$1 73½	
Molasses, . .	1 73	Cheapest form of the saccharine.
Rye meal, . . .	1 04¾	
Indian meal, . .	0 99¾	Cheaper than rye.
Pork, ...	0 22	

3. Ancient capital of Upper Egypt, a standard symbol of grandeur.
4. Roman architect and author of a book on design, *De Architectura*, first century B.C.E.

Flour, ...	0 88	} Costs more than Indian meal, both money and trouble.
Sugar, . . .	0 80	
Lard, ...	0 65	
Apples, . . .	0 25	
Dried apple, . .	0 22	
Sweet potatoes, .	0 10	
One pumpkin, .	0 6	
One watermelon,	0 2	
Salt, ...	0 3	

All experiments which failed

Yes, I did eat $8 74 all told; but I should not thus unblushingly publish my guilt, if I did not know that most of my readers were equally guilty with myself, and that their deeds would look no better in print. The next year I sometimes caught a mess of fish for my dinner, and once I went so far as to slaughter a woodchuck which ravaged my bean-field,—effect his transmigration, as a Tartar[5] would say,—and devour him, partly for experiment's sake; but though it afforded me a momentary enjoyment, notwithstanding a musky flavor, I saw that the longest use would not make that a good practice, however it might seem to have your woodchucks ready dressed by the village butcher.

Clothing and some incidental expenses within the same dates, though little can be inferred from this item, amounted to

$8 40¾

Oil and some household utensils, ... 2 00

So that all the pecuniary outgoes, excepting for washing and mending, which for the most part were done out of the house, and their bills have not yet been received,—and these are all and more than all the ways by which money necessarily goes out in this part of the world,—were

House, ...	$28 12½
Farm one year, ...	14 72½
Food eight months, ...	8 74
Clothing, &c., eight months, . . .	8 40¾
Oil, &c., eight months, ...	2 00
In all,	$61 99¾

I address myself now to those of my readers who have a living to get. And to meet this I have for farm produce sold

---

5. A resident of Tartary, a region of Central Asia, and believer in the transmigration of souls.

$23 44

Earned by day-labor, ...   13 34

In all, ... $36 78,

which subtracted from the sum of the outgoes leaves a balance of $25 21¾ on the one side,—this being very nearly the means with which I started, and the measure of expenses to be incurred,—and on the other, beside the leisure and independence and health thus secured, a comfortable house for me as long as I choose to occupy it.

These statistics, however accidental and therefore uninstructive they may appear, as they have a certain completeness, have a certain value also. Nothing was given me of which I have not rendered some account. It appears from the above estimate, that my food alone cost me in money about twenty-seven cents a week. It was, for nearly two years after this, rye and Indian meal without yeast, potatoes, rice, a very little salt pork, molasses, and salt, and my drink water. It was fit that I should live on rice, mainly, who loved so well the philosophy of India. To meet the objections of some inveterate cavillers, I may as well state, that if I dined out occasionally, as I always had done, and I trust shall have opportunities to do again, it was frequently to the detriment of my domestic arrangements. But the dining out, being, as I have stated, a constant element, does not in the least affect a comparative statement like this.

I learned from my two years' experience that it would cost incredibly little trouble to obtain one's necessary food, even in this latitude; that a man may use as simple a diet as the animals, and yet retain health and strength. I have made a satisfactory dinner, satisfactory on several accounts, simply off a dish of purslane (*Portulaca oleracea*) which I gathered in my cornfield, boiled and salted. I give the Latin on account of the savoriness of the trivial name. And pray what more can a reasonable man desire, in peaceful times, in ordinary noons, than a sufficient number of ears of green sweet-corn boiled, with the addition of salt? Even the little variety which I used was a yielding to the demands of appetite, and not of health. Yet men have come to such a pass that they frequently starve, not for want of necessaries, but for want of luxuries; and I know a good woman who thinks that her son lost his life because he took to drinking water only.

The reader will perceive that I am treating the subject rather from an economic than a dietetic point of view, and he will not venture to put my abstemiousness to the test unless he has a well-stocked larder.

Bread I at first made of pure Indian meal and salt, genuine hoe-cakes, which I baked before my fire out of doors on a shingle or the end of a stick of timber sawed off in building my house; but it was

wont to get smoked and to have a piny flavor. I tried flour also; but
have at last found a mixture of rye and Indian meal most convenient and agreeable. In cold weather it was no little amusement to
bake several small loaves of this in succession, tending and turning
them as carefully as an Egyptian his hatching eggs. They were a
real cereal fruit which I ripened, and they had to my senses a fragrance like that of other noble fruits, which I kept in as long as possible by wrapping them in cloths. I made a study of the ancient and
indispensable art of bread-making, consulting such authorities as
offered, going back to the primitive days and first invention of the
unleavened kind, when from the wildness of nuts and meats men
first reached the mildness and refinement of this diet, and travelling gradually down in my studies through that accidental souring
of the dough which, it is supposed, taught the leavening process,
and through the various fermentations thereafter, till I came to
"good, sweet, wholesome bread," the staff of life. Leaven, which
some deem the soul of bread, the *spiritus* which fills its cellular tissue, which is religiously preserved like the vestal fire,—some precious bottle-full, I suppose, first brought over in the Mayflower, did
the business for America, and its influence is still rising, swelling,
spreading, in cerealian billows over the land,—this seed I regularly
and faithfully procured from the village, till at length one morning
I forgot the rules, and scalded my yeast; by which accident I discovered that even this was not indispensable,—for my discoveries were
not by the synthetic but analytic process,—and I have gladly omitted it since, though most housewives earnestly assured me that safe
and wholesome bread without yeast might not be, and elderly people prophesied a speedy decay of the vital forces. Yet I find it not to
be an essential ingredient, and after going without it for a year am
still in the land of the living; and I am glad to escape the trivialness
of carrying a bottle-full in my pocket, which would sometimes pop
and discharge its contents to my discomfiture. It is simpler and
more respectable to omit it. Man is an animal who more than any
other can adapt himself to all climates and circumstances. Neither
did I put any sal soda, or other acid or alkali, into my bread. It
would seem that I made it according to the recipe which Marcus
Porcius Cato gave about two centuries before Christ. "Panem dep-
sticium sic facito. Manus mortariumque bene lavato. Farinam in
mortarium indito, aquæ paulatim addito, subigitoque pulchre. Ubi
bene subegeris, defingito, coquitoque sub testu."[6] Which I take to
mean—"Make kneaded bread thus. Wash your hands and trough
well. Put the meal into the trough, add water gradually, and knead

---

6. Roman statesman and agriculturalist (239–149 B.C.E.); from his *De Agri Cultura*; also
called *De Re Rustica*.

it thoroughly. When you have kneaded it well, mould it, and bake it under a cover," that is, in a baking-kettle. Not a word about leaven. But I did not always use this staff of life. At one time, owing to the emptiness of my purse, I saw none of it for more than a month.

Every New Englander might easily raise all his own breadstuffs in this land of rye and Indian corn, and not depend on distant and fluctuating markets for them. Yet so far are we from simplicity and independence that, in Concord, fresh and sweet meal is rarely sold in the shops, and hominy and corn in a still coarser form are hardly used by any. For the most part the farmer gives to his cattle and hogs the grain of his own producing, and buys flour, which is at least no more wholesome, at a greater cost, at the store. I saw that I could easily raise my bushel or two of rye and Indian corn, for the former will grow on the poorest land, and the latter does not require the best, and grind them in a handmill, and so do without rice and pork; and if I must have some concentrated sweet, I found by experiment that I could make a very good molasses either of pumpkins or beets, and I knew that I needed only to set out a few maples to obtain it more easily still, and while these were growing I could use various substitutes beside those which I have named. "For," as the Forefathers sang,—

> "we can make liquor to sweeten our lips
> Of pumpkins and parsnips and walnut-tree chips."[7]

Finally, as for salt, that grossest of groceries, to obtain this might be a fit occasion for a visit to the seashore, or, if I did without it altogether, I should probably drink the less water. I do not learn that the Indians ever troubled themselves to go after it.

Thus I could avoid all trade and barter, so far as my food was concerned, and having a shelter already, it would only remain to get clothing and fuel. The pantaloons which I now wear were woven in a farmer's family,—thank Heaven there is so much virtue still in man; for I think the fall from the farmer to the operative as great and memorable as that from the man to the farmer;—and in a new country fuel is an encumbrance. As for a habitat, if I were not permitted still to squat, I might purchase one acre at the same price for which the land I cultivated was sold—namely, eight dollars and eight cents. But as it was, I considered that I enhanced the value of the land by squatting on it.

There is a certain class of unbelievers who sometimes ask me such questions as, if I think that I can live on vegetable food alone; and to strike at the root of the matter at once,—for the root is faith,—I am accustomed to answer such, that I can live on board nails. If they

7. From John Warner Barber, *Historical Collections* (1839).

cannot understand that, they cannot understand much that I have to say. For my part, I am glad to hear of experiments of this kind being tried; as that a young man tried for a fortnight to live on hard, raw corn on the ear, using his teeth for all mortar. The squirrel tribe tried the same and succeeded. The human race is interested in these experiments, though a few old women who are incapacitated for them, or who own their thirds[8] in mills, may be alarmed.

My furniture, part of which I made myself, and the rest cost me nothing of which I have not rendered an account, consisted of a bed, a table, a desk, three chairs, a looking-glass three inches in diameter, a pair of tongs and andirons, a kettle, a skillet, and a frying-pan, a dipper, a wash-bowl, two knives and forks, three plates, one cup, one spoon, a jug for oil, a jug for molasses, and a japanned lamp. None is so poor that he need sit on a pumpkin. That is shift-lessness. There is a plenty of such chairs as I like best in the village garrets to be had for taking them away. Furniture! Thank God, I can sit and I can stand without the aid of a furniture warehouse. What man but a philosopher would not be ashamed to see his furniture packed in a cart and going up country exposed to the light of heaven and the eyes of men, a beggarly account of empty boxes? That is Spaulding's furniture. I could never tell from inspecting such a load whether it belonged to a so called rich man or a poor one; the owner always seemed poverty-stricken. Indeed, the more you have of such things the poorer you are. Each load looks as if it contained the contents of a dozen shanties; and if one shanty is poor, this is a dozen times as poor. Pray, for what do we *move* ever but to get rid of our furniture, our *exuviæ*;[9] at last to go from this world to another newly furnished, and leave this to be burned? It is the same as if all these traps were buckled to a man's belt, and he could not move over the rough country where our lines are cast without dragging them,—dragging his trap. He was a lucky fox that left his tail in the trap. The muskrat will gnaw his third leg off to be free. No wonder man has lost his elasticity. How often he is at a dead set! "Sir, if I may be so bold, what do you mean by a dead set?" If you are a seer, whenever you meet a man you will see all that he owns, ay, and much that he pretends to disown, behind him, even to his kitchen furniture and all the trumpery which he saves and will not burn, and he will appear to be harnessed to it and making what headway he can. I think that the man is at a dead set who has got through a knot hole or gateway where his sledge load of furniture cannot follow him. I cannot but feel compassion when I hear

8. A widow's legal share of an inheritance was one-third.
9. Things cast off, especially skins or shells, whether recent or fossil.

some trig, compact-looking man, seemingly free, all girded and ready, speak of his "furniture," as whether it is insured or not. "But what shall I do with my furniture?" My gay butterfly is entangled in a spider's web then. Even those who seem for a long while not to have any, if you inquire more narrowly you will find have some stored in somebody's barn. I look upon England to-day as an old gentleman who is travelling with a great deal of baggage, trumpery which has accumulated from long housekeeping, which he has not the courage to burn; great trunk, little trunk, bandbox and bundle. Throw away the first three at least. It would surpass the powers of a well man nowadays to take up his bed and walk,[1] and I should certainly advise a sick one to lay down his bed and run. When I have met an immigrant tottering under a bundle which contained his all—looking like an enormous wen which had grown out of the nape of his neck—I have pitied him, not because that was his all, but because he had all *that* to carry. If I have got to drag my trap, I will take care that it be a light one and do not nip me in a vital part. But perchance it would be wisest never to put one's paw into it.

I would observe, by the way, that it costs me nothing for curtains, for I have no gazers to shut out but the sun and moon, and I am willing that they should look in. The moon will not sour milk nor taint meat of mine, nor will the sun injure my furniture or fade my carpet, and if he is sometimes too warm a friend, I find it still better economy to retreat behind some curtain which nature has provided, than to add a single item to the details of housekeeping. A lady once offered me a mat, but as I had no room to spare within the house, nor time to spare within or without to shake it, I declined it, preferring to wipe my feet on the sod before my door. It is best to avoid the beginnings of evil.

Not long since I was present at the auction of a deacon's effects, for his life had not been ineffectual:—

> "The evil that men do lives after them."[2]

As usual, a great proportion was trumpery which had begun to accumulate in his father's day. Among the rest was a dried tapeworm. And now, after lying half a century in his garret and other dust holes, these things were not burned; instead of a *bonfire*, or purifying destruction of them, there was an *auction*, or increasing of them. The neighbors eagerly collected to view them, bought them all, and carefully transported them to their garrets and dust holes, to lie there till their estates are settled, when they will start again. When a man dies he kicks the dust.

---

1. Allusion to Jesus's words to a sick man in John 5:8: "Arise, take up thy bed, and walk."
2. From Antony's speech after the death of Caesar in Shakespeare's *Julius Caesar* 3.3.

The customs of some savage nations might, perchance, be profitably imitated by us, for they at least go through the semblance of casting their slough annually; they have the idea of the thing, whether they have the reality or not. Would it not be well if we were to celebrate such a "busk," or "feast of first fruits," as Bartram describes to have been the custom of the Mucclasse Indians? "When a town celebrates the busk," says he, "having previously provided themselves with new clothes, new pots, pans, and other household utensils and furniture, they collect all their worn out clothes and other despicable things, sweep and cleanse their houses, squares, and the whole town, of their filth, which with all the remaining grain and other old provisions they cast together into one common heap, and consume it with fire. After having taken medicine, and fasted for three days, all the fire in the town is extinguished. During this fast they abstain from the gratification of every appetite and passion whatever. A general amnesty is proclaimed; all malefactors may return to their town.—"

"On the fourth morning, the high priest, by rubbing dry wood together, produces new fire in the public square, from whence every habitation in the town is supplied with the new and pure flame."

They then feast on the new corn and fruits and dance and sing for three days, "and the four following days they receive visits and rejoice with their friends from neighboring towns who have in like manner purified and prepared themselves."[3]

The Mexicans also practised a similar purification at the end of every fifty-two years, in the belief that it was time for the world to come to an end.

I have scarcely heard of a truer sacrament, that is, as the dictionary defines it, "outward and visible sign of an inward and spiritual grace," than this, and I have no doubt that they were originally inspired directly from Heaven to do thus, though they have no biblical record of the revelation.

For more than five years I maintained myself thus solely by the labor of my hands, and I found, that by working about six weeks in a year, I could meet all the expenses of living. The whole of my winters, as well as most of my summers, I had free and clear for study. I have thoroughly tried school-keeping, and found that my expenses were in proportion, or rather out of proportion, to my income, for I was obliged to dress and train, not to say think and believe, accordingly, and I lost my time into the bargain. As I did not teach for the good of my fellow-men, but simply for a livelihood, this was a fail-

3. William Bartram (1739–1823), early American naturalist; from his *Travels through North and South Carolina . . .* (1791).

ure. I have tried trade; but I found that it would take ten years to get under way in that, and that then I should probably be on my way to the devil. I was actually afraid that I might by that time be doing what is called a good business. When formerly I was looking about to see what I could do for a living, some sad experience in conforming to the wishes of friends being fresh in my mind to tax my ingenuity, I thought often and seriously of picking huckleberries; that surely I could do, and its small profits might suffice,—for my greatest skill has been to want but little,—so little capital it required, so little distraction from my wonted moods, I foolishly thought. While my acquaintances went unhesitatingly into trade or the professions, I contemplated this occupation as most like theirs; ranging the hills all summer to pick the berries which came in my way, and thereafter carelessly dispose of them; so, to keep the flocks of Admetus.[4] I also dreamed that I might gather the wild herbs, or carry evergreens to such villagers as loved to be reminded of the woods, even to the city, by hay-cart loads. But I have since learned that trade curses every thing it handles; and though you trade in messages from heaven, the whole curse of trade attaches to the business.

As I preferred some things to others, and especially valued my freedom, as I could fare hard and yet succeed well, I did not wish to spend my time in earning rich carpets or other fine furniture, or delicate cookery, or a house in the Grecian or the Gothic[5] style just yet. If there are any to whom it is no interruption to acquire these things, and who know how to use them when acquired, I relinquish to them the pursuit. Some are "industrious," and appear to love labor for its own sake, or perhaps because it keeps them out of worse mischief; to such I have at present nothing to say. Those who would not know what to do with more leisure than they now enjoy, I might advise to work twice as hard as they do,—work till they pay for themselves, and get their free papers. For myself I found that the occupation of a day-laborer was the most independent of any, especially as it required only thirty or forty days in a year to support one. The laborer's day ends with the going down of the sun, and he is then free to devote himself to his chosen pursuit, independent of his labor; but his employer, who speculates from month to month, has no respite from one end of the year to the other.

In short, I am convinced, both by faith and experience, that to maintain one's self on this earth is not a hardship but a pastime, if we will live simply and wisely; as the pursuits of the simpler nations

---

4. In Greek mythology, Apollo, the god of music, poetry, and prophecy, was forced to tend the flocks of Admetus, king of Pherae, when the god was banished from heaven for nine years.
5. Architectural styles popular in the nineteenth century—revivals of classical Greek and medieval European architecture, respectively.

are still the sports of the more artificial. It is not necessary that a man should earn his living by the sweat of his brow, unless he sweats easier than I do.

One young man of my acquaintance, who has inherited some acres, told me that he thought he should live as I did, *if he had the means*. I would not have any one adopt *my* mode of living on any account; for, beside that before he has fairly learned it I may have found out another for myself, I desire that there may be as many different persons in the world as possible; but I would have each one be very careful to find out and pursue *his own* way, and not his father's or his mother's or his neighbor's instead. The youth may build or plant or sail, only let him not be hindered from doing that which he tells me he would like to do. It is by a mathematical point only that we are wise, as the sailor or the fugitive slave keeps the polestar in his eye; but that is sufficient guidance for all our life. We may not arrive at our port within a calculable period, but we would preserve the true course.

Undoubtedly, in this case, what is true for one is truer still for a thousand, as a large house is not proportionally more expensive than a small one, since one roof may cover, one cellar underlie, and one wall separate several apartments. But for my part, I preferred the solitary dwelling. Moreover, it will commonly be cheaper to build the whole yourself than to convince another of the advantage of the common wall; and when you have done this, the common partition, to be much cheaper, must be a thin one, and that other may prove a bad neighbor, and also not keep his side in repair. The only cooperation which is commonly possible is exceedingly partial and superficial; and what little true coöperration there is, is as if it were not, being a harmony inaudible to men. If a man has faith he will coöperate with equal faith every where; if he has not faith, he will continue to live like the rest of the world, whatever company he is joined to. To coöperate, in the highest as well as the lowest sense, means *to get our living together*. I heard it proposed lately that two young men should travel together over the world, the one without money, earning his means as he went, before the mast and behind the plough, the other carrying a bill of exchange in his pocket. It was easy to see that they could not long be companions or coöperate, since one would not *operate* at all. They would part at the first interesting crisis in their adventures. Above all, as I have implied, the man who goes alone can start to-day; but he who travels with another must wait till that other is ready, and it may be a long time before they get off.

But all this is very selfish, I have heard some of my townsmen say. I confess that I have hitherto indulged very little in philanthropic enterprises. I have made some sacrifices to a sense of duty, and among others have sacrificed this pleasure also. There are those who have used all their arts to persuade me to undertake the support of some poor family in the town; and if I had nothing to do,—for the devil finds employment for the idle,—I might try my hand at some such pastime as that. However, when I have thought to indulge myself in this respect, and lay their Heaven under an obligation by maintaining certain poor persons in all respects as comfortably as I maintain myself, and have even ventured so far as to make them the offer, they have one and all unhesitatingly preferred to remain poor. While my townsmen and women are devoted in so many ways to the good of their fellows, I trust that one at least may be spared to other and less humane pursuits. You must have a genius for charity as well as for any thing else. As for Doing-good, that is one of the professions which are full. Moreover, I have tried it fairly, and, strange as it may seem, am satisfied that it does not agree with my constitution. Probably I should not consciously and deliberately forsake my particular calling to do the good which society demands of me, to save the universe from annihilation; and I believe that a like but infinitely greater steadfastness elsewhere is all that now preserves it. But I would not stand between any man and his genius; and to him who does this work, which I decline, with his whole heart and soul and life, I would say, Persevere, even if the world call it doing evil, as it is most likely they will.

I am far from supposing that my case is a peculiar one; no doubt many of my readers would make a similar defence. At doing something,—I will not engage that my neighbors shall pronounce it good,—I do not hesitate to say that I should be a capital fellow to hire; but what that is, it is for my employer to find out. What *good* I do, in the common sense of that word, must be aside from my main path, and for the most part wholly unintended. Men say, practically, Begin where you are and such as you are, without aiming mainly to become of more worth, and with kindness aforethought go about doing good. If I were to preach at all in this strain, I should say rather, Set about being good. As if the sun should stop when he had kindled his fires up to the splendor of a moon or a star of the sixth magnitude, and go about like a Robin Goodfellow,[6] peeping in at every cottage window, inspiring lunatics, and tainting meats, and making darkness visible, instead of steadily increasing his genial heat and beneficence till he is of such brightness that no mortal can look him in the face, and then, and in the mean while too, going about the world in his own orbit, doing it good, or rather, as a truer philosophy has discovered, the world going about him

6. In English folklore, a mischievous elf; also known as Puck.

getting good. When Phaeton,[7] wishing to prove his heavenly birth by his beneficence, had the sun's chariot but one day, and drove out of the beaten track, he burned several blocks of houses in the lower streets of heaven, and scorched the surface of the earth, and dried up every spring, and made the great desert of Sahara, till at length Jupiter hurled him headlong to the earth with a thunderbolt, and the sun, through grief at his death, did not shine for a year.[8]

There is no odor so bad as that which arises from goodness tainted. It is human, it is divine, carrion. If I knew for a certainty that a man was coming to my house with the conscious design of doing me good, I should run for my life, as from that dry and parching wind of the African deserts called the simoom, which fills the mouth and nose and ears and eyes with dust till you are suffocated, for fear that I should get some of his good done to me,—some of its virus mingled with my blood. No,—in this case I would rather suffer evil the natural way. A man is not a good *man* to me because he will feed me if I should be starving, or warm me if I should be freezing, or pull me out of a ditch if I should ever fall into one. I can find you a Newfoundland dog that will do as much. Philanthropy is not love for one's fellow-man in the broadest sense. Howard[9] was no doubt an exceedingly kind and worthy man in his way, and has his reward; but, comparatively speaking, what are a hundred Howards to *us*, if their philanthropy do not help *us* in our best estate, when we are most worthy to be helped? I never heard of a philanthropic meeting in which it was sincerely proposed to do any good to me, or the like of me.

The Jesuits[1] were quite balked by those Indians who, being burned at the stake, suggested new modes of torture to their tormentors. Being superior to physical suffering, it sometimes chanced that they were superior to any consolation which the missionaries could offer; and the law to do as you would be done by fell with less persuasiveness on the ears of those, who, for their part, did not care how they were done by, who loved their enemies after a new fashion, and came very near freely forgiving them all they did.

Be sure that you give the poor the aid they most need, though it be your example which leaves them far behind. If you give money, spend yourself with it, and do not merely abandon it to them. We make curious mistakes sometimes. Often the poor man is not so cold and hungry as he is dirty and ragged and gross. It is partly his

---

7. In Greek mythology, the son of Helios (the sun).
8. From Ovid's *Metamorphoses* 2.1—400; Jupiter is the chief god in Roman mythology.
9. John Howard (1726?–1790), English prison reformer.
1. A religious order of the Roman Catholic faith, which attempted to convert the Indians to Christianity.

taste, and not merely his misfortune. If you give him money, he will perhaps buy more rags with it. I was wont to pity the clumsy Irish laborers who cut ice on the pond, in such mean and ragged clothes, while I shivered in my more tidy and somewhat more fashionable garments, till, one bitter cold day, one who had slipped into the water came to my house to warm him, and I saw him strip off three pairs of pants and two pairs of stockings ere he got down to the skin, though they were dirty and ragged enough, it is true, and that he could afford to refuse the *extra* garments which I offered him, he had so many *intra* ones. This ducking was the very thing he needed. Then I began to pity myself, and I saw that it would be a greater charity to bestow on me a flannel shirt than a whole slop-shop on him. There are a thousand hacking at the branches of evil to one who is striking at the root, and it may be that he who bestows the largest amount of time and money on the needy is doing the most by his mode of life to produce that misery which he strives in vain to relieve. It is the pious slave-breeder devoting the proceeds of every tenth slave to buy a Sunday's liberty for the rest. Some show their kindness to the poor by employing them in their kitchens. Would they not be kinder if they employed themselves there? You boast of spending a tenth part of your income in charity; may be you should spend the nine tenths so, and done with it. Society recovers only a tenth part of the property then. Is this owing to the generosity of him in whose possession it is found, or to the remissness of the officers of justice?

Philanthropy is almost the only virtue which is sufficiently appreciated by mankind. Nay, it is greatly overrated; and it is our selfishness which overrates it. A robust poor man, one sunny day here in Concord, praised a fellow-townsman to me, because, as he said, he was kind to the poor; meaning himself. The kind uncles and aunts of the race are more esteemed than its true spiritual fathers and mothers. I once heard a reverend lecturer on England, a man of learning and intelligence, after enumerating her scientific, literary, and political worthies, Shakspeare, Bacon, Cromwell, Milton, Newton, and others, speak next of her Christian heroes, whom, as if his profession required it of him, he elevated to a place far above all the rest, as the greatest of the great. They were Penn, Howard, and Mrs. Fry.[2] Every one must feel the falsehood and cant of this. The last were not England's best men and women; only, perhaps, her best philanthropists.

I would not subtract any thing from the praise that is due to phi-

---

2. William Penn (1644–1718), humanitarian and founder of Pennsylvania; John Howard (1726?–1790), English prison reformer; Elizabeth Fry (1780–1845), English prison reformer.

lanthropy, but merely demand justice for all who by their lives and works are a blessing to mankind. I do not value chiefly a man's uprightness and benevolence, which are, as it were, his stem and leaves. Those plants of whose greenness withered we make herb tea for the sick, serve but a humble use, and are most employed by quacks. I want the flower and fruit of a man; that some fragrance be wafted over from him to me, and some ripeness flavor our intercourse. His goodness must not be a partial and transitory act, but a constant superfluity, which costs him nothing and of which he is unconscious. This is a charity that hides a multitude of sins. The philanthropist too often surrounds mankind with the remembrance of his own cast-off griefs as an atmosphere, and calls it sympathy. We should impart our courage, and not our despair, our health and ease, and not our disease, and take care that this does not spread by contagion. From what southern plains comes up the voice of wailing? Under what latitudes reside the heathen to whom we would send light? Who is that intemperate and brutal man whom we would redeem? If any thing ail a man, so that he does not perform his functions, if he have a pain in his bowels even,—for that is the seat of sympathy,—he forthwith sets about reforming—the world. Being a microcosm himself, he discovers, and it is a true discovery, and he is the man to make it,—that the world has been eating green apples; to his eyes, in fact, the globe itself is a great green apple, which there is danger awful to think of that the children of men will nibble before it is ripe; and straightway his drastic philanthropy seeks out the Esquimaux and the Patagonian,[3] and embraces the populous Indian and Chinese villages; and thus, by a few years of philanthropic activity, the powers in the mean while using him for their own ends, no doubt, he cures himself of his dyspepsia, the globe acquires a faint blush on one or both of its cheeks, as if it were beginning to be ripe, and life loses its crudity and is once more sweet and wholesome to live. I never dreamed of any enormity greater than I have committed. I never knew, and never shall know, a worse man than myself.

I believe that what so saddens the reformer is not his sympathy with his fellows in distress, but, though he be the holiest son of God, is his private ail. Let this be righted, let the spring come to him, the morning rise over his couch, and he will forsake his generous companions without apology. My excuse for not lecturing against the use of tobacco is, that I never chewed it; that is a penalty which reformed tobacco-chewers have to pay; though there are things enough I have chewed, which I could lecture against. If you should ever be betrayed into any of these philanthropies, do

3. A native of the southernmost part of South America.

not let your left hand know what your right hand does, for it is not worth knowing. Rescue the drowning and tie your shoe-strings. Take your time, and set about some free labor.

Our manners have been corrupted by communication with the saints. Our hymn-books resound with a melodious cursing of God and enduring him forever. One would say that even the prophets and redeemers had rather consoled the fears than confirmed the hopes of man. There is nowhere recorded a simple and irrepressible satisfaction with the gift of life, any memorable praise of God. All health and success does me good, however far off and withdrawn it may appear; all disease and failure helps to make me sad and does me evil, however much sympathy it may have with me or I with it. If, then, we would indeed restore mankind by truly Indian, botanic, magnetic, or natural means, let us first be as simple and well as Nature ourselves, dispel the clouds which hang over our own brows, and take up a little life into our pores. Do not stay to be an overseer of the poor, but endeavor to become one of the worthies of the world.

I read in the Gulistan, or Flower Garden, of Sheik Sadi of Shiraz, that "They asked a wise man, saying; Of the many celebrated trees which the Most High God has created lofty and umbrageous, they call none azad, or free, excepting the cypress, which bears no fruit; what mystery is there in this? He replied; Each has its appropriate produce, and appointed season, during the continuance of which it is fresh and blooming, and during their absence dry and withered; to neither of which states is the cypress exposed, being always flourishing; and of this nature are the azads, or religious independents.—Fix not thy heart on that which is transitory; for the Dijlah, or Tigris, will continue to flow through Bagdad after the race of caliphs[4] is extinct: if thy hand has plenty, be liberal as the date tree; but if it affords nothing to give away, be an azad, or free man, like the cypress."[5]

COMPLEMENTAL VERSES[6]

THE PRETENSIONS OF POVERTY.

"Thou dost presume too much, poor needy wretch,
    To claim a station in the firmament,
Because thy humble cottage, or thy tub,

4. Bagdad (or Baghdad) is the capital of Iraq, located on the Dijlah (or Tigris) River; a caliph is a Moslem ruler.
5. Muslih-ud-Din (Saadi) (1184?–1291), Persian poet; from his *The Gulistan, or Rose Garden*.
6. By Thomas Carew (1595?–1645), from *Coelum Britannicum*; Thoreau added the title and modernized the spelling.

Nurses some lazy or pedantic virtue
In the cheap sunshine or by shady springs,
With roots and pot-herbs; where thy right hand,
Tearing those humane passions from the mind,
Upon whose stocks fair blooming virtues flourish,
Degradeth nature, and benumbeth sense,
And, Gorgon-like, turns active men to stone.
We not require the dull society
Of your necessitated temperance,
Or that unnatural stupidity
That knows nor joy nor sorrow; nor your forc'd
Falsely exalted passive fortitude
Above the active. This low abject brood,
That fix their seats in mediocrity,
Become your servile minds; but we advance
Such virtues only as admit excess,
Brave, bounteous acts, regal magnificence,
All-seeing prudence, magnanimity
That knows no bound, and that heroic virtue
For which antiquity hath left no name,
But patterns only, such as Hercules,
Achilles, Theseus. Back to thy loath'd cell;
And when thou seest the new enlightened sphere,
Study to know but what those worthies were."

T. Carew.

Where I Lived, and What I Lived for

At a certain season of our life we are accustomed to consider
every spot as the possible site of a house. I have thus surveyed the
country on every side within a dozen miles of where I live. In imagination I have bought all the farms in succession, for all were to be
bought, and I knew their price. I walked over each farmer's premises, tasted his wild apples, discoursed on husbandry with him, took
his farm at his price, at any price, mortgaging it to him in my mind;
even put a higher price on it,—took every thing but a deed of it,—
took his word for his deed, for I dearly love to talk,—cultivated it,
and him too to some extent, I trust, and withdrew when I had enjoyed it long enough, leaving him to carry it on. This experience entitled me to be regarded as a sort of real-estate broker by my
friends. Wherever I sat, there I might live, and the landscape radiated from me accordingly. What is a house but a *sedes*, a seat?—
better if a country seat. I discovered many a site for a house not
likely to be soon improved, which some might have thought too far
from the village, but to my eyes the village was too far from it. Well,

there I might live, I said; and there I did live, for an hour, a summer and a winter life; saw how I could let the years run off, buffet the winter through, and see the spring come in. The future inhabitants of this region, wherever they may place their houses, may be sure that they have been anticipated. An afternoon sufficed to lay out the land into orchard, woodlot, and pasture, and to decide what fine oaks or pines should be left to stand before the door, and whence each blasted tree could be seen to the best advantage; and then I let it lie, fallow perchance, for a man is rich in proportion to the number of things which he can afford to let alone.

My imagination carried me so far that I even had the refusal of several farms,—the refusal was all I wanted,—but I never got my fingers burned by actual possession. The nearest that I came to actual possession was when I bought the Hollowell place, and had begun to sort my seeds, and collected materials with which to make a wheelbarrow to carry it on or off with; but before the owner gave me a deed of it, his wife—every man has such a wife—changed her mind and wished to keep it, and he offered me ten dollars to release him. Now, to speak the truth, I had but ten cents in the world, and it surpassed my arithmetic to tell, if I was that man who had ten cents, or who had a farm, or ten dollars, or all together. However, I let him keep the ten dollars and the farm too, for I had carried it far enough; or rather, to be generous, I sold him the farm for just what I gave for it, and, as he was not a rich man, made him a present of ten dollars, and still had my ten cents, and seeds, and materials for a wheelbarrow left. I found thus that I had been a rich man without any damage to my poverty. But I retained the landscape, and I have since annually carried off what it yielded without a wheelbarrow. With respect to landscapes,—

"I am monarch of all I *survey*,
    My right there is none to dispute."[1]

I have frequently seen a poet withdraw, having enjoyed the most valuable part of a farm, while the crusty farmer supposed that he had got a few wild apples only. Why, the owner does not know it for many years when a poet has put his farm in rhyme, the most admirable kind of invisible fence, has fairly impounded it, milked it, skimmed it, and got all the cream, and left the farmer only the skimmed milk.

The real attractions of the Hollowell farm, to me, were; its complete retirement, being about two miles from the village, half a mile from the nearest neighbor, and separated from the highway by a

---

1. William Cowper (1731–1800), from his "Verses Supposed to Be Written by Alexander Selkirk"; Selkirk was Daniel Defoe's model for Robinson Crusoe. Thoreau, a surveyor, italicized the final word of the first line to emphasize the pun.

broad field; its bounding on the river, which the owner said protected it by its fogs from frosts in the spring, though that was nothing to me; the gray color and ruinous state of the house and barn,
and the dilapidated fences, which put such an interval between me
and the last occupant; the hollow and lichen-covered apple trees,
gnawed by rabbits, showing what kind of neighbors I should have;
but above all, the recollection I had of it from my earliest voyages
up the river, when the house was concealed behind a dense grove
of red maples, through which I heard the house-dog bark. I was in
haste to buy it, before the proprietor finished getting out some
rocks, cutting down the hollow apple trees, and grubbing up some
young birches which had sprung up in the pasture, or, in short, had
made any more of his improvements. To enjoy these advantages I
was ready to carry it on; like Atlas,[2] to take the world on my shoulders,—I never heard what compensation he received for that,—and
do all those things which had no other motive or excuse but that I
might pay for it and be unmolested in my possession of it; for I
knew all the while that it would yield the most abundant crop of
the kind I wanted if I could only afford to let it alone. But it turned
out as I have said.

All that I could say, then, with respect to farming on a large
scale, (I have always cultivated a garden,) was, that I had had my
seeds ready. Many think that seeds improve with age. I have no
doubt that time discriminates between the good and the bad; and
when at last I shall plant, I shall be less likely to be disappointed.
But I would say to my fellows, once for all, As long as possible live
free and uncommitted. It makes but little difference whether you
are committed to a farm or the county jail.

Old Cato, whose "De Re Rusticâ" is my "Cultivator,"[3] says, and
the only translation I have seen makes sheer nonsense of the passage, "When you think of getting a farm, turn it thus in your mind,
not to buy greedily; nor spare your pains to look at it, and do not
think it enough to go round it once. The oftener you go there the
more it will please you, if it is good." I think I shall not buy greedily, but go round and round it as long as I live, and be buried in it
first, that it may please me the more at last.

The present was my next experiment of this kind, which I purpose to describe more at length; for convenience, putting the experience of two years into one. As I have said, I do not propose to
write an ode to dejection, but to brag as lustily as chanticleer in the

---

2. According to Greek mythology, Atlas supported the sky on his shoulders as punishment
   for having taken part in the revolt of the Titans against Zeus.
3. See n. 6, p. 46; "Cultivator": common name for nineteenth-century agricultural
   journal.

morning, standing on his roost, if only to wake my neighbors up.

When first I took up my abode in the woods, that is, began to spend my nights as well as days there, which, by accident, was on Independence day, or the fourth of July, 1845, my house was not finished for winter, but was merely a defence against the rain, without plastering or chimney, the walls being of rough weatherstained boards, with wide chinks, which made it cool at night. The upright white hewn studs and freshly planed door and window casings gave it a clean and airy look, especially in the morning, when its timbers were saturated with dew, so that I fancied that by noon some sweet gum would exude from them. To my imagination it retained throughout the day more or less of this auroral character, reminding me of a certain house on a mountain which I had visited the year before. This was an airy and unplastered cabin, fit to entertain a travelling god, and where a goddess might trail her garments. The winds which passed over my dwelling were such as sweep over the ridges of mountains, bearing the broken strains, or celestial parts only, of terrestrial music. The morning wind forever blows, the poem of creation is uninterrupted; but few are the ears that hear it. Olympus[4] is but the outside of the earth every where.

The only house I had been the owner of before, if I except a boat, was a tent, which I used occasionally when making excursions in the summer, and this is still rolled up in my garret; but the boat, after passing from hand to hand, has gone down the stream of time. With this more substantial shelter about me, I had made some progress toward settling in the world. This frame, so slightly clad, was a sort of crystallization around me, and reacted on the builder. It was suggestive somewhat as a picture in outlines. I did not need to go out doors to take the air, for the atmosphere within had lost none of its freshness. It was not so much within doors as behind a door where I sat, even in the rainiest weather. The Harivansa[5] says, "An abode without birds is like a meat without seasoning." Such was not my abode, for I found myself suddenly neighbor to the birds; not by having imprisoned one, but having caged myself near them. I was not only nearer to some of those which commonly frequent the garden and the orchard, but to those wilder and more thrilling songsters of the forest which never, or rarely, serenade a villager,—the wood-thrush, the veery, the scarlet tanager, the field-sparrow, the whippoorwill, and many others.

I was seated by the shore of a small pond, about a mile and a half south of the village of Concord and somewhat higher than it, in the midst of an extensive wood between that town and Lincoln, and

4. Mount Olympus; in Greek mythology, the residence of the gods.
5. Hindu epic poem concerning the god Krishna, written about the fifth century C.E.

about two miles south of that our only field known to fame, Concord Battle Ground;[6] but I was so low in the woods that the opposite
shore, half a mile off, like the rest, covered with wood, was my most
distant horizon. For the first week, whenever I looked out on the
pond it impressed me like a tarn high up on the side of a mountain,
its bottom far above the surface of other lakes, and, as the sun
arose, I saw it throwing off its nightly clothing of mist, and here and
there, by degrees, its soft ripples or its smooth reflecting surface was
revealed, while the mists, like ghosts, were stealthily withdrawing in
every direction into the woods, as at the breaking up of some nocturnal conventicle. The very dew seemed to hang upon the trees
later into the day than usual, as on the sides of mountains.

This small lake was of most value as a neighbor in the intervals of
a gentle rain storm in August, when, both air and water being perfectly still, but the sky overcast, mid-afternoon had all the serenity
of evening, and the wood-thrush sang around, and was heard from
shore to shore. A lake like this is never smoother than at such a
time; and the clear portion of the air above it being shallow and
darkened by clouds, the water, full of light and reflections, becomes
a lower heaven itself so much the more important. From a hill top
near by, where the wood had been recently cut off, there was a
pleasing vista southward across the pond, through a wide indenta-
tion in the hills which form the shore there, where their opposite
sides sloping toward each other suggested a stream flowing out in
that direction through a wooded valley, but stream there was none.
That way I looked between and over the near green hills to some
distant and higher ones in the horizon, tinged with blue. Indeed, by
standing on tiptoe I could catch a glimpse of some of the peaks of
the still bluer and more distant mountain ranges in the north-west,
those true-blue coins from heaven's own mint, and also of some
portion of the village. But in other directions, even from this point,
I could not see over or beyond the woods which surrounded me. It
is well to have some water in your neighborhood, to give buoyancy
to and float the earth. One value even of the smallest well is, that
when you look into it you see that earth is not continent but insu-
lar. This is as important as that it keeps butter cool. When I looked
across the pond from this peak toward the Sudbury meadows,
which in time of flood I distinguished elevated perhaps by a mirage
in their seething valley, like a coin in a basin, all the earth beyond
the pond appeared like a thin crust insulated and floated even by
this small sheet of intervening water, and I was reminded that this
on which I dwelt was but *dry land*.

Though the view from my door was still more contracted, I did

6. Site of the opening battle of the American Revolution, April 19, 1775.

not feel crowded or confined in the least. There was pasture enough for my imagination. The low shrub-oak plateau to which the opposite shore arose, stretched away toward the prairies of the West and the steppes of Tartary, affording ample room for all the roving families of men. "There are none happy in the world but beings who enjoy freely a vast horizon,"—said Damodara,[7] when his herds required new and larger pastures.

Both place and time were changed, and I dwelt nearer to those parts of the universe and to those eras in history which had most attracted me. Where I lived was as far off as many a region viewed nightly by astronomers. We are wont to imagine rare and delectable places in some remote and more celestial corner of the system, behind the constellation of Cassiopeia's Chair, far from noise and disturbance. I discovered that my house actually had its site in such a withdrawn, but forever new and unprofaned, part of the universe. If it were worth the while to settle in those parts near to the Pleiades or the Hyades, to Aldebaran or Altair,[8] then I was really there, or at an equal remoteness from the life which I had left behind, dwindled and twinkling with as fine a ray to my nearest neighbor, and to be seen only in moonless nights by him. Such was that part of creation where I had squatted;—

> "There was a shepherd that did live,
>   And held his thoughts as high
> As were the mounts whereon his flocks
>   Did hourly feed him by."[9]

What should we think of the shepherd's life if his flocks always wandered to higher pastures than his thoughts?

Every morning was a cheerful invitation to make my life of equal simplicity, and I may say innocence, with Nature herself. I have been as sincere a worshipper of Aurora as the Greeks. I got up early and bathed in the pond; that was a religious exercise, and one of the best things which I did. They say that characters were engraven on the bathing tub of king Tching-thang to this effect: "Renew thyself completely each day; do it again, and again, and forever again."[1] I can understand that. Morning brings back the heroic ages. I was as much affected by the faint hum of a mosquito making its invisible and unimaginable tour through my apartment at earliest dawn, when I was sitting with door and windows open, as I could be by any trumpet that ever sang of fame. It was Homer's requiem; itself an Iliad and Odyssey in the air, singing its own wrath

---

7. Quoted from the *Harivansa*. Damodara is another name for Krishna.
8. Like Cassiopeia's Chair, Pleiades and Aldebaran are constellations of stars.
9. An anonymous Jacobean poem set to music and published in *The Muses Garden* (1610).
1. Confucius, *The Great Learning*.

and wanderings. There was something cosmical about it; a standing advertisement, till forbidden, of the everlasting vigor and fertility of the world. The morning, which is the most memorable season of the day, is the awakening hour. Then there is least somnolence in us; and for an hour, at least, some part of us awakes which slumbers all the rest of the day and night. Little is to be expected of that day, if it can be called a day, to which we are not awakened by our Genius, but by the mechanical nudgings of some servitor, are not awakened by our own newly-acquired force and aspirations from within, accompanied by the undulations of celestial music, instead of factory bells, and a fragrance filling the air—to a higher life than we fell asleep from; and thus the darkness bear its fruit, and prove itself to be good, no less than the light. That man who does not believe that each day contains an earlier, more sacred, and auroral hour than he has yet profaned, has despaired of life, and is pursuing a descending and darkening way. After a partial cessation of his sensuous life, the soul of man, or its organs rather, are reinvigorated each day, and his Genius tries again what noble life it can make. All memorable events, I should say, transpire in morning time and in a morning atmosphere. The Vedas[2] say, "All intelligences awake with the morning." Poetry and art, and the fairest and most memorable of the actions of men, date from such an hour. All poets and heroes, like Memnon, are the children of Aurora, and emit their music at sunrise. To him whose elastic and vigorous thought keeps pace with the sun, the day is a perpetual morning. It matters not what the clocks say or the attitudes and labors of men. Morning is when I am awake and there is a dawn in me. Moral reform is the effort to throw off sleep. Why is it that men give so poor an account of their day if they have not been slumbering? They are not such poor calculators. If they had not been overcome with drowsiness they would have performed something. The millions are awake enough for physical labor; but only one in a million is awake enough for effective intellectual exertion, only one in a hundred millions to a poetic or divine life. To be awake is to be alive. I have never yet met a man who was quite awake. How could I have looked him in the face?

We must learn to reawaken and keep ourselves awake, not by mechanical aids, but by an infinite expectation of the dawn, which does not forsake us in our soundest sleep. I know of no more encouraging fact than the unquestionable ability of man to elevate his life by a conscious endeavor. It is something to be able to paint a particular picture, or to carve a statue, and so to make a few objects

2. Ancient Hindu scriptures.

beautiful; but it is far more glorious to carve and paint the very atmosphere and medium through which we look, which morally we can do. To affect the quality of the day, that is the highest of arts. Every man is tasked to make his life, even in its details, worthy of the contemplation of his most elevated and critical hour. If we refused, or rather used up, such paltry information as we get, the oracles would distinctly inform us how this might be done.

I went to the woods because I wished to live deliberately, to front only the essential facts of life, and see if I could not learn what it had to teach, and not, when I came to die, discover that I had not lived. I did not wish to live what was not life, living is so dear; nor did I wish to practise resignation, unless it was quite necessary. I wanted to live deep and suck out all the marrow of life, to live so sturdily and Spartan-like[3] as to put to rout all that was not life, to cut a broad swath and shave close, to drive life into a corner, and reduce it to its lowest terms, and, if it proved to be mean, why then to get the whole and genuine meanness of it, and publish its meanness to the world; or if it were sublime, to know it by experience, and be able to give a true account of it in my next excursion. For most men, it appears to me, are in a strange uncertainty about it, whether it is of the devil or of God, and have *somewhat hastily* concluded that it is the chief end of man here to "glorify God and enjoy him forever."[4]

Still we live meanly, like ants; though the fable tells us that we were long ago changed into men; like pygmies we fight with cranes;[5] it is error upon error, and clout upon clout, and our best virtue has for its occasion a superfluous and evitable wretchedness. Our life is frittered away by detail. An honest man has hardly need to count more than his ten fingers, or in extreme cases he may add his ten toes, and lump the rest. Simplicity, simplicity, simplicity! I say, let your affairs be as two or three, and not a hundred or a thousand; instead of a million count half a dozen, and keep your accounts on your thumb nail. In the midst of this chopping sea of civilized life, such are the clouds and storms and quicksands and thousand-and-one items to be allowed for, that a man has to live, if he would not founder and go to the bottom and not make his port at all, by dead reckoning, and he must be a great calculator indeed who succeeds. Simplify, simplify. Instead of three meals a day, if it be necessary eat but one; instead of a hundred dishes, five; and

3. The Spartans of ancient Greece were courageous warriors who lived hardy and rigorous lives.
4. Quoted from the Shorter Catechism; see n. 2, p. 9.
5. According to Greek mythology, Zeus turned ants into men. The Trojans are compared to cranes fighting pygmies in the *Iliad*, Book 3.

reduce other things in proportion. Our life is like a German Confederacy,[6] made up of petty states, with its boundary forever fluctuating, so that even a German cannot tell you how it is bounded at any moment. The nation itself, with all its so called internal improvements, which, by the way, are all external and superficial, is just such an unwieldy and overgrown establishment, cluttered with furniture and tripped up by its own traps, ruined by luxury and heedless expense, by want of calculation and a worthy aim, as the million households in the land; and the only cure for it as for them is in a rigid economy, a stern and more than Spartan simplicity of life and elevation of purpose. It lives too fast. Men think that it is essential that the *Nation* have commerce, and export ice, and talk through a telegraph, and ride thirty miles an hour, without a doubt, whether *they* do or not; but whether we should live like baboons or like men, is a little uncertain. If we do not get out sleepers,[7] and forge rails, and devote days and nights to the work, but go to tinkering upon our *lives* to improve *them*, who will build railroads? And if railroads are not built, how shall we get to heaven in season? But if we stay at home and mind our business, who will want railroads? We do not ride on the railroad; it rides upon us. Did you ever think what those sleepers are that underlie the railroad? Each one is a man, an Irishman, or a Yankee man. The rails are laid on them, and they are covered with sand, and the cars run smoothly over them. They are sound sleepers, I assure you. And every few years a new lot is laid down and run over; so that, if some have the pleasure of riding on a rail, others have the misfortune to be ridden upon. And when they run over a man that is walking in his sleep, a supernumerary sleeper in the wrong position, and wake him up, they suddenly stop the cars, and make a hue and cry about it, as if this were an exception. I am glad to know that it takes a gang of men for every five miles to keep the sleepers down and level in their beds as it is, for this is a sign that they may sometime get up again.

Why should we live with such hurry and waste of life? We are determined to be starved before we are hungry. Men say that a stitch in time saves nine, and so they take a thousand stitches to-day to save nine to-morrow. As for *work*, we haven't any of any consequence. We have the Saint Vitus' dance,[8] and cannot possibly keep our heads still. If I should only give a few pulls at the parish bell-

6. A loose collection of states from 1815 to 1866, Germany was unified later in the century under Prince Otto von Bismarck.
7. Wooden railroad ties.
8. Chorea, a nervous disease accompanied by involuntary movements, depression, and emotional instability.

rope, as for a fire, that is, without setting the bell, there is hardly a
man on his farm in the outskirts of Concord, notwithstanding that
press of engagements which was his excuse so many times this
morning, nor a boy, nor a woman, I might almost say, but would
forsake all and follow that sound, not mainly to save property from
the flames, but, if we will confess the truth, much more to see it
burn, since burn it must, and we, be it known, did not set it on
fire,—or to see it put out, and have a hand in it, if that is done as
handsomely; yes, even if it were the parish church itself. Hardly a
man takes a half hour's nap after dinner, but when he wakes he
holds up his head and asks, "What's the news?" as if the rest of
mankind had stood his sentinels. Some give directions to be waked
every half hour, doubtless for no other purpose; and then, to pay for
it, they tell what they have dreamed. After a night's sleep the news
is as indispensable as the breakfast. "Pray tell me any thing new
that has happened to a man any where on this globe,"—and he
reads it over his coffee and rolls, that a man has had his eyes
gouged out this morning on the Wachito River;[9] never dreaming the
while that he lives in the dark unfathomed mammoth cave of this
world, and has but the rudiment of an eye himself.

For my part, I could easily do without the post-office. I think that
there are very few important communications made through it. To
speak critically, I never received more than one or two letters in my
life—I wrote this some years ago—that were worth the postage.
The penny-post is, commonly, an institution through which you seriously offer a man that penny for his thoughts which is so often
safely offered in jest. And I am sure that I never read any memorable news in a newspaper. If we read of one man robbed, or murdered, or killed by accident, or one house burned, or one vessel
wrecked, or one steamboat blown up, or one cow run over on the
Western Railroad, or one mad dog killed, or one lot of grasshoppers
in the winter,—we never need read of another. One is enough. If
you are acquainted with the principle, what do you care for a myriad instances and applications? To a philosopher all *news*, as it is
called, is gossip, and they who edit and read it are old women over
their tea. Yet not a few are greedy after this gossip. There was such
a rush, as I hear, the other day at one of the offices to learn the foreign news by the last arrival, that several large squares of plate glass
belonging to the establishment were broken by the pressure,—news
which I seriously think a ready wit might write a twelvemonth or
twelve years beforehand with sufficient accuracy. As for Spain, for

9. Now called the Ouachita River; it begins in Arkansas and empties into the Red River in
Louisiana.

instance, if you know how to throw in Don Carlos and the Infanta, and Don Pedro and Seville and Granada,[1] from time to time in the right proportions,—they may have changed the names a little since I saw the papers,—and serve up a bull-fight when other entertainments fail, it will be true to the letter, and give us as good an idea of the exact state or ruin of things in Spain as the most succinct and lucid reports under this head in the newspapers: and as for England, almost the last significant scrap of news from that quarter was the revolution of 1649; and if you have learned the history of her crops for an average year, you never need attend to that thing again, unless your speculations are of a merely pecuniary character. If one may judge who rarely looks into the newspapers, nothing new does ever happen in foreign parts, a French revolution not excepted.

What news! how much more important to know what that is which was never old! "Kieou-he-yu (great dignitary of the state of Wei) sent a man to Khoung-tseu to know his news. Khoung-tseu caused the messenger to be seated near him, and questioned him in these terms: What is your master doing? The messenger answered with respect: My master desires to diminish the number of his faults, but he cannot accomplish it. The messenger being gone, the philosopher remarked: What a worthy messenger! What a worthy messenger!"[2] The preacher, instead of vexing the ears of drowsy farmers on their day of rest at the end of the week,—for Sunday is the fit conclusion of an ill-spent week, and not the fresh and brave beginning of a new one,—with this one other draggletail of a sermon, should shout with thundering voice,—"Pause! Avast! Why so seeming fast, but deadly slow?"

Shams and delusions are esteemed for soundest truths, while reality is fabulous. If men would steadily observe realities only, and not allow themselves to be deluded, life, to compare it with such things as we know, would be like a fairy tale and the Arabian Nights' Entertainments.[3] If we respected only what is inevitable and has a right to be, music and poetry would resound along the streets. When we are unhurried and wise, we perceive that only great and worthy things have any permanent and absolute existence,—that petty fears and petty pleasures are but the shadow of the reality. This is always exhilarating and sublime. By closing the eyes and slumbering, and consenting to be deceived by shows, men establish

---

1. Thoreau names persons involved in Portuguese and Spanish politics in the 1830s and '40s: Dom Pedro was emperor of Brazil whose daughter became queen of Portugal; Don Carlos connived against his niece, the Infanta, for the Spanish throne.
2. Confucius, *Analects* 14.
3. A collection of ancient Persian, Indian, and Arabian tales compiled about the tenth century and including, among others, tales of Aladdin, Ali Baba, and Sinbad the Sailor.

and confirm their daily life of routine and habit every where, which still is built on purely illusory foundations. Children, who play life, discern its true law and relations more clearly than men, who fail to live it worthily, but who think that they are wiser by experience, that is, by failure. I have read in a Hindoo book, that "there was a king's son, who, being expelled in infancy from his native city, was brought up by a forester, and, growing up to maturity in that state, imagined himself to belong to the barbarous race with which he lived. One of his father's ministers having discovered him, revealed to him what he was, and the misconception of his character was removed, and he knew himself to be a prince. So soul," continues the Hindoo philosopher, "from the circumstances in which it is placed, mistakes its own character, until the truth is revealed to it by some holy teacher, and then it knows itself to be *Brahme*."[4] I perceive that we inhabitants of New England live this mean life that we do because our vision does not penetrate the surface of things. We think that that *is* which *appears* to be. If a man should walk through this town and see only the reality, where, think you, would the "Milldam"[5] go to? If he should give us an account of the realities he beheld there, we should not recognize the place in his description. Look at a meeting-house, or a court-house, or a jail, or a shop, or a dwelling-house, and say what that thing really is before a true gaze, and they would all go to pieces in your account of them. Men esteem truth remote, in the outskirts of the system, behind the farthest star, before Adam and after the last man. In eternity there is indeed something true and sublime. But all these times and places and occasions are now and here. God himself culminates in the present moment, and will never be more divine in the lapse of all the ages. And we are enabled to apprehend at all what is sublime and noble only by the perpetual instilling and drenching of the reality that surrounds us. The universe constantly and obediently answers to our conceptions; whether we travel fast or slow, the track is laid for us. Let us spend our lives in conceiving then. The poet or the artist never yet had so fair and noble a design but some of his posterity at least could accomplish it.

Let us spend one day as deliberately as Nature, and not be thrown off the track by every nutshell and mosquito's wing that falls on the rails. Let us rise early and fast, or break fast, gently and without perturbation; let company come and let company go, let the bells ring and the children cry,—determined to make a day of it. Why should we knock under and go with the stream? Let us not be upset and overwhelmed in that terrible rapid and whirlpool called a

4. The essence of spiritual being in Hindu thought.
5. The general meeting place and business center of Concord.

dinner, situated in the meridian shallows. Weather this danger and you are safe, for the rest of the way is down hill. With unrelaxed nerves, with morning vigor, sail by it, looking another way, tied to the mast like Ulysses.[6] If the engine whistles, let it whistle till it is hoarse for its pains. If the bell rings, why should we run? We will consider what kind of music they are like. Let us settle ourselves, and work and wedge our feet downward through the mud and slush of opinion, and prejudice, and tradition, and delusion, and appearance, that alluvion which covers the globe, through Paris and London, through New York and Boston and Concord, through church and state, through poetry and philosophy and religion, till we come to a hard bottom and rocks in place, which we can call *reality*, and say, This is, and no mistake; and then begin, having a *point d'appui*,[7] below freshet and frost and fire, a place where you might found a wall or a state, or set a lamp-post safely, or perhaps a gauge, not a Nilometer,[8] but a Realometer, that future ages might know how deep a freshet of shams and appearances had gathered from time to time. If you stand right fronting and face to face to a fact, you will see the sun glimmer on both its surfaces, as if it were a cimeter, and feel its sweet edge dividing you through the heart and marrow, and so you will happily conclude your mortal career. Be it life or death, we crave only reality. If we are really dying, let us hear the rattle in our throats and feel cold in the extremities; if we are alive, let us go about our business.

Time is but the stream I go a-fishing in. I drink at it; but while I drink I see the sandy bottom and detect how shallow it is. Its thin current slides away, but eternity remains. I would drink deeper; fish in the sky, whose bottom is pebbly with stars. I cannot count one. I know not the first letter of the alphabet. I have always been regretting that I was not as wise as the day I was born. The intellect is a cleaver; it discerns and rifts its way into the secret of things. I do not wish to be any more busy with my hands than is necessary. My head is hands and feet. I feel all my best faculties concentrated in it. My instinct tells me that my head is an organ for burrowing, as some creatures use their snout and fore-paws, and with it I would mine and burrow my way through these hills. I think that the richest vein is somewhere hereabouts; so by the divining rod and thin rising vapors I judge; and here I will begin to mine.

6. The Roman name of Odysseus, who had himself tied to the mast so that he might both hear and resist the alluring and fatal song of the Sirens.
7. A base; a point of support.
8. An ancient instrument for recording the rise and fall of the Nile River in Egypt.

Reading

With a little more deliberation in the choice of their pursuits, all men would perhaps become essentially students and observers, for certainly their nature and destiny are interesting to all alike. In accumulating property for ourselves or our posterity, in founding a family or a state, or acquiring fame even, we are mortal; but in dealing with truth we are immortal, and need fear no change nor accident. The oldest Egyptian or Hindoo philosopher raised a corner of the veil from the statue of the divinity; and still the trembling robe remains raised, and I gaze upon as fresh a glory as he did, since it was I in him that was then so bold, and it is he in me that now reviews the vision. No dust has settled on that robe; no time has elapsed since that divinity was revealed. That time which we really improve, or which is improvable, is neither past, present, nor future.

My residence was more favorable, not only to thought, but to serious reading, than a university; and though I was beyond the range of the ordinary circulating library, I had more than ever come within the influence of those books which circulate round the world, whose sentences were first written on bark, and are now merely copied from time to time on to linen paper. Says the poet Mîr Camar Uddîn Mast,[1] "Being seated to run through the region of the spiritual world; I have had this advantage in books. To be intoxicated by a single glass of wine; I have experienced this pleasure when I have drunk the liquor of the esoteric doctrines." I kept Homer's Iliad on my table through the summer, though I looked at his page only now and then. Incessant labor with my hands, at first, for I had my house to finish and my beans to hoe at the same time, made more study impossible. Yet I sustained myself by the prospect of such reading in future. I read one or two shallow books of travel in the intervals of my work, till that employment made me ashamed of myself, and I asked where it was then that *I* lived.

The student may read Homer or Æschylus[2] in the Greek without danger of dissipation or luxuriousness, for it implies that he in some measure emulate their heroes, and consecrate morning hours to their pages. The heroic books, even if printed in the character of our mother tongue, will always be in a language dead to degenerate times; and we must laboriously seek the meaning of each word and line, conjecturing a larger sense than common use permits out of what wisdom and valor and generosity we have. The modern cheap and fertile press, with all its translations, has done little to bring us

---

1. An eighteenth-century Persian poet; quoted from Garcin de Tassy, *Histoire de la Littera-ture Hindoui* (1839).
2. Greek dramatist (525-456 B.C.E.) whose tragedies *Prometheus Bound* and *Seven Against Thebes* Thoreau translated in the early 1840s.

nearer to the heroic writers of antiquity. They seem as solitary, and the letter in which they are printed as rare and curious, as ever. It is worth the expense of youthful days and costly hours, if you learn only some words of an ancient language, which are raised out of the trivialness of the street, to be perpetual suggestions and provocations. It is not in vain that the farmer remembers and repeats the few Latin words which he has heard. Men sometimes speak as if the study of the classics would at length make way for more modern and practical studies; but the adventurous student will always study classics, in whatever language they may be written and however ancient they may be. For what are the classics but the noblest recorded thoughts of man? They are the only oracles which are not decayed, and there are such answers to the most modern inquiry in them as Delphi and Dodona[3] never gave. We might as well omit to study Nature because she is old. To read well, that is, to read true books in a true spirit, is a noble exercise, and one that will task the reader more than any exercise which the customs of the day esteem. It requires a training such as the athletes underwent, the steady intention almost of the whole life to this object. Books must be read as deliberately and reservedly as they were written. It is not enough even to be able to speak the language of that nation by which they are written, for there is a memorable interval between the spoken and the written language, the language heard and the language read. The one is commonly transitory, a sound, a tongue, a dialect merely, almost brutish, and we learn it unconsciously, like the brutes, of our mothers. The other is the maturity and experience of that; if that is our mother tongue, this is our father tongue, a reserved and select expression, too significant to be heard by the ear, which we must be born again in order to speak. The crowds of men who merely *spoke* the Greek and Latin tongues in the middle ages were not entitled by the accident of birth to *read* the works of genius written in those languages; for these were not written in that Greek or Latin which they knew, but in the select language of literature. They had not learned the nobler dialects of Greece and Rome, but the very materials on which they were written were waste paper to them, and they prized instead a cheap contemporary literature. But when the several nations of Europe had acquired distinct though rude written languages of their own, sufficient for the purposes of their rising literatures, then first learning revived, and scholars were enabled to discern from that remoteness the treasures of antiquity. What the Roman and Grecian multitude could not *hear*, after the lapse of ages a few scholars *read*, and a few scholars only are still reading it.

3. Famous oracles of ancient Greece.

However much we may admire the orator's occasional bursts of eloquence, the noblest written words are commonly as far behind or above the fleeting spoken language as the firmament with its stars is behind the clouds. *There* are the stars, and they who can may read them. The astronomers forever comment on and observe them. They are not exhalations like our daily colloquies and vaporous breath. What is called eloquence in the forum is commonly found to be rhetoric in the study. The orator yields to the inspiration of a transient occasion, and speaks to the mob before him, to those who can *hear* him; but the writer, whose more equable life is his occasion, and who would be distracted by the event and the crowd which inspire the orator, speaks to the intellect and heart of mankind, to all in any age who can *understand* him.

No wonder that Alexander[4] carried the Iliad with him on his expeditions in a precious casket. A written word is the choicest of relics. It is something at once more intimate with us and more universal than any other work of art. It is the work of art nearest to life itself. It may be translated into every language, and not only be read but actually breathed from all human lips;—not be represented on canvas or in marble only, but be carved out of the breath of life itself. The symbol of an ancient man's thought becomes a modern man's speech. Two thousand summers have imparted to the monuments of Grecian literature, as to her marbles, only a maturer golden and autumnal tint, for they have carried their own serene and celestial atmosphere into all lands to protect them against the corrosion of time. Books are the treasured wealth of the world and the fit inheritance of generations and nations. Books, the oldest and the best, stand naturally and rightfully on the shelves of every cottage. They have no cause of their own to plead, but while they enlighten and sustain the reader his common sense will not refuse them. Their authors are a natural and irresistible aristocracy in every society, and, more than kings or emperors, exert an influence on mankind. When the illiterate and perhaps scornful trader has earned by enterprise and industry his coveted leisure and independence, and is admitted to the circles of wealth and fashion, he turns inevitably at last to those still higher but yet inaccessible circles of intellect and genius, and is sensible only of the imperfection of his culture and the vanity and insufficiency of all his riches, and further proves his good sense by the pains which he takes to secure for his children that intellectual culture whose want he so keenly feels; and thus it is that he becomes the founder of a family.

Those who have not learned to read the ancient classics in the

---

4. Alexander the Great of Macedon (356–323 B.C.E.), king and conqueror of the Persian empire. The practice Thoreau describes is recorded in Plutarch's *Lives*.

language in which they were written must have a very imperfect knowledge of the history of the human race; for it is remarkable that no transcript of them has ever been made into any modern tongue, unless our civilization itself may be regarded as such a transcript. Homer has never yet been printed in English, nor Æschylus, nor Virgil even,—works as refined, as solidly done, and as beautiful almost as the morning itself; for later writers, say what we will of their genius, have rarely, if ever, equalled the elaborate beauty and finish and the lifelong and heroic literary labors of the ancients. They only talk of forgetting them who never knew them. It will be soon enough to forget them when we have the learning and the genius which will enable us to attend to and appreciate them. That age will be rich indeed when those relics which we call Classics, and the still older and more than classic but even less known Scriptures of the nations, shall have still further accumulated, when the Vaticans shall be filled with Vedas and Zendavestas[5] and Bibles, with Homers and Dantes and Shakspeares, and all the centuries to come shall have successively deposited their trophies in the forum of the world. By such a pile we may hope to scale heaven at last.

The works of the great poets have never yet been read by mankind, for only great poets can read them. They have only been read as the multitude read the stars, at most astrologically, not astronomically. Most men have learned to read to serve a paltry convenience, as they have learned to cipher in order to keep accounts and not be cheated in trade; but of reading as a noble intellectual exercise they know little or nothing; yet this only is reading, in a high sense, not that which lulls us as a luxury and suffers the nobler faculties to sleep the while, but what we have to stand on tiptoe to read and devote our most alert and wakeful hours to.

I think that having learned our letters we should read the best that is in literature, and not be forever repeating our a b abs, and words of one syllable, in the fourth or fifth classes, sitting on the lowest and foremost form all our lives.[6] Most men are satisfied if they read or hear read, and perchance have been convicted by the wisdom of one good book, the Bible, and for the rest of their lives vegetate and dissipate their faculties in what is called easy reading. There is a work in several volumes in our Circulating Library entitled Little Reading, which I thought referred to a town of that name which I had not been to. There are those who, like cormorants and ostriches, can digest all sorts of this, even after the

---

5. The scripture of Zoroastrianism, a religion that began in Iran in the sixth or seventh century B.C.E.
6. I.e., with the youngest children on the front row of the schoolroom.

fullest dinner of meats and vegetables, for they suffer nothing to be wasted. If others are the machines to provide this provender, they are the machines to read it. They read the nine thousandth tale about Zebulon and Sephronia, and how they loved as none had ever loved before, and neither did the course of their true love run smooth,—at any rate, how it did run and stumble, and get up again and go on! how some poor unfortunate got up on to a steeple, who had better never have gone up as far as the belfry; and then, having needlessly got him up there, the happy novelist rings the bell for all the world to come together and hear, O dear! how he did get down again! For my part, I think that they had better metamorphose all such aspiring heroes of universal noveldom into man weathercocks, as they used to put heroes among the constellations, and let them swing round there till they are rusty, and not come down at all to bother honest men with their pranks. The next time the novelist rings the bell I will not stir though the meeting-house burn down. "The Skip of the Tip-Toe-Hop, a Romance of the Middle Ages, by the celebrated author of 'Tittle-Tol-Tan,' to appear in monthly parts; a great rush; don't all come together." All this they read with saucer eyes, and erect and primitive curiosity, and with unwearied gizzard, whose corrugations even yet need no sharpening, just as some little four-year-old bencher his two-cent gilt-covered edition of Cinderella,—without any improvement, that I can see, in the pronunciation, or accent, or emphasis, or any more skill in extracting or inserting the moral. The result is dulness of sight, a stagnation of the vital circulations, and a general deliquium and sloughing off of all the intellectual faculties. This sort of ginger-bread is baked daily and more sedulously than pure wheat or rye-and-Indian in almost every oven, and finds a surer market.

The best books are not read even by those who are called good readers. What does our Concord culture amount to? There is in this town, with a very few exceptions, no taste for the best or for very good books even in English literature, whose words all can read and spell. Even the college-bred and so called liberally educated men here and elsewhere have really little or no acquaintance with the English classics; and as for the recorded wisdom of mankind, the ancient classics and Bibles, which are accessible to all who will know of them, there are the feeblest efforts any where made to become acquainted with them. I know a woodchopper, of middle age, who takes a French paper, not for news as he says, for he is above that, but to "keep himself in practice," he being a Canadian by birth; and when I asked him what he considers the best thing he can do in this world, he says, beside this, to keep up and add to his English. This is about as much as the college bred generally do or aspire to do, and they take an English paper for the pur-

pose. One who has just come from reading perhaps one of the best
English books will find how many with whom he can converse
about it? Or suppose he comes from reading a Greek or Latin classic in the original, whose praises are familiar even to the so called
illiterate; he will find nobody at all to speak to, but must keep silence about it. Indeed, there is hardly the professor in our colleges,
who, if he has mastered the difficulties of the language, has proportionally mastered the difficulties of the wit and poetry of a Greek
poet, and has any sympathy to impart to the alert and heroic
reader; and as for the sacred Scriptures, or Bibles of mankind, who
in this town can tell me even their titles? Most men do not know
that any nation but the Hebrews have had a scripture. A man, any
man, will go considerably out of his way to pick up a silver dollar;
but here are golden words, which the wisest men of antiquity have
uttered, and whose worth the wise of every succeeding age have assured us of,—and yet we learn to read only as far as Easy Reading,
the primers and class-books, and when we leave school, the "Little
Reading," and story books, which are for boys and beginners; and
our reading, our conversation and thinking, are all on a very low
level, worthy only of pygmies and manikins.

I aspire to be acquainted with wiser men than this our Concord
soil has produced, whose names are hardly known here. Or shall I
hear the name of Plato and never read his book? As if Plato were
my townsman and I never saw him,—my next neighbor and I never
heard him speak or attended to the wisdom of his words. But how
actually is it? His Dialogues, which contain what was immortal in
him, lie on the next shelf, and yet I never read them. We are underbred and low-lived and illiterate; and in this respect I confess I do
not make any very broad distinction between the illiterateness of
my townsman who cannot read at all, and the illiterateness of him
who has learned to read only what is for children and feeble intellects. We should be as good as the worthies of antiquity, but partly
by first knowing how good they were. We are a race of tit-men,[7] and
soar but little higher in our intellectual flights than the columns of
the daily paper.

It is not all books that are as dull as their readers. There are
probably words addressed to our condition exactly, which, if we
could really hear and understand, would be more salutary than the
morning or the spring to our lives, and possibly put a new aspect on
the face of things for us. How many a man has dated a new era in
his life from the reading of a book. The book exists for us perchance which will explain our miracles and reveal new ones. The at
present unutterable things we may find somewhere uttered. These

7. Runts, intellectually small.

same questions that disturb and puzzle and confound us have in their turn occurred to all the wise men; not one has been omitted; and each has answered them, according to his ability, by his words and his life. Moreover, with wisdom we shall learn liberality. The solitary hired man on a farm in the outskirts of Concord, who has had his second birth and peculiar religious experience, and is driven as he believes into silent gravity and exclusiveness by his faith, may think it is not true; but Zoroaster, thousands of years ago, travelled the same road and had the same experience; but he, being wise, knew it to be universal, and treated his neighbors accordingly, and is even said to have invented and established worship among men. Let him humbly commune with Zoroaster then, and, through the liberalizing influence of all the worthies, with Jesus Christ himself, and let "our church" go by the board.

We boast that we belong to the nineteenth century and are making the most rapid strides of any nation. But consider how little this village does for its own culture. I do not wish to flatter my townsmen, nor to be flattered by them, for that will not advance either of us. We need to be provoked,—goaded like oxen, as we are, into a trot. We have a comparatively decent system of common schools, schools for infants only; but excepting the half-starved Lyceum[8] in the winter, and latterly the puny beginning of a library suggested by the state, no school for ourselves. We spend more on almost any article of bodily aliment or ailment than on our mental aliment. It is time that we had uncommon schools, that we did not leave off our education when we begin to be men and women. It is time that villages were universities, and their elder inhabitants the fellows of universities, with leisure—if they are indeed so well off—to pursue liberal studies the rest of their lives. Shall the world be confined to one Paris or one Oxford forever? Cannot students be boarded here and get a liberal education under the skies of Concord? Can we not hire some Abelard[9] to lecture to us? Alas! what with foddering the cattle and tending the store, we are kept from school too long, and our education is sadly neglected. In this country, the village should in some respects take the place of the nobleman of Europe. It should be the patron of the fine arts. It is rich enough. It wants only the magnanimity and refinement. It can spend money enough on such things as farmers and traders value, but it is thought Utopian to propose spending money for things which more intelligent men know to be of far more worth. This town has spent seventeen thousand dollars on a town-house, thank fortune or politics,

---

8. An organization that sponsored public lectures which, as a young man, Thoreau had helped to organize.
9. Peter Abelard (1079–1142), a French philosopher, theologian, and teacher.

but probably it will not spend so much on living wit, the true meat to put into that shell, in a hundred years. The one hundred and twenty-five dollars annually subscribed for a Lyceum in the winter is better spent than any other equal sum raised in the town. If we live in the nineteenth century, why should we not enjoy the advantages which the nineteenth century offers? Why should our life be in any respect provincial? If we will read newspapers, why not skip the gossip of Boston and take the best newspaper in the world at once?—not be sucking the pap of "neutral family" papers, or browsing "Olive-Branches"[1] here in New England. Let the reports of all the learned societies come to us, and we will see if they know any thing. Why should we leave it to Harper & Brothers and Redding & Co.[2] to select our reading? As the nobleman of cultivated taste surrounds himself with whatever conduces to his culture,—genius—learning—wit—books—paintings—statuary—music—philosophical instruments, and the like; so let the village do,—not stop short at a pedagogue, a parson, a sexton, a parish library, and three selectmen, because our pilgrim forefathers got through a cold winter once on a bleak rock with these. To act collectively is according to the spirit of our institutions; and I am confident that, as our circumstances are more flourishing, our means are greater than the nobleman's. New England can hire all the wise men in the world to come and teach her, and board them round the while, and not be provincial at all. That is the *uncommon* school we want. Instead of noblemen, let us have noble villages of men. If it is necessary, omit one bridge over the river, go round a little there, and throw one arch at least over the darker gulf of ignorance which surrounds us.

Sounds

But while we are confined to books, though the most select and classic, and read only particular written languages, which are themselves but dialects and provincial, we are in danger of forgetting the language which all things and events speak without metaphor, which alone is copious and standard. Much is published, but little printed. The rays which stream through the shutter will be no longer remembered when the shutter is wholly removed. No method nor discipline can supersede the necessity of being forever on the alert. What is a course of history, or philosophy, or poetry, no matter how well selected, or the best society, or the most admirable

1. A Methodist weekly newspaper; neutral family newspapers avoided discussion of political issues in favor of family entertainment.
2. Book publishers, located in New York and Boston, respectively.

routine of life, compared with the discipline of looking always at what is to be seen? Will you be a reader, a student merely, or a seer? Read your fate, see what is before you, and walk on into futurity.

I did not read books the first summer; I hoed beans. Nay, I often did better than this. There were times when I could not afford to sacrifice the bloom of the present moment to any work, whether of the head or hands. I love a broad margin to my life. Sometimes, in a summer morning, having taken my accustomed bath, I sat in my sunny doorway from sunrise till noon, rapt in a revery, amidst the pines and hickories and sumachs, in undisturbed solitude and still-ness, while the birds sang around or flitted noiseless through the house, until by the sun falling in at my west window, or the noise of some traveller's wagon on the distant highway, I was reminded of the lapse of time. I grew in those seasons like corn in the night, and they were far better than any work of the hands would have been. They were not time subtracted from my life, but so much over and above my usual allowance. I realized what the Orientals mean by contemplation and the forsaking of works. For the most part, I minded not how the hours went. The day advanced as if to light some work of mine; it was morning, and lo, now it is evening, and nothing memorable is accomplished. Instead of singing like the birds, I silently smiled at my incessant good fortune. As the sparrow had its trill, sitting on the hickory before my door, so had I my chuckle or suppressed warble which he might hear out of my nest. My days were not days of the week, bearing the stamp of any hea-then deity, nor were they minced into hours and fretted by the tick-ing of a clock; for I lived like the Puri Indians, of whom it is said that "for yesterday, to-day, and to-morrow they have only one word, and they express the variety of meaning by pointing backward for yesterday, forward for to-morrow, and overhead for the passing day."[1] This was sheer idleness to my fellow-townsmen, no doubt; but if the birds and flowers had tried me by their standard, I should not have been found wanting. A man must find his occasions in himself, it is true. The natural day is very calm, and will hardly re-prove his indolence.

I had this advantage, at least, in my mode of life, over those who were obliged to look abroad for amusement, to society and the the-atre, that my life itself was become my amusement and never ceased to be novel. It was a drama of many scenes and without an end. If we were always indeed getting our living, and regulating our lives according to the last and best mode we had learned, we should never be troubled with ennui. Follow your genius closely enough,

---

1. From Ida Pfeiffer, *A Lady's Voyage Round the World* (1852); the Puris are a tribe in east-ern Brazil.

and it will not fail to show you a fresh prospect every hour. House-work was a pleasant pastime. When my floor was dirty, I rose early, and, setting all my furniture out of doors on the grass, bed and bed-stead making but one budget, dashed water on the floor, and sprin-kled white sand from the pond on it, and then with a broom scrubbed it clean and white; and by the time the villagers had bro-ken their fast the morning sun had dried my house sufficiently to allow me to move in again, and my meditations were almost unin-terrupted. It was pleasant to see my whole household effects out on the grass, making a little pile like a gypsy's pack, and my three-legged table, from which I did not remove the books and pen and ink, standing amid the pines and hickories. They seemed glad to get out themselves, and as if unwilling to be brought in. I was some-times tempted to stretch an awning over them and take my seat there. It was worth the while to see the sun shine on these things, and hear the free wind blow on them; so much more interesting most familiar objects look out of doors than in the house. A bird sits on the next bough, life-everlasting grows under the table, and blackberry vines run round its legs; pine cones, chestnut burs, and strawberry leaves are strewn about. It looked as if this was the way these forms came to be transferred to our furniture, to tables, chairs, and bedsteads,—because they once stood in their midst.

My house was on the side of a hill, immediately on the edge of the larger wood, in the midst of a young forest of pitch pines and hickories, and half a dozen rods from the pond, to which a narrow footpath led down the hill. In my front yard grew the strawberry, blackberry, and life-everlasting, johnswort and goldenrod, shrub-oaks and sand-cherry, blueberry and groundnut. Near the end of May, the sand-cherry, (*Cerasus pumila,*) adorned the sides of the path with its delicate flowers arranged in umbels cylindrically about its short stems, which last, in the fall, weighed down with good sized and handsome cherries, fell over in wreaths like rays on every side. I tasted them out of compliment to Nature, though they were scarcely palatable. The sumach, (*Rhus glabra,*) grew luxuriantly about the house, pushing up through the embankment which I had made, and growing five or six feet the first season. Its broad pinnate tropical leaf was pleasant though strange to look on. The large buds, suddenly pushing out late in the spring from dry sticks which had seemed to be dead, developed themselves as by magic into graceful green and tender boughs, an inch in diameter; and some-times, as I sat at my window, so heedlessly did they grow and tax their weak joints, I heard a fresh and tender bough suddenly fall like a fan to the ground, when there was not a breath of air stirring, broken off by its own weight. In August, the large masses of berries, which, when in flower, had attracted many wild bees, gradually assumed their bright velvety crimson hue, and by their weight again bent down and broke the tender limbs.

As I sit at my window this summer afternoon, hawks are circling about my clearing; the tantivy of wild pigeons, flying by twos and threes athwart my view, or perching restless on the white-pine boughs behind my house, gives a voice to the air; a fishhawk dimples the glassy surface of the pond and brings up a fish; a mink steals out of the marsh before my door and seizes a frog by the shore; the sedge is bending under the weight of the reed-birds flitting hither and thither; and for the last half hour I have heard the rattle of railroad cars, now dying away and then reviving like the beat of a partridge, conveying travellers from Boston to the country. For I did not live so out of the world as that boy, who, as I hear, was put out to a farmer in the east part of the town, but ere long ran away and came home again, quite down at the heel and homesick. He had never seen such a dull and out-of-the-way place; the folks were all gone off; why, you couldn't even hear the whistle! I doubt if there is such a place in Massachusetts now:—

> "In truth, our village has become a butt
> For one of those fleet railroad shafts, and o'er
> Our peaceful plain its soothing sound is—Concord."[2]

The Fitchburg Railroad touches the pond about a hundred rods south of where I dwell. I usually go to the village along its causeway, and am, as it were, related to society by this link. The men on the freight trains, who go over the whole length of the road, bow to me as to an old acquaintance, they pass me so often, and apparently they take me for an employee; and so I am. I too would fain be a track-repairer somewhere in the orbit of the earth.

The whistle of the locomotive penetrates my woods summer and winter, sounding like the scream of a hawk sailing over some farmer's yard, informing me that many restless city merchants are arriving within the circle of the town, or adventurous country traders from the other side. As they come under one horizon, they shout their warning to get off the track to the other, heard sometimes through the circles of two towns. Here come your groceries, country; your rations, countrymen! Nor is there any man so independent on his farm that he can say them nay. And here's your pay for them! screams the countryman's whistle; timber like long battering rams going twenty miles an hour against the city's walls, and chairs enough to seat all the weary and heavy laden that dwell

2. From "Walden Spring," in *The Woodman and Other Poems* (1849), by Ellery Channing (1818–1901), Thoreau's close friend and biographer.

within them. With such huge and lumbering civility the country hands a chair to the city. All the Indian huckleberry hills are stripped, all the cranberry meadows are raked into the city. Up comes the cotton, down goes the woven cloth; up comes the silk, down goes the woollen; up come the books, but down goes the wit that writes them.

When I meet the engine with its train of cars moving off with planetary motion,—or, rather, like a comet, for the beholder knows not if with that velocity and with that direction it will ever revisit this system, since its orbit does not look like a returning curve,—with its steam cloud like a banner streaming behind in golden and silver wreaths, like many a downy cloud which I have seen, high in the heavens, unfolding its masses to the light,—as if this travelling demigod, this cloud-compeller, would ere long take the sunset sky for the livery of his train; when I hear the iron horse make the hills echo with his snort like thunder, shaking the earth with his feet, and breathing fire and smoke from his nostrils, (what kind of winged horse or fiery dragon they will put into the new Mythology I don't know,) it seems as if the earth had got a race now worthy to inhabit it. If all were as it seems, and men made the elements their servants for noble ends! If the cloud that hangs over the engine were the perspiration of heroic deeds, or as beneficent as that which floats over the farmer's fields, then the elements and Nature herself would cheerfully accompany men on their errands and be their escort.

I watch the passage of the morning cars with the same feeling that I do the rising of the sun, which is hardly more regular. Their train of clouds stretching far behind and rising higher and higher, going to heaven while the cars are going to Boston, conceals the sun for a minute and casts my distant field into the shade, a celestial train beside which the petty train of cars which hugs the earth is but the barb of the spear. The stabler of the iron horse was up early this winter morning by the light of the stars amid the mountains, to fodder and harness his steed. Fire, too, was awakened thus early to put the vital heat in him and get him off. If the enterprise were as innocent as it is early! If the snow lies deep, they strap on his snow-shoes, and with the giant plough plough a furrow from the mountains to the seaboard, in which the cars, like a following drill-barrow, sprinkle all the restless men and floating merchandise in the country for seed. All day the fire-steed flies over the country, stopping only that his master may rest, and I am awakened by his tramp and defiant snort at midnight, when in some remote glen in the woods he fronts the elements incased in ice and snow; and he will reach his stall only with the morning star, to start once more on his travels without rest or slumber. Or perchance, at evening, I hear him in his stable blowing off the superfluous energy of the day, that he may calm his nerves and cool his liver and brain for a few hours of iron slumber. If the enterprise were as heroic and commanding as it is protracted and unwearied!

Far through unfrequented woods on the confines of towns, where once only the hunter penetrated by day, in the darkest night dart these bright saloons without the knowledge of their inhabitants; this moment stopping at some brilliant station-house in town or city, where a social crowd is gathered, the next in the Dismal Swamp,[3] scaring the owl and fox. The startings and arrivals of the cars are now the epochs in the village day. They go and come with such regularity and precision, and their whistle can be heard so far, that the farmers set their clocks by them, and thus one well conducted institution regulates a whole country. Have not men improved somewhat in punctuality since the railroad was invented? Do they not talk and think faster in the depot than they did in the stage-office? There is something electrifying in the atmosphere of the former place. I have been astonished at the miracles it has wrought; that some of my neighbors, who, I should have prophesied, once for all, would never get to Boston by so prompt a conveyance, were on hand when the bell rang. To do things "railroad fashion" is now the by-word; and it is worth the while to be warned so often and so sincerely by any power to get off its track. There is no stopping to read the riot act, no firing over the heads of the mob, in this case. We have constructed a fate, an *Atropos*,[4] that never turns aside. (Let that be the name of your engine.) Men are advertised that at a certain hour and minute these bolts will be shot toward particular points of the compass; yet it interferes with no man's business, and the children go to school on the other track. We live the steadier for it. We are all educated thus to be sons of Tell.[5] The air is full of invisible bolts. Every path but your own is the path of fate. Keep on your own track, then.

What recommends commerce to me is its enterprise and bravery. It does not clasp its hands and pray to Jupiter. I see these men every day go about their business with more or less courage and content, doing more even than they suspect, and perchance better employed than they could have consciously devised. I am less affected by their heroism who stood up for half an hour in the front line at Buena Vista,[6] than by the steady and cheerful valor of the men who inhabit

---

3. A coastal swamp in southeastern Virginia and northeastern North Carolina.
4. In Greek mythology, one of the three Fates who determined when a person was to die.
5. I.e., one of the sons of William Tell who, according to legend, shot an arrow through an apple that rested on his son's head.
6. Site of a victory in 1847, celebrated by many of Thoreau's contemporaries, of the United States' forces over those of Mexico during the Mexican War.

the snow-plough for their winter quarters; who have not merely the
three-o'-clock in the morning courage, which Bonaparte[7] thought
was the rarest, but whose courage does not go to rest so early, who
go to sleep only when the storm sleeps or the sinews of their iron
steed are frozen. On this morning of the Great Snow,[8] perchance,
which is still raging and chilling men's blood, I hear the muffled
tone of their engine bell from out the fog bank of their chilled
breath, which announces that the cars *are coming*, without long delay, notwithstanding the veto of a New England north-east snow
storm, and I behold the ploughmen covered with snow and rime,
their heads peering above the mould-board which is turning down
other than daisies and the nests of field-mice, like bowlders of the
Sierra Nevada, that occupy an outside place in the universe.

Commerce is unexpectedly confident and serene, alert, adventurous, and unwearied. It is very natural in its methods withal, far
more so than many fantastic enterprises and sentimental experiments, and hence its singular success. I am refreshed and expanded when the freight train rattles past me, and I smell the
stores which go dispensing their odors all the way from Long Wharf
to Lake Champlain,[9] reminding me of foreign parts, of coral reefs,
and Indian oceans, and tropical climes, and the extent of the globe.
I feel more like a citizen of the world at the sight of the palm-leaf
which will cover so many flaxen New England heads the next summer, the Manilla hemp and cocoa-nut husks, the old junk, gunny
bags, scrap iron, and rusty nails. This car-load of torn sails is more
legible and interesting now than if they should be wrought into paper and printed books. Who can write so graphically the history of
the storms they have weathered as these rents have done? They are
proof-sheets which need no correction. Here goes lumber from the
Maine woods, which did not go out to sea in the last freshet, risen
four dollars on the thousand because of what did go out or was split
up; pine, spruce, cedar,—first, second, third and fourth qualities,
so lately all of one quality, to wave over the bear, and moose, and
caribou. Next rolls Thomaston[1] lime, a prime lot, which will get far
among the hills before it gets slacked. These rags in bales, of all
hues and qualities, the lowest condition to which cotton and linen
descend, the final result of dress,—of patterns which are now no
longer, cried up, unless it be in Milwaukie, as those splendid articles, English, French, or American prints, ginghams, muslins, &c.,
gathered from all quarters both of fashion and poverty, going to become paper of one color or a few shades only, on which forsooth

7. I.e., spontaneous courage.
8. According to Walter Harding, the "Great Snow" of February 1717, described by Cotton
Mather.
9. I.e., from Boston Harbor to the New York-Vermont border.
1. A town in southern Maine, known for its lime deposits.

will be written tales of real life, high and low, and founded on fact! This closed car smells of salt fish, the strong New England and commercial scent, reminding me of the Grand Banks[2] and the fisheries. Who has not seen a salt fish, thoroughly cured for this world, so that nothing can spoil it, and putting the perseverance of the saints to the blush? with which you may sweep or pave the streets, and split your kindlings, and the teamster shelter himself and his lading against sun wind and rain behind it,—and the trader, as a Concord trader once did, hang it up by his door for a sign when he commences business, until at last his oldest customer cannot tell surely whether it be animal, vegetable, or mineral, and yet it shall be as pure as a snowflake, and if it be put into a pot and boiled, will come out an excellent dun fish for a Saturday's dinner. Next Spanish hides, with the tails still preserving their twist and the angle of elevation they had when the oxen that wore them were careering over the pampas of the Spanish main,—a type of all obstinacy, and evincing how almost hopeless and incurable are all constitutional vices. I confess, that practically speaking, when I have learned a man's real disposition, I have no hopes of changing it for the better or worse in this state of existence. As the Orientals say, "A cur's tail may be warmed, and pressed, and bound round with ligatures, and after a twelve years' labor bestowed upon it, still it will retain its natural form."[3] The only effectual cure for such inveteracies as these tails exhibit is to make glue of them, which I believe is what is usually done with them, and then they will stay put and stick. Here is a hogshead of molasses or of brandy directed to John Smith, Cuttingsville, Vermont, some trader among the Green Mountains, who imports for the farmers near his clearing, and now perchance stands over his bulk-head and thinks of the last arrivals on the coast, how they may affect the price for him, telling his customers this moment, as he has told them twenty times before this morning, that he expects some by the next train of prime quality. It is advertised in the Cuttingsville Times.

While these things go up other things come down. Warned by the whizzing sound, I look up from my book and see some tall pine, hewn on far northern hills, which has winged its way over the Green Mountains and the Connecticut, shot like an arrow through the township within ten minutes, and scarce another eye beholds it; going

> "to be the mast
> Of some great ammiral."[4]

2. A major fishing ground in the northern Atlantic Ocean, southeast of Newfoundland.
3. Quoted from Charles Wilkins's translation of *Hitopadesa: Fables and Proverbs from the Sanskrit* (1787), the fable of the lion and the rabbit.
4. John Milton, *Paradise Lost* 1.293–94.

And hark! here comes the cattle-train bearing the cattle of a thousand hills, sheepcots, stables, and cowyards in the air, drovers with their sticks, and shepherd boys in the midst of their flocks, all but the mountain pastures, whirled along like leaves blown from the mountains by the September gales. The air is filled with the bleating of calves and sheep, and the hustling of oxen, as if a pastoral valley were going by. When the old bell-weather at the head rattles his bell, the mountains do indeed skip like rams and the little hills like lambs. A car-load of drovers, too, in the midst, on a level with their droves now, their vocation gone, but still clinging to their useless sticks as their badge of office. But their dogs, where are they? It is a stampede to them; they are quite thrown out; they have lost the scent. Methinks I hear them barking behind the Peterboro' Hills, or panting up the western slope of the Green Mountains.[5] They will not be in at the death. Their vocation, too, is gone. Their fidelity and sagacity are below par now. They will slink back to their kennels in disgrace, or perchance run wild and strike a league with the wolf and the fox. So is your pastoral life whirled past and away. But the bell rings, and I must get off the track and let the cars go by;—

> What's the railroad to me?
> I never go to see
> Where it ends.
> It fills a few hollows,
> And makes banks for the swallows,
> It sets the sand a-blowing,
> And the blackberries a-growing,

but I cross it like a cart-path in the woods. I will not have my eyes put out and my ears spoiled by its smoke and steam and hissing.

Now that the cars are gone by and all the restless world with them, and the fishes in the pond no longer feel their rumbling, I am more alone than ever. For the rest of the long afternoon, perhaps, my meditations are interrupted only by the faint rattle of a carriage or team along the distant highway.

Sometimes, on Sundays, I heard the bells, the Lincoln, Acton, Bedford,[6] or Concord bell, when the wind was favorable, a faint, sweet, and, as it were, natural melody, worth importing into the wilderness. At a sufficient distance over the woods this sound acquires a certain vibratory hum, as if the pine needles in the horizon were the strings of a harp which it swept. All sound heard at the greatest possible distance produces one and the same effect, a vibration of the universal lyre, just as the intervening atmosphere

5. The Peterboro' Hills are in southern New Hampshire, visible from Concord; the Green Mountains run from northern Vermont to western Massachusetts.
6. Towns near Concord.

makes a distant ridge of earth interesting to our eyes by the azure tint it imparts to it. There came to me in this case a melody which the air had strained, and which had conversed with every leaf and needle of the wood, that portion of the sound which the elements had taken up and modulated and echoed from vale to vale. The echo is, to some extent, an original sound, and therein is the magic and charm of it. It is not merely a repetition of what was worth repeating in the bell, but partly the voice of the wood; the same trivial words and notes sung by a wood-nymph.

At evening, the distant lowing of some cow in the horizon beyond the woods sounded sweet and melodious, and at first I would mistake it for the voices of certain minstrels by whom I was sometimes serenaded, who might be straying over hill and dale; but soon I was not unpleasantly disappointed when it was prolonged into the cheap and natural music of the cow. I do not mean to be satirical, but to express my appreciation of those youths' singing, when I state that I perceived clearly that it was akin to the music of the cow, and they were at length one articulation of Nature.

Regularly at half past seven, in one part of the summer, after the evening train had gone by, the whippoorwills chanted their vespers for half an hour, sitting on a stump by my door, or upon the ridge pole of the house. They would begin to sing almost with as much precision as a clock, within five minutes of a particular time, referred to the setting of the sun, every evening. I had a rare opportunity to become acquainted with their habits. Sometimes I heard four or five at once in different parts of the wood, by accident one a bar behind another, and so near me that I distinguished not only the cluck after each note, but often that singular buzzing sound like a fly in a spider's web, only proportionally louder. Sometimes one would circle round and round me in the woods a few feet distant as if tethered by a string, when probably I was near its eggs. They sang at intervals throughout the night, and were again as musical as ever just before and about dawn.

When other birds are still the screech owls take up the strain, like mourning women their ancient u-lu-lu. Their dismal scream is truly Ben Jonsonian.[7] Wise midnight hags! It is no honest and blunt tu-whit tu-who of the poets, but, without jesting, a most solemn graveyard ditty, the mutual consolations of suicide lovers remembering the pangs and the delights of supernal love in the infernal groves. Yet I love to hear their wailing, their doleful responses, trilled along the woodside; reminding me sometimes of music and singing birds; as if it were the dark and tearful side of music, the regrets and sighs that would fain be sung. They are the spirits, the

---

7. Ben Jonson (1572–1637), English dramatist; the reference may be to his "Witches' Song."

low spirits and melancholy forebodings, of fallen souls that once in human shape night-walked the earth and did the deeds of darkness, now expiating their sins with their wailing hymns or threnodies in the scenery of their transgressions. They give me a new sense of the variety and capacity of that nature which is our common dwelling. *Oh-o-o-o-o that I never had been bor-r-r-r-n!* sighs one on this side of the pond, and circles with the restlessness of despair to some new perch on the gray oaks. Then—*that I never had been bor-r-r-r-n!* echoes another on the farther side with tremulous sincerity, and—*bor-r-r-r-n!* comes faintly from far in the Lincoln woods.

I was also serenaded by a hooting owl. Near at hand you could fancy it the most melancholy sound in Nature, as if she meant by this to stereotype and make permanent in her choir the dying moans of a human being,—some poor weak relic of mortality who has left hope behind, and howls like an animal, yet with human sobs, on entering the dark valley, made more awful by a certain gurgling melodiousness,—I find myself beginning with the letters gl when I try to imitate it,—expressive of a mind which has reached the gelatinous mildewy stage in the mortification of all healthy and courageous thought. It reminded me of ghouls and idiots and insane howlings. But now one answers from far woods in a strain made really melodious by distance,—*Hoo hoo hoo, hoorer hoo*; and indeed for the most part it suggested only pleasing associations, whether heard by day or night, summer or winter.

I rejoice that there are owls. Let them do the idiotic and maniacal hooting for men. It is a sound admirably suited to swamps and twilight woods which no day illustrates, suggesting a vast and undeveloped nature which men have not recognized. They represent the stark twilight and unsatisfied thoughts which all have. All day the sun has shone on the surface of some savage swamp, where the double spruce stands hung with usnea lichens, and small hawks circulate above, and the chicadee lisps amid the evergreens, and the partridge and rabbit skulk beneath; but now a more dismal and fitting day dawns, and a different race of creatures awakes to express the meaning of Nature there.

Late in the evening I heard the distant rumbling of wagons over bridges,—a sound heard farther than almost any other at night,—the baying of dogs, and sometimes again the lowing of some disconsolate cow in a distant barn-yard. In the mean while all the shore rang with the trump of bullfrogs, the sturdy spirits of ancient winebibbers and wassailers, still unrepentant, trying to sing a catch in their Stygian lake,[8]—if the Walden nymphs will pardon the com-

8. I.e., any gloomy lake; in Greek mythology, the Styx was one of five rivers surrounding the land of the dead.

parison, for though there are almost no weeds, there are frogs
there,—who would fain keep up the hilarious rules of their old fes-
tal tables, though their voices have waxed hoarse and solemnly
grave, mocking at mirth, and the wine has lost its flavor, and become only liquor to distend their paunches, and sweet intoxication
never comes to drown the memory of the past, but mere saturation
and waterloggedness and distention. The most aldermanic, with
his chin upon a heart-leaf, which serves for a napkin to his drool-
ing chaps, under this northern shore quaffs a deep draught of the
once scorned water, and passes round the cup with the ejaculation
tr-r-r-oonk, tr-r-r-oonk, tr-r-r-oonk! and straightway comes over the
water from some distant cove the same password repeated, where
the next in seniority and girth has gulped down to his mark; and
when this observance has made the circuit of the shores, then ejac-
ulates the master of ceremonies, with satisfaction, *tr-r-r-oonk!* and
each in his turn repeats the same down to the least distended,
leakiest, and flabbiest paunched, that there be no mistake; and
then the bowl goes round again and again, until the sun disperses
the morning mist, and only the patriarch is not under the pond,
but vainly bellowing *troonk* from time to time, and pausing for a
reply.

I am not sure that I ever heard the sound of cock-crowing from
my clearing, and I thought that it might be worth the while to keep
a cockerel for his music merely, as a singing bird. The note of this
once wild Indian pheasant is certainly the most remarkable of any
bird's, and if they could be naturalized without being domesticated,
it would soon become the most famous sound in our woods, surpassing the clangor of the goose and the hooting of the owl; and
then imagine the cackling of the hens to fill the pauses when their
lords' clarions rested! No wonder that man added this bird to his
tame stock,—to say nothing of the eggs and drumsticks. To walk in
a winter morning in a wood where these birds abounded, their native woods, and hear the wild cockerels crow on the trees, clear and
shrill for miles over the resounding earth, drowning the feebler
notes of other birds,—think of it! It would put nations on the alert.
Who would not be early to rise, and rise earlier and earlier every
successive day of his life, till he became unspeakably healthy,
wealthy, and wise? This foreign bird's note is celebrated by the poets of all countries along with the notes of their native songsters.
All climates agree with brave Chanticleer. He is more indigenous
even than the natives. His health is ever good, his lungs are sound,
his spirits never flag. Even the sailor on the Atlantic and Pacific is
awakened by his voice; but its shrill sound never roused me from
my slumbers. I kept neither dog, cat, cow, pig, nor hens, so that you
would have said there was a deficiency of domestic sounds; neither

the churn, nor the spinning wheel, nor even the singing of the kettle, nor the hissing of the urn, nor children crying, to comfort one. An old-fashioned man would have lost his senses or died of ennui before this. Not even rats in the wall, for they were starved out, or rather were never baited in,—only squirrels on the roof and under the floor, a whippoorwill on the ridge pole, a blue-jay screaming beneath the window, a hare or woodchuck under the house, a screech-owl or a cat-owl behind it, a flock of wild geese or a laughing loon on the pond, and a fox to bark in the night. Not even a lark or an oriole, those mild plantation birds, ever visited my clearing. No cockerels to crow nor hens to cackle in the yard. No yard! but unfenced Nature reaching up to your very sills. A young forest growing up under your windows, and wild sumachs and blackberry vines breaking through into your cellar; sturdy pitch-pines rubbing and creaking against the shingles for want of room, their roots reaching quite under the house. Instead of a scuttle or a blind blown off in the gale,—a pine tree snapped off or torn up by the roots behind your house for fuel. Instead of no path to the front-yard gate in the Great Snow,—no gate—no front-yard,—and no path to the civilized world!

Solitude

This is a delicious evening, when the whole body is one sense, and imbibes delight through every pore. I go and come with a strange liberty in Nature, a part of herself. As I walk along the stony shore of the pond in my shirt sleeves, though it is cool as well as cloudy and windy, and I see nothing special to attract me, all the elements are unusually congenial to me. The bullfrogs trump to usher in the night, and the note of the whippoorwill is borne on the rippling wind from over the water. Sympathy with the fluttering alder and poplar leaves almost takes away my breath; yet, like the lake, my serenity is rippled but not ruffled. These small waves raised by the evening wind are as remote from storm as the smooth reflecting surface. Though it is now dark, the wind still blows and roars in the wood, the waves still dash, and some creatures lull the rest with their notes. The repose is never complete. The wildest animals do not repose, but seek their prey now; the fox, and skunk, and rabbit, now roam the fields and woods without fear. They are Nature's watchmen,—links which connect the days of animated life.

When I return to my house I find that visitors have been there and left their cards, either a bunch of flowers, or a wreath of evergreen, or a name in pencil on a yellow walnut leaf or a chip. They who come rarely to the woods take some little piece of the forest into their hands to play with by the way, which they leave, either intentionally or accidentally. One has peeled a willow wand, woven it into a ring, and dropped it on my table. I could always tell if visitors had called in my absence, either by the bended twigs or grass, or the print of their shoes, and generally of what sex or age or quality they were by some slight trace left, as a flower dropped, or a bunch of grass plucked and thrown away, even as far off as the railroad, half a mile distant, or by the lingering odor of a cigar or pipe. Nay, I was frequently notified of the passage of a traveller along the highway sixty rods off by the scent of his pipe.

There is commonly sufficient space about us. Our horizon is never quite at our elbows. The thick wood is not just at our door, nor the pond, but somewhat is always clearing, familiar and worn by us, appropriated and fenced in some way, and reclaimed from Nature. For what reason have I this vast range and circuit, some square miles of unfrequented forest, for my privacy, abandoned to me by men? My nearest neighbor is a mile distant, and no house is visible from any place but the hill-tops within half a mile of my own. I have my horizon bounded by woods all to myself; a distant view of the railroad where it touches the pond on the one hand, and of the fence which skirts the woodland road on the other. But for the most part it is as solitary where I live as on the prairies. It is as much Asia or Africa as New England. I have, as it were, my own sun and moon and stars, and a little world all to myself. At night there was never a traveller passed my house, or knocked at my door, more than if I were the first or last man; unless it were in the spring, when at long intervals some came from the village to fish for pouts,—they plainly fished much more in the Walden Pond of their own natures, and baited their hooks with darkness,—but they soon retreated, usually with light baskets, and left "the world to darkness and to me,"[1] and the black kernel of the night was never profaned by any human neighborhood. I believe that men are generally still a little afraid of the dark, though the witches are all hung, and Christianity and candles have been introduced.

Yet I experienced sometimes that the most sweet and tender, the most innocent and encouraging society may be found in any natural object, even for the poor misanthrope and most melancholy man. There can be no very black melancholy to him who lives in the midst of Nature and has his senses still. There was never yet such a storm but it was Æolian music[2] to a healthy and innocent

---

1. From Thomas Gray, "Elegy Written in a Country Churchyard."
2. Music produced by a stringed instrument when placed in a window casement or otherwise exposed to a current of air; in Greek mythology Aeolus was the god of the winds.

ear. Nothing can rightly compel a simple and brave man to a vulgar sadness. While I enjoy the friendship of the seasons I trust that nothing can make life a burden to me. The gentle rain which waters my beans and keeps me in the house to-day is not drear and melancholy, but good for me too. Though it prevents my hoeing them, it is of far more worth than my hoeing. If it should continue so long as to cause the seeds to rot in the ground and destroy the potatoes in the low lands, it would still be good for the grass on the uplands, and, being good for the grass, it would be good for me. Sometimes, when I compare myself with other men, it seems as if I were more favored by the gods than they, beyond any deserts that I am conscious of; as if I had a warrant and surety at their hands which my fellows have not, and were especially guided and guarded. I do not flatter myself, but if it be possible they flatter me. I have never felt lonesome, or in the least oppressed by a sense of solitude, but once, and that was a few weeks after I came to the woods, when, for an hour, I doubted if the near neighborhood of man was not essential to a serene and healthy life. To be alone was something unpleasant. But I was at the same time conscious of a slight insanity in my mood, and seemed to foresee my recovery. In the midst of a gentle rain while these thoughts prevailed, I was suddenly sensible of such sweet and beneficent society in Nature, in the very pattering of the drops, and in every sound and sight around my house, an infinite and unaccountable friendliness all at once like an atmosphere sustaining me, as made the fancied advantages of human neighborhood insignificant, and I have never thought of them since. Every little pine needle expanded and swelled with sympathy and befriended me. I was so distinctly made aware of the presence of something kindred to me, even in scenes which we are accustomed to call wild and dreary, and also that the nearest of blood to me and humanest was not a person nor a villager, that I thought no place could ever be strange to me again.—

> "Mourning untimely consumes the sad;
> Few are their days in the land of the living,
> Beautiful daughter of Toscar."[3]

Some of my pleasantest hours were during the long rain storms in the spring or fall, which confined me to the house for the afternoon as well as the forenoon, soothed by their ceaseless roar and pelting; when an early twilight ushered in a long evening in which many thoughts had time to take root and unfold themselves. In those driving north-east rains which tried the village houses so,

---

3. From "Croma," in *The Genuine Remains of Ossian* by James Macpherson; the poem's hero is attempting to console Malvina, daughter of Toscar, after the death of her lover.

when the maids stood ready with mop and pail in front entries to keep the deluge out, I sat behind my door in my little house, which was all entry, and thoroughly enjoyed its protection. In one heavy thunder shower the lightning struck a large pitch-pine across the pond, making a very conspicuous and perfectly regular spiral groove from top to bottom, an inch or more deep, and four or five inches wide, as you would groove a walking-stick. I passed it again the other day, and was struck with awe on looking up and behold-ing that mark, now more distinct than ever, where a terrific and re-sistless bolt came down out of the harmless sky eight years ago. Men frequently say to me, "I should think you would feel lonesome down there, and want to be nearer to folks, rainy and snowy days and nights especially." I am tempted to reply to such,—This whole earth which we inhabit is but a point in space. How far apart, think you, dwell the two most distant inhabitants of yonder star, the breadth of whose disk cannot be appreciated by our instruments? Why should I feel lonely? is not our planet in the Milky Way? This which you put seems to me not to be the most important question. What sort of space is that which separates a man from his fellows and makes him solitary? I have found that no exertion of the legs can bring two minds much nearer to one another. What do we want most to dwell near to? Not to many men surely, the depot, the post-office, the bar-room, the meeting-house, the school-house, the gro-cery, Beacon Hill, or the Five Points,[4] where men most congregate, but to the perennial source of our life, whence in all our experience we have found that to issue, as the willow stands near the water and sends out its roots in that direction. This will vary with differ-ent natures, but this is the place where a wise man will dig his cel-lar. . . . I one evening overtook one of my townsmen, who has accumulated what is called "a handsome property,"—though I never got a *fair* view of it,—on the Walden road, driving a pair of cattle to market, who inquired of me how I could bring my mind to give up so many of the comforts of life. I answered that I was very sure I liked it passably well; I was not joking. And so I went home to my bed, and left him to pick his way through the darkness and the mud to Brighton,[5]—or Bright-town,—which place he would reach some time in the morning.

Any prospect of awakening or coming to life to a dead man makes indifferent all times and places. The place where that may occur is always the same, and indescribably pleasant to all our senses. For the most part we allow only outlying and transient cir-

4. Beacon Hill was the fashionable section of Boston; Five Points, in New York City, was known for its crime.
5. A suburb of Boston.

cumstances to make our occasions. They are, in fact, the cause of our distraction. Nearest to all things is that power which fashions their being. *Next* to us the grandest laws are continually being executed. *Next* to us is not the workman whom we have hired, with whom we love so well to talk, but the workman whose work we are.

"How vast and profound is the influence of the subtile powers of Heaven and of Earth!"

"We seek to perceive them, and we do not see them; we seek to hear them, and we do not hear them; identified with the substance of things, they cannot be separated from them."

"They cause that in all the universe men purify and sanctify their hearts, and clothe themselves in their holiday garments to offer sacrifices and oblations to their ancestors. It is an ocean of subtile intelligences. They are every where, above us, on our left, on our right; they environ us on all sides."[6]

We are the subjects of an experiment which is not a little interesting to me. Can we not do without the society of our gossips a little while under these circumstances,—have our own thoughts to cheer us? Confucius says truly, "Virtue does not remain as an abandoned orphan; it must of necessity have neighbors."[7]

With thinking we may be beside ourselves in a sane sense. By a conscious effort of the mind we can stand aloof from actions and their consequences; and all things, good and bad, go by us like a torrent. We are not wholly involved in Nature. I may be either the driftwood in the stream, or Indra[8] in the sky looking down on it. I *may* be affected by a theatrical exhibition; on the other hand, I *may not* be affected by an actual event which appears to concern me much more. I only know myself as a human entity; the scene, so to speak, of thoughts and affections; and am sensible of a certain doubleness by which I can stand as remote from myself as from another. However intense my experience, I am conscious of the presence and criticism of a part of me, which, as it were, is not a part of me, but spectator, sharing no experience, but taking note of it; and that is no more I than it is you. When the play, it may be the tragedy, of life is over, the spectator goes his way. It was a kind of fiction, a work of the imagination only, so far as he was concerned. This doubleness may easily make us poor neighbors and friends sometimes.

I find it wholesome to be alone the greater part of the time. To be in company, even with the best, is soon wearisome and dissipating. I love to be alone. I never found the companion that was so compan-

6. Confucius, *The Doctrine of the Mean* 14.
7. *Analects* 4.
8. In the Hindu Vedas, the god of air, thunder, and rain.

ionable as solitude. We are for the most part more lonely when we go abroad among men than when we stay in our chambers. A man thinking or working is always alone, let him be where he will. Solitude is not measured by the miles of space that intervene between a man and his fellows. The really diligent student in one of the crowded hives of Cambridge College is as solitary as a dervis in the desert. The farmer can work alone in the field or the woods all day, hoeing or chopping, and not feel lonesome, because he is employed; but when he comes home at night he cannot sit down in a room alone, at the mercy of his thoughts, but must be where he can "see the folks," and recreate, and as he thinks remunerate himself for his day's solitude; and hence he wonders how the student can sit alone in the house all night and most of the day without ennui and "the blues;" but he does not realize that the student, though in the house, is still at work in *his* field, and chopping in *his* woods, as the farmer in his, and in turn seeks the same recreation and society that the latter does, though it may be a more condensed form of it.

Society is commonly too cheap. We meet at very short intervals, not having had time to acquire any new value for each other. We meet at meals three times a day, and give each other a new taste of that old musty cheese that we are. We have had to agree on a certain set of rules, called etiquette and politeness, to make this frequent meeting tolerable and that we need not come to open war. We meet at the post-office, and at the sociable, and about the fireside every night; we live thick and are in each other's way, and stumble over one another, and I think that we thus lose some respect for one another. Certainly less frequency would suffice for all important and hearty communications. Consider the girls in a factory,—never alone, hardly in their dreams. It would be better if there were but one inhabitant to a square mile, as where I live. The value of a man is not in his skin, that we should touch him.

I have heard of a man lost in the woods and dying of famine and exhaustion at the foot of a tree, whose loneliness was relieved by the grotesque visions with which, owing to bodily weakness, his diseased imagination surrounded him, and which he believed to be real. So also, owing to bodily and mental health and strength, we may be continually cheered by a like but more normal and natural society, and come to know that we are never alone.

I have a great deal of company in my house; especially in the morning, when nobody calls. Let me suggest a few comparisons, that some one may convey an idea of my situation. I am no more lonely than the loon in the pond that laughs so loud, or than Walden Pond itself. What company has that lonely lake, I pray? And yet it has not the blue devils, but the blue angels in it, in the azure tint of its waters. The sun is alone, except in thick weather, when there sometimes appear to be two, but one is a mock sun. God is alone,—but the devil, he is far from being alone; he sees a great deal of company; he is legion. I am no more lonely than a single mullein or dandelion in a pasture, or a bean leaf, or sorrel, or a horse-fly, or a humble-bee. I am no more lonely than the Mill Brook, or a weathercock, or the north star, or the south wind, or an April shower, or a January thaw, or the first spider in a new house.

I have occasional visits in the long winter evenings, when the snow falls fast and the wind howls in the wood, from an old settler and original proprietor, who is reported to have dug Walden Pond, and stoned it, and fringed it with pine woods; who tells me stories of old time and of new eternity; and between us we manage to pass a cheerful evening with social mirth and pleasant views of things, even without apples or cider,—a most wise and humorous friend, whom I love much, who keeps himself more secret than ever did Goffe or Whalley;[9] and though he is thought to be dead, none can show where he is buried. An elderly dame, too, dwells in my neighborhood, invisible to most persons, in whose odorous herb garden I love to stroll sometimes, gathering simples and listening to her fables; for she has a genius of unequalled fertility, and her memory runs back farther than mythology, and she can tell me the original of every fable, and on what fact every one is founded, for the incidents occurred when she was young. A ruddy and lusty old dame, who delights in all weathers and seasons, and is likely to outlive all her children yet.

The indescribable innocence and beneficence of Nature,—of sun and wind and rain, of summer and winter,—such health, such cheer, they afford forever! and such sympathy have they ever with our race, that all Nature would be affected, and the sun's brightness fade, and the winds would sigh humanely, and the clouds rain tears, and the woods shed their leaves and put on mourning in midsummer, if any man should ever for a just cause grieve. Shall I not have intelligence with the earth? Am I not partly leaves and vegetable mould myself?

What is the pill which will keep us well, serene, contented? Not my or thy great-grandfather's, but our great-grandmother Nature's universal, vegetable, botanic medicines, by which she has kept herself young always, outlived so many old Parrs[1] in her day, and fed her health with their decaying fatness. For my panacea, instead of one of those quack vials of a mixture dipped from Acheron[2] and the

9. William Goffe (d. ca. 1679) and Edward Whalley (1615?–1675?), two of the men indicted for killing Charles I of England, fled to America, where they lived in hiding.
1. Thomas Parr, an Englishman born in 1483 who reputedly lived 152 years.
2. In Greek mythology, Acheron was one of the five rivers surrounding the land of the dead; the Dead Sea is a large salt lake on the Israel-Jordan border.

Dead Sea, which come out of those long shallow black-schooner looking wagons which we sometimes see made to carry bottles, let me have a draught of undiluted morning air. Morning air! If men will not drink of this at the fountainhead of the day, why, then, we must even bottle up some and sell it in the shops, for the benefit of those who have lost their subscription ticket to morning time in this world. But remember, it will not keep quite till noonday even in the coolest cellar, but drive out the stopples long ere that and follow westward the steps of Aurora. I am no worshipper of Hygeia,[3] who was the daughter of that old herb-doctor Æsculapius, and who is represented on monuments holding a serpent in one hand, and in the other a cup out of which the serpent sometimes drinks; but rather of Hebe,[4] cupbearer to Jupiter, who was the daughter of Juno and wild lettuce, and who had the power of restoring gods and men to the vigor of youth. She was probably the only thoroughly sound-conditioned, healthy, and robust young lady that ever walked the globe, and wherever she came it was spring.

Visitors

I think that I love society as much as most, and am ready enough to fasten myself like a bloodsucker for the time to any full-blooded man that comes in my way. I am naturally no hermit, but might possibly sit out the sturdiest frequenter of the bar-room, if my business called me thither.

I had three chairs in my house; one for solitude, two for friendship, three for society. When visitors came in larger and unexpected numbers there was but the third chair for them all, but they generally economized the room by standing up. It is surprising how many great men and women a small house will contain. I have had twenty-five or thirty souls, with their bodies, at once under my roof, and yet we often parted without being aware that we had come very near to one another. Many of our houses, both public and private, with their almost innumerable apartments, their huge halls and their cellars for the storage of wines and other munitions of peace, appear to me extravagantly large for their inhabitants. They are so vast and magnificent that the latter seem to be only vermin which infest them. I am surprised when the herald blows his summons before some Tremont or Astor or Middlesex House,[1] to see come

---

3. In Greek mythology, the goddess of health and daughter of Æsculapius, the god of medical arts.
4. In Greek mythology, Hebe was the goddess of youth, the daughter of Zeus (called "Jupiter" by the Romans) and Hera (called "Juno" by the Romans); according to some legends, Hebe was conceived after Hera ate some wild lettuce.
1. Prosperous hotels in Boston, New York, and Concord, respectively.

creeping out over the piazza for all inhabitants a ridiculous mouse, which soon again slinks into some hole in the pavement.

One inconvenience I sometimes experienced in so small a house, the difficulty of getting to a sufficient distance from my guest when we began to utter the big thoughts in big words. You want room for your thoughts to get into sailing trim and run a course or two before they make their port. The bullet of your thought must have overcome its lateral and ricochet motion and fallen into its last and steady course before it reaches the ear of the hearer, else it may plough out again through the side of his head. Also, our sentences wanted room to unfold and form their columns in the interval. Individuals, like nations, must have suitable broad and natural boundaries, even a considerable neutral ground, between them. I have found it a singular luxury to talk across the pond to a companion on the opposite side. In my house we were so near that we could not begin to hear,—we could not speak low enough to be heard; as when you throw two stones into calm water so near that they break each other's undulations. If we are merely loquacious and loud talkers, then we can afford to stand very near together, cheek by jowl, and feel each other's breath; but if we speak reservedly and thoughtfully, we want to be farther apart, that all animal heat and moisture may have a chance to evaporate. If we would enjoy the most intimate society with that in each of us which is without, or above, being spoken to, we must not only be silent, but commonly so far apart bodily that we cannot possibly hear each other's voice in any case. Referred to this standard, speech is for the convenience of those who are hard of hearing; but there are many fine things which we cannot say if we have to shout. As the conversation began to assume a loftier and grander tone, we gradually shoved our chairs farther apart till they touched the wall in opposite corners, and then commonly there was not room enough.

My "best" room, however, my withdrawing room, always ready for company, on whose carpet the sun rarely fell, was the pine wood behind my house. Thither in summer days, when distinguished guests came, I took them, and a priceless domestic swept the floor and dusted the furniture and kept the things in order.

If one guest came he sometimes partook of my frugal meal, and it was no interruption to conversation to be stirring a hasty-pudding, or watching the rising and maturing of a loaf of bread in the ashes, in the mean while. But if twenty came and sat in my house there was nothing said about dinner, though there might be bread enough for two, more than if eating were a forsaken habit; but we naturally practised abstinence; and this was never felt to be an offence against hospitality, but the most proper and considerate course. The waste and decay of physical life, which so often needs

repair, seemed miraculously retarded in such a case, and the vital
vigor stood its ground. I could entertain thus a thousand as well as
twenty; and if any ever went away disappointed or hungry from my
house when they found me at home, they may depend upon it that
I sympathized with them at least. So easy is it, though many housekeepers doubt it, to establish new and better customs in the place
of the old. You need not rest your reputation on the dinners you
give. For my own part, I was never so effectually deterred from fre-
quenting a man's house, by any kind of Cerberus[2] whatever, as by
the parade one made about dining me, which I took to be a very polite and roundabout hint never to trouble him so again. I think I
shall never revisit those scenes. I should be proud to have for the
motto of my cabin those lines of Spenser which one of my visitors
inscribed on a yellow walnut leaf for a card:—

> "Arrivéd there, the little house they fill,
>   Ne looke for entertainment where none was;
> Rest is their feast, and all things at their will:
>   The noblest mind the best contentment has."[3]

When Winslow afterward governor of the Plymouth Colony, went
with a companion on a visit of ceremony to Massassoit on foot
through the woods, and arrived tired and hungry at his lodge, they
were well received by the king, but nothing was said about eating
that day. When the night arrived, to quote their own words,—"He
laid us on the bed with himself and his wife, they at the one end
and we at the other, it being only plank, laid a foot from the
ground, and a thin mat upon them. Two more of his chief men, for
want of room, pressed by and upon us; so that we were worse weary
of our lodging than of our journey." At one o'clock the next day
Massassoit "brought two fishes that he had shot," about thrice as
big as a bream; "these being boiled, there were at least forty looked
for a share in them. The most ate of them. This meal only we had
in two nights and a day; and had not one of us bought a partridge,
we had taken our journey fasting." Fearing that they would be light-
headed for want of food and also sleep, owing to "the savages' barbarous singing, (for they used to sing themselves asleep,)" and that
they might get home while they had strength to travel, they departed.[4] As for lodging, it is true they were but poorly entertained,
though what they found an inconvenience was no doubt intended
for an honor; but as far as eating was concerned, I do not see how

---

2. In Greek mythology, a three-headed dog who guarded the entrance to the land of the
   dead.
3. Edmund Spenser, *The Fairie Queen* 1.1.35.
4. From Edward Winslow, *The English Plantation at Plymouth* (1622); Massassoit
   (1590–1661) was a Wampanoag chief friendly to the Plymouth settlers.

the Indians could have done better. They had nothing to eat themselves, and they were wiser than to think that apologies could supply the place of food to their guests; so they drew their belts tighter
and said nothing about it. Another time when Winslow visited
them, it being a season of plenty with them, there was no deficiency in this respect.

As for men, they will hardly fail one any where. I had more visitors while I lived in the woods than at any other period of my life; I
mean that I had some. I met several there under more favorable
circumstances than I could any where else. But fewer came to see
me upon trivial business. In this respect, my company was winnowed by my mere distance from town. I had withdrawn so far
within the great ocean of solitude, into which the rivers of society
empty, that for the most part, so far as my needs were concerned,
only the finest sediment was deposited around me. Beside, there
were wafted to me evidences of unexplored and uncultivated continents on the other side.

Who should come to my lodge this morning but a true Homeric
or Paphlagonian[5] man,—he had so suitable and poetic a name that
I am sorry I cannot print it here,—a Canadian, a woodchopper and
post-maker, who can hole fifty posts in a day, who made his last
supper on a woodchuck which his dog caught. He, too, has heard
of Homer, and, "if it were not for books," would "not know what to
do rainy days," though perhaps he has not read one wholly through
for many rainy seasons. Some priest who could pronounce the
Greek itself taught him to read his verse in the testament in his native parish far away; and now I must translate to him, while he
holds the book, Achilles' reproof to Patroclus for his sad countenance.—"Why are you in tears, Patroclus, like a young girl?"—

"Or have you alone heard some news from Phthia?
   They say that Menœtius lives yet, son of Actor,
   And Peleus lives, son of Æacus, among the Myrmidons,
   Either of whom having died, we should greatly grieve."[6]

He says, "That's good." He has a great bundle of white-oak bark under his arm for a sick man, gathered this Sunday morning. "I suppose there's no harm in going after such a thing to-day," says he. To
him Homer was a great writer, though what his writing was about
he did not know. A more simple and natural man it would be hard
to find. Vice and disease, which cast such a sombre moral hue over
the world, seemed to have hardly any existence for him. He was
about twenty-eight years old, and had left Canada and his father's

5. Paphlagonia was a heavily wooded country in northern Asia Minor whose inhabitants
   were known for their heaviness and dullness; the woodchopper was Alek Therien.
6. The *Iliad* 16.13–16; Patroclus is Achilles' closest friend, whose death Achilles avenges.

house a dozen years before to work in the States, and earn money to buy a farm with at last, perhaps in his native country. He was cast in the coarsest mould; a stout but sluggish body, yet gracefully carried, with a thick sunburnt neck, dark bushy hair, and dull sleepy blue eyes, which were occasionally lit up with expression. He wore a flat gray cloth cap, a dingy wool-colored greatcoat, and cowhide boots. He was a great consumer of meat, usually carrying his dinner to his work a couple of miles past my house,—for he chopped all summer,—in a tin pail; cold meats, often cold wood-chucks, and coffee in a stone bottle which dangled by a string from his belt; and sometimes he offered me a drink. He came along early, crossing my bean-field, though without anxiety or haste to get to his work, such as Yankees exhibit. He wasn't a-going to hurt himself. He didn't care if he only earned his board. Frequently he would leave his dinner in the bushes, when his dog had caught a woodchuck by the way, and go back a mile and a half to dress it and leave it in the cellar of the house where he boarded, after deliberating first for half an hour whether he could not sink it in the pond safely till nightfall,—loving to dwell long upon these themes. He would say, as he went by in the morning, "How thick the pigeons are! If working every day were not my trade, I could get all the meat I should want by hunting,—pigeons, woodchucks, rabbits, partridges,—by gosh! I could get all I should want for a week in one day."

He was a skilful chopper, and indulged in some flourishes and ornaments in his art. He cut his trees level and close to the ground, that the sprouts which came up afterward might be more vigorous and a sled might slide over the stumps; and instead of leaving a whole tree to support his corded wood, he would pare it away to a slender stake or splinter which you could break off with your hand at last.

He interested me because he was so quiet and solitary and so happy withal; a well of good humor and contentment which overflowed at his eyes. His mirth was without alloy. Sometimes I saw him at his work in the woods, felling trees, and he would greet me with a laugh of inexpressible satisfaction, and a salutation in Canadian French, though he spoke English as well. When I approached him he would suspend his work, and with half-suppressed mirth lie along the trunk of a pine which he had felled, and, peeling off the inner bark, roll it up into a ball and chew it while he laughed and talked. Such an exuberance of animal spirits had he that he sometimes tumbled down and rolled on the ground with laughter at any thing which made him think and tickled him. Looking round upon the trees he would exclaim,—"By George! I can enjoy myself well enough here chopping; I want no better sport." Sometimes, when at leisure, he amused himself all day in the woods with a pocket pistol, firing salutes to himself at regular intervals as he walked. In the winter he had a fire by which at noon he warmed his coffee in a kettle; and as he sat on a log to eat his dinner the chicadees would sometimes come round and alight on his arm and peck at the potato in his fingers; and he said that he "liked to have the little *fellers* about him."

In him the animal man chiefly was developed. In physical endurance and contentment he was cousin to the pine and the rock. I asked him once if he was not sometimes tired at night, after working all day; and he answered, with a sincere and serious look, "Gorrappit, I never was tired in my life." But the intellectual and what is called spiritual man in him were slumbering as in an infant. He had been instructed only in that innocent and ineffectual way in which the Catholic priests teach the aborigines, by which the pupil is never educated to the degree of consciousness, but only to the degree of trust and reverence, and a child is not made a man, but kept a child. When Nature made him, she gave him a strong body and contentment for his portion, and propped him on every side with reverence and reliance, that he might live out his threescore years and ten a child. He was so genuine and unsophisticated that no introduction would serve to introduce him, more than if you introduced a woodchuck to your neighbor. He had got to find him out as you did. He would not play any part. Men paid him wages for work, and so helped to feed and clothe him; but he never exchanged opinions with them. He was so simply and naturally humble—if he can be called humble who never aspires—that humility was no distinct quality in him, nor could he conceive of it. Wiser men were demigods to him. If you told him that such a one was coming, he did as if he thought that any thing so grand would expect nothing of himself, but take all the responsibility on itself, and let him be forgotten still. He never heard the sound of praise. He particularly reverenced the writer and the preacher. Their performances were miracles. When I told him that I wrote considerably, he thought for a long time that it was merely the handwriting which I meant, for he could write a remarkably good hand himself. I sometimes found the name of his native parish handsomely written in the snow by the highway, with the proper French accent, and knew that he had passed. I asked him if he ever wished to write his thoughts. He said that he had read and written letters for those who could not, but he never tried to write thoughts,—no, he could not, he could not tell what to put first, it would kill him, and then there was spelling to be attended to at the same time!

I heard that a distinguished wise man and reformer asked him if he did not want the world to be changed; but he answered with a chuckle of surprise in his Canadian accent, not knowing that the question had ever been entertained before, "No, I like it well enough." It would have suggested many things to a philosopher to have dealings with him. To a stranger he appeared to know nothing of things in general; yet I sometimes saw in him a man whom I had not seen before, and I did not know whether he was as wise as Shakspeare or as simply ignorant as a child, whether to suspect him of a fine poetic consciousness or of stupidity. A townsman told me that when he met him sauntering through the village in his small close-fitting cap, and whistling to himself, he reminded him of a prince in disguise.

His only books were an almanac and an arithmetic, in which last he was considerably expert. The former was a sort of cyclopædia to him, which he supposed to contain an abstract of human knowledge, as indeed it does to a considerable extent. I loved to sound him on the various reforms of the day, and he never failed to look at them in the most simple and practical light. He had never heard of such things before. Could he do without factories? I asked. He had worn the home-made Vermont gray, he said, and that was good. Could he dispense with tea and coffee? Did this country afford any beverage beside water? He had soaked hemlock leaves in water and drank it, and thought that was better than water in warm weather. When I asked him if he could do without money, he showed the convenience of money in such a way as to suggest and coincide with the most philosophical accounts of the origin of this institution, and the very derivation of the word *pecunia*.[7] If an ox were his property, and he wished to get needles and thread at the store, he thought it would be inconvenient and impossible soon to go on mortgaging some portion of the creature each time to that amount. He could defend many institutions better than any philosopher, because, in describing them as they concerned him, he gave the true reason for their prevalence, and speculation had not suggested to him any other. At another time, hearing Plato's definition of a man,—a biped without feathers,—and that one exhibited a cock plucked and called it Plato's man, he thought it an important difference that the *knees* bent the wrong way. He would sometimes exclaim, "How I love to talk! By George, I could talk all day!" I asked him once, when I had not seen him for many months, if he had got a new idea this summer. "Good Lord," said he, "a man that has to work as I do, if he does not forget the ideas he has had, he will do well. May be the man you hoe with is inclined to race; then, by gorry, your mind must be there; you think of weeds." He would sometimes ask me first on such occasions, if I had made any im-

7. Latin for "money"; derived from *pecus*, "cattle."

provement. One winter day I asked him if he was always satisfied
with himself, wishing to suggest a substitute within him for the
priest without, and some higher motive for living. "Satisfied!" said
he; "some men are satisfied with one thing, and some with another.
One man, perhaps, if he has got enough, will be satisfied to sit all
day with his back to the fire and his belly to the table, by George!"
Yet I never, by any manœuvring, could get him to take the spiritual
view of things; the highest that he appeared to conceive of was a
simple expediency, such as you might expect an animal to appreciate; and this, practically, is true of most men. If I suggested any improvement in his mode of life, he merely answered, without
expressing any regret, that it was too late. Yet he thoroughly believed in honesty and the like virtues.

There was a certain positive originality, however slight, to be detected in him, and I occasionally observed that he was thinking for
himself and expressing his own opinion, a phenomenon so rare that
I would any day walk ten miles to observe it, and it amounted to the
re-origination of many of the institutions of society. Though he hesitated, and perhaps failed to express himself distinctly, he always
had a presentable thought behind. Yet his thinking was so primitive
and immersed in his animal life, that, though more promising than
a merely learned man's, it rarely ripened to any thing which can be
reported. He suggested that there might be men of genius in the
lowest grades of life, however permanently humble and illiterate,
who take their own view always, or do not pretend to see at all; who
are as bottomless even as Walden Pond was thought to be, though
they may be dark and muddy.

Many a traveller came out of his way to see me and the inside of
my house, and, as an excuse for calling, asked for a glass of water. I
told them that I drank at the pond, and pointed thither, offering to
lend them a dipper. Far off as I lived, I was not exempted from that
annual visitation which occurs, methinks, about the first of April,
when every body is on the move; and I had my share of good luck,
though there were some curious specimens among my visitors. Half-
witted men from the almshouse and elsewhere came to see me; but
I endeavored to make them exercise all the wit they had, and make
their confessions to me; in such cases making wit the theme of our
conversation; and so was compensated. Indeed, I found some of
them to be wiser than the so called *overseers* of the poor and selectmen of the town, and thought it was time that the tables were
turned. With respect to wit, I learned that there was not much difference between the half and the whole. One day, in particular, an
inoffensive, simple-minded pauper, whom with others I had often
seen used as fencing stuff, standing or sitting on a bushel in the
fields to keep cattle and himself from straying, visited me, and ex-

pressed a wish to live as I did. He told me, with the utmost simplicity and truth, quite superior, or rather *inferior*, to any thing that is called humility, that he was "deficient in intellect." These were his words. The Lord had made him so, yet he supposed the Lord cared as much for him as for another. "I have always been so," said he, "from my childhood; I never had much mind; I was not like other children; I am weak in the head. It was the Lord's will, I suppose." And there he was to prove the truth of his words. He was a metaphysical puzzle to me. I have rarely met a fellow-man on such promising ground,—it was so simple and sincere and so true all that he said. And, true enough, in proportion as he appeared to humble himself was he exalted. I did not know at first but it was the result of a wise policy. It seemed that from such a basis of truth and frankness as the poor weak-headed pauper had laid, our intercourse might go forward to something better than the intercourse of sages.

I had some guests from those not reckoned commonly among the town's poor, but who should be; who are among the world's poor, at any rate; guests who appeal, not to your hospitality, but to your *hospitalality*; who earnestly wish to be helped, and preface their appeal with the information that they are resolved, for one thing, never to help themselves. I require of a visitor that he be not actually starving, though he may have the very best appetite in the world, however he got it. Objects of charity are not guests. Men who did not know when their visit had terminated, though I went about my business again, answering them from greater and greater remoteness. Men of almost every degree of wit called on me in the migrating season. Some who had more wits than they knew what to do with; runaway slaves with plantation manners, who listened from time to time, like the fox in the fable, as if they heard the hounds a-baying on their track, and looked at me beseechingly, as much as to say,—

"O Christian, will you send me back?"[8]

One real runaway slave, among the rest, whom I helped to forward toward the northstar. Men of one idea, like a hen with one chicken, and that a duckling; men of a thousand ideas, and unkempt heads, like those hens which are made to take charge of a hundred chickens, all in pursuit of one bug, a score of them lost in every morning's dew,—and become frizzled and mangy in consequence; men of ideas instead of legs, a sort of intellectual centipede that made you crawl all over. One man proposed a book in which visitors should write their names, as at the White Mountains; but, alas! I have too good a memory to make that necessary.

I could not but notice some of the peculiarities of my visitors.

---

8. Refrain in "The Fugitive Slave to the Christian" by Elizur Wright (1804–85), American actuary and anti-slavery leader.

Girls and boys and young women generally seemed glad to be in the woods. They looked in the pond and at the flowers, and improved their time. Men of business, even farmers, thought only of solitude and employment, and of the great distance at which I dwelt from something or other; and though they said that they loved a ramble in the woods occasionally, it was obvious that they did not. Restless committed men, whose time was all taken up in getting a living or keeping it; ministers who spoke of God as if they enjoyed a monopoly of the subject, who could not bear all kinds of opinions; doctors, lawyers, uneasy housekeepers who pried into my cupboard and bed when I was out,—how came Mrs.—to know that my sheets were not as clean as hers?—young men who had ceased to be young, and had concluded that it was safest to follow the beaten track of the professions,—all these generally said that it was not possible to do so much good in my position. Ay! there was the rub. The old and infirm and the timid, of whatever age or sex, thought most of sickness, and sudden accident and death; to them life seemed full of danger,—what danger is there if you don't think of any?—and they thought that a prudent man would carefully select the safest position, where Dr. B.[9] might be on hand at a moment's warming. To them the village was literally a *com-munity*, a league for mutual defence, and you would suppose that they would not go a-huckleberrying without a medicine chest. The amount of it is, if a man is alive, there is always *danger* that he may die, though the danger must be allowed to be less in proportion as he is dead-and-alive to begin with. A man sits as many risks as he runs. Finally, there were the self-styled reformers, the greatest bores of all, who thought that I was forever singing,—

> This is the house that I built;
> This is the man that lives in the house that I built;

but they did not know that the third line was,—

> These are the folks that worry the man
> That lives in the house that I built.

I did not fear the hen-harriers, for I kept no chickens; but I feared the men-harriers rather.

I had more cheering visitors than the last. Children come aberrying, railroad men taking a Sunday morning walk in clean shirts, fishermen and hunters, poets and philosophers, in short, all honest pilgrims, who came out to the woods for freedom's sake, and really left the village behind, I was ready to greet with,—"Welcome, Englishmen! welcome, Englishmen!"[1] for I had had communication with that race.

9. Josiah Bartlett II, a physician from Concord.
1. Reputedly the greeting of the Indian, Samoset, to the Pilgrims who landed at Plymouth.

The Bean-Field

Meanwhile my beans, the length of whose rows, added together, was seven miles already planted, were impatient to be hoed, for the earliest had grown considerably before the latest were in the ground; indeed they were not easily to be put off. What was the meaning of this so steady and self-respecting, this small Herculean labor, I knew not. I came to love my rows, my beans, though so many more than I wanted. They attached me to the earth, and so I got strength like Antæus.[1] But why should I raise them? Only Heaven knows. This was my curious labor all summer,—to make this portion of the earth's surface, which had yielded only cinque-foil, blackberries, johnswort, and the like, before, sweet wild fruits and pleasant flowers, produce instead this pulse. What shall I learn of beans or beans of me? I cherish them, I hoe them, early and late I have an eye to them; and this is my day's work. It is a fine broad leaf to look on. My auxiliaries are the dews and rains which water this dry soil, and what fertility is in the soil itself, which for the most part is lean and effete. My enemies are worms, cool days, and most of all woodchucks. The last have nibbled for me a quarter of an acre clean. But what right had I to oust johnswort and the rest, and break up their ancient herb garden? Soon, however, the remaining beans will be too tough for them, and go forward to meet new foes.

When I was four years old, as I well remember, I was brought from Boston to this my native town, through these very woods and this field, to the pond. It is one of the oldest scenes stamped on my memory. And now to-night my flute has waked the echoes over that very water. The pines still stand here older than I; or, if some have fallen, I have cooked my supper with their stumps, and a new growth is rising all around, preparing another aspect for new infant eyes. Almost the same johnswort springs from the same perennial root in this pasture, and even I have at length helped to clothe that fabulous landscape of my infant dreams, and one of the results of my presence and influence is seen in these bean leaves, corn blades, and potato vines.

I planted about two acres and a half of upland; and as it was only about fifteen years since the land was cleared, and I myself had got out two or three cords of stumps, I did not give it any manure; but in the course of the summer it appeared by the arrow-heads which I turned up in hoeing, that an extinct nation had anciently dwelt here and planted corn and beans ere white men came to clear the land, and so, to some extent, had exhausted the soil for this very crop.

---

1. A mythical giant in Greek mythology who got his strength from touching the earth; he was strangled by Hercules, who held him off the ground.

Before yet any woodchuck or squirrel had run across the road, or the sun had got above the shrub-oaks, while all the dew was on, though the farmers warned me against it,—I would advise you to do all your work if possible while the dew is on,—I began to level the ranks of haughty weeds in my bean-field and throw dust upon their heads. Early in the morning I worked barefooted, dabbling like a plastic artist in the dewy and crumbling sand, but later in the day the sun blistered my feet. There the sun lighted me to hoe beans, pacing slowly backward and forward over that yellow gravelly upland, between the long green rows, fifteen rods, the one end terminating in a shrub oak copse where I could rest in the shade, the other in a blackberry field where the green berries deepened their tints by the time I had made another bout. Removing the weeds, putting fresh soil about the bean stems, and encouraging this weed which I had sown, making the yellow soil express its summer thought in bean leaves and blossoms rather than in wormwood and piper and millet grass, making the earth say beans instead of grass,—this was my daily work. As I had little aid from horses or cattle, or hired men or boys, or improved implements of husbandry, I was much slower, and became much more intimate with my beans than usual. But labor of the hands, even when pursued to the verge of drudgery, is perhaps never the worst form of idleness. It has a constant and imperishable moral, and to the scholar it yields a classic result. A very *agricola laboriosus*[2] was I to travellers bound westward through Lincoln and Wayland to nobody knows where; they sitting at their ease in gigs, with elbows on knees, and reins loosely hanging in festoons; I the home-staying, laborious native of the soil. But soon my homestead was out of their sight and thought. It was the only open and cultivated field for a great distance on either side of the road; so they made the most of it; and sometimes the man in the field heard more of travellers' gossip and comment than was meant for his ear: "Beans so late! peas so late!"—for I continued to plant when others had began to hoe,— the ministerial husbandman had not suspected it. "Corn, my boy, for fodder; corn for fodder." "Does he *live* there?" asks the black bonnet of the gray coat; and the hard-featured farmer reins up his grateful dobbin to inquire what you are doing where he sees no manure in the furrow, and recommends a little chip dirt, or any little waste stuff, or it may be ashes or plaster. But here were two acres and a half of furrows, and only a hoe for cart and two hands to draw it,—there being an aversion to other carts and horses,—and chip dirt far away. Fellow-travellers as they rattled by compared it aloud with the fields which they had passed, so that I came to know how I

2. "Hard-working farmer"; Lincoln and Wayland are towns near Concord.

stood in the agricultural world. This was one field not in Mr. Coleman's report.[3] And, by the way, who estimates the value of the crop
which Nature yields in the still wilder fields unimproved by man?
The crop of *English* hay is carefully weighed, the moisture calculated, the silicates and the potash; but in all dells and pond holes in
the woods and pastures and swamps grows a rich and various crop
only unreaped by man. Mine was, as it were, the connecting link between wild and cultivated fields; as some states are civilized, and
others half-civilized, and others savage or barbarous, so my field
was, though not in a bad sense, a half-cultivated field. They were
beans cheerfully returning to their wild and primitive state that I
cultivated, and my hoe played the *Rans des Vaches*[4] for them.

Near at hand, upon the topmost spray of a birch, sings the
brown-thrasher—or red mavis, as some love to call him—all the
morning, glad of your society, that would find out another farmer's
field if yours were not here. While you are planting the seed, he
cries,—"Drop it, drop it,—cover it up, cover it up,—pull it up, pull
it up, pull it up." But this was not corn, and so it was safe from
such enemies as he. You may wonder what his rigmarole, his ama-
teur Paganini[5] performances on one string or on twenty, have to do
with your planting, and yet prefer it to leached ashes or plaster. It
was a cheap sort of top dressing in which I had entire faith.

As I drew a still fresher soil about the rows with my hoe, I disturbed the ashes of unchronicled nations who in primeval years
lived under these heavens, and their small implements of war and
hunting were brought to the light of this modern day. They lay mingled with other natural stones, some of which bore the marks of
having been burned by Indian fires, and some by the sun, and also
bits of pottery and glass brought hither by the recent cultivators of
the soil. When my hoe tinkled against the stones, that music
echoed to the woods and the sky, and was an accompaniment to my
labor which yielded an instant and immeasurable crop. It was no
longer beans that I hoed, nor I that hoed beans; and I remembered
with as much pity as pride, if I remembered at all, my acquaintances who had gone to the city to attend the oratorios. The night-
hawk circled overhead in the sunny afternoons—for I sometimes
made a day of it—like a mote in the eye, or in heaven's eye, falling
from time to time with a swoop and a sound as if the heavens were
rent, torn at last to very rags and tatters, and yet a seamless cope
remained; small imps that fill the air and lay their eggs on the
ground on bare sand or rocks on the tops of hills, where few have

3. Henry Coleman (1785–1849), State Commissioner for the Agricultural Survey of Mass-
    achusetts.
4. A song for calling cattle, sung or played by Swiss cowherds.
5. Nicolo Paganini (1782–1840), Italian violinist and composer.

found them; graceful and slender like ripples caught up from the pond, as leaves are raised by the wind to float in the heavens; such kindredship is in Nature. The hawk is aerial brother of the wave which he sails over and surveys, those his perfect air-inflated wings answering to the elemental unfledged pinions of the sea. Or sometimes I watched a pair of hen-hawks circling high in the sky, alternately soaring and descending, approaching and leaving one another, as if they were the imbodiment of my own thoughts. Or I was attracted by the passage of wild pigeons from this wood to that, with a slight quivering winnowing sound and carrier haste; or from under a rotten stump my hoe turned up a sluggish portentous and outlandish spotted salamander, a trace of Egypt and the Nile, yet our contemporary. When I paused to lean on my hoe, these sounds and sights I heard and saw any where in the row, a part of the inexhaustible entertainment which the country offers.

On gala days the town fires its great guns, which echo like pop-guns to these woods, and some waifs of martial music occasionally penetrate thus far. To me, away there in my bean-field at the other end of the town, the big guns sounded as if a puff ball had burst; and when there was a military turnout of which I was ignorant, I have sometimes had a vague sense all the day of some sort of itching and disease in the horizon, as if some eruption would break out there soon, either scarlatina or canker-rash, until at length some more favorable puff of wind, making haste over the fields and up the Wayland road, brought me information of the "trainers."[6] It seemed by the distant hum as if somebody's bees had swarmed, and that the neighbors, according to Virgil's advice, by a faint *tintinnabulum* upon the most sonorous of their domestic utensils, were endeavoring to call them down into the hive again. And when the sound died quite away, and the hum had ceased, and the most favorable breezes told no tale, I knew that they had got the last drone of them all safely into the Middlesex hive, and that now their minds were bent on the honey with which it was smeared.

I felt proud to know that the liberties of Massachusetts and of our fatherland were in such safe keeping; and as I turned to my hoeing again I was filled with an inexpressible confidence, and pursued my labor cheerfully with a calm trust in the future.

When there were several bands of musicians, it sounded as if all the village was a vast bellows, and all the buildings expanded and collapsed alternately with a din. But sometimes it was a really noble and inspiring strain that reached these woods, and the trumpet that sings of fame, and I felt as if I could spit a Mexican with a good relish,—for why should we always stand for trifles?—and looked

6. Members of the Concord Artillery, a unit of the state militia.

round for a woodchuck or a skunk to exercise my chivalry upon. These martial strains seemed as far away as Palestine, and reminded me of a march of crusaders in the horizon, with a slight tantivy and tremulous motion of the elm-tree tops which overhang the village. This was one of the *great* days; though the sky had from my clearing only the same everlastingly great look that it wears daily, and I saw no difference in it.

It was a singular experience that long acquaintance which I cultivated with beans, what with planting, and hoeing, and harvesting, and threshing, and picking over, and selling them,—the last was the hardest of all,—I might add eating, for I did taste. I was determined to know beans. When they were growing, I used to hoe from five o'clock in the morning till noon, and commonly spent the rest of the day about other affairs. Consider the intimate and curious acquaintance one makes with various kinds of weeds,—it will bear some iteration in the account, for there was no little iteration in the labor,—disturbing their delicate organizations so ruthlessly, and making such invidious distinctions with his hoe, levelling whole ranks of one species, and sedulously cultivating another. That's Roman wormwood,—that's pigweed,—that's sorrel,—that's pipergrass,—have at him, chop him up, turn his roots upward to the sun, don't let him have a fibre in the shade, if you do he'll turn himself t'other side up and be as green as a leek in two days. A long war, not with cranes, but with weeds, those Trojans who had sun and rain and dews on their side. Daily the beans saw me come to their rescue armed with a hoe, and thin the ranks of their enemies, filling up the trenches with weedy dead. Many a lusty crest-waving Hector,[7] that towered a whole foot above his crowding comrades, fell before my weapon and rolled in the dust.

Those summer days which some of my contemporaries devoted to the fine arts in Boston or Rome, and others to contemplation in India, and others to trade in London or New York, I thus, with the other farmers of New England, devoted to husbandry. Not that I wanted beans to eat, for I am by nature a Pythagorean,[8] so far as beans are concerned, whether they mean porridge or voting, and exchanged them for rice; but, perchance, as some must work in fields if only for the sake of tropes and expression, to serve a parable-maker one day. It was on the whole a rare amusement, which continued too long, might have become a dissipation. Though I gave them no manure, and did not hoe them all once, I hoed them unusually well as far as I went, and was paid for it in the end, "there

---

7. In the *Iliad*, the bravest of the Trojan warriors, killed by Achilles.
8. A follower of the Greek philosopher and mathematician, Pythagoras (582–507? B.C.E.), who reputedly forbade his disciples to eat beans.

being in truth," as Evelyn says, "no compost or lætation whatsoever comparable to this continual motion, repastination, and turning of the mould with the spade." "The earth," he adds elsewhere, "especially if fresh, has a certain magnetism in it, by which it attracts the salt, power, or virtue (call it either) which gives it life, and is the logic of all the labor and stir we keep about it, to sustain us; all dungings and other sordid temperings being but the vicars succedaneous to this improvement."[9] Moreover, this being one of those "worn-out and exhausted lay fields which enjoy their sabbath," had perchance, as Sir Kenelm Digby[1] thinks likely, attracted "vital spirits" from the air. I harvested twelve bushels of beans.

But to be more particular, for it is complained that Mr. Coleman has reported chiefly the expensive experiments of gentlemen farmers, my outgoes were,—

For a hoe, ...	$ 0 54
Ploughing, harrowing, and furrowing,	7 50, Too much.
Beans for seed, ...	3 12½
Potatoes "	1 33
Peas "	0 40
Turnip seed, ...	0 06
White line for crow fence, . . .	0 02
Horse cultivator and boy three hours,	1 00
Horse and cart to get crop, . . .	0 75
In all, ...	$14 72½

My income was, (patrem familias vendacem, non emacem esse oportet,)[2] from

Nine bushels and twelve quarts of beans sold, .	$ 16 94
Five " large potatoes, ...	2 50
Nine " small, ...	2 25
Grass, ...	1 00
Stalks, ...	0 75
In all, ...	$23 44

Leaving a pecuniary profit, as I have elsewhere said, of $8 71½.

This is the result of my experience in raising beans. Plant the common small white bush bean about the first of June, in rows three feet by eighteen inches apart, being careful to select fresh round and unmixed seed. First look out for worms, and supply va-

9. John Evelyn (1620–1706), English horticulturalist and author; from *Terra, a Philosophical Discourse of Earth* (1729).
1. English philosopher and naturalist (1603–1665); quoted in Evelyn's *Sylva, or a Discourse of Forest-Trees* (1679), 303.
2. "A householder should be one who sells, not one who buys" (from Cato, *De Agri Cultura*); see n. 6, p. 46.

cancies by planting anew. Then look out for woodchucks, if it is an exposed place, for they will nibble off the earliest tender leaves almost clean as they go; and again, when the young tendrils make their appearance, they have notice of it, and will shear them off with both buds and young pods, sitting erect like a squirrel. But above all harvest as early as possible, if you would escape frosts and have a fair and salable crop; you may save much loss by this means.

This further experience also I gained. I said to myself, I will not plant beans and corn with so much industry another summer, but such seeds, if the seed is not lost, as sincerity, truth, simplicity, faith, innocence, and the like, and see if they will not grow in this soil, even with less toil and manurance, and sustain me, for surely it has not been exhausted for these crops. Alas! I said this to myself; but now another summer is gone, and another, and another, and I am obliged to say to you, Reader, that the seeds which I planted, if indeed they *were* the seeds of those virtues, were wormeaten or had lost their vitality, and so did not come up. Commonly men will only be brave as their fathers were brave, or timid. This generation is very sure to plant corn and beans each new year precisely as the Indians did centuries ago and taught the first settlers to do, as if there were a fate in it. I saw an old man the other day, to my astonishment, making the holes with a hoe for the seventieth time at least, and not for himself to lie down in! But why should not the New Englander try new adventures, and not lay so much stress on his grain, his potato and grass crop, and his orchards,—raise other crops than these? Why concern ourselves so much about our beans for seed, and not be concerned at all about a new generation of men? We should really be fed and cheered if when we met a man we were sure to see that some of the qualities which I have named, which we all prize more than those other productions, but which are for the most part broadcast and floating in the air, had taken root and grown in him. Here comes such a subtle and ineffable quality, for instance, as truth or justice, though the slightest amount or new variety of it, along the road. Our ambassadors should be instructed to send home such seeds as these, and Congress help to distribute them over all the land. We should never stand upon ceremony with sincerity. We should never cheat and insult and banish one another by our meanness, if there were present the kernel of worth and friendliness. We should not meet thus in haste. Most men I do not meet at all, for they seem not to have time; they are busy about their beans. We would not deal with a man thus plodding ever, leaning on a hoe or a spade as a staff between his work, not as a mushroom, but partially risen out of the earth, something more than erect, like swallows alighted and walking on the ground:—

"And as he spake, his wings would now and then
    Spread, as he meant to fly, then close again."[3]

so that we should suspect that we might be conversing with an angel. Bread may not always nourish us; but it always does us good, it even takes stiffness out of our joints, and makes us supple and buoyant, when we knew not what ailed us, to recognize any generosity in man or Nature, to share any unmixed and heroic joy.

Ancient poetry and mythology suggest, at least, that husbandry was once a sacred art; but it is pursued with irreverent haste and heedlessness by us, our object being to have large farms and large crops merely. We have no festival, nor procession, nor ceremony, not excepting our Cattle-shows and so called Thanksgivings, by which the farmer expresses a sense of the sacredness of his calling, or is reminded of its sacred origin. It is the premium and the feast which tempt him. He sacrifices not to Ceres and the Terrestrial Jove, but to the infernal Plutus rather.[4] By avarice and selfishness, and a grovelling habit, from which none of us is free, of regarding the soil as property, or the means of acquiring property chiefly, the landscape is deformed, husbandry is degraded with us, and the farmer leads the meanest of lives. He knows Nature but as a robber. Cato says that the profits of agriculture are particularly pious or just, (*maximeque pius quæstus,*) and according to Varro[5] the old Romans "called the same earth Mother and Ceres, and thought that they who cultivated it led a pious and useful life, and that they alone were left of the race of King Saturn."[6]

We are wont to forget that the sun looks on our cultivated fields and on the prairies and forests without distinction. They all reflect and absorb his rays alike, and the former make but a small part of the glorious picture which he beholds in his daily course. In his view the earth is all equally cultivated like a garden. Therefore we should receive the benefit of his light and heat with a corresponding trust and magnanimity. What though I value the seed of these beans, and harvest that in the fall of the year? This broad field which I have looked at so long looks not to me as the principal cultivator, but away from me to influences more genial to it, which water and make it green. These beans have results which are not harvested by me. Do they not grow for woodchucks partly? The ear of wheat, (in Latin *spica*, obsoletely *speca*, from *spe*, hope,) should not be the only hope of the husbandman; its kernel or grain

---

3. Francis Quarles (1592–1644), English poet; from "The Shepherd's Oracles," eclogue 5.
4. In Roman mythology, the goddess of corn and harvests; "Jove" is another name for the Roman "Jupiter"; Plutus is the god of riches.
5. Marcus Terentius Varro (116–27 B.C.E.), Roman scholar and satirist; from his *Rerum Rusticarum.*
6. In Roman mythology, the god of agriculture (called "Cronus" by the Greeks).

(*granum*, from *gerendo*, bearing,) is not all that it bears. How, then, can our harvest fail? Shall I not rejoice also at the abundance of the weeds whose seeds are the granary of the birds? It matters little comparatively whether the fields fill the farmer's barns. The true husbandman will cease from anxiety, as the squirrels manifest no concern whether the woods will bear chestnuts this year or not, and finish his labor with every day, relinquishing all claim to the produce of his fields, and sacrificing in his mind not only his first but his last fruits also.

The Village

After hoeing, or perhaps reading and writing, in the forenoon, I usually bathed again in the pond, swimming across one of its coves for a stint, and washed the dust of labor from my person, or smoothed out the last wrinkle which study had made, and for the afternoon was absolutely free. Every day or two I strolled to the village to hear some of the gossip which is incessantly going on there, circulating either from mouth to mouth, or from newspaper to newspaper, and which, taken in homœopathic doses, was really as refreshing in its way as the rustle of leaves and the peeping of frogs. As I walked in the woods to see the birds and squirrels, so I walked in the village to see the men and boys; instead of the wind among the pines I heard the carts rattle. In one direction from my house there was a colony of muskrats in the river meadows; under the grove of elms and buttonwoods in the other horizon was a village of busy men, as curious to me as if they had been prairie dogs, each sitting at the mouth of its burrow, or running over to a neighbor's to gossip. I went there frequently to observe their habits. The village appeared to me a great news room; and on one side, to support it, as once at Redding & Company's on State Street, they kept nuts and raisins, or salt and meal and other groceries. Some have such a vast appetite for the former commodity, that is, the news, and such sound digestive organs, that they can sit forever in public avenues without stirring, and let it simmer and whisper through them like the Etesian winds,[1] or as if inhaling ether, it only producing numbness and insensibility to pain,—otherwise it would often be painful to hear,—without affecting the consciousness. I hardly ever failed, when I rambled through the village, to see a row of such worthies, either sitting on a ladder sunning themselves, with their bodies inclined forward and their eyes glancing along the line this way and that, from time to time, with a voluptuous expression, or else lean-

1. Northerly Mediterranean summer winds that recur annually.

ing against a barn with their hands in their pockets, like caryatides, as if to prop it up. They, being commonly out of doors, heard whatever was in the wind. These are the coarsest mills, in which all gossip is first rudely digested or cracked up before it is emptied into finer and more delicate hoppers within doors. I observed that the vitals of the village were the grocery, the bar-room, the post-office, and the bank; and, as a necessary part of the machinery, they kept a bell, a big gun, and a fire-engine, at convenient places; and the houses were so arranged as to make the most of mankind, in lanes and fronting one another, so that every traveller had to run the gantlet, and every man, woman, and child might get a lick at him. Of course, those who were stationed nearest to the head of the line, where they could most see and be seen, and have the first blow at him, paid the highest prices for their places; and the few straggling inhabitants in the outskirts, where long gaps in the line began to occur, and the traveller could get over walls or turn aside into cow paths, and so escape, paid a very slight ground or window tax. Signs were hung out on all sides to allure him; some to catch him by the appetite, as the tavern and victualling cellar; some by the fancy, as the dry goods store and the jeweller's; and others by the hair or the feet or the skirts, as the barber, the shoemaker, or the tailor. Besides, there was a still more terrible standing invitation to call at every one of these houses, and company expected about these times. For the most part I escaped wonderfully from these dangers, either by proceeding at once boldly and without deliberation to the goal, as is recommended to those who run the gantlet, or by keeping my thoughts on high things, like Orpheus,[2] who, "loudly singing the praises of the gods to his lyre, drowned the voices of the Sirens, and kept out of danger." Sometimes I bolted suddenly, and nobody could tell my whereabouts, for I did not stand much about gracefulness, and never hesitated at a gap in a fence. I was even accustomed to make an irruption into some houses, where I was well entertained, and after learning the kernels and very last sieve-ful of news, what had subsided, the prospects of war and peace, and whether the world was likely to hold together much longer, I was let out through the rear avenues, and so escaped to the woods again.

It was very pleasant, when I staid late in town, to launch myself into the night, especially if it was dark and tempestuous, and set sail from some bright village parlor or lecture room, with a bag of rye or Indian meal upon my shoulder, for my snug harbor in the

2. In Greek mythology, the son of a Muse whose music had supernatural powers and whose singing could charm animals and inanimate objects.

woods, having made all tight without and withdrawn under hatches
with a merry crew of thoughts, leaving only my outer man at the
helm, or even tying up the helm when it was plain sailing. I had
many a genial thought by the cabin fire "as I sailed." I was never
cast away nor distressed in any weather, though I encountered
some severe storms. It is darker in the woods, even in common
nights, than most suppose. I frequently had to look up at the opening between the trees above the path in order to learn my route,
and, where there was no cart-path, to feel with my feet the faint
track which I had worn, or steer by the known relation of particular
trees which I felt with my hands, passing between two pines for instance, not more than eighteen inches apart, in the midst of the
woods, invariably, in the darkest night. Sometimes, after coming
home thus late in a dark and muggy night, when my feet felt the
path which my eyes could not see, dreaming and absent-minded all
the way, until I was aroused by having to raise my hand to lift the
latch, I have not been able to recall a single step of my walk, and I
have thought that perhaps my body would find its way home if its
master should forsake it, as the hand finds its way to the mouth
without assistance. Several times, when a visitor chanced to stay
into evening, and it proved a dark night, I was obliged to conduct
him to the cart-path in the rear of the house, and then point out to
him the direction he was to pursue, and in keeping which he was to
be guided rather by his feet than his eyes. One very dark night I directed thus on their way two young men who had been fishing in
the pond. They lived about a mile off through the woods, and were
quite used to the route. A day or two after one of them told me that
they wandered about the greater part of the night, close by their
own premises, and did not get home till toward morning, by which
time, as there had been several heavy showers in the mean while,
and the leaves were very wet, they were drenched to their skins. I
have heard of many going astray even in the village streets, when
the darkness was so thick that you could cut it with a knife, as the
saying is. Some who live in the outskirts, having come to town
a-shopping in their wagons, have been obliged to put up for the
night; and gentlemen and ladies making a call have gone half a mile
out of their way, feeling the sidewalk only with their feet, and not
knowing when they turned. It is a surprising and memorable, as
well as valuable experience, to be lost in the woods any time. Often
in a snow storm, even by day, one will come out upon a well-known
road and yet find it impossible to tell which way leads to the village.
Though he knows that he has travelled it a thousand times, he cannot recognize a feature in it, but it is as strange to him as if it were
a road in Siberia. By night, of course, the perplexity is infinitely

greater. In our most trivial walks, we are constantly, though unconsciously, steering like pilots by certain well-known beacons and
headlands, and if we go beyond our usual course we still carry in
our minds the bearing of some neighboring cape; and not till we are
completely lost, or turned round,—for a man needs only to be
turned round once with his eyes shut in this world to be lost,—do
we appreciate the vastness and strangeness of Nature. Every man
has to learn the points of compass again as often as he awakes,
whether from sleep or any abstraction. Not till we are lost, in other
words, not till we have lost the world, do we begin to find ourselves,
and realize where we are and the infinite extent of our relations.

One afternoon, near the end of the first summer, when I went to
the village to get a shoe from the cobbler's, I was seized and put
into jail, because, as I have elsewhere related,[3] I did not pay a tax
to, or recognize the authority of, the state which buys and sells
men, women, and children, like cattle at the door of its senate-
house. I had gone down to the woods for other purposes. But,
wherever a man goes, men will pursue and paw him with their dirty
institutions, and, if they can, constrain him to belong to their desperate odd-fellow society. It is true, I might have resisted forcibly
with more or less effect, might have run "amok" against society; but
I preferred that society should run "amok" against me, it being the
desperate party. However, I was released the next day, obtained my
mended shoe, and returned to the woods in season to get my dinner of huckleberries on Fair-Haven Hill. I was never molested by
any person but those who represented the state. I had no lock nor
bolt but for the desk which held my papers, not even a nail to put
over my latch or windows. I never fastened my door night or day,
though I was to be absent several days; not even when the next fall
I spent a fortnight in the woods of Maine. And yet my house was
more respected than if it had been surrounded by a file of soldiers.
The tired rambler could rest and warm himself by my fire, the literary amuse himself with the few books on my table, or the curious,
by opening my closet door, see what was left of my dinner, and
what prospect I had of a supper. Yet, though many people of every
class came this way to the pond, I suffered no serious inconvenience from these sources, and I never missed any thing but one
small book, a volume of Homer, which perhaps was improperly
gilded, and this I trust a soldier of our camp has found by this time.
I am convinced, that if all men were to live as simply as I then did,
thieving and robbery would be unknown. These take place only in
communities where some have got more than is sufficient while

---

3. I.e., in "Resistance to Civil Government" (1849) and "Civil Disobedience" (1866).
  Thoreau was arrested on July 24, 1846, for several years' nonpayment of poll tax.

others have not enough. The Pope's Homers[4] would soon get properly distributed.—

> "Nec bella fuerunt,
> Faginus astabat dum scyphus ante dapes."[5]
> "Nor wars did men molest,
> When only beechen bowls were in request."

"You who govern public affairs, what need have you to employ punishments? Love virtue, and the people will be virtuous. The virtues of a superior man are like the wind; the virtues of a common man are like the grass; the grass, when the wind passes over it, bends."[6]

The Ponds

Sometimes, having had a surfeit of human society and gossip, and worn out all my village friends, I rambled still farther westward than I habitually dwell, into yet more unfrequented parts of the town, "to fresh woods and pastures new,"[1] or, while the sun was setting, made my supper of huckleberries and blueberries on Fair Haven Hill, and laid up a store for several days. The fruits do not yield their true flavor to the purchaser of them, nor to him who raises them for the market. There is but one way to obtain it, yet few take that way. If you would know the flavor of huckleberries, ask the cow-boy or the partridge. It is a vulgar error to suppose that you have tasted huckleberries who never plucked them. A huckleberry never reaches Boston; they have not been known there since they grew on her three hills. The ambrosial and essential part of the fruit is lost with the bloom which is rubbed off in the market cart, and they become mere provender. As long as Eternal Justice reigns, not one innocent huckleberry can be transported thither from the country's hills.

Occasionally, after my hoeing was done for the day, I joined some impatient companion who had been fishing on the pond since morning, as silent and motionless as a duck or a floating leaf, and, after practising various kinds of philosophy, had concluded commonly, by the time I arrived, that he belonged to the ancient sect of Coenobites.[2] There was one older man, an excellent fisher and skilled in all kinds of woodcraft, who was pleased to look upon my house as a building erected for the convenience of fishermen; and I

---

4. Alexander Pope (1688–1744) translated Homer's *Iliad* and *Odyssey* into English.
5. From Albius Tibullus, *Elegies* 3.11.7–8.
6. From Confucius, *Analects* 12.
1. John Milton, "Lycidas" 194.
2. A religious community, and a pun ("See no bites").

was equally pleased when he sat in my doorway to arrange his lines. Once in a while we sat together on the pond, he at one end of the boat, and I at the other; but not many words passed between us, for he had grown deaf in his later years, but he occasionally hummed a psalm, which harmonized well enough with my philosophy. Our intercourse was thus altogether one of unbroken harmony, far more pleasing to remember than if it had been carried on by speech. When, as was commonly the case, I had none to commune with, I used to raise the echoes by striking with a paddle on the side of my boat, filling the surrounding woods with circling and dilating sound, stirring them up as the keeper of a menagerie his wild beasts, until I elicited a growl from every wooded vale and hill-side.

In warm evenings I frequently sat in the boat playing the flute, and saw the perch, which I seemed to have charmed, hovering around me, and the moon travelling over the ribbed bottom, which was strewed with the wrecks of the forest. Formerly I had come to this pond adventurously, from time to time, in dark summer nights, with a companion, and making a fire close to the water's edge, which we thought attracted the fishes, we caught pouts with a bunch of worms strung on a thread; and when we had done, far in the night, threw the burning brands high into the air like skyrockets, which, coming down into the pond, were quenched with a loud hissing, and we were suddenly groping in total darkness. Through this, whistling a tune, we took our way to the haunts of men again. But now I had made my home by the shore.

Sometimes, after staying in a village parlor till the family had all retired, I have returned to the woods, and, partly with a view to the next day's dinner, spent the hours of midnight fishing from a boat by moonlight, serenaded by owls and foxes, and hearing, from time to time, the creaking note of some unknown bird close at hand. These experiences were very memorable and valuable to me,—anchored in forty feet of water, and twenty or thirty rods from the shore, surrounded sometimes by thousands of small perch and shiners, dimpling the surface with their tails in the moonlight, and communicating by a long flaxen line with mysterious nocturnal fishes which had their dwelling forty feet below, or sometimes dragging sixty feet of line about the pond as I drifted in the gentle night breeze, now and then feeling a slight vibration along it, indicative of some life prowling about its extremity, of dull uncertain blundering purpose there, and slow to make up its mind. At length you slowly raise, pulling hand over hand, some horned pout squeaking and squirming to the upper air. It was very queer, especially in dark nights, when your thoughts had wandered to vast and cosmogonal themes in other spheres, to feel this faint jerk, which came to interrupt your dreams and link you to Nature again. It seemed as if I might next cast my line upward into the air, as well as downward into this element which was scarcely more dense. Thus I caught two fishes as it were with one hook.

The scenery of Walden is on a humble scale, and, though very beautiful, does not approach to grandeur, nor can it much concern one who has not long frequented it or lived by its shore; yet this pond is so remarkable for its depth and purity as to merit a particular description. It is a clear and deep green well, half a mile long and a mile and three quarters in circumference, and contains about sixty-one and a half acres; a perennial spring in the midst of pine and oak woods, without any visible inlet or outlet except by the clouds and evaporation. The surrounding hills rise abruptly from the water to the height of forty to eighty feet, though on the southeast and east they attain to about one hundred and one hundred and fifty feet respectively, within a quarter and a third of a mile. They are exclusively woodland. All our Concord waters have two colors at least, one when viewed at a distance, and another, more proper, close at hand. The first depends more on the light, and follows the sky. In clear weather, in summer, they appear blue at a little distance, especially if agitated, and at a great distance all appear alike. In stormy weather they are sometimes of a dark slate color. The sea, however, is said to be blue one day and green another without any perceptible change in the atmosphere. I have seen our river, when, the landscape being covered with snow, both water and ice were almost as green as grass. Some consider blue "to be the color of pure water, whether liquid or solid."[3] But, looking directly down into our waters from a boat, they are seen to be of very different colors. Walden is blue at one time and green at another, even from the same point of view. Lying between the earth and the heavens, it partakes of the color of both. Viewed from a hill-top it reflects the color of the sky, but near at hand it is of a yellowish tint next the shore where you can see the sand, then a light green, which gradually deepens to a uniform dark green in the body of the pond. In some lights, viewed even from a hill-top, it is of a vivid green next the shore. Some have referred this to the reflection of the verdure; but it is equally green there against the railroad sandbank, and in the spring, before the leaves are expanded, and it may be simply the result of the prevailing blue mixed with the yellow of the sand. Such is the color of its iris. This is that portion, also, where in the spring, the ice being warmed by the heat of the sun reflected from the bottom, and also transmitted through the earth, melts first and forms a narrow canal about the still frozen middle.

3. From James David Forbes, *Travels through the Alps of Savoy* (1843).

Like the rest of our waters, when much agitated, in clear weather, so that the surface of the waves may reflect the sky at the right angle, or because there is more light mixed with it, it appears at a little distance of a darker blue than the sky itself; and at such a time, being on its surface, and looking with divided vision, so as to see the reflection, I have discerned a matchless and indescribable light blue, such as watered or changeable silks and sword blades suggest, more cerulean than the sky itself, alternating with the original dark green on the opposite sides of the waves, which last appeared but muddy in comparison. It is a vitreous greenish blue, as I remember it, like those patches of the winter sky seen through cloud vistas in the west before sundown. Yet a single glass of its water held up to the light is as colorless as an equal quantity of air. It is well known that a large plate of glass will have a green tint, owing, as the makers say, to its "body," but a small piece of the same will be colorless. How large a body of Walden water would be required to reflect a green tint I have never proved. The water of our river is black or a very dark brown to one looking directly down on it, and, like that of most ponds, imparts to the body of one bathing in it a yellowish tinge; but this water is of such crystalline purity that the body of the bather appears of an alabaster whiteness, still more unnatural, which, as the limbs are magnified and distorted withal, produces a monstrous effect, making fit studies for a Michael Angelo.[4]

The water is so transparent that the bottom can easily be discerned at the depth of twenty-five or thirty feet. Paddling over it, you may see many feet beneath the surface the schools of perch and shiners, perhaps only an inch long, yet the former easily distinguished by their transverse bars, and you think that they must be ascetic fish that find a subsistence there. Once, in the winter, many years ago, when I had been cutting holes through the ice in order to catch pickerel, as I stepped ashore I tossed my axe back on to the ice, but, as if some evil genius had directed it, it slid four or five rods directly into one of the holes, where the water was twenty-five feet deep. Out of curiosity, I lay down on the ice and looked through the hole, until I saw the axe a little on one side, standing on its head, with its helve erect and gently swaying to and fro with the pulse of the pond; and there it might have stood erect and swaying till in the course of time the handle rotted off, if I had not disturbed it. Making another hole directly over it with an ice chisel which I had, and cutting down the longest birch which I could find in the neighborhood with my knife, I made a slip-noose, which I attached to its end, and, letting it down carefully, passed it over the

---

4. Italian painter, sculptor, and architect (1475–1564). Known for oversized and muscular figures.

knob of the handle, and drew it by a line along the birch, and so pulled the axe out again.

The shore is composed of a belt of smooth rounded white stones like paving stones, excepting one or two short sand beaches, and is so steep that in many places a single leap will carry you into water over your head; and were it not for its remarkable transparency, that would be the last to be seen of its bottom till it rose on the opposite side. Some think it is bottomless. It is nowhere muddy, and a casual observer would say that there were no weeds at all in it; and of noticeable plants, except in the little meadows recently overflowed, which do not properly belong to it, a closer scrutiny does not detect a flag nor a bulrush, nor even a lily, yellow or white, but only a few small heart-leaves and potamogetons, and perhaps a water-target or two; all which however a bather might not perceive; and these plants are clean and bright like the element they grow in. The stones extend a rod or two into the water, and then the bottom is pure sand, except in the deepest parts, where there is usually a little sediment, probably from the decay of the leaves which have been wafted on to it so many successive falls, and a bright green weed is brought up on anchors even in midwinter.

We have one other pond just like this, White Pond in Nine Acre Corner, about two and a half miles westerly; but, though I am acquainted with most of the ponds within a dozen miles of this centre, I do not know a third of this pure and well-like character. Successive nations perchance have drank at, admired, and fathomed it, and passed away, and still its water is green and pellucid as ever. Not an intermitting spring! Perhaps on that spring morning when Adam and Eve were driven out of Eden Walden Pond was already in existence, and even then breaking up in a gentle spring rain accompanied with mist and a southerly wind, and covered with myriads of ducks and geese, which had not heard of the fall, when still such pure lakes sufficed them. Even then it had commenced to rise and fall, and had clarified its waters and colored them of the hue they now wear, and obtained a patent of heaven to be the only Walden Pond in the world and distiller of celestial dews. Who knows in how many unremembered nations' literatures this has been the Castalian Fountain?[5] or what nymphs presided over it in the Golden Age? It is a gem of the first water which Concord wears in her coronet.

Yet perchance the first who came to this well have left some trace of their footsteps. I have been surprised to detect encircling the pond, even where a thick wood has just been cut down on the shore, a narrow shelf-like path in the steep hill-side, alternately ris-

5. In Greek mythology, a fountain on Mount Parnassus, the source of poetic inspiration.

ing and falling, approaching and receding from the water's edge, as old probably as the race of man here, worn by the feet of aboriginal hunters, and still from time to time unwittingly trodden by the present occupants of the land. This is particularly distinct to one standing on the middle of the pond in winter, just after a light snow has fallen, appearing as a clear undulating white line, unobscured by weeds and twigs, and very obvious a quarter of a mile off in many places where in summer it is hardly distinguishable close at hand. The snow reprints it, as it were, in clear white type alto-relievo.[6] The ornamented grounds of villas which will one day be built here may still preserve some trace of this.

The pond rises and falls, but whether regularly or not, and within what period, nobody knows, though, as usual, many pretend to know. It is commonly higher in the winter and lower in the summer, though not corresponding to the general wet and dryness. I can remember when it was a foot or two lower, and also when it was at least five feet higher, than when I lived by it. There is a narrow sand-bar running into it, with very deep water on one side, on which I helped boil a kettle of chowder, some six rods from the main shore, about the year 1824, which it has not been possible to do for twenty-five years; and on the other hand, my friends used to listen with incredulity when I told them, that a few years later I was accustomed to fish from a boat in a secluded cove in the woods, fifteen rods from the only shore they knew, which place was long since converted into a meadow. But the pond has risen steadily for two years, and now, in the summer of '52, is just five feet higher than when I lived there, or as high as it was thirty years ago, and fishing goes on again in the meadow. This makes a difference of level, at the outside, of six or seven feet; and yet the water shed by the surrounding hills is insignificant in amount, and this overflow must be referred to causes which affect the deep springs. This same summer the pond has begun to fall again. It is remarkable that this fluctuation, whether periodical or not, appears thus to require many years for its accomplishment. I have observed one rise and a part of two falls, and I expect that a dozen or fifteen years hence the water will again be as low as I have ever known it. Flint's Pond, a mile eastward, allowing for the disturbance occasioned by its inlets and outlets, and the smaller intermediate ponds also, sympathize with Walden, and recently attained their greatest height at the same time with the latter. The same is true, as far as my observation goes, of White Pond.

This rise and fall of Walden at long intervals serves this use at

---

6. A sculptural term referring to the projection of a figure from the background; also called "high relief."

least; the water standing at this great height for a year or more, though it makes it difficult to walk round it, kills the shrubs and trees which have sprung up about its edge since the last rise, pitch-pines, birches, alders, aspens, and others, and, falling again, leaves an unobstructed shore; for, unlike many ponds and all waters which are subject to a daily tide, its shore is cleanest when the water is lowest. On the side of the pond next my house, a row of pitch pines fifteen feet high has been killed and tipped over as if by a lever, and thus a stop put to their encroachments; and their size indicates how many years have elapsed since the last rise to this height. By this fluctuation the pond asserts its title to a shore, and thus the *shore* is *shorn*, and the trees cannot hold it by right of possession. These are the lips of the lake on which no beard grows. It licks its chaps from time to time. When the water is at its height, the alders, willows, and maples send forth a mass of fibrous red roots several feet long from all sides of their stems in the water, and to the height of three or four feet from the ground, in the effort to maintain themselves; and I have known the high-blueberry bushes about the shore, which commonly produce no fruit, bear an abundant crop under these circumstances.

Some have been puzzled to tell how the shore became so regularly paved. My townsmen have all heard the tradition, the oldest people tell me that they heard it in their youth, that anciently the Indians were holding a pow-wow upon a hill here, which rose as high into the heavens as the pond now sinks deep into the earth, and they used much profanity, as the story goes, though this vice is one of which the Indians were never guilty, and while they were thus engaged the hill shook and suddenly sank, and only one old squaw, named Walden, escaped, and from her the pond was named.[7] It has been conjectured that when the hill shook these stones rolled down its side and became the present shore. It is very certain, at any rate, that once there was no pond here, and now there is one; and this Indian fable does not in any respect conflict with the account of that ancient settler whom I have mentioned, who remembers so well when he first came here with his divining rod, saw a thin vapor rising from the sward, and the hazel pointed steadily downward, and he concluded to dig a well here. As for the stones, many still think that they are hardly to be accounted for by the action of the waves on these hills; but I observe that the surrounding hills are remarkably full of the same kind of stones, so that they have been obliged to pile them up in walls on both sides of the railroad cut nearest the pond; and, moreover, there are most

---

7. This is told of Alexander's Lake in Killingly Ct. by Barber. v *his* Con. Hist. Coll. [*Thoreau's note*].

stones where the shore is most abrupt; so that, unfortunately, it is no longer a mystery to me. I detect the paver. If the name was not derived from that of some English locality,—Saffron Walden,[8] for instance,—one might suppose that it was called, originally, *Walled-in* Pond.

The pond was my well ready dug. For four months in the year its water is as cold as it is pure at all times; and I think that it is then as good as any, if not the best, in the town. In the winter, all water which is exposed to the air is colder than springs and wells which are protected from it. The temperature of the pond water which had stood in the room where I sat from five o'clock in the afternoon till noon the next day, the sixth of March, 1846, the thermometer having been up to 65° or 70° some of the time, owing partly to the sun on the roof, was 42°, or one degree colder than the water of one of the coldest wells in the village just drawn. The temperature of the Boiling Spring[9] the same day was 45°, or the warmest of any water tried, though it is the coldest that I know of in summer, when, beside, shallow and stagnant surface water is not mingled with it. Moreover, in summer, Walden never becomes so warm as most water which is exposed to the sun, on account of its depth. In the warmest weather I usually placed a pailful in my cellar, where it became cool in the night, and remained so during the day; though I also resorted to a spring in the neighborhood. It was as good when a week old as the day it was dipped, and had no taste of the pump. Whoever camps for a week in summer by the shore of a pond, needs only bury a pail of water a few feet deep in the shade of his camp to be independent on the luxury of ice.

There have been caught in Walden, pickerel, one weighing seven pounds, to say nothing of another which carried off a reel with great velocity, which the fisherman safely set down at eight pounds because he did not see him, perch and pouts, some of each weighing over two pounds, shiners, chivins or roach, (*Leuciscus pulchellus,*) a very few breams, (*Pomotis obesus,*) one trout weighing a little over five pounds,[1] and a couple of eels, one weighing four pounds,—I am thus particular because the weight of a fish is commonly its only title to fame, and these are the only eels I have heard of here;—also, I have a faint recollection of a little fish some five inches long, with silvery sides and a greenish back, somewhat dace-like in its character, which I mention here chiefly to link my facts

<hr/>

8. Evelyn in his Diary (1654) mentions "the parish of Saffron Walden, famous for the abundance of Saffron there cultivated, and esteemed the best of any foreign country" [*Thoreau's note*]. Saffron Walden is a town forty miles from London, England.
9. A "bubbling" spring (not a "hot spring") located half a mile west of Walden Pond.
1. *Pomotis obesus* [v Nov 26–58] one trout weighing a little over 5 lbs—(Nov. 14–57) [*Thoreau's note*].

to fable. Nevertheless, this pond is not very fertile in fish. Its pickerel, though not abundant, are its chief boast. I have seen at one
time lying on the ice pickerel of at least three different kinds; a long
and shallow one, steel-colored, most like those caught in the river;
a bright golden kind, with greenish reflections and remarkably
deep, which is the most common here; and another, golden-
colored, and shaped like the last, but peppered on the sides with
small dark brown or black spots, intermixed with a few faint blood-
red ones, very much like a trout. The specific name *reticulatus*
would not apply to this; it should be *guttatus* rather. These are all
very firm fish, and weigh more than their size promises. The shiners, pouts, and perch also, and indeed all the fishes which inhabit
this pond, are much cleaner, handsomer, and firmer fleshed than
those in the river and most other ponds, as the water is purer, and
they can easily be distinguished from them. Probably many ichthy-
ologists would make new varieties of some of them. There are also
a clean race of frogs and tortoises, and a few muscles in it; muskrats and minks leave their trace about it, and occasionally a travelling mud-turtle visits it. Sometimes, when I pushed off my boat in
the morning, I disturbed a great mud-turtle which had secreted
himself under the boat in the night. Ducks and geese frequent it in
the spring and fall, the white-bellied swallows (*Hirundo bicolor*)
skim over it, kingfishers dart away from its coves, and the peet-
weets (*Totanus macularius*) "teter" along its stony shores all summer. I have sometimes disturbed a fishhawk sitting on a white-pine
over the water; but I doubt if it is ever profaned by the wing of a
gull, like Fair Haven.[2] At most, it tolerates one annual loon. These
are all the animals of consequence which frequent it now.

You may see from a boat, in calm weather, near the sandy eastern
shore, where the water is eight or ten feet deep, and also in some
other parts of the pond, some circular heaps half a dozen feet in diameter by a foot in height, consisting of small stones less than a
hen's egg in size, where all around is bare sand. At first you wonder
if the Indians could have formed them on the ice for any purpose,
and so, when the ice melted, they sank to the bottom; but they are
too regular and some of them plainly too fresh for that. They are
similar to those found in rivers; but as there are no suckers nor
lampreys here, I know not by what fish they could be made. Perhaps they are the nests of the chivin. These lend a pleasing mystery
to the bottom.

The shore is irregular enough not to be monotonous. I have in
my mind's eye the western indented with deep bays, the bolder
northern, and the beautifully scolloped southern shore, where suc-

2. A wide bay in the Sudbury River about a mile south of Walden Pond.

cessive capes overlap each other and suggest unexplored coves between. The forest has never so good a setting, nor is so distinctly beautiful, as when seen from the middle of a small lake amid hills which rise from the water's edge; for the water in which it is reflected not only makes the best foreground in such a case, but, with its winding shore, the most natural and agreeable boundary to it. There is no rawness nor imperfection in its edge there, as where the axe has cleared a part, or a cultivated field abuts on it. The trees have ample room to expand on the water side, and each sends forth its most vigorous branch in that direction. There Nature has woven a natural selvage, and the eye rises by just gradations from the low shrubs of the shore to the highest trees. There are few traces of man's hand to be seen. The water laves the shore as it did a thousand years ago.

A lake is the landscape's most beautiful and expressive feature. It is earth's eye; looking into which the beholder measures the depth of his own nature. The fluviatile trees next the shore are the slender eyelashes which fringe it, and the wooded hills and cliffs around are its overhanging brows.

Standing on the smooth sandy beach at the east end of the pond, in a calm September afternoon, when a slight haze makes the opposite shore line indistinct, I have seen whence came the expression, "the glassy surface of a lake." When you invert your head, it looks like a thread of finest gossamer stretched across the valley, and gleaming against the distant pine woods, separating one stratum of the atmosphere from another. You would think that you could walk dry under it to the opposite hills, and that the swallows which skim over might perch on it. Indeed, they sometimes dive below the line, as it were by mistake, and are undeceived. As you look over the pond westward you are obliged to employ both your hands to defend your eyes against the reflected as well as the true sun, for they are equally bright; and if, between the two, you survey its surface critically, it is literally as smooth as glass, except where the skater insects at equal intervals scattered over its whole extent, by their motions in the sun produce the finest imaginable sparkle on it, or, perchance, a duck plumes itself, or, as I have said, a swallow skims so low as to touch it. It may be that in the distance a fish describes an arc of three or four feet in the air, and there is one bright flash where it emerges, and another where it strikes the water; sometimes the whole silvery arc is revealed; or here and there, perhaps, is a thistle-down floating on its surface, which the fishes dart at and so dimple it again. It is like molten glass cooled but not congealed, and the few motes in it are pure and beautiful like the imperfections in glass. You may often detect a yet smoother and darker water, separated from the rest as if by an invisible cobweb, boom of the water nymphs, resting on it. From a hill-top you can see a fish leap in almost any part; for not a pickerel or shiner picks an insect from this smooth surface but it manifestly disturbs the equilibrium of the whole lake. It is wonderful with what elaborateness this simple fact is advertised,—this piscine murder will out,—and from my distant perch I distinguish the circling undulations when they are half a dozen rods in diameter. You can even detect a water-bug (*Gyrinus*) ceaselessly progressing over the smooth surface a quarter of a mile off; for they furrow the water slightly, making a conspicuous ripple bounded by two diverging lines, but the skaters glide over it without rippling it perceptibly. When the surface is considerably agitated there are no skaters nor water-bugs on it, but apparently, in calm days, they leave their havens and adventurously glide forth from the shore by short impulses till they completely cover it. It is a soothing employment, on one of those fine days in the fall when all the warmth of the sun is fully appreciated, to sit on a stump on such a height as this, overlooking the pond, and study the dimpling circles which are incessantly inscribed on its otherwise invisible surface amid the reflected skies and trees. Over this great expanse there is no disturbance but it is thus at once gently smoothed away and assuaged, as, when a vase of water is jarred, the trembling circles seek the shore and all is smooth again. Not a fish can leap or an insect fall on the pond but it is thus reported in circling dimples, in lines of beauty, as it were the constant welling up of its fountain, the gentle pulsing of its life, the heaving of its breast. The thrills of joy and thrills of pain are undistinguishable. How peaceful the phenomena of the lake! Again the works of man shine as in the spring. Ay, every leaf and twig and stone and cobweb sparkles now at mid-afternoon as when covered with dew in a spring morning. Every motion of an oar or an insect produces a flash of light; and if an oar falls, how sweet the echo!

In such a day, in September or October, Walden is a perfect forest mirror, set round with stones as precious to my eye as if fewer or rarer. Nothing so fair, so pure, and at the same time so large, as a lake, perchance, lies on the surface of the earth. Sky water. It needs no fence. Nations come and go without defiling it. It is a mirror which no stone can crack, whose quicksilver will never wear off, whose gilding Nature continually repairs; no storms, no dust, can dim its surface ever fresh;—a mirror in which all impurity presented to it sinks, swept and dusted by the sun's hazy brush,—this the light dust-cloth,—which retains no breath that is breathed on it, but sends its own to float as clouds high above its surface, and be reflected in its bosom still.

A field of water betrays the spirit that is in the air. It is continually receiving new life and motion from above. It is intermediate in its nature between land and sky. On land only the grass and trees wave, but the water itself is rippled by the wind. I see where the breeze dashes across it by the streaks or flakes of light. It is remarkable that we can look down on its surface. We shall, perhaps, look down thus on the surface of air at length, and mark where a still subtler spirit sweeps over it.

The skaters and water-bugs finally disappear in the latter part of October, when the severe frosts have come; and then and in November, usually, in a calm day, there is absolutely nothing to ripple the surface. One November afternoon, in the calm at the end of a rain storm of several days' duration, when the sky was still completely overcast and the air was full of mist, I observed that the pond was remarkably smooth, so that it was difficult to distinguish its surface; though it no longer reflected the bright tints of October, but the sombre November colors of the surrounding hills. Though I passed over it as gently as possible, the slight undulations produced by my boat extended almost as far as I could see, and gave a ribbed appearance to the reflections. But, as I was looking over the surface, I saw here and there at a distance a faint glimmer, as if some skater insects which had escaped the frosts might be collected there, or, perchance, the surface, being so smooth, betrayed where a spring welled up from the bottom. Paddling gently to one of these places, I was surprised to find myself surrounded by myriads of small perch, about five inches long, of a rich bronze color in the green water, sporting there and constantly rising to the surface and dimpling it, sometimes leaving bubbles on it. In such transparent and seemingly bottomless water, reflecting the clouds, I seemed to be floating through the air as in a balloon, and their swimming impressed me as a kind of flight or hovering, as if they were a compact flock of birds passing just beneath my level on the right or left, their fins, like sails, set all around them. There were many such schools in the pond, apparently improving the short season before winter would draw an icy shutter over their broad skylight, sometimes giving to the surface an appearance as if a slight breeze struck it, or a few rain-drops fell there. When I approached carelessly and alarmed them, they make a sudden plash and rippling with their tails, as if one had struck the water with a brushy bough, and instantly took refuge in the depths. At length the wind rose, the mist increased, and the waves began to run, and the perch leaped much higher than before, half out of water, a hundred black points, three inches long, at once above the surface. Even as late as the fifth of December, one year, I saw some dimples on the surface, and thinking it was going to rain hard immediately, the air being full of mist, I made haste to take my place at the oars and row homeward; already the rain seemed rapidly increasing, though I felt none on my cheek, and I anticipated a thorough soaking. But suddenly the dimples ceased, for they were produced by the perch, which the noise of my oars had scared into the depths, and I saw their schools dimly disappearing; so I spent a dry afternoon after all.

An old man who used to frequent this pond nearly sixty years ago, when it was dark with surrounding forests, tells me that in those days he sometimes saw it all alive with ducks and other water fowl, and that there were many eagles about it. He came here a-fishing, and used an old log canoe which he found on the shore. It was made of two white-pine logs dug out and pinned together, and was cut off square at the ends. It was very clumsy, but lasted a great many years before it became water-logged and perhaps sank to the bottom. He did not know whose it was; it belonged to the pond. He used to make a cable for his anchor of strips of hickory bark tied together. An old man, a potter, who lived by the pond before the Revolution, told him once that there was an iron chest at the bottom, and that he had seen it. Sometimes it would come floating up to the shore; but when you went toward it, it would go back into deep water and disappear. I was pleased to hear of the old log canoe, which took the place of an Indian one of the same material but more graceful construction, which perchance had first been a tree on the bank, and then, as it were, fell into the water, to float there for a generation, the most proper vessel for the lake. I remember that when I first looked into these depths there were many large trunks to be seen indistinctly lying on the bottom, which had either been blown over formerly, or left on the ice at the last cutting, when wood was cheaper; but now they have mostly disappeared.

When I first paddled a boat on Walden, it was completely surrounded by thick and lofty pine and oak woods, and in some of its coves grape vines had run over the trees next the water and formed bowers under which a boat could pass. The hills which form its shores are so steep, and the woods on them were then so high, that, as you looked down from the west end, it had the appearance of an amphitheatre for some kind of sylvan spectacle. I have spent many an hour, when I was younger, floating over its surface as the zephyr willed, having paddled my boat to the middle, and lying on my back across the seats, in a summer forenoon, dreaming awake, until I was aroused by the boat touching the sand, and I arose to see what shore my fates had impelled me to; days when idleness was the most attractive and productive industry. Many a forenoon have I stolen away, preferring to spend thus the most valued part of the day; for I was rich, if not in money, in sunny hours and summer days, and spent them lavishly; nor do I regret that I did not waste more of them in the workshop or the teacher's desk. But since I left those shores the woodchoppers have still further laid them waste, and now for many a year there will be no more rambling through the aisles of the wood, with occasional vistas through which you see the water. My Muse may be excused if she is silent henceforth. How can you expect the birds to sing when their groves are cut down?

Now the trunks of trees on the bottom, and the old log canoe, and the dark surrounding woods, are gone, and the villagers, who scarcely know where it lies, instead of going to the pond to bathe or drink, are thinking to bring its water, which should be as sacred as the Ganges[3] at least, to the village in a pipe, to wash their dishes with!—to earn their Walden by the turning of a cock or drawing of a plug! That devilish Iron Horse, whose ear-rending neigh is heard throughout the town, has muddied the Boiling Spring with his foot, and he it is that has browsed off all the woods on Walden shore; that Trojan horse, with a thousand men in his belly, introduced by mercenary Greeks! Where is the country's champion, the Moore of Moore Hall,[4] to meet him at the Deep Cut and thrust an avenging lance between the ribs of the bloated pest?

Nevertheless, of all the characters I have known, perhaps Walden wears best, and best preserves its purity. Many men have been likened to it, but few deserve that honor. Though the wood-choppers have laid bare first this shore and then that, and the Irish have built their sties by it, and the railroad has infringed on its border, and the ice-men have skimmed it once, it is itself unchanged, the same water which my youthful eyes fell on; all the change is in me. It has not acquired one permanent wrinkle after all its ripples. It is perennially young, and I may stand and see a swallow dip apparently to pick an insect from its surface as of yore. It struck me again to-night, as if I had not seen it almost daily for more than twenty years,—Why, here is Walden, the same woodland lake that I discovered so many years ago; where a forest was cut down last winter another is springing up by its shore as lustily as ever; the same thought is welling up to its surface that was then; it is the same liquid joy and happiness to itself and its Maker, ay, and it *may* be to me. It is the work of a brave man surely, in whom there was no guile! He rounded this water with his hand, deepened and clarified it in his thought, and in his will bequeathed it to Concord. I see by its face that it is visited by the same reflection; and I can almost say, Walden, is it you?

3. A river in northern India, believed to be sacred by the Hindus.
4. According to an old English ballad, "The Dragon of Wantley," a hero who killed a dragon.

It is no dream of mine,
To ornament a line;
I cannot come nearer to God and Heaven
Than I live to Walden even.
I am its stony shore,
And the breeze that passes o'er;
In the hollow of my hand
Are its water and its sand,
And its deepest resort
Lies high in my thought.

The cars never pause to look at it; yet I fancy that the engineers and firemen and brakemen, and those passengers who have a season ticket and see it often, are better men for the sight. The engineer does not forget at night, or his nature does not, that he has beheld this vision of serenity and purity once at least during the day. Though seen but once, it helps to wash out State-street[5] and the engine's soot. One proposes that it be called "God's Drop."

I have said that Walden has no visible inlet nor outlet, but it is on the one hand distantly and indirectly related to Flint's Pond, which is more elevated, by a chain of small ponds coming from that quarter, and on the other directly and manifestly to Concord River, which is lower, by a similar chain of ponds through which in some other geological period it may have flowed, and by a little digging, which God forbid, it can be made to flow thither again. If by living thus reserved and austere, like a hermit in the woods, so long, it has acquired such wonderful purity, who would not regret that the comparatively impure waters of Flint's Pond should be mingled with it, or itself should ever go to waste its sweetness in the ocean wave?

Flint's, or Sandy Pond, in Lincoln, our greatest lake and inland sea, lies about a mile east of Walden. It is much larger, being said to contain one hundred and ninety-seven acres, and is more fertile in fish; but it is comparatively shallow, and not remarkably pure. A walk through the woods thither was often my recreation. It was worth the while, if only to feel the wind blow on your cheek freely, and see the waves run, and remember the life of mariners. I went a-chestnutting there in the fall, on windy days, when the nuts were dropping into the water and were washed to my feet; and one day, as I crept along its sedgy shore, the fresh spray blowing in my face, I came upon the mouldering wreck of a boat, the sides gone, and hardly more than the impression of its flat bottom left amid the rushes; yet its model was sharply defined, as if it were a large de-

---

5. The financial district of Boston.

cayed pad, with its veins. It was as impressive a wreck as one could imagine on the sea-shore, and had as good a moral. It is by this time mere vegetable mould and undistinguishable pond shore, through which rushes and flags have pushed up. I used to admire the ripple marks on the sandy bottom, at the north end of this pond, made firm and hard to the feet of the wader by the pressure of the water, and the rushes which grew in Indian file, in waving lines, corresponding to these marks, rank behind rank, as if the waves had planted them. There also I have found, in considerable quantities, curious balls, composed apparently of fine grass or roots, of pipewort perhaps, from half an inch to four inches in diameter, and perfectly spherical. These wash back and forth in shallow water on a sandy bottom, and are sometimes cast on the shore. They are either solid grass, or have a little sand in the middle. At first you would say that they were formed by the action of the waves, like a pebble; yet the smallest are made of equally coarse materials, half an inch long, and they are produced only at one season of the year. Moreover, the waves, I suspect, do not so much construct as wear down a material which has already acquired consistency. They preserve their form when dry for an indefinite period.

Flint's Pond! Such is the poverty of our nomenclature. What right had the unclean and stupid farmer, whose farm abutted on this sky water, whose shores he has ruthlessly laid bare, to give his name to it? Some skin-flint, who loved better the reflecting surface of a dollar, or a bright cent, in which he could see his own brazen face; who regarded even the wild ducks which settled in it as trespassers; his fingers grown into crooked and horny talons from the long habit of grasping harpy-like;—so it is not named for me. I go not there to see him nor to hear of him; who never *saw* it, who never bathed in it, who never loved it, who never protected it, who never spoke a good word for it, nor thanked God that he had made it. Rather let it be named from the fishes that swim in it, the wild fowl or quadrupeds which frequent it, the wild flowers which grow by its shores, or some wild man or child the thread of whose history is interwoven with its own; not from him who could show no title to it but the deed which a like-minded neighbor or legislature gave him,—him who thought only of its money value; whose presence perchance cursed all the shore; who exhausted the land around it, and would fain have exhausted the waters within it; who regretted only that it was not English hay or cranberry meadow,—there was nothing to redeem it, forsooth, in his eyes,—and would have drained and sold it for the mud at its bottom. It did not turn his mill, and it was no *privilege* to him to behold it. I respect not his labors, his farm where every thing has its price; who would carry the landscape, who would carry his God, to market, if he could get any thing for him; who goes to market *for* his god as it is; on whose farm nothing grows free, whose fields bear no crops, whose meadows no flowers, whose trees no fruits, but dollars; who loves not the beauty of his fruits, whose fruits are not ripe for him till they are turned to dollars. Give me the poverty that enjoys true wealth. Farmers are respectable and interesting to me in proportion as they are poor,—poor farmers. A model farm! where the house stands like a fungus in a muck-heap, chambers for men, horses, oxen, and swine, cleansed and uncleansed, all contiguous to one another! Stocked with men! A great grease-spot, redolent of manures and buttermilk! Under a high state of cultivation, being manured with the hearts and brains of men! As if you were to raise your potatoes in the church-yard! Such is a model farm.

No, no; if the fairest features of the landscape are to be named after men, let them be the noblest and worthiest men alone. Let our lakes receive as true names at least as the Icarian Sea, where "still the shore" a "brave attempt resounds."[6]

Goose Pond, of small extent, is on my way to Flint's; Fair-Haven, an expansion of Concord River, said to contain some seventy acres, is a mile south-west; and White Pond, of about forty acres, is a mile and a half beyond Fair-Haven. This is my lake country.[7] These, with Concord River, are my water privileges; and night and day, year in year out, they grind such grist as I carry to them.

Since the woodcutters, and the railroad, and I myself have profaned Walden, perhaps the most attractive, if not the most beautiful, of all our lakes, the gem of the woods, is White Pond;—a poor name from its commonness, whether derived from the remarkable purity of its waters or the color of its sands. In these as in other respects, however, it is a lesser twin of Walden. They are so much alike that you would say they must be connected under ground. It has the same stony shore, and its waters are of the same hue. As at Walden, in sultry dog-day weather, looking down through the woods on some of its bays which are not so deep but that the reflection from the bottom tinges them, its waters are of a misty bluish-green or glaucous color. Many years since I used to go there to collect the sand by cart-loads, to make sand-paper with, and I have continued to visit it ever since. One who frequents it proposes to call it Virid Lake. Perhaps it might be called Yellow-Pine Lake, from the following circumstance. About fifteen years ago you could see the top of a pitch-pine, of the kind called yellow-pine here-

6. According to Greek mythology, the Icarian Sea was named for Icarus, who, while attempting to escape Crete on wings made of wax, fell into the sea when he flew too near the sun; Thoreau quotes from "Icarus" by William of Hawthomden (1585–1649).
7. The English Lake Country, associated with William Wordsworth and other English Romantic poets.

abouts, though it is not a distinct species, projecting above the surface in deep water, many rods from the shore. It was even supposed by some that the pond had sunk, and this was one of the primitive forest that formerly stood there. I find that even so long ago as 1792, in a "Topographical Description of the Town of Concord," by one of its citizens, in the Collections of the Massachusetts Historical Society, the author,[8] after speaking of Walden and White Ponds, adds: "In the middle of the latter may be seen, when the water is very low, a tree which appears as if it grew in the place where it now stands, although the roots are fifty feet below the surface of the water; the top of this tree is broken off, and at that place measures fourteen inches in diameter." In the spring of '49 I talked with the man who lives nearest the pond in Sudbury, who told me that it was he who got out this tree ten or fifteen years before. As near as he could remember, it stood twelve or fifteen rods from the shore, where the water was thirty or forty feet deep. It was in the winter, and he had been getting out ice in the forenoon, and had resolved that in that afternoon, with the aid of his neighbors, he would take out the old yellow-pine. He sawed a channel in the ice toward the shore, and hauled it over and along and out on to the ice with oxen; but, before he had gone far in his work, he was surprised to find that it was wrong end upward, with the stumps of the branches pointing down, and the small end firmly fastened in the sandy bottom. It was about a foot in diameter at the big end, and he had expected to get a good saw-log, but it was so rotten as to be fit only for fuel, if for that. He had some of it in his shed then. There were marks of an axe and of woodpeckers on the but. He thought that it might have been a dead tree on the shore, but was finally blown over into the pond, and after the top had become water-logged, while the but-end was still dry and light, had drifted out and sunk wrong end up. His father, eighty years old, could not remember when it was not there. Several pretty large logs may still be seen lying on the bottom, where, owing to the undulation of the surface, they look like huge water snakes in motion.

This pond has rarely been profaned by a boat, for there is little in it to tempt a fisherman. Instead of the white lily, which requires mud, or the common sweet flag, the blue flag (*Iris versicolor*) grows thinly in the pure water, rising from the stony bottom all around the shore, where it is visited by humming birds in June, and the color both of its bluish blades and its flowers, and especially their reflections, are in singular harmony with the glaucous water.

White Pond and Walden are great crystals on the surface of the earth, Lakes of Light. If they were permanently congealed, and

8. William Jones.

small enough to be clutched, they would, perchance, be carried off by slaves, like precious stones, to adorn the heads of emperors; but being liquid, and ample, and secured to us and our successors forever, we disregard them, and run after the diamond of Kohinoor.[9] They are too pure to have a market value; they contain no muck. How much more beautiful than our lives, how much more transparent than our characters, are they! We never learned meanness of them. How much fairer than the pool before the farmer's door, in which his ducks swim! Hither the clean wild ducks come. Nature has no human inhabitant who appreciates her. The birds with their plumage and their notes are in harmony with the flowers, but what youth or maiden conspires with the wild luxuriant beauty of Nature? She flourishes most alone, far from the towns where they reside. Talk of heaven! ye disgrace earth.

Baker Farm

Sometimes I rambled to pine groves, standing like temples, or like fleets at sea, full-rigged, with wavy boughs, and rippling with light, so soft and green and shady that the Druids[1] would have forsaken their oaks to worship in them; or to the cedar wood beyond Flint's Pond, where the trees, covered with hoary blue berries, spiring higher and higher, are fit to stand before Valhalla,[2] and the creeping juniper covers the ground with wreaths full of fruit; or to swamps where the usnea lichen hangs in festoons from the black-spruce trees, and toad-stools, round tables of the swamp gods, cover the ground, and more beautiful fungi adorn the stumps, like butterflies or shells, vegetable winkles; where the swamp-pink and dogwood grow, the red alder-berry glows like eyes of imps, the waxwork grooves and crushes the hardest woods in its folds, and the wild-holly berries make the beholder forget his home with their beauty, and he is dazzled and tempted by nameless other wild forbidden fruits, too fair for mortal taste. Instead of calling on some scholar, I paid many a visit to particular trees, of kinds which are rare in this neighborhood, standing far away in the middle of some pasture, or in the depths of a wood or swamp, or on a hill-top; such as the black-birch, of which we have some handsome specimens two feet in diameter; its cousin the yellow-birch, with its loose golden vest, perfumed like the first; the beech, which has so neat a bole and beautifully lichen-painted, perfect in all its details, of

9. A famous diamond from India, weighing 106 carats, now part of the British crown jewels.
1. An ancient Celtic priesthood that worshipped in oak groves.
2. In Norse mythology, a great hall in which the souls of dead warriors live.

which, excepting scattered specimens, I know but one small grove
of sizable trees left in the township, supposed by some to have been
planted by the pigeons that were once baited with beech nuts near
by; it is worth the while to see the silver grain sparkle when you
split this wood; the bass; the hornbeam; the *Celtis occidentalis*, or
false elm, of which we have but one well-grown; some taller mast of
a pine, a shingle tree, or a more perfect hemlock than usual, standing like a pagoda in the midst of the woods; and many others I
could mention. These were the shrines I visited both summer and
winter.

Once it chanced that I stood in the very abutment of a rainbow's
arch, which filled the lower stratum of the atmosphere, tinging the
grass and leaves around, and dazzling me as if I looked through colored crystal. It was a lake of rainbow light, in which, for a short
while, I lived like a dolphin. If it had lasted longer it might have
tinged my employments and life. As I walked on the railroad causeway, I used to wonder at the halo of light around my shadow, and
would fain fancy myself one of the elect. One who visited me declared that the shadows of some Irishmen before him had no halo
about them, that it was only natives that were so distinguished.
Benvenuto Cellini[3] tells us in his memoirs, that, after a certain terrible dream or vision which he had during his confinement in the
castle of St. Angelo, a resplendent light appeared over the shadow
of his head at morning and evening, whether he was in Italy or
France, and it was particularly conspicuous when the grass was
moist with dew. This was probably the same phenomenon to which
I have referred, which is especially observed in the morning, but
also at other times, and even by moonlight. Though a constant one,
it is not commonly noticed, and, in the case of an excitable imagination like Cellini's, it would be basis enough for superstition. Beside, he tells us that he showed it to very few. But are they not
indeed distinguished who are conscious that they are regarded at
all?

I set out one afternoon to go a-fishing to Fair-Haven, through the
woods, to eke out my scanty fare of vegetables. My way led through
Pleasant Meadow, an adjunct of the Baker Farm, that retreat of
which a poet has since sung, beginning,—

> "Thy entry is a pleasant field,
>   Which some mossy fruit trees yield
>   Partly to a ruddy brook,

3. Italian sculptor and goldsmith (1500–1571), known for his autobiography.

By gliding musquash undertook,
And mercurial trout,
Darting about."[4]

I thought of living there before I went to Walden. I "hooked" the apples, leaped the brook, and scared the musquash and the trout. It was one of those afternoons which seem indefinitely long before one, in which many events may happen, a large portion of our natural life, though it was already half spent when I started. By the way there came up a shower, which compelled me to stand half an hour under a pine, piling boughs over my head, and wearing my handkerchief for a shed; and when at length I had made one cast over the pickerel-weed, standing up to my middle in water, I found myself suddenly in the shadow of a cloud, and the thunder began to rumble with such emphasis that I could do no more than listen to it. The gods must be proud, thought I, with such forked flashes to rout a poor unarmed fisherman. So I made haste for shelter to the nearest hut, which stood half a mile from any road, but so much the nearer to the pond, and had long been uninhabited:—

"And here a poet builded,
In the completed years,
For behold a trival cabin
That to destruction steers."

So the Muse fables. But therein, as I found, dwelt now John Field, an Irishman, and his wife, and several children, from the broad-faced boy who assisted his father at his work, and now came running by his side from the bog to escape the rain, to the wrinkled, sibyl-like,[5] cone-headed infant that sat upon its father's knee as in the palaces of nobles, and looked out from its home in the midst of wet and hunger inquisitively upon the stranger, with the privilege of infancy, not knowing but it was the last of a noble line, and the hope and cynosure of the world, instead of John Field's poor starveling brat. There we sat together under that part of the roof which leaked the least, while it showered and thundered without. I had sat there many times of old before the ship was built that floated this family to America. An honest, hard-working, but shiftless man plainly was John Field; and his wife, she too was brave to cook so many successive dinners in the recesses of that lofty stove; with round greasy face and bare breast, still thinking to improve her condition one day; with the never absent mop in one hand, and

---

4. All the poetic excerpts in this chapter are from "Baker Farm," in *The Woodman and Other Poems* (1849), by Ellery Channing.
5. In ancient Greece, a sibyl was a fortune-teller who lived to be very old.

yet no effects of it visible any where. The chickens, which had also taken shelter here from the rain, stalked about the room like members of the family, too humanized methought to roast well. They stood and looked in my eye or pecked at my shoe significantly. Meanwhile my host told me his story, how hard he worked "bogging" for a neighboring farmer, turning up a meadow with a spade or bog hoe at the rate of ten dollars an acre and the use of the land with manure for one year, and his little broad-faced son worked cheerfully at his father's side the while, not knowing how poor a bargain the latter had made. I tried to help him with my experience, telling him that he was one of my nearest neighbors, and that I too, who came a-fishing here, and looked like a loafer, was getting my living like himself; that I lived in a tight, light, and clean house, which hardly cost more than the annual rent of such a ruin as his commonly amounts to; and how, if he chose, he might in a month or two build himself a palace of his own; that I did not use tea, nor coffee, nor butter, nor milk, nor fresh meat, and so did not have to work to get them; again, as I did not work hard, I did not have to eat hard, and it cost me but a trifle for my food; but as he began with tea, and coffee, and butter, and milk, and beef, he had to work hard to pay for them, and when he had worked hard he had to eat hard again to repair the waste of his system,—and so it was as broad as it was long, indeed it was broader than it was long, for he was discontented and wasted his life into the bargain; and yet he had rated it as a gain in coming to America, that here you could get tea, and coffee, and meat every day. But the only true America is that country where you are at liberty to pursue such a mode of life as may enable you to do without these, and where the state does not endeavor to compel you to sustain the slavery and war and other superfluous expenses which directly or indirectly result from the use of such things. For I purposely talked to him as if he were a philosopher, or desired to be one. I should be glad if all the meadows on the earth were left in a wild state, if that were the consequence of men's beginning to redeem themselves. A man will not need to study history to find out what is best for his own culture. But alas! the culture of an Irishman is an enterprise to be undertaken with a sort of moral bog hoe. I told him, that as he worked so hard at bogging, he required thick boots and stout clothing, which yet were soon soiled and worn out, but I wore light shoes and thin clothing, which cost not half so much, though he might think that I was dressed like a gentleman, (which, however, was not the case,) and in an hour or two, without labor, but as a recreation, I could, if I wished, catch as many fish as I should want for two days, or earn enough money to support me a week. If he and his family would live simply, they might all go a-huckle-berrying in the summer for their amusement. John heaved a sigh at this, and his wife stared with arms a-kimbo, and both appeared to be wondering if they had capital enough to begin such a course with, or arithmetic enough to carry it through. It was sailing by dead reckoning to them, and they saw not clearly how to make their port so; therefore I suppose they still take life bravely, after their fashion, face to face, giving it tooth and nail, not having skill to split its massive columns with any fine entering wedge, and rout it in detail;—thinking to deal with it roughly, as one should handle a thistle. But they fight at an overwhelming disadvantage,—living, John Field, alas! without arithmetic, and failing so.

"Do you ever fish?" I asked. "O yes, I catch a mess now and then when I am lying by; good perch I catch." "What's your bait?" "I catch shiners with fish-worms, and bait the perch with them." "You'd better go now, John," said his wife with glistening and hopeful face; but John demurred.

The shower was now over, and a rainbow above the eastern woods promised a fair evening; so I took my departure. When I had got without I asked for a dish, hoping to get a sight of the well bottom, to complete my survey of the premises; but there, alas! are shallows and quicksands, and rope broken withal, and bucket irrecoverable. Meanwhile the right culinary vessel was selected, water was seemingly distilled, and after consultation and long delay passed out to the thirsty one,—not yet suffered to cool, not yet to settle. Such gruel sustains life here, I thought; so, shutting my eyes, and excluding the motes by a skilfully directed undercurrent, I drank to genuine hospitality the heartiest draught I could. I am not squeamish in such cases when manners are concerned.

As I was leaving the Irishman's roof after the rain, bending my steps again to the pond, my haste to catch pickerel, wading in retired meadows, in sloughs and bog-holes, in forlorn and savage places, appeared for an instant trivial to me who had been sent to school and college; but as I ran down the hill toward the reddening west, with the rainbow over my shoulder, and some faint tinkling sounds borne to my ear through the cleansed air, from I know not what quarter, my Good Genius seemed to say,—Go fish and hunt far and wide day by day,—farther and wider,—and rest thee by many brooks and hearth-sides without misgiving. Remember thy Creator in the days of thy youth.[6] Rise free from care before the dawn, and seek adventures. Let the noon find thee by other lakes, and the night overtake thee every where at home. There are no larger fields

6. Ecclesiastes 12.1.

than these, no worthier games than may here be played. Grow wild according to thy nature, like these sedges and brakes, which will never become English hay. Let the thunder rumble; what if it threaten ruin to farmers crops? that is not its errand to thee. Take shelter under the cloud, while they flee to carts and sheds. Let not to get a living be thy trade, but thy sport. Enjoy the land, but own it not. Through want of enterprise and faith men are where they are, buying and selling, and spending their lives like serfs.

O Baker Farm!

> "Landscape where the richest element
>   Is a little sunshine innocent." **
>
> "No one runs to revel
>   On thy rail-fenced lea." * *
>
> "Debate with no man hast thou,
>   With questions art never perplexed,
>   As tame at the first sight as now,
>   In thy plain russet gabardine dressed." * *
>
> "Come ye who love,
>   And ye who hate,
>   Children of the Holy Dove,
>   And Guy Faux[7] of the state,
>   And hang conspiracies
>   From the tough rafters of the trees!"

Men come tamely home at night only from the next field or street, where their household echoes haunt, and their life pines because it breathes its own breath over again; their shadows morning and evening reach farther than their daily steps. We should come home from far, from adventures, and perils, and discoveries every day, with new experience and character.

Before I had reached the pond some fresh impulse had brought out John Field, with altered mind, letting go "bogging" ere this sunset. But he, poor man, disturbed only a couple of fins while I was catching a fair string, and he said it was his luck; but when we changed seats in the boat luck changed seats too. Poor John Field!—I trust he does not read this, unless he will improve by it,— thinking to live by some derivative old country mode in this primitive new country,—to catch perch with shiners. It is good bait sometimes, I allow. With his horizon all his own, yet he a poor man, born to be poor, with his inherited Irish poverty or poor life, his

---

7. Guy Fawkes (1570–1606) was an English Catholic executed for attempting to blow up the House of Lords.

Adam's grandmother and boggy ways, not to rise in this world, he
nor his posterity, till their wading webbed bog-trotting feet get *ta-
laria*[8] to their heels.

Higher Laws

As I came home through the woods with my string of fish, trailing my pole, it being now quite dark, I caught a glimpse of a woodchuck stealing across my path, and felt a strange thrill of savage
delight, and was strongly tempted to seize and devour him raw; not
that I was hungry then, except for that wildness which he represented. Once or twice, however, while I lived at the pond, I found
myself ranging the woods, like a half-starved hound, with a strange
abandonment, seeking some kind of venison which I might devour,
and no morsel could have been too savage for me. The wildest
scenes had become unaccountably familiar. I found in myself, and
still find, an instinct toward a higher, or, as it is named, spiritual
life, as do most men, and another toward a primitive rank and savage one, and I reverence them both. I love the wild not less than
the good. The wildness and adventure that are in fishing still recommended it to me. I like sometimes to take rank hold on life and
spend my day more as the animals do. Perhaps I have owed to this
employment and to hunting, when quite young, my closest acquaintance with Nature. They early introduce us to and detain us
in scenery with which otherwise, at that age, we should have little
acquaintance. Fishermen, hunters, woodchoppers, and others,
spending their lives in the fields and woods, in a peculiar sense a
part of Nature themselves, are often in a more favorable mood for
observing her, in the intervals of their pursuits, than philosophers
or poets even, who approach her with expectation. She is not afraid
to exhibit herself to them. The traveller on the prairie is naturally a
hunter, on the head waters of the Missouri and Columbia a trapper,
and at the Falls of St. Mary[1] a fisherman. He who is only a traveller
learns things at secondhand and by the halves, and is poor authority. We are most interested when science reports what those men
already know practically or instinctively, for that alone is a true *humanity*, or account of human experience.

They mistake who assert that the Yankee has few amusements,
because he has not so many public holidays, and men and boys do
not play so many games as they do in England, for here the more

---

8. Winged sandals, or wings growing directly from the ankles.
1. St. Marys River flows out of Lake Superior, forming part of the boundary between
   Michigan and Ontario; the Sault Sainte Marie Canals now permit ships to circumvent
   the falls and the rapids.

primitive but solitary amusements of hunting fishing and the like have not yet given place to the former. Almost every New England boy among my contemporaries shouldered a fowling piece between the ages of ten and fourteen; and his hunting and fishing grounds were not limited like the preserves of an English nobleman, but were more boundless even than those of a savage. No wonder, then, that he did not oftener stay to play on the common. But already a change is taking place, owing, not to an increased humanity, but to an increased scarcity of game, for perhaps the hunter is the greatest friend of the animals hunted, not excepting the Humane Society.

Moreover, when at the pond, I wished sometimes to add fish to my fare for variety. I have actually fished from the same kind of necessity that the first fishers did. Whatever humanity I might conjure up against it was all factitious, and concerned my philosophy more than my feelings. I speak of fishing only now, for I had long felt differently about fowling, and sold my gun before I went to the woods. Not that I am less humane than others, but I did not perceive that my feelings were much affected. I did not pity the fishes nor the worms. This was habit. As for fowling, during the last years that I carried a gun my excuse was that I was studying ornithology, and sought only new or rare birds. But I confess that I am now inclined to think that there is a finer way of studying ornithology than this. It requires so much closer attention to the habits of the birds, that, if for that reason only, I have been willing to omit the gun. Yet notwithstanding the objection on the score of humanity, I am compelled to doubt if equally valuable sports are ever substituted for these; and when some of my friends have asked me anxiously about their boys, whether they should let them hunt, I have answered, yes,—remembering that it was one of the best parts of my education,—*make* them hunters, though sportsmen only at first, if possible, mighty hunters at last, so that they shall not find game large enough for them in this or any vegetable wilderness,—hunters as well as fishers of men.[2] Thus far I am of the opinion of Chaucer's nun, who

> "yave not of the text a pulled hen
> That saith that hunters ben not holy men."[3]

There is a period in the history of the individual, as of the race, when the hunters are the "best men," as the Algonquins[4] called

---

2. Jesus' call to the fishermen Simon and Andrew in Mark 1.17: "Come ye after me, and I will make you to become fishers of men."
3. From the "Prologue" to Geoffrey Chaucer's *Canterbury Tales*; the lines (177–78) describe the monk, however, not the nun.
4. A tribe of Indians formerly inhabiting the area north of the St. Lawrence River in Canada.

them. We cannot but pity the boy who has never fired a gun; he is no more humane, while his education has been sadly neglected. This was my answer with respect to those youths who were bent on this pursuit, trusting that they would soon outgrow it. No humane being, past the thoughtless age of boyhood, will wantonly murder any creature, which holds its life by the same tenure that he does. The hare in its extremity cries like a child. I warn you, mothers, that my sympathies do not always make the usual phil-*anthropic* distinctions.

Such is oftenest the young man's introduction to the forest, and the most original part of himself. He goes thither at first as a hunter and fisher, until at last, if he has the seeds of a better life in him, he distinguishes his proper objects, as a poet or naturalist it may be, and leaves the gun and fish-pole behind. The mass of men are still and always young in this respect. In some countries a hunting parson is no uncommon sight. Such a one might make a good shepherd's dog, but is far from being the Good Shepherd. I have been surprised to consider that the only obvious employment, except wood-chopping, ice-cutting, or the like business, which ever to my knowledge detained at Walden Pond for a whole half day any of my fellow-citizens, whether fathers or children of the town, with just one exception, was fishing. Commonly they did not think that they were lucky, or well paid for their time, unless they got a long string of fish, though they had the opportunity of seeing the pond all the while. They might go there a thousand times before the sediment of fishing would sink to the bottom and leave their purpose pure; but no doubt such a clarifying process would be going on all the while. The governor and his council faintly remember the pond, for they went a-fishing there when they were boys; but now they are too old and dignified to go a-fishing, and so they know it no more forever. Yet even they expect to go to heaven at last. If the legislature regards it, it is chiefly to regulate the number of hooks to be used there; but they know nothing about the hook of hooks with which to angle for the pond itself, impaling the legislature for a bait. Thus, even in civilized communities, the embryo man passes through the hunter stage of development.

I have found repeatedly, of late years, that I cannot fish without falling a little in self-respect. I have tried it again and again. I have skill at it, and, like many of my fellows, a certain instinct for it, which revives from time to time, but always when I have done I feel that it would have been better if I had not fished. I think that I do not mistake. It is a faint intimation, yet so are the first streaks of morning. There is unquestionably this instinct in me which belongs to the lower orders of creation; yet with every year I am less a fisherman, though without more humanity or even wisdom; at present I am no fisherman at all. But I see that if I were to live in a wilderness I should again be tempted to become a fisher and hunter in earnest. Beside, there is something essentially unclean about this diet and all flesh, and I began to see where housework commences, and whence the endeavor, which costs so much, to wear a tidy and respectable appearance each day, to keep the house sweet and free from all ill odors and sights. Having been my own butcher and scullion and cook, as well as the gentleman for whom the dishes were served up, I can speak from an unusually complete experience. The practical objection to animal food in my case was its uncleanness; and, besides, when I had caught and cleaned and cooked and eaten my fish, they seemed not to have fed me essentially. It was insignificant and unnecessary, and cost more than it came to. A little bread or a few potatoes would have done as well, with less trouble and filth. Like many of my contemporaries, I had rarely for many years used animal food, or tea, or coffee, &c.; not so much because of any ill effects which I had traced to them, as because they were not agreeable to my imagination. The repugnance to animal food is not the effect of experience, but is an instinct. It appeared more beautiful to live low and fare hard in many respects; and though I never did so, I went far enough to please my imagination. I believe that every man who has ever been earnest to preserve his higher or poetic faculties in the best condition has been particularly inclined to abstain from animal food, and from much food of any kind. It is a significant fact, stated by entomologists, I find it in Kirby and Spence, that "some insects in their perfect state, though furnished with organs of feeding, make no use of them;" and they lay it down as "a general rule, that almost all insects in this state eat much less than in that of larvæ. The voracious caterpillar when transformed into a butterfly," . . "and the gluttonous maggot when become a fly," content themselves with a drop or two of honey or some other sweet liquid.[5] The abdomen under the wings of the butterfly still represents the larva. This is the tid-bit which tempts his insectivorous fate. The gross feeder is a man in the larva state; and there are whole nations in that condition, nations without fancy or imagination, whose vast abdomens betray them.

It is hard to provide and cook so simple and clean a diet as will not offend the imagination; but this, I think, is to be fed when we feed the body; they should both sit down at the same table. Yet perhaps this may be done. The fruits eaten temperately need not make us ashamed of our appetites, nor interrupt the worthiest pursuits. But put an extra condiment into your dish, and it will poison you. It is not worth the while to live by rich cookery. Most men would feel

---

5. From William Kirby and William Spence, *An Introduction to Entomology* (1815–1826).

shame if caught preparing with their own hands precisely such a dinner, whether of animal or vegetable food, as is every day prepared for them by others. Yet till this is otherwise we are not civilized, and, if gentlemen and ladies, are not true men and women. This certainly suggests what change is to be made. It may be vain to ask why the imagination will not be reconciled to flesh and fat. I am satisfied that it is not. Is it not a reproach that man is a carnivorous animal? True, he can and does live, in a great measure, by preying on other animals; but this is a miserable way,—as any one who will go to snaring rabbits, or slaughtering lambs, may learn,—and he will be regarded as a benefactor of his race who shall teach man to confine himself to a more innocent and wholesome diet. Whatever my own practice may be, I have no doubt that it is a part of the destiny of the human race, in its gradual improvement, to leave off eating animals, as surely as the savage tribes have left off eating each other when they came in contact with the more civilized.

If one listens to the faintest but constant suggestions of his genius, which are certainly true, he sees not to what extremes, or even insanity, it may lead him; and yet that way, as he grows more resolute and faithful, his road lies. The faintest assured objection which one healthy man feels will at length prevail over the arguments and customs of mankind. No man ever followed his genius till it misled him. Though the result were bodily weakness, yet perhaps no one can say that the consequences were to be regretted, for these were a life in conformity to higher principles. If the day and the night are such that you greet them with joy, and life emits a fragrance like flowers and sweet-scented herbs, is more elastic, more starry, more immortal,—that is your success. All nature is your congratulation, and you have cause momentarily to bless yourself. The greatest gains and values are farthest from being appreciated. We easily come to doubt if they exist. We soon forget them. They are the highest reality. Perhaps the facts most astounding and most real are never communicated by man to man. The true harvest of my daily life is somewhat as intangible and indescribable as the tints of morning or evening. It is a little stardust caught, a segment of the rainbow which I have clutched.

Yet, for my part, I was never unusually squeamish; I could sometimes eat a fried rat with a good relish, if it were necessary. I am glad to have drunk water so long, for the same reason that I prefer the natural sky to an opium-eater's heaven. I would fain keep sober always; and there are infinite degrees of drunkenness. I believe that water is the only drink for a wise man; wine is not so noble a liquor; and think of dashing the hopes of a morning with a cup of warm coffee, or of an evening with a dish of tea! Ah, how low I fall when I am tempted by them! Even music may be intoxicating. Such apparently slight causes destroyed Greece and Rome, and will destroy England and America. Of all ebriosity, who does not prefer to be intoxicated by the air he breathes? I have found it to be the most serious objection to coarse labors long continued, that they compelled me to eat and drink coarsely also. But to tell the truth, I find myself at present somewhat less particular in these respects. I carry less religion to the table, ask no blessing; not because I am wiser than I was, but, I am obliged to confess, because, however much it is to be regretted, with years I have grown more coarse and indifferent. Perhaps these questions are entertained only in youth, as most believe of poetry. My practice is "nowhere," my opinion is here. Nevertheless I am far from regarding myself as one of those privileged ones to whom the Ved refers when it says, that "he who has true faith in the Omnipresent Supreme Being may eat all that exists," that is, is not bound to inquire what is his food, or who prepares it; and even in their case it is to be observed, as a Hindoo commentator has remarked, that the Vedant limits this privilege to "the time of distress."[6]

Who has not sometimes derived an inexpressible satisfaction from his food in which appetite had no share? I have been thrilled to think that I owed a mental perception to the commonly gross sense of taste, that I have been inspired through the palate, that some berries which I had eaten on a hill-side had fed my genius. "The soul not being mistress of herself," says Thseng-tseu, "one looks, and one does not see; one listens, and one does not hear; one eats, and one does not know the savor of food."[7] He who distinguishes the true savor of his food can never be a glutton; he who does not cannot be otherwise. A puritan may go to his brown-bread crust with as gross an appetite as ever an alderman to his turtle. Not that food which entereth into the mouth defileth a man, but the appetite with which it is eaten.[8] It is neither the quality nor the quantity, but the devotion to sensual savors; when that which is eaten is not a viand to sustain our animal, or inspire our spiritual life, but food for the worms that possess us. If the hunter has a taste for mud-turtles, muskrats, and other such savage tid-bits, the fine lady indulges a taste for jelly made of a calf's foot, or for sardines from over the sea, and they are even. He goes to the mill-pond, she to her preserve-pot. The wonder is how they, how you and I, can live this slimy beastly life, eating and drinking.

Our whole life is startlingly moral. There is never an instant's truce between virtue and vice. Goodness is the only investment

6. From *Translation of . . . the Veds* (1832) by Raja Rammohun Roy.
7. Confucius, *The Great Learning* 7.
8. Compare Matthew 15.11: "Not that which goeth into the mouth defileth a man: but that which cometh out of the mouth, this defileth a man."

that never fails. In the music of the harp which trembles round the world it is the insisting on this which thrills us. The harp is the travelling patterer for the Universe's Insurance Company, recommending its laws, and our little goodness is all the assessment that we pay. Though the youth at last grows indifferent, the laws of the universe are not indifferent, but are forever on the side of the most sensitive. Listen to every zephyr for some reproof, for it is surely there, and he is unfortunate who does not hear it. We cannot touch a string or move a stop but the charming moral transfixes us. Many an irksome noise, go a long way off, is heard as music, a proud sweet satire on the meanness of our lives.

We are conscious of an animal in us, which awakens in proportion as our higher nature slumbers. It is reptile and sensual, and perhaps cannot be wholly expelled; like the worms which, even in life and health, occupy our bodies. Possibly we may withdraw from it, but never change its nature. I fear that it may enjoy a certain health of its own; that we may be well, yet not pure. The other day I picked up the lower jaw of a hog, with white and sound teeth and tusks, which suggested that there was an animal health and vigor distinct from the spiritual. This creature succeeded by other means than temperance and purity. "That in which men differ from brute beasts," says Mencius,[9] "is a thing very inconsiderable; the common herd lose it very soon; superior men preserve it carefully." Who knows what sort of life would result if we had attained to purity? If I knew so wise a man as could teach me purity I would go to seek him forthwith. "A command over our passions, and over the external senses of the body, and good acts, are declared by the Ved to be indispensable in the mind's approximation to God." Yet the spirit can for the time pervade and control every member and function of the body, and transmute what in form is the grossest sensuality into purity and devotion. The generative energy, which, when we are loose, dissipates and makes us unclean, when we are continent invigorates and inspires us. Chastity is the flowering of man; and what are called Genius, Heroism, Holiness, and the like, are but various fruits which succeed it. Man flows at once to God when the channel of purity is open. By turns our purity inspires and our impurity casts us down. He is blessed who is assured that the animal is dying out in him day by day, and the divine being established. Perhaps there is none but has cause for shame on account of the inferior and brutish nature to which he is allied. I fear that we are such gods or demigods only as fauns and satyrs, the divine allied to beasts, the creatures of appetite, and that, to some extent, our very life is our disgrace.—

9. Latinized name of Meng-tse, Chinese philosopher (d. 289? B.C.E.); from his *Works*.

"How happy's he who hath due place assigned
To his beasts and disaforested his mind!
            *   *   *   *   *
Can use his horse, goat, wolf, and ev'ry beast,
And is not ass himself to all the rest!
Else man not only is the herd of swine,
But he's those devils too which did incline
Them to a headlong rage, and made them worse."[1]

All sensuality is one, though it takes many forms; all purity is one.
It is the same whether a man eat, or drink, or cohabit, or sleep sen-
sually. They are but one appetite, and we only need to see a person
do any one of these things to know how great a sensualist he is. The
impure can neither stand nor sit with purity. When the reptile is attacked at one mouth of his burrow, he shows himself at another. If
you would be chaste, you must be temperate. What is chastity? How
shall a man know if he is chaste? He shall not know it. We have
heard of this virtue, but we know not what it is. We speak con-
formably to the rumor which we have heard. From exertion come
wisdom and purity; from sloth ignorance and sensuality. In the student sensuality is a sluggish habit of mind. An unclean person is
universally a slothful one, one who sits by a stove, whom the sun
shines on prostrate, who reposes without being fatigued. If you
would avoid uncleanness, and all the sins, work earnestly, though it
be at cleaning a stable. Nature is hard to be overcome, but she must
be overcome. What avails it that you are Christian, if you are not
purer than the heathen, if you deny yourself no more, if you are not
more religious? I know of many systems of religion esteemed heathenish whose precepts fill the reader with shame, and provoke him
to new endeavors, though it be to the performance of rites merely.

I hesitate to say these things, but it is not because of the subject,—I care not how obscene my *words* are,—but because I cannot
speak of them without betraying my impurity. We discourse freely
without shame of one form of sensuality, and are silent about another. We are so degraded that we cannot speak simply of the necessary functions of human nature. In earlier ages, in some countries,
every function was reverently spoken of and regulated by law. Nothing was too trivial for the Hindoo lawgiver, however offensive it may
be to modern taste. He teaches how to eat, drink, cohabit, void ex-
crement and urine, and the like, elevating what is mean, and does
not falsely excuse himself by calling these things trifles.

Every man is the builder of a temple, called his body, to the god
he worships, after a style purely his own, nor can he get off by hammering marble instead. We are all sculptors and painters, and our

1. From "To Sir Edward Herbert," by John Donne (1573–1631).

material is our own flesh and blood and bones. Any nobleness begins at once to refine a man's features, any meanness or sensuality
to imbrute them.

John Farmer sat at his door one September evening, after a hard
day's work, his mind still running on his labor more or less. Having
bathed he sat down to recreate his intellectual man. It was a rather
cool evening, and some of his neighbors were apprehending a frost.
He had not attended to the train of his thoughts long when he
heard some one playing on a flute, and that sound harmonized with
his mood. Still he thought of his work; but the burden of his
thought was, that though this kept running in his head, and he
found himself planning and contriving it against his will, yet it concerned him very little. It was no more than the scurf of his skin,
which was constantly shuffled off. But the notes of the flute came
home to his ears out of a different sphere from that he worked in,
and suggested work for certain faculties which slumbered in him.
They gently did away with the street, and the village, and the state
in which he lived. A voice said to him,—Why do you stay here and
live this mean moiling life, when a glorious existence is possible for
you? Those same stars twinkle over other fields than these.—But
how to come out of this condition and actually migrate thither? All
that he could think of was to practise some new austerity, to let his
mind descend into his body and redeem it, and treat himself with
ever increasing respect.

Brute Neighbors

Sometimes I had a companion in my fishing,[1] who came through
the village to my house from the other side of the town, and the
catching of the dinner was as much a social exercise as the eating
of it.

Hermit. I wonder what the world is doing now. I have not heard
so much as a locust over the sweet-fern these three hours. The pigeons are all asleep upon their roosts,—no flutter from them. Was
that a farmer's noon horn which sounded from beyond the woods
just now? The hands are coming in to boiled salt beef and cider and
Indian bread. Why will men worry themselves so? He that does not
eat need not work. I wonder how much they have reaped. Who
would live there where a body can never think for the barking of
Bose?[2] And O, the housekeeping! to keep bright the devil's door-

---

1. Thoreau's frequent companion, and the model for the poet of the following dialogue,
   was Ellery Channing.
2. In Thoreau's time, a generic name for any dog.

knobs, and scour his tubs this bright day! Better not keep a house. Say, some hollow tree; and then for morning calls and dinner-parties! Only a wood-pecker tapping. O, they swarm; the sun is too warm there; they are born too far into life for me. I have water from the spring, and a loaf of brown bread on the shelf.—Hark! I hear a rustling of the leaves. Is it some ill-fed village hound yielding to the instinct of the chase? or the lost pig which is said to be in these woods, whose tracks I saw after the rain? It comes on apace; my sumachs and sweet-briars tremble.—Eh, Mr. Poet, is it you? How do you like the world to-day?

Poet. See those clouds; how they hang! That's the greatest thing I have seen to-day. There's nothing like it in old paintings, nothing like it in foreign lands,—unless when we were off the coast of Spain. That's a true Mediterranean sky. I thought, as I have my liv-ing to get, and have not eaten to-day, that I might go a fishing. That's the true industry for poets. It is the only trade I have learned. Come, let's along.

Hermit. I cannot resist. My brown bread will soon be gone. I will go with you gladly soon, but I am just concluding a serious medita-tion. I think that I am near the end of it. Leave me alone, then, for a while. But that we may not be delayed, you shall be digging the bait meanwhile. Angle-worms are rarely to be met with in these parts, where the soil was never fattened with manure; the race is nearly extinct. The sport of digging the bait is nearly equal to that of catching the fish, when one's appetite is not too keen; and this you may have all to yourself to-day. I would advise you to set in the spade down yonder among the ground-nuts, where you see the johnswort waving. I think that I may warrant you one worm to every three sods you turn up, if you look well in among the roots of the grass, as if you were weeding. Or, if you choose to go farther, it will not be unwise, for I have found the increase of fair bait to be very nearly as the squares of the distances.

Hermit alone. Let me see; where was I? Methinks I was nearly in this frame of mind; the world lay about at this angle. Shall I go to heaven or a-fishing? If I should soon bring this meditation to an end, would another so sweet occasion be likely to offer? I was as near being resolved into the essence of things as ever I was in my life. I fear my thoughts will not come back to me. If it would do any good, I would whistle for them. When they make us an offer, is it wise to say, We will think of it? My thoughts have left no track, and I cannot find the path again. What was it that I was thinking of? It was a very hazy day. I will just try these three sentences of Con-fut-see;[3] they may fetch that state about again. I know not whether it

3. Confucius.

was the dumps or a budding ecstasy. Mem.[4] There never is but one opportunity of a kind.

Poet. How now, Hermit, is it too soon? I have got just thirteen whole ones, beside several which are imperfect or undersized; but they will do for the smaller fry; they do not cover up the hook so much. Those village worms are quite too large; a shiner may make a meal off one without finding the skewer.

Hermit. Well, then, let's be off. Shall we to the Concord? There's good sport there if the water be not too high.

Why do precisely these objects which we behold make a world? Why has man just these species of animals for his neighbors; as if nothing but a mouse could have filled this crevice? I suspect that Pilpay & Co.[5] have put animals to their best use, for they are all beasts of burden, in a sense, made to carry some portion of our thoughts.

The mice which haunted my house were not the common ones, which are said to have been introduced into the country, but a wild native kind (*Mus leucopus*) not found in the village. I sent one to a distinguished naturalist,[6] and it interested him much. When I was building, one of these had its nest underneath the house, and before I had laid the second floor, and swept out the shavings, would come out regularly at lunch time and pick up the crumbs at my feet. It probably had never seen a man before; and it soon became quite familiar, and would run over my shoes and up my clothes. It could readily ascend the sides of the room by short impulses, like a squirrel, which it resembled in its motions. At length, as I leaned with my elbow on the bench one day, it ran up my clothes, and along my sleeve, and round and round the paper which held my dinner, while I kept the latter close, and dodged and played at bo-peep with it; and when at last I held still a piece of cheese between my thumb and finger, it came and nibbled it, sitting in my hand, and afterward cleaned its face and paws, like a fly, and walked away.

A phoebe soon built in my shed, and a robin for protection in a pine which grew against the house. In June the partridge, (*Tetrao umbellus*,) which is so shy a bird, led her brood past my windows, from the woods in the rear to the front of my house, clucking and calling to them like a hen, and in all her behavior proving herself the hen of the woods. The young suddenly disperse on your approach, at a signal from the mother, as if a whirlwind had swept them away, and they so exactly resemble the dried leaves and twigs

4. Memorandum.
5. Pilpay was erroneously supposed to have been the author of a collection of Sanskrit fables translated by Charles Wilkins, the *Hitopadesa*. Hence, tellers of fables.
6. Louis Agassiz (1807–1873), for whom Thoreau occasionally worked as a collector of specimens.

that many a traveller has placed his foot in the midst of a brood, and heard the whir of the old bird as she flew off, and her anxious calls and mewing, or seen her trail her wings to attract his attention, without suspecting their neighborhood. The parent will sometimes roll and spin round before you in such a dishabille, that you cannot, for a few moments, detect what kind of creature it is. The young squat still and flat, often running their heads under a leaf, and mind only their mother's directions given from a distance, nor will your approach make them run again and betray themselves. You may even tread on them, or have your eyes on them for a minute, without discovering them. I have held them in my open hand at such a time, and still their only care, obedient to their mother and their instinct, was to squat there without fear or trembling. So perfect is this instinct, that once, when I had laid them on the leaves again, and one accidentally fell on its side, it was found with the rest in exactly the same position ten minutes afterward. They are not callow like the young of most birds, but more perfectly developed and precocious even than chickens. The remarkably adult yet innocent expression of their open and serene eyes is very memorable. All intelligence seems reflected in them. They suggest not merely the purity of infancy, but a wisdom clarified by experience. Such an eye was not born when the bird was, but is coeval with the sky it reflects. The woods do not yield another such a gem. The traveller does not often look into such a limpid well. The ignorant or reckless sportsman often shoots the parent at such a time, and leaves these innocents to fall a prey to some prowling beast or bird, or gradually mingle with the decaying leaves which they so much resemble. It is said that when hatched by a hen they will directly disperse on some alarm, and so are lost, for they never hear the mother's call which gathers them again. These were my hens and chickens.

It is remarkable how many creatures live wild and free though secret in the woods, and still sustain themselves in the neighborhood of towns, suspected by hunters only. How retired the otter manages to live here! He grows to be four feet long, as big as a small boy, perhaps without any human being getting a glimpse of him. I formerly saw the raccoon in the woods behind where my house is built, and probably still heard their whinnering at night. Commonly I rested an hour or two in the shade at noon, after planting, and ate my lunch, and read a little by a spring which was the source of a swamp and of a brook, oozing from under Brister's Hill, half a mile from my field. The approach to this was through a succession of descending grassy hollows, full of young pitch-pines, into a larger wood about the swamp. There, in a very secluded and shaded spot, under a spreading white-pine, there was yet a clean firm sward to sit on. I had dug out the spring and made a well of clear gray water, where I could dip up a pailful without roiling it, and thither I went for this purpose almost every day in midsummer, when the pond was warmest. Thither too the wood-cock led her brood, to probe the mud for worms, flying but a foot above them down the bank, while they ran in a troop beneath; but at last, spying me, she would leave her young and circle round and round me, nearer and nearer till within four or five feet, pretending broken wings and legs, to attract my attention, and get off her young, who would already have taken up their march, with faint wiry peep, single file through the swamp, as she directed. Or I heard the peep of the young when I could not see the parent bird. There too the turtle-doves sat over the spring, or fluttered from bough to bough of the soft white-pines over my head; or the red squirrel, coursing down the nearest bough, was particularly familiar and inquisitive. You only need sit still long enough in some attractive spot in the woods that all its inhabitants may exhibit themselves to you by turns.

I was witness to events of a less peaceful character. One day when I went out to my wood-pile, or rather my pile of stumps, I observed two large ants, the one red, the other much larger, nearly half an inch long, and black, fiercely contending with one another. Having once got hold they never let go, but struggled and wrestled and rolled on the chips incessantly. Looking farther, I was surprised to find that the chips were covered with such combatants, that it was not a *duellum*, but a *bellum*,[7] a war between two races of ants, the red always pitted against the black, and frequently two red ones to one black. The legions of these Myrmidons[8] covered all the hills and vales in my wood-yard, and the ground was already strewn with the dead and dying, both red and black. It was the only battle which I have ever witnessed, the only battle-field I ever trod while the battle was raging; internecine war; the red republicans on the one hand, and the black imperialists on the other. On every side they were engaged in deadly combat, yet without any noise that I could hear, and human soldiers never fought so resolutely. I watched a couple that were fast locked in each other's embraces, in a little sunny valley amid the chips, now at noon-day prepared to fight till the sun went down, or life went out. The smaller red champion had fastened himself like a vice to his adversary's front, and through all the tumblings on that field never for an instant ceased to gnaw at one of his feelers near the root, having already caused the other to go by the board; while the stronger black one dashed him from side to side, and, as I saw on looking nearer, had

7. Not a duel, "a combat between two," but a war.
8. In Greek legend, a warlike people who fought with Achilles in the Trojan War.

already divested him of several of his members. They fought with more pertinacity than bull-dogs. Neither manifested the least disposition to retreat. It was evident that their battle-cry was Conquer or die. In the mean while there came along a single red ant on the hill-side of this valley, evidently full of excitement, who either had despatched his foe, or had not yet taken part in the battle; probably the latter, for he had lost none of his limbs; whose mother had charged him to return with his shield or upon it. Or perchance he was some Achilles, who had nourished his wrath apart, and had now come to avenge or rescue his Patroclus. He saw this unequal combat from afar,—for the blacks were nearly twice the size of the red,—he drew near with rapid pace till he stood on his guard within half an inch of the combatants; then, watching his opportunity, he sprang upon the black warrior, and commenced his operations near the root of his right fore-leg, leaving the foe to select among his own members; and so there were three united for life, as if a new kind of attraction had been invented which put all other locks and cements to shame. I should not have wondered by this time to find that they had their respective musical bands stationed on some eminent chip, and playing their national airs the while, to excite the slow and cheer the dying combatants. I was myself excited somewhat even as if they had been men. The more you think of it, the less the difference. And certainly there is not the fight recorded in Concord history, at least, if in the history of America, that will bear a moment's comparison with this, whether for the numbers engaged in it, or for the patriotism and heroism displayed. For numbers and for carnage it was an Austerlitz or Dresden.[9] Concord Fight! Two killed on the patriots' side, and Luther Blanchard wounded! Why here every ant was a Buttrick,—"Fire! for God's sake fire!"—and thousands shared the fate of Davis and Hosmer.[1] There was not one hireling there. I have no doubt that it was a principle they fought for, as much as our ancestors, and not to avoid a three-penny tax on their tea; and the results of this battle will be as important and memorable to those whom it concerns as those of the battle of Bunker Hill, at least.

I took up the chip on which the three I have particularly described were struggling, carried it into my house, and placed it under a tumbler on my window-sill, in order to see the issue. Holding a microscope to the first-mentioned red ant, I saw that, though he was assiduously gnawing at the near fore-leg of his enemy, having severed his remaining feeler, his own breast was all torn away, ex-

9. Two battles fought by Napoleon.
1. The first major battle of the American Revolution. The five hundred "minutemen" were under the command of Major John Buttrick; Isaac Davis and David Hosmer were the only two Americans killed.

posing what vitals he had there to the jaws of the black warrior, whose breast-plate was apparently too thick for him to pierce; and the dark carbuncles of the sufferer's eyes shone with ferocity such as war only could excite. They struggled half an hour longer under the tumbler, and when I looked again the black soldier had severed the heads of his foes from their bodies, and the still living heads were hanging on either side of him like ghastly trophies at his saddle-bow, still apparently as firmly fastened as ever, and he was endeavoring with feeble struggles, being without feelers and with only the remnant of a leg, and I know not how many other wounds, to divest himself of them; which at length, after half an hour more, he accomplished. I raised the glass, and he went off over the window-sill in that crippled state. Whether he finally survived that combat, and spent the remainder of his days in some Hotel des Invalides,[2] I do not know; but I thought that his industry would not be worth much thereafter. I never learned which party was victorious, nor the cause of the war; but I felt for the rest of that day as if I had had my feelings excited and harrowed by witnessing the struggle, the ferocity and carnage, of a human battle before my door.

Kirby and Spence tell us that the battles of ants have long been celebrated and the date of them recorded, though they say that Huber[3] is the only modern author who appears to have witnessed them. "Æneas Sylvius,"[4] say they, "after giving a very circumstantial account of one contested with great obstinacy by a great and small species on the trunk of a pear tree," adds that " 'This action was fought in the pontificate of Eugenius the Fourth,[5] in the presence of Nicholas Pistoriensis, an eminent lawyer, who related the whole history of the battle with the greatest fidelity.' A similar engagement between great and small ants is recorded by Olaus Magnus,[6] in which the small ones, being victorious, are said to have buried the bodies of their own soldiers, but left those of their giant enemies a prey to the birds. This event happened previous to the expulsion of the tyrant Christiern the Second from Sweden." The battle which I witnessed took place in the Presidency of Polk, five years before the passage of Webster's Fugitive-Slave Bill.[7]

Many a village Bose, fit only to course a mud-turtle in a victualling cellar, sported his heavy quarters in the woods, without the

2. A veterans' hospital in Paris.
3. Pierre Huber (1777–1840), a Swiss entomologist.
4. The pen name of Pope Pius II (1405–1464), poet and historian.
5. Pope from 1431 to 1437.
6. Swedish historian (1490–1558).
7. James K. Polk (1795–1849), president from 1845 to 1849. Daniel Webster (1782–1852), senator from Massachusetts; he did not introduce the Fugitive Slave Bill, passed in 1850, but he assisted in its passage.

knowledge of his master, and ineffectually smelled at old fox burrows and woodchucks' holes; led perchance by some slight cur
which nimbly threaded the wood, and might still inspire a natural
terror in its denizens;—now far behind his guide, barking like a ca-
nine bull toward some small squirrel which had treed itself for
scrutiny, then, cantering off, bending the bushes with his weight,
imagining that he is on the track of some stray member of the jer-
billa family. Once I was surprised to see a cat walking along the
stony shore of the pond, for they rarely wander so far from home.
The surprise was mutual. Nevertheless the most domestic cat,
which has lain on a rug all her days, appears quite at home in the
woods, and, by her sly and stealthy behavior, proves herself more
native there than the regular inhabitants. Once, when berrying, I
met with a cat with young kittens in the woods, quite wild, and they
all, like their mother, had their backs up and were fiercely spitting
at me. A few years before I lived in the woods there was what was
called a "winged cat" in one of the farm-houses in Lincoln nearest
the pond, Mr. Gilian Baker's. When I called to see her in June,
1842, she was gone a-hunting in the woods, as was her wont, (I am
not sure whether it was a male or female, and so use the more common pronoun,) but her mistress told me that she came into the
neighborhood a little more than a year before, in April, and was finally taken into their house; that she was of a dark brownish-gray
color, with a white spot on her throat, and white feet, and had a
large bushy tail like a fox; that in the winter the fur grew thick and
flatted out along her sides, forming strips ten or twelve inches long
by two and a half wide, and under her chin like a muff, the upper
side loose, the under matted like felt, and in the spring these ap-
pendages dropped off. They gave me a pair of her "wings," which I
keep still. There is no appearance of a membrane about them.
Some thought it was part flying-squirrel or some other wild animal,
which is not impossible, for, according to naturalists, prolific hybrids have been produced by the union of the marten and domestic
cat. This would have been the right kind of cat for me to keep, if I
had kept any; for why should not a poet's cat be winged as well as
his horse?[8]

In the fall the loon (*Colymbus glacialis*) came, as usual, to moult
and bathe in the pond, making the woods ring with his wild laughter before I had risen. At rumor of his arrival all the Mill-dam
sportsmen are on the alert, in gigs and on foot, two by two and
three by three, with patent rifles and conical balls and spy-glasses.
They come rustling through the woods like autumn leaves, at least
ten men to one loon. Some station themselves on this side of the

8. Inspired poets are said to ride on Pegasus, a winged horse in Greek mythology.

pond, some on that, for the poor bird cannot be omnipresent; if he dive here he must come up there. But now the kind October wind rises, rustling the leaves and rippling the surface of the water, so that no loon can be heard or seen, though his foes sweep the pond with spy-glasses, and make the woods resound with their discharges. The waves generously rise and dash angrily, taking sides with all waterfowl, and our sportsmen must beat a retreat to town and shop and unfinished jobs. But they were too often successful. When I went to get a pail of water early in the morning I frequently saw this stately bird sailing out of my cove within a few rods. If I endeavored to overtake him in a boat, in order to see how he would manœuver, he would dive and be completely lost, so that I did not discover him again, sometimes, till the latter part of the day. But I was more than a match for him on the surface. He commonly went off in a rain.

As I was paddling along the north shore one very calm October afternoon, for such days especially they settle on to the lakes, like the milkweed down, having looked in vain over the pond for a loon, suddenly one, sailing out from the shore toward the middle a few rods in front of me, set up his wild laugh and betrayed himself. I pursued with a paddle and he dived, but when he came up I was nearer than before. He dived again, but I miscalculated the direction he would take, and we were fifty rods apart when he came to the surface this time, for I had helped to widen the interval; and again he laughed long and loud, and with more reason than before. He manœuvred so cunningly that I could not get within half a dozen rods of him. Each time, when he came to the surface, turning his head this way and that, he coolly surveyed the water and the land, and apparently chose his course so that he might come up where there was the widest expanse of water and at the greatest distance from the boat. It was surprising how quickly he made up his mind and put his resolve into execution. He led me at once to the widest part of the pond, and could not be driven from it. While he was thinking one thing in his brain, I was endeavoring to divine his thought in mine. It was a pretty game, played on the smooth surface of the pond, a man against a loon. Suddenly your adversary's checker disappears beneath the board, and the problem is to place yours nearest to where his will appear again. Sometimes he would come up unexpectedly on the opposite side of me, having apparently passed directly under the boat. So long-winded was he and so unweariable, that when he had swum farthest he would immediately plunge again, nevertheless; and then no wit could divine where in the deep pond, beneath the smooth surface, he might be speeding his way like a fish, for he had time and ability to visit the bottom of the pond in its deepest part. It is said that loons have been caught in the New York lakes eighty feet beneath the surface, with hooks set for trout,—though Walden is deeper than that. How surprised must the fishes be to see this ungainly visitor from another sphere speeding his way amid their schools! Yet he appeared to know his course as surely under water as on the surface, and swam much faster there. Once or twice I saw a ripple where he approached the surface, just put his head out to reconnoitre, and instantly dived again. I found that it was as well for me to rest on my oars and wait his reappearing as to endeavor to calculate where he would rise; for again and again, when I was straining my eyes over the surface one way, I would suddenly be startled by his unearthly laugh behind me. But why, after displaying so much cunning, did he invariably betray himself the moment he came up by that loud laugh? Did not his white breast enough betray him? He was indeed a silly loon, I thought. I could commonly hear the plash of the water when he came up, and so also detected him. But after an hour he seemed as fresh as ever, dived as willingly and swam yet farther than at first. It was surprising to see how serenely he sailed off with unruffled breast when he came to the surface, doing all the work with his webbed feet beneath. His usual note was this demoniac laughter, yet somewhat like that of a water-fowl; but occasionally, when he had balked me most successfully and come up a long way off, he uttered a long-drawn unearthly howl, probably more like that of a wolf than any bird; as when a beast puts his muzzle to the ground and deliberately howls. This was his looning,—perhaps the wildest sound that is ever heard here, making the woods ring far and wide. I concluded that he laughed in derision of my efforts, confident of his own resources. Though the sky was by this time overcast, the pond was so smooth that I could see where he broke the surface when I did not hear him. His white breast, the stillness of the air, and the smoothness of the water were all against him. At length, having come up fifty rods off, he uttered one of those prolonged howls, as if calling on the god of loons to aid him, and immediately there came a wind from the east and rippled the surface, and filled the whole air with misty rain, and I was impressed as if it were the prayer of the loon answered, and his god was angry with me; and so I left him disappearing far away on the tumultuous surface.

For hours, in fall days, I watched the ducks cunningly tack and veer and hold the middle of the pond, far from the sportsman; tricks which they will have less need to practice in Louisiana bayous. When compelled to rise they would sometimes circle round and round and over the pond at a considerable height, from which they could easily see to other ponds and the river, like black motes in the sky; and, when I thought they had gone off thither long since, they would settle down by a slanting flight of a quarter of a mile on to a distant part which was left free; but what beside safety they got by sailing in the middle of Walden I do not know, unless they love its water for the same reason that I do.

House-Warming

In October I went a-graping to the river meadows, and loaded myself with clusters more precious for their beauty and fragrance than for food. There too I admired, though I did not gather, the cranberries, small waxen gems, pendants of the meadow grass, pearly and red, which the farmer plucks with an ugly rake, leaving the smooth meadow in a snarl, heedlessly measuring them by the bushel and the dollar only, and sells the spoils of the meads to Boston and New York; destined to be *jammed*, to satisfy the tastes of lovers of Nature there. So butchers rake the tongues of bison out of the prairie grass, regardless of the torn and drooping plant. The barberry's brilliant fruit was likewise food for my eyes merely; but I collected a small store of wild apples for coddling, which the proprietor and travellers had overlooked. When chestnuts were ripe I laid up half a bushel for winter. It was very exciting at that season to roam the then boundless chestnut woods of Lincoln,—they now sleep their long sleep under the railroad,—with a bag on my shoulder, and a stick to open burrs with in my hand, for I did not always wait for the frost, amid the rustling of leaves and the loud reproofs of the red-squirrels and the jays, whose half-consumed nuts I sometimes stole, for the burrs which they had selected were sure to contain sound ones. Occasionally I climbed and shook the trees. They grew also behind my house, and one large tree which almost overshadowed it, was, when in flower, a bouquet which scented the whole neighborhood, but the squirrels and the jays got most of its fruit; the last coming in flocks early in the morning and picking the nuts out of the burrs before they fell. I relinquished these trees to them and visited the more distant woods composed wholly of chestnut. These nuts, as far as they went, were a good substitute for bread. Many other substitutes might, perhaps, be found. Digging one day for fish-worms I discovered the ground-nut (*Apios tuberosa*) on its string, the potato of the aborigines, a sort of fabulous fruit, which I had begun to doubt if I had ever dug and eaten in childhood, as I had told, and had not dreamed it. I had often since seen its crimpled red velvety blossom supported by the stems of other plants without knowing it to be the same. Cultivation has well nigh exterminated it. It has a sweetish taste, much like that of a frostbitten potato, and I found it better boiled than roasted. This tuber seemed like a faint promise of Nature to rear her own children and feed them simply here at some future period. In these days of fatted cattle and waving grain-fields, this humble root, which was once the *totem* of an Indian tribe,[1] is quite forgotten, or known only by its flowering vine; but let wild Nature reign here once more, and the tender and luxurious English grains will probably disappear before a myriad of foes, and without the care of man the crow may carry back even the last seed of corn to the great corn-field of the Indian's God in the south-west, whence he is said to have brought it; but the now almost exterminated ground-nut will perhaps revive and flourish in spite of frosts and wildness, prove itself indigenous, and resume its ancient importance and dignity as the diet of the hunter tribe. Some Indian Ceres or Minerva[2] must have been the inventor and bestower of it; and when the reign of poetry commences here, its leaves and string of nuts may be represented on our works of art.

Already, by the first of September, I had seen two or three small maples turned scarlet across the pond, beneath where the white stems of three aspens diverged, at the point of a promontory, next the water. Ah, many a tale their color told! And gradually from week to week the character of each tree came out, and it admired itself reflected in the smooth mirror of the lake. Each morning the manager of this gallery substituted some new picture, distinguished by more brilliant or harmonious coloring, for the old upon the walls.

The wasps came by thousands to my lodge in October, as to winter quarters, and settled on my windows within and on the walls over-head, sometimes deterring visitors from entering. Each morning, when they were numbed with cold, I swept some of them out, but I did not trouble myself much to get rid of them; I even felt complimented by their regarding my house as a desirable shelter. They never molested me seriously, though they bedded with me; and they gradually disappeared, into what crevices I do not know, avoiding winter and unspeakable cold.

Like the wasps, before I finally went into winter quarters in November, I used to resort to the north-east side of Walden, which the sun, reflected from the pitch-pine woods and the stony shore, made the fire-side of the pond; it is so much pleasanter and wholesomer to be warmed by the sun while you can be, than by an artificial fire. I thus warmed myself by the still glowing embers which the summer, like a departed hunter, had left.

When I came to build my chimney I studied masonry. My bricks being second-hand ones required to be cleaned with a trowel, so

---

1. According to some authorities, the potato was believed by some Indians to bear a spiritual relation to their tribe.
2. In Roman mythology, goddesses of agriculture and wisdom, respectively.

that I learned more than usual of the qualities of bricks and trow-els. The mortar on them was fifty years old, and was said to be still growing harder; but this is one of those sayings which men love to repeat whether they are true or not. Such sayings themselves grow harder and adhere more firmly with age, and it would take many blows with a trowel to clean an old wiseacre of them. Many of the villages of Mesopotamia are built of secondhand bricks of a very good quality, obtained from the ruins of Babylon, and the cement on them is older and probably harder still. However that may be, I was struck by the peculiar toughness of the steel which bore so many violent blows without being worn out. As my bricks had been in a chimney before, though I did not read the name of Nebuchad-nezzar[3] on them, I picked out as many fireplace bricks as I could find, to save work and waste, and I filled the spaces between the bricks about the fireplace with stones from the pond shore, and also made my mortar with the white sand from the same place. I lingered most about the fireplace, as the most vital part of the house. Indeed, I worked so deliberately, that though I commenced at the ground in the morning, a course of bricks raised a few inches above the floor served for my pillow at night; yet I did not get a stiff neck for it that I remember; my stiff neck is of older date. I took a poet[4] to board for a fortnight about those times, which caused me to be put to it for room. He brought his own knife, though I had two, and we used to scour them by thrusting them into the earth. He shared with me the labors of cooking. I was pleased to see my work rising so square and solid by degrees, and reflected, that, if it proceeded slowly, it was calculated to endure a long time. The chimney is to some extent an independent structure, standing on the ground and rising through the house to the heavens; even after the house is burned it still stands sometimes, and its importance and independence are apparent. This was toward the end of sum-mer. It was now November.

The north wind had already begun to cool the pond, though it took many weeks of steady blowing to accomplish it, it is so deep. When I began to have a fire at evening, before I plastered my house, the chimney carried smoke particularly well, because of the numerous chinks between the boards. Yet I passed some cheer-ful evenings in that cool and airy apartment, surrounded by the rough brown boards full of knots, and rafters with the bark on high over-head. My house never pleased my eye so much after it was plastered, though I was obliged to confess that it was more com-

3. King of ancient Babylonia (604–561 B.C.E.).
4. Ellery Channing.

fortable. Should not every apartment in which man dwells be lofty enough to create some obscurity over-head, where flickering shadows may play at evening about the rafters? These forms are more agreeable to the fancy and imagination than fresco paintings or other the most expensive furniture. I now first began to inhabit my house, I may say, when I began to use it for warmth as well as shelter. I had got a couple of old fire-dogs to keep the wood from the hearth, and it did me good to see the soot form on the back of the chimney which I had built, and I poked the fire with more right and more satisfaction than usual. My dwelling was small, and I could hardly entertain an echo in it; but it seemed larger for being a single apartment and remote from neighbors. All the attractions of a house were concentrated in one room; it was kitchen, chamber, parlor, and keeping-room;[5] and whatever satisfaction parent or child, master or servant, derive from living in a house, I enjoyed it all. Cato says, the master of a family (*patremfamilias*) must have in his rustic villa "cellam oleariam, vinariam, dolia multa, uti lubeat caritatem expectare, et rei, et virtuti, et gloriæ erit," that is, "an oil and wine cellar, many casks, so that it may be pleasant to expect hard times; it will be for his advantage, and virtue, and glory."[6] I had in my cellar a firkin of potatoes, about two quarts of peas with the weevil in them, and on my shelf a little rice, a jug of molasses, and of rye and Indian meal a peck each.

I sometimes dream of a larger and more populous house, standing in a golden age, of enduring materials, and without ginger-bread work, which shall still consist of only one room, a vast, rude, substantial, primitive hall, without ceiling or plastering, with bare rafters and purlins supporting a sort of lower heaven over one's head,—useful to keep off rain and snow; where the king and queen posts stand out to receive your homage, when you have done reverence to the prostrate Saturn[7] of an older dynasty on stepping over the sill; a cavernous house, wherein you must reach up a torch upon a pole to see the roof; where some may live in the fire-place, some in the recess of a window, and some on settles, some at one end of the hall, some at another, and some aloft on rafters with the spiders, if they choose; a house which you have got into when you have opened the outside door, and the ceremony is over; where the weary traveller may wash, and eat, and converse, and sleep, without further journey; such a shelter as you would be glad to reach in a tempestuous night, containing all the essentials of a house, and nothing for house-keeping; where you can see all the treasures of the house

---

5. A New England dialect term for a sitting-room.
6. From *De Agri Cultura*; see n. 6, p. 46.
7. A Roman god (known to the Greeks as "Cronus"), overthrown by Jupiter (Greek: "Zeus").

at one view, and every thing hangs upon its peg that a man should use; at once kitchen, pantry, parlor, chamber, store-house, and garret; where you can see so necessary a thing as a barrel or a ladder, so convenient a thing as a cupboard, and hear the pot boil, and pay your respects to the fire that cooks your dinner and the oven that bakes your bread, and the necessary furniture and utensils are the chief ornaments; where the washing is not put out, nor the fire, nor the mistress, and perhaps you are sometimes requested to move from off the trap-door, when the cook would descend into the cellar, and so learn whether the ground is solid or hollow beneath you without stamping. A house whose inside is as open and manifest as a bird's nest, and you cannot go in at the front door and out at the back without seeing some of its inhabitants; where to be a guest is to be presented with the freedom of the house, and not to be carefully excluded from seven eighths of it, shut up in a particular cell, and told to make yourself at home there,—in solitary confinement. Nowadays the host does not admit you to *his* hearth, but has got the mason to build one for yourself somewhere in his alley, and hospitality is the art of *keeping* you at the greatest distance. There is as much secrecy about the cooking as if he had a design to poison you. I am aware that I have been on many a man's premises, and might have been legally ordered off, but I am not aware that I have been in many men's houses. I might visit in my old clothes a king and queen who lived simply in such a house as I have described, if I were going their way; but backing out of a modern palace will be all that I shall desire to learn, if ever I am caught in one.

It would seem as if the very language of our parlors would lose all its nerve and degenerate into *parlaver*[8] wholly, our lives pass at such remoteness from its symbols, and its metaphors and tropes are necessarily so far fetched, through slides and dumb-waiters, as it were; in other words, the parlor is so far from the kitchen and workshop. The dinner even is only the parable of a dinner, commonly. As if only the savage dwelt near enough to Nature and Truth to borrow a trope from them. How can the scholar, who dwells away in the North West Territory[9] or the Isle of Man, tell what is parliamentary in the kitchen?

However, only one or two of my guests were ever bold enough to stay and eat a hasty-pudding with me; but when they saw that crisis approaching they beat a hasty retreat rather, as if it would shake the house to its foundations. Nevertheless, it stood through a great many hasty-puddings.

8. A punning combination of "parlor" and "palaver," i.e., empty, profuse talk.
9. The area included within the current states of Ohio, Indiana, Michigan, Wisconsin, and Minnesota. The Isle of Man is in the Irish Sea.

I did not plaster till it was freezing weather. I brought over some whiter and cleaner sand for this purpose from the opposite shore of the pond in a boat, a sort of conveyance which would have tempted me to go much farther if necessary. My house had in the mean while been shingled down to the ground on every side. In lathing I was pleased to be able to send home each nail with a single blow of the hammer, and it was my ambition to transfer the plaster from the board to the wall neatly and rapidly. I remembered the story of a conceited fellow, who, in fine clothes, was wont to lounge about the village once, giving advice to workmen. Venturing one day to substitute deeds for words, he turned up his cuffs, seized a plasterer's board, and having loaded his trowel without mishap, with a complacent look toward the lathing overhead, made a bold gesture thitherward; and straightway, to his complete discomfiture, received the whole contents in his ruffled bosom. I admired anew the economy and convenience of plastering, which so effectually shuts out the cold and takes a handsome finish, and I learned the various casualties to which the plasterer is liable. I was surprised to see how thirsty the bricks were which drank up all the moisture in my plaster before I had smoothed it, and how many pailfuls of water it takes to christen a new hearth. I had the previous winter made a small quantity of lime by burning the shells of the *Unio fluviatilis*, which our river affords, for the sake of the experiment; so that I knew where my materials came from. I might have got good limestone within a mile or two and burned it myself, if I had cared to do so.

The pond had in the mean while skimmed over in the shadiest and shallowest coves, some days or even weeks before the general freezing. The first ice is especially interesting and perfect, being hard, dark, and transparent, and affords the best opportunity that ever offers for examining the bottom where it is shallow; for you can lie at your length on ice only an inch thick, like a skater insect on the surface of the water, and study the bottom at your leisure, only two or three inches distant, like a picture behind a glass, and the water is necessarily always smooth then. There are many furrows in the sand where some creature has travelled about and doubled on its tracks; and, for wrecks, it is strewn with the cases of cadis worms made of minute grains of white quartz. Perhaps these have creased it, for you find some of their cases in the furrows, though they are deep and broad for them to make. But the ice itself is the object of most interest, though you must improve the earliest opportunity to study it. If you examine it closely the morning after it freezes, you find that the greater part of the bubbles, which at first appeared to be within it, are against its under surface, and that more are continually rising from the bottom; while the ice is as yet comparatively solid and dark, that is, you see the water through it.

These bubbles are from an eightieth to an eighth of an inch in diameter, very clear and beautiful, and you see your face reflected in them through the ice. There may be thirty or forty of them to a square inch. There are also already within the ice narrow oblong perpendicular bubbles about half an inch long, sharp cones with the apex upward; or oftener, if the ice is quite fresh, minute spherical bubbles one directly above another, like a string of beads. But these within the ice are not so numerous nor obvious as those beneath. I sometimes used to cast on stones to try the strength of the ice, and those which broke through carried in air with them, which formed very large and conspicuous white bubbles beneath. One day when I came to the same place forty-eight hours afterward, I found that those large bubbles were still perfect, though an inch more of ice had formed, as I could see distinctly by the seam in the edge of a cake. But as the last two days had been very warm, like an Indian summer, the ice was not now transparent, showing the dark green color of the water, and the bottom, but opaque and whitish or gray, and though twice as thick was hardly stronger than before, for the air bubbles had greatly expanded under this heat and run together, and lost their regularity; they were no longer one directly over another, but often like silvery coins poured from a bag, one overlapping another, or in thin flakes, as if occupying slight cleavages. The beauty of the ice was gone, and it was too late to study the bottom. Being curious to know what position my great bubbles occupied with regard to the new ice, I broke out a cake containing a middling sized one, and turned it bottom upward. The new ice had formed around and under the bubble, so that it was included between the two ices. It was wholly in the lower ice, but close against the upper, and was flattish, or perhaps slightly lenticular, with a rounded edge, a quarter of an inch deep by four inches in diameter; and I was surprised to find that directly under the bubble the ice was melted with great regularity in the form of a saucer reversed, to the height of five eighths of an inch in the middle, leaving a thin partition there between the water and the bubble, hardly an eighth of an inch thick; and in many places the small bubbles in this partition had burst out downward, and probably there was no ice at all under the largest bubbles, which were a foot in diameter. I inferred that the infinite number of minute bubbles which I had first seen against the under surface of the ice were now frozen in likewise, and that each, in its degree, had operated like a burning glass on the ice beneath to melt and rot it. These are the little air-guns which contribute to make the ice crack and whoop.

At length the winter set in in good earnest, just as I had finished plastering, and the wind began to howl around the house as it had not had permission to do so till then. Night after night the geese came lumbering in in the dark with a clangor and a whistling of wings, even after the ground was covered with snow, some to alight in Walden, and some flying low over the woods toward Fair Haven, bound for Mexico. Several times, when returning from the village at ten or eleven o'clock at night, I heard the tread of a flock of geese, or else ducks, on the dry leaves in the woods by a pond-hole behind my dwelling, where they had come up to feed, and the faint honk or quack of their leader as they hurried off. In 1845 Walden froze entirely over for the first time on the night of the 22d of December, Flint's and other shallower ponds and the river having been frozen ten days or more; in '46, the 16th; in '49, about the 31st; and in '50, about the 27th of December; in '52, the 5th of January; in '53, the 31st of December. The snow had already covered the ground since the 25th of November, and surrounded me suddenly with the scenery of winter. I withdrew yet farther into my shell, and endeavored to keep a bright fire both within my house and within my breast. My employment out of doors now was to collect the dead wood in the forest, bringing it in my hands or on my shoulders, or sometimes trailing a dead pine tree under each arm to my shed. An old forest fence which had seen its best days was a great haul for me. I sacrificed it to Vulcan, for it was past serving the god Terminus.[1] How much more interesting an event is that man's supper who has just been forth in the snow to hunt, nay, you might say, steal, the fuel to cook it with! His bread and meat are sweet. There are enough fagots and waste wood of all kinds in the forests of most of our towns to support many fires, but which at present warm none, and, some think, hinder the growth of the young wood. There was also the drift-wood of the pond. In the course of the summer I had discovered a raft of pitch-pine logs with the bark on, pinned together by the Irish when the railroad was built. This I hauled up partly on the shore. After soaking two years and then lying high six months it was perfectly sound, though waterlogged past drying. I amused myself one winter day with sliding this piece-meal across the pond, nearly half a mile, skating behind with one end of a log fifteen feet long on my shoulder, and the other on the ice; or I tied several logs together with a birch withe, and then, with a longer birch or alder which had a hook at the end, dragged them across. Though completely waterlogged and almost as heavy as lead, they not only burned long, but made a very hot fire; nay, I thought that they burned better for the soaking, as if the pitch, being confined by the water, burned longer as in a lamp.

Gilpin, in his account of the forest borderers of England, says that "the encroachments of trespassers, and the houses and fences thus raised on the borders of the forest," were "considered as great

---

1. In Roman mythology, the gods of fire and boundaries, respectively.

nuisances by the old forest law, and were severely punished under the name of *purprestures*, as tending *ad terrorem ferarum—ad nocumentum forestæ*, &c.," to the frightening of the game and the detriment of the forest.[2] But I was interested in the preservation of the venison and the vert more than the hunters or wood-choppers, and as much as though I had been the Lord Warden[3] himself; and if any part was burned, though I burned it myself by accident, I grieved with a grief that lasted longer and was more inconsolable than that of the proprietors; nay, I grieved when it was cut down by the proprietors themselves. I would that our farmers when they cut down a forest felt some of that awe which the old Romans did when they came to thin, or let in the light to, a consecrated grove, (*lucum conlucare*,) that is, would believe that it is sacred to some god. The Roman made an expiatory offering, and prayed, Whatever god or goddess thou art to whom this grove is sacred, be propitious to me, my family, and children, &c.

It is remarkable what a value is still put upon wood even in this age and in this new country, a value more permanent and universal than that of gold. After all our discoveries and inventions no man will go by a pile of wood. It is as precious to us as it was to our Saxon and Norman ancestors. If they made their bows of it, we make our gun-stocks of it. Michaux, more than thirty years ago, says that the price of wood for fuel in New York and Philadelphia "nearly equals, and sometimes exceeds, that of the best wood in Paris, though this immense capital annually requires more than three hundred thousand cords, and is surrounded to the distance of three hundred miles by cultivated plains."[4] In this town the price of wood rises almost steadily, and the only question is, how much higher it is to be this year than it was the last. Mechanics and tradesmen who come in person to the forest on no other errand, are sure to attend the wood auction, and even pay a high price for the privilege of gleaning after the wood-chopper. It is now many years that men have resorted to the forest for fuel and the materials of the arts; the New Englander and the New Hollander, the Parisian and the Celt, the farmer and Robinhood, Goody Blake and Harry Gill,[5] in most parts of the world the prince and the peasant, the scholar and the savage, equally require still a few sticks from the forest to warm them and cook their food. Neither could I do without them.

Every man looks at his wood-pile with a kind of affection. I loved

2. William Gilpin (1724–1804), English author and landscape artist; from his *Remarks on Forest Scenery* (1834).
3. A person who has the responsibility of protecting the wildlife and preserving the greenery of a forest.
4. François André Michaux (1770–1855), French naturalist, from his *North American Sylva* (1819).
5. In a poem of this title by William Wordsworth (1770–1850), Harry Gill denies fuel to Goody Blake, whereupon she curses him to eternal cold.

to have mine before my window, and the more chips the better to remind me of my pleasing work. I had an old axe which nobody claimed, with which by spells in winter days, on the sunny side of the house, I played about the stumps which I had got out of my bean-field. As my driver prophesied when I was ploughing, they warmed me twice, once while I was splitting them, and again when they were on the fire, so that no fuel could give out more heat. As for the axe, I was advised to get the village blacksmith to "jump" it;[6] but I jumped him, and, putting a hickory helve from the woods into it, made it do. If it was dull, it was at least hung true.

A few pieces of fat pine were a great treasure. It is interesting to remember how much of this food for fire is still concealed in the bowels of the earth. In previous years I had often gone "prospecting" over some bare hill-side, where a pitch-pine wood had formerly stood, and got out the fat pine roots. They are almost indestructible. Stumps thirty or forty years old, at least, will still be sound at the core, though the sap-wood has all become vegetable mould, as appears by the scales of the thick bark forming a ring level with the earth four or five inches distant from the heart. With axe and shovel you explore this mine, and follow the marrowy store, yellow as beef tallow, or as if you had struck on a vein of gold, deep into the earth. But commonly I kindled my fire with the dry leaves of the forest, which I had stored up in my shed before the snow came. Green hickory finely split makes the wood-chopper's kindlings, when he has a camp in the woods. Once in a while I got a little of this. When the villagers were lighting their fires beyond the horizon, I too gave notice to the various wild inhabitants of Walden vale, by a smoky streamer from my chimney, that I was awake.—

> Light-winged Smoke, Icarian bird,
> Melting thy pinions in thy upward flight,
> Lark without song, and messenger of dawn,
> Circling above the hamlets as thy nest;
> Or else, departing dream, and shadowy form
> Of midnight vision, gathering up thy skirts;
> By night star-veiling, and by day
> Darkening the light and blotting out the sun;
> Go thou my incense upward from this hearth,
> And ask the gods to pardon this clear flame.

Hard green wood just cut, though I used but little of that, answered my purpose better than any other. I sometimes left a good fire when I went to take a walk in a winter afternoon; and when I

---

6. To flatten or lengthen the end of a piece of metal by hammering it.

returned, three or four hours afterward, it would be still alive and glowing. My house was not empty though I was gone. It was as if I had left a cheerful housekeeper behind. It was I and Fire that lived there; and commonly my housekeeper proved trustworthy. One day, however, as I was splitting wood, I thought that I would just look in at the window and see if the house was not on fire; it was the only time I remember to have been particularly anxious on this score; so I looked and saw that a spark had caught my bed, and I went in and extinguished it when it had burned a place as big as my hand. But my house occupied so sunny and sheltered a position, and its roof was so low, that I could afford to let the fire go out in the middle of almost any winter day.

The moles nested in my cellar, nibbling every third potato, and making a snug bed even there of some hair left after plastering and of brown paper; for even the wildest animals love comfort and warmth as well as man, and they survive the winter only because they are so careful to secure them. Some of my friends spoke as if I was coming to the woods on purpose to freeze myself. The animal merely makes a bed, which he warms with his body in a sheltered place; but man, having discovered fire, boxes up some air in a spacious apartment, and warms that, instead of robbing himself, makes that his bed, in which he can move about divested of more cumbrous clothing, maintain a kind of summer in the midst of winter, and by means of windows even admit the light, and with a lamp lengthen out the day. Thus he goes a step or two beyond instinct, and saves a little time for the fine arts. Though, when I had been exposed to the rudest blasts a long time, my whole body began to grow torpid, when I reached the genial atmosphere of my house I soon recovered my faculties and prolonged my life. But the most luxuriously housed has little to boast of in this respect, nor need we trouble ourselves to speculate how the human race may be at last destroyed. It would be easy to cut their threads any time with a little sharper blast from the north. We go on dating from Cold Fridays and Great Snows; but a little colder Friday, or greater snow, would put a period to man's existence on the globe.

The next winter I used a small cooking-stove for economy, since I did not own the forest; but it did not keep fire so well as the open fire-place. Cooking was then, for the most part, no longer a poetic, but merely a chemic process. It will soon be forgotten, in these days of stoves, that we used to roast potatoes in the ashes, after the Indian fashion. The stove not only took up room and scented the house, but it concealed the fire, and I felt as if I had lost a companion. You can always see a face in the fire. The laborer, looking into it at evening, purifies his thoughts of the dross and earthiness which they have accumulated during the day. But I could no longer sit and look into the fire, and the pertinent words of a poet recurred to me with new force.—

"Never, bright flame, may be denied to me
Thy dear, life imaging, close sympathy.
What but my hopes shot upward e'er so bright?
What but my fortunes sunk so low in night?

Why art thou banished from our hearth and hall,
Thou who art welcomed and beloved by all?
Was thy existence then too fanciful
For our life's common light, who are so dull?
Did thy bright gleam mysterious converse hold
With our congenial souls? secrets too bold?
Well, we are safe and strong, for now we sit
Beside a hearth where no dim shadows flit,
Where nothing cheers nor saddens, but a fire
Warms feet and hands—nor does to more aspire;
By whose compact utilitarian heap
The present may sit down and go to sleep,
Nor fear the ghosts who from the dim past walked,
And with us by the unequal light of the old wood fire talked."

(Mrs. Hooper)[7]

Former Inhabitants; and Winter Visitors

I weathered some merry snow storms, and spent some cheerful winter evenings by my fire-side, while the snow whirled wildly without, and even the hooting of the owl was hushed. For many weeks I met no one in my walks but those who came occasionally to cut wood and sled it to the village. The elements, however, abetted me in making a path through the deepest snow in the woods, for when I had once gone through the wind blew the oak leaves into my tracks, where they lodged, and by absorbing the rays of the sun melted the snow, and so not only made a dry bed for my feet, but in the night their dark line was my guide. For human society I was obliged to conjure up the former occupants of these woods. Within the memory of many of my townsmen the road near which my house stands resounded with the laugh and gossip of inhabitants, and the woods which border it were notched and dotted here and there with their little gardens and dwellings, though it was then much more shut in by the forest than now. In some places, within

---

7. From "The Wood-Fire" by Ellen Sturgis Hooper (1812–1848), an American poet widely admired by the Transcendentalists.

my own remembrance, the pines would scrape both sides of a chaise at once, and women and children who were compelled to go this way to Lincoln alone and on foot did it with fear, and often ran a good part of the distance. Though mainly but a humble route to neighboring villages, or for the woodman's team, it once amused the traveller more than now by its variety, and lingered longer in his memory. Where now firm open fields stretch from the village to the woods, it then ran through a maple swamp on a foundation of logs, the remnants of which, doubtless, still underlie the present dusty highway, from the Stratton, now the Alms House, Farm to Brister's Hill.

East of my bean-field, across the road, lived Cato Ingraham, slave of Duncan Ingraham, Esquire, gentleman of Concord village; who built his slave a house, and gave him permission to live in Walden Woods;—Cato, not Uticensis, but Concordiensis.[1] Some say that he was a Guinea Negro. There are a few who remember his little patch among the walnuts, which he let grow up till he should be old and need them; but a younger and whiter speculator got them at last. He too, however, occupies an equally narrow house at present. Cato's half-obliterated cellar hole still remains, though known to few, being concealed from the traveller by a fringe of pines. It is now filled with the smooth sumach, (*Rhus glabra*,) and one of the earliest species of goldenrod (*Solidago stricta*) grows there luxuriantly.

Here, by the very corner of my field, still nearer to town, Zilpha, a colored woman, had her little house, where she spun linen for the townsfolk, making the Walden Woods ring with her shrill singing, for she had a loud and notable voice. At length, in the war of 1812, her dwelling was set on fire by English soldiers, prisoners on parole, when she was away, and her cat and dog and hens were all burned up together. She led a hard life, and somewhat inhumane. One old frequenter of these woods remembers, that as he passed her house one noon he heard her muttering to herself over her gurgling pot,— "Ye are all bones, bones!" I have seen bricks amid the oak copse there.

Down the road, on the right hand, on Brister's Hill, lived Brister Freeman, "a handy Negro," slave of Squire Cummings once,— there where grow still the apple-trees which Brister planted and tended; large old trees now, but their fruit still wild and ciderish to my taste. Not long since I read his epitaph in the old Lincoln burying-ground, a little on one side, near the unmarked graves of some British grenadiers who fell in the retreat from Concord,—

1. I.e., not the Roman statesman, Marcus Porcius Cato (95–46 B.C.E.), who died in the town of Utica in north Africa, but Cato of Concord.

where he is styled "Sippio Brister,"—Scipio Africanus[2] he had some title to be called,—"a man of color," as if he were discolored. It also told me, with staring emphasis, when he died; which was but an indirect way of informing me that he ever lived. With him dwelt Fenda, his hospitable wife, who told fortunes, yet pleasantly,—large, round, and black, blacker than any of the children of night, such a dusky orb as never rose on Concord before or since.

Farther down the hill, on the left, on the old road in the woods, are marks of some homestead of the Stratton family; whose orchard once covered all the slope of Brister's Hill, but was long since killed out by pitch-pines, excepting a few stumps, whose old roots furnish still the wild stocks of many a thrifty village tree.[3]

Nearer yet to town, you come to Breed's location, on the other side of the way, just on the edge of the wood; ground famous for the pranks of a demon not distinctly named in old mythology, who has acted a prominent and astounding part in our New England life, and deserves, as much as any mythological character, to have his biography written one day; who first comes in the guise of a friend or hired man, and then robs and murders the whole family,—New-England Rum. But history must not yet tell the tragedies enacted here; let time intervene in some measure to assuage and lend an azure tint to them. Here the most indistinct and dubious tradition says that once a tavern stood; the well the same, which tempered the traveller's beverage and refreshed his steed. Here then men saluted one another, and heard and told the news, and went their ways again.

Breed's hut was standing only a dozen years ago, though it had long been unoccupied. It was about the size of mine. It was set on fire by mischievous boys, one Election night, if I do not mistake. I lived on the edge of the village then, and had just lost myself over Davenant's Gondibert,[4] that winter that I labored with a lethargy,—which, by the way, I never knew whether to regard as a family complaint, having an uncle who goes to sleep shaving himself, and is obliged to sprout potatoes in a cellar Sundays, in order to keep awake and keep the Sabbath, or as the consequence of my attempt to read Chalmers' collection of English poetry[5] without skipping. It

2. Roman general (237–183 B.C.E.) who was awarded the honorary name "Africanus" after he defeated the Carthaginian general, Hannibal.
3. Surveying for Cyrus Jarvis Dec. 23d 56—he shows me a deed of this lot containing 6 A. 52 rods all on the W. of the Wayland Road—& "consisting of plowland, orcharding & woodland" sold by Joseph Stratton to Samuel Swan of Concord In holder Aug. 11th 1777 [Thoreau's note].
4. William D'Avenant (1606–1668), English dramatist and poet; Gondibert is an unfinished romantic epic of chivalry.
5. Alexander Chalmers, The Works of the English Poets from Chaucer to Cowper (1810), 21 vols.

fairly overcame my Nervii.[6] I had just sunk my head on this when the bells rung fire, and in hot haste the engines rolled that way, led by a straggling troop of men and boys, and I among the foremost, for I had leaped the brook. We thought it was far south over the woods,—we who had run to fires before,—barn, shop, or dwelling-house, or all together. "It's Baker's barn," cried one. "It is the Codman Place," affirmed another. And then fresh sparks went up above the wood, as if the roof fell in, and we all shouted "Concord to the rescue!" Wagons shot past with furious speed and crushing loads, bearing, perchance, among the rest, the agent of the Insurance Company, who was bound to go however far; and ever and anon the engine bell tinkled behind, more slow and sure, and rearmost of all, as it was afterward whispered, came they who set the fire and gave the alarm. Thus we kept on like true idealists, rejecting the evidence of our senses, until at a turn in the road we heard the crackling and actually felt the heat of the fire from over the wall, and realized, alas! that we were there. The very nearness of the fire but cooled our ardor. At first we thought to throw a frog-pond on to it; but concluded to let it burn, it was so far gone and so worthless. So we stood round our engine, jostled one another, expressed our sentiments through speaking trumpets, or in lower tone referred to the great conflagrations which the world has witnessed, including Bascom's shop, and, between ourselves, we thought that, were we there in season with our "tub,"[7] and a full frog-pond by, we could turn that threatened last and universal one into another flood. We finally retreated without doing any mischief,—returned to sleep and Gondibert. But as for Gondibert, I would except that passage in the preface about wit being the soul's powder,—"but most of mankind are strangers to wit, as Indians are to powder."[8]

It chanced that I walked that way across the fields the following night, about the same hour, and hearing a low moaning at this spot, I drew near in the dark, and discovered the only survivor of the family that I know, the heir of both its virtues and its vices, who alone was interested in this burning, lying on his stomach and looking over the cellar wall at the still smouldering cinders beneath, muttering to himself, as is his wont. He had been working far off in the river meadows all day, and had improved the first moments that he could call his own to visit the home of his fathers and his youth. He gazed into the cellar from all sides and points of view by turns, always lying down to it, as if there was some treasure, which he remembered, concealed between the stones, where there was ab-

6. A punning reference to a northern European tribe that was defeated by Julius Caesar in 57 B.C.E.
7. A hand-drawn fire engine.
8. From "The Author's Preface."

solutely nothing but a heap of bricks and ashes. The house being gone, he looked at what there was left. He was soothed by the sympathy which my mere presence implied, and showed me, as well as the darkness permitted, where the well was covered up; which, thank Heaven, could never be burned; and he groped long about the wall to find the well-sweep which his father had cut and mounted, feeling for the iron hook or staple by which a burden had been fastened to the heavy end,—all that he could now cling to,—to convince me that it was no common "rider."[9] I felt it, and still remark it almost daily in my walks, for by it hangs the history of a family.

Once more, on the left, where are seen the well and lilac bushes by the wall, in the now open field, lived Nutting and Le Grosse. But to return toward Lincoln.

Farther in the woods than any of these, where the road approaches nearest to the pond, Wyman the potter squatted, and furnished his townsmen with earthen ware, and left descendants to succeed him. Neither were they rich in worldly goods, holding the land by sufferance while they lived; and there often the sheriff came in vain to collect the taxes, and "attached a chip,"[1] for form's sake, as I have read in his accounts, there being nothing else that he could lay his hands on. One day in midsummer, when I was hoeing, a man who was carrying a load of pottery to market stopped his horse against my field and inquired concerning Wyman the younger. He had long ago bought a potter's wheel of him, and wished to know what had become of him. I had read of the potter's clay and wheel in Scripture,[2] but it had never occurred to me that the pots we use were not such as had come down unbroken from those days, or grown on trees like gourds somewhere, and I was pleased to hear that so fictile an art was ever practised in my neighborhood.

The last inhabitant of these woods before me was an Irishman, Hugh Quoil, (if I have spelt his name with coil enough,) who occupied Wyman's tenement,—Col. Quoil, he was called. Rumor said that he had been a soldier at Waterloo.[3] If he had lived I should have made him fight his battles over again. His trade here was that of a ditcher. Napoleon went to St. Helena; Quoil came to Walden Woods. All I know of him is tragic. He was a man of manners, like one who had seen the world, and was capable of more civil speech than you could well attend to. He wore a great coat in mid-summer, being affected with the trembling delirium, and his face was the color of carmine. He died in the road at the foot of Brister's Hill shortly after I came to the woods, so that I have not remembered

---

9. The top rail of a fence.
1. Confiscated a worthless item.
2. Jeremiah 18: 3–6.
3. A Belgian village, scene of Napoleon's defeat by the duke of Wellington, June 18, 1815.

him as a neighbor. Before his house was pulled down, when his comrades avoided it as "an unlucky castle," I visited it. There lay his old clothes curled up by use, as if they were himself, upon his raised plank bed. His pipe lay broken on the hearth, instead of a bowl broken at the fountain. The last could never have been the symbol of his death, for he confessed to me that, though he had heard of Brister's Spring, he had never seen it; and soiled cards, kings of diamonds spades and hearts, were scattered over the floor. One black chicken which the administrator could not catch, black as night and as silent, not even croaking, awaiting Reynard,[4] still went to roost in the next apartment. In the rear there was the dim outline of a garden, which had been planted but had never received its first hoeing, owing to those terrible shaking fits, though it was now harvest time. It was over-run with Roman wormwood and beggar-ticks, which last stuck to my clothes for all fruit. The skin of a woodchuck was freshly stretched upon the back of the house, a trophy of his last Waterloo; but no warm cap or mittens would he want more.

Now only a dent in the earth marks the site of these dwellings, with buried cellar stones, and strawberries, raspberries, thimbleberries, hazel-bushes, and sumachs growing in the sunny sward there; some pitch-pine or gnarled oak occupies what was the chimney nook, and a sweet-scented black-birch, perhaps, waves where the door-stone was. Sometimes the well dent is visible, where once a spring oozed; now dry and tearless grass; or it was covered deep,— not to be discovered till some late day,—with a flat stone under the sod, when the last of the race departed. What a sorrowful act must that be,—the covering up of wells! coincident with the opening of wells of tears. These cellar dents, like deserted fox burrows, old holes, are all that is left where once were the stir and bustle of human life, and "fate, free-will, foreknowledge absolute,"[5] in some form and dialect or other were by turns discussed. But all I can learn of their conclusions amounts to just this, that "Cato and Brister pulled wool;"[6] which is about as edifying as the history of more famous schools of philosophy.

Still grows the vivacious lilac a generation after the door and lintel and the sill are gone, unfolding its sweet-scented flowers each spring, to be plucked by the musing traveller; planted and tended once by children's hands, in front-yard plots,—now standing by wall-sides in retired pastures, and giving place to new-rising forests;—the last of that stirp, sole survivor of that family. Little did the dusky children think that the puny slip with its two eyes only,

---

4. Literary name for the fox.
5. Milton, *Paradise Lost* 2.560.
6. I.e., performed menial tasks.

which they stuck in the ground in the shadow of the house and daily watered, would root itself so, and outlive them, and house itself in the rear that shaded it, and grown man's garden and orchard, and tell their story faintly to the lone wanderer a half century after they had grown up and died,—blossoming as fair, and smelling as sweet, as in that first spring. I mark its still tender, civil, cheerful, lilac colors.

But this small village, germ of something more, why did it fail while Concord keeps its ground? Were there no natural advantages,—no water privileges, forsooth? Ay, the deep Walden Pond and cool Brister's Spring,—privilege to drink long and healthy draughts at these, all unimproved by these men but to dilute their glass. They were universally a thirsty race. Might not the basket, stable-broom, mat-making, corn-parching, linen-spinning, and pottery business have thrived here, making the wilderness to blossom like the rose, and a numerous posterity have inherited the land of their fathers? The sterile soil would at least have been proof against a low-land degeneracy. Alas! how little does the memory of these human inhabitants enhance the beauty of the landscape! Again, perhaps, Nature will try, with me for a first settler, and my house raised last spring to be the oldest in the hamlet.

I am not aware that any man has ever built on the spot which I occupy. Deliver me from a city built on the site of a more ancient city, whose materials are ruins, whose gardens cemeteries. The soil is blanched and accursed there, and before that becomes necessary the earth itself will be destroyed. With such reminiscences I re-peopled the woods and lulled myself asleep.

At this season I seldom had a visitor. When the snow lay deepest no wanderer ventured near my house for a week or fortnight at a time, but there I lived as snug as a meadow mouse, or as cattle and poultry which are said to have survived for a long time buried in drifts, even without food; or like that early settler's family in the town of Sutton, in this state, whose cottage was completely covered by the great snow of 1717 when he was absent, and an Indian found it only by the hole which the chimney's breath made in the drift, and so relieved the family. But no friendly Indian concerned himself about me; nor needed he, for the master of the house was at home. The Great Snow! How cheerful it is to hear of! When the farmers could not get to the woods and swamps with their teams, and were obliged to cut down the shade trees before their houses, and when the crust was harder cut off the trees in the swamps ten feet from the ground, as it appeared the next spring.

In the deepest snows, the path which I used from the highway to my house, about half a mile long, might have been represented by a meandering dotted line, with wide intervals between the dots. For a week of even weather I took exactly the same number of steps, and of the same length, coming and going, stepping deliberately and with the precision of a pair of dividers in my own deep tracks,—to such routine the winter reduces us,—yet often they were filled with heaven's own blue. But no weather interfered fatally with my walks, or rather my going abroad, for I frequently tramped eight or ten miles through the deepest snow to keep an appointment with a beech-tree, or a yellow-birch, or an old acquaintance among the pines; when the ice and snow causing their limbs to droop, and so sharpening their tops, had changed the pines into fir-trees; wading to the tops of the highest hills when the snow was nearly two feet deep on a level, and shaking down another snow-storm on my head at every step; or sometimes creeping and floundering thither on my hands and knees, when the hunters had gone into winter quarters. One afternoon I amused myself by watching a barred owl (*Strix nebulosa*) sitting on one of the lower dead limbs of a white-pine, close to the trunk, in broad daylight, I standing within a rod of him. He could hear me when I moved and cronched the snow with my feet, but could not plainly see me. When I made most noise he would stretch out his neck, and erect his neck feathers, and open his eyes wide; but their lids soon fell again, and he began to nod. I too felt a slumberous influence after watching him half an hour, as he sat thus with his eyes half open, like a cat, winged brother of the cat. There was only a narrow slit left between their lids, by which he preserved a peninsular relation to me; thus, with half-shut eyes, looking out from the land of dreams, and endeavoring to realize me, vague object or mote that interrupted his visions. At length, on some louder noise or my nearer approach, he would grow uneasy and sluggishly turn about on his perch, as if impatient at having his dreams disturbed; and when he launched himself off and flapped through the pines, spreading his wings to unexpected breadth, I could not hear the slightest sound from them. Thus, guided amid the pine boughs rather by a delicate sense of their neighborhood than by sight, feeling his twilight way as it were with his sensitive pinions, he found a new perch, where he might in peace await the dawning of his day.

As I walked over the long causeway made for the railroad through the meadows, I encountered many a blustering and nipping wind, for nowhere has it freer play; and when the frost had smitten me on one cheek, heathen as I was, I turned to it the other also.[7] Nor was it much better by the carriage road from Brister's

---

7. Compare Jesus' Sermon on the Mount: "I say unto you, That ye resist not evil: but whosoever shall smite thee on thy right cheek, turn to him the other also" (Matthew 5.39).

Hill. For I came to town still, like a friendly Indian, when the contents of the broad open fields were all piled up between the walls of the Walden road, and half an hour sufficed to obliterate the tracks of the last traveller. And when I returned new drifts would have formed, through which I floundered, where the busy north-west wind had been depositing the powdery snow round a sharp angle in the road, and not a rabbit's track, nor even the fine print, the small type, of a deer mouse was to be seen. Yet I rarely failed to find, even in mid-winter, some warm and springy swamp where the grass and the skunk-cabbage still put forth with perennial verdure, and some hardier bird occasionally awaited the return of spring.

Sometimes, notwithstanding the snow, when I returned from my walk at evening I crossed the deep tracks of a woodchopper leading from my door, and found his pile of whittlings on the hearth, and my house filled with the odor of his pipe. Or on a Sunday afternoon, if I chanced to be at home, I heard the cronching of the snow made by the step of a long-headed farmer, who from far through the woods sought my house, to have a social "crack;" one of the few of his vocation who are "men on their farms;"[8] who donned a frock instead of a professor's gown, and is as ready to extract the moral out of church or state as to haul a load of manure from his barn-yard. We talked of rude and simple times, when men sat about large fires in cold bracing weather, with clear heads; and when other dessert failed, we tried our teeth on many a nut which wise squirrels have long since abandoned, for those which have the thickest shells are commonly empty.

The one who came from farthest to my lodge, through deepest snows and most dismal tempests, was a poet.[9] A farmer, a hunter, a soldier, a reporter, even a philosopher, may be daunted; but nothing can deter a poet, for he is actuated by pure love. Who can predict his comings and goings? His business calls him out at all hours, even when doctors sleep. We made that small house ring with boisterous mirth and resound with the murmur of much sober talk, making amends then to Walden vale for the long silences. Broadway was still and deserted in comparison. At suitable intervals there were regular salutes of laughter, which might have been referred indifferently to the last uttered or the forth-coming jest. We made many a "bran new" theory of life over a thin dish of gruel, which combined the advantages of conviviality with the clear-headedness which philosophy requires.

I should not forget that during my last winter at the pond there

---

8. In "The American Scholar," Ralph Waldo Emerson distinguishes the ideal individual ("Man on the farm") from the social being (the farmer).
9. Ellery Channing.

was another welcome visitor,[1] who at one time came through the village, through snow and rain and darkness, till he saw my lamp through the trees, and shared with me some long winter evenings. One of the last of the philosophers,—Connecticut gave him to the world,—he peddled first her wares, afterwards, as he declares, his brains. These he peddles still, prompting God and disgracing man, bearing for fruit his brain only, like the nut its kernel. I think that he must be the man of the most faith of any alive. His words and attitude always suppose a better state of things than other men are acquainted with, and he will be the last man to be disappointed as the ages revolve. He has no venture in the present. But though comparatively disregarded now, when his day comes, laws unsuspected by most will take effect, and masters of families and rulers will come to him for advice.—

"How blind that cannot see serenity!"[2]

A true friend of man; almost the only friend of human progress. An Old Mortality,[3] say rather an Immortality, with unwearied patience and faith making plain the image engraven in men's bodies, the God of whom they are but defaced and leaning monuments. With his hospitable intellect he embraces children, beggars, insane, and scholars, and entertains the thought of all, adding to it commonly some breadth and elegance. I think that he should keep a caravansary on the world's highway, where philosophers of all nations might put up, and on his sign should be printed, "Entertainment for man, but not for his beast. Enter ye that have leisure and a quiet mind, who earnestly seek the right road." He is perhaps the sanest man and has the fewest crotchets of any I chance to know; the same yesterday and to-morrow. Of yore we had sauntered and talked, and effectually put the world behind us; for he was pledged to no institution in it, freeborn, *ingenuus*. Whichever way we turned, it seemed that the heavens and the earth had met together, since he enhanced the beauty of the landscape. A blue-robed man, whose fittest roof is the overarching sky which reflects his serenity. I do not see how he can ever die; Nature cannot spare him.

Having each some shingles of thought well dried, we sat and whittled them, trying our knives, and admiring the clear yellowish grain of the pumpkin pine. We waded so gently and reverently, or we pulled together so smoothly, that the fishes of thought were not scared from the stream, nor feared any angler on the bank, but came and went grandly, like the clouds which float through the

---

1. Amos Bronson Alcott (1799–1888), Transcendentalist and educator.
2. From *The Life and Death of Thomas Wolsey*, Cardinal (1599) by Thomas Storer.
3. The title of a novel by Sir Walter Scott (1771–1832); the leading character wanders through Scotland repairing and cleaning gravestones.

western sky, and the mother-o'-pearl flocks which sometimes form and dissolve there. There we worked, revising mythology, rounding a fable here and there, and building castles in the air for which earth offered no worthy foundation. Great Looker! Great Expecter! to converse with whom was a New England Night's Entertainment. Ah! such discourse we had, hermit and philosopher, and the old settler I have spoken of,—we three,—it expanded and racked my little house; I should not dare to say how many pounds' weight there was above the atmospheric pressure on every circular inch; it opened its seams so that they had to be calked with much dulness thereafter to stop the consequent leak;—but I had enough of that kind of oakum already picked.

There was one other[4] with whom I had "solid seasons," long to be remembered, at his house in the village, and who looked in upon me from time to time; but I had no more for society there.

There too, as every where, I sometimes expected the Visitor who never comes. The Vishnu Purana[5] says, "The house-holder is to remain at eventide in his court-yard as long as it takes to milk a cow, or longer if he pleases, to await the arrival of a guest." I often performed this duty of hospitality, waited long enough to milk a whole herd of cows, but did not see the man approaching from the town.

Winter Animals

When the ponds were firmly frozen, they afforded not only new and shorter routes to many points, but new views from their surfaces of the familiar landscape around them. When I crossed Flint's Pond, after it was covered with snow, though I had often paddled about and skated over it, it was so unexpectedly wide and so strange that I could think of nothing but Baffin's Bay.[1] The Lincoln hills rose up around me at the extremity of a snowy plain, in which I did not remember to have stood before; and the fishermen, at an indeterminable distance over the ice, moving slowly about with their wolfish dogs, passed for sealers or Esquimaux, or in misty weather loomed like fabulous creatures, and I did not know whether they were giants or pygmies. I took this course when I went to lecture in Lincoln in the evening, travelling in no road and passing no house between my own hut and the lecture room. In Goose Pond, which lay in my way, a colony of muskrats dwelt, and raised their cabins high above the ice, though none could be seen abroad when I

4. Ralph Waldo Emerson (1803–1882), a leading Transcendentalist and a close friend of Thoreau.
5. A Hindu scripture.
1. A part of the north Atlantic Ocean between Greenland and Canada.

crossed it. Walden, being like the rest usually bare of snow, or with only shallow and interrupted drifts on it, was my yard, where I could walk freely when the snow was nearly two feet deep on a level elsewhere and the villagers were confined to their streets. There, far from the village street, and except at very long intervals, from the jingle of sleigh-bells, I slid and skated, as in a vast moose-yard well trodden, overhung by oak woods and solemn pines bent down with snow or bristling with icicles.

For sounds in winter nights, and often in winter days, I heard the forlorn but melodious note of a hooting owl indefinitely far; such a sound as the frozen earth would yield if struck with a suitable plectrum, the very *lingua vernacula*[2] of Walden Wood, and quite familiar to me at last, though I never saw the bird while it was making it. I seldom opened my door in a winter evening without hearing it; *Hoo hoo hoo, hoorer hoo*, sounded sonorously, and the first three syllables accented somewhat like *how der do*; or sometimes *hoo hoo* only. One night in the beginning of winter, before the pond froze over, about nine o'clock, I was startled by the loud honking of a goose, and, stepping to the door, heard the sound of their wings like a tempest in the woods as they flew low over my house. They passed over the pond toward Fair Haven, seemingly deterred from settling by my light, their commodore honking all the while with a regular beat. Suddenly an unmistakable cat-owl from very near me, with the most harsh and tremendous voice I ever heard from any inhabitant of the woods, responded at regular intervals to the goose, as if determined to expose and disgrace this intruder from Hudson's Bay[3] by exhibiting a greater compass and volume of voice in a native, and *boo-hoo* him out of Concord horizon. What do you mean by alarming the citadel at this time of night consecrated to me? Do you think I am ever caught napping at such an hour, and that I have not got lungs and a larynx as well as yourself? *Boo-hoo, boo-hoo, boo-hoo!* It was one of the most thrilling discords I ever heard. And yet, if you had a discriminating ear, there were in it the elements of a concord such as these plains never saw nor heard.

I also heard the whooping of the ice in the pond, my great bedfellow in that part of Concord, as if it were restless in its bed and would fain turn over, were troubled with flatulency and bad dreams; or I was waked by the cracking of the ground by the frost, as if some one had driven a team against my door, and in the morning would find a crack in the earth a quarter of a mile long and a third of an inch wide.

Sometimes I heard the foxes as they ranged over the snow crust,

2. The native language of a locality.
3. An inland sea in north central Canada.

in moonlight nights, in search of a partridge or other game, barking
raggedly and demoniacally like forest dogs, as if laboring with some
anxiety, or seeking expression, struggling for light and to be dogs
outright and run freely in the streets; for if we take the ages into
our account, may there not be a civilization going on among brutes
as well as men? They seemed to me to be rudimental, burrowing
men, still standing on their defence, awaiting their transformation.
Sometimes one came near to my window, attracted by my light,
barked a vulpine curse at me, and then retreated.

Usually the red squirrel (*Sciurus Hudsonius*) waked me in the
dawn, coursing over the roof and up and down the sides of the
house, as if sent out of the woods for this purpose. In the course of
the winter I threw out half a bushel of ears of sweetcorn, which
had not got ripe, on to the snow crust by my door, and was amused
by watching the motions of the various animals which were baited
by it. In the twilight and the night the rabbits came regularly and
made a hearty meal. All day long the red squirrels came and went,
and afforded me much entertainment by their manœuvres. One
would approach at first warily through the shrub-oaks, running over
the snow crust by fits and starts like a leaf blown by the wind, now
a few paces this way, with wonderful speed and waste of energy,
making inconceivable haste with his "trotters," as if it were for a
wager, and now as many paces that way, but never getting on more
than half a rod at a time; and then suddenly pausing with a ludicrous expression and a gratuitous somerset, as if all the eyes in the
universe were fixed on him,—for all the motions of a squirrel, even
in the most solitary recesses of the forest, imply spectators as much
as those of a dancing girl,—wasting more time in delay and circumspection than would have sufficed to walk the whole distance,—I
never saw one walk,—and then suddenly, before you could say Jack
Robinson, he would be in the top of a young pitch-pine, winding up
his clock and chiding all imaginary spectators, soliloquizing and
talking to all the universe at the same time,—for no reason that I
could ever detect, or he himself was aware of, I suspect. At length
he would reach the corn, and selecting a suitable ear, frisk about in
the same uncertain trigonometrical way to the top-most stick of my
wood-pile, before my window, where he looked me in the face, and
there sit for hours, supplying himself with a new ear from time to
time, nibbling at first voraciously and throwing the half-naked cobs
about; till at length he grew more dainty still and played with his
food, tasting only the inside of the kernel, and the ear, which was
held balanced over the stick by one paw, slipped from his careless
grasp and fell to the ground, when he would look over at it with a
ludicrous expression of uncertainty, as if suspecting that it had life,
with a mind not made up whether to get it again, or a new one, or

be off; now thinking of corn, then listening to hear what was in the wind. So the little impudent fellow would waste many an ear in a forenoon; till at last, seizing some longer and plumper one, considerably bigger than himself, and skilfully balancing it, he would set out with it to the woods, like a tiger with a buffalo, by the same zigzag course and frequent pauses, scratching along with it as if it were too heavy for him and falling all the while, making its fall a diagonal between a perpendicular and horizontal, being determined to put it through at any rate;—a singularly frivolous and whimsical fellow;—and so he would get off with it to where he lived, perhaps carry it to the top of a pine tree forty or fifty rods distant, and I would afterwards find the cobs strewn about the woods in various directions.

At length the jays arrive, whose discordant screams were heard long before, as they were warily making their approach an eighth of a mile off, and in a stealthy and sneaking manner they flit from tree to tree, nearer and nearer, and pick up the kernels which the squirrels have dropped. Then, sitting on a pitch-pine bough, they attempt to swallow in their haste a kernel which is too big for their throats and chokes them; and after great labor they disgorge it, and spend an hour in the endeavor to crack it by repeated blows with their bills. They were manifestly thieves, and I had not much respect for them; but the squirrels, though at first shy, went to work as if they were taking what was their own.

Meanwhile also came the chicadees in flocks, which, picking up the crumbs the squirrels had dropped, flew to the nearest twig, and, placing them under their claws, hammered away at them with their little bills, as if it were an insect in the bark, till they were sufficiently reduced for their slender throats. A little flock of these titmice came daily to pick a dinner out of my wood-pile, or the crumbs at my door, with faint flitting lisping notes, like the tinkling of icicles in the grass, or else with sprightly *day day day*, or more rarely, in spring-like days, a wiry summery *phe-be* from the woodside. They were so familiar that at length one alighted on an armful of wood which I was carrying in, and pecked at the sticks without fear. I once had a sparrow alight upon my shoulder for a moment while I was hoeing in a village garden, and I felt that I was more distinguished by that circumstance than I should have been by any epaulet I could have worn. The squirrels also grew at last to be quite familiar, and occasionally stepped upon my shoe, when that was the nearest way.

When the ground was not yet quite covered, and again near the end of winter, when the snow was melted on my south hillside and about my wood-pile, the partridges came out of the woods morning and evening to feed there. Whichever side you walk in the woods the partridge bursts away on whirring wings, jarring the snow from the dry leaves and twigs on high, which comes sifting down in the sun-beams like golden dust; for this brave bird is not to be scared by winter. It is frequently covered up by drifts, and, it is said, "sometimes plunges from on wing into the soft snow, where it remains concealed for a day or two." I used to start them in the open land also, where they had come out of the woods at sunset to "bud" the wild apple-trees. They will come regularly every evening to particular trees, where the cunning sportsman lies in wait for them, and the distant orchards next the woods suffer thus not a little. I am glad that the partridge gets fed, at any rate. It is Nature's own bird which lives on buds and diet-drink.

In dark winter mornings, or in short winter afternoons, I sometimes heard a pack of hounds threading all the woods with hounding cry and yelp, unable to resist the instinct of the chase, and the note of the hunting horn at intervals, proving that man was in the rear. The woods ring again, and yet no fox bursts forth on to the open level of the pond, nor following pack pursuing their Actæon.[4] And perhaps at evening I see the hunters returning with a single brush trailing from their sleigh for a trophy, seeking their inn. They tell me that if the fox would remain in the bosom of the frozen earth he would be safe, or if he would run in a straight line away no foxhound could overtake him; but, having left his pursuers far behind, he stops to rest and listen till they come up, and when he runs he circles round to his old haunts, where the hunters await him. Sometimes, however, he will run upon a wall many rods, and then leap off far to one side, and he appears to know that water will not retain his scent. A hunter told me that he once saw a fox pursued by hounds burst out on to Walden when the ice was covered with shallow puddles, run part way across, and then return to the same shore. Ere long the hounds arrived, but here they lost the scent. Sometimes a pack hunting by themselves would pass my door, and circle round my house, and yelp and hound without regarding me, as if afflicted by a species of madness, so that nothing could divert them from the pursuit. Thus they circle until they fall upon the recent trail of a fox, for a wise hound will forsake every thing else for this. One day a man came to my hut from Lexington to inquire after his hound that made a large track, and had been hunting for a week by himself. But I fear that he was not the wiser for all I told him, for every time I attempted to answer his questions he interrupted me by asking, "What do you do here?" He had lost a dog, but found a man.

One old hunter who has a dry tongue, who used to come to

4. In Greek mythology a hunter who was transformed into a stag, then pursued and killed by his own dogs.

bathe in Walden once every year when the water was warmest, and at such times looked in upon me, told me, that many years ago he took his gun one afternoon and went out for a cruise in Walden Wood; and as he walked the Wayland road he heard the cry of hounds approaching, and ere long a fox leaped the wall into the road, and as quick as thought leaped the other wall out of the road, and his swift bullet had not touched him. Some way behind came an old hound and her three pups in full pursuit, hunting on their own account, and disappeared again in the woods. Late in the afternoon, as he was resting in the thick woods south of Walden, he heard the voice of the hounds far over toward Fair Haven still pursuing the fox; and on they came, their hounding cry which made all the woods ring sounding nearer and nearer, now from Well-Meadow, now from the Baker Farm. For a long time he stood still and listened to their music, so sweet to a hunter's ear, when suddenly the fox appeared, threading the solemn aisles with an easy coursing pace, whose sound was concealed by a sympathetic rustle of the leaves, swift and still, keeping the ground, leaving his pursuers far behind; and, leaping upon a rock amid the woods, he sat erect and listening, with his back to the hunter. For a moment compassion restrained the latter's arm; but that was a short-lived mood, and as quick as thought can follow thought his piece was levelled, and *whang*!—the fox rolling over the rock lay dead on the ground. The hunter still kept his place and listened to the hounds. Still on they came, and now the near woods resounded through all their aisles with their demoniac cry. At length the old hound burst into view with muzzle to the ground, and snapping the air as if possessed, and ran directly to the rock; but spying the dead fox she suddenly ceased her hounding, as if struck dumb with amazement, and walked round and round him in silence; and one by one her pups arrived, and, like their mother, were sobered into silence by the mystery. Then the hunter came forward and stood in their midst, and the mystery was solved. They waited in silence while he skinned the fox, then followed the brush a while, and at length turned off into the woods again. That evening a Weston[5] Squire came to the Concord hunter's cottage to inquire for his hounds, and told how for a week they had been hunting on their own account from Weston woods. The Concord hunter told him what he knew and offered him the skin; but the other declined it and departed. He did not find his hounds that night, but the next day learned that they had crossed the river and put up at a farm-house for the night, whence, having been well fed, they took their departure early in the morning.

5. A town near Concord.

The hunter who told me this could remember one Sam Nutting, who used to hunt bears on Fair Haven Ledges, and exchange their skins for rum in Concord village; who told him, even, that he had seen a moose there. Nutting had a famous fox-hound named Burgoyne,—he pronounced it Bugine,—which my informant used to borrow. In the "Wast Book"[6] of an old trader of this town, who was also a captain, town-clerk, and representative, I find the following entry. Jan. 18th, 1742–3, "John Melven Cr. by 1 Grey Fox 0—2—3;" they are not now found here; and in his ledger, Feb. 7th, 1743, Hezekiah Stratton has credit "by ½ a Catt[7] skin 0—1—4½;" of course, a wild-cat, for Stratton was a sergeant in the old French war, and would not have got credit for hunting less noble game. Credit is given for deer skins also, and they were daily sold. One man still preserves the horns of the last deer that was killed in this vicinity, and another has told me the particulars of the hunt in which his uncle was engaged. The hunters were formerly a numerous and merry crew here. I remember well one gaunt Nimrod[8] who would catch up a leaf by the roadside and play a strain on it wilder and more melodious, if my memory serves me, than any hunting horn.

At midnight, when there was a moon, I sometimes met with hounds in my path prowling about the woods, which would skulk out of my way, as if afraid, and stand silent amid the bushes till I had passed.

Squirrels and wild mice disputed for my store of nuts. There were scores of pitch-pines around my house, from one to four inches in diameter, which had been gnawed by mice the previous winter,—a Norwegian winter for them, for the snow lay long and deep, and they were obliged to mix a large proportion of pine bark with their other diet. These trees were alive and apparently flourishing at mid-summer, and many of them had grown a foot, though completely girdled; but after another winter such were without exception dead. It is remarkable that a single mouse should thus be allowed a whole pine tree for its dinner, gnawing round instead of up and down it; but perhaps it is necessary in order to thin these trees, which are wont to grow up densely.

The hares (*Lepus Americanus*) were very familiar. One had her form under my house all winter, separated from me only by the flooring, and she startled me each morning by her hasty departure when I began to stir,—thump, thump, thump, striking her head against the floor timbers in her hurry. They used to come round my door at dusk to nibble the potato parings which I had thrown out,

6. An account book, or daybook.
7. can it be Calf? v. Mott ledger near beginning [*Thoreau's note*]. Thoreau also underlined the word "Catt" in his copy.
8. Described in Genesis 10.9 as "a mighty hunter."

and were so nearly the color of the ground that they could hardly be distinguished when still. Sometimes in the twilight I alternately lost and recovered sight of one sitting motionless under my window. When I opened my door in the evening, off they would go with a squeak and a bounce. Near at hand they only excited my pity. One evening one sat by my door two paces from me, at first trembling with fear, yet unwilling to move; a poor wee thing, lean and bony, with ragged ears and sharp nose, scant tail and slender paws. It looked as if Nature no longer contained the breed of nobler bloods, but stood on her last toes. Its large eyes appeared young and unhealthy, almost dropsical. I took a step, and lo, away it scud with an elastic spring over the snow crust, straightening its body and its limbs into graceful length, and soon put the forest between me and itself,—the wild free venison, asserting its vigor and the dignity of Nature. Not without reason was its slenderness. Such then was its nature. (*Lepus, levipes*, light-foot, some think.)

What is a country without rabbits and partridges? They are among the most simple and indigenous animal products; ancient and venerable families known to antiquity as to modern times; of the very hue and substance of Nature, nearest allied to leaves and to the ground,—and to one another; it is either winged or it is legged. It is hardly as if you had seen a wild creature when a rabbit or a partridge bursts away, only a natural one, as much to be expected as rustling leaves. The partridge and the rabbit are still sure to thrive, like true natives of the soil, whatever revolutions occur. If the forest is cut off, the sprouts and bushes which spring up afford them concealment, and they become more numerous than ever. That must be a poor country indeed that does not support a hare. Our woods teem with them both, and around every swamp may be seen the partridge or rabbit walk, beset with twiggy fences and horse-hair snares, which some cowboy tends.

The Pond in Winter

After a still winter night I awoke with the impression that some question had been put to me, which I had been endeavoring in vain to answer in my sleep, as what—how—when—where? But there was dawning Nature, in whom all creatures live, looking in at my broad windows with serene and satisfied face, and no question on *her* lips. I awoke to an answered question, to Nature and daylight. The snow lying deep on the earth dotted with young pines, and the very slope of the hill on which my house is placed, seemed to say, Forward! Nature puts no question and answers none which we mortals ask. She has long ago taken her resolution. "O Prince, our eyes contemplate with admiration and transmit to the soul the wonderful and varied spectacle of this universe. The night veils without doubt a part of this glorious creation; but day comes to reveal to us this great work, which extends from earth even into the plains of the ether."[1]

Then to my morning work. First I take an axe and pail and go in search of water, if that be not a dream. After a cold and snowy night it needed a divining rod to find it. Every winter the liquid and trembling surface of the pond, which was so sensitive to every breath, and reflected every light and shadow, becomes solid to the depth of a foot or a foot and a half, so that it will support the heaviest teams, and perchance the snow covers it to an equal depth, and it is not to be distinguished from any level field. Like the marmots in the surrounding hills, it closes its eye-lids and becomes dormant for three months or more. Standing on the snow-covered plain, as if in a pasture amid the hills, I cut my way first through a foot of snow, and then a foot of ice, and open a window under my feet, where, kneeling to drink, I look down into the quiet parlor of the fishes, pervaded by a softened light as through a window of ground glass, with its bright sanded floor the same as in summer; there a perennial waveless serenity reigns as in the amber twilight sky, corresponding to the cool and even temperament of the inhabitants. Heaven is under our feet as well as over our heads.

Early in the morning, while all things are crisp with frost, men come with fishing reels and slender lunch, and let down their fine lines through the snowy field to take pickerel and perch; wild men, who instinctively follow other fashions and trust other authorities than their townsmen, and by their goings and comings stitch towns together in parts where else they would be ripped. They sit and eat their luncheon in stout fear-naughts[2] on the dry oak leaves on the shore, as wise in natural lore as the citizen is in artificial. They never consulted with books, and know and can tell much less than they have done. The things which they practise are said not yet to be known. Here is one fishing for pickerel with grown perch for bait. You look into his pail with wonder as into a summer pond, as if he kept summer locked up at home, or knew where she had retreated. How, pray, did he get these in midwinter? O, he got worms out of rotten logs since the ground froze, and so he caught them. His life itself passes deeper in Nature than the studies of the naturalist penetrate; himself a subject for the naturalist. The latter raises the moss and bark gently with his knife in search of insects;

1. From *Mahabharata. Harivansa, ou Historie de la Famille de Hari* (1834–1835), translated by S. A. Langlois.
2. A coat made of heavy woolen material.

the former lays open logs to their core with his axe, and moss and
bark fly far and wide. He gets his living by barking trees. Such a
man has some right to fish, and I love to see Nature carried out in
him. The perch swallows the grub-worm, the pickerel swallows the
perch, and the fisherman swallows the pickerel; and so all the
chinks in the scale of being are filled.

When I strolled around the pond in misty weather I was sometimes amused by the primitive mode which some ruder fisherman
had adopted. He would perhaps have placed alder branches over
the narrow holes in the ice, which were four or five rods apart and
an equal distance from the shore, and having fastened the end of
the line to a stick to prevent its being pulled through, have passed
the slack line over a twig of the alder, a foot or more above the ice,
and tied a dry oak leaf to it, which, being pulled down, would show
when he had a bite. These alders loomed through the mist at regular intervals as you walked half way round the pond.

Ah, the pickerel of Walden! when I see them lying on the ice, or
in the well which the fisherman cuts in the ice, making a little hole
to admit the water, I am always surprised by their rare beauty, as if
they were fabulous fishes, they are so foreign to the streets, even to
the woods, foreign as Arabia to our Concord life. They possess a
quite dazzling and transcendent beauty which separates them by a
wide interval from the cadaverous cod and haddock whose fame is
trumpeted[3] in our streets. They are not green like the pines, nor
gray like the stones, nor blue like the sky; but they have, to my eyes,
if possible, yet rarer colors, like flowers and precious stones, as if
they were the pearls, the animalized *nuclei* or crystals of the
Walden water. They, of course, are Walden all over and all through;
are themselves small Waldens in the animal kingdom, Waldenses.[4]
It is surprising that they are caught here,—that in this deep and capacious spring, far beneath the rattling teams and chaises and tinkling sleighs that travel the Walden road, this great gold and
emerald fish swims. I never chanced to see its kind in any market;
it would be the cynosure of all eyes there. Easily, with a few convul-
sive quirks, they give up their watery ghosts, like a mortal translated
before his time to the thin air of heaven.

As I was desirous to recover the long lost bottom of Walden
Pond, I surveyed it carefully, before the ice broke up, early in '46,
with compass and chain and sounding line. There have been many
stories told about the bottom, or rather no bottom, of this pond,
which certainly had no foundation for themselves. It is remarkable

3. In the nineteenth century, fish sellers blew horns as they went through the streets.
4. A sect of religious dissenters founded about 1170 by Peter Waldo in France.

how long men will believe in the bottomlessness of a pond without taking the trouble to sound it. I have visited two such Bottomless Ponds in one walk in this neighborhood. Many have believed that Walden reached quite through to the other side of the globe. Some who have lain flat on the ice for a long time, looking down through the illusive medium, perchance with watery eyes into the bargain, and driven to hasty conclusions by the fear of catching cold in their breasts, have seen vast holes "into which a load of hay might be driven," if there were any body to drive it, the undoubted source of the Styx and entrance to the Infernal Regions from these parts. Others have gone down from the village with a "fifty-six"[5] and a wagon load of inch rope, but yet have failed to find any bottom; for while the "fifty-six" was resting by the way, they were paying out the rope in the vain attempt to fathom their truly immeasurable capacity for marvellousness. But I can assure my readers that Walden has a reasonably tight bottom at a not unreasonable, though at an unusual, depth. I fathomed it easily with a cod-line and a stone weighing about a pound and a half, and could tell accurately when the stone left the bottom, by having to pull so much harder before the water got underneath to help me. The greatest depth was exactly one hundred and two feet; to which may be added the five feet which it has risen since, making one hundred and seven. This is a remarkable depth for so small an area; yet not an inch of it can be spared by the imagination. What if all ponds were shallow? Would it not react on the minds of men? I am thankful that this pond was made deep and pure for a symbol. While men believe in the infinite some ponds will be thought to be bottomless.

A factory owner, hearing what depth I had found, thought that it could not be true, for, judging from his acquaintance with dams, sand would not lie at so steep an angle. But the deepest ponds are not so deep in proportion to their area as most suppose, and, if drained, would not leave very remarkable valleys. They are not like cups between the hills; for this one, which is so unusually deep for its area, appears in a vertical section through its centre not deeper than a shallow plate. Most ponds, emptied, would leave a meadow no more hollow than we frequently see. William Gilpin, who is so admirable in all that relates to landscapes, and usually so correct, standing at the head of Loch Fyne, in Scotland, which he describes as "a bay of salt water, sixty or seventy fathoms deep, four miles in breadth," and about fifty miles long, surrounded by mountains, observes, "If we could have seen it immediately after the diluvian crash, or whatever convulsion of Nature occasioned it, before the waters gushed in, what a horrid chasm it must have appeared!

---

5. A fifty-six-pound iron weight.

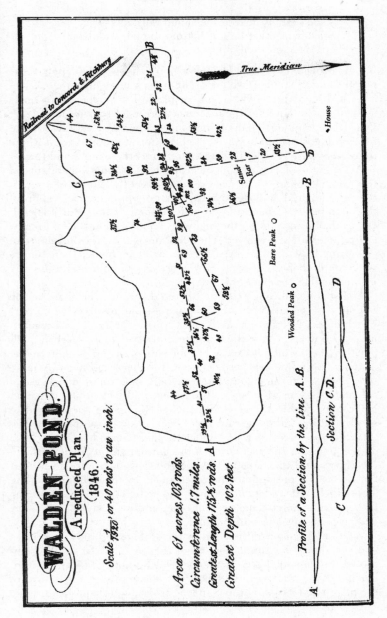

So high as heaved the tumid hills, so low
Down sunk a hollow bottom, broad, and deep,
Capacious bed of waters—."[6]

But if, using the shortest diameter of Loch Fyne, we apply these proportions to Walden, which, as we have seen, appears already in a vertical section only like a shallow plate, it will appear four times as shallow. So much for the *increased* horrors of the chasm of Loch Fyne when emptied. No doubt many a smiling valley with its stretching cornfields occupies exactly such a "horrid chasm," from which the waters have receded, though it requires the insight and the far sight of the geologist to convince the unsuspecting inhabitants of this fact. Often an inquisitive eye may detect the shores of a primitive lake in the low horizon hills, and no subsequent elevation of the plain has been necessary to conceal their history. But it is easiest, as they who work on the highways know, to find the hollows by the puddles after a shower. The amount of it is, the imagination, give it the least license, dives deeper and soars higher than Nature goes. So, probably, the depth of the ocean will be found to be very inconsiderable compared with its breadth.

As I sounded through the ice I could determine the shape of the bottom with greater accuracy than is possible in surveying harbors which do not freeze over, and I was surprised at its general regularity. In the deepest part there are several acres more level than almost any field which is exposed to the sun wind and plough. In one instance, on a line arbitrarily chosen, the depth did not vary more than one foot in thirty rods; and generally, near the middle, I could calculate the variation for each one hundred feet in any direction beforehand within three or four inches. Some are accustomed to speak of deep and dangerous holes even in quiet sandy ponds like this, but the effect of water under these circumstances is to level all inequalities. The regularity of the bottom and its conformity to the shores and the range of the neighboring hills were so perfect that a distant promontory betrayed itself in the soundings quite across the pond; and its direction could be determined by observing the opposite shore. Cape becomes bar, and plain shoal, and valley and gorge deep water and channel.

When I had mapped the pond by the scale of ten rods to an inch, and put down the soundings, more than a hundred in all, I observed this remarkable coincidence. Having noticed that the number indicating the greatest depth was apparently in the centre of the map, I laid a rule on the map lengthwise, and then breadthwise,

6. From *Observation on Several Parts of Great Britain* (1808); Gilpin quotes from Milton, *Paradise Lost*, 7.288–90.

and found, to my surprise, that the line of greatest length inter-
sected the line of greatest breadth *exactly* at the point of greatest
depth, notwithstanding that the middle is so nearly level, the outline of the pond far from regular, and the extreme length and
breadth were got by measuring into the coves; and I said to myself,
Who knows but this hint would conduct to the deepest part of the
ocean as well as of a pond or puddle? Is not this the rule also for
the height of mountains, regarded as the opposite of valleys? We
know that a hill is not highest at its narrowest part.

Of five coves, three, or all which had been sounded, were observed to have a bar quite across their mouths and deeper water
within, so that the bay tended to be an expansion of water within
the land not only horizontally but vertically, and to form a basin or
independent pond, the direction of the two capes showing the
course of the bar. Every harbor on the sea-coast, also, has its bar at
its entrance. In proportion as the mouth of the cove was wider
compared with its length, the water over the bar was deeper compared with that in the basin. Given, then, the length and breadth of
the cove, and the character of the surrounding shore, and you have
almost elements enough to make out a formula for all cases.

In order to see how nearly I could guess, with this experience, at
the deepest point in a pond, by observing the outlines of its surface
and the character of its shores alone, I made a plan of White Pond,
which contains about forty-one acres, and, like this, has no island
in it, nor any visible inlet or outlet; and as the line of greatest
breadth fell very near the line of least breadth, where two opposite
capes approached each other and two opposite bays receded, I ventured to mark a point a short distance from the latter line, but still
on the line of greatest length, as the deepest. The deepest part was
found to be within one hundred feet of this, still farther in the direction to which I had inclined, and was only one foot deeper,
namely, sixty feet. Of course, a stream running through, or an island in the pond, would make the problem much more complicated.

If we knew all the laws of Nature, we should need only one fact,
or the description of one actual phenomenon, to infer all the particular results at that point. Now we know only a few laws, and our
result is vitiated, not, of course, by any confusion or irregularity in
Nature, but by our ignorance of essential elements in the calculation. Our notions of law and harmony are commonly confined to
those instances which we detect; but the harmony which results
from a far greater number of seemingly conflicting, but really con-
curring, laws, which we have not detected, is still more wonderful.
The particular laws are as our points of view, as, to the traveller, a

mountain outline varies with every step, and it has an infinite number of profiles, though absolutely but one form. Even when cleft or
bored through it is not comprehended in its entireness.

What I have observed of the pond is no less true in ethics. It is
the law of average. Such a rule of the two diameters not only guides
us toward the sun in the system and the heart in man, but draw
lines through the length and breadth of the aggregate of a man's
particular daily behaviors and waves of life into his coves and inlets,
and where they intersect will be the height or depth of his character. Perhaps we need only to know how his shores trend and his adjacent country or circumstances, to infer his depth and concealed
bottom. If he is surrounded by mountainous circumstances, an
Achillean shore,[7] whose peaks overshadow and are reflected in his
bosom, they suggest a corresponding depth in him. But a low and
smooth shore proves him shallow on that side. In our bodies, a bold
projecting brow falls off to and indicates a corresponding depth of
thought. Also there is a bar across the entrance of our every cove,
or particular inclination; each is our harbor for a season, in which
we are detained and partially land-locked. These inclinations are
not whimsical usually, but their form, size, and direction are determined by the promontories of the shore, the ancient axes of elevation. When this bar is gradually increased by storms, tides, or
currents, or there is a subsidence of the waters, so that it reaches to
the surface, that which was at first but an inclination in the shore
in which a thought was harbored becomes an individual lake, cut
off from the ocean, wherein the thought secures its own conditions, changes, perhaps, from salt to fresh, becomes a sweet sea,
dead sea, or a marsh. At the advent of each individual into this life,
may we not suppose that such a bar has risen to the surface somewhere? It is true, we are such poor navigators that our thoughts, for
the most part, stand off and on upon a harborless coast, are conversant only with the bights of the bays of poesy, or steer for the public ports of entry, and go into the dry docks of science, where they
merely refit for this world, and no natural currents concur to indi-
vidualize them.

As for the inlet or outlet of Walden, I have not discovered any
but rain and snow and evaporation, though perhaps, with a thermometer and a line, such places may be found, for where the water
flows into the pond it will probably be coldest in summer and
warmest in winter. When the ice-men were at work here in '46–7,
the cakes sent to the shore were one day rejected by those who
were stacking them up there, not being thick enough to lie side by

---

7. The Greek hero Achilles was reportedly born in Thessaly, a mountainous region in
    northeastern Greece.

side with the rest; and the cutters thus discovered that the ice over a small space was two or three inches thinner than elsewhere, which made them think that there was an inlet there. They also showed me in another place what they thought was a "leach hole," through which the pond leaked out under a hill into a neighboring meadow, pushing me out on a cake of ice to see it. It was a small cavity under ten feet of water; but I think that I can warrant the pond not to need soldering till they find a worse leak than that. One has suggested, that if such a "leach hole" should be found, its connection with the meadow, if any existed, might be proved by conveying some colored powder or sawdust to the mouth of the hole, and then putting a strainer over the spring in the meadow, which would catch some of the particles carried through by the current.

While I was surveying, the ice, which was sixteen inches thick, undulated under a slight wind like water. It is well known that a level cannot be used on ice. At one rod from the shore its greatest fluctuation, when observed by means of a level on land directed toward a graduated staff on the ice, was three quarters of an inch, though the ice appeared firmly attached to the shore. It was probably greater in the middle. Who knows but if our instruments were delicate enough we might detect an undulation in the crust of the earth? When two legs of my level were on the shore and the third on the ice, and the sights were directed over the latter, a rise or fall of the ice of an almost infinitesimal amount made a difference of several feet on a tree across the pond. When I began to cut holes for sounding, there were three or four inches of water on the ice under a deep snow which had sunk it thus far; but the water began immediately to run into these holes, and continued to run for two days in deep streams, which wore away the ice on every side, and contributed essentially, if not mainly, to dry the surface of the pond; for, as the water ran in, it raised and floated the ice. This was somewhat like cutting a hole in the bottom of a ship to let the water out. When such holes freeze, and a rain succeeds, and finally a new freezing forms a fresh smooth ice over all, it is beautifully mottled internally by dark figures, shaped somewhat like a spider's web, what you may call ice rosettes, produced by the channels worn by the water flowing from all sides to a centre. Sometimes, also, when the ice was covered with shallow puddles, I saw a double shadow of myself, one standing on the head of the other, one on the ice, the other on the trees or hill-side.

While yet it is cold January, and snow and ice are thick and solid, the prudent landlord comes from the village to get ice to cool his summer drink; impressively, even pathetically wise, to foresee the heat and thirst of July now in January,—wearing a thick coat and mittens! when so many things are not provided for. It may be that he lays up no treasures in this world which will cool his summer drink in the next.[8] He cuts and saws the solid pond, unroofs the house of fishes, and carts off their very element and air, held fast by chains and stakes like corded wood, through the favoring winter air, to wintry cellars, to underlie the summer there. It looks like solidified azure, as, far off, it is drawn through the streets. These ice-cutters are a merry race, full of jest and sport, and when I went among them they were wont to invite me to saw pit-fashion with them, I standing underneath.

In the winter of '46–7 there came a hundred men of Hyperborean[9] extraction swoop down on to our pond one morning, with many car-loads of ungainly-looking farming tools, sleds, ploughs, drill-barrows, turf-knives, spades, saws, rakes, and each man was armed with a double-pointed pike-staff, such as is not described in the New-England Farmer or the Cultivator.[1] I did not know whether they had come to sow a crop of winter rye, or some other kind of grain recently introduced from Iceland. As I saw no manure, I judged that they meant to skim the land, as I had done, thinking the soil was deep and had lain fallow long enough. They said that a gentleman farmer, who was behind the scenes, wanted to double his money, which, as I understood, amounted to half a million already; but in order to cover each one of his dollars with another, he took off the only coat, ay, the skin itself, of Walden Pond in the midst of a hard winter. They went to work at once, ploughing, harrowing, rolling, furrowing, in admirable order, as if they were bent on making this a model farm; but when I was looking sharp to see what kind of seed they dropped into the furrow, a gang of fellows by my side suddenly began to hook up the virgin mould itself, with a peculiar jerk, clean down to the sand, or rather the water,—for it was a very springy soil,—indeed all the *terra firma*[2] there was,—and haul it away on sleds, and then I guessed that they must be cutting peat in a bog. So they came and went every day, with a peculiar shriek from the locomotive, from and to some point of the polar regions, as it seemed to me, like a flock of arctic snow-birds. But sometimes Squaw Walden had her revenge, and a hired man, walking behind his team, slipped through a crack in the ground down toward Tartarus,[3] and he who was so brave before suddenly became but the ninth part of a man, almost gave up

---

8. Matthew 6.19–21.
9. According to Greek mythology, a tribe that lived far north of Greece.
1. Nineteenth-century farm journals.
2. Solid ground.
3. In Greek mythology, a dark region far beneath the surface of the earth.

his animal heat, and was glad to take refuge in my house, and acknowledge that there was some virtue in a stove; or sometimes the frozen soil took a piece of steel out of a plough-share, or a plough got set in the furrow and had to be cut out.

To speak literally, a hundred Irishmen, with Yankee overseers, came from Cambridge every day to get out the ice. They divided it into cakes by methods too well known to require description, and these, being sledded to the shore, were rapidly hauled off on to an ice platform, and raised by grappling irons and block and tackle, worked by horses, on to a stack, as surely as so many barrels of flour, and there placed evenly side by side, and row upon row, as if they formed the solid base of an obelisk designed to pierce the clouds. They told me that in a good day they could get out a thousand tons, which was the yield of about one acre. Deep ruts and "cradle holes" were worn in the ice, as on *terra firma*, by the passage of the sleds over the same track, and the horses invariably ate their oats out of cakes of ice hollowed out like buckets. They stacked up the cakes thus in the open air in a pile thirty-five feet high on one side and six or seven rods square, putting hay between the outside layers to exclude the air; for when the wind, though never so cold, finds a passage through, it will wear large cavities, leaving slight supports or studs only here and there, and finally topple it down. At first it looked like a vast blue fort or Valhalla; but when they began to tuck the coarse meadow hay into the crevices, and this became covered with rime and icicles, it looked like a venerable moss-grown and hoary ruin, built of azure-tinted marble, the abode of Winter, that old man we see in the almanac,—his shanty, as if he had a design to estivate with us. They calculated that not twenty-five per cent. of this would reach its destination, and that two or three per cent. would be wasted in the cars. However, a still greater part of this heap had a different destiny from what was intended; for, either because the ice was found not to keep so well as was expected, containing more air than usual, or for some other reason, it never got to market. This heap, made in the winter of '46–7 and estimated to contain ten thousand tons, was finally covered with hay and boards; and though it was unroofed the following July, and a part of it carried off, the rest remaining exposed to the sun, it stood over that summer and the next winter, and was not quite melted till September 1848. Thus the pond recovered the greater part.

Like the water, the Walden ice, seen near at hand, has a green tint, but at a distance is beautifully blue, and you can easily tell it from the white ice of the river, or the merely greenish ice of some ponds, a quarter of a mile off. Sometimes one of those great cakes slips from the ice-man's sled into the village street, and lies there for a week like a great emerald, an object of interest to all passers. I have noticed that a portion of Walden which in the state of water was green will often, when frozen, appear from the same point of view blue. So the hollows about this pond will, sometimes, in the winter, be filled with a greenish water somewhat like its own, but the next day will have frozen blue. Perhaps the blue color of water and ice is due to the light and air they contain, and the most transparent is the bluest. Ice is an interesting subject for contemplation. They told me that they had some in the ice-houses at Fresh Pond five years old which was as good as ever. Why is it that a bucket of water soon becomes putrid, but frozen remains sweet forever? It is commonly said that this is the difference between the affections and the intellect.

Thus for sixteen days I saw from my window a hundred men at work like busy husbandmen, with teams and horses and apparently all the implements of farming, such a picture as we see on the first page of the almanac; and as often as I looked out I was reminded of the fable of the lark and the reapers, or the parable of the sower, and the like;[4] and now they are all gone, and in thirty days more, probably, I shall look from the same window on the pure sea-green Walden water there, reflecting the clouds and the trees, and sending up its evaporations in solitude, and no traces will appear that a man has ever stood there. Perhaps I shall hear a solitary loon laugh as he dives and plumes himself, or shall see a lonely fisher in his boat, like a floating leaf, beholding his form reflected in the waves, where lately a hundred men securely labored.

Thus it appears that the sweltering inhabitants of Charleston and New Orleans, of Madras and Bombay and Calcutta,[5] drink at my well. In the morning I bathe my intellect in the stupendous and cosmogonal philosophy of the Bhagvat Geeta, since whose composition years of the gods have elapsed, and in comparison with which our modern world and its literature seem puny and trivial; and I doubt if that philosophy is not to be referred to a previous state of existence, so remote is its sublimity from our conceptions. I lay down the book and go to my well for water, and lo! there I meet the servant of the Bramin, priest of Brahma and Vishnu and Indra,[6] who still sits in his temple on the Ganges reading the Vedas, or dwells at the root of a tree with his crust and water jug. I meet his servant come to draw water for his master, and our buckets as it were grate together in the same well. The pure Walden water is

---

4. The Lark and Her Young, in Jean La Fontaine's *Fables* (4.22); and the Parable of the Sower, Matthew 13.3–9, 18–23.
5. Madras, Bombay, and Calcutta, all major cities in India, were three of the many places that bought ice from New England merchants.
6. The three major Hindu deities.

mingled with the sacred water of the Ganges. With favoring winds it is wafted past the site of the fabulous islands of Atlantis and the Hesperides,[7] makes the periplus of Hanno, and, floating by Ternate and Tidore[8] and the mouth of the Persian Gulf, melts in the tropic gales of the Indian seas, and is landed in ports of which Alexander[9] only heard the names.

Spring

The opening of large tracts by the ice-cutters commonly causes a pond to break up earlier; for the water, agitated by the wind, even in cold weather, wears away the surrounding ice. But such was not the effect on Walden that year, for she had soon got a thick new garment to take the place of the old. This pond never breaks up so soon as the others in this neighborhood, on account both of its greater depth and its having no stream passing through it to melt or wear away the ice. I never knew it to open in the course of a winter, not excepting that of '52–3, which gave the ponds so severe a trial. It commonly opens about the first of April, a week or ten days later than Flint's Pond and Fair-Haven, beginning to melt on the north side and in the shallower parts where it began to freeze. It indicates better than any water hereabouts the absolute progress of the season, being least affected by transient changes of temperature. A severe cold of a few days' duration in March may very much retard the opening of the former ponds, while the temperature of Walden increases almost uninterruptedly. A thermometer thrust into the middle of Walden on the 6th of March, 1847, stood at 32°, or freezing point; near the shore at 33°; in the middle of Flint's Pond, the same day, at 32½°; at a dozen rods from the shore, in shallow water, under ice a foot thick, at 36°. This difference of three and a half degrees between the temperature of the deep water and the shallow in the latter pond, and the fact that a great proportion of it is comparatively shallow, show why it should break up so much sooner than Walden. The ice in the shallowest part was at this time several inches thinner than in the middle. In mid-winter the middle had been the warmest and the ice thinnest there. So, also, every one who has waded about the shores of a pond in summer must have perceived how much warmer the water is close to the shore,

---

7. Paradisiacal islands of the west in Greek mythology.
8. Follows the route of the Carthaginian explorer Hanno, who traveled to west Africa: Ternate and Tidore are islands in the Molucca Sea, south of the Philippines.
9. Alexander the Great (356–323 B.C.E.) extended his empire, and Greek culture, into northwestern India. There he heard fabulous stories of the Ganges in eastern India but was unable to reach it.

where only three or four inches deep, than a little distance out, and on the surface where it is deep, than near the bottom. In spring the sun not only exerts an influence through the increased temperature of the air and earth, but its heat passes through ice a foot or more thick, and is reflected from the bottom in shallow water, and so also warms the water and melts the under side of the ice, at the same time that it is melting it more directly above, making it uneven, and causing the air bubbles which it contains to extend themselves upward and downward until it is completely honey-combed, and at last disappears suddenly in a single spring rain. Ice has its grain as well as wood, and when a cake begins to rot or "comb," that is, assume the appearance of honey-comb, whatever may be its position, the air cells are at right angles with what was the water surface. Where there is a rock or a log rising near to the surface the ice over it is much thinner, and is frequently quite dissolved by this reflected heat; and I have been told that in the experiment at Cambridge to freeze water in a shallow wooden pond, though the cold air circulated underneath, and so had access to both sides, the reflection of the sun from the bottom more than counterbalanced this advantage. When a warm rain in the middle of the winter melts off the snow-ice from Walden, and leaves a hard dark or transparent ice on the middle, there will be a strip of rotten though thicker white ice, a rod or more wide, about the shores, created by this reflected heat. Also, as I have said, the bubbles themselves within the ice operate as burning glasses to melt the ice beneath.

The phenomena of the year take place every day in a pond on a small scale. Every morning, generally speaking, the shallow water is being warmed more rapidly than the deep, though it may not be made so warm after all, and every evening it is being cooled more rapidly until the morning. The day is an epitome of the year. The night is the winter, the morning and evening are the spring and fall, and the noon is the summer. The cracking and booming of the ice indicate a change of temperature. One pleasant morning after a cold night, February 24th, 1850, having gone to Flint's Pond to spend the day, I noticed with surprise, that when I struck the ice with the head of my axe, it resounded like a gong for many rods around, or as if I had struck on a tight drum-head. The pond began to boom about an hour after sunrise, when it felt the influence of the sun's rays slanted upon it from over the hills; it stretched itself and yawned like a waking man with a gradually increasing tumult, which was kept up three or four hours. It took a short siesta at noon, and boomed once more toward night, as the sun was withdrawing his influence. In the right stage of the weather a pond fires its evening gun with great regularity. But in the middle of the day, being full of cracks, and the air also being less elastic, it had completely lost its resonance, and probably fishes and muskrats could not then have been stunned by a blow on it. The fishermen say that the "thundering of the pond" scares the fishes and prevents their biting. The pond does not thunder every evening, and I cannot tell surely when to expect its thundering; but though I may perceive no difference in the weather, it does. Who would have suspected so large and cold and thick-skinned a thing to be so sensitive? Yet it has its law to which it thunders obedience when it should as surely as the buds expand in the spring. The earth is all alive and covered with papillæ. The largest pond is as sensitive to atmospheric changes as the globule of mercury in its tube.

One attraction in coming to the woods to live was that I should have leisure and opportunity to see the spring come in. The ice in the pond at length begins to be honey-combed, and I can set my heel in it as I walk. Fogs and rains and warmer suns are gradually melting the snow; the days have grown sensibly longer; and I see how I shall get through the winter without adding to my woodpile, for large fires are no longer necessary. I am on the alert for the first signs of spring, to hear the chance note of some arriving bird, or the striped squirrel's chirp, for his stores must be now nearly exhausted, or see the woodchuck venture out of his winter quarters. On the 13th of March, after I had heard the bluebird, song-sparrow, and red-wing, the ice was still nearly a foot thick. As the weather grew warmer, it was not sensibly worn away by the water, nor broken up and floated off as in rivers, but, though it was completely melted for half a rod in width about the shore, the middle was merely honey-combed and saturated with water, so that you could put your foot through it when six inches thick; but by the next day evening, perhaps, after a warm rain followed by fog, it would have wholly disappeared, all gone off with the fog, spirited away. One year I went across the middle only five days before it disappeared entirely. In 1845 Walden was first completely open on the 1st of April; in '46, the 25th of March; in '47, the 8th of April; in '51, the 28th of March; in '52, the 18th of April; in '53, the 23d of March; in '54, about the 7th of April.

Every incident connected with the breaking up of the rivers and ponds and the settling of the weather is particularly interesting to us who live in a climate of so great extremes. When the warmer days come, they who dwell near the river hear the ice crack at night with a startling whoop as loud as artillery, as if its icy fetters were rent from end to end, and within a few days see it rapidly going out. So the alligator comes out of the mud with quakings of the earth. One old man, who has been a close observer of Nature, and seems as thoroughly wise in regard to all her operations as if she had been

put upon the stocks when he was a boy, and he had helped to lay
her keel,—who has come to his growth, and can hardly acquire
more of natural lore if he should live to the age of Methuselah,[1]—
told me, and I was surprised to hear him express wonder at any of
Nature's operations, for I thought that there were no secrets between them, that one spring day he took his gun and boat, and
thought that he would have a little sport with the ducks. There was
ice still on the meadows, but it was all gone out of the river, and he
dropped down without obstruction from Sudbury, where he lived,
to Fair-Haven Pond, which he found, unexpectedly, covered for the
most part with a firm field of ice. It was a warm day, and he was
surprised to see so great a body of ice remaining. Not seeing any
ducks, he hid his boat on the north or back side of an island in the
pond, and then concealed himself in the bushes on the south side,
to await them. The ice was melted for three or four rods from the
shore, and there was a smooth and warm sheet of water, with a
muddy bottom, such as the ducks love, within, and he thought it
likely that some would be along pretty soon. After he had lain still
there about an hour he heard a low and seemingly very distant
sound, but singularly grand and impressive, unlike any thing he had
ever heard, gradually swelling and increasing as if it would have a
universal and memorable ending, a sullen rush and roar, which
seemed to him all at once like the sound of a vast body of fowl coming in to settle there, and, seizing his gun, he started up in haste
and excited; but he found, to his surprise, that the whole body of
the ice had started while he lay there, and drifted in to the shore,
and the sound he had heard was made by its edge grating on the
shore,—at first gently nibbled and crumbled off, but at length heaving up and scattering its wrecks along the island to a considerable
height before it came to a stand still.

At length the sun's rays have attained the right angle, and warm
winds blow up mist and rain and melt the snow banks, and the sun
dispersing the mist smiles on a checkered landscape of russet and
white smoking with incense, through which the traveller picks his
way from islet to islet, cheered by the music of a thousand tinkling
rills and rivulets whose veins are filled with the blood of winter
which they are bearing off.

Few phenomena gave me more delight than to observe the forms
which thawing sand and clay assume in flowing down the sides of a
deep cut on the railroad through which I passed on my way to the
village, a phenomenon not very common on so large a scale, though
the number of freshly exposed banks of the right material must
have been greatly multiplied since railroads were invented. The ma-

---

1. According to Genesis 5.27, Methuselah lived to be 969 years old.

terial was sand of every degree of fineness and of various rich colors, commonly mixed with a little clay. When the frost comes out in the spring, and even in a thawing day in the winter, the sand begins to flow down the slopes like lava, sometimes bursting out through the snow and overflowing it where no sand was to be seen before. Innumerable little streams overlap and interlace one with another, exhibiting a sort of hybrid product, which obeys half way the law of currents, and half way that of vegetation. As it flows it takes the forms of sappy leaves or vines, making heaps of pulpy sprays a foot or more in depth, and resembling, as you look down on them, the laciniated lobed and imbricated thalluses of some lichens; or you are reminded of coral, of leopards' paws or birds' feet, of brains or lungs or bowels, and excrements of all kinds. It is a truly *grotesque* vegetation, whose forms and color we see imitated in bronze, a sort of architectural foliage more ancient and typical than acanthus, chiccory, ivy, vine, or any vegetable leaves; destined perhaps, under some circumstances, to become a puzzle to future geologists. The whole cut impressed me as if it were a cave with its stalactites laid open to the light. The various shades of the sand are singularly rich and agreeable, embracing the different iron colors, brown, gray, yellowish, and reddish. When the flowing mass reaches the drain at the foot of the bank it spreads out flatter into *strands*, the separate streams losing their semi-cylindrical form and gradually becoming more flat and broad, running together as they are more moist, till they form an almost flat *sand*, still variously and beautifully shaded, but in which you can trace the original forms of vegetation; till at length, in the water itself, they are converted into *banks*, like those formed off the mouths of rivers, and the forms of vegetation are lost in the ripple marks on the bottom.

The whole bank, which is from twenty to forty feet high, is sometimes overlaid with a mass of this kind of foliage, or sandy rupture, for a quarter of a mile on one or both sides, the produce of one spring day. What makes this sand foliage remarkable is its springing into existence thus suddenly. When I see on the one side the inert bank,—for the sun acts on one side first,—and on the other this luxuriant foliage, the creation of an hour, I am affected as if in a peculiar sense I stood in the laboratory of the Artist who made the world and me,—had come to where he was still at work, sporting on this bank, and with excess of energy strewing his fresh designs about. I feel as if I were nearer to the vitals of the globe, for this sandy overflow is something such a foliaceous mass as the vitals of the animal body. You find thus in the very sands an anticipation of the vegetable leaf. No wonder that the earth expresses itself outwardly in leaves, it so labors with the idea inwardly. The atoms have already learned this law, and are pregnant by it. The overhanging leaf sees here its prototype. *Internally*, whether in the globe or animal body, it is a moist thick *lobe*, a word especially applicable to the liver and lungs and the *leaves* of fat, (λείβω, *labor, lapsus*, to flow or slip downward, a lapsing; λοβος, *globus*, lobe, globe; also lap, flap, and many other words,) *externally* a dry thin *leaf*, even as the *f* and *v* are a pressed and dried *b*. The radicals of lobe are *lb*, the soft mass of the *b* (single lobed, or B, double lobed,) with a liquid *l* behind it pressing it forward. In globe, *glb*, the guttural *g* adds to the meaning the capacity of the throat. The feathers and wings of birds are still drier and thinner leaves. Thus, also, you pass from the lumpish grub in the earth to the airy and fluttering butterfly. The very globe continually transcends and translates itself, and becomes winged in its orbit. Even ice begins with delicate crystal leaves, as if it had flowed into moulds which the fronds of water plants have impressed on the watery mirror. The whole tree itself is but one leaf, and rivers are still vaster leaves whose pulp is intervening earth, and towns and cities are the ova of insects in their axils.

When the sun withdraws the sand ceases to flow, but in the morning the streams will start once more and branch and branch again into a myriad of others. You here see perchance how blood vessels are formed. If you look closely you observe that first there pushes forward from the thawing mass a stream of softened sand with a drop-like point, like the ball of the finger, feeling its way slowly and blindly downward, until at last with more heat and moisture, as the sun gets higher, the most fluid portion, in its effort to obey the law to which the most inert also yields, separates from the latter and forms for itself a meandering channel or artery within that, in which is seen a little silvery stream glancing like lightning from one stage of pulpy leaves or branches to another, and ever and anon swallowed up in the sand. It is wonderful how rapidly yet perfectly the sand organizes itself as it flows, using the best material its mass affords to form the sharp edges of its channel. Such are the sources of rivers. In the silicious matter which the water deposits is perhaps the bony system, and in the still finer soil and organic matter the fleshy fibre or cellular tissue. What is man but a mass of thawing clay? The ball of the human finger is but a drop congealed. The fingers and toes flow to their extent from the thawing mass of the body. Who knows what the human body would expand and flow out to under a more genial heaven? Is not the hand a spreading *palm* leaf with its lobes and veins? The ear may be regarded, fancifully, as a lichen, *umbilicaria*, on the side of the head, with its lobe or drop. The lip—*labium*, from *labor* (?)—laps or lapses from the sides of the cavernous mouth. The nose is a manifest congealed drop or stalactite. The chin is a still larger drop, the confluent dripping of the face. The cheeks are a slide from the brows into the valley of the face, opposed and diffused by the cheek bones. Each rounded lobe of the vegetable leaf, too, is a thick and now loitering drop, larger or smaller; the lobes are the fingers of the leaf; and as many lobes as it has, in so many directions it tends to flow, and more heat or other genial influences would have caused it to flow yet farther.

Thus it seemed that this one hillside illustrated the principle of all the operations of Nature. The Maker of this earth but patented a leaf. What Champollion[2] will decipher this hieroglyphic for us, that we may turn over a new leaf at last? This phenomenon is more exhilarating to me than the luxuriance and fertility of vineyards. True, it is somewhat excrementitious in its character, and there is no end to the heaps of liver lights and bowels, as if the globe were turned wrong side outward; but this suggests at least that Nature has some bowels, and there again is mother of humanity. This is the frost coming out of the ground; this is Spring. It precedes the green and flowery spring, as mythology precedes regular poetry. I know of nothing more purgative of winter fumes and indigestions. It convinces me that Earth is still in her swaddling clothes, and stretches forth baby fingers on every side. Fresh curls spring from the baldest brow. There is nothing inorganic. These foliaceous heaps lie along the bank like the slag of a furnace, showing that Nature is "in full blast" within. The earth is not a mere fragment of dead history, stratum upon stratum like the leaves of a book, to be studied by geologists and antiquaries chiefly, but living poetry like the leaves of a tree, which precede flowers and fruit,—not a fossil earth, but a living earth; compared with whose great central life all animal and vegetable life is merely parasitic. Its throes will heave our exuviæ[3] from their graves. You may melt your metals and cast them into the most beautiful moulds you can; they will never excite me like the forms which this molten earth flows out into. And not only it, but the institutions upon it, are plastic like clay in the hands of the potter.

Ere long, not only on these banks, but on every hill and plain and in every hollow, the frost comes out of the ground like a dormant quadruped from its burrow, and seeks the sea with music, or migrates to other climes in clouds. Thaw with his gentle persuasion is more powerful than Thor[4] with his hammer. The one melts, the other but breaks in pieces.

When the ground was partially bare of snow, and a few warm

---

2. Jean François Champollion (1790–1832), French Egyptologist, deciphered the Rosetta stone that provided a key to the ancient inscriptions of Egypt.
3. See n. 9, p. 48.
4. In Norse mythology, the god of war and thunder.

days had dried its surface somewhat, it was pleasant to compare the
first tender signs of the infant year just peeping forth with the
stately beauty of the withered vegetation which had withstood
the winter,—life-everlasting, golden-rods, pinweeds, and graceful
wild grasses, more obvious and interesting frequently than in summer even, as if their beauty was not ripe till then; even cotton-
grass, cat-tails, mulleins, johns-wort, hard-hack, meadow-sweet,
and other strong stemmed plants, those unexhausted granaries
which entertain the earliest birds,—decent weeds, at least, which
widowed Nature wears. I am particularly attracted by the arching
and sheaf-like top of the wool-grass; it brings back the summer to
our winter memories, and is among the forms which art loves to
copy, and which, in the vegetable kingdom, have the same relation
to types already in the mind of man that astronomy has. It is an antique style older than Greek or Egyptian. Many of the phenomena
of Winter are suggestive of an inexpressible tenderness and fragile
delicacy. We are accustomed to hear this king described as a rude
and boisterous tyrant; but with the gentleness of a lover he adorns
the tresses of Summer.

At the approach of spring the red-squirrels got under my house,
two at a time, directly under my feet as I sat reading or writing, and
kept up the queerest chuckling and chirruping and vocal pirouet-
ting and gurgling sounds that ever were heard; and when I stamped
they only chirruped the louder, as if past all fear and respect in
their mad pranks, defying humanity to stop them. No you don't—
chickaree—chickaree. They were wholly deaf to my arguments, or
failed to perceive their force, and fell into a strain of invective that
was irresistible.

The first sparrow of spring! The year beginning with younger
hope than ever! The faint silvery warblings heard over the partially
bare and moist fields from the blue-bird, the song-sparrow, and the
red-wing, as if the last flakes of winter tinkled as they fell! What at
such a time are histories, chronologies, traditions, and all written
revelations? The brooks sing carols and glees to the spring. The
marsh-hawk sailing low over the meadow is already seeking the first
slimy life that awakes. The sinking sound of melting snow is heard
in all dells, and the ice dissolves apace in the ponds. The grass
flames up on the hillsides like a spring fire,—"et primitus oritur
herba imbribus primoribus evocata,"[5] as if the earth sent forth an
inward heat to greet the returning sun; not yellow but green is the
color of its flame;—the symbol of perpetual youth, the grass-blade,
like a long green ribbon, streams from the sod into the summer,

---

5. From Varro, *Rerum Rusticarum*: "And for the first time, the grass rises, called forth by
the first rains."

checked indeed by the frost, but anon pushing on again, lifting its spear of last year's hay with the fresh life below. It grows as steadily as the rill oozes out of the ground. It is almost identical with that, for in the growing days of June, when the rills are dry, the grass blades are their channels, and from year to year the herds drink at this perennial green stream, and the mower draws from it betimes their winter supply. So our human life but dies down to its root, and still puts forth its green blade to eternity.

Walden is melting apace. There is a canal two rods wide along the northerly and westerly sides, and wider still at the east end. A great field of ice has cracked off from the main body. I hear a song-sparrow singing from the bushes on the shore,—*olit, olit, olit,*—*chip, chip, chip, che char,*—*che wiss, wiss, wiss.* He too is helping to crack it. How handsome the great sweeping curves in the edge of the ice, answering somewhat to those of the shore, but more regular! It is unusually hard, owing to the recent severe but transient cold, and all watered or waved like a palace floor. But the wind slides eastward over its opaque surface in vain, till it reaches the living surface beyond. It is glorious to behold this ribbon of water sparkling in the sun, the bare face of the pond full of glee and youth, as if it spoke the joy of the fishes within it, and of the sands on its shore,—a silvery sheen as from the scales of a *leuciscus*,[6] as it were all one active fish. Such is the contrast between winter and spring. Walden was dead and is alive again. But this spring it broke up more steadily, as I have said.

The change from storm and winter to serene and mild weather, from dark and sluggish hours to bright and elastic ones, is a memorable crisis which all things proclaim. It is seemingly instantaneous at last. Suddenly an influx of light filled my house, though the evening was at hand, and the clouds of winter still overhung it, and the eaves were dripping with sleety rain. I looked out the window, and lo! where yesterday was cold gray ice there lay the transparent pond already calm and full of hope as on a summer evening, reflecting a summer evening sky in its bosom, though none was visible overhead, as if it had intelligence with some remote horizon. I heard a robin in the distance, the first I had heard for many a thousand years, methought, whose note I shall not forget for many a thousand more,—the same sweet and powerful song as of yore. O the evening robin, at the end of a New England summer day! If I could ever find the twig he sits upon! I mean *he*; I mean *the twig*. This at least is not the *Turdus migratorius.*[7] The pitch-pines and shrub-oaks about my house, which had so long drooped, suddenly resumed

---

6. A small freshwater fish, probably the shiner.
7. Migratory thrush.

their several characters, looked brighter, greener, and more erect and alive, as if effectually cleansed and restored by the rain. I knew that it would not rain any more. You may tell by looking at any twig of the forest, ay, at your very wood-pile, whether its winter is past or not. As it grew darker, I was startled by the *honking* of geese flying low over the woods, like weary travellers getting in late from southern lakes, and indulging at last in unrestrained complaint and mutual consolation. Standing at my door, I could hear the rush of their wings; when, driving toward my house, they suddenly spied my light, and with hushed clamor wheeled and settled in the pond. So I came in, and shut the door, and passed my first spring night in the woods.

In the morning I watched the geese from the door through the mist, sailing in the middle of the pond, fifty rods off, so large and tumultuous that Walden appeared like an artificial pond for their amusement. But when I stood on the shore they at once rose up with a great flapping of wings at the signal of their commander, and when they had got into rank circled about over my head, twenty-nine of them, and then steered straight to Canada, with a regular *honk* from the leader at intervals, trusting to break their fast in muddier pools. A "plump" of ducks rose at the same time and took the route to the north in the wake of their noisier cousins.

For a week I heard the circling groping clangor of some solitary goose in the foggy mornings, seeking its companion, and still peopling the woods with the sound of a larger life than they could sustain. In April the pigeons were seen again flying express in small flocks, and in due time I heard the martins twittering over my clearing, though it had not seemed that the township contained so many that it could afford me any, and I fancied that they were peculiarly of the ancient race that dwelt in hollow trees ere white men came. In almost all climes the tortoise and the frog are among the precursors and heralds of this season, and birds fly with song and glancing plumage, and plants spring and bloom, and winds blow, to correct this slight oscillation of the poles and preserve the equilibrium of Nature.

As every season seems best to us in its turn, so the coming in of spring is like the creation of Cosmos out of Chaos and the realization of the Golden Age.—[8]

> "Eurus ad Auroram, Nabathæaque regna recessit,
>   Persidaque, et radiis juga subdita matutinis."

8. According to Greek mythology, the universe ("Cosmos") was created from some unformed original state ("Chaos"); the Golden Age of innocence, peace and happiness occurred soon after creation.

"The East-Wind withdrew to Aurora and the Nabathæan
        kingdom,
And the Persian, and the ridges placed under the morning rays.

       *   *   *   *

Man was born. Whether that Artificer of things,
The origin of a better world, made him from the divine seed;
Or the earth being recent and lately sundered from the high
Ether, retained some seeds of cognate heaven."[9]

A single gentle rain makes the grass many shades greener. So our prospects brighten on the influx of better thoughts. We should be blessed if we lived in the present always, and took advantage of every accident that befell us, like the grass which confesses the influence of the slightest dew that falls on it; and did not spend our time in atoning for the neglect of past opportunities, which we call doing our duty. We loiter in winter while it is already spring. In a pleasant spring morning all men's sins are forgiven. Such a day is a truce to vice. While such a sun holds out to burn, the vilest sinner may return. Through our own recovered innocence we discern the innocence of our neighbors. You may have known your neighbor yesterday for a thief, a drunkard, or a sensualist, and merely pitied or despised him, and despaired of the world; but the sun shines bright and warm this first spring morning, recreating the world, and you meet him at some serene work, and see how his exhausted and debauched veins expand with still joy and bless the new day, feel the spring influence with the innocence of infancy, and all his faults are forgotten. There is not only an atmosphere of good will about him, but even a savor of holiness groping for expression, blindly and ineffectually perhaps, like a new-born instinct, and for a short hour the south hill-side echoes to no vulgar jest. You see some innocent fair shoots preparing to burst from his gnarled rind and try another year's life, tender and fresh as the youngest plant. Even he has entered into the joy of his Lord. Why the jailer does not leave open his prison doors,—why the judge does not dismiss his case,—why the preacher does not dismiss his congregation! It is because they do not obey the hint which God gives them, nor accept the pardon which he freely offers to all.

"A return to goodness produced each day in the tranquil and beneficent breath of the morning, causes that in respect to the love of virtue and the hatred of vice, one approaches a little the primitive nature of man, as the sprouts of the forest which has been felled. In like manner the evil which one does in the interval of a day prevents the germs of virtues which began to spring up again from developing themselves and destroys them.

9. Ovid, *Metamorphoses* 1.61–62, 78–81.

"After the germs of virtue have thus been prevented many times from developing themselves, then the beneficent breath of evening does not suffice to preserve them. As soon as the breath of evening does not suffice longer to preserve them, then the nature of man does not differ much from that of the brute. Men seeing the nature of this man like that of the brute, think that he has never possessed the innate faculty of reason. Are those the true and natural sentiments of man?"[1]

"The Golden Age was first created, which without any avenger
Spontaneously without law cherished fidelity and rectitude.
Punishment and fear were not; nor were threatening words read
On suspended brass; nor did the suppliant crowd fear
The words of their judge; but were safe without an avenger.
Not yet the pine felled on its mountains had descended
To the liquid waves that it might see a foreign world,
And mortals knew no shores but their own.

    *   *   *   *

There was eternal spring, and placid zephyrs with warm
Blasts soothed the flowers born without seed."[2]

On the 29th of April, as I was fishing from the bank of the river near the Nine-Acre-Corner bridge, standing on the quaking grass and willow roots, where the muskrats lurk, I heard a singular rattling sound, somewhat like that of the sticks which boys play with their fingers, when, looking up, I observed a very slight and graceful hawk, like a night-hawk, alternately soaring like a ripple and tumbling a rod or two over and over, showing the underside of its wings, which gleamed like a satin ribbon in the sun, or like the pearly inside of a shell. This sight reminded me of falconry and what nobleness and poetry are associated with that sport. The Merlin it seemed to me it might be called: but I care not for its name. It was the most ethereal flight I had ever witnessed. It did not simply flutter like a butterfly, nor soar like the larger hawks, but it sported with proud reliance in the fields of air; mounting again and again with its strange chuckle, it repeated its free and beautiful fall, turning over and over like a kite, and then recovering from its lofty tumbling, as if it had never set its foot on *terra firma*. It appeared to have no companion in the universe,—sporting there alone,—and to need none but the morning and the ether with which it played. It was not lonely, but made all the earth lonely beneath it. Where was the parent which hatched it, its kindred, and its father in the heavens? The tenant of the air, it seemed related to the earth but by an egg hatched some time in the crevice of a crag;—or was its native

---

1. From the Chinese philosopher Meng-tse; *Works* 6.1
2. Ovid, *Metamorphoses* 1.89–96, 107–8.

nest made in the angle of a cloud, woven of the rainbow's trim-
mings and the sunset sky, and lined with some soft midsummer
haze caught up from earth? Its eyry now some cliffy cloud.

Beside this I got a rare mess of golden and silver and bright
cupreous fishes, which looked like a string of jewels. Ah! I have
penetrated to those meadows on the morning of many a first spring
day, jumping from hummock to hummock, from willow root to willow root, when the wild river valley and the woods were bathed in
so pure and bright a light as would have waked the dead, if they
had been slumbering in their graves, as some suppose. There needs
no stronger proof of immortality. All things must live in such a
light. O Death, where was thy sting? O Grave, where was thy victory, then?[3]

Our village life would stagnate if it were not for the unexplored
forests and meadows which surround it. We need the tonic of wildness,—to wade sometimes in marshes where the bittern and the
meadow-hen lurk, and hear the booming of the snipe; to smell the
whispering sedge where only some wilder and more solitary fowl
builds her nest, and the mink crawls with its belly close to the
ground. At the same time that we are earnest to explore and learn
all things, we require that all things be mysterious and unexplorable, that land and sea be infinitely wild, unsurveyed and unfathomed by us because unfathomable. We can never have enough
of Nature. We must be refreshed by the sight of inexhaustible vigor,
vast and Titanic features, the sea-coast with its wrecks, the wilderness with its living and its decaying trees, the thunder cloud, and
the rain which lasts three weeks and produces freshets. We need to
witness our own limits transgressed, and some life pasturing freely
where we never wander. We are cheered when we observe the vul-
ture feeding on the carrion which disgusts and disheartens us and
deriving health and strength from the repast. There was a dead
horse in the hollow by the path to my house, which compelled me
sometimes to go out of my way, especially in the night when the air
was heavy, but the assurance it gave me of the strong appetite and
inviolable health of Nature was my compensation for this. I love to
see that Nature is so rife with life that myriads can be afforded to
be sacrificed and suffered to prey on one another; that tender organizations can be so serenely squashed out of existence like
pulp,—tadpoles which herons gobble up, and tortoises and toads
run over in the road; and that sometimes it has rained flesh and
blood![4] With the liability to accident, we must see how little ac-

3. 1 Corinthians 15.55.
4. Probably an allusion to newspaper accounts in 1850 of a "shower of flesh and blood," or
"blood rain," of small organisms in Virginia thought to have been transported by high
winds. See *Proceedings of the Boston Society of Natural History* 3 (November 1850): 289.

count is to be made of it. The impression made on a wise man is that of universal innocence. Poison is not poisonous after all, nor are any wounds fatal. Compassion is a very untenable ground. It must be expeditious. Its pleadings will not bear to be stereotyped.

Early in May, the oaks, hickories, maples, and other trees, just putting out amidst the pine woods around the pond, imparted a brightness like sunshine to the landscape, especially in cloudy days, as if the sun were breaking through mists and shining faintly on the hill-sides here and there. On the third or fourth of May I saw a loon in the pond, and during the first week of the month I heard the whippoorwill, the brown-thrasher, the veery, the wood-pewee, the chewink, and other birds. I had heard the wood-thrush long before. The phœbe had already come once more and looked in at my door and window, to see if my house was cavern-like enough for her, sustaining herself on humming wings with clinched talons, as if she held by the air, while she surveyed the premises. The sulphur-like pollen of the pitch-pine soon covered the pond and the stones and rotten wood along the shore, so that you could have collected a barrel-ful. This is the "sulphur showers" we hear of. Even in Calidas' drama of Sacontala, we read of "rills dyed yellow with the golden dust of the lotus."[5] And so the seasons went rolling on into summer, as one rambles into higher and higher grass.

Thus was my first year's life in the woods completed; and the second year was similar to it. I finally left Walden September 6th, 1847.

Conclusion

To the sick the doctors wisely recommend a change of air and scenery. Thank Heaven, here is not all the world. The buck-eye does not grow in New England, and the mocking-bird is rarely heard here. The wild-goose is more of a cosmopolite than we; he breaks his fast in Canada, takes a luncheon in the Ohio, and plumes himself for the night in a southern bayou. Even the bison, to some extent, keeps pace with the seasons, cropping the pastures of the Colorado only till a greener and sweeter grass awaits him by the Yellowstone. Yet we think that if rail-fences are pulled down, and stone-walls piled up on our farms, bounds are henceforth set to our lives and our fates decided. If you are chosen town-clerk, forsooth, you cannot go to Tierra del Fuego this summer: but you may go to the land of infernal fire nevertheless. The universe is wider than our views of it.

---

5. From Sir William Jones's translation of *Sacontala* by Calidas, a fifth-century Hindu poet and dramatist.

Yet we should oftener look over the tafferel of our craft, like curious passengers, and not make the voyage like stupid sailors picking oakum.[1] The other side of the globe is but the home of our correspondent. Our voyaging is only great-circle sailing,[2] and the doctors prescribe for diseases of the skin merely. One hastens to Southern Africa to chase the giraffe; but surely that is not the game he would be after. How long, pray, would a man hunt giraffes if he could? Snipes and woodcocks also may afford rare sport; but I trust it would be nobler game to shoot one's self.—

> "Direct your eye right inward, and you'll find
> A thousand regions in your mind
> Yet undiscovered. Travel them, and be
> Expert in home-cosmography."[3]

What does Africa,—what does the West stand for? Is not our own interior white on the chart? black though it may prove, like the coast, when discovered. Is it the source of the Nile, or the Niger, or the Mississippi, or a North-West Passage around this continent, that we would find? Are these the problems which most concern mankind? Is Franklin the only man who is lost, that his wife should be so earnest to find him? Does Mr. Grinnell[4] know where he himself is? Be rather the Mungo Park, the Lewis and Clarke and Frobisher,[5] of your own streams and oceans; explore your own higher latitudes,—with shiploads of preserved meats to support you, if they be necessary; and pile the empty cans sky-high for a sign. Were preserved meats invented to preserve meat merely? Nay, be a Columbus to whole new continents and worlds within you, opening new channels, not of trade, but of thought. Every man is the lord of a realm beside which the earthly empire of the Czar is but a petty state, a hummock left by the ice. Yet some can be patriotic who have no *self*-respect, and sacrifice the greater to the less. They love the soil which makes their graves, but have no sympathy with the spirit which may still animate their clay. Patriotism is a maggot in their heads. What was the meaning of that South-Sea Exploring

---

1. Oakum, a hemp fiber obtained by untwisting and picking out the fibers of old rope, is used for caulking seams in a ship; picking oakum is a dull and monotonous job.
2. In geometry, a great circle is a circle formed on the surface of a sphere by a plane that passes through the center of the sphere; great-circle sailing is navigation along the arc of any great circle on the earth's surface.
3. William Habbington (1605–1664), "To My Honoured Friend Sir Ed. P. Knight." Thoreau modernized the spelling and changed "eye-sight" to "eye right."
4. John Franklin (1786–1847), English explorer who disappeared in 1847 attempting to find the Northwest Passage; his remains were finally discovered in 1859. Henry Grinnell (1799–1874), a wealthy New York merchant, financed two searches for Franklin, in 1850 and 1853.
5. Mungo Park (1771–1806), Scottish explorer who traced the course of the Niger River; Meriwether Lewis (1774–1809) and William Clark (1770–1838) led an expedition to discover a land route to the Pacific Ocean (1804–1806); Martin Frobisher (1535?–1594), English explorer who attempted three times to find the Northwest Passage.

Expedition,[6] with all its parade and expense, but an indirect recognition of the fact, that there are continents and seas in the moral world, to which every man is an isthmus or an inlet, yet unexplored by him, but that it is easier to sail many thousand miles through cold and storm and cannibals, in a government ship, with five hundred men and boys to assist one, than it is to explore the private sea, the Atlantic and Pacific Ocean of one's being alone.—

"Erret, et extremos alter scrutetur Iberos.
Plus habet hic vitæ, plus habet ille viæ."[7]

Let them wander and scrutinize the outlandish Australians.
I have more of God, they more of the road.

It is not worth the while to go round the world to count the cats in Zanzibar.[8] Yet do this even till you can do better, and you may perhaps find some "Symmes' Hole"[9] by which to get at the inside at last. England and France, Spain and Portugal, Gold Coast and Slave Coast, all front on this private sea; but no bark from them has ventured out of sight of land, though it is without doubt the direct way to India. If you would learn to speak all tongues and conform to the customs of all nations, if you would travel farther than all travellers, be naturalized in all climes, and cause the Sphinx[1] to dash her head against a stone, even obey the precept of the old philospher,[2] and Explore thyself. Herein are demanded the eye and the nerve. Only the defeated and deserters go to the wars, cowards that run away and enlist. Start now on that farthest western way, which does not pause at the Mississippi or the Pacific, nor conduct toward a worn-out China or Japan, but leads on direct a tangent to this sphere, summer and winter, day and night, sun down, moon down, and at last earth down too.

It is said that Mirabeau[3] took to highway robbery "to ascertain what degree of resolution was necessary in order to place one's self in formal opposition to the most sacred laws of society." He declared that "a soldier who fights in the ranks does not require half

6. An expedition sponsored by the U.S. Navy and led by Charles Wilkes (1798–1877), which explored the South Pacific and Antarctic Oceans in 1838–1842.
7. From Claudian (fl. 400 c.e.). "The Old Man of Verona." In his translation, Thoreau substitutes "Australians" for "Iberians" (i.e., those living in the part of Europe now comprising Spain and Portugal).
8. An island off the coast of eastern Africa; Thoreau read about Zanzibar cats in Charles Pickering's The Races of Man (1851).
9. According to John Symmes, a retired army officer, "the earth is hollow and habitable within"; from 1818 until his death in 1829, he tried to raise support for an expedition.
1. In Greek mythology, a winged monster with a woman's head and a lion's body that destroyed anyone unable to guess her riddle; according to legend, Oedipus guessed the riddle, and the Sphinx killed herself.
2. The dictum "Know thyself" has been attributed to several Greek philosophers.
3. Honore Riqueti, Count de Mirabeau (1749–1791), French revolutionary statesman.

so much courage as a foot-pad,"—"that honor and religion have never stood in the way of a well-considered and a firm resolve." This was manly, as the world goes; and yet it was idle, if not desperate. A saner man would have found himself often enough "in formal opposition" to what are deemed "the most sacred laws of society," through obedience to yet more sacred laws, and so have tested his resolution without going out of his way. It is not for a man to put himself in such an attitude to society, but to maintain himself in whatever attitude he find himself through obedience to the laws of his being, which will never be one of opposition to a just government, if he should chance to meet with such.

I left the woods for as good a reason as I went there. Perhaps it seemed to me that I had several more lives to live, and could not spare any more time for that one. It is remarkable how easily and insensibly we fall into a particular route, and make a beaten track for ourselves. I had not lived there a week before my feet wore a path from my door to the pond-side; and though it is five or six years since I trod it, it is still quite distinct. It is true, I fear that others may have fallen into it, and so helped to keep it open. The surface of the earth is soft and impressible by the feet of men; and so with the paths which the mind travels. How worn and dusty, then, must be the highways of the world, how deep the ruts of tradition and conformity! I did not wish to take a cabin passage, but rather to go before the mast and on the deck of the world, for there I could best see the moonlight amid the mountains. I do not wish to go below now.

I learned this, at least, by my experiment; that if one advances confidently in the direction of his dreams, and endeavors to live the life which he has imagined, he will meet with a success unexpected in common hours. He will put some things behind, will pass an invisible boundary; new, universal, and more liberal laws will begin to establish themselves around and within him; or the old laws be expanded, and interpreted in his favor in a more liberal sense, and he will live with the license of a higher order of beings. In proportion as he simplifies his life, the laws of the universe will appear less complex, and solitude will not be solitude, nor poverty poverty, nor weakness weakness. If you have built castles in the air, your work need not be lost; that is where they should be. Now put the foundations under them.

It is a ridiculous demand which England and America make, that you shall speak so that they can understand you. Neither men nor toad-stools grow so. As if that were important, and there were not enough to understand you without them. As if Nature could support but one order of understandings, could not sustain birds as well as quadrupeds, flying as well as creeping things, and *hush* and

who, which Bright[4] can understand, were the best English. As if
there were safety in stupidity alone. I fear chiefly lest my expression
may not be *extra- vagant* enough, may not wander far enough beyond the narrow limits of my daily experience, so as to be adequate
to the truth of which I have been convinced. *Extra vagance!* it depends on how you are yarded. The migrating buffalo, which seeks
new pastures in another latitude, is not extravagant like the cow
which kicks over the pail, leaps the cow-yard fence, and runs after
her calf, in milking time. I desire to speak somewhere *without*
bounds; like a man in a waking moment, to men in their waking
moments; for I am convinced that I cannot exaggerate enough even
to lay the foundation of a true expression. Who that has heard a
strain of music feared then lest he should speak extravagantly any
more forever? In view of the future or possible, we should live quite
laxly and undefined in front, our outlines dim and misty on that
side; as our shadows reveal an insensible perspiration toward the
sun. The volatile truth of our words should continually betray the
inadequacy of the residual statement. Their truth is instantly *translated;* its literal monument alone remains. The words which express
our faith and piety are not definite; yet they are significant and fragrant like frankincense to superior natures.

Why level downward to our dullest perception always, and praise
that as common sense? The commonest sense is the sense of men
asleep, which they express by snoring. Sometimes we are inclined
to class those who are once-and-a-half witted with the half-witted,
because we appreciate only a third part of their wit. Some would
find fault with the morning-red, if they ever got up early enough.
"They pretend," as I hear, "that the verses of Kabir have four different senses; illusion, spirit, intellect, and the exoteric doctrine of the
Vedas;"[5] but in this part of the world it is considered a ground for
complaint if a man's writings admit of more than one interpretation. While England endeavors to cure the potato-rot, will not any
endeavor to cure the brain-rot, which prevails so much more widely
and fatally?

I do not suppose that I have attained to obscurity, but I should be
proud if no more fatal fault were found with my pages on this score
than was found with the Walden ice. Southern customers objected
to its blue color, which is the evidence of its purity, as if it were
muddy, and preferred the Cambridge ice, which is white, but tastes
of weeds. The purity men love is like the mists which envelop the
earth, and not like the azure ether beyond.

---

4. A common name for an ox.
5. From Garcin de Tassy, *History of Hindu Literature* (1839); Kabir was an Indian mystic of
the fifteenth century who tried to reconcile the religions of the Hindus and Moslems.

Some are dinning in our ears that we Americans, and moderns generally, are intellectual dwarfs compared with the ancients, or even the Elizabethan men. But what is that to the purpose? A living dog is better than a dead lion.[6] Shall a man go and hang himself because he belongs to the race of pygmies, and not be the biggest pygmy that he can? Let every one mind his own business, and endeavor to be what he was made.

Why should we be in such desperate haste to succeed, and in such desperate enterprises? If a man does not keep pace with his companions, perhaps it is because he hears a different drummer. Let him step to the music which he hears, however measured or far away. It is not important that he should mature as soon as an apple-tree or an oak. Shall he turn his spring into summer? If the condition of things which we were made for is not yet, what were any reality which we can substitute? We will not be shipwrecked on a vain reality. Shall we with pains erect a heaven of blue glass over ourselves, though when it is done we shall be sure to gaze still at the true ethereal heaven far above, as if the former were not?

There was an artist[7] in the city of Kouroo who was disposed to strive after perfection. One day it came into his mind to make a staff. Having considered that in an imperfect work time is an ingredient, but into a perfect work time does not enter, he said to himself, It shall be perfect in all respects, though I should do nothing else in my life. He proceeded instantly to the forest for wood, being resolved that it should not be made of unsuitable material; and as he searched for and rejected stick after stick, his friends gradually deserted him, for they grew old in their works and died, but he grew not older by a moment. His singleness of purpose and resolution, and his elevated piety, endowed him, without his knowledge, with perennial youth. As he made no compromise with Time, Time kept out of his way, and only sighed at a distance because he could not overcome him. Before he had found a stock in all respects suitable the city of Kouroo was a hoary ruin, and he sat on one of its mounds to peel the stick. Before he had given it the proper shape the dynasty of the Candahars was at an end, and with the point of the stick he wrote the name of the last of that race in the sand, and then resumed his work. By the time he had smoothed and polished the staff Kalpa was no longer the pole-star; and ere he had put on the ferule and the head adorned with precious stones,

6. Ecclesiastes 9.4.
7. Scholars generally agree that this "legend" was probably composed by Thoreau. In the Hindu scripture, Bhagavad-Gita, there is a nation of Kooroo; Kalpa is not a star but the period of time between the creation and destruction of the world, said to be more than four billion years; Brahma, the supreme Hindu deity, reputedly has a day and night equal to one Kalpa: at the end of every Kalpa, the world is absorbed into Brahma and then recreated.

Brahma had awoke and slumbered many times. But why do I stay to mention these things? When the finishing stroke was put to his work, it suddenly expanded before the eyes of the astonished artist into the fairest of all the creations of Brahma. He had made a new system in making a staff, a world with full and fair proportions; in which, though the old cities and dynasties had passed away, fairer and more glorious ones had taken their places. And now he saw by the heap of shavings still fresh at his feet, that, for him and his work, the former lapse of time had been an illusion, and that no more time had elapsed than is required for a single scintillation from the brain of Brahma to fall on and inflame the tinder of a mortal brain. The material was pure, and his art was pure; how could the result be other than wonderful?

No face which we can give to a matter will stead us so well at last as the truth. This alone wears well. For the most part, we are not where we are, but in a false position. Through an infirmity of our natures, we suppose a case, and put ourselves into it, and hence are in two cases at the same time, and it is doubly difficult to get out. In sane moments we regard only the facts, the case that is. Say what you have to say, not what you ought. Any truth is better than make-believe. Tom Hyde, the tinker, standing on the gallows, was asked if he had any thing to say. "Tell the tailors," said he, "to remember to make a knot in their thread before they take the first stitch." His companion's prayer is forgotten.

However mean your life is, meet it and live it; do not shun it and call it hard names. It is not so bad as you are. It looks poorest when you are richest. The fault-finder will find faults even in paradise. Love your life, poor as it is. You may perhaps have some pleasant, thrilling, glorious hours, even in a poor-house. The setting sun is reflected from the windows of the alms-house as brightly as from the rich man's abode; the snow melts before its door as early in the spring. I do not see but a quiet mind may live as contentedly there, and have as cheering thoughts, as in a palace. The town's poor seem to me often to live the most independent lives of any. May be they are simply great enough to receive without misgiving. Most think that they are above being supported by the town; but it oftener happens that they are not above supporting themselves by dishonest means, which should be more disreputable. Cultivate poverty like a garden herb, like sage. Do not trouble yourself much to get new things, whether clothes or friends. Turn the old; return to them. Things do not change; we change. Sell your clothes and keep your thoughts. God will see that you do not want society. If I were confined to a corner of a garret all my days, like a spider, the world would be just as large to me while I had my thoughts about me. The philosopher said: "From an army of three divisions one can take away its general, and put it in disorder; from the man the most abject and vulgar one cannot take away his thought."[8] Do not seek so anxiously to be developed, to subject yourself to many influences to be played on; it is all dissipation. Humility like darkness reveals the heavenly lights. The shadows of poverty and meanness gather around us, "and lo! creation widens to our view."[9] We are often reminded that if there were bestowed on us the wealth of Crœsus,[1] our aims must still be the same, and our means essentially the same. Moreover, if you are restricted in your range by poverty, if you cannot buy books and newspapers, for instance, you are but confined to the most significant and vital experiences; you are compelled to deal with the material which yields the most sugar and the most starch. It is life near the bone where it is sweetest. You are defended from being a trifler. No man loses ever on a lower level by magnanimity on a higher. Superfluous wealth can buy superfluities only. Money is not required to buy one necessary of the soul.

I live in the angle of a leaden wall, into whose composition was poured a little alloy of bell metal. Often, in the repose of my midday, there reaches my ears a confused *tintinnabulum*[2] from without. It is the noise of my contemporaries. My neighbors tell me of their adventures with famous gentlemen and ladies, what notabilities they met at the dinner-table; but I am no more interested in such things than in the contents of the Daily Times. The interest and the conversation are about costume and manners chiefly; but a goose is a goose still, dress it as you will. They tell me of California and Texas, of England and the Indies, of the Hon. Mr. —— of Georgia or of Massachusetts, all transient and fleeting phenomena, till I am ready to leap from their court-yard like the Mameluke bey.[3] I delight to come to my bearings,—not walk in procession with pomp and parade, in a conspicuous place, but to walk even with the Builder of the universe, if I may,—not to live in this restless, nervous, bustling, trivial Nineteenth Century, but stand or sit thoughtfully while it goes by. What are men celebrating? They are all on a committee of arrangements, and hourly expect a speech from somebody. God is only the president of the day, and Webster[4] is his orator. I love to weigh, to settle, to gravitate toward that which most strongly and rightfully attracts me;—not hang by the beam of the

---

8. Confucius, *Analects* 9.25.
9. From "Night and Death," by Joseph Blanco White, English ecclesiastic and poet (1775–1841). According to White, both night and death reveal knowledge of a wider universe to us. In the poem, the line is "lo! creation widened in man's view."
1. King of Lydia, in western Asia Minor, in the sixth century B.C.E., famed for his wealth.
2. Literally, a small tinkling bell; here, a ringing of bells.
3. The Mamelukes, a military caste in Egypt, were massacred in 1811 by Mehemet Ali, viceroy of Egypt; a story holds that one man, an officer (or "bey"), leaped from a wall to his horse and escaped.
4. Daniel Webster, senator from Massachusetts and a noted orator; see n. 7, p. 157.

scale and try to weigh less,—not suppose a case, but take the case
that is; to travel the only path I can, and that on which no power
can resist me. It affords me no satisfaction to commence to spring
an arch before I have got a solid foundation. Let us not play at kittly-
benders.[5] There is a solid bottom every where. We read that the
traveller asked the boy if the swamp before him had a hard bottom.
The boy replied that it had. But presently the traveller's horse sank
in up to the girths, and he observed to the boy, "I thought you said
that this bog had a hard bottom." "So it has," answered the latter,
"but you have not got half way to it yet." So it is with the bogs and
quicksands of society; but he is an old boy that knows it. Only what
is thought said or done at a certain rare coincidence is good. I
would not be one of those who will foolishly drive a nail into mere
lath and plastering; such a deed would keep me awake nights. Give
me a hammer, and let me feel for the furrowing. Do not depend on
the putty. Drive a nail home and clinch it so faithfully that you can
wake up in the night and think of your work with satisfaction,—a
work at which you would not be ashamed to invoke the Muse.[6] So
will help you God, and so only. Every nail driven should be as another rivet in the machine of the universe, you carrying on the
work.

Rather than love, than money, than fame, give me truth. I sat at
a table where were rich food and wine in abundance, and obse-
quious attendance, but sincerity and truth were not; and I went
away hungry from the inhospitable board. The hospitality was as
cold as the ices. I thought that there was no need of ice to freeze
them. They talked to me of the age of the wine and the fame of the
vintage; but I thought of an older, a newer, and purer wine, of a
more glorious vintage, which they had not got, and could not buy.
The style, the house and grounds and "entertainment" pass for
nothing with me. I called on the king, but he made me wait in his
hall, and conducted like a man incapacitated for hospitality. There
was a man in my neighborhood who lived in a hollow tree. His
manners were truly regal. I should have done better had I called on
him.

How long shall we sit in our porticoes practising idle and musty
virtues, which any work would make impertinent? As if one were to
begin the day with long-suffering, and hire a man to hoe his potatoes; and in the afternoon go forth to practise Christian meekness
and charity with goodness aforethought! Consider the China pride[7]
and stagnant self-complacency of mankind. This generation re-

5. A game in which children attempt to run or skate on thin ice without breaking it.
6. In Greek mythology, one of the nine goddesses of poetry, music, dance, and other arts;
   epic poems traditionally begin with an invocation of the Muse.
7. The Chinese empire was commonly believed to be smug and self-satisfied.

clines a little to congratulate itself on being the last of an illustrious line; and in Boston and London and Paris and Rome, thinking of its long descent, it speaks of its progress in art and science and literature with satisfaction. There are the Records of the Philosophical Societies, and the public Eulogies of *Great Men!* It is the good Adam contemplating his own virtue. "Yes, we have done great deeds, and sung divine songs, which shall never die,"—that is, as long as *we* can remember them. The learned societies and great men of Assyria,[8]—where are they? What youthful philosophers and experimentalists we are! There is not one of my readers who has yet lived a whole human life. These may be but the spring months in the life of the race. If we have had the seven-years' itch, we have not seen the seventeen-year locust yet in Concord. We are acquainted with a mere pellicle of the globe on which we live. Most have not delved six feet beneath the surface, nor leaped as many above it. We know not where we are. Beside, we are sound asleep nearly half our time. Yet we esteem ourselves wise, and have an established order on the surface. Truly, we are deep thinkers, we are ambitious spirits! As I stand over the insect crawling amid the pine needles on the forest floor, and endeavoring to conceal itself from my sight, and ask myself why it will cherish those humble thoughts, and hide its head from me who might, perhaps, be its benefactor, and impart to its race some cheering information, I am reminded of the greater Benefactor and Intelligence that stands over me the human insect.

There is an incessant influx of novelty into the world, and yet we tolerate incredible dulness. I need only suggest what kind of sermons are still listened to in the most enlightened countries. There are such words as joy and sorrow, but they are only the burden of a psalm, sung with a nasal twang, while we believe in the ordinary and mean. We think that we can change our clothes only. It is said that the British Empire is very large and respectable, and that the United States are a first-rate power. We do not believe that a tide rises and falls behind every man which can float the British Empire like a chip, if he should ever harbor it in his mind. Who knows what sort of seventeen-year locust will next come out of the ground? The government of the world I live in was not framed, like that of Britain, in after-dinner conversations over the wine.

The life in us is like the water in the river. It may rise this year higher than man has ever known it, and flood the parched uplands; even this may be the eventful year, which will drown out all our muskrats. It was not always dry land where we dwell. I see far inland the banks which the stream anciently washed, before science

8. An ancient empire in western Asia.

began to record its freshets. Every one has heard the story which has gone the rounds of New England, of a strong and beautiful bug which came out of the dry leaf of an old table of apple-tree wood, which had stood in a farmer's kitchen for sixty years, first in Connecticut, and afterward in Massachusetts,—from an egg deposited in the living tree many years earlier still, as appeared by counting the annual layers beyond it; which was heard gnawing out for several weeks, hatched perchance by the heat of an urn. Who does not feel his faith in a resurrection and immortality strengthened by hearing of this? Who knows what beautiful and winged life, whose egg has been buried for ages under many concentric layers of woodenness in the dead dry life of society, deposited at first in the alburnum of the green and living tree, which has been gradually converted into the semblance of its well-seasoned tomb,—heard perchance gnawing out now for years by the astonished family of man, as they sat round the festive board,—may unexpectedly come forth from amidst society's most trivial and handselled furniture, to enjoy its perfect summer life at last!

I do not say that John or Jonathan[9] will realize all this; but such is the character of that morrow which mere lapse of time can never make to dawn. The light which puts out our eyes is darkness to us. Only that day dawns to which we are awake. There is more day to dawn. The sun is but a morning star.

THE END.

---

9. Common mid-nineteenth-century names for an Englishman and an American, respectively.

TEXTUAL APPENDIX TO *WALDEN*

The present text is based on the first edition of *Walden*, published by Ticknor and Fields on August 9, 1854. Emendations have been made either according to Thoreau's corrections and additions to his own copy of the first edition (and, in the case of the title, Thoreau's correspondence with his publisher requesting that the subtitle be dropped in future printings) or in a few cases according to the editor's judgment. Decisions to emend have been made after consulting and comparing the proof sheets corrected by Thoreau and relevant manuscript versions with a copy of the first edition in the Knight Library, University of Oregon. All changes to the 1854 edition of *Walden*, whether initiated by Thoreau or by the editor, are summarized in the list below.

Annotations Thoreau made in his copy of *Walden* are included among the editor's annotations at the foot of pages 126, 174, and 188, identified by the bracketed statement: [*Thoreau's note*]. One of these annotations ("breams, . . . 5lbs—" on 126) contains material apparently intended as an addition to the *Walden* text, for in Thoreau's copy the note is marked for insertion with a caret. For the present edition, therefore, the scientific name for the bream, the trout, and its weight have been treated as additions to the text and rendered to conform to printing conventions and the surrounding text, while Thoreau's bracketed and parenthetical cross-references to the Journal in his note have been treated as annotations and not included in the *Walden* text.

In addition to these emendations, there are a few nonsubstantive differences between the present text and the first edition of *Walden*. Since the Norton edition was completely reset, end-line hyphens generally do not conform in placement to those found in the 1854 edition, and one possibly substantive hyphenation in the first edition ("re-/create") has been resolved to nonhyphenated form ("recreate," 151.06). Five misspellings not detected by Thoreau or his printer have been corrected ("occasionally," 106.06; "neighbor-hood," 122.41; "sweet-briars," 152.09; "crumbs," 153.22, 185.26, 185.31; and "ledger," 188.09), as has a grammatical error ("have" corrected to "has," 194.15) and an error in spelling a family name ("Stratton," 173.10). In the latter case, Thoreau made the correction in his copy at 174.09 but neglected to correct the previous occurrence at 173.10. Other variant or irregular spellings have been preserved since they might reflect Thoreau's preferences. A period inadvertently omitted in the 1854 edition has been restored (162.39).

Textual Variants

All variants between the Norton Critical Edition and the first edition of *Walden* are summarized in the table below. Page and line number and the word or phrase as printed in the Norton Critical Edition are in boldface, followed by the first edition reading. (T) refers to changes authorized by Thoreau's corrections or additions in his copy of the first edition, now in the Abernethy Library, Middlebury College, Middlebury, Vermont, or by his correspondence with the publisher; (Ed) refers to changes made by the present editor for reasons explained above.

Title page Walden   *Walden; Or, Life in the Woods* (T)
18.01 port   post (T)
21.10 wheat is said to have been handed   wheat was handed (T)
41.13 there   There (Ed)
68.20 accomplish it   come to the end of them (T)
83.21 were   are (T)
83.21 rang   rings (T)
88.31 double   single (T)
95.11 remunerate   remunerate, (T)
106.06 occasionally   occcasionally (Ed)
117.12 invariably,   invariably (T)
122.41 neighborhood   neighborhood (Ed)
126.33 breams, (Pomotis obesus,) one trout weighing a little over five pounds,   breams (T/Ed)
127.23 it, kingfishers dart away from its coves,   it, (T)
137.26 black   white (T)
151.06 recreate   rec/reate (Ed)
152.09 sweet-briars   sweet-briers (Ed)
153.18 kind (Mus leucopus)   kind (T)
153.22 crumbs   crums (Ed)
162.39 masonry.   masonry (Ed)
172.22 (Mrs. Hooper)   (T)
173.10 Stratton   Stratten (Ed)
174.09 Stratton   Stratten (T)
180.08 deer   meadow (T)
184.35 frisk   brisk (T)
185.26 crumbs   crums (Ed)
185.31 crumbs   crums (Ed)
188.09 ledger   leger (Ed)
194.15 has   have (Ed)
209.33 on   in (T)

Civil Disobedience

I heartily accept the motto,—"That government is best which governs least";[1] and I should like to see it acted up to more rapidly and systematically. Carried out, it finally amounts to this, which also I believe,—"That government is best which governs not at all"; and when men are prepared for it, that will be the kind of government which they will have. Government is at best but an expedient; but most governments are usually, and all governments are sometimes, inexpedient. The objections which have been brought against a standing army, and they are many and weighty, and deserve to prevail, may also at last be brought against a standing government. The standing army is only an arm of the standing government. The government itself, which is only the mode which the people have chosen to execute their will, is equally liable to be abused and perverted before the people can act through it. Witness the present Mexican war,[2] the work of comparatively a few individuals using the standing government as their tool; for, in the outset, the people would not have consented to this measure.

This American government,—what is it but a tradition, though a recent one, endeavoring to transmit itself unimpaired to posterity, but each instant losing some of its integrity? It has not the vitality and force of a single living man; for a single man can bend it to his will. It is a sort of wooden gun to the people themselves.[3] But it is not the less necessary for this; for the people must have some complicated machinery or other, and hear its din, to satisfy that idea of government which they have. Governments show thus how successfully men can be imposed on, even impose on themselves, for their own advantage. It is excellent, we must all allow. Yet this government never of itself furthered any enterprise, but by the alacrity with which it got out of its way. *It* does not keep the country free. *It* does not settle the West. *It* does not educate. The character inher-

---

1. The motto of the *United States Magazine and Democratic Review*, a monthly literary-political journal; a similar statement occurs in Emerson's essay "Politics."
2. Between Mexico and the United States (1846–1848), taking place when Thoreau was arrested for non payment of the poll tax; the issues included slavery and the annexation of Texas.
3. In the 1849 printing, this sentence continues: ". . . and, if ever they should use it in earnest as a real one against each other, it will surely split."

ent in the American people has done all that has been accomplished; and it would have done somewhat more, if the government had not sometimes got in its way. For government is an expedient by which men would fain succeed in letting one another alone; and, as has been said, when it is most expedient, the governed are most let alone by it. Trade and commerce, if they were not made of India-rubber,[4] would never manage to bounce over the obstacles which legislators are continually putting in their way; and, if one were to judge these men wholly by the effects of their actions and not partly by their intentions, they would deserve to be classed and punished with those mischievous persons who put obstructions on the railroads.

But, to speak practically and as a citizen, unlike those who call themselves no-government men, I ask for, not at once no government, but *at once* a better government. Let every man make known what kind of government would command his respect, and that will be one step toward obtaining it.

After all, the practical reason why, when the power is once in the hands of the people, a majority are permitted, and for a long period continue, to rule, is not because they are most likely to be in the right, nor because this seems fairest to the minority, but because they are physically the strongest. But a government in which the majority rule in all cases cannot be based on justice, even as far as men understand it. Can there not be a government in which majorities do not virtually decide right and wrong, but conscience?—in which majorities decide only those questions to which the rule of expediency is applicable? Must the citizen ever for a moment, or in the least degree, resign his conscience to the legislator? Why has every man a conscience, then? I think that we should be men first, and subjects afterward. It is not desirable to cultivate a respect for the law, so much as for the right. The only obligation which I have a right to assume, is to do at any time what I think right. It is truly enough said, that a corporation has no conscience; but a corporation of conscientious men is a corporation *with* a conscience. Law never made men a whit more just; and, by means of their respect for it, even the well-disposed are daily made the agents of injustice. A common and natural result of an undue respect for law is, that you may see a file of soldiers, colonel, captain, corporal, privates, powder-monkeys,[5] and all, marching in admirable order over hill and dale to the wars, against their wills, ay, against their common sense and consciences, which makes it very steep marching indeed, and produces a palpitation of the heart. They have no doubt that it is a

4. A form of crude rubber made from latex.
5. Young boys in military service who carry gunpowder from a storehouse to the guns.

damnable business in which they are concerned; they are all peace-ably inclined. Now, what are they? Men at all? or small movable forts and magazines, at the service of some unscrupulous man in power? Visit the Navy-Yard,[6] and behold a marine, such a man as an American government can make, or such as it can make a man with its black arts,—a mere shadow and reminiscence of humanity, a man laid out alive and standing, and already, as one may say, buried under arms with funeral accompaniments, though it may be,—

> "Not a drum was heard, not a funeral note,
>   As his corse to the rampart we hurried;
> Not a soldier discharged his farewell shot
>   O'er the grave where our hero we buried."[7]

The mass of men serve the state thus, not as men mainly, but as machines, with their bodies. They are the standing army, and the militia, jailers, constables, posse comitatus,[8] &c. In most cases there is no free exercise whatever of the judgment or of the moral sense; but they put themselves on a level with wood and earth and stones; and wooden men can perhaps be manufactured that will serve the purpose as well. Such command no more respect than men of straw or a lump of dirt. They have the same sort of worth only as horses and dogs. Yet such as these even are commonly esteemed good citizens. Others,—as most legislators, politicians, lawyers, ministers, and office-holders,—serve the state chiefly with their heads; and, as they rarely make any moral distinctions, they are as likely to serve the Devil, without *intending* it, as God. A very few, as heroes, patriots, martyrs, reformers in the great sense, and *men*, serve the state with their consciences also, and so necessarily resist it for the most part; and they are commonly treated as ene-mies by it. A wise man will only be useful as a man, and will not submit to be "clay," and "stop a hole to keep the wind away,"[9] but leave that office to his dust at least:—

> "I am too high born to be propertied,
> To be a secondary at control,
> Or useful serving-man and instrument
> To any sovereign state throughout the world."[1]

He who gives himself entirely to his fellow-men appears to them useless and selfish; but he who gives himself partially to them is pronounced a benefactor and philanthropist.

6. Probably the U.S. Navy Yard in Boston, Massachusetts.
7. From "The Burial of Sir John Moore at Corunna" by Charles Wolfe (1791–1823).
8. A body of men summoned by a sheriff to assist in keeping peace.
9. Shakespeare, *Hamlet* 5.1.236–7.
1. Shakespeare, *King John* 5.2.79–82.

How does it become a man to behave toward this American government to-day? I answer, that he cannot without disgrace be associated with it. I cannot for an instant recognize that political organization as *my* government which is the *slave's* government also.

All men recognize the right of revolution; that is, the right to refuse allegiance to, and to resist, the government, when its tyranny or its inefficiency are great and unendurable. But almost all say that such is not the case now. But such was the case, they think, in the Revolution of '75.[2] If one were to tell me that this was a bad government because it taxed certain foreign commodities brought to its ports, it is most probable that I should not make an ado about it, for I can do without them. All machines have their friction; and possibly this does enough good to counterbalance the evil. At any rate, it is a great evil to make a stir about it. But when the friction comes to have its machine, and oppression and robbery are organized, I say, let us not have such a machine any longer. In other words, when a sixth of the population of a nation which has undertaken to be the refuge of liberty are slaves, and a whole country is unjustly overrun and conquered by a foreign army, and subjected to military law, I think that it is not too soon for honest men to rebel and revolutionize. What makes this duty the more urgent is the fact, that the country so overrun is not our own, but ours is the invading army.

Paley, a common authority with many on moral questions, in his chapter on the "Duty of Submission to Civil Government," resolves all civil obligation into expediency; and he proceeds to say, "that so long as the interest of the whole society requires it, that is, so long as the established government cannot be resisted or changed without public inconveniency, it is the will of God that the established government be obeyed, and no longer. . . . . This principle being admitted, the justice of every particular case of resistance is reduced to a computation of the quantity of the danger and grievance on the one side, and of the probability and expense of redressing it on the other."[3] Of this, he says, every man shall judge for himself. But Paley appears never to have contemplated those cases to which the rule of expediency does not apply, in which a people, as well as an individual, must do justice, cost what it may. If I have unjustly wrested a plank from a drowning man, I must restore it to him though I drown myself. This, according to Paley, would be inconvenient. But he that would save his life, in such a case, shall lose

2. The American Revolution, begun with the Battle of Lexington and Concord on April 19, 1775.
3. William Paley (1743–1805), English theologian and philosopher; from his *Principles of Moral and Political Philosophy* (1785).

it.[4] This people must cease to hold slaves, and to make war on Mexico, though it cost them their existence as a people.

In their practice, nations agree with Paley; but does any one think that Massachusetts does exactly what is right at the present crisis?

> "A drab of state, a cloth-o'-silver slut,
> To have her train borne up, and her soul trail in the dirt."[5]

Practically speaking, the opponents to a reform in Massachusetts are not a hundred thousand politicians at the South, but a hundred thousand merchants and farmers here, who are more interested in commerce and agriculture than they are in humanity, and are not prepared to do justice to the slave and to Mexico, *cost what it may*. I quarrel not with far-off foes, but with those who, near at home, co-operate with, and do the bidding of, these far away, and without whom the latter would be harmless. We are accustomed to say, that the mass of men are unprepared; but improvement is slow, because the few are not materially wiser or better than the many. It is not so important that many should be as good as you, as that there be some absolute goodness somewhere; for that will leaven the whole lump.[6] There are thousands who are *in opinion* opposed to slavery and to the war, who yet in effect do nothing to put an end to them; who, esteeming themselves children of Washington and Franklin, sit down with their hands in their pockets, and say that they know not what to do, and do nothing; who even postpone the question of freedom to the question of free-trade, and quietly read the prices-current along with the latest advices from Mexico, after dinner, and, it may be, fall asleep over them both. What is the price-current of an honest man and patriot to-day? They hesitate, and they regret, and sometimes they petition; but they do nothing in earnest and with effect. They will wait, well disposed, for others to remedy the evil, that they may no longer have it to regret. At most, they give only a cheap vote, and a feeble countenance and God-speed, to the right, as it goes by them. There are nine hundred and ninety-nine patrons of virtue to one virtuous man. But it is easier to deal with the real possessor of a thing than with the temporary guardian of it.

All voting is a sort of gaming, like checkers or backgammon, with a slight moral tinge to it, a playing with right and wrong, with moral questions; and betting naturally accompanies it. The character of the voters is not staked. I cast my vote, perchance, as I think right; but I am not vitally concerned that that right should prevail. I am

---

4. Luke 9.24.
5. Cyril Tourneur (1575?–1626), *The Revenger's Tragedy* 4.4.72–73.
6. 1 Corinthians 5.6–8.

willing to leave it to the majority. Its obligation, therefore, never exceeds that of expediency. Even voting *for the right* is *doing* nothing for it. It is only expressing to men feebly your desire that it should prevail. A wise man will not leave the right to the mercy of chance, nor wish it to prevail through the power of the majority. There is but little virtue in the action of masses of men. When the majority shall at length vote for the abolition of slavery, it will be because they are indifferent to slavery, or because there is but little slavery left to be abolished by their vote. *They* will then be the only slaves. Only *his* vote can hasten the abolition of slavery who asserts his own freedom by his vote.

I hear of a convention to be held at Baltimore, or elsewhere, for the selection of a candidate for the Presidency, made up chiefly of editors, and men who are politicians by profession; but I think, what is it to any independent, intelligent, and respectable man what decision they may come to? Shall we not have the advantage of his wisdom and honesty, nevertheless? Can we not count upon some independent votes? Are there not many individuals in the country who do not attend conventions? But no: I find that the respectable man, so called, has immediately drifted from his position, and despairs of his country, when his country has more reason to despair of him. He forthwith adopts one of the candidates thus selected as the only *available* one, thus proving that he is himself *available* for any purposes of the demagogue. His vote is of no more worth than that of any unprincipled foreigner or hireling native, who may have been bought. O for a man who is a *man*, and, as my neighbor says, has a bone in his back which you cannot pass your hand through! Our statistics are at fault: the population has been returned too large. How many *men* are there to a square thousand miles in this country? Hardly one. Does not America offer any inducement for men to settle here? The American has dwindled into an Odd Fellow,[7]—one who may be known by the development of his organ of gregariousness, and a manifest lack of intellect and cheerful self-reliance; whose first and chief concern, on coming into the world, is to see that the Almshouses are in good repair; and, before yet he has lawfully donned the virile garb,[8] to collect a fund for the support of the widows and orphans that may be; who, in short, ventures to live only by the aid of the Mutual Insurance company, which has promised to bury him decently.

It is not a man's duty, as a matter of course, to devote himself to the eradication of any, even the most enormous wrong; he may still properly have other concerns to engage him; but it is his duty, at

7. A member of the Independent Order of Odd Fellows, a secret fraternal organization.
8. Adult clothing a Roman boy was permitted to wear upon reaching age fourteen.

least, to wash his hands of it, and, if he gives it no thought longer, not to give it practically his support. If I devote myself to other pursuits and contemplations, I must first see, at least, that I do not pursue them sitting upon another man's shoulders. I must get off him first, that he may pursue his contemplations too. See what gross inconsistency is tolerated. I have heard some of my townsmen say, "I should like to have them order me out to help put down an insurrection of the slaves, or to march to Mexico;—see if I would go"; and yet these very men have each, directly by their allegiance, and so indirectly, at least, by their money, furnished a substitute. The soldier is applauded who refuses to serve in an unjust war by those who do not refuse to sustain the unjust government which makes the war; is applauded by those whose own act and authority he disregards and sets at naught; as if the State were penitent to that degree that it hired one to scourge it while it sinned, but not to that degree that it left off sinning for a moment. Thus, under the name of Order and Civil Government, we are all made at last to pay homage to and support our own meanness. After the first blush of sin comes its indifference; and from immoral it becomes, as it were, *un*moral, and not quite unnecessary to that life which we have made.

The broadest and most prevalent error requires the most disinterested virtue to sustain it. The slight reproach to which the virtue of patriotism is commonly liable, the noble are most likely to incur. Those who, while they disapprove of the character and measures of a government, yield to it their allegiance and support, are undoubtedly its most conscientious supporters, and so frequently the most serious obstacles to reform. Some are petitioning the State to dissolve the Union, to disregard the requisitions of the President. Why do they not dissolve it themselves,—the union between themselves and the State,—and refuse to pay their quota into its treasury? Do not they stand in the same relation to the State, that the State does to the Union? And have not the same reasons prevented the State from resisting the Union, which have prevented them from resisting the State?

How can a man be satisfied to entertain an opinion merely, and enjoy *it*? Is there any enjoyment in it, if his opinion is that he is aggrieved? If you are cheated out of a single dollar by your neighbor, you do not rest satisfied with knowing that you are cheated, or with saying that you are cheated, or even with petitioning him to pay you your due; but you take effectual steps at once to obtain the full amount, and see that you are never cheated again. Action from principle, the perception and the performance of right, changes things and relations; it is essentially revolutionary, and does not consist wholly with anything which was. It not only divides states and churches, it divides families; ay, it divides the *individual*, separating the diabolical in him from the divine.

Unjust laws exist: shall we be content to obey them, or shall we endeavor to amend them, and obey them until we have succeeded, or shall we transgress them at once? Men generally, under such a government as this, think that they ought to wait until they have persuaded the majority to alter them. They think that, if they should resist, the remedy would be worse than the evil. But it is the fault of the government itself that the remedy *is* worse than the evil. *It* makes it worse. Why is it not more apt to anticipate and provide for reform? Why does it not cherish its wise minority? Why does it cry and resist before it is hurt? Why does it not encourage its citizens to be on the alert to point out its faults, and *do* better than it would have them? Why does it always crucify Christ, and excommunicate Copernicus and Luther,[9] and pronounce Washington and Franklin rebels?

One would think, that a deliberate and practical denial of its authority was the only offence never contemplated by government; else, why has it not assigned its definite, its suitable and proportionate penalty? If a man who has no property refuses but once to earn nine shillings for the State, he is put in prison for a period unlimited by any law that I know, and determined only by the discretion of those who placed him there; but if he should steal ninety times nine shillings[1] from the State, he is soon permitted to go at large again.

If the injustice is part of the necessary friction of the machine of government, let it go, let it go: perchance it will wear smooth,—certainly the machine will wear out. If the injustice has a spring, or a pulley, or a rope, or a crank, exclusively for itself, then perhaps you may consider whether the remedy will not be worse than the evil; but if it is of such a nature that it requires you to be the agent of injustice to another, then, I say, break the law. Let your life be a counter friction to stop the machine. What I have to do is to see, at any rate, that I do not lend myself to the wrong which I condemn.

As for adopting the ways which the State has provided for remedying the evil, I know not of such ways. They take too much time, and a man's life will be gone. I have other affairs to attend to. I came into this world, not chiefly to make this a good place to live in, but to live in it, be it good or bad. A man has not everything to do, but something; and because he cannot do *everything*, it is not necessary that he should do *something* wrong. It is not my business to be petitioning the Governor or the Legislature any more than it

9. Nicolaus Copernicus (1473–1543), Polish astronomer; he was not excommunicated, but his dissertation on the solar system was banned by the Roman Catholic Church; Martin Luther (1483–1546), German theologian, leader of the Protestant Reformation.
1. The approximate amount of poll tax Thoreau refused to pay.

is theirs to petition me; and, if they should not hear my petition, what should I do then? But in this case the State has provided no way: its very Constitution is the evil. This may seem to be harsh and stubborn and unconciliatory; but it is to treat with the utmost kindness and consideration the only spirit that can appreciate or deserves it. So is all change for the better, like birth and death, which convulse the body.

I do not hesitate to say, that those who call themselves Abolitionists should at once effectually withdraw their support, both in person and property, from the government of Massachusetts, and not wait till they constitute a majority of one, before they suffer the right to prevail through them. I think that it is enough if they have God on their side, without waiting for that other one. Moreover, any man more right than his neighbors constitutes a majority of one already.

I meet this American government, or its representative, the State government, directly, and face to face, once a year—no more—in the person of its tax-gatherer; this is the only mode in which a man situated as I am necessarily meets it; and it then says distinctly, Recognize me; and the simplest, the most effectual, and, in the present posture of affairs, the indispensablest mode of treating with it on this head, of expressing your little satisfaction with and love for it, is to deny it then. My civil neighbor, the tax-gatherer, is the very man I have to deal with,—for it is, after all, with men and not with parchment that I quarrel,—and he has voluntarily chosen to be an agent of the government. How shall he ever know well what he is and does as an officer of the government, or as a man, until he is obliged to consider whether he shall treat me, his neighbor, for whom he has respect, as a neighbor and well-disposed man, or as a maniac and disturber of the peace, and see if he can get over this obstruction to his neighborliness without a ruder and more impetuous thought or speech corresponding with his action. I know this well, that if one thousand, if one hundred, if ten men whom I could name,—if ten *honest* men only,—ay, if *one* HONEST man, in this State of Massachusetts, *ceasing to hold slaves*, were actually to withdraw from this copartnership, and be locked up in the county jail therefor, it would be the abolition of slavery in America. For it matters not how small the beginning may seem to be: what is once well done is done forever. But we love better to talk about it: that we say is our mission. Reform keeps many scores of newspapers in its service, but not one man. If my esteemed neighbor, the State's ambassador,[2] who will devote his days to the settlement of the ques-

---

2. Samuel Hoar (1778–1856), a congressman from Concord, was sent to Charleston, South Carolina, to protest the treatment accorded Negro seamen from Massachusetts. Hoar was expelled from Charleston by the legislature of South Carolina.

tion of human rights in the Council Chamber, instead of being threatened with the prisons of Carolina, were to sit down the prisoner of Massachusetts, that State which is so anxious to foist the sin of slavery upon her sister,—though at present she can discover only an act of inhospitality to be the ground of a quarrel with her,— the Legislature would not wholly waive the subject the following winter.

Under a government which imprisons any unjustly, the true place for a just man is also a prison. The proper place to-day, the only place which Massachusetts has provided for her freer and less desponding spirits, is in her prisons, to be put out and locked out of the State by her own act, as they have already put themselves out by their principles. It is there that the fugitive slave, and the Mexican prisoner on parole, and the Indian come to plead the wrongs of his race, should find them; on that separate, but more free and honorable ground, where the State places those who are not *with* her, but *against* her,—the only house in a slave State in which a free man can abide with honor. If any think that their influence would be lost there, and their voices no longer afflict the ear of the State, that they would not be as an enemy within its walls, they do not know by how much truth is stronger than error, nor how much more eloquently and effectively he can combat injustice who has experienced a little in his own person. Cast your whole vote, not a strip of paper merely, but your whole influence. A minority is powerless while it conforms to the majority; it is not even a minority then; but it is irresistible when it clogs by its whole weight. If the alternative is to keep all just men in prison, or give up war and slavery, the State will not hesitate which to choose. If a thousand men were not to pay their tax-bills this year, that would not be a violent and bloody measure, as it would be to pay them, and enable the State to commit violence and shed innocent blood. This is, in fact, the definition of a peaceable revolution, if any such is possible. If the tax-gatherer, or any other public officer, asks me, as one has done, "But what shall I do?" my answer is, "If you really wish to do anything, resign your office." When the subject has refused allegiance, and the officer has resigned his office, then the revolution is accomplished. But even suppose blood should flow. Is there not a sort of blood shed when the conscience is wounded? Through this wound a man's real manhood and immortality flow out, and he bleeds to an everlasting death. I see this blood flowing now.

I have contemplated the imprisonment of the offender, rather than the seizure of his goods,—though both will serve the same purpose,—because they who assert the purest right, and consequently are most dangerous to a corrupt State, commonly have not spent much time in accumulating property. To such the State renders comparatively small service, and a slight tax is wont to appear exorbitant, particularly if they are obliged to earn it by special labor with their hands. If there were one who lived wholly without the use of money, the State itself would hesitate to demand it of him. But the rich man,—not to make any invidious comparison,—is always sold to the institution which makes him rich. Absolutely speaking, the more money, the less virtue; for money comes between a man and his objects, and obtains them for him; and it was certainly no great virtue to obtain it. It puts to rest many questions which he would otherwise be taxed to answer; while the only new question which it puts is the hard but superfluous one, how to spend it. Thus his moral ground is taken from under his feet. The opportunities of living are diminished in proportion as what are called the "means" are increased. The best thing a man can do for his culture when he is rich is to endeavor to carry out those schemes which he entertained when he was poor. Christ answered the Herodians according to their condition. "Show me the tribute-money," said he;—and one took a penny out of his pocket;—if you use money which has the image of Cæsar on it, and which he has made current and valuable, that is, *if you are men of the State*, and gladly enjoy the advantages of Cæsar's government, then pay him back some of his own when he demands it; "Render therefore to Cæsar that which is Cæsar's, and to God those things which are God's,"[3]—leaving them no wiser than before as to which was which; for they did not wish to know.

When I converse with the freest of my neighbors, I perceive that, whatever they may say about the magnitude and seriousness of the question, and their regard for the public tranquillity, the long and the short of the matter is, that they cannot spare the protection of the existing government, and they dread the consequences to their property and families of disobedience to it. For my own part, I should not like to think that I ever rely on the protection of the State. But, if I deny the authority of the State when it presents its tax-bill, it will soon take and waste all my property, and so harass me and my children without end. This is hard. This makes it impossible for a man to live honestly, and at the same time comfortably, in outward respects. It will not be worth the while to accumulate property; that would be sure to go again. You must hire or squat somewhere, and raise but a small crop, and eat that soon. You must live within yourself, and depend upon yourself always tucked up and ready for a start, and not have many affairs. A man may grow rich in Turkey even, if he will be in all respects a good subject of

3. Matthew 22.15–22. Herodians were followers of Herod Antipas, tetrarch of Galilee from 4 B.C.E. to 39 C.E.

the Turkish government. Confucius said: "If a state is governed by the principles of reason, poverty and misery are subjects of shame; if a state is not governed by the principles of reason, riches and honors are the subjects of shame."[4] No: until I want the protection of Massachusetts to be extended to me in some distant Southern port, where my liberty is endangered, or until I am bent solely on building up an estate at home by peaceful enterprise, I can afford to refuse allegiance to Massachusetts, and her right to my property and life. It costs me less in every sense to incur the penalty of disobedience to the State, than it would to obey. I should feel as if I were worth less in that case.

Some years ago, the State met me in behalf of the Church, and commanded me to pay a certain sum toward the support of a clergyman whose preaching my father attended, but never I myself. "Pay," it said, "or be locked up in the jail." I declined to pay. But, unfortunately, another man saw fit to pay it. I did not see why the schoolmaster should be taxed to support the priest, and not the priest the schoolmaster; for I was not the State's schoolmaster, but I supported myself by voluntary subscription. I did not see why the lyceum should not present its tax-bill, and have the State to back its demand, as well as the Church. However, at the request of the selectmen, I condescended to make some such statement as this in writing:—"Know all men by these presents, that I, Henry Thoreau, do not wish to be regarded as a member of any incorporated society which I have not joined." This I gave to the town clerk; and he has it. The State, having thus learned that I did not wish to be regarded as a member of that church, has never made a like demand on me since; though it said that it must adhere to its original presumption that time. If I had known how to name them, I should then have signed off in detail from all the societies which I never signed on to; but I did not know where to find a complete list.

I have paid no poll-tax for six years. I was put into a jail once on this account, for one night; and, as I stood considering the walls of solid stone, two or three feet thick, the door of wood and iron, a foot thick, and the iron grating which strained the light, I could not help being struck with the foolishness of that institution which treated me as if I were mere flesh and blood and bones, to be locked up. I wondered that it should have concluded at length that this was the best use it could put me to, and had never thought to avail itself of my services in some way. I saw that, if there was a wall of stone between me and my townsmen, there was a still more difficult one to climb or break through, before they could get to be as free as I was. I did not for a moment feel confined, and the walls

4. *Analects* 8.13.

seemed a great waste of stone and mortar. I felt as if I alone of all my townsmen had paid my tax. They plainly did not know how to treat me, but behaved like persons who are underbred. In every threat and in every compliment there was a blunder; for they thought that my chief desire was to stand the other side of that stone wall. I could not but smile to see how industriously they locked the door on my meditations, which followed them out again without let or hindrance, and *they* were really all that was dangerous. As they could not reach me, they had resolved to punish my body; just as boys, if they cannot come at some person against whom they have a spite, will abuse his dog. I saw that the State was half-witted, that it was timid as a lone woman with her silver spoons, and that it did not know its friends from its foes, and I lost all my remaining respect for it, and pitied it.

Thus the State never intentionally confronts a man's sense, intellectual or moral, but only his body, his senses. It is not armed with superior wit or honesty, but with superior physical strength. I was not born to be forced. I will breathe after my own fashion. Let us see who is the strongest. What force has a multitude? They only can force me who obey a higher law than I. They force me to become like themselves. I do not hear of *men* being *forced* to live this way or that by masses of men. What sort of life were that to live? When I meet a government which says to me, "Your money or your life," why should I be in haste to give it my money? It may be in a great strait, and not know what to do: I cannot help that. It must help itself; do as I do. It is not worth the while to snivel about it. I am not responsible for the successful working of the machinery of society. I am not the son of the engineer. I perceive that, when an acorn and a chestnut fall side by side, the one does not remain inert to make way for the other, but both obey their own laws, and spring and grow and flourish as best they can, till one, perchance, overshadows and destroys the other. If a plant cannot live according to its nature, it dies; and so a man.

The night in prison was novel and interesting enough. The prisoners in their shirt-sleeves were enjoying a chat and the evening air in the doorway, when I entered. But the jailer said, "Come, boys, it is time to lock up"; and so they dispersed, and I heard the sound of their steps returning into the hollow apartments. My room-mate was introduced to me by the jailer, as "a first-rate fellow and a clever man." When the door was locked, he showed me where to hang my hat, and how he managed matters there. The rooms were whitewashed once a month; and this one, at least, was the whitest, most simply furnished, and probably the neatest apartment in the town. He naturally wanted to know where I came from, and what brought me there; and, when I had told him, I asked him in my turn how he came there, presuming him to be an honest man, of course; and, as the world goes, I believe he was. "Why," said he, "they accuse me of burning a barn; but I never did it." As near as I could discover, he had probably gone to bed in a barn when drunk, and smoked his pipe there; and so a barn was burnt. He had the reputation of being a clever man, had been there some three months waiting for his trial to come on, and would have to wait as much longer; but he was quite domesticated and contented, since he got his board for nothing, and thought that he was well treated.

He occupied one window, and I the other; and I saw, that, if one stayed there long, his principal business would be to look out the window. I had soon read all the tracts that were left there, and examined where former prisoners had broken out, and where a grate had been sawed off, and heard the history of the various occupants of that room; for I found that even here there was a history and a gossip which never circulated beyond the walls of the jail. Probably this is the only house in the town where verses are composed, which are afterward printed in a circular form, but not published. I was shown quite a long list of verses which were composed by some young men who had been detected in an attempt to escape, who avenged themselves by singing them.

I pumped my fellow-prisoner as dry as I could, for fear I should never see him again; but at length he showed me which was my bed, and left me to blow out the lamp.

It was like travelling into a far country, such as I had never expected to behold, to lie there for one night. It seemed to me that I never had heard the town-clock strike before, nor the evening sounds of the village; for we slept with the windows open, which were inside the grating. It was to see my native village in the light of the Middle Ages, and our Concord was turned into a Rhine stream, and visions of knights and castles passed before me. They were the voices of old burghers that I heard in the streets. I was an involuntary spectator and auditor of whatever was done and said in the kitchen of the adjacent village-inn,—a wholly new and rare experience to me. It was a closer view of my native town. I was fairly inside of it. I never had seen its institutions before. This is one of its peculiar institutions; for it is a shire[5] town. I began to comprehend what its inhabitants were about.

In the morning, our breakfasts were put through the hole in the door, in small oblong-square tin pans, made to fit, and holding a pint of chocolate, with brown bread, and an iron

5. The seat of government in a county.

spoon. When they called for the vessels again, I was green enough to return what bread I had left; but my comrade seized it, and said that I should lay that up for lunch or dinner. Soon after he was let out to work at haying in a neighboring field, whither he went every day, and would not be back till noon; so he bade me good-day, saying that he doubted if he should see me again.

When I came out of prison,—for some one[6] interfered, and paid that tax,—I did not perceive that great changes had taken place on the common, such as he observed who went in a youth, and emerged a tottering and gray-headed man; and yet a change had to my eyes come over the scene,—the town, and State, and country,—greater than any that mere time could effect. I saw yet more distinctly the State in which I lived. I saw to what extent the people among whom I lived could be trusted as good neighbors and friends; that their friendship was for summer weather only; that they did not greatly propose to do right; that they were a distinct race from me by their prejudices and superstitions, as the Chinamen and Malays are; that, in their sacrifices to humanity, they ran no risks, not even to their property; that, after all, they were not so noble but they treated the thief as he had treated them, and hoped, by a certain outward observance and a few prayers, and by walking in a particular straight though useless path from time to time, to save their souls. This may be to judge my neighbors harshly; for I believe that many of them are not aware that they have such an institution as the jail in their village.

It was formerly the custom in our village, when a poor debtor came out of jail, for his acquaintances to salute him, looking through their fingers, which were crossed to represent the grating of a jail window, "How do ye do?" My neighbors did not thus salute me, but first looked at me, and then at one another, as if I had returned from a long journey. I was put into jail as I was going to the shoemaker's to get a shoe which was mended. When I was let out the next morning, I proceeded to finish my errand, and having put on my mended shoe, joined a huckleberry party, who were impatient to put themselves under my conduct; and in half an hour,—for the horse was soon tackled,[7]—was in the midst of a huckleberry field, on one of our highest hills, two miles off, and then the State was nowhere to be seen.

This is the whole history of "My Prisons."[8]

6. Probably Thoreau's aunt, Maria Thoreau.
7. Harnessed.
8. An ironic reference to *Le Mie Prigioni*, the memoirs of Italian patriot Silvio Pellico (1789–1854).

I have never declined paying the highway tax, because I am as desirous of being a good neighbor as I am of being a bad subject; and, as for supporting schools, I am doing my part to educate my fellow-countrymen now. It is for no particular item in the tax-bill that I refuse to pay it. I simply wish to refuse allegiance to the State, to withdraw and stand aloof from it effectually. I do not care to trace the course of my dollar, if I could, till it buys a man or a musket to shoot one with,—the dollar is innocent,—but I am concerned to trace the effects of my allegiance. In fact, I quietly declare war with the State, after my fashion, though I will still make what use and get what advantage of her I can, as is usual in such cases.

If others pay the tax which is demanded of me, from a sympathy with the State, they do but what they have already done in their own case, or rather they abet injustice to a greater extent than the State requires. If they pay the tax from a mistaken interest in the individual taxed, to save his property, or prevent his going to jail, it is because they have not considered wisely how far they let their private feelings interfere with the public good.

This, then, is my position at present. But one cannot be too much on his guard in such a case, lest his action be biassed by obstinacy, or an undue regard for the opinions of men. Let him see that he does only what belongs to himself and to the hour.

I think sometimes, Why, this people mean well; they are only ignorant; they would do better if they knew how: why give your neighbors this pain to treat you as they are not inclined to? But I think again, this is no reason why I should do as they do, or permit others to suffer much greater pain of a different kind. Again, I sometimes say to myself, When many millions of men, without heat, without ill will, without personal feeling of any kind, demand of you a few shillings only, without the possibility, such is their constitution, of retracting or altering their present demand, and without the possibility, on your side, of appeal to any other millions, why expose yourself to this overwhelming brute force? You do not resist cold and hunger, the winds and the waves, thus obstinately; you quietly submit to a thousand similar necessities. You do not put your head into the fire. But just in proportion as I regard this as not wholly a brute force, but partly a human force, and consider that I have relations to those millions as to so many millions of men, and not of mere brute or inanimate things, I see that appeal is possible, first and instantaneously, from them to the Maker of them, and, secondly, from them to themselves. But, if I put my head deliberately into the fire, there is no appeal to fire or to the Maker of fire, and I have only myself to blame. If I could convince myself that I have any right to be satisfied with men as they are, and to treat them accordingly, and not according, in some respects, to my requisitions and expectations of what they and I ought to be, then, like a good Mussulman[9] and fatalist, I should endeavor to be satisfied with things as they are, and say it is the will of God. And, above all, there is this difference between resisting this and a purely brute or natural force, that I can resist this with some effect; but I cannot expect, like Orpheus,[1] to change the nature of the rocks and trees and beasts.

I do not wish to quarrel with any man or nation. I do not wish to split hairs, to make fine distinctions, or set myself up as better than my neighbors. I seek rather, I may say, even an excuse for conforming to the laws of the land. I am but too ready to conform to them. Indeed, I have reason to suspect myself on this head; and each year, as the tax-gatherer comes round, I find myself disposed to review the acts and position of the general and State governments, and the spirit of the people, to discover a pretext for conformity.

> "We must affect our country as our parents;
> And if at any time we alienate
> Our love or industry from doing it honor,
> We must respect effects and teach the soul
> Matter of conscience and religion,
> And not desire of rule or benefit."[2]

I believe that the State will soon be able to take all my work of this sort out of my hands, and then I shall be no better a patriot than my fellow-countrymen. Seen from a lower point of view, the Constitution, with all its faults, is very good; the law and the courts are very respectable; even this State and this American government are, in many respects, very admirable and rare things, to be thankful for, such as a great many have described them; but seen from a point of view a little higher, they are what I have described them; seen from a higher still, and the highest, who shall say what they are, or that they are worth looking at or thinking of at all?

However, the government does not concern me much, and I shall bestow the fewest possible thoughts on it. It is not many moments that I live under a government, even in this world. If a man is thought-free, fancy-free, imagination-free, that which *is not* never for a long time appearing *to be* to him, unwise rulers or reformers cannot fatally interrupt him.

I know that most men think differently from myself; but those whose lives are by profession devoted to the study of these or kin-

---

9. A Muslim, a Mohammedan.
1. The Greek mythology Orpheus, son of the Muse Calliope, charmed wild animals and moved stones and trees with his music and singing.
2. George Peele (1558?–1598?) *The Battle of Alcazar* 2.2.425–30, slightly altered.

dred subjects, content me as little as any. Statesmen and legislators, standing so completely within the institution, never distinctly and nakedly behold it. They speak of moving society, but have no resting-place without it. They may be men of a certain experience and discrimination, and have no doubt invented ingenious and even useful systems, for which we sincerely thank them; but all their wit and usefulness lie within certain not very wide limits. They are wont to forget that the world is not governed by policy and expediency. Webster[3] never goes behind government, and so cannot speak with authority about it. His words are wisdom to those legislators who contemplate no essential reform in the existing government; but for thinkers, and those who legislate for all time, he never once glances at the subject. I know of those whose serene and wise speculations on this theme would soon reveal the limits of his mind's range and hospitality. Yet, compared with the cheap professions of most reformers, and the still cheaper wisdom and eloquence of politicians in general, his are almost the only sensible and valuable words, and we thank Heaven for him. Comparatively, he is always strong, original, and, above all, practical. Still his quality is not wisdom, but prudence. The lawyer's truth is not Truth, but consistency, or a consistent expediency. Truth is always in harmony with herself, and is not concerned chiefly to reveal the justice that may consist with wrong-doing. He well deserves to be called, as he has been called, the Defender of the Constitution. There are really no blows to be given by him but defensive ones. He is not a leader, but a follower. His leaders are the men of '87.[4] "I have never made an effort," he says, "and never propose to make an effort; I have never countenanced an effort, and never mean to countenance an effort, to disturb the arrangement as originally made, by which the various States came into the Union."[5] Still thinking of the sanction which the Constitution gives to slavery, he says, "Because it was a part of the original compact,—let it stand."[6] Notwithstanding his special acuteness and ability, he is unable to take a fact out of its merely political relations, and behold it as it lies absolutely to be disposed of by the intellect,—what, for instance, it behooves a man to do here in America today with regard to slavery, but ventures, or is driven, to make some such desperate answer as

---

3. Daniel Webster (1782–1852), senator from Massachusetts, noted orator, and supporter of a compromise with the South.
4. Members of the Federal Constitutional Convention, held in Philadelphia in 1787 and presided over by George Washington.
5. From Webster's speech in the Senate, "The Admission of Texas," delivered December 22, 1845.
6. No source in Webster's works has been found for this quotation. In *Reform Papers* (Princeton: Princeton University Press, 1973), editor Wendell Glick suggests that Thoreau may be quoting from memory a line in Webster's speech, "The Constitution and the Union," delivered in the Senate, March 7, 1850 (p. 325).

the following, while professing to speak absolutely, and as a private man,—from which what new and singular code of social duties might be inferred? "The manner," says he, "in which the governments of those States where slavery exists are to regulate it, is for their own consideration, under their responsibility to their constituents, to the general laws of propriety, humanity, and justice, and to God. Associations formed elsewhere, springing from a feeling of humanity, or any other cause, have nothing whatever to do with it. They have never received any encouragement from me, and they never will."[7]

They who know of no purer sources of truth, who have traced up its stream no higher, stand, and wisely stand, by the Bible and the Constitution, and drink at it there with reverence and humility; but they who behold where it comes trickling into this lake or that pool, gird up their loins once more, and continue their pilgrimage toward its fountain-head.

No man with a genius for legislation has appeared in America. They are rare in the history of the world. There are orators, politicians, and eloquent men, by the thousand; but the speaker has not yet opened his mouth to speak, who is capable of settling the much-vexed questions of the day. We love eloquence for its own sake, and not for any truth which it may utter, or any heroism it may inspire. Our legislators have not yet learned the comparative value of free-trade and of freedom, of union, and of rectitude, to a nation. They have no genius or talent for comparatively humble questions of taxation and finance, commerce and manufactures and agriculture. If we were left solely to the wordy wit of legislators in Congress for our guidance, uncorrected by the seasonable experience and the effectual complaints of the people, America would not long retain her rank among the nations. For eighteen hundred years, though perchance I have no right to say it, the New Testament has been written; yet where is the legislator who has wisdom and practical talent enough to avail himself of the light which it sheds on the science of legislation?

The authority of government, even such as I am willing to submit to,—for I will cheerfully obey those who know and can do better than I, and in many things even those who neither know nor can do so well,—is still an impure one: to be strictly just, it must have the sanction and consent of the governed. It can have no pure right over my person and property but what I concede to it. The progress from an absolute to a limited monarchy, from a limited monarchy

---

7. These extracts have been inserted since the Lecture was read [*Thoreau's note*], I.e., "The manner . . . will"; quoted, slightly modified, from Webster's speech, "Exclusion of Slavery from the Territories," delivered August 12, 1848.

to a democracy, is a progress toward a true respect for the individual. Even the Chinese philosopher was wise enough to regard the
individual as the basis of the empire.[8] Is a democracy, such as we
know it, the last improvement possible in government? Is it not
possible to take a step further towards recognizing and organizing
the rights of man? There will never be a really free and enlightened
State, until the State comes to recognize the individual as a higher
and independent power, from which all its own power and authority are derived, and treats him accordingly. I please myself with
imagining a State at last which can afford to be just to all men, and
to treat the individual with respect as a neighbor; which even would
not think it inconsistent with its own repose, if a few were to live
aloof from it, not meddling with it, nor embraced by it, who fulfilled all the duties of neighbors and fellow-men. A State which
bore this kind of fruit, and suffered it to drop off as fast as it
ripened, would prepare the way for a still more perfect and glorious
State, which also I have imagined, but not yet anywhere seen.

8. Menicus (see n. 9, p. 149); from *Works* 4.

Slavery in Massachusetts[†]

I lately attended a meeting of the citizens of Concord, expecting, as one among many, to speak on the subject of slavery in Massachusetts; but I was surprised and disappointed to find that what had called my townsmen together was the destiny of Nebraska[1], and not of Massachusetts, and that what I had to say would be entirely out of order. I had thought that the house was on fire, and not the prairie; but though several of the citizens of Massachusetts are now in prison for attempting to rescue a slave[2] from her own clutches, not one of the speakers at that meeting expressed regret for it, not one even referred to it. It was only the disposition of some wild lands a thousand miles off, which appeared to concern them. The inhabitants of Concord are not prepared to stand by one of their own bridges, but talk only of taking up a position on the highlands beyond the Yellowstone river. Our Buttricks, and Davises, and Hosmers are retreating thither, and I fear that they will have no Lexington Common between them and the enemy[3]. There is not one slave in Nebraska; there are perhaps a million slaves in Massachusetts.

They who have been bred in the school of politics fail now and always to face the facts. Their measures are half measures and make-shifts, merely. They put off the day of settlement indefinitely, and meanwhile, the debt accumulates. Though the Fugitive Slave

---

† First published in a shorter version in *The Liberator* for July 21, 1854, with the subtitle "An Address, Delivered at the Anti-Slavery Celebration at Framingham, July 4, 1854." For an account of the Framingham counter-demonstration, see Albert J. von Frank, "Fourth of July," reprinted in this volume; for an incisive recent study of the essay's composition, see Sandra Harbert Petrulionis, "Editorial Savoir Faire: Thoreau Transforms His Journal into "Slavery in Massachusetts," *Resources for American Literary Study* 25.2 (1999):206–31. From *The Writings of Henry D. Thoreau* by Henry David Thoreau. © 1973 Princeton University Press, 2001 renewed PUP. Reprinted by permission of Princeton University Press.

1. The Kansas-Nebraska Act, passed by Congress on May 24, 1854, left the decision to allow slavery in these territories to their residents. It thus repealed the Missouri Compromise (Thoreau's "compromise pact of 1820"), which prohibited slavery in new states north of latitude 36°30'.

2. On May 25, 1854, nine men were arrested in Boston for attempting to rescue Anthony Burns, a fugitive slave from Virginia, including Thoreau's friend, Thomas Wentworth Higginson (1823–1911), a Unitarian minister and anti-slavery activist.

3. Concord militiamen who successfully defended the North Bridge against the British in the Battle of Concord, April 19, 1775 (see n. 1, p. 156). Fighting had begun earlier that morning on nearby Lexington common.

Law[4] had not been the subject of discussion on that occasion, it was at length faintly resolved by my townsmen, at an adjourned meeting, as I learn, that the compromise compact of 1820 having been repudiated by one of the parties, 'Therefore, . . . the Fugitive Slave Law must be repealed.' But this is not the reason why an iniquitous law should be repealed. The fact which the politician faces is merely, that there is less honor among thieves than was supposed, and not the fact that they are thieves.

As I had no opportunity to express my thoughts at that meeting, will you allow me to do so here?

Again[5] it happens that the Boston Court House is full of armed men, holding prisoner and trying a MAN, to find out if he is not really a SLAVE. Does any one think that Justice or God awaits Mr. Loring's decision?[6] For him to sit there deciding still, when this question is already decided from eternity to eternity, and the unlettered slave himself, and the multitude around, have long since heard and assented to the decision, is simply to make himself ridiculous. We may be tempted to ask from whom he received his commission, and who he is that received it; what novel statutes he obeys, and what precedents are to him of authority. Such an arbiter's very existence is an impertinence. We do not ask him to make up his mind, but to make up his pack.

I listen to hear the voice of a Governor, Commander-in-Chief of the forces of Massachusetts. I hear only the creaking of crickets and the hum of insects which now fill the summer air. The Governor's exploit is to review the troops on muster days. I have seen him on horseback, with his hat off, listening to a chaplain's prayer. It chances that is all I have ever seen of a Governor. I think that I could manage to get along without one. If *he* is not of the least use to prevent my being kidnapped, pray of what important use is he likely to be to me? When freedom is most endangered, he dwells in the deepest obscurity. A distinguished clergyman told me that he chose the profession of a clergyman, because it afforded the most leisure for literary pursuits. I would recommend to him the profession of a Governor.

Three years ago, also, when the Simm's tragedy was acted, I said to myself, there is such an officer, if not such a man, as the Governor of Massachusetts,—what has he been about the last fortnight? Has he had as much as he could do to keep on the fence during

---

4. Passed by Congress in 1850, the Fugitive Slave Law required that escaped slaves be returned to their masters, if necessary with assistance from state and federal troops.
5. Like Anthony Burns, another fugitive slave, Thomas Sims had been imprisoned in the Boston courthouse. On April 12, 1851, federal troops assisted his return to Savannah, Georgia, where he was publicly whipped.
6. U.S. Commissioner Edward Greely Loring, who upheld the Fugitive Slave Law. Burns was returned to Virginia on June 5, 1854.

this moral earthquake? It seemed to me that no keener satire could
have been aimed at, no more cutting insult have been offered to
that man, than just what happened—the absence of all inquiry after him in that crisis. The worst and the most I chance to know of
him is, that he did not improve that opportunity to make himself
known, and worthily known. He could at least have *resigned* himself into fame. It appeared to be forgotten that there was such a
man, or such an office. Yet no doubt he was endeavoring to fill the
gubernatorial chair all the while. He was no Governor of mine. He
did not govern me.

But at last, in the present case, the Governor was heard from. After he and the United States Government had perfectly succeeded
in robbing a poor innocent black man of his liberty for life, and, as
far as they could, of his Creator's likeness in his breast, he made a
speech to his accomplices, at a congratulatory supper!

I have read a recent law of this State, making it penal for 'any officer of the Commonwealth' to 'detain, or aid in the . . . detention,'
any where within its limits, 'of any person, for the reason that he is
claimed as a fugitive slave.'[7] Also, it was a matter of notoriety that a
writ of replevin to take the fugitive out of the custody of the United
States Marshal could not be served, for want of sufficient force to
aid the officer.[8]

I had thought that the Governor was in some sense the executive
officer of the State; that it was his business, as a Governor, to see
that the laws of the State were executed; while, as a man, he took
care that he did not, by so doing, break the laws of humanity; but
when there is any special important use for him, he is useless, or
worse than useless, and permits the laws of the State to go unexe-
cuted. Perhaps I do not know what are the duties of a Governor;
but if to be a Governor requires to subject one's self to so much ig-
nominy without remedy, if it is to put a restraint upon my manhood, I shall take care never to be Governor of Massachusetts. I
have not read far in the statutes of this Commonwealth. It is not
profitable reading. They do not always say what is true; and they do
not always mean what they say. What I am concerned to know is,
that that man's influence and authority were on the side of the
slaveholder, and not of the slave—of the guilty, and not of the innocent—of injustice, and not of justice. I never saw him of whom I
speak; indeed, I did not know that he was Governor until this event
occurred. I heard of him and Anthony Burns at the same time, and
thus, undoubtedly, most will hear of him. So far am I from being

7. One of the Massachusetts Personal Liberty Laws, this statue was passed in 1843 to prohibit the state from aiding the capture and return of slaves.
8. By state law, a writ of replevin called for a jury trial to determine the legality of holding
   a detainee. But federal authorities ignored such writs.

governed by him. I do not mean that it was any thing to his discredit that I had not heard of him, only that I heard what I did. The worst I shall say of him is, that he proved no better than the majority of his constituents would be likely to prove. In my opinion, he was not equal to the occasion.

The whole military force of the State is at the service of a Mr. Suttle,[9] a slaveholder from Virginia, to enable him to catch a man whom he calls his property; but not a soldier is offered to save a citizen of Massachusetts from being kidnapped! Is this what all these soldiers, all this *training* has been for these seventy-nine years past? Have they been trained merely to rob Mexico,[1] and carry back fugitive slaves to their masters?

These very nights, I heard the sound of a drum in our streets. There were men *training* still; and for what? I could with an effort pardon the cockerels of Concord for crowing still, for they, perchance, had not been beaten that morning; but I could not excuse this rub-a-dub of the 'trainers.' The slave was carried back by exactly such as these, i.e., by the soldier, of whom the best you can say in this connection is, that he is a fool made conspicuous by a painted coat.

Three years ago, also, just a week after the authorities of Boston assembled to carry back a perfectly innocent man, and one whom they knew to be innocent, into slavery, the inhabitants of Concord caused the bells to be rung and the cannons to be fired, to celebrate their liberty—and the courage and love of liberty of their ancestors who fought at the bridge. As if *those* three millions had fought for the right to be free themselves, but to hold in slavery three million others. Now-a-days, men wear a fool's cap, and call it a liberty cap. I do not know but there are some, who, if they were tied to a whipping-post, and could but get one hand free, would use it to ring the bells and fire the cannons, to celebrate *their* liberty. So some of my townsmen took the liberty to ring and fire; that was the extent of their freedom; and when the sound of the bells died away, their liberty died away also; when the powder was all expended, their liberty went off with the smoke.

The joke could be no broader, if the inmates of the prisons were to subscribe for all the powder to be used in such salutes, and hire the jailers to do the firing and ringing for them, while they enjoyed it through the grating.

This is what I thought about my neighbors.

Every humane and intelligent inhabitant of Concord, when he or

9. Charles Suttle, Anthony Burns's master.
1. Territory acquired through the war with Mexico (1846–48), which Thoreau protested in "Resistance to Civil Government." Seventy-nine years had passed since the Lexington and Concord battles.

she heard those bells and those cannons, thought not with pride of the events of the 19th of April, 1775, but with shame of the events of the 12th of April, 1851. But now we have half buried that old shame under a new one.

Massachusetts sat waiting Mr. Loring's decision, as if it could in any way affect her own criminality. Her crime, the most conspicuous and fatal crime of all, was permitting him to be the umpire in such a case. It was really the trial of Massachusetts. Every moment that she hesitated to set this man free—every moment that she now hesitates to atone for her crime, she is convicted. The Commissioner on her case is God; not Edward G. God, but simple God.

I wish my countrymen to consider, that whatever the human law may be, neither an individual nor a nation can ever commit the least act of injustice against the obscurest individual, without having to pay the penalty for it. A government which deliberately enacts injustice, and persists in it, will at length ever become the laughing-stock of the world.

Much has been said about American slavery, but I think that we do not even yet realize what slavery is. If I were seriously to propose to Congress to make mankind into sausages, I have no doubt that most of the members would smile at my proposition, and if any believed me to be in earnest, they would think that I proposed something much worse than Congress had ever done. But if any of them will tell me that to make a man into a sausage would be much worse,—would be any worse, than to make him into a slave,—than it was to enact the Fugitive Slave Law, I will accuse him of foolishness, of intellectual incapacity, of making a distinction without a difference. The one is just as sensible a proposition as the other.

I hear a good deal said about trampling this law under foot. Why, one need not go out of his way to do that. This law rises not to the level of the head or the reason; its natural habitat is in the dirt. It was born and bred, and has its life only in the dust and mire, on a level with the feet, and he who walks with freedom, and does not with Hindoo mercy avoid treading on every venomous reptile, will inevitably tread on it, and so trample it under foot,—and Webster,[2] its maker, with it, like the dirt-bug and its ball.

Recent events will be valuable as a criticism on the administration of justice in our midst, or, rather, as showing what are the true resources of justice in any community. It has come to this, that the friends of liberty, the friends of the slave, have shuddered when they have understood that his fate was left to the legal tribunals of the country to be decided. Free men have no faith that justice will

---

2. Daniel Webster [see n. 3, p. 244]. Webster supported the Compromise of 1850, which included the Fugitive Slave Law. "Dirt-bug": dung beetle.

be awarded in such a case; the judge may decide this way or that; it is a kind of accident, at best. It is evident that he is not a competent authority in so important a case. It is no time, then, to be judging according to his precedents, but to establish a precedent for the future. I would much rather trust to the sentiment of the people. In their vote, you would get something of some value, at least, however small; but, in the other case, only the trammelled judgment of an individual, of no significance, be it which way it might.

It is to some extent fatal to the courts, when the people are compelled to go behind them. I do not wish to believe that the courts were made for fair weather, and for very civil cases merely,—but think of leaving it to any court in the land to decide whether more than three millions of people, in this case, a sixth part of a nation, have a right to be freemen or not! But it has been left to the courts of *justice*, so-called—to the Supreme Court of the land—and, as you all know, recognizing no authority but the Constitution, it has decided that the three millions are, and shall continue to be, slaves. Such judges as these are merely the inspectors of a pick-lock and murderer's tools, to tell him whether they are in working order or not, and there they think that their responsibility ends. There was a prior case on the docket, which they, as judges appointed by God, had no right to skip, which having been justly settled, they would have been saved from this humiliation. It was the case of the murderer himself.

The law will never make men free; it is men who have got to make the law free. They are the lovers of law and order, who observe the law when the government breaks it.

Among human beings, the judge whose words seal the fate of a man furthest into eternity, is not he who merely pronounces the verdict of the law, but he, whoever he may be, who, from a love of truth, and unprejudiced by any custom or enactment of men, utters a true opinion or *sentence* concerning him. He it is that *sentences* him. Whoever has discerned truth, has received his commission from a higher source than the chiefest justice in the world, who can discern only law. He finds himself constituted judge of the judge.— Strange that it should be necessary to state such simple truths.

I am more and more convinced that, with reference to any public question, it is more important to know what the country thinks of it, than what the city thinks. The city does not *think* much. On any moral question, I would rather have the opinion of Boxboro than of Boston and New York put together. When the former speaks, I feel as if somebody *had* spoken, as if *humanity* was yet, and a reasonable being had asserted its rights,—as if some unprejudiced men among the country's hills had at length turned their attention to the subject, and by a few sensible words redeemed the reputation of the race. When, in some obscure country town, the farmers come together to a special town meeting, to express their opinion on some subject which is vexing the land, that, I think, is the true Congress, and the most respectable one that is ever assembled in the United States.

It is evident that there are, in this Commonwealth, at least, two parties, becoming more and more distinct—the party of the city, and the party of the country. I know that the country is mean enough, but I am glad to believe that there is a slight difference in her favor. But as yet, she has few, if any organs, through which to express herself. The editorials which she reads, like the news, come from the sea-board. Let us, the inhabitants of the country, cultivate self-respect. Let us not send to the city for aught more essential than our broadcloths and groceries, or, if we read the opinions of the city, let us entertain opinions of our own.

Among measures to be adopted, I would suggest to make as earnest and vigorous an assault on the Press as has already been made, and with effect, on the Church. The Church has much improved within a few years; but the Press is almost, without exception, corrupt. I believe that, in this country, the press exerts a greater and a more pernicious influence than the Church did in its worst period. We are not a religious people, but we are a nation of politicians. We do not care for the Bible, but we do care for the newspaper. At any meeting of politicians,—like that at Concord the other evening, for instance,—how impertinent it would be to quote from the Bible! how pertinent to quote from a newspaper or from the Constitution! The newspaper is a Bible which we read every morning and every afternoon, standing and sitting, riding and walking. It is a Bible which every man carries in his pocket, which lies on every table and counter, and which the mail, and thousands of missionaries, are continually dispensing. It is, in short, the only book which America has printed, and which America reads. So wide is its influence. The editor is a preacher whom you voluntarily support. Your tax is commonly one cent daily, and it costs nothing for pew hire.[3] But how many of these preachers preach the truth? I repeat the testimony of many an intelligent foreigner, as well as my own convictions, when I say, that probably no country was ever ruled by so mean a class of tyrants as, with a few noble exceptions, are the editors of the periodical press in *this* country. And as they live and rule only by their servility, and appealing to the worst, and not the better nature of man, the people who read them are in the condition of the dog that returns to his vomit.[4]

---

3. Annual rent for a church pew.
4. Proverbs 26:11: "Like a dog that returns to his vomit is a fool that repeats his folly."

The *Liberator* and the *Commonwealth* were the only papers in Boston, as far as I know, which made themselves heard in condemnation of the cowardice and meanness of the authorities of that city, as exhibited in '51. The other journals, almost without exception, by their manner of referring to and speaking of the Fugitive Slave Law, and the carrying back of the slave Simms, insulted the common sense of the country, at least. And, for the most part, they did this, one would say, because they thought so to secure the approbation of their patrons, not being aware that a sounder sentiment prevailed to any extent in the heart of the Commonwealth. I am told that some of them have improved of late; but they are still eminently time-serving.[5] Such is the character they have won.

But, thank fortune, this preacher can be even more easily reached by the weapons of the reformer than could the recreant priest. The free men of New England have only to refrain from purchasing and reading these sheets, have only to withhold their cents, to kill a score of them at once. One whom I respect told me that he purchased Mitchell's *Citizen* in the cars, and then threw it out the window. But would not his contempt have been more fatally expressed, if he had not bought it?

Are they Americans? are they New Englanders? are they inhabitants of Lexington, and Concord, and Framingham, who read and support the Boston *Post*, *Mail*, *Journal*, *Advertiser*, *Courier*, and *Times*? Are these the Flags of our Union? I am not a newspaper reader, and may omit to name the worst.

Could slavery suggest a more complete servility than some of these journals exhibit? Is there any dust which their conduct does not lick, and make fouler still with its slime? I do not know whether the Boston *Herald* is still in existence, but I remember to have seen it about the streets when Simms was carried off. Did it not act its part well—serve its master faithfully? How could it have gone lower on its belly? How can a man stoop lower than he is low? do more than put his extremities in the place of the head he has? than make his head his lower extremity? When I have taken up this paper with my cuffs turned up, I have heard the gurgling of the sewer through every column. I have felt that I was handling a paper picked out of the public gutters, a leaf from the gospel of the gambling-house, the groggery and the brothel, harmonizing with the gospel of the Merchants' Exchange.

The majority of the men of the North, and of the South, and East, and West, are not men of principle. If they vote, they do not send men to Congress on errands of humanity, but while their brothers and sisters are being scourged and hung for loving liberty, while——I might here insert all that slavery implies and is,——it is

---

5. Opportunistic, serving dominant powers.

the mismanagement of wood and iron and stone and gold which concerns them. Do what you will, O Government! with my wife and children, my mother and brother, my father and sister, I will obey your commands to the letter. It will indeed grieve me if you hurt them, if you deliver them to overseers to be hunted by hounds or to be whipped to death; but nevertheless, I will peaceably pursue my chosen calling on this fair earth, until perchance, one day, when I have put on mourning for them dead, I shall have persuaded you to relent. Such is the attitude, such are the words of Massachusetts.

Rather than do thus, I need not say what match I would touch, what system endeavor to blow up,—but as I love my life, I would side with the light, and let the dark earth roll from under me, calling my mother and my brother to follow.

I would remind my countrymen, that they are to be men first, and Americans only at a late and convenient hour. No matter how valuable law may be to protect your property, even to keep soul and body together, if it do not keep you and humanity together.

I am sorry to say, that I doubt if there is a judge in Massachusetts who is prepared to resign his office, and get his living innocently, whenever it is required of him to pass sentence under a law which is merely contrary to the law of God. I am compelled to see that they put themselves, or rather, are by character, in this respect, exactly on a level with the marine who discharges his musket in any direction he is ordered to. They are just as much tools and as little men. Certainly, they are not the more to be respected, because their master enslaves their understandings and consciences, instead of their bodies.

The judges and lawyers,—simply as such, I mean,—and all men of expediency, try this case by a very low and incompetent standard. They consider, not whether the Fugitive Slave Law is right, but whether it is what they call *constitutional*. Is virtue constitutional, or vice? Is equity constitutional, or iniquity? In important moral and vital questions like this, it is just as impertinent to ask whether a law is constitutional or not, as to ask whether it is profitable or not. They persist in being the servants of the worst of men, and not the servants of humanity. The question is not whether you or your grandfather, seventy years ago, did not enter into an agreement to serve the devil, and that service is not accordingly now due; but whether you will not now, for once and at last, serve God,—in spite of your own past recreancy, or that of your ancestor,—by obeying that eternal and only just CONSTITUTION, which He, and not any Jefferson or Adams,[6] has written in your being.

6. Thomas Jefferson (1743–1826) and John Adams (1735–1826), two members of the committee that drafted the Declaration of Independence in 1776, not the Constitution; "agreement with the devil" paraphrases *The Liberator's* view of the Constitution as a proslavery document: "a covenant with death and an agreement with hell."

The amount of it is, if the majority vote the devil to be God, the minority will live and behave accordingly, and obey the successful candidate, trusting that some time or other, by some Speaker's casting vote, perhaps, they may reinstate God. This is the highest principle I can get out of or invent for my neighbors. These men act as if they believed that they could safely slide down hill a little way— or a good way—and would surely come to a place, by and by, where they could begin to slide up again. This is expediency, or choosing that course which offers the slightest obstacles to the feet, that is, a down-hill one. But there is no such thing as accomplishing a righteous reform by the use of 'expediency.' There is no such thing as sliding up hill. In morals, the only sliders are backsliders.

Thus we steadily worship Mammon,[7] both School, and State, and Church, and the Seventh Day curse God with a tintamar from one end of the Union to the other.

Will mankind never learn that policy is not morality—that it never secures any moral right, but considers merely what is expedient? chooses the available candidate, who is invariably the devil,—and what right have his constituents to be surprised, because the devil does not behave like an angel of light? What is wanted is men, not of policy, but of probity—who recognize a higher law than the Constitution, or the decision of the majority. The fate of the country does not depend on how you vote at the polls—the worst man is as strong as the best at that game; it does not depend on what kind of paper you drop into the ballot-box once a year, but on what kind of man you drop from your chamber into the street every morning.

What should concern Massachusetts is not the Nebraska Bill, nor the Fugitive Slave Bill, but her own slaveholding and servility. Let the State dissolve her union with the slaveholder. She may wriggle and hesitate, and ask leave to read the Constitution once more; but she can find no respectable law or precedent which sanctions the continuance of such a Union for an instant.

Let each inhabitant of the State dissolve his union with her, as long as she delays to do her duty.

The events of the past month teach me to distrust Fame. I see that she does not finely discriminate, but coarsely hurrahs. She considers not the simple heroism of an action, but only as it is connected with its apparent consequences. She praises till she is hoarse the easy exploit of the Boston tea party, but will be comparatively silent about the braver and more disinterestedly heroic

---

7. Riches, worldly gain. Luke 16:13: "No servant can serve two masters; for either he will hate the one and love the other, or he will be devoted to the one and despise the other. You cannot serve God and mammon." "Tintamar": confused noise or uproar.

attack on the Boston Court-House, simply because it was unsuccessful!

Covered with disgrace, the State has sat down coolly to try for their lives and liberties the men who attempted to do its duty for it. And this is called *justice!* They who have shown that they can behave particularly well may perchance be put under bonds for *their good behavior.* They whom truth requires at present to plead guilty, are of all the inhabitants of the State, pre-eminently innocent. While the Governor, and the Mayor, and countless officers of the Commonwealth, are at large, the champions of liberty are imprisoned.

Only they are guiltless, who commit the crime of contempt of such a Court. It behoves every man to see that his influence is on the side of justice, and let the courts make their own characters. My sympathies in this case are wholly with the accused, and wholly against the accusers and their judges. Justice is sweet and musical; but injustice is harsh and discordant. The judge still sits grinding at his organ, but it yields no music, and we hear only the sound of the handle. He believes that all the music resides in the handle, and the crowd toss him their coppers the same as before.

Do you suppose that that Massachusetts which is now doing these things,—which hesitates to crown these men, some of whose lawyers, and even judges, perchance, may be driven to take refuge in some poor quibble, that they may not wholly outrage their instinctive sense of justice,—do you suppose that she is any thing but base and servile? that she is the champion of liberty?

Show me a free State, and a court truly of justice, and I will fight for them, if need be; but show me Massachusetts, and I refuse her my allegiance, and express contempt for her courts.

The effect of a good government is to make life more valuable,—of a bad one, to make it less valuable. We can afford that railroad, and all merely material stock, should lose some of its value, for that only compels us to live more simply and economically; but suppose that the value of life itself should be diminished! How can we make a less demand on man and nature, how live more economically in respect to virtue and all noble qualities, than we do? I have lived for the last month,—and I think that every man in Massachusetts capable of the sentiment of patriotism must have had a similar experience,—with the sense of having suffered a vast and indefinite loss. I did not know at first what ailed me. At last it occurred to me that what I had lost was a country. I had never respected the Government near to which I had lived, but I had foolishly thought that I might manage to live here, minding my private affairs, and forget it. For my part, my old and worthiest pursuits have lost I cannot say how much of their attraction, and I feel that my investment in life

here is worth many per cent. less since Massachusetts last deliberately sent back an innocent man, Anthony Burns, to slavery. I dwelt
before, perhaps, in the illusion that my life passed somewhere only
between heaven and hell, but now I cannot persuade myself that I
do not dwell *wholly within* hell. The site of that political organization called Massachusetts is to me morally covered with volcanic
scoriæ[8] and cinders, such as Milton describes in the infernal regions. If there is any hell more unprincipled than our rulers, and
we, the ruled, I feel curious to see it. Life itself being worth less, all
things with it, which minister to it, are worth less. Suppose you
have a small library, with pictures to adorn the walls—a garden laid
out around—and contemplate scientific and literary pursuits, &c.,
and discover all at once that your villa, with all its contents, is located in hell, and that the justice of the peace has a cloven foot and
a forked tail—do not these things suddenly lose their value in your
eyes?

I feel that, to some extent, the State has fatally interfered with
my lawful business. It has not only interrupted me in my passage
through Court street[9] on errands of trade, but it has interrupted me
and every man on his onward and upward path, on which he had
trusted soon to leave Court street far behind. What right had it to
remind me of Court street? I have found that hollow which even I
had relied on for solid.

I am surprised to see men going about their business as if nothing had happened. I say to myself—Unfortunates! they have not
heard the news. I am surprised that the man whom I just met on
horseback should be so earnest to overtake his newly-bought cows
running away—since all property is insecure—and if they do not
run away again, they may be taken away from him when he gets
them. Fool! does he not know that his seed-corn is worth less this
year—that all beneficent harvests fail as you approach the empire
of hell? No prudent man will build a stone house under these circumstances, or engage in any peaceful enterprise which it requires
a long time to accomplish. Art is as long as ever, but life is more interrupted and less available for a man's proper pursuits. It is not an
era of repose. We have used up all our inherited freedom. If we
would save our lives, we must fight for them.

I walk toward one of our ponds, but what signifies the beauty of
nature when men are base? We walk to lakes to see our serenity reflected in them; when we are not serene, we go not to them. Who
can be serene in a country where both the rulers and the ruled are

---

8. Hardened lava. Thoreau's imagery recalls the geology of Milton's hell in *Paradise Lost*,
   Book 1.
9. Site of the Boston State Courthouse, where Burns was imprisoned, a courthouse guard
   killed, and nine Massachusetts citizens arrested in the effort to rescue Burns.

without principle? The remembrance of my country spoils my walk. My thoughts are murder to the State, and involuntarily go plotting against her.

But it chanced the other day that I scented a white water-lily, and a season I had waited for had arrived. It is the emblem of purity. It bursts up so pure and fair to the eye, and so sweet to the scent, as if to show us what purity and sweetness reside in, and can be extracted from, the slime and muck of earth. I think I have plucked the first one that has opened for a mile. What confirmation of our hopes is in the fragrance of this flower! I shall not so soon despair of the world for it, notwithstanding slavery, and the cowardice and want of principle of Northern men. It suggests what kind of laws have prevailed longest and widest, and still prevail, and that the time may come when man's deeds will smell as sweet. Such is the odor which the plant emits. If Nature can compound this fragrance still annually, I shall believe her still young and full of vigor, her integrity and genius unimpaired, and that there is virtue even in man, too, who is fitted to perceive and love it. It reminds me that Nature has been partner to no Missouri Compromise. I scent no compromise in the fragrance of the water-lily. It is not a *Nymphœa Douglassii*.[1] In it, the sweet, and pure, and innocent, are wholly sundered from the obscene and baleful. I do not scent in this the time-serving irresolution of a Massachusetts Governor, nor of a Boston Mayor. So behave that the odor of your actions may enhance the general sweetness of the atmosphere, that when we behold or scent a flower, we may not be reminded how inconsistent your deeds are with it; for all odor is but one form of advertisement of a moral quality, and if fair actions had not been performed, the lily would not smell sweet. The foul slime stands for the sloth and vice of man, the decay of humanity; the fragrant flower that springs from it, for the purity and courage which are immortal.

Slavery and servility have produced no sweet-scented flower annually, to charm the senses of men, for they have no real life: they are merely a decaying and a death, offensive to all healthy nostrils. We do not complain that they *live*, but that they do not *get buried*. Let the living bury them; even they are good for manure.

---

1. An invented species. Thoreau puns on the name of Stephen A. Douglas (1813–1861), Democratic senator from Illinois, who proposed the Kansas-Nebraska Act and supported the Compromise of 1850, including the Fugitive Slave Law.

Walking[†]

I wish to speak a word for Nature, for absolute freedom and wildness, as contrasted with a freedom and culture merely civil,—to regard man as an inhabitant, or a part and parcel of Nature, rather than a member of society. I wish to make an extreme statement, if so I may make an emphatic one, for there are enough champions of civilization: the minister, and the school-committee, and every one of you will take care of that.

I have met with but one or two persons in the course of my life who understood the art of Walking, that is, of taking walks,—who had a genius, so to speak, for *sauntering*: which word is beautifully derived "from idle people who roved about the country, in the Middle Ages, and asked charity, under pretence of going *à la Sainte Terre*," to the Holy Land, till the children exclaimed, "There goes a *Sainte-Terrer*," a Saunterer,—a Holy Lander.[1] They who never go to the Holy Land in their walks, as they pretend, are indeed mere idlers and vagabonds; but they who do go there are saunterers in the good sense, such as I mean. Some, however, would derive the word from *sans terre*, without land or a home, which, therefore, in the good sense, will mean, having no particular home, but equally at home everywhere. For this is the secret of successful sauntering. He who sits still in a house all the time may be the greatest vagrant of all; but the saunterer, in the good sense, is no more vagrant than the meandering river, which is all the while sedulously seeking the shortest course to the sea. But I prefer the first, which, indeed, is the most probable derivation. For every walk is a sort of crusade, preached by some Peter the Hermit[2] in us, to go forth and reconquer this Holy Land from the hands of the Infidels.

It is true, we are but faint-hearted crusaders, even the walkers, nowadays, who undertake no persevering, never-ending enterprises. Our expeditions are but tours, and come round again at evening to

---

† Reprinted from the *Atlantic Monthly* 9.56 (June 1862): 657–74.
1. A false etymology, taken from Samuel Johnson's *A Dictionary of the English Language* (1755).
2. Pieter of Amiens (1050–1115), French monk and leader of the First Crusade.

the old hearth-side from which we set out. Half the walk is but retracing our steps. We should go forth on the shortest walk, perchance, in the spirit of undying adventure, never to return,— prepared to send back our embalmed hearts only as relics to our desolate kingdoms.[3] If you are ready to leave father and mother, and brother and sister, and wife and child and friends, and never see them again,[4]—if you have paid your debts, and made your will, and settled all your affairs, and are a free man, then you are ready for a walk.

To come down to my own experience, my companion and I, for I sometimes have a companion, take pleasure in fancying ourselves knights of a new, or rather an old, order,—not Equestrians or Chevaliers, not Ritters or Riders, but Walkers, a still more ancient and honorable class, I trust. The chivalric and heroic spirit which once belonged to the Rider seems now to reside in, or perchance to have subsided into, the Walker,—not the Knight, but Walker Errant. He is a sort of fourth estate, outside of Church and State and People.

We have felt that we almost alone hereabouts practised this noble art; though, to tell the truth, at least, if their own assertions are to be received, most of my townsmen would fain walk sometimes, as I do, but they cannot. No wealth can buy the requisite leisure, freedom, and independence, which are the capital in this profession. It comes only by the grace of God. It requires a direct dispensation from Heaven to become a walker. You must be born into the family of the Walkers. *Ambulator nascitur, non fit.*[5] Some of my townsmen, it is true, can remember and have described to me some walks which they took ten years ago, in which they were so blessed as to lose themselves for half an hour in the woods; but I know very well that they have confined themselves to the highway ever since, whatever pretensions they may make to belong to this select class. No doubt they were elevated for a moment as by the reminiscence of a previous state of existence, when even they were foresters and outlaws.

"When he came to grene wode,
In a mery mornynge,
There he herde the notes small
Of byrdes mery syngynge.

"It is ferre gone, sayd Robyn,
That I was last here;

3. The hearts of wealthy crusaders were sometimes returned to Europe, along with their remaining possessions, when their bodies could not be.
4. Thoreau alludes to Jesus' words to his disciples: "every one who has left houses or brothers or sisters or father or mother or children or lands, for my name's sake, will . . . inherit eternal life" (Matthew 19:29).
5. "The walker is born, not made;" adapted from the classical adage "Poeta [the poet] nascitur, non fit."

Me lyste a lytell for to shote
At the donne dere."[6]

I think that I cannot preserve my health and spirits, unless I
spend four hours a day at least—and it is commonly more than
that—sauntering through the woods and over the hills and fields,
absolutely free from all worldly engagements. You may safely say, A
penny for your thoughts, or a thousand pounds. When sometimes I
am reminded that the mechanics and shopkeepers stay in their
shops not only all the forenoon, but all the afternoon too, sitting
with crossed legs, so many of them,—as if the legs were made to sit
upon, and not to stand or walk upon,—I think that they deserve
some credit for not having all committed suicide long ago.

I, who cannot stay in my chamber for a single day without acquiring some rust, and when sometimes I have stolen forth for a
walk at the eleventh hour of four o'clock in the afternoon, too late
to redeem the day, when the shades of night were already beginning
to be mingled with the daylight, have felt as if I had committed
some sin to be atoned for,—I confess that I am astonished at the
power of endurance, to say nothing of the moral insensibility, of my
neighbors who confine themselves to shops and offices the whole
day for weeks and months, ay, and years almost together. I know
not what manner of stuff they are of,—sitting there now at three
o'clock in the afternoon, as if it were three o'clock in the morning.
Bonaparte may talk of the three-o'clock-in-the-morning courage,[7]
but it is nothing to the courage which can sit down cheerfully at
this hour in the afternoon over against one's self whom you have
known all the morning, to starve out a garrison to whom you are
bound by such strong ties of sympathy. I wonder that about this
time, or say between four and five o'clock in the afternoon, too late
for the morning papers and too early for the evening ones, there is
not a general explosion heard up and down the street, scattering a
legion of antiquated and house-bred notions and whims to the four
winds for an airing,—and so the evil cure itself.

How womankind, who are confined to the house still more than
men, stand it I do not know; but I have ground to suspect that most
of them do not *stand* it at all. When, early in a summer afternoon,
we have been shaking the dust of the village from the skirts of our
garments, making haste past those houses with purely Doric or
Gothic fronts, which have such an air of repose about them, my
companion whispers that probably about these times their occupants are all gone to bed. Then it is that I appreciate the beauty

6. "A Lytell Geste of Robyn Hode," in Joseph Ritson, *Robin Hood: A Collection of All the
   Ancient Poems, Songs and Ballads* (1795), 1:78, ll. 105–12.
7. See n. 7, p. 84.

and the glory of architecture, which itself never turns in, but forever stands out and erect, keeping watch over the slumberers.

No doubt temperament, and, above all, age, have a good deal to do with it. As a man grows older, his ability to sit still and follow indoor occupations increases. He grows vespertinal in his habits as the evening of life approaches, till at last he comes forth only just before sundown, and gets all the walk that he requires in half an hour.

But the walking of which I speak has nothing in it akin to taking exercise, as it is called, as the sick take medicine at stated hours,— as the swinging of dumbbells or chairs; but is itself the enterprise and adventure of the day. If you would get exercise, go in search of the springs of life. Think of a man's swinging dumbbells for his health, when those springs are bubbling up in far-off pastures unsought by him!

Moreover, you must walk like a camel, which is said to be the only beast which ruminates when walking. When a traveller asked Wordsworth's[8] servant to show him her master's study, she answered, "Here is his library, but his study is out of doors."

Living much out of doors, in the sun and wind, will no doubt produce a certain roughness of character,—will cause a thicker cuticle to grow over some of the finer qualities of our nature, as on the face and hands, or as severe manual labor robs the hands of some of their delicacy of touch. So staying in the house, on the other hand, may produce a softness and smoothness, not to say thinness of skin, accompanied by an increased sensibility to certain impressions. Perhaps we should be more susceptible to some influences important to our intellectual and moral growth, if the sun had shone and the wind blown on us a little less; and no doubt it is a nice matter to proportion rightly the thick and thin skin. But methinks that is a scurf that will fall off fast enough,—that the natural remedy is to be found in the proportion which the night bears to the day, the winter to the summer, thought to experience. There will be so much the more air and sunshine in our thoughts. The callous palms of the laborer are conversant with finer tissues of self-respect and heroism, whose touch thrills the heart, than the languid fingers of idleness. That is mere sentimentality that lies abed by day and thinks itself white, far from the tan and callus of experience.

When we walk, we naturally go to the fields and woods: what would become of us, if we walked only in a garden or a mall?[9] Even some sects of philosophers have felt the necessity of importing the woods to themselves, since they did not go to the woods. "They

8. William Wordsworth (1770–1850), English Romantic poet.
9. A shady public walk.

planted groves and walks of Platanes," where they took *subdiales ambulationes* in porticos open to the air. Of course it is of no use to direct our steps to the woods, if they do not carry us thither. I am alarmed when it happens that I have walked a mile into the woods bodily, without getting there in spirit. In my afternoon walk I would fain forget all my morning occupations and my obligations to society. But it sometimes happens that I cannot easily shake off the village. The thought of some work will run in my head, and I am not where my body is,—I am out of my senses. In my walks I would fain return to my senses. What business have I in the woods, if I am thinking of something out of the woods? I suspect myself, and cannot help a shudder, when I find myself so implicated even in what are called good works,—for this may sometimes happen.

My vicinity affords many good walks; and though for so many years I have walked almost every day, and sometimes for several days together, I have not yet exhausted them. An absolutely new prospect is a great happiness, and I can still get this any afternoon. Two or three hours' walking will carry me to as strange a country as I expect ever to see. A single farm-house which I had not seen before is sometimes as good as the dominions of the King of Dahomey.[1] There is in fact a sort of harmony discoverable between the capabilities of the landscape within a circle of ten miles' radius, or the limits of an afternoon walk, and the threescore years and ten of human life. It will never become quite familiar to you.

Nowadays almost all man's improvements, so called, as the building of houses, and the cutting down of the forest and of all large trees, simply deform the landscape, and make it more and more tame and cheap. A people who would begin by burning the fences and let the forest stand! I saw the fences half consumed, their ends lost in the middle of the prairie, and some worldly miser with a surveyor looking after his bounds, while heaven had taken place around him, and he did not see the angels going to and fro, but was looking for an old post-hole in the midst of paradise. I looked again, and saw him standing in the middle of a boggy, stygian fen, surrounded by devils, and he had found his bounds without a doubt, three little stones, where a stake had been driven, and looking nearer, I saw that the Prince of Darkness was his surveyor.

I can easily walk ten, fifteen, twenty, any number of miles, commencing at my own door, without going by any house, without crossing a road except where the fox and the mink do: first along by the river, and then the brook, and then the meadow and the wood-

---

1. Monarchs of the west African country of Dahomey (now Benin) successfully expanded their domains, from the sixteenth to the nineteenth centuries, in part by cooperating with European slave traders.

side. There are square miles in my vicinity which have no inhabitant. From many a hill I can see civilization and the abodes of man afar. The farmers and their works are scarcely more obvious than woodchucks and their burrows. Man and his affairs, church and state and school, trade and commerce, and manufacturers and agriculture, even politics, the most alarming of them all,—I am pleased to see how little space they occupy in the landscape. Politics is but a narrow field, and that still narrower highway yonder leads to it. I sometimes direct the traveller thither. If you would go to the political world, follow the great road,—follow that market-man, keep his dust in your eyes, and it will lead you straight to it; for it, too, has its place merely, and does not occupy all space. I pass from it as from a bean-field into the forest, and it is forgotten. In one half-hour I can walk off to some portion of the earth's surface where a man does not stand from one year's end to another, and there, consequently, politics are not, for they are but as the cigar-smoke of a man.

The village is the place to which the roads tend, a sort of expansion of the highway, as a lake of a river. It is the body of which roads are the arms and legs,—a trivial or quadrivial place, the thoroughfare and ordinary of travellers. The word is from the Latin *villa*, which, together with *via*, a way or more anciently *ved* and *vella*, Varro[2] derives from *veho*, to carry, because the villa is the place to and from which things are carried. They who got their living by teaming were said *vellaturam facere*. Hence, too, apparently, the Latin word *vilis* and our vile; also *villain*. This suggests what kind of degeneracy villagers are liable to. They are wayworn by the travel that goes by and over them, without travelling themselves.

Some do not walk at all; others walk in the highways; a few walk across lots. Roads are made for horses and men of business. I do not travel in them much, comparatively, because I am not in a hurry to get to any tavern or grocery or livery-stable or depot to which they lead. I am a good horse to travel, but not from choice a roadster. The landscape-painter uses the figures of men to mark a road. He would not make that use of my figure. I walk out into a Nature such as the old prophets and poets, Menu,[3] Moses, Homer, Chaucer, walked in. You may name it America, but it is not America: neither Americus Vespucius, nor Columbus, nor the rest were the discoverers of it. There is a truer account of it in mythology than in any history of America, so called, that I have seen.

However, there are a few old roads that may be trodden with profit, as if they led somewhere now that they are nearly discontin-

2. Marcus Terentius Varro. See n. 5, p. 114.
3. Or "Manu," mythical Hindu lawgiver to whom the Sanskrit "Laws of Manu," which give social, moral, and ethical precepts, are attributed.

ued. There is the Old Marlborough Road,[4] which does not go to
Marlborough now, methinks, unless that is Marlborough where it
carries me. I am the bolder to speak of it here, because I presume
that there are one or two such roads in every town.

The Old Marlborough Road.

WHERE they once dug for money,
But never found any;
Where sometimes Martial Miles
Singly files,
And Elijah Wood,
I fear for no good:
No other man,
Save Elisha Dugan,—
O man of wild habits,
Partridges and rabbits,
Who hast no cares
Only to set snares,
Who liv'st all alone,
Close to the bone,
And where life is sweetest
Constantly eatest.
When the spring stirs my blood
  With the instinct to travel,
  I can get enough gravel
On the Old Marlborough Road.
  Nobody repairs it,
  For nobody wears it;
  It is a living way,
  As the Christians say.
Not many there be
  Who enter therein,
Only the guests of the
  Irishman Quin.
What is it, what is it,
  But a direction out there,
And the bare possibility
  Of going somewhere?
  Great guide-boards of stone,
  But travellers none;
  Cenotaphs of the towns
  Named on their crowns.
  It is worth going to see

4. Road running southwest from Concord to Marlborough, Massachusetts; see the map of
    Concord, pp. xii–xiii.

Where you *might* be.
What king
Did the thing,
I am still wondering;
Set up how or when,
By what selectmen,
Gourgas or Lee,
Clark or Darby?
They 're a great endeavor
To be something forever;
Blank tablets of stone,
Where a traveller might groan,
And in one sentence
Grave[5] all that is known;
Which another might read,
In his extreme need.
I know one or two
Lines that would do,
Literature that might stand
All over the land,
Which a man could remember
Till next December,
And read again in the spring,
After the thawing.
If with fancy unfurled
    You leave your abode,
You may go round the world
    By the Old Marlborough Road.

At present, in this vicinity, the best part of the land is not private property; the landscape is not owned, and the walker enjoys comparative freedom. But possibly the day will come when it will be partitioned off into so-called pleasure-grounds, in which a few will take a narrow and exclusive pleasure only,—when fences shall be multiplied, and man-traps and other engines invented to confine men to the *public* road, and walking over the surface of God's earth shall be construed to mean trespassing on some gentleman's grounds. To enjoy a thing exclusively is commonly to exclude yourself from the true enjoyment of it. Let us improve our opportunities, then, before the evil days come.

What is it that makes it so hard sometimes to determine whither we will walk? I believe that there is a subtile magnetism in Nature, which, if we unconsciously yield to it, will direct us aright. It is not indifferent to us which way we walk. There is a right way; but we are very liable from heedlessness and stupidity to take the wrong

5. Engrave.

one. We would fain take that walk, never yet taken by us through this actual world, which is perfectly symbolical of the path which we love to travel in the interior and ideal world; and sometimes, no doubt, we find it difficult to choose our direction, because it does not yet exist distinctly in our idea.

When I go out of the house for a walk, uncertain as yet whither I will bend my steps, and submit myself to my instinct to decide for me, I find, strange and whimsical as it may seem, that I finally and inevitably settle southwest, toward some particular wood or meadow or deserted pasture or hill in that direction. My needle is slow to settle,—varies a few degrees, and does not always point due southwest, it is true, and it has good authority for this variation, but it always settles between west and south-southwest. The future lies that way to me, and the earth seems more unexhausted and richer on that side. The outline which would bound my walks would be, not a circle, but a parabola, or rather like one of those cometary orbits which have been thought to be non-returning curves, in this case opening westward, in which my house occupies the place of the sun. I turn round and round irresolute sometimes for a quarter of an hour, until I decide, for the thousandth time, that I will walk into the southwest or west. Eastward I go only by force; but westward I go free. Thither no business leads me. It is hard for me to believe that I shall find fair landscapes or sufficient wildness and freedom behind the eastern horizon. I am not excited by the prospect of a walk thither; but I believe that the forest which I see in the western horizon stretches uninterruptedly towards the setting sun, and that there are no towns nor cities in it of enough consequence to disturb me. Let me live where I will, on this side is the city, on that the wilderness, and ever I am leaving the city more and more, and withdrawing into the wilderness. I should not lay so much stress on this fact, if I did not believe that something like this is the prevailing tendency of my countrymen. I must walk toward Oregon, and not toward Europe. And that way the nation is moving, and I may say that mankind progress from east to west. Within a few years we have witnessed the phenomenon of a southeastward migration, in the settlement of Australia; but this affects us as a retrograde movement, and, judging from the moral and physical character of the first generation of Australians, has not yet proved a successful experiment. The eastern Tartars think that there is nothing west beyond Thibet. "The world ends there," say they; "beyond there is nothing but a shoreless sea."[6] It is unmitigated East where they live.

We go eastward to realize history and study the works of art and literature, retracing the steps of the race; we go westward as into

6. Évariste Régis Huc, (1813–1860), French missionary-traveler; from *Recollections of a Journey through Tartary, Thibet, and China, during the Years 1844, 1845, and 1846* (1852).

the future, with a spirit of enterprise and adventure. The Atlantic is a Lethean[7] stream, in our passage over which we have had an opportunity to forget the Old World and its institutions. If we do not succeed this time, there is perhaps one more chance for the race left before it arrives on the banks of the Styx;[8] and that is in the Lethe of the Pacific, which is three times as wide.

I know not how significant it is, or how far it is an evidence of singularity, that an individual should thus consent in his pettiest walk with the general movement of the race; but I know that something akin to the migratory instinct in birds and quadrupeds,—which, in some instances, is known to have affected the squirrel tribe, impelling them to a general and mysterious movement, in which they were seen, say some, crossing the broadest rivers, each on its particular chip, with its tail raised for a sail, and bridging narrower streams with their dead,—that something like the *furor* which affects the domestic cattle in the spring, and which is referred to a worm in their tails,—affects both nations and individuals, either perennially or from time to time. Not a flock of wild geese cackles over our town, but it to some extent unsettles the value of real estate here, and, if I were a broker, I should probably take that disturbance into account.

> "Than longen folk to gon on pilgrimages,
> And palmeres for to seken strange strondes."[9]

Every sunset which I witness inspires me with the desire to go to a West as distant and as fair as that into which the sun goes down. He appears to migrate westward daily, and tempt us to follow him. He is the Great Western Pioneer whom the nations follow. We dream all night of those mountain-ridges in the horizon, though they may be of vapor only, which were last gilded by his rays. The island of Atlantis, and the islands and gardens of the Hesperides,[1] a sort of terrestrial paradise, appear to have been the Great West of the ancients, enveloped in mystery and poetry. Who has not seen in imagination, when looking into the sunset sky, the gardens of the Hesperides, and the foundation of all those fables?

Columbus felt the westward tendency more strongly than any before. He obeyed it, and found a New World for Castile and Leon.[2] The herd of men in those days scented fresh pastures from afar.

---

7. In Greek mythology, souls who drank from the river Lethe in Hades forgot their former lives.
8. In Greek mythology, a river in Hades across which the dead were ferried.
9. Geoffrey Chaucer, "General Prologue" to *The Canterbury Tales*, 12–13.
1. In Greek mythology, seven nymphs who guarded the golden fruit of an apple tree that grew in the far West. The tree was a wedding gift to queen Hera from Gaia, goddess of Earth. Atlantis: a legendary lost island civilization described in Plato's *Timaeus*.
2. Spanish kingdoms ruled by Isabella I and Ferdinand V, who sponsored the voyages of Columbus.

"And now the sun had stretched out all the hills,
And now was dropped into the western bay;
At last *he* rose, and twitched his mantle blue;
To-morrow to fresh woods and pastures new."[3]

Where on the globe can there be found an area of equal extent with that occupied by the bulk of our States, so fertile and so rich and varied in its productions, and at the same time so habitable by the European, as this is? Michaux, who knew but part of them, says that "the species of large trees are much more numerous in North America than in Europe; in the United States there are more than one hundred and forty species that exceed thirty feet in height; in France there are but thirty that attain this size."[4] Later botanists more than confirm his observations. Humboldt[5] came to America to realize his youthful dreams of a tropical vegetation, and he beheld it in its greatest perfection in the primitive forests of the Amazon, the most gigantic wilderness on the earth, which he has so eloquently described. The geographer Guyot, himself a European, goes far- ther,—farther than I am ready to follow him; yet not when he says,—"As the plant is made for the animal, as the vegetable world is made for the animal world, America is made for the man of the Old World. . . . . The man of the Old World sets out upon his way. Leaving the highlands of Asia, he descends from station to station towards Europe. Each of his steps is marked by a new civilization superior to the preceding, by a greater power of development. Ar- rived at the Atlantic, he pauses on the shore of this unknown ocean, the bounds of which he knows not, and turns upon his footprints for an instant." When he has exhausted the rich soil of Europe, and reinvigorated himself, "then recommences his adventurous career westward as in the earliest ages." So far Guyot.[6]

From this western impulse coming in contact with the barrier of the Atlantic sprang the commerce and enterprise of modern times. The younger Michaux, in his "Travels West of the Alleghanies in 1802," says that the common inquiry in the newly settled West was, " 'From what part of the world have you come?' As if these vast and fertile regions would naturally be the place of meeting and common country of all the inhabitants of the globe."[7]

3. John Milton, "Lycidas," 190–94.
4. Francois André Michaux (see n. 4, p. 169); from *North American Sylva*.
5. Friedrich Heinrich Alexander, Baron von Humboldt (1769–1859), German naturalist and traveler.
6. Arnold Henry Guyot (1807–1884), American geographer, born in Switzerland; from *The Earth and Man: Lectures on Comparative Physical Geography, in Its Relation to the History of Mankind* (1851).
7. Francois André Michaux (see n. 4, p. 169); from *Voyage à l'Ouest des Monts Alléghanys* (1808). Michaux was the son of André Michaux (1746–1803), famous French botanist and explorer.

To use an obsolete Latin word, I might say, *Ex Oriente lux; ex Occidente* FRUX. From the East light; from the West fruit.

Sir Francis Head, an English traveller and a Governor-General of Canada, tells us that "in both the northern and southern hemispheres of the New World, Nature has not only outlined her works on a larger scale, but has painted the whole picture with brighter and more costly colors than she used in delineating and in beautifying the Old World. . . . . The heavens of America appear infinitely higher, the sky is bluer, the air is fresher, the cold is intenser, the moon looks larger, the stars are brighter, the thunder is louder, the lightning is vivider, the wind is stronger, the rain is heavier, the mountains are higher, the rivers longer, the forests bigger, the plains broader."[8] This statement will do at least to set against Buffon's account[9] of this part of the world and its productions.

Linnæus said long ago, "Nescio quæ facies *læta, glabra* plantis Americanis: I know not what there is of joyous and smooth in the aspect of American plants";[1] and I think that in this country there are no, or at most very few, *Africanæ bestiæ*, African beasts, as the Romans called them, and that in this respect also it is peculiarly fitted for the habitation of man. We are told that within three miles of the centre of the East-Indian city of Singapore, some of the inhabitants are annually carried off by tigers; but the traveller can lie down in the woods at night almost anywhere in North America without fear of wild beasts.

These are encouraging testimonies. If the moon looks larger here than in Europe, probably the sun looks larger also. If the heavens of America appear infinitely higher, and the stars brighter, I trust that these facts are symbolical of the height to which the philosophy and poetry and religion of her inhabitants may one day soar. At length, perchance, the immaterial heaven will appear as much higher to the American mind, and the intimations that star it as much brighter. For I believe that climate does thus react on man,— as there is something in the mountain-air that feeds the spirit and inspires. Will not man grow to greater perfection intellectually as well as physically under these influences? Or is it unimportant how many foggy days there are in his life? I trust that we shall be more imaginative, that our thoughts will be clearer, fresher, and more ethereal, as our sky,—our understanding more comprehen-

8. Sir Francis Bond Head (1793–1875), Lieutenant-Governor of Ontario; from *The Emigrant* (1847).
9. French naturalist Georges Louis Leclerc, Comte de Buffon (1707–1785) had argued that North American animals represented smaller, degenerated forms of those found in Europe, a theory Thomas Jefferson attempted to refute in his *Notes on the State of Virginia* (1787).
1. Carl von Linné (1707–1778), Swedish botanist and inventor of binomial classification; from *Philosophia Botanica* (1763).

sive and broader, like our plains,—our intellect generally on a
grander scale, like our thunder and lightning, our rivers and mountains and forests,—and our hearts shall even correspond in breadth
and depth and grandeur to our inland seas. Perchance there will
appear to the traveller something, he knows not what, of *læta* and
glabra, of joyous and serene, in our very faces. Else to what end
does the world go on, and why was America discovered?

To Americans I hardly need to say,—

"Westward the star of empire takes its way."[2]

As a true patriot, I should be ashamed to think that Adam in
paradise was more favorably situated on the whole than the backwoodsman in this country.

Our sympathies in Massachusetts are not confined to New England; though we may be estranged from the South, we sympathize
with the West. There is the home of the younger sons, as among
the Scandinavians they took to the sea for their inheritance. It is
too late to be studying Hebrew; it is more important to understand
even the slang of to-day.

Some months ago I went to see a panorama[3] of the Rhine. It was
like a dream of the Middle Ages. I floated down its historic stream
in something more than imagination, under bridges built by the Romans, and repaired by later heroes, past cities and castles whose
very names were music to my ears, and each of which was the subject of a legend. There were Ehrenbreitstein and Rolandseck[4] and
Coblentz,[5] which I knew only in history. They were ruins that interested me chiefly. There seemed to come up from its waters and its
vine-clad hills and valleys a hushed music as of Crusaders depart-
ing for the Holy Land. I floated along under the spell of enchant-
ment, as if I had been transported to an heroic age, and breathed
an atmosphere of chivalry.

Soon after, I went to see a panorama of the Mississippi, and as I
worked my way up the river in the light of to-day, and saw the
steamboats wooding up, counted the rising cities, gazed on the
fresh ruins of Nauvoo,[6] beheld the Indians moving west across
the stream, and, as before I had looked up the Moselle, now looked

---

2. The slogan of mid-nineteenth-century American expansionism and manifest destiny, derived from George Berkeley's famous line in "Verses on the Prospect of Planting Arts and
   Learning in America" (1752): "Westward the course of empire takes its way."
3. A large painting wound on massive rollers and unscrolled in a theater, creating the illusion that the audience was moving through space and time.
4. Castle ruins above the Rhine village of Rolandseck, traditionally associated with Charle-
   magne's knight, Roland.
5. City at the confluence of the Rhine and Moselle Rivers in western Germany; Ehrenbreitstein: a massive cliff opposite Koblenz, famous for its fortifications.
6. Town in western Illinois founded by Joseph Smith, Jr., but abandoned in 1846 when its
   Mormon population was driven westward.

up the Ohio and the Missouri, and heard the legends of Dubuque and of Wenona's Cliff,[7]—still thinking more of the future than of the past or present,—I saw that this was a Rhine stream of a different kind; that the foundations of castles were yet to be laid, and the famous bridges were yet to be thrown over the river; and I felt that *this was the heroic age itself,* though we know it not, for the hero is commonly the simplest and obscurest of men.

The West of which I speak is but another name for the Wild; and what I have been preparing to say is, that in Wildness is the preservation of the world. Every tree sends its fibres forth in search of the Wild. The cities import it at any price. Men plough and sail for it. From the forest and wilderness come the tonics and barks which brace mankind. Our ancestors were savages. The story of Romulus and Remus[8] being suckled by a wolf is not a meaningless fable. The founders of every State which has risen to eminence have drawn their nourishment and vigor from a similar wild source. It was because the children of the Empire were not suckled by the wolf that they were conquered and displaced by the children of the Northern forests who were.

I believe in the forest, and in the meadow, and in the night in which the corn grows. We require an infusion of hemlock-spruce or arbor-vitæ in our tea. There is a difference between eating and drinking for strength and from mere gluttony. The Hottentots[9] eagerly devour the marrow of the koodoo and other antelopes raw, as a matter of course. Some of our Northern Indians eat raw the marrow of the Arctic reindeer, as well as various other parts, including the summits of the antlers, as long as they are soft. And herein, perchance, they have stolen a march on the cooks of Paris. They get what usually goes to feed the fire. This is probably better than stall-fed beef and slaughter-house pork to make a man of. Give me a wildness whose glance no civilization can endure,—as if we lived on the marrow of koodoos devoured raw.

There are some intervals which border the strain of the woodthrush, to which I would migrate,—wild lands where no settler has squatted; to which, methinks, I am already acclimated.

The African hunter Cumming tells us that the skin of the eland, as well as that of most other antelopes just killed, emits the most delicious perfume of trees and grass. I would have every man so

---

7. American Indian legends set near Dubuque, in northeastern Iowa, and the cliffs above Winona, Minnesota, on the Mississippi River.
8. In Roman mythology, twin brothers cast on the Tiber River as babies, then rescued by a she-wolf; Romulus became the founder of Rome.
9. White colonists' name for the aboriginal Khoikhoi people of southwestern Africa. Thoreau's source is *Five Years of a Hunter's Life in the Far Interior of South Africa* (1850) by Roualeyn George Gordon-Cumming, "the African hunter Cumming" below.

much like a wild antelope, so much a part and parcel of Nature, that his very person should thus sweetly advertise our senses of his presence, and remind us of those parts of Nature which he most haunts. I feel no disposition to be satirical, when the trapper's coat emits the odor of musquash[1] even; it is a sweeter scent to me than that which commonly exhales from the merchant's or the scholar's garments. When I go into their wardrobes and handle their vestments, I am reminded of no grassy plains and flowery meads which they have frequented, but of dusty merchants' exchanges and libraries rather.

A tanned skin is something more than respectable, and perhaps olive is a fitter color than white for a man,—a denizen of the woods. "The pale white man!" I do not wonder that the African pitied him. Darwin the naturalist says, "A white man bathing by the side of a Tahitian was like a plant bleached by the gardener's art, compared with a fine, dark green one, growing vigorously in the open fields."[2]

Ben Jonson[3] exclaims,—

"How near to good is what is fair!"

So I would say,—

How near to good is what is *wild!*

Life consists with wildness. The most alive is the wildest. Not yet subdued to man, its presence refreshes him. One who pressed forward incessantly and never rested from his labors, who grew fast and made infinite demands on life, would always find himself in a new country or wilderness, and surrounded by the raw material of life. He would be climbing over the prostrate stems of primitive forest-trees.

Hope and the future for me are not in lawns and cultivated fields, not in towns and cities, but in the impervious and quaking swamps. When, formerly, I have analyzed my partiality for some farm which I had contemplated purchasing, I have frequently found that I was attracted solely by a few square rods of impermeable and unfathomable bog,—a natural sink in one corner of it. That was the jewel which dazzled me. I derive more of my subsistence from the swamps which surround my native town than from the cultivated gardens in the village. There are no richer parterres[4] to my eyes than the dense beds of dwarf andromeda (*Cassandra*

1. Muskrat.
2. Charles Darwin (see n. 8, p. 12); from *Journal of Researches . . . during the Voyage of H.M.S. Beagle* (1846).
3. Ben Jonson (1574–1637), English dramatist and poet; from Jonson's masque, "Love Freed from Ignorance and Folly" 348.
4. Ornamental flower gardens with beds and paths arranged in patterns.

calyculata) which cover these tender places on the earth's surface. Botany cannot go farther than tell me the names of the shrubs which grow there,—the high-blueberry, panicled andromeda, lamb-kill, azalea, and rhodora,—all standing in the quaking sphagnum. I often think that I should like to have my house front on this mass of dull red bushes, omitting other flower plots and borders, trans-planted spruce and trim box, even gravelled walks,—to have this fertile spot under my windows, not a few imported barrow-fulls of soil only to cover the sand which was thrown out in digging the cel-lar. Why not put my house, my parlor, behind this plot, instead of behind that meagre assemblage of curiosities, that poor apology for a Nature and Art, which I call my front-yard? It is an effort to clear up and make a decent appearance when the carpenter and mason have departed, though done as much for the passer-by as the dweller within. The most tasteful front-yard fence was never an agreeable object of study to me; the most elaborate ornaments, acorn-tops, or what not, soon wearied and disgusted me. Bring your sills up to the very edge of the swamp, then, (though it may not be the best place for a dry cellar,) so that there be no access on that side to citizens. Front-yards are not made to walk in, but, at most, through, and you could go in the back way.

Yes, though you may think me perverse, if it were proposed to me to dwell in the neighborhood of the most beautiful garden that ever human art contrived, or else of a dismal swamp, I should certainly decide for the swamp. How vain, then, have been all your labors, citizens, for me!

My spirits infallibly rise in proportion to the outward dreariness. Give me the ocean, the desert, or the wilderness! In the desert, pure air and solitude compensate for want of moisture and fertility. The traveller Burton[5] says of it,—"Your *morale* improves; you be-come frank and cordial, hospitable and single-minded. . . . . In the desert, spirituous liquors excite only disgust. There is a keen enjoy-ment in a mere animal existence." They who have been travelling long on the steppes of Tartary[6] say,—"On reëntering cultivated lands, the agitation, perplexity, and turmoil of civilization oppressed and suffocated us; the air seemed to fail us, and we felt every mo-ment as if about to die of asphyxia." When I would recreate myself, I seek the darkest wood, the thickest and most interminable, and, to the citizen, most dismal swamp. I enter a swamp as a sacred place,—a *sanctum sanctorum*.[7] There is the strength, the marrow of Nature. The wild-wood covers the virgin mould,—and the same soil

5. Sir Richard Francis Burton (1821–1890), English explorer, writer, and ethnologist; from *Personal Narrative of a Pilgrimage to El Medinah and Meccah* (1856).
6. In western China and Tibet; Thoreau again quotes Father Huc's *Recollections* (see n. 6, p. 268).
7. Holy of holies.

is good for men and for trees. A man's health requires as many acres of meadow to his prospect as his farm does loads of muck. There are the strong meats on which he feeds. A town is saved, not more by the righteous men in it than by the woods and swamps, that surround it. A township where one primitive forest waves above, while another primitive forest rots below,—such a town is fitted to raise not only corn and potatoes, but poets and philosophers for the coming ages. In such a soil grew Homer and Confucius and the rest, and out of such a wilderness comes the Reformer eating locusts and wild honey.[8]

To preserve wild animals implies generally the creation of a forest for them to dwell in or resort to. So is it with man. A hundred years ago they sold bark in our streets peeled from our own woods. In the very aspect of those primitive and rugged trees, there was, methinks, a tanning principle which hardened and consolidated the fibres of men's thoughts. Ah! already I shudder for these comparatively degenerate days of my native village, when you cannot collect a load of bark of good thickness,—and we no longer produce tar and turpentine.

The civilized nations—Greece, Rome, England—have been sustained by the primitive forests which anciently rotted where they stand. They survive as long as the soil is not exhausted. Alas for human culture! little is to be expected of a nation, when the vegetable mould is exhausted, and it is compelled to make manure of the bones of its fathers. There the poet sustains himself merely by his own superfluous fat, and the philosopher comes down on his marrow-bones.

It is said to be the task of the American "to work the virgin soil," and that "agriculture here already assumes proportions unknown everywhere else."[9] I think that the farmer displaces the Indian even because he redeems the meadow, and so makes himself stronger and in some respects more natural. I was surveying for a man the other day a single straight line one hundred and thirty-two rods long, through a swamp, at whose entrance might have been written the words which Dante read over the entrance to the infernal regions,—"Leave all hope, ye that enter,"[1]—that is, of ever getting out again; where at one time I saw my employer actually up to his neck and swimming for his life in his property, though it was still winter. He had another similar swamp which I could not survey at all, because it was completely under water, and nevertheless, with regard to a third swamp, which I did *survey* from a distance, he remarked

---

8. The biblical description of John the Baptist, who "came . . . preaching in the wilderness of Judea" and whose "meat was locusts and wild honey" (Matthew 3.1–4).
9. Guyot, *Earth and Man*; see n. 6, p. 270.
1. Dante Alighieri (1265–1321), Italian poet; from *The Inferno* 3.1.9.

to me, true to his instincts, that he would not part with it for any consideration, on account of the mud which it contained. And that man intends to put a girdling ditch round the whole in the course of forty months, and so redeem it by the magic of his spade. I refer to him only as the type of a class.

The weapons with which we have gained our most important victories, which should be handed down as heirlooms from father to son, are not the sword and the lance, but the bush-whack, the turf-cutter, the spade, and the bog-hoe, rusted with the blood of many a meadow, and begrimed with the dust of many a hard-fought field. The very winds blew the Indian's cornfield into the meadow, and pointed out the way which he had not the skill to follow. He had no better implement with which to intrench himself in the land than a clamshell. But the farmer is armed with plough and spade.

In Literature it is only the wild that attracts us. Dulness is but another name for tameness. It is the uncivilized free and wild thinking in "Hamlet" and the "Iliad," in all the Scriptures and Mythologies, not learned in the schools, that delights us. As the wild duck is more swift and beautiful than the tame, so is the wild—the mallard—thought, which 'mid falling dews wings its way above the fens. A truly good book is something as natural, and as unexpectedly and unaccountably fair and perfect, as a wild flower discovered on the prairies of the West or in the jungles of the East. Genius is a light which makes the darkness visible, like the lightning's flash, which perchance shatters the temple of knowledge itself,—and not a taper lighted at the hearth-stone of the race, which pales before the light of common day.

English literature, from the days of the minstrels to the Lake Poets,[2]—Chaucer and Spenser and Milton, and even Shakespeare, included,—breathes no quite fresh and in this sense wild strain. It is an essentially tame and civilized literature, reflecting Greece and Rome. Her wilderness is a green-wood,—her wild man a Robin Hood. There is plenty of genial love of Nature, but not so much of Nature herself. Her chronicles inform us when her wild animals, but not when the wild man in her, became extinct.

The science of Humboldt is one thing, poetry is another thing. The poet to-day, notwithstanding all the discoveries of science, and the accumulated learning of mankind, enjoys no advantage over Homer.

Where is the literature which gives expression to Nature? He would be a poet who could impress the winds and streams into his service, to speak for him; who nailed words to their primitive

---

2. English Romantic poets who lived in the Lake District of northwestern England, especially William Wordsworth and Samuel Taylor Coleridge.

senses, as farmers drive down stakes in the spring, which the frost
has heaved; who derived his words as often as he used them,—
transplanted them to his page with earth adhering to their roots;
whose words were so true and fresh and natural that they would
appear to expand like the buds at the approach of spring, though
they lay half-smothered between two musty leaves in a library,—ay,
to bloom and bear fruit there, after their kind, annually, for the
faithful reader, in sympathy with surrounding Nature.

I do not know of any poetry to quote which adequately expresses
this yearning for the Wild. Approached from this side, the best poetry is tame. I do not know where to find in any literature, ancient
or modern, any account which contents me of that Nature with
which even I am acquainted. You will perceive that I demand something which no Augustan nor Elizabethan age,[3] which no *culture*, in
short, can give. Mythology comes nearer to it than anything. How
much more fertile a Nature, at least, has Grecian mythology its
root in than English literature! Mythology is the crop which the
Old World bore before its soil was exhausted, before the fancy and
imagination were affected with blight; and which it still bears,
wherever its pristine vigor is unabated. All other literatures endure
only as the elms which overshadow our houses; but this is like the
great dragon-tree[4] of the Western Isles, as old as mankind, and,
whether that does or not, will endure as long; for the decay of other
literatures makes the soil in which it thrives.

The West is preparing to add its fables to those of the East. The
valleys of the Ganges, the Nile, and the Rhine, having yielded their
crop, it remains to be seen what the valleys of the Amazon, the
Plate, the Orinoco, the St. Lawrence, and the Mississippi will produce. Perchance, when, in the course of ages, American liberty has
become a fiction of the past,—as it is to some extent a fiction of the
present,—the poets of the world will be inspired by American
mythology.

The wildest dreams of wild men, even, are not the less true,
though they may not recommend themselves to the sense which is
most common among Englishmen and Americans to-day. It is not
every truth that recommends itself to the common sense. Nature
has a place for the wild clematis as well as for the cabbage. Some
expressions of truth are reminiscent,—others merely *sensible*, as
the phrase is,—others prophetic. Some forms of disease, even, may
prophesy forms of health. The geologist has discovered that the figures of serpents, griffins, flying dragons, and other fanciful embell-
ishments of heraldry, have their prototypes in the forms of fossil

3. Golden ages in western European culture; the reigns of Augustus Caesar (63 B.C.E.–
   14 C.E.) in Rome and Elizabeth I (1533–1603) in England.
4. Massive tree, *Dracaena draco*, in the Canary Islands.

species which were extinct before man was created, and hence "indicate a faint and shadowy knowledge of a previous state of organic existence."[5] The Hindoos dreamed that the earth rested on an elephant, and the elephant on a tortoise, and the tortoise on a serpent; and though it may be an unimportant coincidence, it will not be out of place here to state, that a fossil tortoise has lately been discovered in Asia large enough to support an elephant. I confess that I am partial to these wild fancies, which transcend the order of time and development. They are the sublimest recreation of the intellect. The partridge loves peas, but not those that go with her into the pot.

In short, all good things are wild and free. There is something in a strain of music, whether produced by an instrument or by the human voice,—take the sound of a bugle in a summer night, for instance,—which by its wildness, to speak without satire, reminds me of the cries emitted by wild beasts in their native forests. It is so much of their wildness as I can understand. Give me for my friends and neighbors wild men, not tame ones. The wildness of the savage is but a faint symbol of the awful ferity with which good men and lovers meet.

I love even to see the domestic animals reassert their native rights,—any evidence that they have not wholly lost their original wild habits and vigor; as when my neighbor's cow breaks out of her pasture early in the spring and boldly swims the river, a cold, gray tide, twenty-five or thirty rods wide, swollen by the melted snow. It is the buffalo crossing the Mississippi. This exploit confers some dignity on the herd in my eyes,—already dignified. The seeds of instinct are preserved under the thick hides of cattle and horses, like seeds in the bowels of the earth, an indefinite period.

Any sportiveness in cattle is unexpected. I saw one day a herd of a dozen bullocks and cows running about and frisking in unwieldy sport, like huge rats, even like kittens. They shook their heads, raised their tails, and rushed up and down a hill, and I perceived by their horns, as well as by their activity, their relation to the deer tribe. But, alas! a sudden loud *Whoa!* would have damped their ardor at once, reduced them from venison to beef, and stiffened their sides and sinews like the locomotive. Who but the Evil One has cried, "Whoa!" to mankind? Indeed, the life of cattle, like that of many men, is but a sort of locomotiveness; they move a side at a time, and man, by his machinery, is meeting the horse and ox half-way. Whatever part the whip has touched is thenceforth palsied. Who would ever think of a *side* of any of the supple cat tribe, as we speak of a *side* of beef?

5. From Robert Hunt, *The Poetry of Science* (1850).

I rejoice that horses and steers have to be broken before they can be made the slaves of men, and that men themselves have some wild oats still left to sow before they become submissive members of society. Undoubtedly, all men are not equally fit subjects for civilization; and because the majority, like dogs and sheep, are tame by inherited disposition, this is no reason why the others should have their natures broken that they may be reduced to the same level. Men are in the main alike, but they were made several in order that they might be various. If a low use is to be served, one man will do nearly or quite as well as another; if a high one, individual excellence is to be regarded. Any man can stop a hole to keep the wind away, but no other man could serve so rare a use as the author[6] of this illustration did. Confucius says,—"The skins of the tiger and the leopard, when they are tanned, are as the skins of the dog and the sheep tanned."[7] But it is not the part of a true culture to tame tigers, any more than it is to make sheep ferocious; and tanning their skins for shoes is not the best use to which they can be put.

When looking over a list of men's names in a foreign language, as of military officers, or of authors who have written on a particular subject, I am reminded once more that there is nothing in a name. The name Menschikoff,[8] for instance, has nothing in it to my ears more human than a whisker, and it may belong to a rat. As the names of the Poles and Russians are to us, so are ours to them. It is as if they had been named by the child's rigmarole,—*Iery wiery ichery van, tittle-tol-tan.* I see in my mind a herd of wild creatures swarming over the earth, and to each the herdsman has affixed some barbarous sound in his own dialect. The names of men are of course as cheap and meaningless as *Bose* and *Tray*, the names of dogs.

Methinks it would be some advantage to philosophy, if men were named merely in the gross, as they are known. It would be necessary only to know the genus, and perhaps the race or variety, to know the individual. We are not prepared to believe that every private soldier in a Roman army had a name of his own,—because we have not supposed that he had a character of his own. At present our only true names are nicknames. I knew a boy who, from his peculiar energy, was called "Buster" by his playmates, and this rightly supplanted his Christian name. Some travellers tell us that an In-

---

6. William Shakespeare in *Hamlet*: "Imperious Caesar dead and turn'd to clay, / Might stop a hole to keep the wind away" (5.l.235).
7. *The Analects* 12.8; Thoreau quotes from Jean-Pierre-Guillaume Pauthier, *Confucius et Mencius: Les Quatre Livres de Philosophie Morale et Politique de la Chine* (1841).
8. Possibly Prince Aleksandr Sergeyevich Menshikov (1787–1869), Russian military commander and statesman.

dian had no name given him at first, but earned it, and his name was his fame; and among some tribes he acquired a new name with every new exploit. It is pitiful when a man bears a name for convenience merely, who has earned neither name nor fame.

I will not allow mere names to make distinctions for me, but still see men in herds for all them. A familiar name cannot make a man less strange to me. It may be given to a savage who retains in secret his own wild title earned in the woods. We have a wild savage in us, and a savage name is perchance somewhere recorded as ours. I see that my neighbor, who bears the familiar epithet William, or Edwin, takes it off with his jacket. It does not adhere to him when asleep or in anger, or aroused by any passion or inspiration. I seem to hear pronounced by some of his kin at such a time his original wild name in some jawbreaking or else melodious tongue.

Here is this vast, savage, howling mother of ours, Nature, lying all around, with such beauty, and such affection for her children, as the leopard; and yet we are so early weaned from her breast to society, to that culture which is exclusively an interaction of man on man,—a sort of breeding in and in, which produces at most a merely English nobility, a civilization destined to have a speedy limit.

In society, in the best institutions of men, it is easy to detect a certain precocity. When we should still be growing children, we are already little men. Give me a culture which imports much muck from the meadows, and deepens the soil,—not that which trusts to heating manures, and improved implements and modes of culture only!

Many a poor sore-eyed student that I have heard of would grow faster, both intellectually and physically, if, instead of sitting up so very late, he honestly slumbered a fool's allowance.

There may be an excess even of informing light. Niépce,[9] a Frenchman, discovered "actinism," that power in the sun's rays which produces a chemical effect,—that granite rocks, and stone structures, and statues of metal, "are all alike destructively acted upon during the hours of sunshine, and, but for provisions of Nature no less wonderful, would soon perish under the delicate touch of the most subtile of the agencies of the universe." But he observed that "those bodies which underwent this change during the daylight possessed the power of restoring themselves to their original conditions during the hours of night, when this excitement was no longer influencing them." Hence it has been inferred that "the

9. Joseph Nicéphore Niépce (1765–1833), French photographer and inventor; from Hunt, *Poetry of Science* (see n. 5, p. 279).

hours of darkness are as necessary to the inorganic creation as we
know night and sleep are to the organic kingdom." Not even does
the moon shine every night, but gives place to darkness.

I would not have every man nor every part of a man cultivated,
any more than I would have every acre of earth cultivated: part will
be tillage, but the greater part will be meadow and forest, not only
serving an immediate use, but preparing a mould against a distant
future, by the annual decay of the vegetation which it supports.

There are other letters for the child to learn than those which
Cadmus[1] invented. The Spaniards have a good term to express this
wild and dusky knowledge,—*Gramática parda*, tawny grammar,—
kind of mother-wit derived from that same leopard to which I have
referred.

We have heard of a Society for the Diffusion of Useful Knowledge.[2] It is said that knowledge is power; and the like. Methinks
there is equal need of a Society for the Diffusion of Useful Ignorance, what we will call Beautiful Knowledge, a knowledge useful
in a higher sense: for what is most of our boasted so-called knowledge but a conceit that we know something, which robs us of the
advantage of our actual ignorance? What we call knowledge is often our positive ignorance; ignorance our negative knowledge. By
long years of patient industry and reading of the newspapers—for
what are the libraries of science but files of newspapers?—a man
accumulates a myriad facts, lays them up in his memory, and then
when in some spring of his life he saunters abroad into the Great
Fields of thought, he, as it were, goes to grass like a horse, and
leaves all his harness behind in the stable. I would say to the Society for the Diffusion of Useful Knowledge, sometimes,—Go to
grass. You have eaten hay long enough. The spring has come with
its green crop. The very cows are driven to their country pastures
before the end of May; though I have heard of one unnatural
farmer who kept his cow in the barn and fed her on hay all the
year round. So, frequently, the Society for the Diffusion of Useful
Knowledge treats its cattle.

A man's ignorance sometimes is not only useful, but beautiful,—
while his knowledge, so called, is oftentimes worse than useless,
besides being ugly. Which is the best man to deal with,—he who
knows nothing about a subject, and, what is extremely rare, knows
that he knows nothing, or he who really knows something about it,
but thinks that he knows all?

My desire for knowledge is intermittent; but my desire to bathe

1. In Greek mythology, Cadmus brought the alphabet to Greece from Phoenicia.
2. Founded in England in 1826, and three years later in Boston, the Society championed
    popular education and issued inexpensive monthly treatises promoting utilitarian doc-
    trines.

my head in atmospheres unknown to my feet is perennial and constant. The highest that we can attain to is not Knowledge, but Sympathy with Intelligence. I do not know that this higher knowledge
amounts to anything more definite than a novel and grand surprise
on a sudden revelation of the insufficiency of all that we called
Knowledge before,—a discovery that there are more things in
heaven and earth than are dreamed of in our philosophy.[3] It is the
lighting up of the mist by the sun. Man cannot *know* in any higher
sense than this, any more than be can look serenely and with impunity in the face of the sun: Ὡς τὶ νοῶν, οὐ κεῖνον νοήσεις,—"You
will not perceive that, as perceiving a particular thing," say the
Chaldean Oracles.[4]

There is something servile in the habit of seeking after a law
which we may obey. We may study the laws of matter at and for our
convenience, but a successful life knows no law. It is an unfortunate discovery certainly, that of a law which binds us where we did
not know before that we were bound. Live free, child of the mist,—
and with respect to knowledge we are all children of the mist. The
man who takes the liberty to live is superior to all the laws, by
virtue of his relation to the law-maker. "That is active duty," says
the Vishnu Purana,[5] "which is not for our bondage; that is knowledge which is for our liberation: all other duty is good only unto
weariness; all other knowledge is only the cleverness of an artist."

It is remarkable how few events or crises there are in our histories; how little exercised we have been in our minds; how few experiences we have had. I would fain be assured that I am growing
apace and rankly, though my very growth disturb this dull equanimity,—though it be with struggle through long, dark, muggy nights or
seasons of gloom. It would be well, if all our lives were a divine
tragedy even, instead of this trivial comedy or farce. Dante, Bunyan,[6] and others, appear to have been exercised in their minds more
than we: they were subjected to a kind of culture such as our district schools and colleges do not contemplate. Even Mahomet,[7]
though many may scream at his name, had a good deal more to live
for, ay, and to die for, than they have commonly.

When, at rare intervals, some thought visits one, as perchance he

3. *Hamlet* l.5.166–7.
4. "The Oracles of Zoroaster," from *The Phenix: A Collection of Old and Rare Fragments*
   (1835). Zoroaster, or Zarathustra, was an ancient Iranian prophet, founder of the religion of Zoroastrianism. See n. 5, p. 74.
5. A sacred Hindu text; from James Elliot Cabot, "The Philosophy of the Ancient Hindoos,"
   Massachusetts Quarterly Review 1 (September 1848).
6. John Bunyan (1628–1688), English preacher and author of *The Pilgrim's Progress*.
   Dante: see n. 1, p. 276.
7. Muhammad (570?–632), the prophet of Islam.

is walking on a railroad, then indeed the cars go by without his
hearing them. But soon, by some inexorable law, our life goes by
and the cars return.

> "Gentle breeze, that wanderest unseen,
>   And bendest the thistles round Loira of storms,
>   Traveller of the windy glens,
>   Why hast thou left my ear so soon?"[8]

While almost all men feel an attraction drawing them to society,
few are attracted strongly to Nature. In their relation to Nature
men appear to me for the most part, notwithstanding their arts,
lower than the animals. It is not often a beautiful relation, as in the
case of the animals. How little appreciation of the beauty of the
landscape there is among us! We have to be told that the Greeks
called the world Κόσμος, Beauty, or Order, but we do not see
clearly why they did so, and we esteem it at best only a curious
philological fact.

For my part, I feel that with regard to Nature I live a sort of border life, on the confines of a world into which I make occasional
and transient forays only, and my patriotism and allegiance to the
State into whose territories I seem to retreat are those of a moss-
trooper.[9] Unto a life which I call natural I would gladly follow even
a will-o'-the-wisp through bogs and sloughs unimaginable, but no
moon nor fire-fly has shown me the causeway to it. Nature is a personality so vast and universal that we have never seen one of her
features. The walker in the familiar fields which stretch around my
native town sometimes finds himself in another land than is described in their owners' deeds, as it were in some faraway field on
the confines of the actual Concord, where her jurisdiction ceases,
and the idea which the word Concord suggests ceases to be suggested. These farms which I have myself surveyed, these bounds
which I have set up appear dimly still as through a mist; but they
have no chemistry to fix them; they fade from the surface of the
glass; and the picture which the painter painted stands out dimly
from beneath. The world with which we are commonly acquainted
leaves no trace, and it will have no anniversary.

I took a walk on Spaulding's Farm the other afternoon. I saw the
setting sun lighting up the opposite side of a stately pine wood. Its
golden rays straggled into the aisles of the wood as into some noble
hall. I was impressed as if some ancient and altogether admirable
and shining family had settled there in that part of the land called
Concord, unknown to me,—to whom the sun was servant,—who

---

8. "Ca-Lodin," 2–5, in Patrick Macgregor, *The Genuine Remains of Ossian, Literally Translated with a Preliminary Dissertation* (1841).
9. In the seventeenth century a marauder along the border of England and Scotland.

had not gone into society in the village,—who had not been called on. I saw their park, their pleasure-ground, beyond through the wood, in Spaulding's cranberry-meadow. The pines furnished them with gables as they grew. Their house was not obvious to vision; the trees grew through it. I do not know whether I heard the sounds of a suppressed hilarity or not. They seemed to recline on the sunbeams. They have sons and daughters. They are quite well. The farmer's cart-path, which leads directly through their hall, does not in the least put them out,—as the muddy bottom of a pool is sometimes seen through the reflected skies. They never heard of Spaulding, and do not know that he is their neighbor,—notwithstanding I heard him whistle as he drove his team through the house. Nothing can equal the serenity of their lives. Their coat of arms is simply a lichen. I saw it painted on the pines and oaks. Their attics were in the tops of the trees. They are of no politics. There was no noise of labor. I did not perceive that they were weaving or spinning. Yet I did detect, when the wind lulled and hearing was done away, the finest imaginable sweet musical hum,—as of a distant hive in May, which perchance was the sound of their thinking. They had no idle thoughts, and no one without could see their work, for their industry was not as in knots and excrescences embayed.

But I find it difficult to remember them. They fade irrevocably out of my mind even now while I speak and endeavor to recall them, and recollect myself. It is only after a long and serious effort to recollect my best thoughts that I become again aware of their cohabitancy. If it were not for such families as this, I think I should move out of Concord.

We are accustomed to say in New England that few and fewer pigeons visit us every year. Our forests furnish no mast[1] for them. So, it would seem, few and fewer thoughts visit each growing man from year to year, for the grove in our minds is laid waste,—sold to feed unnecessary fires of ambition, or sent to mill, and there is scarcely a twig left for them to perch on. They no longer build nor breed with us. In some more genial season, perchance, a faint shadow flits across the landscape of the mind, cast by the *wings* of some thought in its vernal or autumnal migration, but, looking up, we are unable to detect the substance of the thought itself. Our winged thoughts are turned to poultry. They no longer soar, and they attain only to a Shanghai and Cochin-China[2] grandeur. Those *gra-a-ate thoughts*, those *gra-a-ate men* you hear of!

1. Fruit of beech, oak, chestnut, and other woodland trees.
2. Breeds of poultry imported from Asia.

We hug the earth,—how rarely we mount! Methinks we might elevate ourselves a little more. We might climb a tree, at least. I found my account in climbing a tree once. It was a tall white pine, on the top of a hill; and though I got well pitched, I was well paid for it, for I discovered new mountains in the horizon which I had never seen before,—so much more of the earth and the heavens. I might have walked about the foot of the tree for threescore years and ten, and yet I certainly should never have seen them. But, above all, I discovered around me,—it was near the end of June,—on the ends of the topmost branches only, a few minute and delicate red cone-like blossoms, the fertile flower of the white pine looking heavenward. I carried straightway to the village the topmost spire, and showed it to stranger jurymen who walked the streets,—for it was court-week,—and to farmers and lumber-dealers and wood-choppers and hunters, and not one had ever seen the like before, but they wondered as at a star dropped down. Tell of ancient architects finishing their works on the tops of columns as perfectly as on the lower and more visible parts! Nature has from the first expanded the minute blossoms of the forest only toward the heavens, above men's heads and unobserved by them. We see only the flowers that are under our feet in the meadows. The pines have developed their delicate blossoms on the highest twigs of the wood every summer for ages, as well over the heads of Nature's red children as of her white ones; yet scarcely a farmer or hunter in the land has ever seen them.

Above all, we cannot afford not to live in the present. He is blessed over all mortals who loses no moment of the passing life in remembering the past. Unless our philosophy hears the cock crow in every barn-yard within our horizon, it is belated. That sound commonly reminds us that we are growing rusty and antique in our employments and habits of thought. His philosophy comes down to a more recent time than ours. There is something suggested by it that is a newer testament,—the gospel according to this moment. He has not fallen astern; he has got up early, and kept up early, and to be where he is is to be in season, in the foremost rank of time. It is an expression of the health and soundness of Nature, a brag for all the world,—healthiness as of a spring burst forth, a new fountain of the Muses,[3] to celebrate this last instant of time. Where he lives no fugitive slave laws[4] are passed. Who has not betrayed his master many times since last he heard that note?[5]

---

3. In Greek mythology, after Apollo transformed the nymph Castalia into a fountain at Delphi, whoever drank from the Castalian spring was inspired with the genius of poetry.
4. Laws requiring the return of escaped slaves to their masters, the injustice Thoreau addresses in "Slavery in Massachusetts."
5. Peter denies having known his master three times before the cock crows, as Jesus had predicted before his arrest (Matthew 26.69–75).

The merit of this bird's strain is in its freedom from all plaintiveness. The singer can easily move us to tears or to laughter, but where is he who can excite in us a pure morning joy? When, in doleful dumps, breaking the awful stillness of our wooden sidewalk on a Sunday, or, perchance, a watcher in the house of mourning, I hear a cockerel crow far or near, I think to myself, "There is one of us well, at any rate,"—and with a sudden gush return to my senses.

We had a remarkable sunset one day last November. I was walking in a meadow, the source of a small brook, when the sun at last, just before setting, after a cold gray day, reached a clear stratum in the horizon, and the softest, brightest morning sunlight fell on the dry grass and on the stems of the trees in the opposite horizon, and on the leaves of the shrub-oaks on the hill-side, while our shadows stretched long over the meadow eastward, as if we were the only motes in its beams. It was such a light as we could not have imagined a moment before, and the air also was so warm and serene that nothing was wanting to make a paradise of that meadow. When we reflected that this was not a solitary phenomenon, never to happen again, but that it would happen forever and ever an infinite number of evenings, and cheer and reassure the latest child that walked there, it was more glorious still.

The sun sets on some retired meadow, where no house is visible, with all the glory and splendor that it lavishes on cities, and, perchance, as it has never set before,—where there is but a solitary marsh-hawk to have his wings gilded by it, or only a musquash looks out from his cabin, and there is some little black-veined brook in the midst of the marsh, just beginning to meander, winding slowly round a decaying stump. We walked in so pure and bright a light, gilding the withered grass and leaves, so softly and serenely bright, I thought I had never bathed in such a golden flood, without a ripple or a murmur to it. The west side of every wood and rising ground gleamed like the boundary of Elysium,[6] and the sun on our backs seemed like a gentle herdsman driving us home at evening.

So we saunter toward the Holy Land, till one day the sun shall shine more brightly than ever he has done, shall perchance shine into our minds and hearts, and light up our whole lives with a great awakening light, as warm and serene and golden as on a bank-side in autumn.

---

6. In Greek mythology, the final resting place of heroic and virtuous souls, located by Hesiod in the far western ocean.

Wild Apples[†]

The History of the Apple-Tree

It is remarkable how closely the history of the Apple-tree is connected with that of man. The geologist tells us that the order of the *Rosaceæ*, which includes the Apple, also the true Grasses, and the *Labiatæ*, or Mints, were introduced only a short time previous to the appearance of man on the globe.[1]

It appears that apples made a part of the food of that unknown primitive people whose traces have lately been found at the bottom of the Swiss lakes, supposed to be older than the foundation of Rome, so old that they had no metallic implements. An entire black and shrivelled Crab-Apple has been recovered from their stores.

Tacitus says of the ancient Germans, that they satisfied their hunger with wild apples (*agrestia poma*) among other things.[2]

Niebuhr observes that "the words for a house, a field, a plough, ploughing, wine, oil, milk, sheep, apples, and others relating to agriculture and the gentler way of life, agree in Latin and Greek, while the Latin words for all objects pertaining to war or the chase are utterly alien from the Greek."[3] Thus the apple-tree may be considered a symbol of peace no less than the olive.

The apple was early so important, and generally distributed, that its name traced to its root in many languages signifies fruit in general. Μῆλον, in Greek, means an apple, also the fruit of other trees, also a sheep and any cattle, and finally riches in general.

The apple-tree has been celebrated by the Hebrews, Greeks, Romans, and Scandinavians. Some have thought that the first human pair were tempted by its fruit. Goddesses are fabled to have contended for it, dragons were set to watch it, and heroes were employed to pluck it.

The tree is mentioned in at least three places in the Old Testa-

---

† Reprinted from the *Atlantic Monthly* 10.61 (November 1862): 513–26.
1. Louis Agassiz (1807–1873), Harvard naturalist born in Switzerland, as cited in Hugh Miller, *The Testimony of the Rocks* (1857).
2. Cornelius Tacitus (55?–120?), Roman historian; from *De Germania in Cornelii Taciti Opera ex Recensione Io. Augusti Ernesti* (1817).
3. Barthold Georg Niebuhr (1776–1831), German philologist and historian; from *The History of Rome* (1835).

ment, and its fruit in two or three more. Solomon sings,—"As the apple-tree among the trees of the wood, so is my beloved among the sons." And again,—"Stay me with flagons, comfort me with apples." The noblest part of man's noblest feature is named from this fruit, "the apple of the eye."[4]

The apple-tree is also mentioned by Homer and Herodotus. Ulysses saw in the glorious garden of Alcinoüs "pears and pomegranates, and apple-trees bearing beautiful fruit" (καὶ μηλέαι ἀγλαόκαρποι). And according to Homer, apples were among the fruits which Tantalus could not pluck, the wind ever blowing their boughs away from him.[5] Theophrastus[6] knew and described the apple-tree as a botanist.

According to the Prose Edda,[7] "Iduna keeps in a box the apples which the gods, when they feel old age approaching, have only to taste of to become young again. It is in this manner that they will be kept in renovated youth until Ragnarök" (or the destruction of the gods).

I learn from Loudon[8] that "the ancient Welsh bards were rewarded for excelling in song by the token of the apple-spray"; and "in the Highlands of Scotland the apple-tree is the badge of the clan Lamont."

The apple-tree (Pyrus malus) belongs chiefly to the northern temperate zone. Loudon says, that "it grows spontaneously in every part of Europe except the frigid zone, and throughout Western Asia, China, and Japan." We have also two or three varieties of the apple indigenous in North America. The cultivated apple-tree was first introduced into this country by the earliest settlers, and it is thought to do as well or better here than anywhere else. Probably some of the varieties which are now cultivated were first introduced into Britain by the Romans.

Pliny,[9] adopting the distinction of Theophrastus, says,—"Of trees there are some which are altogether wild (sylvestres), some more civilized (urbaniores)." Theophrastus includes the apple among the last; and, indeed, it is in this sense the most civilized of all trees. It is as harmless as a dove, as beautiful as a rose, and as valuable as flocks and herds. It has been longer cultivated than any other, and so is more humanized; and who knows but, like the dog, it will at length be no longer traceable to its wild original? It migrates with

---

4. Song of Solomon 2.3 and 2.5; Psalms 17.8.
5. Herodotus, fifth-century B.C.E. Greek historian; Homer, The Odyssey, 7.589; 11.585.
6. Greek philosopher and natural historian (372?–287 B.C.E.).
7. A collection of ancient Scandinavian myths; Iduna is the goddess of spring. From Snorri Sturluson, The Prose Edda in Paul Henri Mallet, Northern Antiquities (1847).
8. John Claudius Loudon (1783–1843), Scottish botanist and landscape architect; from Arboretum et Fruticetum Britannicum (1844).
9. Pliny the Elder (23–79), Roman naturalist; from Historiae Mundi (1593).

man, like the dog and horse and cow: first, perchance, from Greece to Italy, thence to England, thence to America; and our Western emigrant is still marching steadily toward the setting sun with the seeds of the apple in his pocket, or perhaps a few young trees strapped to his load. At least a million apple-trees are thus set farther westward this year than any cultivated ones grew last year. Consider how the Blossom-Week, like the Sabbath, is thus annually spreading over the prairies; for when man migrates, he carries with him not only his birds, quadrupeds, insects, vegetables, and his very sward, but his orchard also.

The leaves and tender twigs are an agreeable food to many domestic animals, as the cow, horse, sheep, and goat; and the fruit is sought after by the first, as well as by the hog. Thus there appears to have existed a natural alliance between these animals and this tree from the first. "The fruit of the Crab in the forests of France" is said to be "a great resource for the wild-boar."

Not only the Indian, but many indigenous insects, birds, and quadrupeds, welcomed the apple-tree to these shores. The tent-caterpillar saddled her eggs on the very first twig that was formed, and it has since shared her affections with the wild cherry; and the canker-worm also in a measure abandoned the elm to feed on it. As it grew apace, the blue-bird, robin, cherry-bird, king-bird, and many more, came with haste and built their nests and warbled in its boughs, and so became orchard-birds, and multiplied more than ever. It was an era in the history of their race. The downy woodpecker found such a savory morsel under its bark, that he perforated it in a ring quite round the tree, before he left it,—a thing which he had never done before, to my knowledge. It did not take the partridge long to find out how sweet its buds were, and every winter eve she flew, and still flies, from the wood, to pluck them, much to the farmer's sorrow. The rabbit, too, was not slow to learn the taste of its twigs and bark; and when the fruit was ripe, the squirrel half-rolled, half-carried it to his hole; and even the musquash crept up the bank from the brook at evening, and greedily devoured it, until he had worn a path in the grass there; and when it was frozen and thawed, the crow and the jay were glad to taste it occasionally. The owl crept into the first apple-tree that became hollow, and fairly hooted with delight, finding it just the place for him; so, settling down into it, he has remained there ever since.

My theme being the Wild Apple, I will merely glance at some of the seasons in the annual growth of the cultivated apple, and pass on to my special province.

The flowers of the apple are perhaps the most beautiful of any tree's, so copious and so delicious to both sight and scent. The walker is frequently tempted to turn and linger near some more than usually handsome one, whose blossoms are two-thirds expanded. How superior it is in these respects to the pear, whose blossoms are neither colored nor fragrant!

By the middle of July, green apples are so large as to remind us of coddling, and of the autumn. The sward is commonly strewed with little ones which fall still-born, as it were,—Nature thus thinning them for us. The Roman writer Palladius[1] said,—"If apples are inclined to fall before their time, a stone placed in a split root will retain them." Some such notion, still surviving, may account for some of the stones which we see placed to be overgrown in the forks of trees. They have a saying in Suffolk, England,—

> "At Michaelmas time, or a little before,
> Half an apple goes to the core."

Early apples begin to be ripe about the first of August; but I think that none of them are so good to eat as some to smell. One is worth more to scent your handkerchief with than any perfume which they sell in the shops. The fragrance of some fruits is not to be forgotten, along with that of flowers. Some gnarly apple which I pick up in the road reminds me by its fragrance of all the wealth of Pomona,[2]—carrying me forward to those days when they will be collected in golden and ruddy heaps in the orchards and about the cider-mills.

A week or two later, as you are going by orchards or gardens, especially in the evenings, you pass through a little region possessed by the fragrance of ripe apples, and thus enjoy them without price, and without robbing anybody.

There is thus about all natural products a certain volatile and ethereal quality which represents their highest value, and which cannot be vulgarized, or bought and sold. No mortal has ever enjoyed the perfect flavor of any fruit, and only the god-like among men begin to taste its ambrosial qualities. For nectar and ambrosia are only those fine flavors of every earthly fruit which our coarse palates fail to perceive,—just as we occupy the heaven of the gods without knowing it. When I see a particularly mean man carrying a load of fair and fragrant early apples to market, I seem to see a contest going on between him and his horse, on the one side, and the apples on the other, and, to my mind, the apples always gain it. Pliny says that apples are the heaviest of all things, and that the oxen begin to sweat at the mere sight of a load of them. Our driver begins to lose his load the moment he tries to transport them to

---

1. Rutilius Taurus Aemilianus Palladius, fourth-century Roman agricultural writer; from *Scriptores Rei Rusticae, Rei Rusticae Auctores Latine Veteres* (1595).
2. Roman goddess of fruit trees.

where they do not belong, that is, to any but the most beautiful. Though he gets out from time to time, and feels of them, and thinks they are all there, I see the stream of their evanescent and celestial qualities going to heaven from his cart, while the pulp and skin and core only are going to market. They are not apples, but pomace. Are not these still Iduna's apples, the taste of which keeps the gods forever young? and think you that they will let Loki or Tjassi carry them off to Jötunheim, while they grow wrinkled and gray? No, for Ragnarök, or the destruction of the gods, is not yet.[3]

There is another thinning of the fruit, commonly near the end of August or in September, when the ground is strewn with windfalls; and this happens especially when high winds occur after rain. In some orchards you may see fully three-quarters of the whole crop on the ground, lying in a circular form beneath the trees, yet hard and green,—or, if it is a hill-side, rolled far down the hill. However, it is an ill wind that blows nobody any good. All the country over, people are busy picking up the windfalls, and this will make them cheap for early apple-pies.

In October, the leaves falling, the apples are more distinct on the trees. I saw one year in a neighboring town some trees fuller of fruit than I remembered to have ever seen before, small yellow apples hanging over the road. The branches were gracefully drooping with their weight, like a barberry-bush, so that the whole tree acquired a new character. Even the topmost branches, instead of standing erect, spread and drooped in all directions; and there were so many poles supporting the lower ones, that they looked like pictures of banian-trees. As an old English manuscript says, "The mo appelen the tree bereth, the more sche boweth to the folk."

Surely the apple is the noblest of fruits. Let the most beautiful or the swiftest have it. That should be the "going" price of apples.

Between the fifth and twentieth of October I see the barrels lie under the trees. And perhaps I talk with one who is selecting some choice barrels to fulfil an order. He turns a specked one over many times before he leaves it out. If I were to tell what is passing in my mind, I should say that every one was specked which he had handled; for he rubs off all the bloom, and those fugacious ethereal qualities leave it. Cool evenings prompt the farmers to make haste, and at length I see only the ladders here and there left leaning against the trees.

It would be well, if we accepted these gifts with more joy and gratitude, and did not think it enough simply to put a fresh load of

3. According to Norse mythology, the evil spirit Loki and Thjassi, a giant, hid the goddess Iduna and her apple tree in a forest in Jötunheim, the land of the giants. Without Iduna's apples the gods began to age, until Loki was forced to return Iduna's tree, and their youth was restored.

compost about the tree. Some old English customs are suggestive at least. I find them described chiefly in Brand's "Popular Antiquities."[4] It appears that "on Christmas eve the farmers and their men in Devonshire take a large bowl of cider, with a toast in it, and carrying it in state to the orchard, they salute the apple-trees with much ceremony, in order to make them bear well the next season." This salutation consists in "throwing some of the cider about the roots of the tree, placing bits of the toast on the branches," and then, "encircling one of the best bearing trees in the orchard, they drink the following toast three several times:—

> 'Here's to thee, old apple-tree,
> Whence thou mayst bud, and whence thou mayst blow,
> And whence thou mayst bear apples enow!
> Hats-full! caps-full!
> Bushel, bushel, sacks-full!
> And my pockets full, too! Hurra!' "

Also what was called "apple-howling" used to be practised in various counties of England on New Year's eve. A troop of boys visited the different orchards, and, encircling the apple-trees, repeated the following words:—

> "Stand fast, root! bear well, top!
> Pray God send us a good howling crop:
> Every twig, apples big;
> Every bough, apples enow!"

"They then shout in chorus, one of the boys accompanying them on a cow's horn. During this ceremony they rap the trees with their sticks." This is called "wassailing" the trees, and is thought by some to be "a relic of the heathen sacrifice to Pomona."

Herrick[5] sings,—

> "Wassaile the trees that they may beare
> You many a plum and many a peare;
> For more or less fruits they will bring
> As you so give them wassailing."

Our poets have as yet a better right to sing of cider than of wine; but it behooves them to sing better than English Phillips[6] did, else they will do no credit to their Muse.

---

4. John Brand (1744–1806), English antiquarian; from *Observations on Popular Antiquities* (1813), Thoreau's source in this and the next two paragraphs.
5. Robert Herrick (1591–1674), English poet. From "Another" in *Hesperides* (1648); also quoted in Brand's *Popular Antiquities*.
6. John Philips (1676–1709), English poet, wrote *Cider, A Poem in Two Books* (1708), in imitation of Virgil's *Georgics*.

The Wild Apple

So much for the more civilized apple-trees (*urbaniores*, as Pliny calls them).[7] I love better to go through the old orchards of un-grafted apple-trees, at whatever season of the year,—so irregularly planted: sometimes two trees standing close together; and the rows so devious that you would think that they not only had grown while the owner was sleeping, but had been set out by him in a somnambulic state. The rows of grafted fruit will never tempt me to wander amid them like these. But I now, alas, speak rather from memory than from any recent experience, such ravages have been made!

Some soils, like a rocky tract called the Easterbrooks Country in my neighborhood, are so suited to the apple, that it will grow faster in them without any care, or if only the ground is broken up once a year, than it will in many places with any amount of care. The own-ers of this tract allow that the soil is excellent for fruit, but they say that it is so rocky that they have not patience to plough it, and that, together with the distance, is the reason why it is not cultivated. There are, or were recently, extensive orchards there standing with-out order. Nay, they spring up wild and bear well there in the midst of pines, birches, maples, and oaks. I am often surprised to see ris-ing amid these trees the rounded tops of apple-trees glowing with red or yellow fruit, in harmony with the autumnal tints of the forest.

Going up the side of a cliff about the first of November, I saw a vigorous young apple-tree, which, planted by birds or cows, had shot up amid the rocks and open woods there, and had now much fruit on it, uninjured by the frosts, when all cultivated apples were gathered. It was a rank wild growth, with many green leaves on it still, and made an impression of thorniness. The fruit was hard and green, but looked as if it would be palatable in the winter. Some was dangling on the twigs, but more half-buried in the wet leaves under the tree, or rolled far down the hill amid the rocks. The owner knows nothing of it. The day was not observed when it first blossomed, nor when it first bore fruit, unless by the chickadee. There was no dancing on the green beneath it in its honor, and now there is no hand to pluck its fruit,—which is only gnawed by squir-rels, as I perceive. It has done double duty,—not only borne this crop, but each twig has grown a foot into the air. And this is *such* fruit! bigger than many berries, we must admit, and carried home will be sound and palatable next spring. What care I for Iduna's ap-ples so long as I can get these?

7. See n. 9, p. 289.

When I go by this shrub thus late and hardy, and see its dangling fruit, I respect the tree, and I am grateful for Nature's bounty, even though I cannot eat it. Here on this rugged and woody hill-side has grown an apple-tree, not planted by man, no relic of a former orchard, but a natural growth, like the pines and oaks. Most fruits which we prize and use depend entirely on our care. Corn and grain, potatoes, peaches, melons, etc., depend altogether on our planting; but the apple emulates man's independence and enterprise. It is not simply carried, as I have said, but, like him, to some extent, it has migrated to this New World, and is even, here and there, making its way amid the aboriginal trees; just as the ox and dog and horse sometimes run wild and maintain themselves.

Even the sourest and crabbedest apple, growing in the most unfavorable position, suggests such thoughts as these, it is so noble a fruit.

The Crab

Nevertheless, *our* wild apple is wild only like myself, perchance, who belong not to the aboriginal race here, but have strayed into the woods from the cultivated stock. Wilder still, as I have said, there grows elsewhere in this country a native and aboriginal Crab-Apple, *Malus coronaria*, "whose nature has not yet been modified by cultivation." It is found from Western New-York to Minnesota, and southward. Michaux[8] says that its ordinary height "is fifteen or eighteen feet, but it is sometimes found twenty-five or thirty feet high," and that the large ones "exactly resemble the common apple-tree." "The flowers are white mingled with rose-color, and are collected in corymbs." They are remarkable for their delicious odor. The fruit, according to him, is about an inch and a half in diameter, and is intensely acid. Yet they make fine sweetmeats, and also cider of them. He concludes, that, "if, on being cultivated, it does not yield new and palatable varieties, it will at least be celebrated for the beauty of its flowers, and for the sweetness of its perfume."

I never saw the Crab-Apple till May, 1861. I had heard of it through Michaux, but more modern botanists, so far as I know, have not treated it as of any peculiar importance. Thus it was a half-fabulous tree to me. I contemplated a pilgrimage to the "Glades," a portion of Pennsylvania where it was said to grow to perfection. I thought of sending to a nursery for it, but doubted if they had it, or would distinguish it from European varieties. At last I had occasion to go to Minnesota, and on entering Michigan I be-

8. See n. 4, p. 169.

gan to notice from the cars a tree with handsome rose-colored flowers. At first I thought it some variety of thorn; but it was not long before the truth flashed on me, that this was my long-sought Crab-Apple. It was the prevailing flowering shrub or tree to be seen from the cars at that season of the year,—about the middle of May. But the cars never stopped before one, and so I was launched on the bosom of the Mississippi without having touched one, experiencing the fate of Tantalus. On arriving at St. Anthony's Falls, I was sorry to be told that I was too far north for the Crab-Apple. Nevertheless I succeeded in finding it about eight miles west of the Falls; touched it and smelled it, and secured a lingering corymb of flowers for my herbarium. This must have been near its northern limit.

How The Wild Apple Grows

But though these are indigenous, like the Indians, I doubt whether they are any hardier than those backwoodsmen among the apple-trees, which, though descended from cultivated stocks, plant themselves in distant fields and forests, where the soil is favorable to them. I know of no trees which have more difficulties to contend with, and which more sturdily resist their foes. These are the ones whose story we have to tell. It oftentimes reads thus:—

Near the beginning of May, we notice little thickets of apple-trees just springing up in the pastures where cattle have been,—as the rocky ones of our Easterbrooks Country, or the top of Nobscot Hill, in Sudbury. One or two of these perhaps survive the drought and other accidents,—their very birthplace defending them against the encroaching grass and some other dangers, at first.

> In two years' time 't had thus
>   Reached the level of the rocks,
> Admired the stretching world,
>   Nor feared the wandering flocks.
>
> But at this tender age
>   Its sufferings began:
> There came a browsing ox
>   And cut it down a span.

This time, perhaps, the ox does not notice it amid the grass; but the next year, when it has grown more stout, he recognizes it for a fellow-emigrant from the old country, the flavor of whose leaves and twigs he well knows; and though at first he pauses to welcome it, and express his surprise, and gets for answer, "The same cause that brought you here brought me,"[9] he nevertheless browses it again, reflecting, it may be, that he has some title to it.

Thus cut down annually, it does not despair; but, putting forth two short twigs for every one cut off, it spreads out low along the ground in the hollows or between the rocks, growing more stout and scrubby, until it forms, not a tree as yet, but a little pyramidal, stiff, twiggy mass, almost as solid and impenetrable as a rock. Some of the densest and most impenetrable clumps of bushes that I have ever seen, as well on account of the closeness and stubbornness of their branches as of their thorns, have been these wild-apple scrubs. They are more like the scrubby fir and black spruce on which you stand, and sometimes walk, on the tops of mountains, where cold is the demon they contend with, than anything else. No wonder they are prompted to grow thorns at last, to defend themselves against such foes. In their thorniness, however, there is no malice, only some malic acid.

The rocky pastures of the tract I have referred to—for they maintain their ground best in a rocky field—are thickly sprinkled with these little tufts, reminding you often of some rigid gray mosses or lichens, and you see thousands of little trees just springing up between them, with the seed still attached to them.

Being regularly clipped all around each year by the cows, as a hedge with shears, they are often of a perfect conical or pyramidal form, from one to four feet high, and more or less sharp, as if trimmed by the gardener's art. In the pastures on Nobscot Hill and its spurs, they make fine dark shadows when the sun is low. They are also an excellent covert from hawks for many small birds that roost and build in them. Whole flocks perch in them at night, and I have seen three robins' nests in one which was six feet in diameter.

No doubt many of these are already old trees, if you reckon from the day they were planted, but infants still when you consider their development and the long life before them. I counted the annual rings of some which were just one foot high, and as wide as high, and found that they were about twelve years old, but quite sound and thrifty! They were so low that they were unnoticed by the walker, while many of their contemporaries from the nurseries were already bearing considerable crops. But what you gain in time is perhaps in this case, too, lost in power,—that is, in the vigor of the tree. This is their pyramidal state.

The cows continue to browse them thus for twenty years or more, keeping them down and compelling them to spread, until at

9. Thoreau adapts the final line of Emerson's poem, "The Rhodora: On Being Asked, Whence Is the Flower?": "The self-same Power that brought me there brought you."

last they are so broad that they become their own fence, when some interior shoot, which their foes cannot reach, darts upward with joy: for it has not forgotten its high calling, and bears its own peculiar fruit in triumph.

Such are the tactics by which it finally defeats its bovine foes. Now, if you have watched the progress of a particular shrub, you will see that it is no longer a simple pyramid or cone, but that out of its apex there rises a sprig or two, growing more lustily perchance than an orchard-tree, since the plant now devotes the whole of its repressed energy to these upright parts. In a short time these become a small tree, an inverted pyramid resting on the apex of the other, so that the whole has now the form of a vast hour-glass. The spreading bottom, having served its purpose, finally disappears, and the generous tree permits the now harmless cows to come in and stand in its shade, and rub against and redden its trunk, which has grown in spite of them, and even to taste a part of its fruit, and so disperse the seed.

Thus the cows create their own shade and food; and the tree, its hour-glass being inverted, lives a second life, as it were.

It is an important question with some nowadays, whether you should trim young apple-trees as high as your nose or as high as your eyes. The ox trims them up as high as he can reach, and that is about the right height, I think.

In spite of wandering kine, and other adverse circumstances, that despised shrub, valued only by small birds as a covert and shelter from hawks, has its blossom-week at last, and in course of time its harvest, sincere, though small.

By the end of some October, when its leaves have fallen, I frequently see such a central sprig, whose progress I have watched, when I thought it had forgotten its destiny, as I had, bearing its first crop of small green or yellow or rosy fruit, which the cows cannot get at over the bushy and thorny hedge which surrounds it, and I make haste to taste the new and undescribed variety. We have all heard of the numerous varieties of fruit invented by Van Mons and Knight.[1] This is the system of Van Cow, and she has invented far more and more memorable varieties than both of them.

Through what hardships it may attain to bear a sweet fruit! Though somewhat small, it may prove equal, if not superior, in flavor to that which has grown in a garden,—will perchance be all the sweeter and more palatable for the very difficulties it has had to contend with. Who knows but this chance wild fruit, planted by a cow or a bird on some remote and rocky hill-side, where it is as yet

---

1. Jean-Baptiste Van Mons (1765–1842) and Thomas Andrew Knight (1759–1838), European horticulturists.

unobserved by man, may be the choicest of all its kind, and foreign potentates shall hear of it, and royal societies seek to propagate it, though the virtues of the perhaps truly crabbed owner of the soil may never be heard of,—at least, beyond the limits of his village? It was thus the Porter and the Baldwin[2] grew.

Every wild-apple shrub excites our expectation thus, somewhat as every wild child. It is perhaps, a prince in disguise. What a lesson to man! So are human beings, referred to the highest standard, the celestial fruit which they suggest and aspire to bear, browsed on by fate; and only the most persistent and strongest genius defends itself and prevails, sends a tender scion upward at last, and drops its perfect fruit on the ungrateful earth. Poets and philosophers and statesmen thus spring up in the country pastures, and outlast the hosts of unoriginal men.

Such is always the pursuit of knowledge. The celestial fruits, the golden apples of the Hesperides,[3] are ever guarded by a hundred-headed dragon which never sleeps, so that it is an Herculean labor to pluck them.[4]

This is one, and the most remarkable way, in which the wild apple is propagated; but commonly it springs up at wide intervals in woods and swamps, and by the sides of roads, as the soil may suit it, and grows with comparative rapidity. Those which grow in dense woods are very tall and slender. I frequently pluck from these trees a perfectly mild and tamed fruit. As Palladius[5] says, "*Et injussu consternitur ubere mali*": And the ground is strewn with the fruit of an unbidden apple-tree.

It is an old notion, that, if these wild trees do not bear a valuable fruit of their own, they are the best stocks by which to transmit to posterity the most highly prized qualities of others. However, I am not in search of stocks, but the wild fruit itself, whose fierce gust has suffered no "inteneration."[6] It is not my

> "highest plot
> To plant the Bergamot."[7]

---

2. Well-known apple varieties.
3. See n. 1, p. 269.
4. One of Hercules' last labors was to steal apples from the Garden of the Hesperides.
5. See n. 1, p. 291.
6. The act of softening or making tender.
7. Andrew Marvell (1621–1678), "An Horatian Ode upon Cromwell's Return from Ireland" 31–32.

The Fruit, And Its Flavor

The time for wild apples is the last of October and the first of November. They then get to be palatable, for they ripen late, and they are still perhaps as beautiful as ever. I make a great account of these fruits, which the farmers do not think it worth the while to gather,—wild flavors of the Muse, vivacious and inspiriting. The farmer thinks that he has better in his barrels, but he is mistaken, unless he has a walker's appetite and imagination, neither of which can he have.

Such as grow quite wild, and are left out till the first of November, I presume that the owner does not mean to gather. They belong to children as wild as themselves,—to certain active boys that I know,—to the wild-eyed woman of the fields, to whom nothing comes amiss, who gleans after all the world,—and, moreover, to us walkers. We have met with them, and they are ours. These rights, long enough insisted upon, have come to be an institution in some old countries, where they have learned how to live. I hear that "the custom of grippling, which may be called apple-gleaning, is, or was formerly, practised in Herefordshire. It consists in leaving a few apples, which are called the gripples, on every tree, after the general gathering, for the boys, who go with climbing-poles and bags to collect them."[8]

As for those I speak of, I pluck them as a wild fruit, native to this quarter of the earth,—fruit of old trees that have been dying ever since I was a boy and are not yet dead, frequented only by the woodpecker and the squirrel, deserted now by the owner, who has not faith enough to look under their boughs. From the appearance of the tree-top, at a little distance, you would expect nothing but lichens to drop from it, but your faith is rewarded by finding the ground strewn with spirited fruit,—some of it, perhaps, collected at squirrel-holes, with the marks of their teeth by which they carried them,—some containing a cricket or two silently feeding within, and some, especially in damp days, a shelless snail. The very sticks and stones lodged in the tree-top might have convinced you of the savoriness of the fruit which has been so eagerly sought after in past years.

I have seen no account of these among the "Fruits and Fruit-Trees of America,"[9] though they are more memorable to my taste than the grafted kinds; more racy and wild American flavors do they possess, when October and November, when December and January, and perhaps February and March even, have assuaged them

8. Loudon, Arboretum; see n. 8, p. 289.
9. Andrew Jackson Downing, The Fruits and Fruit-Trees of America (1845).

somewhat. An old farmer in my neighborhood, who always selects the right word, says that "they have a kind of bow-arrow tang."

Apples for grafting appear to have been selected commonly, not so much for their spirited flavor, as for their mildness, their size, and bearing qualities,—not so much for their beauty, as for their fairness and soundness. Indeed, I have no faith in the selected lists of pomological gentlemen. Their "Favorites" and "None-suches" and "Seek-no-farthers," when I have fruited them, commonly turn out very tame and forgetable. They are eaten with comparatively little zest, and have no real *tang* nor *smack* to them.

What if some of these wildings are acrid and puckery, genuine *verjuice*,[1] do they not still belong to the *Pomaceœ*, which are uniformly innocent and kind to our race? I still begrudge them to the cider-mill. Perhaps they are not fairly ripe yet.

No wonder that these small and high-colored apples are thought to make the best cider. Loudon quotes from the "Herefordshire Report," that "apples of a small size are always, if equal in quality, to be preferred to those of a larger size, in order that the rind and kernel may bear the greatest proportion to the pulp, which affords the weakest and most watery juice." And he says, that, "to prove this, Dr. Symonds, of Hereford, about the year 1800, made one hogshead of cider entirely from the rinds and cores of apples, and another from the pulp only, when the first was found of extraordinary strength and flavor, while the latter was sweet and insipid."[2]

Evelyn[3] says that the "Red-strake" was the favorite cider-apple in his day; and he quotes one Dr. Newburg as saying, "In Jersey 't is a general observation, as I hear, that the more of red any apple has in its rind, the more proper it is for this use. Pale-faced apples they exclude as much as may be from their cider-vat." This opinion still prevails.

All apples are good in November. Those which the farmer leaves out as unsalable, and unpalatable to those who frequent the markets, are choicest fruit to the walker. But it is remarkable that the wild apple, which I praise as so spirited and racy when eaten in the fields or woods, being brought into the house, has frequently a harsh and crabbed taste. The Saunterer's Apple not even the saunterer can eat in the house. The palate rejects it there, as it does haws and acorns, and demands a tamed one; for there you miss the November air, which is the sauce it is to be eaten with. Accordingly, when Tityrus, seeing the lengthening shadows, invites Melibœus[4]

1. The acidic juice of unripe grapes, crab-apples, or other sour fruit, made into a liquor.
2. Loudon, *Arboretum*; see n. 8, p. 289.
3. John Evelyn, *Sylva* (1679); see n. 4, p. 10.
4. Tityrus and Meliboeus are shepherds in Virgil's first *Eclogue*. In the final scene, which Thoreau quotes (lines 80–81), Tityrus, whose land has been restored following a recent civil war, offers shelter, apples, and chestnuts to Meliboeus, an exile whose flock is now dying.

to go home and pass the night with him, he promises him *mild* apples and soft chestnuts,—*mitia poma, castaneae molles.* I frequently pluck wild apples of so rich and spicy a flavor that I wonder all orchardists do not get a scion from that tree, and I fail not to bring home my pockets full. But perchance, when I take one out of my desk and taste it in my chamber, I find it unexpectedly crude,—sour enough to set a squirrel's teeth on edge and make a jay scream.

These apples have hung in the wind and frost and rain till they have absorbed the qualities of the weather or season, and thus are highly *seasoned*, and they *pierce* and *sting* and *permeate* us with their spirit. They must be eaten in *season*, accordingly,—that is, out-of-doors.

To appreciate the wild and sharp flavors of these October fruits, it is necessary that you be breathing the sharp October or November air. The out-door air and exercise which the walker gets give a different tone to his palate, and he craves a fruit which the sedentary would call harsh and crabbed. They must be eaten in the fields, when your system is all aglow with exercise, when the frosty weather nips your fingers, the wind rattles the bare boughs or rustles the few remaining leaves, and the jay is heard screaming around. What is sour in the house a bracing walk makes sweet. Some of these apples might be labelled, "To be eaten in the wind."

Of course no flavors are thrown away; they are intended for the taste that is up to them. Some apples have two distinct flavors, and perhaps one-half of them must be eaten in the house, the other outdoors. One Peter Whitney wrote from Northborough in 1782, for the Proceedings of the Boston Academy, describing an apple-tree in that town "producing fruit of opposite qualities, part of the same apple being frequently sour and the other sweet"; also some all sour, and others all sweet, and this diversity on all parts of the tree.[5]

There is a wild apple on Nawshawtuct Hill in my town which has to me a peculiarly pleasant bitter tang, not perceived till it is three-quarters tasted. It remains on the tongue. As you eat it, it smells exactly like a squash-bug. It is a sort of triumph to eat and relish it.

I hear that the fruit of a kind of plumtree in Provence is "called *Prunes sibarelles*, because it is impossible to whistle after having eaten them, from their sourness."[6] But perhaps they were only eaten in the house and in summer, and if tried out-of-doors in a stinging atmosphere, who knows but you could whistle an octave higher and clearer?

5. Peter Whitney, "An Account of a Singular Apple-Tree," *Memoirs of the American Academy of Arts and Sciences* 1 (1785).
6. Loudon, *Arboretum*; see n. 8, p. 289.

In the fields only are the sours and bitters of Nature appreciated; just as the wood-chopper eats his meal in a sunny glade, in the middle of a winter day, with content, basks in a sunny ray there and dreams of summer in a degree of cold which, experienced in a chamber, would make a student miserable. They who are at work abroad are not cold, but rather it is they who sit shivering in houses. As with temperatures, so with flavors; as with cold and heat, so with sour and sweet. This natural raciness, the sours and bitters which the diseased palate refuses, are the true condiments.

Let your condiments be in the condition of your senses. To appreciate the flavor of these wild apples requires vigorous and healthy senses, *papillae* firm and erect on the tongue and palate, not easily flattened and tamed.

From my experience with wild apples, I can understand that there may be reason for a savage's preferring many kinds of food which the civilized man rejects. The former has the palate of an out-door man. It takes a savage or wild taste to appreciate a wild fruit.

What a healthy out-of-door appetite it takes to relish the apple of life, the apple of the world, then!

> "Nor is it every apple I desire,
>   Nor that which pleases every palate best;
> 'T is not the lasting Deuxan I require,
>   Nor yet the red-cheeked Greening I request,
> Nor that which first beshrewed the name of wife,
> Nor that whose beauty caused the golden strife:
> No, no! bring me an apple from the tree of life!"[7]

So there is one *thought* for the field, another for the house. I would have my thoughts, like wild apples, to be food for walkers, and will not warrant them to be palatable, if tasted in the house.

Their Beauty

Almost all wild apples are handsome. They cannot be too gnarly and crabbed and rusty to look at. The gnarliest will have some redeeming traits even to the eye. You will discover some evening redness dashed or sprinkled on some protuberance or in some cavity. It is rare that the summer lets an apple go without streaking or spotting it on some part of its sphere. It will have some red stains, commemorating the mornings and evenings it has witnessed; some dark

---

7. Francis Quarles, *Emblems, Divine and Moral* (1825), 5.2.

and rusty blotches, in memory of the clouds and foggy, mildewy days that have passed over it; and a spacious field of green reflecting the general face of Nature,—green even as the fields; or a yellow ground, which implies a milder flavor,—yellow as the harvest, or russet as the hills.

Apples, these I mean, unspeakably fair,—apples not of Discord, but of Concord! Yet not so rare but that the homeliest may have a share. Painted by the frosts, some a uniform clear bright yellow, or red, or crimson, as if their spheres had regularly revolved, and enjoyed the influence of the sun on all sides alike,—some with the faintest pink blush imaginable,—some brindled with deep red streaks like a cow, or with hundreds of fine blood-red rays running regularly from the stem-dimple to the blossom-end, like meridional lines, on a straw-colored ground,—some touched with a greenish rust, like a fine lichen, here and there, with crimson blotches or eyes more or less confluent and fiery when wet,—and others gnarly, and freckled or peppered all over on the stem side with fine crimson spots on a white ground, as if accidentally sprinkled from the brush of Him who paints the autumn leaves. Others, again, are sometimes red inside, perfused with a beautiful blush, fairy food, too beautiful to eat,—apple of the Hesperides, apple of the evening sky! But like shells and pebbles on the sea-shore, they must be seen as they sparkle amid the withering leaves in some dell in the woods, in the autumnal air, or as they lie in the wet grass, and not when they have wilted and faded in the house.

The Naming of Them

It would be a pleasant pastime to find suitable names for the hundred varieties which go to a single heap at the cidermill. Would it not tax a man's invention,—no one to be named after a man, and all in the *lingua vernacula*?[8] Who shall stand godfather at the christening of the wild apples? It would exhaust the Latin and Greek languages, if they were used, and make the *lingua vernacula* flag. We should have to call in the sunrise and the sunset, the rainbow and the autumn woods and the wild flowers, and the woodpecker and the purple finch and the squirrel and the jay and the butterfly, the November traveller and the truant boy, to our aid.

In 1836 there were in the garden of the London Horticultural Society more than fourteen hundred distinct sorts. But here are species which they have not in their catalogue, not to mention the varieties which our Crab might yield to cultivation.

8. See n. 2, p. 183.

Let us enumerate a few of these. I find myself compelled, after all, to give the Latin names of some for the benefit of those who live where English is not spoken,—for they are likely to have a world-wide reputation.

There is, first of all, the Wood-Apple (*Malus sylvatica*); the Blue-Jay Apple; the Apple which grows in Dells in the Woods, (*sylvestrivallis*,) also in Hollows in Pastures (*campestrivallis*); the Apple that grows in an old Cellar-Hole (*Malus cellaris*); the Meadow-Apple; the Partridge-Apple; the Truant's Apple, (*Cessatoris*,) which no boy will ever go by without knocking off some, however *late* it may be; the Saunterer's Apple,—you must lose yourself before you can find the way to that; the Beauty of the Air (*Decus Aëris*); December-Eating; the Frozen-Thawed, (*gelato-soluta*,) good only in that state; the Concord Apple, possibly the same with the *Musketaquidensis*; the Assabet Apple; the Brindled Apple; Wine of New England; the Chickaree Apple; the Green Apple (*Malus viridis*);—this has many synonymes; in an imperfect state, it is the *Cholera morbifera aut dysenterifera, puerulis dilectissima*;—the Apple which Atlanta stopped to pick up; the Hedge-Apple (*Malus sepium*); the Slug-Apple (*limacea*); the Railroad-Apple, which perhaps came from a core thrown out of the cars; the Apple whose Fruit we tasted in our Youth; our Particular Apple, not to be found in any catalogue,—*Pedestrium solatium*; also the Apple where hangs the Forgotten Scythe; Iduna's Apples, and the Apples which Loki found in the Wood; and a great many more I have on my list, too numerous to mention,—all of them good. As Bodæus[9] exclaims, referring to the cultivated kinds, and adapting Virgil to his case, so I, adapting Bodæus,—

> "Not if I had a hundred tongues, a hundred mouths,
> An iron voice, could I describe all the forms
> And reckon up all the names of these *wild apples*."

The Last Gleaning

By the middle of November the wild apples have lost some of their brilliancy, and have chiefly fallen. A great part are decayed on the ground, and the sound ones are more palatable than before. The note of the chickadee sounds now more distinct, as you wander amid the old trees, and the autumnal dandelion is half-closed and tearful. But still, if you are a skilful gleaner, you may get many a pocket-full even of grafted fruit, long after apples are supposed

---

9. Johannes Bodaeus, *Theophrasti Eresii De Historia Plantarum Libri Decem, Graece et La-tine* (1644). Bodaeus adapts Virgil's *Georgics* 2: 42–44; and Thoreau substitutes "wild apples" for Bodaeus's "fruits" in the last line.

to be gone out-of-doors. I know a Blue-Pearmain tree, growing within the edge of a swamp, almost as good as wild. You would not suppose that there was any fruit left there, on the first survey, but you must look according to system. Those which lie exposed are quite brown and rotten now, or perchance a few still show one blooming cheek here and there amid the wet leaves. Nevertheless, with experienced eyes, I explore amid the bare alders and the huckleberry-bushes and the withered sedge, and in the crevices of the rocks, which are full of leaves, and pry under the fallen and decaying ferns, which, with apple and alder leaves, thickly strew the ground. For I know that they lie concealed, fallen into hollows long since and covered up by the leaves of the tree itself,—a proper kind of packing. From these lurking-places, anywhere within the circumference of the tree, I draw forth the fruit, all wet and glossy, maybe nibbled by rabbits and hollowed out by crickets and perhaps with a leaf or two cemented to it, (as Curzon[1] an old manuscript from a monastery's mouldy cellar,) but still with a rich bloom on it, and at least as ripe and well kept, if not better than those in barrels, more crisp and lively than they. If these resources fail to yield anything, I have learned to look between the bases of the suckers which spring thickly from some horizontal limb, for now and then one lodges there, or in the very midst of an alder-clump, where they are covered by leaves, safe from cows which may have smelled them out. If I am sharp-set, for I do not refuse the Blue-Pearmain, I fill my pockets on each side; and as I retrace my steps in the frosty eve, being perhaps four or five miles from home, I eat one first from this side, and then from that, to keep my balance.

I learn from Topsell's Gesner,[2] whose authority appears to be Albertus,[3] that the following is the way in which the hedgehog collects and carries home his apples. He says,—"His meat is apples, worms, or grapes: when he findeth apples or grapes on the earth, he rolleth himself upon them, until he have filled all his prickles, and then carrieth them home to his den, never bearing above one in his mouth; and if it fortune that one of them fall off by the way, he likewise shaketh off all the residue, and walloweth upon them afresh, until they be all settled upon his back again. So, forth he goeth, making a noise like a cart-wheel; and if he have any young

1. Robert Curzon, Fourteenth Baron Zouche (1810–1872), describes his discovery of rotting manuscripts in an Egyptian monastery in *The Monasteries of the Levant* (1849).
2. Edward Topsell (ca. 1572–1625), English cleric and naturalist; from *The Historie of Foure-Footed Beasts and Serpents* (1607). Topsell's work is a translation of *Historiae Animalium* (1551–87) by Konrad Gesner (1516–1565), a Swiss naturalist.
3. Albertus Magnus (1193–1280), German scholastic philosopher, theologian, and scientist.

ones in his nest, they pull off his load wherewithal he is loaded, eating thereof what they please, and laying up the residue for the time to come."

The "Frozen-Thawed" Apple

Toward the end of November, though some of the sound ones are yet more mellow and perhaps more edible, they have generally, like the leaves, lost their beauty, and are beginning to freeze. It is finger-cold, and prudent farmers get in their barrelled apples, and bring you the apples and cider which they have engaged; for it is time to put them into the cellar. Perhaps a few on the ground show their red cheeks above the early snow, and occasionally some even preserve their color and soundness under the snow throughout the winter. But generally at the beginning of the winter they freeze hard, and soon, though undecayed, acquire the color of a baked apple.

Before the end of December, generally, they experience their first thawing. Those which a month ago were sour, crabbed, and quite unpalatable to the civilized taste, such at least as were frozen while sound, let a warmer sun come to thaw them, for they are extremely sensitive to its rays, are found to be filled with a rich sweet cider, better than any bottled cider that I know of, and with which I am better acquainted than with wine. All apples are good in this state, and your jaws are the cider-press. Others, which have more substance, are a sweet and luscious food,—in my opinion of more worth than the pine-apples which are imported from the West Indies. Those which lately even I tasted only to repent of it,—for I am semi-civilized,—which the farmer willingly left on the tree, I am now glad to find have the property of hanging on like the leaves of the young oaks. It is a way to keep cider sweet without boiling. Let the frost come to freeze them first, solid as stones, and then the rain or a warm winter day to thaw them, and they will seem to have borrowed a flavor from heaven through the medium of the air in which they hang. Or perchance you find, when you get home, that those which rattled in your pocket have thawed, and the ice is turned to cider. But after the third or fourth freezing and thawing they will not be found so good.

What are the imported half-ripe fruits of the torrid South, to this fruit matured by the cold of the frigid North? These are those crabbed apples with which I cheated my companion, and kept a smooth face that I might tempt him to eat. Now we both greedily fill our pockets with them,—bending to drink the cup and save our lappets from the overflowing juice,—and grow more social with their wine. Was there one that hung so high and sheltered by the tangled branches that our sticks could not dislodge it?

It is a fruit never carried to market, that I am aware of,—quite distinct from the apple of the markets, as from dried apple and cider,—and it is not every winter that produces it in perfection.

The era of the Wild Apple will soon be past. It is a fruit which will probably become extinct in New England. You may still wander through old orchards of native fruit of great extent, which for the most part went to the cider-mill, now all gone to decay. I have heard of an orchard in a distant town, on the side of a hill, where the apples rolled down and lay four feet deep against a wall on the lower side, and this the owner cut down for fear they should be made into cider. Since the temperance reform and the general introduction of grafted fruit, no native apple-trees, such as I see everywhere in deserted pastures, and where the woods have grown up around them, are set out. I fear that he who walks over these fields a century hence will not know the pleasure of knocking off wild apples. Ah, poor man, there are many pleasures which he will not know! Notwithstanding the prevalence of the Baldwin and the Porter, I doubt if so extensive orchards are set out to-day in my town as there were a century ago, when those vast straggling cider-orchards were planted, when men both ate and drank apples, when the pomace-heap was the only nursery, and trees cost nothing but the trouble of setting them out. Men could afford then to stick a tree by every wall-side and let it take its chance. I see nobody planting trees to-day in such out-of-the-way places, along the lonely roads and lanes, and at the bottom of dells in the wood. Now that they have grafted trees, and pay a price for them, they collect them into a plat by their houses, and fence them in,—and the end of it all will be that we shall be compelled to look for our apples in a barrel.

This is "The word of the Lord that came to Joel the son of Pethuel.

"Hear this, ye old men, and give ear, all ye inhabitants of the land! Hath this been in your days, or even in the days of your fathers? . . . .

"That which the palmer-worm hath left hath the locust eaten; and that which the locust hath left hath the canker-worm eaten; and that which the canker-worm hath left hath the caterpillar eaten.

"Awake, ye drunkards, and weep! and howl, all ye drinkers of wine, because of the new wine! for it is cut off from your mouth.

"For a nation is come up upon my land, strong, and without number, whose teeth are the teeth of a lion, and he hath the cheek-teeth of a great lion.

"He hath laid my vine waste, and barked my fig-tree; he hath made it clean bare, and cast it away; the branches thereof are made white. . . . .

"Be ye ashamed, O ye husbandmen! howl, O ye vine-dressers! . . . .

"The vine is dried up, and the fig-tree languisheth; the pomegranate-tree, the palm-tree also, and the apple-tree, even all the trees of the field, are withered: because joy is withered away from the sons of men."[4]

4. Joel 1.1–2, 4–7, 11–12.

JOURNAL

THE JOURNAL AND *WALDEN*

Thoreau began keeping a journal in 1837 at the age of twenty, soon after he graduated from Harvard College, and he continued the practice until August 1861, nine months before his death. A massive work to which in the last eleven years of his life he typically devoted numerous hours a week, the Journal is at the same time an illuminating source of information about his imaginative life and published writings and a remarkable literary creation in its own right. The passages that comprise the present collection have been selected from what survives of the twenty-one journal volumes (or over forty-six hundred manuscript pages) Thoreau filled between July 1845, when he moved to Walden Pond, and May 1854, when he sent the last of his *Walden* manuscript to the printer. Although highly selective, this collection may serve to illustrate the central role played by the Journal in Thoreau's creation and recreation of his Walden experience and to suggest the complex, interdependent relation that developed between the two works-in-progress.

During the nine years in which *Walden* developed from journal reflections into lectures and then through a series of drafts, the Journal was undergoing a metamorphosis of its own.[1] Successively, and at times simultaneously, in these years the Journal assumed the forms of a source book for future writings; a draft book for *Walden* and other writing in progress; a record of daily walks and reflections, incorporating Thoreau's increasingly detailed exploration into natural and local history; and, finally, a distinct work with an aesthetic integrity and unconventional life of its own, now broadly conceived as "the record of . . . my affection for any aspect of the world" (355). In the early 1850s Thoreau recognized that as a work perpetually in process the Journal could be more faithful to the "life" he sought to represent than could any conventional literary structure assembled from Journal fragments.[2] In this sense, the Journal project became quite distinct from *Walden*. Yet, the difference between these two works can be overemphasized. To a significant degree, *Walden* turned out as it did because in these years

---

1. Seven partial manuscript versions of *Walden* were first distinguished by J. Lyndon Shanley and analyzed in *The Making of* Walden (Chicago: University of Chicago, 1957), which also prints Shanley's reconstruction of the first version of *Walden*. For two recent studies of the composition of *Walden*, see Stephen Adams and Donald A. Ross, *Revising Mythologies: The Composition of Thoreau's Major Works* (Charlottesville: University Press of Virginia, 1988), 51–63; 165–91; and Robert Sattelmeyer, "The Remaking of *Walden*," in James Barbour and Tom Quirk, eds. *Writing the American Classics* (Chapel Hill: University of North Carolina Press, 1990), 53–78, reprinted on pp. 489–507 of this volume.

2. See Sharon Cameron, *Writing Nature: Henry Thoreau's Journal* (New York: Oxford University Press, 1985) for a persuasive reading of the Journal "against" *Walden*. While acknowledging the different formal qualities and constraints in *Walden* and the Journal, H. Daniel Peck sees them (together with A *Week*) as "emergences one from another, and all of them" part of a larger project he calls Thoreau's "morning work" (x). See *Thoreau's Morning Work: Memory and Perception in* A Week on the Concord and Merrimack Rivers, *the Journal, and* Walden (New Haven: Yale University Press, 1990).

the Journal provided a means of perpetuating, even as it transformed, the *Walden* enterprise and the Walden experiment.

Two circumstances have combined to obscure the Journal's intimate relation to *Walden*: the unavailability until recently of much of the Walden-period Journal, and a prevalent misconception about the kind of work the Journal is. The misconception involves a deep-seated belief that, owing to the supposed spontaneous composition and private character of diaries and journals, this form of writing is "a mode of spontaneous utterance wholly unshaped by convention," and therefore more like a natural production than an artistic or "literary" one.[3] According to this belief, journal writing may therefore provide the stuff of which literature is made, or a useful "background" for understanding literature; but, apparently lacking the formal design of works intended for publication, this writing must be disqualified as literature itself. As a corollary of their supposed mode of production, journals and diaries may be thought as well to mirror raw experience (or "fact," or "nature") more closely. Inevitably, perhaps, this notion of the artless journal mirroring nature has especially colored understanding of a writer famous for wanting to "front" the "facts" of nature, and whose "rare descriptive powers" have long been celebrated.[4] Knowing that Thoreau kept a journal and that *Walden* is in part based on his experiences at the pond, readers have thus often assumed that in writing his book Thoreau simply drew upon the journal record of his thoughts and activities there, filling out the "account" with recollections after his return.[5]

But rather than an artless private record, free from convention, Thoreau's journal was initially, and in important ways remained, the product of a highly refined theory of journal writing shared by other members of the Transcendentalist circle in Concord, one that effectively defined the parameters of both its form and content. Moreover, because members of the circle often exchanged their journals, the writing of them was to a certain extent a public matter, certainly a social one. In Transcendentalist theory, post-Puritan self-examination and romantic self-expression combine in a conception of the primary function of journal composition as a means of giving form to those moments of insight that define the journalist's imaginative and spiritual life. The writer's journal thus bears witness to an on-going process of

---

3. Lawrence Rosenwald, *Emerson and the Art of the Diary* (New York: Oxford University Press, 1988), 21.

4. John Burroughs, *Indoor Studies* (Boston: Houghton Mifflin, 1902), 37. An example of the conclusions to which this notion has led critics is Perry Miller's influential dismissal of the mature Journal as a mere dry compilation of "facts without metaphors." Miller's reading has seemed to serve as presumptive evidence for the argument (already present in Emerson's eulogy) that Thoreau suffered a creative decline after *Walden*, and thus had "a career . . . as tragic as that of King Lear." "Thoreau in the Context of International Romanticism," *The New England Quarterly* 34 (1961): 158.

5. Shanley, for instance, in arguing for the importance of studying the *Walden* manuscript for an understanding of Thoreau's aesthetic achievement, contrasts it with the Journal as follows: "Although the journals made it clear that Thoreau added to *Walden* between 1847 and 1854, and especially after 1850, only the manuscript could reveal to how great an extent *Walden* is the result of a gradual re-creation of his experience rather than simply a recounting of that experience as he had entered it in his journal when it happened" (5).

"self-culture," or the discovery and expression of transpersonal truth in his or her deeper "nature," a process epitomized in the creation of poetry.[6] As Emerson puts it in "The Poet," "The man is only half himself, the other half is his expression."[7]

Thoreau's early journal has been aptly described as a "display case" of such self-consciously crafted thoughts and "moments."[8] But by the time he moved to Walden Pond he had learned to "winnow" for his literary compositions the kernels of insight recorded in his journal—to rely on them, that is, on "sources" in a double sense—as well as to draft new material there for immediate use.[9] Since a primary motive for moving to the Pond was to complete a draft of his first book, *A Week on the Concord and Merrimack Rivers*, hoping to build a literary reputation as well as a hut by the shore of Walden, Thoreau took with him two journal volumes to use as literary workbooks in this way. Initially, he seems to have intended to use a third volume, from which the first nine entries in the present collection are taken (319–28), as a regular dated record of his thoughts. Thoreau may well have gone to Walden with a new literary project in mind, or he may have discovered the literary potential inherent in his new pastoral standpoint after settling in. In any case, rather quickly the distinction between regular journal and draft book, between self-culture and explicitly "literary" composition, began to fade (at least as a matter of journal record) and with it the distance between Thoreau's experience and its literary representation. The Journal shows Thoreau to have begun his new work much earlier than he himself suggests in *Walden*. The "very particular inquiries . . . made by my townsmen concerning my mode of life," which he claims prompted his "simple and sincere account" in response, in actuality only provided him "a convenient rhetorical pretext for explaining the purpose of a lecture [on his life at the Pond which] he had already begun to write" in the fall of 1845.[1]

With respect to work on what was becoming *Walden*, then, the original function of the Journal as a means of cultivating inspiration and insight is transformed with Thoreau's discovery of his "present condition" as subject. And in this way the field of the Journal is also extended to the representation of his engagement with the local and natural history of Concord environs (features that will dominate the

---

6. On Transcendentalist journal-keeping, see *Journal 1: 1837–1844*, ed. Elizabeth Hall Witherell, William L. Howarth, Robert Sattelmeyer, and Thomas Blanding (Princeton University Press, 1981), 592–95; Lawrence Buell, *Literary Transcendentalism: Style and Vision in the American Renaissance* (Ithaca: Cornell University Press, 1973), 265–83; and Rosenwald, *Emerson and the Art of the Diary*, 83–98. An excellent study of Emerson's development of the doctrine of self-culture is David M. Robinson's *Apostle of Culture: Emerson as Preacher and Lecturer* (Philadelphia: University of Pennsylvania Press, 1982). For a more detailed discussion of the Journal and self-culture, see William Rossi, "The Journal, Self-Culture, and the Genesis of 'Walking,' " *Thoreau Quarterly* 16 (1984): 138–55.

7. Ralph Waldo Emerson, *Essays: Second Series*, ed. Alfred R. Ferguson and Jean Ferguson Carr (Cambridge: Harvard University Press, 1983), 4.

8. *Journal 1*, 592.

9. See *Journal 2: 1842–1848*, ed. Robert Sattelmeyer (Princeton: Princeton University Press, 1986), 452–54, and p. 329 in the Journal selections in this volume.

1. *Journal 2: 1842–1848*, 454–55; 457.

mature Journal), in, for instance, his reconstruction of former inhabitants' lives and study of the thawing sandbank (329–30, 345–47). But while the original function is transformed, it is not abandoned. The original disposition may still be seen in the close resemblance between the journal versions of several passages that end up in *Walden* and their final published form, as if Thoreau wished to preserve the bloom of that particular kind of experience the Journal was designed to help cultivate.[2] Yet, if Thoreau took care to preserve these individual kernels in his developing book manuscript (there to expand them further), he apparently did not so treasure the Journal *as* journal at this time. In preparing for publication various writings begun or continued at the Pond, he did not hesitate to remove pages from his journal as he needed them for draft.[3] Apparently, at this point Thoreau thought of his journal primarily as a collection of discrete fragments to be assembled into larger wholes in the process of winnowing them "into Lectures" and then "in due time from Lectures into Essays" (329).

But the commercial failure of *A Week on the Concord and Merrimack Rivers,* evident within a few months of its publication in May 1849, and the debt Thoreau incurred as a result, rendered the *Walden* manuscript he had been working to complete unpublishable for the time being and a conventional literary career doubtful at best. In order to make a living and still to carry out his determination to make "letters my profession," Thoreau fashioned a daily routine of reading, writing, or making pencils for the family business in the morning, while walking and occasionally surveying in the afternoon.[4] Adopting the methods of the serious naturalist he was in fact becoming, Thoreau made field notes on his daily walks, and then anywhere from a few hours to several days later he composed the scrupulously dated accounts of his rambles that characterize the mature Journal. This method appears thus to have satisfied both the working naturalist's requirements for a reliable record of detailed observations and the writer's desire for aesthetic integrity and literary vitality.[5] As a result, the Journal grew and

2. Readers who desire to locate for comparison the final (i.e., the *Walden*) version of Journal passages reprinted in the Norton Critical Edition may do so by consulting the tables of Cross-References to Published Versions in the Princeton Journal volumes beginning with *Journal 2.*

3. See the Historical Introduction and 467–75 in the Textual Introduction of *Journal 2.* In addition to much of *A Week,* two lectures on his Walden life, and a first draft of *Walden,* these various writings included a long essay on "Thomas Carlyle and His Works," published in 1847 in *Graham's American Monthly Magazine*; the excursion "Ktaadn, and the Maine Woods," published the following year in the *Union Magazine of Literature and Art*; and a lecture on each of these two topics.

4. *The Correspondence of Henry David Thoreau,* ed. Walter Harding and Carl Bode (New York: New York University Press, 1958), 249; and see Robert D. Richardson, Jr., *Henry Thoreau: A Life of the Mind* (Berkeley: University of California Press, 1986), 194–97. Thoreau describes his daily routine in a letter dated November 20, 1849 (*Correspondence,* 250–51).

5. See William L. Howarth, *The Book of Concord: Thoreau's Life as a Writer* (New York: Viking, 1982), 59–64. Both the notes and the interval Thoreau deliberately allowed to intervene between the walks and their literary representation were important. "I succeed best," he wrote in May 1852, "when I *recur* to my experience not too late, but within a day or two; when there is some distance, but enough of freshness." *The Journal of Henry D. Thoreau* (1906; New York: Dover, 1962) 4.20.

prospered. "As you *see* so at length will you *say*" (359), Thoreau told himself in November 1851. And this conviction eventually made *Walden*, as it had already begun to make the Journal, the natural beneficiary of that reciprocal deepening of perception and expression.

Considering the observation, thought, and time Thoreau committed to the Journal's keeping in the early 1850s, then, it is not surprising that he began to preserve his volumes intact, making careful indexes and numbering the volumes sequentially. Rather than removing pages for literary draft, as he had done during and for some time after his stay at Walden, he now recopied passages deemed appropriate (and in several cases apparently drafted intentionally) for *Walden* and transferred them to a separate draft-in-progress. The private success of the journal led in January 1852 to Thoreau's recognition that, rather than supplying "parts" from which "wholes" might "at last" be made, the Journal itself supplied the "proper frame" for his "disconnected thoughts" (362). While he continued to transcribe Journal passages for *Walden* and other writings intended for publication, he saw that he could never transcribe all that those passages suggested within their Journal habitat, for there they were "allied to life." "Perhaps I can never find so good a setting for my thoughts as I shall thus have taken them out of" (364). From this time on Thoreau consciously developed this Journal "setting" as an original perspective from which to view present society, history, and, especially, nature, a perspective not subject to the constraints upon vision and representation imposed by conventional literary form and by Thoreau's methods of constructing that form.[6]

But the Journal clearly continued to play a no less crucial role in furthering the *Walden* project. Indeed, that Thoreau's discovery of the Journal's unique form in January 1852 should be accompanied by renewed and intensive work on his book suggests that the independent Journal perspective helped in some way to stimulate the substantial revision and even reconception of *Walden* that followed in the next two years. At the same time, the profuse emergence of *Walden* draft in the Journal about this time also hints at a deeper, long-standing intimacy between the Walden experiment and the Journal, as does the surfacing now of the fundamental question "Why I left the woods?" (361). More than merely unable, Thoreau seems unwilling to answer this question. "Perhaps," he says, "it is none of my business—even if it is your's" (361). And no wonder. For this is the same question, or tension, that the Journal[7] had kept in play, sustaining it as a kind of "vital heat," since late 1849 or early 1850. When, in the wake of the commercial failure of *A Week*, the Journal became an integral part of the new rou-

---

For analyses of Thoreau's literary art in the mature Journal, see Howarth, *The Book of Concord*; Sharon Cameron, *Writing Nature*; Joan Burbick, *Thoreau's Alternative History: Changing Perspectives on Nature, Culture, and Language* (Philadelphia: University of Pennsylvania Press, 1987); and H. Daniel Peck, *Thoreau's Morning Work*.

6. Cameron's book presents a detailed analysis of the Journal form and language as a non-anthropocentric alternative to writing nature. See *Writing Nature*, especially 108–54.

7. Or, more precisely, the whole Journal project—the walking, natural and historical study, field notes, and journal entries—which each act of journal composition provisionally completed and furthered.

tine Thoreau then established, it became the means of perpetuating—now as a potentially revitalizing daily event—precisely the dialectic of pastoral withdrawl and return that was the Walden experiment. The complex dual perspective figured in *Walden* as that of "civilized" so-journer and perpetual Walden dweller is thus inseparable from the maintenance of that vital and necessary duality in the Journal. If, as form and project, the Journal assumed a kind of independent existence, then it did so by virtue of the germinal memory of the Walden experiment and pastoral perspective that Thoreau carried on by means of the Journal and that the Journal, as it were, carried within itself.

Finally, as an accumulating phenological record of seasonal patterns and rhythms, the Journal project fostered in Thoreau an increasingly concrete perception of the seasonal cycle of which he strove to see his own particular life as part and parcel.[8] To the working out of precise correspondences between the larger rhythms of his chosen place and those in his own life and consciousness the Journal is increasingly de-voted in the years after *Walden*. It seems appropriate, therefore, that when the time finally arrived for the book to be published, that "fact" should be registered in the Journal among other late summer phenom-ena: "Walden published. Elder berries. Waxwork yellowing" (375).

Entry dates for the following excerpted Journal passages are given in footnotes. Dates enclosed in brackets represent the Princeton Journal editors' conjectures based on proximity to dated material and other rel-evant information; unbracketed dates are Thoreau's. Thoreau's errors of spelling, grammar, and punctuation have been allowed to stand without comment unless serious ambiguity might result from doing so.

All Journal text is reprinted with permission from the following vol-umes in the Princeton University Press edition of the Writings of Henry D. Thoreau: *Journal 2: 1842–1848*, edited by Robert Sat-telmeyer (1984); *Journal 3: 1848–1851*, edited by Robert Sattelmeyer, Mark R. Patterson, and William Rossi (1990); *Journal 4: 1851–1852*, edited by Leonard N. Neufeldt and Nancy Craig Simmons (1992); *Journal 5: 1852–1853*, edited by Patrick F. O'Connell (1997); *Jour-nal 6: 1853*, edited by William Rossi and Heather Kirk Thomas (2000); *Journal 8: 1854*, edited by Sandra Harbert Petrulionis (2002); and *Journal 7: 1853–1854*, edited by Nancy Craig Simmons and Ron Thomas (in press).

---

8. See Peck, *Thoreau's Morning Work,* 42–49, 112–14.

Selections from the Journal, 1845–54[†]

[†]

Walden Sat. July 5th—45

Yesterday I came here to live. My house makes me think of some mountain houses I have seen, which seemed to have a fresher auroral atmosphere about them as I fancy of the halls of Olympus.[1] I lodged at the house of a saw-miller last summer, on the Caatskills mountains, high up as Pine orchard in the blue-berry & raspberry region, where the quiet and cleanliness & coolness seemed to be all one, which had this ambrosial character. He was the miller of the Kaaterskill Falls, They were a clean & wholesome family inside and out—like their house. The latter was not plastered—only lathed and the inner doors were not hung. The house seemed high placed, airy, and perfumed, fit to entertain a travelling God. It was so high indeed that all the music, the broken strains, the waifs & accompaniments of tunes, that swept over the ridge of the Caatskills, passed through its aisles. Could not man be man in such an abode? And would he ever find out this grovelling life?

It was the very light & atmosphere in which the works of Grecian art were composed, and in which they rest. They have appropriated to themselves a loftier hall than mortals ever occupy, at least on a level with the mountain brows of the world.

There was wanting a little of the glare of the lower vales and in its place a pure twilight as became the precincts of heaven Yet so equable and calm was the season there that you could not tell whether it was morning or noon or evening. Always there was the sound of the morning cricket

July 6th

I wish to meet the facts of life—the vital facts, which where [sic] the phenomena or actuality the Gods meant to show us,—face to

† From *Journal* by Henry David Thoreau, Vol. 2, © 1984 Princeton University Press; Vol. 3, © 1990 Princeton University Press; Vol. 4, © 1992 Princeton University Press; Vol. 5, © 1997 Princeton University Press; Vol. 6, © 2000 Princeton University Press; Vol. 7, © 2008 Princeton University Press; Vol. 8, © 2002 Princeton University Press. Reprinted by permission of the Princeton University Press.
1. Mount Olympus; in Greek mythology the residence of the gods.

face, And so I came down here. Life! who knows what it is—what it does? If I am not quite right here I am less wrong than before—and now let us see what they will have. The preacher, instead of vexing the ears of drowsy farmers on their day of rest, at the end of the week, (for sunday always seemed to me like a fit conclusion of an ill spent week and not the fresh and brave beginning of a new one) with this one other draggletail and postponed affair of a sermon, from thirdly to 15thly, should teach them with a thundering voice—pause & simplicity.

stop—Avast—Why so fast? In all studies we go not forward but rather backward with redoubled pauses, we always study *antiques*—with silence and reflection. Even time has a depth, and below its surface the waves do not lapse and roar. I wonder men can be so frivolous almost as to attend to the gross form of negro slavery—there are so many keen and subtle masters, who subject us both. Self-emancipation in the West Indies of a man's thinking and imagining provinces, which should be more than his island territory One emancipated heart & intellect—It would knock off the fetters from a million slaves.

July 7th

I am glad to remember tonight as I sit by my door that I too am at least a remote descendent of that heroic race of men of whom there is tradition. I too sit here on the shore of my Ithaca a fellow wanderer and survivor of Ulysses.[2] How Symbolical, significant of I know not what the pitch pine stands here before my door unlike any glyph I have seen sculptured or painted yet— One of nature's later designs. Yet perfect as her Grecian art. There it is, a done tree. Who can mend it? And now where is the generation of heroes whose lives are to pass amid these our northern pines? Whose exploits shall appear to posterity pictured amid these strong and shaggy forms?

Shall there be only arrows and bows to go with these pines on some pipe stone quarry at length.

If we can forget we have done somewhat, if we can remember we have done somewhat. Let us remember this

The Great spirit of course makes indifferent all times & places. The place where he is seen is always the same, and indescribably pleasant to all our senses. We had allowed only near-lying and transient circumstances to make our occasions— But nearest to all

---

2. The *Odyssey* tells of the wanderings of Odysseus (Ulysses), returning home to the island of Ithaca after the Trojan War.

things is that which fashions its being. Next to us the grandest laws are being enacted and administered.

Bread may not always nourish us, but it always does us good it even takes stiffness out of our joints and makes us supple and boyant when we knew not what ailed us—to share any heroic joy— to recognise any largeness in man or nature, to see and to know— This is all cure and prevention.

Verily a good house is a temple— A clean house—pure and undefiled, as the saying is. I have seen such made of white pine. Seasoned and seasoning still to eternity. Where a Goddess might trail her garment. The less dust we bring in to nature, the less we shall have to pick up. It was a place where one would go in, expecting to find something agreeable; as to a shade—or to a shelter—a more natural place.

I hear the far off lowing of a cow and it seems to heave the firmament. I at first thought it was the voice of a minstrel whom I know, who might be straying over hill and dale this eve—but soon I was not disappointed when it was prolonged into the sweet and natural and withal cheap tone of the cow. This youths brave music is indeed of kin with the music of the cow. They are but one articulation of nature.

Sound was made not so much for convenience, that we might hear when called, as to regale the sense—and fill one of the avenues of life. A healthy organization will never need what are commonly called the sensual gratifications, but will enjoy the daintiest feasts at those tables where there is nothing to tempt the appetite of the sensual.

There are strange affinities in this universe—strange ties stranger harmonies and relationships, what kin am I to some wildest pond among the mountains—high up ones shaggy side—in the gray morning twilight draped with mist—suspended in low wreathes from the dead willows and bare firs that stand here and there in the water, as if here were the evidence of those old contests between the land and water which we read of. But why should I find anything to welcome me in such a nook as this— This faint reflection this dim watery eye—where in some angle of the hills the woods meet the waters edge and a grey tarn lies sleeping

My beans—whose continuous length of row is 7 miles, already planted and now so impatient of be howed—not easily to be put off. What is the meaning of this service this small Hercules labor— of this small warfare—I know not. I come to love my rows—they attatch me to the earth—and so I get new strength and health like Antaeus

—My beans, so many more than I want. This has been my curious labor— Why only heaven knows—to make this surface of the earth, which yielded only blackberries & Johnswort—& cinqfoil— sweet wild fruits & pleasant flowers produce instead this pulse What shall I learn of beans or beans of me— I cherish them— I hoe them early & late I have an eye to them.— And this is my days work. It is a fine broad leaf to look upon.

My auxiliaries are the dews and rains—to water this dry soil— and genial fatness in the soil itself, which for the most part is lean and effoete. My enemies are worms cool days—and most of all woodchucks. They have nibbled for me an eigth of an acre clean. I plant in faith—and they reap—this is the tax I pay—for ousting jonswort & the rest But soon the surviving beans will be too tough for woodchucks and then—they will go forward to meet new foes.

July 14th 1845

What sweet and tender, the most innocent and divinely encouraging society there is in every natural object, and so in universal nature even for the poor misanthrope and most melancholy man. There can be no really *black* melan-choly to him who lives in the midst of nature, and has still his senses. There never was yet such a storm but it was Aeolian music[3] to the innocent ear. Nothing can compel to a vulgar sadness a simple & brave man. While I enjoy the sweet friendship of the seasons I trust that nothing can make life a burden to me. This rain which is now watering my beans, and keeping me in the house waters me too. I needed it as much. And what if most are not hoed—those who send the rain whom I chiefly respect will pardon me.

Sometimes when I compare myself with other men methinks I am favored by the Gods. They seem to whisper joy to me beyond my deserts and that I do have a solid warrant and surety at their hands, which my fellows do not. I do not flatter myself but if it were possible *they* flatter me. I am especially guided and guarded.

And now I think of it—let me remember—

What was seen true once—and sanctioned by the flash of Jove— will always be true, and nothing can hinder it. I have the warrant that no fair dream I have had need fail of its fulfilment.

Here I know I am in good company—here is the world its centre and metropolis, and all the palms of Asia—and the laurels of Greece—and the firs of the Arctic Zones incline thither.

Here I can read Homer if I would have books, as well as in Ionia, and not wish myself in Boston or New-york or London or Rome or

---

3. Music produced by a stringed instrument when placed in a window casement or otherwise exposed to a current of air; in Greek mythology Aeolus was the god of the winds.

Greece— In such place as this he wrote or sang. Who should come to my lodge just now—but a true Homeric boor—one of those Paphlagonian men?[4] Alek Therien—he called himself— A Canadian now, a woodchopper—a post maker—makes fifty posts—holes them i.e. in a day, and who made his last supper on a woodchuck which his dog caught— And he too has heard of Homer and *if it were not for books would not know what to do*—rainy days. Some priest once who could read glibly from the Greek itself—taught him reading in a measure his verse at least in his turn—at Nicolet away by the Trois Riviers once.

*   *   *

Therien said this morning (July 16th Wednesday) If those beans were mine I should'nt like to hoe them till the dew was off—" He was going to his wood chopping. Ah said I that is one of the notions the farmers have got—but I don't believe it.

"How thick the pigeons are" said he, "if working every day were not my trade I could get all the meat I should want by hunting. Pigeons wood-chucks—Rabbits—Partridges—by George I could get all I should want for a week in one day."

I imagine it to be some advantage to live a primitive and frontier life—though in the midst of an outward civilization. Of course all the improvements of the ages do not carry a man backward nor forward in relation to the great facts of his existence.

Our furniture should be as simple as the Arab's or the Indians'— At first the thoughtful wondering man plucked in haste the fruits which the boughs extended to him—and found in the sticks and stones around him his implements ready. And he still remembered that he was a sojourner in nature. When he was refreshed with food and sleep he contemplated his journey again. He dwelt in a tent in this world. He was either threading the vallies or crossing the plains or climbing the mountain tops

Now the best works of art serve comparatively but to dissipate the mind—for they are themselves transitionary and paroxismal and not free and absolute thoughts.

Men have become the tools of their tools—the man who independently plucked the fruits when he was hungry—is become a *farmer*

There are scores of pitch pine in my field—from one to three inches in diameter, girdled by the mice last winter— A Norwegian winter it was for them—for the snow lay long and deep—and they had to mix much pine meal with their usual diet— Yet these trees

4. Inhabitants of a wooded region in Asia Minor, known for their heaviness and dullness.

have not many of them died even in midsummer—and laid bare for a foot—but have grown a foot. They seem to do all their gnawing beneath the snow. There is not much danger of the mouse tribe becoming extinct in hard winters for their granary is a cheap and extensive one.

Here is one has had her nest under my house, and came when I took my luncheon to pick the crumbs at my feet. It had never seen the race of man before, and so the sooner became familiar— It ran over my shoes and up my pantaloons inside clinging to my flesh with its sharp claws. It would run up the side of the room by short impulses like a squirrel—which resembles—coming between the house mouse and the former— Its belly is a little reddish and its ears a little longer. At length as I leaned my elbow on the bench it ran over my arm and round the paper which contained my dinner. And when I held it a piece of cheese it came and nibled between my fingers and then cleaned its face and paws like a fly.

There[5] is a memorable intervale between the written and the spoken language—the language read and the language heard. The one is transient—a sound—a tongue—a dialect—and all men learn it of their mothers—

It is loquacious, fragmentary—raw material— The other is a reserved select matured expression—a deliberate word addressed to the ear of nations & generations. The one is natural & convenient—the other divine & instructive— The clouds flit here below— genial refreshing with their showers—and gratifying with their tints—alternate sun & shade— A grosser heaven adapted to our trivial wants—but above them—repose the blue firmament and the stars. The stars are written words & stereotyped on the blue parchment of the skies—the fickle clouds that hide them from our view—which we on this side need though heaven does not These are our daily colloquies our vaporous garrulous breath.

Books must be read as deliberately and reservedly as they were written. The herd of men the generations who speak the Greek and Latin, are not entitled by the accident of birth to read the works of Genius whose mother tongue speaks every where, and is learned by every child who hears.

* * *

Walden Aug 6—45

I have just been reading a book called "The Crescent & the Cross"[6] till now I am somewhat ashamed of myself. Am I sick, or

---

5. [After July 16, 1845.]
6. Eliot Warburton, *The Crescent and the Cross; or, Romance and Realities of Eastern Travel* (1845).

idle—that I can sacrifice my energy—America—and to-day—to this mans ill remembered and indolent story— Carnac and Luxor[7] are but names, and still more desert sand and at length a wave of the great ocean itself are needed to wash away the filth that attaches to their grandeur. Carnac—Carnac—this is carnac for me and I behold the columns of a larger and a purer temple.

May our childish and fickle aspirations be divine, while we descend to this mean intercourse. Our reading should be heroic—in an unknown tongue—a dialect always but imperfectly learned—through which we stammer line by line, catching but a glimmering of the sense—and still afterward admiring its unexhausted hieroglyphics—its untranslated columns.

Here grow around me nameless trees and shrubs each morning freshly sculptured—rising new stories day by day—instead of hideous ruins— Their myriad-handed worker—uncompelled as uncompelling.

This is my carnac—that its unmeasured dome—the measuring art man has invented flourishes and dies upon this temples floor nor ever dreams to reach that ceilings height. Carnac & Luxor crumble underneath—their shadowy roofs let in the light once more reflected from the ceiling of the sky

Behold these flowers—let us be up with Time not dreaming of 3000 years ago. Erect ourselves and let those columns lie—not stoop to raise a foil against the sky— Where is the *spirit* of that time but in this present day—this present line 3000 years ago are not agone—they are still lingering here aye every one,

> And Memnon's mother[8] sprightly greets us now
> Wears still her youthful blushes on her brow
> And Carnac's columns why stand they on the plain?
> T'enjoy our Opportunities they would fain remain
>
> This is my Carnac whose unmeasured dome
> Shelters the measuring art & measurer's home
> Whose propylaeum is the system nigh
> And sculptured facade the visible sky

Where there is memory which compelleth time the muse's mother and the muses nine—there are all ages—past and future time unwearied memory that does not forget the actions of the past—that does not forego—to stamp them freshly— That old

7. Sites of ruins of the ancient city of Thebes on the Nile River in Upper Egypt. The ruined temple of Amon-Re at Karnak contains massive columns decorated with hieroglyphics.
8. I.e., Eos, goddess of the dawn in Greek mythology; in Roman mythology called Aurora. Memnon was a Theban king whose statue was supposed to emit musical sounds at dawn.

mortality industrious to retouch the monuments of time, in the world's cemetery through out every clime

The student may read Homer or Aeschylus in the original Greek—for to do so implies to emulate their heroes—the consecration of morning hours to their page—

The heroic books though printed in the character of our mother tongue—are always written in a foreign language dead to idle & degenerate times, and we must laboriously seek the meaning of each word and line, conjecturing a larger sense than the text renders us at last out of our own valor and generosity.

A man must find his own occasions in himself. The natural day is very calm, and will hardly reproove our indolence. If there is no elevation in our spirits—the pond will not seem elevated like a mountain tarn, but a low pool a silent muddy water—a place for fishermen.

I sit here at my window like a priest of Isis[9]—and observe the phenomena of 3000 years ago, yet unimpaired. The tantivy of wild pigeons, an ancient race of birds—gives a voice to the air—flying by twos and threes athwart my view or perching restless on the white pine boughs occasionally—a fish-hawk dimples the glassy surface of the pond and brings up a fish And for the last half hour I have heard the rattle of rail-road cars conveying travellers from Boston to the country.

* * *

All[1] nature is classic and akin to art— The sumack and pine and hickory which surround my house remind me of the most graceful sculpture. Some times the trees do not make merely a vague impression—but their tops or a single limb or leaf seems to have grown to a distinct expression and invites my life to a like distinctness and emphasis.

Poetry Painting Sculpture claim at once and associate with themselves those perfect pieces of art—leaves—vines acorns—

The critic must at last stand as mute though contented before a true poem—as before an acorn or a vine leaf. The perfect work of art is received again into the bosom of nature whence its material proceeded—and that criticism which can only detect its unnaturalness has no longer any office to fulfill.

The choicest maxims that have come down to us are more beautiful or integrally wise—than they are wise to our understandings— This wisdom which we are inclined to pluck from their stalk is the fruit only of a single association. Every natural form—palm leaves

9. An Egyptian goddess capable of transforming herself into any kind of creature; Isis was worshipped until the sixth century C.E.
1. [After August 6, 1845.]

and acorns—oak-leaves and sumack and dodder—are untranslate-
able aphorisms

* * *

Twenty three years since when I was 5 years old, I was brought
from Boston to this pond, away in the country which was then but
another name for the extended world for me—one of the most ancient scenes stamped on the tablets of my memory—the oriental
asiatic valley of my world—whence so many races and inventions
have gone forth in recent times. That woodland vision for a long
time made the drapery of my dreams. That sweet solitude my spirit
seemed so early to require that I might have room to entertain my
thronging guests, and that speaking silence that my ears might distinguish the significant sounds. Some how or other it at once gave
the preference to this recess among the pines where almost sunshine & shadow were the only inhabitants that varied the scene,
over that tumultuous and varied city—as if it had found its proper
nursery.

Well now to-night my flute awakes the echoes over this very water, but one generation of pines has fallen and with their stumps I
have cooked my supper, And a lusty growth of oaks and pines is rising all around its brim and preparing its wilder aspect for new infant eyes.

Almost the same johnswort springs from the same perennial root
in this pasture.—

Even I have at length helped to clothe that fabulous landscape of
my imagination— —and one result of my presence and influence is
seen in the bean leaves and corn blades and potatoe vines.

Seek to preserve the tenderness of your nature as you would the
bloom upon a peach.

Most men are so taken up with the cares and rude practice of
life—that its finer fruits can not be plucked by them. Literally the
laboring man has not leisure for a strict and lofty integrity day by
day   he cannot afford to sustain the fairest and nobelest relations.
His labor will depreciate in the market.

How can he remember well his ignorance who has so often to
use his knowledge

August 15th

The sounds heard at this hour 8½ are the distant rumbling of
wagons over bridges—a sound farthest heard of any human at
night—the baying of dogs—the lowing of cattle in distant yards

What if we were to obey these fine dictates these divine suggestions which are addressed to the mind & not to the body—which
are certainly true—not to eat meat—not to buy or sell or barter &c
&c &c?

I will not plant beans another summer but sincerity—truth—simplicity—faith—trust—innocence—and see if they will not grow in this soil with such manure as I have, and sustain me. When a man meets a man—it should not be some uncertain appearance and falsehood—but the personification of great qualities. Here comes truth perchance personified along the road— Let me see how Truth behaves— I have not seen enough of her— He shall utter no foreign word—no doubtful sentence—and I shall not make haste to part with him.

I would not forget that I deal with infinite and divine qualities in my fellow. All men indeed are divine in their core of light but that is indistinct and distant to me, like the stars of the least magnitude—or the galaxy itself—but my kindred planets show their round disks and even their attendant moons to my eye.

Even the tired laborers I meet on the road, I really meet as travelling Gods, but it is as yet and must be for a long season, without speech.

*   *   *

I[2] find an instinct in me conducting to a mystic spiritual life—and also another—to a primitive savage life—

Toward evening—as the world waxes darker I am permitted to see the woodchuck stealing across my path, and tempted to seize and devour it. The wildest most desolate scenes are strangely familiar to me

Why not live a hard and emphatic life? not to be avoided—full of adventures and work! Learn much—in it. travel much though it be only in these woods I some-times walk across a field with unexpected expansion and long-missed content—as if there were a field worthy of me. The usual daily boundaries of life are dispersed and I see in what field I stand.

*   *   *

Exaggeration[3]—was ever any virtue attributed to a man without exaggeration—was ever any vice—without infinite exagggeration? Do we not exaggerate ourselves to ourselves—or Do we often recognise ourselves for the actual men we are— The lightning is an exaggeration of light. We live by exaggeration Exaggerated history is poetry—and is truth referred to a new standard. To a small man every greater one is an exaggeration. No truth was ever expressed but with this sort of emphasis—so that for the time there was no other truth. The value of what is really valuable can never be exaggerated. You must speak loud to those who are hard of hear-

2. August 23, 1845.
3. [Summer 1845.]

ing—so you acquire a habit of speaking loud to those who are not.
In order to appreciate any even the humblest man—you must not
only understand but you must first love him— And there never was
such an exaggerator as love— Who are we   are we not all of us
great men   And yet what actually— Nothing certainly to speak
of— By an immense exaggeration we appreciate our Greek—Poetry—& Philosophy—Egyptian Ruins—our shakspears & Miltons
our liberty & christianity. We give importance to this hour over all
other hours— We do not live by justice—but[4]

* * *

From all points of the compass from the earth beneath and the
heavens above have come these inspirations and been entered duly
in such order as they came in the Journal. Thereafter when the
time arrived they were winnowed into Lectures—and again in due
time from Lectures into Essays— And at last they stand like the
cubes of Pythagoras firmly on either basis—like statues on their
pedestals—but the statues rarely take hold of hands— There is
only such connexion and series as is attainable in the galleries. And
this affects their immediate practical & popular influence.

* * *

I[5] went over to neighbor Hugh Quoil's the waterloo soldier—the
Colonels house the other day. He lay lately dead at the foot of the
hill—the house locked up—and wife at work in town but before key
reaches padlock or news wife—another door is unlocked for him
and news is carried farther than to wife in town—
In his old house—an "unlucky castle now" pervious to wind &
snow—lay his old clothes his outmost cuticle curled up by habit as
it were like himself upon his raised plank bed. One black chicken
still goes to roost lonely in the next apartment—stepping silent over
the floor—frightened by the sound of its own wings—never—
croaking—black as night and silent too, awaiting reynard—its God
actually dead.
And in his garden never to be harvested where corn and beans
and potatoes had grown tardily unwillingly as if foreknowing that
the planter would die—how how luxurious the weeds—cockles and
burs stick to your clothes, and beans are hard to find—corn never
got its first hoeing
I never was much acquainted with Hugh Quoil—the Ditcher
dubbed Colonel sometime—killed a Colonel in some war and rode
off his horse? Soldier at Waterloo—son of Erin.   though sometimes
I met him in the path, and can vouch for it that he verily lived and
was once an inhabitant of this earth—fought toiled joyed sorrowed

---

4. Two-thirds page removed from manuscript at this point.
5. [Fall 1845.]

drank—experienced life and at length Death—and do believe that a solid shank bone or skull which no longer aches lie somewhere and can still be produced which once with garment of flesh and broadcloth were called and hired to do work as Hugh Quoil.

I say I have met him—got and given the nod—as when man meets man and not ghost— At distance seemingly a ruddy face as of cold biting January—but nearer—clear bright carmine with signs of inward combustion It would have made the ball of your finger burn to touch his cheek—with sober reflecting eye that had seen other sights. Straight-bodied snuff colored coat long familiar with him, he with it, axe or turf knife in hand—no sword nor firelock now—fought his battles through still but did not conquer—on the Napoleon side at last—and exiled to this st Helena Rock— A man of manners—gentleman like—who had seen this world—more civil speech than you could well attend to.

He and I at length came to be neighbors not speaking nor ever visiting hardly seeing neighbors—but nearest inhabitants mutually.

He was thirstier than I—drank more—probably—but not out of the pond— It was never the lower for him—perhaps I ate more than he. The last time I met him the only time I spoke with him it was at the foot of the hill in the highway where I was crossing to the spring one warm afternoon in summer—the pond water being too warm for me— I was crossing pail in hand—when Quoil came down the hill still in snuff colored coat as last winter—shivering as with cold rather with heat—delirium tremens they name it— I greeted him and told him my errand to get water at the spring close by only at the foot of the hill over the fence— he answered with stuttering parched lips—bloodshot eye—staggering gesture—he'd like to see it— Follow me there then. But I had got my pail full and back before he scaled the fence— And he drawing his coat about him to warm him to cool him answered in delirium tremens—hydrophobia dialect not easy to be written here he'd heard of it but had never seen it—and so shivered his way along toward the town—not to work there nor transact special business—but to get whack at a sweet remote hour to liquor & to oblivion.

* * *

Over eastward of my bean field lived Cato Ingraham slave—born slave perhaps of Duncan Ingraham Esqr—gentleman of Concord village—who built him a house and gave him permission to live in Walden woods— —and then on the N E corner Zilpha—colored woman of fame—and down the road on the right hand Bristow— colored man—on Bristow's hill—where grow still those little wild apples he tended now large trees but still wild—and farther still you come to Breeds location and again on the left by well and roadside Hilda lived Farther up the road at the ponds end Wyeman the potter who furnished his towns men earthen ware—the squatter—

Now only a dent in the earth marks the site of most of those human dwellings—sometimes the well dent where a spring oozed now
dry and tearless grass—or covered deep not to be discovered till late
days by accident with a flat stone under the sod.

* * *

For[6] every inferior earthly pleasure we forego a superior celestial
one is substituted.

To purify our lives requires simply to weed out what is foul &
noxious— And the sound and innocent is supplied—as nature purifies the blood—if we will but reject impurities.

Nature and human life are as various to our several experiences
as our constitutions are various— Who shall say what prospect life
offers to another? Could a greater miracle take place than if we
should look through each other's eyes for an instant. What I have
read of Rhapsodists[7]—of the primitive poets—Argonautic expeditions[8]—the life of demigods & heroes—Eleusinian mysteries[9]—
&c—suggests nothing so ineffably grand and informing as this
would be.

We know not what it is to live in the open air—our lives are domestic in more senses than we had thought. From the hearth to the
field is a great distance. A man should always speak as if there were
no obstruction not even a mote or a shadow between him & the celestial bodies. The voices of men sound hoarse and cavernous—tinkling as from out of the recesses of caves—enough to frighten bats
& toads—not like bells—not like the music of birds, not a natural
melody.

Of all the Inhabitants of Concord I know not one that dwells in
nature.— If one were to inhabit her forever he would never meet a
man. This country is not settled nor discovered yet

Circumstances & employment have but little effect on the finer
qualities of our nature. I observe among the rail-road men—
such inextinguishable ineradicable refinement & delicacy of
nature—older and of more worth than the sun & moon. A
genuine magnanimity—more than Greek or Roman—equal to
the least occasion—of unexplored of uncontaminated descent.
Greater traits I observe in them—in the shortest intercourse—
than are recorded of Epaminondas Socrates—or Cato— The
most famous philosophers & poets seem infantile—in comparison
with these easy profligate giants. with faces homely—hard and
scarred like the rocks—but human & wise—embracing—copt &

6. [Fall–Winter 1845–46.]
7. Professional reciters of poetry in ancient Greece.
8. According to Greek mythology, journeys made by fifty Greek heroes and their leader, Jason, aboard the *Argo* in search of a golden ram's fleece.
9. The best known of several such religious cults that flourished in ancient Greece as private forms of worship, available only to specially initiated persons.

musselman—all races & nations. One is a famous pacha—or sultan in disguise

A fineness which is commonly thought to adorn the drawing rooms only There is no more real rudeness in laborers—and washerwomen than in Gentlemen & ladies   Under some ancient wrinkled—almost forlorn visage—as of a Indian chieftain slumber the world famous humanities of man. There is the race—& you need look no farther. You can tell a nobleman's head among a million—though he may be shovelling gravel six rods off in the midst of a gang—with a cotton handkerchief tied about it— Such as are to succeed the worthies of history— It seems no disadvantage, their humble occupation and that they take no airs upon themselves. Civilization seems to make bright the superficial film of the eye

Most men are wrecked upon their consciousness—morally—intellectually—and humanly.

—

A place of pines—of forest scenes and events visited by successive nations of men all of whom have successively fathomed it— And still its water is green & pellucid not an intermittent spring— somewhat perennial in it— While the nations pass away. A true well—a gem of the first water—which concord wears in her coronet.

looking blue as amethyst or solidified azure far off as it is drawn through the streets. Green in the deeps—blue in the shallows— Perhaps the grass is a denser deeper heaven

—

* * *

My house is 10 feet wide by 15 long—with a garret & closet— 2 windows one door at the end—and a fire place   A cellar six feet square and seven deep with shelving sides not stoned—but having never come to the sun the sand still keeps its place.

I laid up a half bushel of chestnuts which were an important item in the winter's store—which cost me only a pleasant ramble in the October woods.

Flints pond lies east a mile or more—a walk to which through the woods by such paths as the Indians used is a pleasant diversion summer or winter— Our greatest lake— Worth the while if only to feel the wind blow—and see the waves run—and remember those that go down upon the sea— I went a nutting there in the fall—one windy day—when the nuts were dropping into the water & were washed ashore— and as I crawled along its long sedgey shore the fresh spray flung in my face—I came upon what seemed a large pad amid the reeds—which proved the mouldering wreck of a boat still distinctly preserving its well modelled outline—as when it was first cast up upon that beach—but ready to furnish the substance of new pads and reeds.

* * *

I expect of any lecturer[1] that he will read me a more or less simple & sincere account of his life—of what he has done & thought. Not so much what he has read or heard of other mens lives—and actions— But some such account as he would put into a letter to his kindred if in a distant land—describing his outward circumstance and any little adventures that he might have—and also his thoughts and feelings about them there.

He who gives us only the results of other men's living though with brilliant temporary success—we may in some measure justly accuse of having defrauded us of our time— We want a man to give us that which was most precious to him—not his lifes blood but even that for which his life's blood circulated what he has got by living—

If any thing ever yielded him pure pleasure or instruction—let him communicate it. The Miser must tell us how much he loves wealth and what means he takes to accumulate it— He must describe those facts which he knows & loves better than any body else.

He must not lecture on Missions & the Temperance The mechanic will naturally lecture about his trade the farmer about his farm and every man about that which he compared with other men—knows best.

Yet incredible mistakes are made— I have heard an Owl lecture with a perverse show of learning upon the solar microscope—and chanticlere upon nebulous stars When both ought to have been sound asleep in a hollow tree—or upon a hen roost. When I lectured here before this winter I heard that some of my towns men had expected of me some account of my life at the pond—this I will endeavor to give tonight.

I find that no way of doing or thinking however ancient is to be trusted. What every body echoes or in silence passes by may turn out to be sheer falsehood at last— As it were the mere smoke of opinion falling back in cinders which some thought—a cloud that would sprinkle fertile rain upon their fields.

One says you cant live so and so—it is madness—on vegetable food solely—or mainly—for it furnishes nothing to make bones with—walking behind his oxen—and so religiously devotes a part of his day to supplying his system with the raw material of bones.

---

1. Lecture draft in the Journal at this point and above indicates that Thoreau expected to lecture on his Walden experience during his first winter there, or about six months after he had moved to the pond. The opportunity to do so, however, did not arrive until the following winter, February 10, 1847, when he spoke before the Concord Lyceum on "The History of Myself."

Certain things are absolute necessaries of life in some circles—
the most helpless and diseased—in others certain other or fewer
things—and in others fewer still—and still what the absolutely indispensable are has never been determined I know a robust and
hearty mother who thinks that her son who died abroad—came to
his end by living too low, as she had since learned that he drank
only water— Men are not inclined to leave off hanging men—to-
day—though they will be to-morrow. I heard of a family in Concord
this winter which would have starved, if it had not been for potatoes—& tea & coffee.

—

It has not been my design to live cheaply but only to live as I
could not devoting much time to getting a living— I made the
most of what means were already got.

—

To determine the character of our life and how adequate it is to
the occasion—just try it by any test—as for instance that this same
sun is seen in Europe & in America at the same time—that these
same stars are visible in 24 hours to ⅔ the inhabitants of the
globe—and who shall say to how many inhabitants of the universe—
What farmer in his field lives according even to this somewhat
trivial material fact.
I just looked up at a fine twinkling star—and thought that a voy-
ager whom I know now many days sail from this coast—might possibly be looking up at that same star with me— The stars are the
apexes of important triangles.
There is always the possibility—the possibility I say of being *all*—
or remaining a particle in the universe

Perhaps we may distribute the necessaries of life under the several heads of food—clothing—shelter—& fuel And this suggests
how nearly the expression "animal heat"—is to being synonymous
with animal life.

* * *

The philosopher is in advance of his age not merely in his discourse but in his life—in the form & outward mode of it. He is not
fed—clothed—warmed—sheltered like other men—
How can a man be a philosopher and not maintain his vital heat
by better methods than other men.
The body is so perfectly subjugated by the mind that it prophe-
cies the sovereignty of the latter over the whole of nature. The instincts are to a certain extent a sort of independent nobility—of
equal date with the crown. They are perhaps the mind of our ancestors subsided in us. The experience of the race—
I have thought sometimes when going home through the woods

at night—star-gazing all the way—till I was aroused from my reflections by finding my door before me—that perhaps my body would find its way home if its master should have forsaken it— As the hand finds its way to the mouth without assistance.

All matter indeed is capable of entertaining thought.

—

Why do men degenerate— what makes families run out? What is the nature of that luxury that ennervates nations and is there none of it in our lives? Are we the founders of a race.

Men frequently say to me I should think you would feel lonely down there— I should think you would want to be nearer to folks rainy days & nights especially. How far apart dwell the most distant inhabitants of those stars the breadth of whose disks cannot be appreciated by our instruments.

But what after all do we want to dwell near to?— not mainly to the depot or to many men—not to the post office or the bar room—or the meeting house or school house—or Beacon hill or the Five points where men are more numerous than any where— —but rather I should say to the source of our life—whence in all our experience we have found that to issue. As the willow stands near the water and sends out its roots in that direction.

But most men are not so wise as a tree or rather are like those trees which being badly located make only wood & leaves and bear no fruit.

This will vary with different natures of course—but this is the place where a wise man will dig his cellar.

What is the great attraction in cities? It is universally admitted that human beings invariably degenerate there—and do not propagate their kind.— Yet the prevailing tendency is to the city life—whether we move to Boston or stay in Concord.

We are restless to pack up our furniture and move into a more bustling neighborhood but we are proportionally slow to rent a new mode of living—or rather to rend the old.

* * *

March 13th 1846   The Songsparrow & Black bird heard today—the snow going off—the ice in the pond 1 foot thick.

—

Men speak—or at least think much of cooperation nowadays—of working together to some worthy end— But what little there is, is as if it were not—being a simple result of which the means are hidden—a harmony inaudible to men— If a man has faith—he will cooperate with equal faith every where— If he has not faith he will continue to live like the rest of the world. To cooperate in the lowest & in the highest sense—thoroughly—is simply to get your living together. I heard it proposed lately that two young men should travel together over the world—the one making his way as he went, seeking his fortune,—before the mast—behind the plow—walking and sleeping on the ground—living from hand to mouth—and so come in immediate contact with all lands and nations—the other carrying a bill of exchange in his pocket as a resource in case of extremity— It was easy to see that they could not be companions to one another—or cooperate. They would part company at the first interesting crisis the most interesting point in their adventures

I live about a mile from my neighbor no house is visible within a quarter of a mile or more—

The pond furnishes my water which 8 or 9 months in the year I think is the best in the town— In the summer I set it in my cellar and found that it became sufficiently cool.—

It seemed to me that it would become colder—than well water under the same circumstances—but I never tried the experiment

* * *

In[2] due time in the spring I heard the martins twittering over my clearing though it had not appeared that the town contained so many that it could afford any to me They were rather of the ancient stock that dwell in hollow trees before the white man came than the modern village race that live in boxes.

Let a man live in any part of the globe and he will hear the same simple spring sounds to cheer him. Along the Nile and the Orinoco and the Mississippi birds of the same genus—migrate. Everywhere the frog and the turtle greet the season The temperate and Frigid salute the Torrid zone again—and birds fly & plants and winds blow to correct this oscillation of the poles and preserve the equilibrium of nature. This slight oscillation how it is painted by the seasons and heralded by the songs and the glancing plumage of migrating birds—

The Pewee (Phoebe?) came and look in at my door or window to see if my house were cave like enough for her—sustaining herself on humming wings—with clenched talons as if she held by the air—while she surveyed the premises.

Girls and boys generally seemed glad to be in the woods & young women they looked in the pond and at the flowers and improved their time.

But men of business only thought of Solitude and employment. though they said they loved a ramble in the woods occasionally it was obvious that they did not.

Restless committed men whose time is all taken up in getting a living—Ministers Doctors—lawyers generally suggested in one way or another the importance of doing good.

2. [After March 13, 1846.]

Conscientious preachers—(the way of their profession)—uneasy house keepers—young men who had ceased to be young and had concluded that it was safest to follow the beaten track of the professions generally said it was not possible to do so much good in my position.

The old and infirm thought of sickness & sudden death—to them life seemed full of danger—any where—and a prudent man would carefully select the safest position

* * *

Husbandry[3] is universally a sacred art—pursued with too much heedlessness and haste by us— To have large farms and large crops is our object. Our thoughts on this subject should be as slow and deliberate as the pace of the ox.

"According to the early laws of Greece, the ploughing ox was held sacred, & was entitled, when past service, to range the pastures in freedom & repose. It was forbidden, by the decrees of Triptolemus, to put to death this faithfully of the labors of the husbandman, who shared the toils of ploughing & threshing. Whenever, therefore, an ox was slaughtered, he must first be consecrated or devoted as a sacrifice (ἱερεῖον), by the sprinkling of the sacrificial barley; this was a precaution against the barbarous practice of eating raw flesh (βουφόαγια). A peculiar sacrifice (Διπόλια) at Athens, at which the slayer of the ox fled, and the guilty axe was thrown into the sea, on the sentence of the Prytanes, yearly placed before the people a visible type of the first beginnings of their social institutions."[4]

Ap 18th The morning must remind every one of his ideal life— Then if ever we can realize the life of the Greeks   We see then Aurora. The morning brings back the heroic ages.

I get up early and bathe in the pond—that is one of the best things I do—so far the day is well spent.

In some unrecorded hours of solitude whether of morning or evening whose stillness was audible—when the atmosphere contained an auroral perfume the hum of a mosquito was a trumpet that recalled what I had read of most ancient history and heroic ages. There was somewhat that I fancy the Greeks meant by ambrosial about it—more than Sybilline or Delphic[5]— It expressed the infinite fertility and fragrance and the everlastingness of the

3. April 17, 1846.
4. According to Greek mythology, Triptolemus was chosen by Demeter, goddess of agriculture, to teach the skills of farming; the Prytanes were members of a governing body chosen each year in ancient Athens. Thoreau's source has not been identified.
5. I.e., prophetic or inspirational.

κοσμος It was θειον[6] Only Homer could name it. The faintest is the most significant sound.

* * *

The[7] struggle in me is between a love of contemplation and a love of action—the life of a philosopher & of a hero. The poetic & philosophic have my constant vote—the practic hinders & unfits me for the former.

How many things that my neighbors do bunglingly could I do skilfully & effectually—but I fain would not have leisure— My tendency is, on the one hand to the poetic life—on the other to the practic—and the result is the indifference[8] of both—or the philosophic.

In the practic the poetic loses its intensity—and fineness but gains in health & assurance—

The practical life is the poetic making for itself a basis—and in proportion to the breadth of the base will be the quantity of material at the apex— The angle of slope for various materials is determined by science. The fabric of life is pyramidal.

The man of practice is laying the foundations of a poetic life

The poet of great sensibility is rearing a superstructure without foundation.

To make a perfect man—the Soul must be much like the body not too unearthly & the body like the soul. The one must not deny & oppress the other.

The line of greatest breadth intersects the line of greatest length at the point of greatest depth or height

A law so universal—and to be read in all material—in Ethics as well as mechanics—that it remains its own most final statement.

—It is the heart in man— It is the sun in the system—it is the result of forces— In the case of the pond it is the law operating without friction. Draw lines through the length & breadth of the aggregate of a man's particular daily experiences and volumes of life into his coves and inlets—and where they intersect will be the height or depth of his character.

You only need to know how his shores trend & the character of the adjacent country to know his depth and concealed bottom.

There is a bar too across the entrance of his every cove—every cove is his harbor for a season—and in each successively is he detained—land locked.

There is no exclusively moral law—there is no exclusively physical law.

* * *

6. κοσμος, cosmos; θειον, divine.
7. [After April 18, 1846.]
8. In magnetism, the indifference point is the middle region of a magnet where the two powers neutralize each other.

For the most part I know not how the hours go. Certainly I am
not living that heroic life I had dreamed of— And yet all my veins
are full of life—and nature whispers no reproach— The day advances as if to light some work of mine—and I defer in my thought
as if there were some where busier men— It was morning & lo! it is
now evening— And nothing memorable is accomplished— Yet my
nature is *almost* content with this— It hears no reproach in nature.

What are these pines & these birds about? What is this pond
a-doing? I must know a little more—& be forever ready. Instead of
singing as the birds I silently smile at my incessant good fortune but
I dont know that I bear any flowers or fruits— Methinks if they try
me by their standards I shall not be found wanting—but men try
one another not so. The elements are working their will with me.

As the fields sparrow has its trill sitting on the hickory before my
door—so have I my chuckle as happy as he—which he may hear
out of my nest.

Man is like a plant and his satisfactions are like those of a vegetable—his rarest life is least his own— One or two persons come
to my house—there being proposed it may be to their vision the
faint possibility of intercourse—& joyous communion. They are as
full as they are silent and wait for your plectrum or your spirit to
stir the strings of their lyre. If they could ever come to the length of
a sentence or hear one—on that ground they are thinking of!! They
speak faintly—they do not obtrude themselves They have heard
some news which none, not even they themselves can impart. What
come they out for to seek? If you will strike my chord?

They come with somethings in their minds no particular fact or
information—which yet is ready to take any form of expression on
the proper impulse   It is a wealth they bear about them which can
be expended in various ways. Laden with its honey the bee straightway flies to the hive to make its treasure common stock— The
poet is impelled to communicate at every risk and at any sacrifice.

I think I have this advantage in my present mode of life over
those who are obliged to look abroad for amusement—to theatres
& society—that my life itself is my amusement and never ceases to
be novel—the commencement of an experiment—or a drama
which will never end.

Sunday May 3d
I heard the whippoorwill last night for the first time.

Carlyle's books[9] are not to be studied but read with a swift satisfaction—rather— Their flavor & charm—their gust is like the

---

9. Thomas Carlyle (1795–1881), Scottish essayist and historian. Thoreau lectured on

froth of wine which can only be tasted once & that hastily. On a review I never can find the pages I had read— The book has done its
work when once I have reached the conclusion, and will never inspire me again.

They are calculated to make one strong and lively impression—
and entertain us for the while more entirely than any—but that is
the last we shall know of them   They have not that stereotyped
success & accomplishment which we name classic—

It is an easy and inexpensive entertainment—and we are not
pained by the author's straining & impoverishing himself to feed his
readers.

It is plain that the reviewers and politicians do not know how to
dispose of him— They take it too easily & must try again a loftier
pitch— They speak of him within the passing hour as if he too
were one other ephemeral man of letters about town who lives under Mr. Somebody's administration. Who will not vex the world
after burial—

But he does not depend on the favor of reviewers—nor the honesty of booksellers—nor on popularity— He has more to impart
than to receive from his generation

He is a strong & finished journeyman in his craft—& reminds us
oftener of Samuel Johnsson[1] than of any other. So few writers are
respectable—ever get out of their apprenticeship—

* * *

When[2] my friends reprove me for not devoting myself to some
trade or profession, and acquiring property I feel not the reproach— I am guiltless & safe comparatively on that score— But
when they remind me of the advantages of society of worthy and
earnest helpful relations to people I am convicted—and yet not I
only but they also.

But I am advised by thee Friend of friends to strive singly for the
highest—without concern for the lower— The integrity of life is
otherwise sacrificed to factitious virtues—and frittered away in
morbid efforts and despair.

Disturb not the sailor with too many details—but let him be sure
that he keep his guiding star in his eye. It is by a mathematical
point that we are wise—but that is a sufficient guidance for all our
lives— The blind are led by the slightest clue.

When I am reproved for being what I am I find the only resource
is being still more entirely what I am.

Carlyle's writings before the Concord Lyceum on February 4, 1846, and published an essay, "Thomas Carlyle and His Works," the following year.
1. Samuel Johnson (1709–1784), English author, lexicographer, and critic.
2. May 15, 1846.

Carry yourself as you should and your garments will trail as they should.

I am useless for keeping flocks & herds, for I am on the trail of a rarer game.

To the mariner the faint star is the chief light though he will avail himself of the light in the binnacle.

* * *

In[3] my short experience of human life I have found that the outward obstacles which stood in my way were not living men—but dead institutions   It has been unspeakably grateful & refreshing to make my way through the crowd of this latest generation honest & dishonest virtuous & vicious as through the dewy grass—men are as innocent as the morning to the early riser—and unsuspicious pilgrim and many an early traveller which he met on his way v poetry[4]—but the institutions as church—state—the school property &c are grim and ghostly phantoms like Moloch & Juggernaut[5] because of the blind reverence paid to them. When I have indulged a poets dream of a terrestrial paradise I have not foreseen that any cossack or Chipeway—would disturb it—but some monster institution would swallow it— The only highway man I ever met was the state itself—When I have refused to pay the tax which it demanded for the protection I did not want itself has robbed me— When I have asserted the freedom it declared it has imprisoned me.

I love mankind   I hate the institutions of their forefathers—

What are the sermons of the church but the Dudleian lectures[6] —against long extinct perhaps always imaginary evils, which the dead generations have *willed* and so the bell still tolls to call us to the funeral services which a generation can rightly demand but once.

It is singular that not the Devil himself—has been in my way but these cobwebs—which tradition says were originally spun to obstruct the fiend.

If I will not fight—if I will not pray—if I will not be taxed—if I will not bury the unsettled prairie—my neighbor will still tolerate me and sometimes even sustains me—but not the state.

And should our piety derive its origin still from that exploit of

---

3. [After July 24, 1846.] Thoreau was arrested for several years' nonpayment of poll tax on July 24, 1846, and, though unwilling, was released the next day.
4. Thoreau's notation to himself to insert lines of an old ballad, "The Lordling Peasant": "The early pilgrim blithe he hailed / That o'er the hills did stray; / And many an early husbandman, / That he met on his way."
5. Gods described in the Old Testament and Hindu myth, respectively, to whose images their devotees blindly sacrificed themselves or others.
6. Lectures given at Harvard by speakers who frequently took conservative positions on religious issues.

pius Aenaeus who bore his father Anchises on his shoulders from the ruins of Troy.

Not thieves & highwaymen but Constables & judges—not sinners but priests—not the ignorant but pedants & pedagogues—not foreign foes but standing armies—not pirates but men of war. Not free malevolence—but organized benevolence.

For instance the jailer or constable as a mere man and neighbor—with life in him intended for this particular 3 score years & ten—maybe a right worthy man with a thought in the brain of him—but as the officer & tool of the state he has no more understanding or heart than his prison key or his staff— This is what is saddest that men should voluntarily assume the character & office of brute nature.— Certainly there are modes enough by which a man may put bread into his mouth which will not prejudice him as a companion & neighbor. There are stones enough in the path of the traveller with out a man's adding his own body to the number.

There probably never were worse crimes committed since time began than in the present Mexican war—to take a single instance— And yet I have not yet learned the name or residence and probably never should of the reckless vilain who should father them— all concerned—from the political contriver to the latest recruit possess an average share of virtue & of vice   the vilainy is in the readiness with which men, doing outrage to their proper natures—lend themselves to perform the office of inferior & brutal ones.

The stern command is—move or ye shall be moved—be the master of your own action—or you shall unawares become the tool of the meanest slave. Any can command him who doth not command himself. Let men be men & stones be stones and we shall see if majorities *do* rule.

Countless reforms are called for because society is not animated or instinct enough with life, but like snakes I have seen in early spring—with alternate portions torpid & flexible—so that they could wriggle neither way.

All men more or less are buried partially in the grave of custom, and of some we see only a few hairs upon the crown above ground.

Better are the physically dead for they more lively rot.

* * *

Of[7] Emerson's Essays I should say that they were not poetry— that they were not written exactly at the right crisis though inconceivably near to it. Poetry is simply a miracle & we only recognize it receding from us not coming toward us— It yields only tints &

---

7. December 2, 1846. Emerson's *Essays* was published in 1841 and *Essays: Second Series* in 1844.

hues of thought like the clouds which reflect the sun—& not distinct propositions—

In poetry the sentence is as one word—whose syllables are words— They do not convey thoughts but some of the health which he had inspired— It does not deal in thoughts—they are indifferent to it—

A poem is one undivided unimpeded expression—fallen ripe into literature   The poet has opened his heart and still lives— And it is undividedly and unimpededly received by those for whom it was matured—but mortal eye can never dissect it— while it sees it is blinded.

The wisest *man*—though he should get all the academies in the world to help him cannot add to or subtract one syllable from a line of poetry.

* * *

When[8] I am stimulated by reading the biographies of literary men to adopt some method of educating myself and directing my studies—I can only resolve to keep unimpaired the freedom & wakefulness of my genius. I will not seek to accomplish much in breadth and bulk and loose my self in industry but keep my celestial relations fresh.

No method or discipline can supersede the necessity of being forever on the alert— What is a course of History—no matter how well selected—or the most admirable routine of life—and fairest relation to society—when one is reminded that he may be a *Seer* that to keep his eye constantly on the true and real is a discipline that will absorb every other.

How can he appear or be seen to be well employed to the mass of men whose profession it is to climb resolutely the heights of life—and never lose a step he has taken

Let the youth seize upon the finest and most memorable experience in his life—that which most reconciled him to his unknown destiny—and seek to discover in it his future path. Let him be sure that that way is his only true and worthy career.

Every mortal sent into this world has a star in the heavens appointed to guide him— Its ray he cannot mistake— It has sent its beam to him either through clouds and mists faintly or through a serene heaven— He knows better than to seek advice of any.

This world is no place for the exercise of what is called common sense. This world would be denied.

Of how much improvement a man is susceptible—and what are the methods?

* * *

8. [After December 2, 1846.] Quotations from the *Auto-Biography* of Johann Wolfgang von Goethe immediately precede this excerpt. See *Journal 2*, 356–57.

The[9] best books are not read even by those who have learned their letters. What does our Concord culture amount to? There is in this town—with a very few exceptions, no taste for the best or the very good books even in English literature which all can read— Even college bred—& so called liberally educated men here & elsewhere have no acquaintance with the English Classics.— and as for the recorded wisdom of mankind—which accessible to all who will know of it—there are but the feeblest efforts made to study or to become acquainted with it. One who has just come from reading perhaps the best of English books will find how few to converse with respecting it! It is for the most part foreign & unheard of. One who comes from reading a Greek—or Latin book—in the original— whose praisies are familiar even to the illiterate will find nobody at all to speak to and must keep silence about it.

Indeed there is hardly the professor in our colleges who if he has mastered the difficulties of the language has in any like proportion mastered the difficulty of the wisdom & the poetry. And the zealous morning reader of Homer or of the Greek Dramatic poets might find no more valuable sympathy in the atmosphere of Cambridge A man—any man will go considerably[1]

your gone—pull it up—pull it up. But this—was Beans and not corn & so it was safe from such enemies as he

—In summer days which some devoted to the fine arts—away in Italy—and others to contemplation away in India and some to trade in London & New York—I with other farmers of N.E. devoted to field-labor.

When my hoe tinkled on a stone it was no longer beans that I hoed nor I that hoed beans.— By such sugar plums they tempt us to live this life of man—however mean and trivial.

Or it was my amusement when I rested in the shrub oaks to watch a pair of hen-hawks circling high in the sky as silently as the humors on my eye—alternately soaring and descending—approaching and leaving one another—the imbodiment of some of my own thoughts which some times soar as high & sail & circle as majestically there.

* * *

Mythology[2] is ancient history or biography   The oldest history still memorable becomes a mythus— It is the fruit which history at last bears— The fable so far from being false contains only the essential parts of the history— What is today a diffuse biography—

9. [Winter 1846–1847.]
1. Thirty-four pages removed from manuscript at this point, some or all of it, perhaps, containing draft for *Walden*.
2. [Spring 1848.]

was anciently before printing was discovered— —a short & pithy tradition a century was equal to a thousand years. To day you have the story told at length with all its accompaniments In mythology you have the essential & memorable parts alone—the you & I the here & there the now & then being omitted— In how few words for instance the Greeks would have told the story of Abelard & Heloise[3] instead of a volume They would have made a mythus of it among the fables of their gods and demigods or mortals—and then have stuck up their names to shine in some corner of the firmament— And who knows what Greeks may come again at last to mythologize their Love.— and our own deeds.

How many Vols folio must the life and labors of Prometheus[4] have filled if perchance it fell in days of cheap printing!— What shape at length will assume the fable of Columbus—to be confounded at last with that of Jason—& the expedition of the Argonauts—and future Homers quoted as authority. And Franklin[5] there may be a line for him in the future Classical dictionary recording what that demigod did.— & referring him to some new genealogy—

I see already the naked fables scattered up & down the history of modern—Europe— A small volume of mythology preparing in the press of time— The hero tell—with his bow—Shakespeare— the new Apollo— —Cromwell—Napoleon.

The most comprehensive the most pithy & significant book is the mythology

Few[6] phenomena give me more delight in the spring of the year than to observe the forms which thawing clay and sand assume on flowing down the sides of a deep cut on the rail road through which I walk.

The clay especially assumes an infinite variety of forms—

There lie the sand and clay all winter on this shelving surface an inert mass but when the spring sun comes to thaw the ice which binds them they begin to flow down the bank like lava—

These little streams & ripples of lava like clay over flow & interlace one another like some mythological vegetation—like the forms which I seem to have seen imitated in bronze— What affects me is

3. The tragic love affair between Peter Abelard (1079–1142), famed teacher and theologian of Notre Dame in Paris, and Heloise (d. 1163), a woman of learning and Abelard's pupil.
4. In Greek mythology, a Titan whose labors included creating humans out of clay and stealing fire for the human race from heaven, against the hostility of the gods.
5. Benjamin Franklin (1706–1790), American statesman, scientist, and philosopher.
6. Thoreau later extensively revised the following description of the thawing sandbank. For these revisions, see *Journal 2*, 576–79.

the presence of the law—between the inert mass and the luxuriant vegetation what interval is there? Here is an artist at work—as it were not at work but—a-playing designing — — It begins to flow & immediately it takes the forms of vines—or of the feet & claws of animals—or of the human brain or lungs or bowels— Now it is bluish clay now clay mixed with reddish sand—now pure iron sand—and sand and clay of every degree of fineness and every shade of color— The whole bank for a quarter of a mile on both sides is sometimes overlaid with a mass of plump & sappy verdure of this kind— I am startled probably because it grows so fast—it is produced in one spring day. The lobe of these leaves—perchance of all leaves—is a thick—now loitering drop like the ball of the finger larger or smaller   so perchance the fingers & toes flow to their extent from the thawing mass of the body—& then are congealed for a night.

—Whither may the sun of new spring lead them on— These roots of ours— In the mornings these resting streams start again and branch & branch again into a myriad others— Here it is coarse red sand & even pebbles—there fine adhesive clay—

—And where the flowing mass reaches the drain at the foot of the bank on either side it spreads out flatter in to sands like those formed at the mouths of rivers—the separate streams losing their semicilindrical form—and gradually growing more and more flat—and running together as it is more moist till they form an almost flat sand—variously & beautifully shaded—& in which you can still trace the forms of vegetation till at length in the water itself they become the ripple marks on the bottom

The lobes are the fingers of the leaf as many lobes as it has in so many directions it inclines to flow—more genial heat or other influences in its springs might have caused it flow farther.

—So it seemed as if this one hill side contained an epitome of all the operations in nature.

So the stream is but a leaf   What is the river with all its branches—but a leaf divested of its pulp— — but its pulp is intervening earth—forests & fields & town & cities— What is the river but a tree on oak or pine—& its leaves perchance are ponds & lakes & meadows innumerable as the springs which feed it.

I perceive that there is the same power that made me my brain my lungs my bowels my fingers & toes working in other clay this very day— I am in the studio of an artist.

This cut is about a quarter of a mile long—& 30 or 40 feet deep—and in several places clay occurs which rises to within a dozen feet of the surface.— Where there is sand only the slope is great & uniform—but the clay being more adhesive inclines to stand out longer from the sand as in boulders—which are continually washing & coming down.

Flowing down it of course runs together and forms masses and conglomerations but if flowed upward it would disperesed itself more—& grow more freely—& unimpeded

* * *

Is[7] it a use I make of my friends which necessarily transcends their privity (consciousness)?— They sometimes even demand to be admitted to my solitary joy—ask why I smile—but I see too plainly—that if I degraded my ideal to an identity with any actual mortal whose hand is to be grasped there would be an end of our fine relations. I would be related to my friend by the most etherial part of our natures alone—and what else is quite obedient to this.

I learned this by my experiments in the woods, of more value perhaps than all the rest—that if one will advance confidently in the direction of his dreams, and live that life which he has imagined— If he will walk the water, if he will step forth on to the clouds if he will heartily embrace the true, if in his life he will transend the temporal— (He shall walk securely—perfect success shall attend him, there shall be the terra firma or the coelum firmior—) If he will do that in which alone he has faith, if he will yield to love and go whither it leads him)   He shall be translated—he shall know no interval he shall be surrounded by new environments, new and more universal & libereal laws shall {MS *torn*} establish themselves around & within[8]

It is not enough that my friend is good—he must be wise— Our intercourse is likely to be a tragedy with that one who cannot measure us   Where there is not discernment the behavior even of a pure soul may in effect amount to coarseness.— In a difference with a friend I have felt that our intercourse was prophaned when that friend made haste come to speech about it. I am more grieved that my friend can so easily give utterance to his wounded feelings—than by what he says. Such a wound cannot be permanently healed. There is a certain vulgarity & coarseness in that sentiment that is liable to a common difference—such wordy reproaches as are heard in street & the kitchen.[9]

as it were in a new world in which these laws prevailed— All things were miraculously changed— Nature was unexpectedly

---

7. [After May 26, 1849.]
8. Two-fifths page removed from the manuscript at this point.
9. Two-fifths page removed from the manuscript at this point. The "friend" with whom Thoreau had a falling-out at this time is believed to have been Emerson. See *Journal 3*, 485–88.

kind. I lived with the license of a higher order of beings— Some restrictions were taken off. I was met. Solitude, was not solitude— nor silence—silence—nor poverty poverty nor weakness weakness. I had travelled things {MS torn}t as they had been. I had died to a life {MS torn} my life,[1]

* * *

The[2] Hindoos by constitution possess in in a wonderful degree the faculty of contemplation—they can speculate—they have imagination & invention & fancy. The western man thinks only with ruinous interruptions & friction—his contemplative faculty is rusty & does not work. He is soon aground in the shallows of the practical— It gives him indigestion to think. His cowardly *legs* run away with him—but the Hindoo bravely cuts off his legs in the first place. To him his imagination is a distinct & honorable faculty as valuable as the understanding or the legs— The legs were made to transport it—& it does not merely direct the legs. How incredibly poor in speculation is the western world!— one would have thought that a drop of thought & a single afternoon would have set afloat more speculations—

What has Europe been *thinking* of these two thousand years. A child put to bed half an hour before its time would have invented more systems—would have had more theories set afloat would have amused itself with more thoughts. But instead of going to bed and thinking Europe has got up and gone to work, and when she goes to bed she goes to sleep. We cannot go to bed & think as children do   The Yankee cannot sit but he sleeps— I have an uncle who is obliged to sprout potatoes on sundays to keep him awake. The Hindoo thinks so vividly & intensely that he can think sitting or on his back—far into a siesta   He can dream awake.

* * *

Feb 24th 1850   Saw red wing blackbirds & heard them sing & whistle—& also cherry birds on the cedar trees by Flints Pond in company with hundreds of lisping robins Feb. 28th heard blue birds & saw a striped squirrel—and a caterpillar

He is a happy man who is assured that the animal is dying out in him day by day & the spiritual being established.

What a strange alliance of the divine & brutish there is in a man

Man has a gross animal & unreasoning nature which puts to shame his spiritual.

We would fain esteem a person for what he is absolutely & not relatively to us alone,—and be so esteemed ourselves. There is

---

1. Three-fifths page removed from the manuscript at this point.
2. [After September 11, 1849.]

no safety or progress in the love which is identical with partiality.

We would love universal and absolute qualities, all other love is transient & factitious & impure

* * *

The[3] calmness & gentleness with which the Hindoo philosophers approach & discourse on forbidden themes is admirable

What extracts from the vedas I have read fall on me like the light of a higher & purer luminary which describes a loftier curve through a purer stratum—free from particulars—simple—universal— It rises on me like the full moon after the stars have come out wading through some far summer stratum of the sky.

The Vedant teaches how "by forsaking religious rites" the votary may "obtain purification of mind."[4]

One wise sentence is worth the state of Massachusetts, many times over.

The Vedas contain a sensible account of God.

The religion & phil. of the Hebrews are those of a wilder & ruder tribe—wanting the civility & intellectual refinements & subtlety of the Hindoos.

Man flows at once to God as soon as the channel of purity, physical, intellectual & moral, is open.

with the Hindoos virtue is an intellectual exercise—not a social & *practical* one— It is a knowing not a doing.

I do not prefer one religion or philosophy to another— I have no sympathy with the bigotry & ignorance which make transient & partial & puerile distinctions between one man's faith or form of faith & anothers—as christian & heathen— I pray to be delivered from narrowness partiality exaggeration—bigotry. To the philosopher all sects all nations are alike. I like Brahma—Hare Buddha—the Great spirit as well as God.

* * *

A page with as true & inevitable & deep a meaning as a hill-side. A book which nature shall own as her own flower her own leaves—with whose leaves her own shall rustle in sympathy imperishable & russet—which shall push out with the skunk cabbage in the spring

I am not offended by the odor of the skunk in passing by sacred places—I am invigorated rather. It is a reminiscence of immortality borne on the gale   O thou partial world, when wilt thou know God?

---

3. [After April 26, 1850.]
4. The Vedas are Hindu scriptures; Thoreau quotes from *Translation of . . . the Veds* (1832) by Raja Rammohun Roy.

I would as soon transplant this vegetable to Polynesia or to heaven with me as the violet.

Shoes are commonly too narrow. If you should take off a gentleman's shoes you would find that his foot was wider than his shoe. Think of his wearing such an engine—walking in it many miles year after year. A shoe which presses aagainst the sides of the foot is to be condemned— To compress the foot like the Chinese is as bad as to compress the head—like the Flat heads—for the Head & the foot are one body. A sensible man will not follow fashion in this respect but reason. Better moccasins or Sandals or even bare feet, than a tight shoe.

A wise man will wear a shoe wide & large enough shaped somewhat like the foot & tied with a leather string.   & so go his way in peace letting his foot fall at every step.

When your shoe chafes your feet put in a mullein leaf.

When I ask for a garment of a particular form my tailoress tells me gravely "They do not make them so now," and I find it difficult to get made what I want—simply because she cannot believe that I mean what I say— It surpasses her credulity— Properly speaking my style is as fashionable as theirs. "They do not make them so now"! as if she quoted the Fates. I am for a moment absorbed in thought—thinking wondering who they are & where *they* live. It is some Oak Hall[5] O Call— O K all correct establishment which she knows but I do not. Oliver Cromwell— I emphasize & in imagination italicize each word separately of that sentence to come at the meaning of it

* * *

Jewett's[6] steam mill is profitable because the planing machine alone while that is running makes shavings & waste enough to feed the engine—to say nothing of the saw-dust—from the saw mill & the Engine had not required the least repair for several years. Perhaps as there is not so much sawing & planing to be done in England they therefore may not find steam so cheap as water.

A single gentle rain in the spring makes the grass look many shades greener.

It is wisest to live without any definite & recognised object from day to day,—any particular object for the world is round and we are not to live on a tangent or a radius to the sphere— As an old poet says Though man proposeth, God disposeth all.

Our thoughts are wont to run in muddy or dusty ruts

5. A Boston clothing store.
6. May 12, 1850.

I too revive as does the grass after rain— We are never so flourishing our day is never so fair but that the sun may come out a little brighter through mists & we yearn to live a better life— What have we to boast of? we are made the very sewers the cloacae of nature.

If the hunter has a taste for mud turtles & muskrats & skunks and other such savage tit bits—the fine lady indulges a taste for some form of potted cheese or jelly made of a calf's foot or anchovies from over the water—& they are even. He goes to the mill pond—she to her preserve pot. I wonder how he—I wonder how I can live this slimy beastly kind of life—eating & drinking—

The fresh foliage of the woods in May—when the leaves are about as big as a mouse's ear—putting out like taller grasses & herbs

In all my rambles I have seen no landscape which can make me forget Fair Haven. I still sit on its Cliff in a new spring day & look over the awakening woods & the river & hear the new birds sing with the same delight as ever— It is as sweet a mystery to me as ever what this world is— Wild Fair Haven lake in the South with its pine covered island & its meadows—the hickories putting out fresh young yellowish leaves—and the oaks light greyish ones while the oven bird thrums his sawyer-like strain & the chewink rustles through the dry leaves or repeats his jingle on a tree top—& the wood thrush, the genius of the wood, whistles for the first time his clear & thrilling strain— It sounds as it did the first time I heard it. The sight of these budding woods intoxicates me—this diet drink.

The strong colored pine—the grass of trees—in the midst of which other trees are but as weeds or flowers. a little exotic.

* * *

Today June 4th I have been tending a burning in the woods. Ray was there. It is a pleasant fact that you will know no man long however low in the social scale however poor miserable, intemperate & worthless he may appear to be a mere burden to society—but you will find at least that there is something which he understands & can do better than any other. I was pleased to hear that one man had sent Ray as the one who had had the most experience in setting fires of any man in Lincoln— He had experience & skill as a burner of brush. You must burn against the wind always & burn slowly— When the fire breaks over the hoed line—a little system & perseverance will accomplish more toward quelling it than any man would believe.

—It fortunately happens that the experience acquired is oftentimes worth more than the wages. When a fire breaks out in the woods & a man fights it too near & on the side—in the heat of the moment without the systematic cooperation of others he is disposed to think it a desperate case & that this relentless fiend will run through the forests till it is glutted with food; but let the company rest from their labors a moment—& then proceed more deliberately & systematically giving the fire a wider berth—and the company will be astonished to find how soon & easily they will subdue it. The woods themselves furnish one of the best weapons with which to contend with the fires that destroy them—a pitch pine bow. It is the best instrument to thrash it with. There are few men who do not love better to give advice than to give assistance.

* * *

Men go to a fire for entertainment. When I see how eagerly men will run to a fire whether in warm or in cold weather by day or by night dragging an engine at their heels, I am astonished to perceive how good a purpose the love of excitement is made to serve.— What other force pray—what offered pay—what disinterested neighborliness could ever effect so much. No these are boys who are to be dealt with—& these are the motives that prevail.

There is no old man or woman dropping into the grave but covets excitement.

* * *

Olive or red seems the fittest color for a man—a denizen of the woods. The *pale white man* I do not wonder that the African pitied him.

The white-pine cones which are earlier than the pitch are now two inches long curved sickle-like from the top most branches—reminding you of the tropical trees which bear their fruit at their heads.

The life in us is like the water in the river, it may rise this year higher than ever it was known to before and flood the uplands— even this may be the eventful year—& drown out all our muskrats There are as many strata at different levels of life as there are leaves in a book   Most men probably have lived in two or three. When on the higher levels we can remember the lower levels, but when on the lower we cannot remember the higher.

My imagination, my love & reverance & admiration, my sense of the miraculous is not so excited by any event as by the remembrance of my youth. Men talk about bible miracles because there is no miracle in their lives. Cease to gnaw that crust. There is ripe fruit over your head   Wo to him who wants a companion—for he is unfit to be the companion even of himself.

We inspire friendship in men when we have contracted friendship with the gods.

When we cease to sympathise with and to be personally related to men, and begin to be universally related—then we are capable of inspiring others with the sentiment of love for us.

I have been into a village and there was not a man of a large soul
in it— In what respect was it better than a village of prairie dogs?

We hug the earth—how rare we mount!   how rarely, we climb a
tree! We might get a little higher methinks   That pine would make
us dizzy. You can see the *Mts* from it as you never did before.

Shall not a man have his spring as well as the plants?

The halo around the shadow is visible both morning & evening.

* * *

However mean your life is meet it & live—do not shun it and call
it hard names. It is not so bad as you are. It looks poorest when you
are richest   The fault finder will find faults even in paradise
Love your life, poor as it is. You may perchance have some pleasant—thrilling glorious hours even in a poor-house— The setting
sun is reflected from the windows of the alms-house as brightly as
from the rich man's house.

The snow melts before its door as early in the spring. I do not see
but a quiet mind may live as contentedly there, and have as cheering thoughts as any where—& indeed the towns poor seem to live
the most independent lives of any.   they are simply great enough
to receive—without misgiving. Cultivate poverty like sage like a garden herb. Do not trouble yourself to get new things—whether
clothes—or friends— That is dissipation. Turn the old—return to
them. Things do not change, we change. If I were confined to a
corner—in a garret all my days like a spider—the world would be
just as large to me—while I had my thoughts

In all my travels I never came to the abode of the present

I live in the angle of a leaden wall into whose alloy was poured a
littl bell metal. Some times in the repose of my midday there
reaches my ears a confused tintinnabulum from without— It is the
noise of my contemporaries.

That the brilliant leaves of Autumn are not withered ones is
proved by the fact, that they wilt when gathered as soon as the
green.

But now, Oct 31st, they are all withered. This has been the most
perfect afternoon in the year. The air quite warm enough—perfectly still & dry & clear, and not a cloud in the sky. Scarcely the
song of a cricket is heard to disturb the stillness   When they
ceased their song I do not know— I wonder that the impetus
which our hearing had got did not hurry us into deafness over a
precipitous silence   There must have been a thick web of cobwebs
on the grass this morning promising this fair day—for I see them
still through the afternoon covering not only the grass but the
bushes & the trees. They are stretched across the unfrequented
roads from weed to weed & broken by the legs of the horses

* * *

This[7] is a peculiar season—peculiar for its stillness—the crickets have ceased their song. The few birds are well nigh silent— The tinted & gay leaves are now sere and dead and the woods wear a sombre aspect. A carpet of snow under the pines & shrub-oaks will make it look more cheerful— Very few plants have now their spring But thoughts still spring in man's brain. There are no flowers nor berries to speak of. The grass begins to die at top— In the morning it is stiff with frost. Ice has been discovered in somebody's tub very early this morn of the thickness of a dollar. The flies are betwixt life & death. The wasps come into the houses & settle on the walls & windows All insects go into crevices. The fly is entangled in a web and struggles vainly to escape—but there is no spider to secure him— The corner of the pane is a deserted camp.

When I lived in the woods the wasps came by thousands to my lodge in November—as to winter quarters, and settled on my—windows & on the walls over my head sometimes deterring visitors from entering— Each morning when they were numbed with cold I swept some of them out. But I did not trouble myself to get rid of them they never molested me, though they bedded with me—and they gradually disappeared into what crevices I do not know.—avoiding winter

I saw a squash-bug go slowly behind a clapboard to avoid winter—as some of these melon-seeds come up in the garden again in the spring—so some of these squash bugs come forth— The flies are for a long time in a somnambulic state— They have too littl energy or vis vitae to clean their wings or heads which are covered with dust. They buzz and bump their heads against the windows or lie on their backs and that is all—two or three short spurts— One of these mornings we shall hear that Mr Minot had to break the ice to water his cow. And so it will go on till the ground freezes. If the race had never lived through a winter what would they think was coming?

Walden Pond has at last fallen a little— It has been so high over the stones quite into the bushes that walkers have been excluded from it. There has been no accessible shore— All Ponds have been high— The water stood higher than usual in the distant ponds which I visited & had never seen before. It has been a peculiar season. At Goose-Pond I notice that the birches of one years growth from the stumps standing in the water are all dead apparently killed by the water—unless like the pine they die down after springing from the stump.

It is warm somewhere anyday in the year— You will find some nook in the woods generally at midforenoon of the most blustering

7. November 8, 1850.

day where you may forget the cold. I used to resort to the North
east shore of Walden where the sun reflected from the pine woods
on the stoney shore made it as warm as a fireside. It is so much
pleasanter and wholsomer to be warmed by the sun when you can
than by a fire.

* * *

The[8] era of wild apples will soon be over— I wander through old
orchards of great extent now all gone to decay all of native fruit
which for the most part went to the cider mill— But since the
temperance reform—and the general introduction of grafted fruit—
no wild apples such as I see every where in deserted pastures and
where the woods have grown up among them—are set out. I fear
that he who walks over these hills a century hence will not know
the pleasure of knocking off wild apples— Ah poor man! there
are many pleasures which he will be debarred from. Notwithstanding the prevalence of the Baldwin & the porter,[9] I doubt if as extensive orchards are set out to day in this town as there were a
century ago when these vast straggling cider orchards were set out.
Men stuck in a tree then by every wall side & let it take its
chance— I see nobody planting trees today in such out of the way
places along almost every road & lane & wall side, and at the bottom of dells in the wood. Now that they have grafted trees & pay a
price for them they collect them into a plot by their houses & fence
them in.

My Journal should be the record of my love. I would write in it
only of the things I love. My affection for any aspect of the world.
What I love to think of. I have no more distinctness or pointedness
in my yearnings than an expanding bud—which does indeed point
to flower & fruit to summer & autumn—but is aware of the warm
sun & spring influence only. I feel ripe for something yet do nothing—cant discover what that thing is. I feel fertile merely. It is seed
time with me— I have lain fallow long enough.

Notwithstanding a sense of unworthiness which possesses me
not without reason—notwithstanding that I regard myself as a good
deal of a scamp—yet for the most part the spirit of the universe is
unaccountably kind to me—and I enjoy perhaps an unusual share
of happiness. Yet I question sometimes if there is not some settlement to come.

* * *

Dec 31st

I observe that in the cut by Walden Pond the sand and stones fall
from the overhanging bank and rest on the snow below— And thus

8. November 16, 1850. Compare "Wild Apples," p. 308.
9. Common varieties of eating apples.

perchance the stratum deposited by the side of the road in the winter can permanently be distinguished from the summer one by some faint seam to be referred to the peculiar conditions under which it was deposited.

The Pond has been frozen over since I was there last.

Certain meadows, as Heywoods, contain warmer water than others and are slow to freeze. I do not remember to have crossed this with impunity in all places. The brook that issues from it is still open completely though the thermometer was down to 8 below zero this morning.

The blue-jays evidently notify each other of the presence of an intruder, and will sometimes make a great chattering about it, & so communicate the alarm to other birds—& to beasts.

* * *

July 19th

Here I am 34 years old, and yet my life is almost wholly unexpanded. How much is in the germ! There is such an interval between my ideal and the actual in many instances that I may say I am unborn. There is the instinct for society—but no society. Life is not long enough for one success. Within another 34 years that miracle can hardly take place. Methinks my seasons revolve more slowly than those of nature, I am differently timed. I am—contented. This rapid revolution of nature even of nature in me—why should it hurry me. Let a man step to the music which he hears however measured. Is it important that I should mature as soon as an apple tree? Ye, as soon as an oak? May not my life in nature, in proportion as it is supernatural, be only the spring & infantile portion of my spirit's life   shall I turn my spring to summer? May I not sacrifice a hasty & petty completeness here—to entireness there? If my curve is large—why bend it to a smaller circle? My spirits unfolding observes not the pace of nature. The society which I was made for is not here, shall I then substitute for the anticipation of that this poor reality. I would have the unmixed expectation of that than this reality.

If life is a waiting—so be it. I will not be shipwrecked on a vain reality. What were any reality which I can substitute. Shall I with pains erect a heaven of blue glass over myself though when it is done I shall be sure to gaze still on the true etherial heaven—far above as if the former were not—that still distant sky oer arching that blue expressive eye of heaven. I am enamored of the blue eyed arch of heaven.

I did not *make* this demand for a more thorough sympathy. This is not my idiosyncrasy or disease. He that made the demand will answer the demand.

My blood flows as slowly as the waves of my native Musketaquid—yet they reach the ocean sooner perchance than those of the Nashua.[1]

Already the golden-rod is budded, but I can make no haste for that.

* * *

It[2] is the fault of some excellent writers—De Quincy's first impressions on seeing London[3] suggest it to me—that they express themselves with too great fullness & detail. They give the most faithful natural & living account of their sensations mental & physical—but they lack moderation and sententiousness—they do not affect us by an ineffectual earnesst and a reserve of meaning—like a stutterer—they say all they mean. Their sentences are not concentrated and nutty. Sentences which suggest far more than they say, which have an atmosphere about them—which do not merely report an old but make a new impression— Sentences which suggest as many things and are as durable as a Roman Acqueduct To frame these that is the *art* of writing. Sentences which are expensive towards which so many volumes—so much life went—which lie like boulders on the page—up & down or across. Not mere repetition but creation. Which a man might sell his grounds & castle to build. If De Quincy had suggested each of his pages in a sentence & passed on it would have been far more excellent writing.— His style is no where kinked and knotted up into something hard & significant which you could swallow like a diamond without digesting.

Aug 23[d] Sat.

To walden to bathe at 5½ AM   Traces of the heavy rains in the night The sand and gravel are beaten hard by them. 3 or 4 showers in succession. But the grass is not so wet as after an ordinary dew. The verbena hastata at the pond has reached the top of its spike— a little in advance of what I noticed yesterday—only one or two flowers are adhering. At the commencement of my walk I saw no traces of fog.   but after detected fogs over particular meadows & high up some brooks' valleys—and far in the deep cut the wood fog 1st muskmelon this morning—

* * *

Sep 19th '51

Perambulated Carlisle line

Large flowered bidens or Beggar ticks or Burr-Marygold now abundant by river side. Found the bound-stones on Carlisle by the

---

1. Rivers that flow north into the Merrimack River (at points in northeastern Massachusetts and southeastern New Hampshire, respectively) before it flows into the Atlantic Ocean at Newburyport, Massachusetts. "Musketaquid" is the Indian name for the Concord River.
2. August 22, 1851.
3. Thomas De Quincey (1785–1859), English writer; his impressions are described in *Literary Reminiscences* (1851).

river—all or mostly tipped over by the ice & water like the pitch
pines about Walden pond. Grapes very abundant along that line.

The soap-wort Gentian now— In an old pasture now grown up
to birches & other trees—followed the cow paths to the old apple
trees. Mr Isaiah Green of Carlisle who lives nearest to the Kibbe
Place—can remember when there were 3 or 4 houses around him
(he is nearly 80 years old & has always lived there & was born
there) now he is quite retired—& the nearest road is scarcely used
at all. He spoke of one old field, now grown up—which were going
through, as the "hog-pasture", formerly. We found the meadows so
dry that it was thought to be a good time to burn out the moss.

Sep. 20th

3 Pm. to Cliffs via Bear Hill. As I go through the fields endeavoring to recover my tone & sanity—& to perceive things truly & simply
again, after having been perambulating the bounds of the town all
the week, and dealing with the most common place and worldly
minded men, and emphatically *trivial* things I feel as if I had committed suicide in a sense. I am again forcibly struck with the truth of
the fable of Apollo serving king Admetus[4]—its universal applicability.
A fatal coarseness is the result of mixing in the trivial affairs of men.
Though I have been associating even with the *select* men[5] of this and
the surrounding towns, I feel inexpressibly begrimmed, my pegasus
has lost his wings, he has turned a reptile and gone on his belly.
Such things are compatible only with a cheap and superficial life

The poet must keep himself unstained and aloof. Let him peram-
bulate the bounds of Imagination's provinces the realms of faery,
and not the insignificant boundaries of towns. The excursions of
the imagination are so boundless—the limits of towns are so petty.

I scare up the great bittern in meadow by the Heywood Brook
near the ivy.— he rises buoyantly as he flies against the wind &
sweep south over the willow with outstretched neck surveying.

* * *

It[6] is a rare qualification to be ably to state a fact simply & adequately. To digest some experience cleanly. To say yes and no with
authority— To make a square edge. To conceive & suffer the truth
to pass through us living & intact—even as a waterfowl an eel—
thus peopling new waters. First of all a man must see, before he
can say.— Statements are made but partially— Things are said
with reference to certain conventions or existing institutions.—
not absolutely. A fact truly & absolutely stated is taken out of the
region of commonsense and acquires a mythologic or universal sig-

---

4. Apollo, the Greek and Roman god of music, poetry, and prophecy, was banished from
   heaven for nine years and forced to tend the flocks of Admetus, king of Pherae.
5. Pun on "selectmen," a board of town officers elected to manage local affairs.
6. November 1, 1851.

nificance. Say it & have done with it. Express it without expressing yourself. See not with the eye of science—which is barren—nor of youthful poetry which is impotent. But taste the world. & digest it. It would seem as if things got said but rarely & by chance— As you *see* so at length will you *say*. When facts are seen superficially they are seen as they lie in relation to certain institution's perchance. But I would have them expressed as more deeply seen with deeper references.— so that the hearer or reader cannot recognize them or apprehend their significance from the platform of common life—but it will be necessary that he be in a sense translated in order to understand them.

When the truth respecting *his* things shall naturally exhale from a man like the odor of the muskrat from the coat of the trapper. At first blush a man is not capable of reporting truth—he must be drenched & saturated with it first. What was *enthusiasm* in the young man must become *temperament* in the mature man. without excitement—heat or passion he will survey the world which excited the youth—& threw him off his balance. As all things are significant; so all words should be significant. It is a fault which attaches to the speaker to speak flippantly or superficially of anything. Of what use are words which do not move the hearer.— are not oracular & fateful?— A style in which the matter is all in all & the manner nothing at all.

In your thoughts no more than in your walks do you meet men— in moods I find such privacy as in dismal swamps & on mountain tops.

Man recognizes laws little enforced & he condescends to obey them. In the moment that he feels his superiority to them as compulsatory he as it were courteously reenacts them but to obey them.

* * *

Friday Nov 14

Surveying the Ministerial lot in the S W part of the town. Unexpectedly find Heywoods pond frozen over thinly it being shallow & coldly placed.

In the evening went to a party. It is a bad place to go to.— 30 or 40 persons mostly young women in a small room—warm & noisy. Was introduced to two young women— The first one was as lively & loquacious as a chic-a-dee—had been accustomed to the society of watering places, and therefore could get no refreshment out of such a dry fellow as I. The other was said to be pretty looking, but I rarely look people in their faces, and moreover I could not hear what she said there was such a clacking—could only see the motion of her lips when I looked that way. I could imagine better places for conversation—where there should be a certain degree of silence surrounding you & less than 40 talking at once. Why this afternoon even I did better. There was old Mr Joseph Hosmer & I ate our luncheon of cracker & cheese together in the woods. I heard all he said, though it was not much to be sure & he could hear me.   & then he talked out of such a glorious repose—taking a leisurely bite at the cracker & cheese between his words—& so some of him was communicated to me & some of me to him.

These parties I think are a part of the machinery of modern society—that young people may be brought together to form marriage connections.

What is the use of going to see people whom yet you never see— & who never see you? I begin to suspect that it is not necessary that we should see one another.

Some of my friends make singular blunders. They go out of their way to talk with certain young women of whom they think or have heard that they are pretty—and take pains to introduce me to them. That may be a reason why they should look at them, but it is not a reason why they should talk with them. I confess that I am lacking a sense perchance in this respect—& I derive no pleasure from talking with a young woman half an hour—simply because she has regular features.

The society of young women is the most unprofitably I have ever tried.

They are so light & flighty that you can never be sure whether they are there or not there. I prefer to talk with the more staid & settled—*settled for life*, in every sense.

* * *

Jan 20th

Walked down the Boston road. It was good to look off over the great unspotted fields of snow the walls & fences almost buried in it—& hardly a turf or stake left bare for the starving crows to alight on. There is no track nor mark to mar its purity beyond the single sled track—except where once in half a mile some traveller has stepped aside for a sleigh to pass.

The farmers now a days can cart out peat & muck over the frozen meadows. Somewhat analogous methinks the scholar does—drives in with tight traced energy & winter cheer—onto his now firm meadowy grounds—& carts hauls off the virgin loads of fertilizing soil which he threw up in the warm soft summer. We now bring our muck out of the meadows, but it was thrown up first in summer. The scholars & the farmers work are strictly analogous.

Easily he now conveys sliding over the snow clad ground—great loads of fuel & of lumber which have grown in many summers— from the forest to the town. *He* deals with the dry hay & cows—the spoils of summer meads & fields—stored in his barns doling it out from day to day, & manufactures milk for men.

When I see the farmer driving into his barn yard with a load of muck—whose blackness contrasts strangely with the white snow, I have the thought which I have described. He is doing like myself. My barn-yard is my journal.

* * *

Jan 22nd

Having occasion to get up & light a lamp in the middle of a sultry night I observed a stream of large black ants passing up and down one of the bare corner posts—those descending having their large white eggs or larva in their mouths—the others making haste up for another load. I supposed that they had found the heat so great just under the roof as to compel them to remove their progeny to a cooler place by night. They had evidently taken & communicated the resolution to improve the coolness of the night to remove their young to a cooler & safer locality. One stream running up another down with great industry.

But Why I changed—? Why I left the woods? I do not think that I can tell, I have often wished myself back— I do not know any better how I ever came to go there—. Perhaps it is none of my business—even if it is your's. Perhaps I wanted a change— There was a little stagnation it may be—about 2 o'clock in the afternoon the world's axle—creaked as if it needed greasing—as if the oxen labored—& could hardly get their load over the ridge of the day— Perhaps if I lived there much longer I might live there forever— One would think twice before he accepted heaven on such terms— A ticket to Heaven must include tickets to Limbo—Purgatory—& Hell. Your ticket to the boxes admits you to the pit also. And if you take a cabin-passage you can smoke at least forward of the engine.— You have the liberty of the whole boat. But no I do not wish for a ticket to the boxes—nor to take a cabin passage. I will rather go before the mast & on the deck of the world. I have no desire to go "abaft the engine"

What is it that I see from a mile to a mile & a half & 2 miles distant in the horizon on all sides of our villages—the woods.— which still almost without exception encircle the towns.— They at least bound almost every view. They have been driven off only so far. Where still wild creatures haunt. How long will these last.? Is this a universal and permanent feature? Is it not an interesting, an important question whether these are decreasing or not. Have the oldest countries retained it?

Look out what window I will my eyes rest in the distance on a forest! Is this fact of no significance— Is this circumstance of no value? Why such pains in old countries to plant gardens & parks?— A certain sample of wild nature—a certain primitiveness.

One man proposed—a book in which visitors should write their names—said he would be at the expense of it!!! Did he consider what the expense of it would be? As if it were of any use when a man had failed to make any memorable impression on you—for him to leave his name. But it may be that he writes a good hand.— who had not left any fame. No! I kept a book to put their fames in— I was at the expense of it.

The milk man is now filling his ice-house.

The towns thus bordered—with a fringed & tasselled border— each has its preserves. Methinks the town should have more super-vision & control over its parks[7] than it has. It concerns us all whether these proprietors—choose to cut down all the woods this winter or not.

I must say that I do not know what made me leave the pond— I left it as unaccountably as I went to it. To speak sincerely, I went there because I had got ready to go— I left it for the same reason.

* * *

To set down such choice experiences that my own writings may inspire me.— and at last I may make wholes of parts.

Certainly it is a distinct profession to rescue from oblivion & to fix the sentiments & thoughts which visit all men more or less gen-erally. That the contemplation of the unfinished picture may sug-gest its harmonious completion. Associate reverently, and as much as you can with your loftiest thoughts. Each thought that is wel-comed and recorded is a nest egg—by the side of which more will be laid. Thoughts accidentally thrown together become a frame—in which more may be developed—& exhibited. Perhaps this is the main value of a habit of writing—of keeping a journal. That so we remember our best hours—& stimulate ourselves. My thoughts are my company— They have a certain individuality & separate exis-tence—aye personality. Having by chance recorded a few discon-nected thoughts and then brought them into juxtaposition—they suggest a whole new field in which it was possible to labor & to think. Thought begat thought.

The mother o' pearl tint is common in the winter sky ½ hour be-fore sundown.

* * *

A[8] tree seen against other trees is a mere dark mass—but against the sky it has parts, has symmetry & expression.

Whatever wit has been produced on the spur of the moment will bear to be reconsidered & reformed with phlegm. The arrow had best not be loosely shot. The most transient & passing remark— must be reconsidered by the writer—made sure & warranted—as if

7. I.e., naturally occurring wooded areas or meadows resembling artificial parks.
8. January 26, 1852.

the earth had rested on its axle to back it,—and all the natural
forces lay behind it. The writer must direct his sentences as carefully & leisurely as the marks-man his rifle—who shoots sitting &
with a rest—with patent sights & conical balls beside. He must not
merely seem to speak the truth. He must really speak it. If you foresee that a part of your essay will topple down after the lapse of
time, throw it down now.   yourself.

The thousand fine points & tops of the trees delight me—they
are the plumes & standards & bayonets of a host that march to victory over the earth. The trees are handsome towards the heavens—
as well as up their boles—they are good for other things than
boards & shingles.

Obey the spur of the moment. These accumulated it is that
makes the impulse & the impetus of the life of genius.— These are
the spongioles or rootlets by which its trunk is fed. If you neglect
the moments—if you cut off your fibrous roots—what but a lan-
guishing life is to be expected. Let the spurs of countless moments
goad us incessantly into life.

* * *

Let all things give way to the impulse of expression. It is the bud
unfolding— The perennial spring. As well stay the spring. Who
shall resist the thaw?

What if all the ponds were shallow!— would it not react on the
minds of men? If there were no physical deeps. I thank God that he
made this pond deep & pure—for a symbol.

The word is well naturalized or rooted that can be traced back to
a celtic originnal. It is like getting out stumps & fat pine roots.

While men believe in the infinite some ponds will be thought
bottomless.

In winter we will think brave & hardy—& most native thoughts—
Then the tender summer birds are flown.

In few countries do they enjoy so fine a contrast of summer &
winter—we really have four seasons.   each incredible to the other.
Winter cannot be mistaken for summer here. Though I see the
boat turned up on the shore & half buried under snow—as I walk
over the invisible river—summer is far away.   with its rustling
reeds. It only suggests the want of thrift—the carelessness of its
owner.

Nature never indulges in exclamations—never says Ah! or alas!
She is not of French descent. She is a plain writer uses few gestures—does not add to her verbs—uses few adverbs.   uses no exple-
tives. I find that I use many words for the sake of emphasis—which
really add nothing to the force of my sentences—and they look relieved the moment I have cancelled these. Words by which I express my mood, my conviction, rather than the simple truth.

Yesterday though warm it was clear enough for water & windows to sparkle.

* * *

I[9] do not know but thoughts written down thus in a journal might be printed in the same form with greater advantage—than if the related ones were brought together into separate essays. They are now allied to life—& are seen by the reader not to be far fetched— It is more simple—less artful— I feel that in the other case I should have no proper frame for my sketches. Mere facts & names & dates communicate more than we suspect— Whether the flower looks better in the nosegay—than in the meadow where it grew—& we had to wet our feet to get it! Is the scholastic air any advantage?

Jan 28

Perhaps I can never find so good a setting for my thoughts as I shall thus have taken them out of. The crystal never sparkles more brightly than in the cavern. The world have always loved best the fable with the moral. The children could read the fable alone—the grown up read both. The truth so told has the best advantages of the most abstract statement—for it is not the less universally applicable. Where also will you ever find the true cement for your thoughts? How will you ever rivet them together without leaving the marks of the file?

Yet Plutarch did not so— Montaigne[1] did not so. Men have written travels in this form—but perhaps no man's daily life has been rich enough to be journalized. Our life should be so active and progressive as to be a journey— Our meals should all be of journey-cake & hasty pudding. We should be more alert—see the sun rise—not keep fashionable hours— Enter a house our own house as a Khan—a caravansery. At noon I did not dine   I ate my journey-cake. I quenched my thirst at a spring or a brook. As I sat at the table the hospitality was so perfect & the repast so sumptuous that I seemed to be breaking my fast upon a bank in the midst of an arduous journey—that the water seemed to be a living spring—the napkins grass, the conversation free as the winds.   & the servants that waited on us were our simple desires.—

Cut off from Pilpay[2] & AEsop the moral alone at the bottom— would that content you?

There will be no more rambling through the aisles of the wood, with occasional vistas through which you see the pond.

---

9. January 27, 1852.
1. Greek biographer, historian, and moral philosopher (46?–120?); and French essayist (1533–1592), respectively. Montaigne modeled his *Essays* on Plutarch's moral history and treatises.
2. Supposed to have been the author of a collection of Sanskrit fables, the *Hitopadesa*.

In those days when how to get my living honestly with freedom left for my proper pursuits, was a question which vexed me even more than it does now—I used to see a large box by the RR, 6 feet long by 3 wide, in which the workmen locked up their tools at night— And it suggested to me that every man who has hard pushed might get him such a one for a dollar, and having bored a few auger holes in it to admit the air at least—get into it when it rained and at night, & so have freedom in his mind and in his soul be free. This did not seem the worst alternative nor by any means a despicable resource. You could sit up as late as you pleased. & you would not have any creditor dogging you for rent. I should not be in a bad box. Many a man is harassed to death to pay the rent of a larger and more luxurious box—who would not have frozen to death in such a box as this. I should not be in so bad a box as many a man is in now.

* * *

The[3] entertaining a single thought of a certain elevation makes all men of one religion. It is always some base alloy that creates the distinction of sects— Thought greets thought over the widest gulfs of time with unerring free-masonry. I know for instance that Sadi[4] entertained once identically the same thought that I do—and thereafter I can find no essential difference between Sadi and myself. He is not Persian—he is not ancient—he is not strange to me. By the identity of his thought with mine he still survives. It makes no odds what atoms serve us. Sadi possessed no greater privacy or individuality than is thrown open to me. He had no more interior & essential & sacred self than can come naked into my thought this moment. Truth and a true man is something essentially public not private. If Sadi were to come back to claim a *personal* identity with the historical Sadi he would find there were too many of us—he could not get a skin that would contain us all. The symbol of a personal identity preserved in this sense is a mummy from the Catacombs—a whole skin it may but no life within it. By living the life of a man is made common property. By sympathy with Sadi I have embowelled him. In his thoughts I have a sample of *him* a slice from his core—which makes it unimportant where certain bones which the thinker once employed may lie—but I could not have got this without being equally entitled to it with himself. The difference between any man and that posterity amid whom he is famous is too insignificant to sanction that he should be set up again in any world as distinct from them.

Methinks I can be as intimate with the essence of an ancient worthy as, so to speak, he was with himself.

3. August 8, 1852.
4. Muslih-ud-Din (Saadi) (1184?–1291), famous Persian poet.

I only know myself as a human entity—the scene, so to speak, of thoughts & affections—and am sensible of a certain doubleness by which I can stand as remote from myself as from another. However intense my experience— I am conscious of the presence & criticism of a part of me which as it were is not a part of me—but spectator sharing no experience, but taking note of it—and that is no more I than it is you.— When the play—it may be the tragedy—is over, the spectator goes his way. It was a kind of fiction—a work of the imagination—so far as he was concerned. A man *may* be affected by a theatrical exhibition; On the other hand he *may* not be affected by an actual event which appears to concern him never so much.

* * *

Pm[5] to Walden.

Storm drawing to a close—crickets sound much louder after the rain in this cloudy weather. They are beginning to dig potatoes in earnest. Hips of the early roses are reddening. I have not seen a rose for a week or two. Lower leaves of the smooth sumach are red. Hear chic-a-day-day-day—& crows— But for music reduced almost to the winter quire. Young partridges ⅔ grown burst away. Globular galls on young oaks green on one side red on the other. Elatina (?) Americana   Small crypta in Walden Pond   Paddled *round* the pond— The shore is composed of a belt of smooth rounded white stones like paving stones a rod or two in width—excepting 1 or 2 short sand beaches—and is so steep that much of the way a single leap will carry you into water over your head.   & the bottom is not to be touched, scarcely even seen again, except for the transparency of the water till it rises on the other side   It is nowhere muddy & a casual observer would say that there were no weeds at all in it, and of noticeable plants a closer scrutiny detects only a few small hearts leaves &—potamogetons—& perchance a water target or two—which yet even a bather might not perceive.— Both fishes and plants are clean & bright like the element they live in. Viewed from a hill top it is blue in the depths & green in the shallows—but from a boat it is seen to be a uniform dark green— I can remember when it was 4 or 5 feet higher—also a foot or two lower than when I lived there   There is a narrow sand bar running into it in one place with very deep water on one side—on which I boiled a kettle of chowder at least 6 rods from the main shore more than 20 years ago which it has not been possible to do since—and my friends used to listen with incredulity when I told them that a year or two later I was accustomed to fish from a boat in a deep cove in the woods, long since converted into a meadow—but since

5. August 27, 1852.

I left it the pond has risen steadily for a year past ap.[6] unaffected by drowth or rain & now in the summer of 52 is as high as it was 20 years ago—& fishing goes on again in the meadow—& yet this water shed by the surrounding hills is insignificant in amount & this overflow must be referred to causes which affect the deep springs— The surrounding hills are from 50 to a hundred & in one place perhaps 200 feet high, covered with wood.

* * *

Nov 2nd

Tall buttercups—red Clover—houstonias Polygonum aviculare still. Those handsome red buds on often red-barked twigs with some red leaves still left appear to be blueberry buds. The prinos berries also now attract me in the scarcity of leaves—its own all gone—its berries are apparently a brighter red for it— The month of chicadees & new swolen buds— At long intervals I see or hear a robin still.

To Walden

In the latter part of Oct. the skaters & water bugs entirely disappear from the surface of the pond & then & in november, when the weather is perfectly calm—it is almost absolutely as smooth as glass. This afternoon a 3 days rain storm is drawing to an end. though still overcast— The air is quite still but misty—& from time to time mizzling—and the pond is very smooth & its surface difficult to distinguish. though it no longer reflects the *bright*-tints of autumn—but sombre colors only.— Calm at the end of a storm. except here and there a slight glimmer or dimple—as if a few skaters which had escaped the frosts were still collected there—or a faint breeze then struck—or a few rain drops fell there, or perchance the surface being remarkably smooth betrayed by circling dimples where a spring welled up from below. I paddled gently toward one of those places & was surprised to find myriads of small perch about 5 inches long sporting there one after another rising to the surface & dimpling it—leaving bubbles on it. They were very handsome as they surrounded the boat with their distinct tranverse stripes—a rich brown color

There were many such schools in the pond—as it were improving the short season before the ice would close their window. When I approached them suddenly with noise—they made a sudden plash & rippling with their tails in fright & then took refuge in the depths

Slate colored snow birds? with a faint note. Suddenly the wind rose the mist increased & the waves rose and still the perch leaped—but much higher half out of water a hundred black points 3 inches long at once above the surface.

6. Apparently.

The pond dark before was now a glorious & indescribable blue—mixed with dark—perhaps the opposite side of the wave—a sort of changeable or watered silk blue, more cerulean if possible than the sky itself which was now seen overhead— It required a certain division of the sight however to discern this.— like the colors on a steel sword blade   The leaves which are not not withered—whose tints are still fresh & bright are now remarked in sheltered places Plucked quite a handsome nose gay from the S side of Heywood's peak. *Wht* & blue stemmed golden rods—asters, undulatus & ?

I do not know whether the perch amuse them selves thus more in the fall than at any other time. In such transparent & apparently bottomless water their swimming impresses the beholder as a kind of flight or hovering like a compact flock of birds passing below one—just beneath his level on the right or left. What a singular experience must be theirs in their winter quarters—their long night—expecting when the sun will open their shutters

If you look discerningly so as to see the reflection only—you see a most glorious light blue in comparison with which the original dark green of the opposite side of the waves is but muddy.

* * *

Jan 6th

Walden froze over apparently last night. It is but little more than an inch thick—& 2 or 3 square rods by Hubbards shore are still open. A dark transparent ice— It would not have frozen entirely over as it were in one night or may be a little more and yet have been so thin next the shore as well as in the middle, if it had not been so late in the winter, & so ready to freeze. It is a dark transparent ice. But will not bear me without much cracking. As I walked along the edge I started out 3 little pickerel no bigger than my finger from *close* to the shore which went wiggling into deeper water like bloodsuckers or pollywogs. When I lie down on it and examine it closely, I find that the greater part of the bubbles which I had thought were within its own substance are against its under surface, and that they are continually rising up from the bottom. perfect spheres apparently & very beautiful & clear in which I see my face through this thin ice (perhaps 1 & $\frac{1}{8}$ inch) from $\frac{1}{80}$ of an inch in diameter or a mere point up to $\frac{1}{8}$ of an inch. There are 30 or 40 of these at least to every square inch— These probably when heated by the sun make it crack & whoop— There are also within the substance of the ice oblong perpendicular bubbles $\frac{1}{2}$ inch long more or less by about $\frac{1}{30}$ of an inch & these are commonly widest at the bottom?[7]   —or oftener separate minute spherical bubbles of equal or smaller diameter one directly above another like a string of

---

7. Thoreau made a drawing of the oblong bubble structure at this point in the manuscript.

beads—perhaps the first stage of the former— But these internal bubbles are not nearly so numerous as those in the water beneath. It may be 24 hours since the ice began to form decidedly.

I see on the sandy bottom a few inches beneath—the white cases of Cadis worms made of the white quartz sand or pebbles— And the bottom is very much creased or furrowed where some creature has travelled about and doubled on its tracks—perhaps the cadis worm, for I find one or two of the same in the furrows—though the latter are deep & broad for them to make.

* * *

Jan 27th

Trench says a wild man is a *willed* man[8] Well then a man of will who does what he wills—or wishes—a man of hope and of the future tense—for not only the obstinate is willed but far more the constant & persevering— The obstinate man properly speaking is one who will not. The perseverance of the saints is positive willedness—not a mere passive willingness— The fates are wild for they *will*—& the Almighty is wild above all.

What are our fields but felds or felled woods—they bear a more recent name than the woods suggesting that previously the earth was covered with woods. Always in the new country a field is a clearing.

* * *

Sunday March 20th

8 Am   Via Walden Goose Flints & Beaver Ponds & the valley of Stony Brook to the south end of Lincoln— A rather cool and breezy morning which was followed by milder day.

We go listening for early birds—with bread & cheese for our dinners * * * It was a question whether we should not go to Fair Haven to see the gulls &c. I notice the downy-swaddled plants now & in the fall, the fragrant life everlasting & the rib-wort—innocents born in a cloud. Those algae I saw the other day in John Hosmers ditch were the most like sea weed of anything I have seen in the county—they made me look at the whole earth as a sea-shore. reminded me of Nereids—sea nymphs triton—Proteus[9] &c &c— made the ditches fabulate in an older than the arrowheaded character. Better learn this strange character which nature speaks to day—than the Sanscrit—books in the brooks— Saw a large dead water bug in walden. I suspect he came out alive. Walden is melting apace— It has a canal 2 rods wide along the northerly side &

---

8. Richard Chenevix Trench (1807–1886), Irish author, philologist, and archbishop of Dublin; from his *On the Study of Words* (1852).
9. In Greek mythology the Nereids, or sea nymphs, were fifty daughters of the sea god Nereus; Triton and Proteus were minor sea gods, the latter capable of transforming himself into various natural forms.

the W end—wider at the E end—yet after running round from
W to E it does not keep the S shore but crosses in front of the deep
cove in a broad crack to where it started—by the Ice ground It is
glorious to behold the life & joy of this ribbon of water sparkling in
the sun— The wind blows eastward over the opaque ice—unusually hard owing to the recent severe though transient cold—all watered or waved like a tesselated floor—a figured carpet— Yet
dead—yet in vain till it slides on to the living water surface, where
it raises a myriad brilliant sparkles on the bare face of the pond—
and expression of glee—of youth—of spring—as if it spoke the joy
of the fishes within it—& of the sands on its shore— A silvery
sheen like the scales of a leuciscus—as if it were all one active fish
in the spring. It is the contrast between life & death— There is the
difference between winter and spring. The bared face of the pond
sparkles with joy. How handsome the curves which the edge of the
ice makes answering somewhat to those of the shore but more regular—sweeping entirely round the pond—as if defined by a vast
bold sweep—

* * *

Dec 22nd 53

A slight whitening of snow last evening—the 2nd whitening of
the winter—just enough to spoil the skating now 10 days old on
the ponds— Walden skimmed over in the widest part, but some
acres still open—will to-night prob. freeze entirely to-night if this
weather holds.

Surveying the last 3 days— They have not yielded much that I
am aware of— All I find is old bound marks—and the slowness &
dullness of farmers reconfirmed— They even complain that I walk
too fast for them. Their legs have become stiff from toil. This
coarse & hurried out door work compels me to live grossly or be
inattentive to my diet—that is the worst of it. Like work—like diet
that I find is the rule. Left to my chosen pursuits I should never
drink tea nor coffee, nor eat meal. The diet of any class or generation is the natural result of its employment and locality. It is remarkable how unprofitable it is for the most part to talk with
farmers.— They commonly stand on their good-behavior & attempt to moralize or philosophize in a serious conversation—.
Sportsmen & loafers are better company. For society a man must
not be too *good* or well disposed to spoil his natural disposition—
The bad are frequently good enough to let you see how bad they
are—but the good as frequently endeavor get between you and
themselves.— I have dined out 5 times & tea'd once within a
week—4 times there was tea on the dinner table always meat but
once—once baked beans—always pie but no puddings. I suspect
tea has taken the place of cider with farmers I am reminded of

Haydon the painter's[1] experience when he went about painting the nobility— I go about to the houses of the farmers & squires in like manner— This is my portrait painting—when I would fain be employed on higher subjects. I have offered myself much more earnestly as a lecturer than a surveyor— Yet I do not get any employment as a lecturer was not invited to lecture once last winter and only once (without pay) this winter—but I can get surveying enough—which a hundred others in this county can do as well as I—though it is not boasting much to say that a hundred others in N. England cannot lecture as well as I on my themes. But they who do not make the highest demand on you shall rue it— It is because they make a low demand on themselves. All the while that they use only your humbler faculties—your higher unemployed faculties— like an invisible cimetar are cutting them in twain. Woe be to the generation that lets any higher faculty in its midst go unemployed—that is to deny God & know him not—& he accordingly will know not of them.

* * *

That[2] sand foliage! It convinces me that nature is still in her youth— That florid fact about which Mythology merely mutters— that the very soil—can fabulate as well as you or I. It stretches forth its baby fingers on every side. Fresh curls spring forth from its bald brow— There is nothing inorganic— This earth is not then a mere fragment of dead history—strata upon strata like the leaves of a book—an object for a museum & an Antiquarian but living poetry like the leaves of a tree— —not a fossil earth—but a living specimen. You may melt your metals & cast them into the most beautiful moulds you can—they will never excite me like the forms which this molten earth flows out into— The very earth—as well as the institutions upon it—is plastic like potters clay in the hands of the artist. These florid heaps lie along the bank like the slag of a furnace—showing that nature is in full-blast within.   but there is No admittance except on business. Ye dead & alive preachers. Ye have no business here. Ye will enter it only as your tomb.

I fear only lest my expressions may not be extravagant enough— may not wander far enough beyond the narrow limits of our ordinary insight & faith—so as to be adequate to the truth of which I have been convinced. I desire to speak somewhere without bounds in order that I may attain to an expression in some degree adequate to truth of which I have been convinced— From a man in a waking moment to men in their waking moments. Wandering toward the

---

1. Benjamin Robert Haydon (1786–1846), ambitious English painter of historical and religious subjects, known for his portraits of William Wordsworth and John Keats, among others. Thoreau alludes to his *Autobiography and Journals* (1853).
2. February 5, 1854.

more distant boundaries of wider pastures— Nothing is so truly bounded & obedient to law as music—yet nothing so surely breaks all petty & narrow bonds.

Whenever I hear any music I fear that I may have spoken tamely & within bounds. And I am convinced that I cannot exaggerate enough even to lay the foundation of a true expression— As for books & the adequateness of their statements to the truth—they are as the tower of Babel[3] to the sky.

* * *

Feb 19

Many College text books which were a weariness & a stumbling block—when *studied* I have since read a little in with pleasure & profit.

For several weeks—the fall has seemed far behind—spring comparatively near— Yet I cannot say that there is any positive sign of spring yet—only we feel that we are sloping toward it. The sky has sometimes a warmth in its colors more like summer— A few birds have possibly strayed northward—further than they have wintered—

Pm to Fair Haven by river, back by RR. Though the wind is cold, the earth feels the heat of the sun higher in the heavens & melts in ploughed fields. The willow twigs rise out of the ice beside the river the silvery down of each Catkin just peeping from under each scale in some places—the work probably of last falls sun—like a mouse peeping from under its covert. I incline to walk now in swamps & on the river ponds—where I cannot walk in summer— I am struck by the greenness of the green briar at this season still covering the alders &c 12 feet high & full of shining & fresh berries— The greenness of the sassafrass shoots makes a similar impression.

The large moths ap.[4] love the neighborhood of water—& are wont to suspend their coccoons over the edge of the meadow & river—places more or less inaccessible to men at least. I saw a button bush with what at first sight looked like the open pods of the locust or of the water asclepias attached— They were the light ash-colored coccoons of the A. Promethea 4 or 5—with the completely withered & faded leaves wrapt around them—& so artfully and admirably secured to the twigs by fine silk wound round the leaf-stalk & the twig—which last add nothing to its strength being deciduous, but aid its deception— They are taken at a little distance for a few curled & withered leaves left on. Though the particular twigs on which you find some coccoons may never or very

---

3. In Genesis 11.1–9, God prevents the completion of this tower by rendering the language shared by its builders incomprehensible to them.
4. Apparently.

rarely retain any leaves the maple for instance—there are enough
leaves left on other shrubs & trees to warrant their adopting this
disguise. Yet it is startling to think that the inference has in this
case been drawn by some mind that as most other plants retain
some leaves the walker will suspect these also to.

Each and all such disguises & other resources remind us that not
some poor worms instinct merely, as we call it, but the mind of the
universe rather which we share has been intended upon each particular object— All the wit in the world was brought to bear on
each case to secure its end— It was long ago in a full senate of all
intellects determined how coccoons had best be suspended—kindred mind with mine that admires & approves decided it so. ***
The snow not only reveals a track but sometimes hands it down—to
the ice that succeeds it. The sled track which I saw in the slight
snow over the ice here Feb. 2nd—though we have had many snows
since—& now there is no snow at all—is still perfectly marked on
the ice.

Much study a weariness of the flesh! eh? But did not they intend
that we should read & ponder—who covered the whole earth with
alphabets—primers or bibles coarse or fine print—the very debris
of the cliffs—the—stivers of the rocks are covered with geograpic
lichens—no surface is permitted to be bare long—as by an inevitable decree we have come to times at last when our very waste
paper is printed. Was not he who creates lichens the abetter of
Cadmus[5] when he invented letters. Types almost arrange themselves into words & sentences as dust arrange itself under the magnet. Print!—it is a close-hugging lichen that forms on a favorable
surface—which paper offers— The linen gets itself wrought into
paper—that the song of the shirt may be printed on it— Who
placed us with eyes between a microscopic and a telescopic
world?***

I wait till sundown on Fair Haven to hear it[6] boom but am disappointed—though I hear much slight crackling—but as for the previous cracking—it is so disruptive & produces such a commotion
that it extends itself through snow drifts six inches deep, and is
even more distinct there than in bare ice even to the sharpest angle
of its forking. Saw an otter track near Walden.

* * *

In[7] correcting my mss—which I do with sufficient phlegm. I find
that I invariably turn out much that is good along with the bad,
which it is then impossible for me to distinguish— —so much for

5. In Greek mythology, the founder of the city of Thebes, who is said to have introduced
    the Phoenician alphabet to Greece.
6. I.e., Fair Haven Pond, about one-half mile southwest of Walden Pond.
7. March 1, 1854; "mss" is the abbreviation for "manuscripts."

keeping bad company—but after the lapse of time having purified the main body & thus created a distinct standard for comparison— I can review the rejected sentence & easily detect those which deserve to be readmitted.

Pm to Walden via R W E's[8]

I am surprised to see how bare Minott's hillside is already— It is already spring there & Minott is puttering outside in the sun— How wise in his Grandfather to select such a site for a house—the summers he has lived have been so much longer.

How pleasant the calm season & the warmth—(The sun is even like a burning glass on my back—) & the sight & sound of melting snow running down the hill. I look in among the withered grass blades for some starting greenness— I listen to hear the first blue-bird in the soft air. I hear the dry clucking of hens which have come abroad.

The ice at Walden is softened—the skating is gone—with a stick you can loosen it to the depth of an inch or the first freezing & turn it up in cakes. Yesterday you could skate here—now only *close* to the *south* shore.

I notice the redness of the andromeda leaves—but not so much as once— The sand foliage is now in its prime.

March 2nd

A Corner man tells me that Witherel has seen a blue-bird & Martial Miles thought that he heard one. I doubt it. It may have been given to Witherel to see the first blue bird—so much has been withholden from him[9]

What produces the peculiar softness of the air yesterday & today—as if it were the air of the south suddenly pillowed amid our wintry hills— We have suddenly a different sky—a dif. atmosphere. It is as if the subtlest possible soft vapor were diffused through the atmosphere Warm Air has come to us from the S, but charged with moisture—which will yet distill in rain or congeal into snow & hail—

The sand foliage is vital in its form—reminding me what are called the vitals of the animal body— I am not sure that its arteries are even hollow   They are rather meandering channels with remarkably distinct sharp edges—formed instantaneously as by magic— How rapidly & perfectly it organizes itself— The material must be sufficiently cohesive. I suspect that a certain portion of clay is necessary. Mixed Sand & clay being saturated with melted ice & snow—the most liquid portion flows downward through the

---

8. Ralph Waldo Emerson's.
9. Thoreau added this sentence later. Both Witherel and Miles were local fishermen and ne'er-do-wells; the Corner (or Nine Acre Corner) was a relatively populous area in southern Middlesex county. See Concord map.

mass forming for itself instantly a perfect canal—using the best materials the mass—affords for its banks— It digs & builds it in a twinkling— The less fluid portions clog the artery change its course and form thick stems & leaves— The lobe principle—lobe of the ear (labor-lapsus?)

On the outside all the life of the earth is expressed in animal or vegetable—but make a deep cut in it & you find it vital— —you find in the very sands an anticipation of the vegetable leaf— No wonder then that plants grow & spring in it— The atoms have already learned the law— Let a vegetable sap convey it upwards and you have a vegetable leaf— No wonder that the earth expresses itself outwardly in leaves—which labors with the idea thus inwardly— The overhanging leaf sees here its prototype. The earth is pregnant with law—

The various shades of this sand foliage are very agreeable to the eye. including all the different colors which iron assumes—brown—grey—yellowish reddish—& clay-color. Perhaps it produces the greater effect by arranged the sands of the same color—side by side—bringing them together.

* * *

Saw[1] several yellow red poles—(sylvia petechia) on the willows by the Hubbard bridge Am not sure I heard their note— May have mistaken it formerly for the Pine warbler—its chestnut crown would distinguish it. Hazel the *very first* male open.

I find that I can criticise my composition best when I stand at a little distance from it—when I do not see it, for instance—. I make a little chapter of contents which enables me to recall it page by page to my mind—& judge it more impartially when my MSS is out of the way. The distraction of surveying enables me rapidly to take new points of view. A day or two surveying is equal to a journey.

Pickerel have darted in shallows for nearly a week.

Some poets mature early & die young. Their fruits have a delicious flavor like strawberries—but do not keep till fall or winter— Others are slower in coming to their growth Their fruits maybe less delicious—but are a more lasting food & are so hardened by the sun of summer & the coolness of autumn that they keep sound over winter— The first are June eatings—early but soon withering—the last are russets which last till June again.

* * *

Wednesday Aug 9th   To Boston
Walden published. Elder berries. Waxwork yellowing.

1. P.M., April 8, 1854.

REVIEWS AND
POSTHUMOUS
ASSESSMENTS

Thanks to vigorous promotion by the publisher James T. Fields, *Walden* seems to have been well received and widely reviewed. To date, sixty-nine contemporary reviews have been located, the majority reported to be "strongly favorable."[1] Sales were brisk in the first year, after which the book sold modestly. *Walden* was reissued after Thoreau's death, in spring 1862.

Between 1863 and 1866, Ticknor and Fields brought out five volumes of Thoreau's travel writings, political and natural history essays, and letters, enlisting Henry's sister, Sophia, and friends William Ellery Channing and Ralph Waldo Emerson as editors. "Walking and "Wild Apples" appeared in the first of these volumes, *Excursions* (Boston: Ticknor and Fields, 1863), edited by Sophia and Channing and containing Emerson's memoir, "Thoreau." As indicated by even the brief selection of *Excursions* reviews reprinted here, Emerson's profile of his friend considerably shaped Thoreau's reception, as it does still.

"Civil Disobedience" and "Slavery in Massachusetts" were collected with other political essays and Thoreau's excursion to Canada in the final volume, *A Yankee in Canada, with Anti-Slavery and Reform Papers* (Boston: Ticknor and Fields, 1866), also edited by Sophia Thoreau and Channing. Appearing after emancipation and in the first months of Reconstruction, these essays seemed mostly irrelevant to reviewers, with perhaps the sole exception of Sydney Morse. Unlike Thoreau the naturist, whose green blade began to reemerge about fifteen years after the author's death (stimulated by the marketing of Houghton Mifflin in the 1880s), his reputation as political writer and social critic lay dormant until it was revived in the 1890s by socialists in England and, in the first decade of the new century, by radicals in the United States.

Readers interested in additional reviews of *Walden* should consult Joel Myerson's *Emerson and Thoreau: The Contemporary Reviews* (Cambridge: Cambridge University Press, 1992). Gary Scharnhorst provides a nearly exhaustive list of nineteenth-century commentary in *Henry David Thoreau: An Annotated Bibliography of Comment and Criticism before 1900* (New York: Garland 1992); less complete but still useful is Raymond Borst, *Henry David Thoreau: A Reference Guide, 1835–1899* (Boston: G. K. Hall, 1987). Selected criticism from

1. See Bradley P. Dean and Gary Scharnhorst, "The Contemporary Reception of *Walden*," *Studies in the American Renaissance 1990*, 293–328, and Bradley P. Dean and Richard E. Winslow III, "Three Newly Discovered Contemporary Reviews of *Walden*," *Thoreau Society Bulletin* 240 (Summer 2002): 1–2.

1848 to 1964 is reprinted in Wendell Glick, *The Recognition of Henry David Thoreau* (Ann Arbor: University of Michigan Press, 1969). On Thoreau's nineteenth-century reputation and late-century canonization, see Gary Scharnhorst, *Henry David Thoreau: A Case Study in Canonization* (Columbia, S.C.: Camden House, 1993); and Lawrence Buell, *The Environmental Imagination: Thoreau, Nature Writing, and the Formation of American Culture* (Cambridge, Mass.: Harvard University Press, 1995), 311–15, 340–69.

[Review of *Walden*]†

This is a remarkable book. The thread of the work is a narrative of the personal experience of the eccentric author as a hermit on the shores of Walden Pond. The body consists of his reflections on life and its pursuits. Mr. Thoreau carried out his ideas of "communism" by building with his own hands an humble hut, cultivating his own garden patch, earning with the sweat of his brow enough of coarse food to sustain life, and living independent of the world and of its circumstances. He continued this selfish existence for two years, and then returned to society, but why, he does not inform his readers. Whether satisfied that he had mistaken the "pleasures of solitude," or whether the self-improvement which the world has charitably supposed was the object of his retirement had been accomplished, it is certain that he was relieved of none of his selfish opinions—that he left behind in the woods of Concord none of his misanthropy, and that he brought back habits of thought which, though profound, are erratic, and often border on the transcendental.

The narrative of the two years hermit life of such a man can hardly fail to be attractive, and the study of the workings of a mind so constituted must possess a peculiar interest. But the attraction is without sympathy—the interest is devoid of admiration. The outré opinions of a mind like that of Mr. Thoreau, while they will attract attention as the eccentric outbursts of real genius, so far from finding a response in the bosom of the reader, will excite a smile, from their very extravagance, and we can easily imagine that if Mr. Thoreau would banish from his mind the idea that man is an oyster, he might become a passable philospher.

Mr. Thoreau has made an attractive book—more attractive than his "Week on the Concord and Merrimack." But while many will be fascinated by its contents, few will be improved. As the pantheistic doctrines of the author marred the beauty of his former work, so does his selfish philosophy darkly tinge the pages of "Walden," and

† From Boston *Daily Journal* (August 10, 1854): 1.

the best that can be said of the work in its probable effects is, that while many will be charmed by the descriptive powers of the author, and will smile at his extravagant ideas, few will be influenced by his opinions. This is a negative virtue in a book which is likely to be widely circulated, and which might do much mischief if the author could establish a bond of sympathy with the reader.

[Review of *Walden*]†

The author of this book—Mr. Henry D. Thoreau—is undoubtedly a man of genius. It is not possible to open twenty pages without finding plentiful indications of that fact. Unfortunately, however, he is an erratic genius, thoroughly impracticable, and apt to confuse rather than arrange the order of things, mental and physical.

Mr. Thoreau, it will be remembered, was one of the earliest contributors to Emerson's remarkable transcendental publication, the *Dial*. His eccentricities constituted one of the features of that very eccentric journal, and were well suited to it. Subsequently he published a volume called *Week on the Concord and Merrimack Rivers*. A great deal of observation and quaintness were incorporated in the latter work, and obtained for it some popularity here and in Europe. Influenced by a peculiar philosophy of his own, Mr. Thoreau abandoned literature in 1845. He was probably disgusted with social life, and thought an experience of its savage phase might be agreeable. With this idea he "borrowed an axe" and went down to Walden Pond, in the vicinity of Concord, with the intention of building a house and living in it. The Cabin was constructed, and Mr. Thoreau occupied it for two years. Why he returned to society after that period he does not inform us. The present book was written in solitude, and occupied those spare moments when the author was not more profitably engaged in the labors of the field.

As a contribution to the Comic Literature of America, *Walden* is worthy of some attention, but in no other respect. The author evidently imagines himself to be a Philosopher, but he is not. He talks constantly of "vast cosmogonal themes," but narrows them all down to the nearest line of self. The mere fact of existence seems to satisfy Mr. Thoreau. He wonders why men aspire to anything higher than the cultivation of a patch of beans, when by that they may live—perhaps grow fat. Mr. Thoreau has been accused of communistic principles. This is his idea of communism: "I would rather sit on a pumpkin, and have it all to myself, than be crowded on a vel-

† From *New York Times* (September 22, 1854): 3.

vet cushion. I would rather ride on earth, in an ox cart, with a free
circulation, than go to Heaven in the fancy car of an excursion
train, and breathe a *malaria* all the way."

This is one of Mr. Thoreau's "vast cosmogonal themes": "While
civilization has been improving our houses, it has not equally improved the men who are to inhabit them. It has created palaces,
but it was not so easy to create noblemen and kings. And *if the civilized man's pursuits are no worthier than the savage's—if he employed the greater part of his life in obtaining gross necessaries and
comforts merely—why should he have a better dwelling than the former?*" In other words, why should he not live like a savage, to save
the trouble of living like a Christian?

Mr. Thoreau denounces everything that indicates progress. Railroads, telegraphs, steam engines, newspapers, and everything else
which the world values, offend him. There is nothing estimable in
his eyes but a log hut and a patch of beans. On the latter he dwells
with infinite delight. It is one of the few things that does not disgust his philosophical mind. Ascetics who have a taste for beans
will find comfort in this volume.

Mr. Thoreau is a good writer, possessed of great comic powers,
and able to describe accurately many peculiar phases of nature. But
the present work will fail to satisfy any class of readers. The literary
man may be pleased with the style, but he will surely lament the
selfish *animus*[1] of the book.

[GAMALIEL BAILEY?]

[Review of *Walden*]†

In its narrative, this book is unique, in its philosophy quite Emersonian. It is marked by genius of a certain order, but just as
strongly, by pride of intellect. It contains many acute observations
on the follies of mankind, but enough of such follies to show that
its author has his full share of the infirmities of human nature,
without being conscious of it. By precept and example he clearly
shows how very little is absolutely necessary to the subsistence of a
man, what a Robinson Crusoe life he may lead in Massachusetts,
how little labor he need perform, if he will but reduce his wants to
the philosophical standard, and how much time he may then have
for meditation and study. To go out and squat, all alone, by a pretty
pond in the woods, dig, lay the foundation of a little cabin, and put

---

1. Animating spirit, hostile character.
† From *National Era* 8 (September 28, 1854): 155.

it up, with borrowed tools, furnish it, raise corn, beans, and potatoes, and do one's own cooking, hermit like, so that the total cost of
the whole building, furnishing, purchasing necessaries, and living
for eight months, shall not exceed forty or fifty dollars, may do for
an experiment, by a highly civilized man, with Yankee versatility,
who has had the full benefit of the best civilization of the age. All
men are not "up to" everything. But, if they were, if they all had the
universal genius of the "Yankee nation," how long would they remain civilized, by squatting upon solitary duck-ponds, eschewing
matrimony, casting off all ties of family, each one setting his wits to
work to see how little he could do with; and how much of that little he could himself accomplish? At the end of eight months, Mr.
Thoreau might remain a ruminating philosopher, but he would
have few but ruminating animals to write books for.

But, with all its extravagances, its sophisms, and its intellectual
pride, the book is acute and suggestive, and contains passages of
great beauty.

ELIZABETH BARSTOW STODDARD

[Review of *Walden*]†

If my limits would allow, the Book I would most like to expatiate
upon, would be Thoreau's *Walden, or Life in the Woods*, published
by Ticknor and Fields, Boston. It is the result of a two or three
years' sojourn in the woods, and it is a most minute history of
Thoreau's external life, and internal speculation. It is the latest ef-
fervescence of the peculiar school, at the head of which stands
Ralph Waldo Emerson. Of *Walden*, Emerson says, that Thoreau has
cornered nature in it. Several years ago Thoreau sought the freedom of the woods, and built him a little house with his two hands,
on the margin of Walden Pond, near Concord, Massachusetts.
There he contemplated, on "cornered" nature, and hoed beans, determined, as he said, to know them. Notwithstanding an apparent
contempt for utility, he seems a sharp accountant, and not a little
interest is attached to his bills of expense, they are so ludicrously
small. Coarse bread, occasional molasses and rice, now and then a
fish taken from Walden Pond, and philosophically matured vegetables, (he sold his beans) were his fare. His ideas of beauty are
positive, but limited. The world of art is beyond his wisdom. Individualism is the altar at which he worships. Philanthropy is an

† From *Daily Alta California* (October 8, 1854): 2.

opposite term, and he does not scruple to affirm that Philanthropy and he are two. The book is full of talent, curious and interesting. I recommend it as a study to all fops, male and female.

CHARLES FREDERICK BRIGGS†

A Yankee Diogenes

The New England character is essentially anti-Diogenic; the Yankee is too shrewd not to comprehend the advantages of living in what we call the world; there are no bargains to be made in the desert, nobody to be taken advantage of in the woods, while the dwellers in tubs and shanties have slender opportunities of bettering their condition by barter. When the New Englander leaves his home, it is not for the pleasure of living by himself; if he is migratory in his habits, it is not from his fondness for solitude, nor from any impatience he feels at living in a crowd. Where there are most men, there is, generally, most money, and there is where the strongest attractions exist for the genuine New Englander. A Yankee Diogenes is a *lusus*,[1] and we feel a peculiar interest in reading the account which an oddity of that kind gives of himself. The name of Thoreau has not a New England sound; but we believe that the author of *Walden* is a genuine New Englander, and of New England antecedents and education. Although he plainly gives the reasons for publishing his book, at the outset, he does not clearly state the causes that led him to live the life of a hermit on the shore of Walden Pond. But we infer from his volume that his aim was the very remarkable one of trying to be something, while he lived upon nothing; in opposition to the general rule of striving to live upon something, while doing nothing. Mr. Thoreau probably tried the experiment long enough to test its success, and then fell back again into his normal condition. But he does not tell us such was the case. He was happy enough to get back among the good people of Concord, we have no doubt; for although he paints his shanty-life in rose-colored tints, we do not believe he liked it, else why not stick to it? We have a mistrust of the sincerity of the St. Simon Stylites',[2] and suspect that they come down from their pillars in the

---

† From *Putnam's Monthly Magazine* 4 (October 1854): 443–48. Lengthy extracts from *Walden* have been omitted.
1. An oddity or freak of nature. Diogenes (c. 400–325 B.C.E.), member of a Greek philosophical sect, the Cynics, who stressed stoic self-sufficiency and rejected luxury and conventionalism; he lived in poverty and is said to have inhabited an earthenware tub [*Editor*].
2. Imitators of Saint Simeon Stylites (c. 390–459), a Syrian monk and reputed miracle worker who lived on a column fifty feet high, from which he counseled and healed pilgrims [*Editor*].

night-time, when nobody is looking at them. Diogenes placed his tub where Alexander would be sure of seeing it, and Mr. Thoreau ingenuously confesses that he occasionally went out to dine, and when the society of woodchucks and chipping-squirrels were insufficient for his amusement, he liked to go into Concord and listen to the village gossips in the stores and taverns. Mr. Thoreau informs us that he lived alone in the woods, by the shore of Walden Pond, in a shanty built by his own hands, a mile from any neighbor, two years and a half. What he did there besides writing the book before us, cultivating beans, sounding Walden Pond, reading Homer, baking johnny-cakes, studying Brahminical theology, listening to chipping-squirrels, receiving visits, and having high imaginations, we do not know. He gives us the results of his bean cultivation with great particularity, and the cost of his shanty; but the actual results of his two years and a half of hermit life he does not give. But there have been a good many lives spent and a good deal of noise made about them, too, from the sum total of whose results not half so much good could be extracted as may be found in this little volume. Many a man will find pleasure in reading it, and many a one, we hope, will be profited by its counsels. A tour in Europe would have cost a good deal more, and not have produced half as much. As a matter of curiosity, to show how cheaply a gentleman of refined tastes, lofty aspirations and cultivated intellect may live, even in these days of high prices, we copy Mr. Thoreau's account of his first year's operations; he did better, he informs us, the second year. The entire cost of his house, which answered all his purposes, and was as comfortable and showy as he desired, was $28 12½. But one cannot live on a house unless he rents it to somebody else, even though he be a philosopher and a believer in Vishnu. Mr. Thoreau felt the need of a little ready money, one of the most convenient things in the world to have by one, even before his house was finished.

"Wishing to earn ten or twelve dollars by some agreeable and honest method," he observes, "I planted about two acres and a half of light and sandy soil, chiefly with beans, but also a small part with potatoes and corn, peas and turnips." As he was a squatter, he paid nothing for rent, and as he was making no calculation for future crops, he expended nothing for manure so that the results of his farming will not be highly instructive to young agriculturists, nor be likely to be held up as excitements to farming pursuits by agricultural periodicals.***

*** according to his figures it cost him twenty-seven cents a week to live, clothes included; and for this sum he lived healthily and happily, received a good many distinguished visitors, who, to humor his style, used to leave their names on a leaf or a chip, when they did not happen to find him at home. But, it strikes us that all the knowledge which the "Hermit of Walden" gained by his singular experiment in living might have been done just as well, and as satisfactorily, without any experiment at all. We know what it costs to feed prisoners, paupers and soldiers; we know what the cheapest and most nutritious food costs, and how little it requires to keep up the bodily health of a full-grown man. A very simple calculation will enable any one to satisfy himself in regard to such points. and those who wish to live upon twenty-seven cents a week, may indulge in that pleasure. The great Abernethy's prescription for the attainment of perfect bodily health was, "live on sixpence a day and earn it." But that would be Sybaritic indulgence compared with Mr. Thoreau's experience, whose daily expenditure hardly amounted to a quarter of that sum. And he lived happily, too, though it don't exactly speak volumes in favor of his system to announce that he only continued his economical mode of life two years. If it was "the thing," why did he not continue it? But, if he did not always live like a hermit, squatting on other people's property, and depending upon chance perch and pickerel for his dinner, he lived enough by his own labor, and carried his system of economy to such a degree of perfection, that he tells us:

> "More than five years I maintained myself thus solely by the labor of my hands, and I found that working about six weeks in a year, I could meet all the expenses of living."

* * *

There is nothing of the mean or sordid in the economy of Mr. Thoreau, though to some his simplicity and abstemiousness may appear trivial and affected; he does not live cheaply for the sake of saving, nor idly to avoid labor; but, that he may live independently and enjoy his great thoughts; that he may read the Hindoo scriptures and commune with the visible forms of nature. We must do him the credit to admit that there is no mock sentiment, nor simulation of piety or philanthropy in his volume. He is not much of a cynic, and though we have called him a Yankee Diogenes, the only personage to whom he bears a decided resemblance is that good humored creation of Dickens, Mark Tapley, whose delight was in being jolly under difficulties.

* * *

There is much excellent good sense delivered in a very comprehensive and by no means unpleasant style in Mr. Thoreau's book, and let people think as they may of the wisdom or propriety of living after his fashion, denying oneself all the luxuries which the earth can afford, for the sake of leading a life of lawless vagabondage, and freedom from starched collars, there are but few readers who will fail to find profit and refreshment in his pages. Perhaps some practical people will think that a philosopher like Mr. Thoreau might have done the world a better service by purchasing a piece of land, and showing how much it might be made to produce, instead of squatting on another man's premises, and proving how little will suffice to keep body and soul together. But we must allow philosophers, and all other men, to fulfill their missions in their own way. If Mr. Thoreau had been a practical farmer, we should not have been favored with his volume; his corn and cabbage would have done but little towards profiting us, and we might never have been the better for his labors. As it is, we see how much more valuable to mankind is our philosophical vagabond than a hundred sturdy agriculturists; any plodder may raise beans, but it is only one in a million who can write a readable volume.

* * *

[Review of *Walden*]†

This is a charming volume by a writer who reminds us of Emerson by his philosophy—of the Elizabethan writers by his quaintness and originality—and by his minuteness and acuteness of observation, of Gilbert White,[1] the author of the Natural History of Selborne. Mr. Thoreau lived alone in the woods for two years, a mile from any neighbor, in a house which he had built himself in Concord, Mass., on the shore of Walden Pond. In the present volume he relates in a lively and sparkling, yet pithy style, his experiences during that period—describing the various natural phenomena, the sights and sounds, as well as the different phases of humanity, that fell under his observation and favoring us with exact statistics of the cost of supporting his hermit life. It is rarely that one finds so much originality and freshness in a modern book—such an entire absence of conventionality and cant—or so much suggestive observation on the philosophy of life. Almost every page abounds in brilliant, and piquant things, which, in spite of the intellectual pride of the author—the intense and occasionally unpleasant egotism with which every line is steeped—lure the reader on with bewitched attention from title-page to finis. Mr. Thoreau has an odd twist in his brains, but, as Hazlitt[2] says of Sir Thomas Browne, they are "all the better for the twist." The best parts of the book, to our mind, are those

† From *Yankee Blade* (October 28, 1854): 3.
1. Gilbert White (1720–1793), English naturalist and ornithologist; author of *The Natural History and Antiquities of Selborne* (1789) [*Editor*].
2. William Hazlitt (1778–1830), English essayist and literary critic; from *Lectures on the Literature of the Age of Elizabeth* (1817), quoting Samuel Taylor Coleridge on English

which treat of Sounds, Solitude, Brute Neighbors, Winter Animals, The Pond in Winter, and Reading; the poorest, the Conclusion, in which he tries to Emersonize, and often "attains" triumphantly to the obscurity which he seems to court.

[LYDIA MARIA CHILD?]

[Review of *A Week on the Concord and Merrimack Rivers* and *Walden*]†

These books spring from a depth of thought which will not suffer them to be put by, and are written in a spirit in striking contrast with that which is uppermost in our time and country. Out of the heart of practical, hard-working, progressive New England comes these Oriental utterances. The life exhibited in them teaches us, much more impressively than any number of sermons could, that this Western activity of which we are so proud, these material improvements, this commercial enterprise, this rapid accumulation of wealth, even our external, associated philanthropic action, are very easily overrated. The true glory of the human soul is not to be reached by the most rapid travelling in car or steamboat, by the instant transmission of intelligence however far, by the most speedy accumulation of a fortune, and however efficient measures we may adopt for the reform of the intemperate, the emancipation of the enslaved, &c., it will avail little unless we are ourselves essentially noble enough to inspire those whom we would so benefit with nobleness. External bondage is trifling compared with the bondage of an ignoble soul. Such things are often said, doubtless, in pulpits and elsewhere, but the men who say them are too apt to live just with the crowd, and so their words come more and more to ring with a hollow sound.

It is refreshing to find in these books the sentiments of one man whose aim manifestly is to *live*, and not to waste his time upon the externals of living. Educated at Cambridge, in the way called liberal, he seems determined to make a liberal life of it, and not to become the slave of any calling, for the sake of earning a reputable livelihood or of being regarded as a useful member of society. He evidently considers it his first business to become more and more a living, advancing soul, knowing that thus alone (though he desires

---

author, Sir Thomas Browne (1605–1682): "In short, he has brains in his head, which is all the more interesting for a little twist in the brains" [*Editor*].
† From the *National Anti-Slavery Standard* (December 16, 1854): 3.

to think as little as possible about that) can he be, in any proper sense, useful to others. Mr. Thoreau's view of life has been called selfish. His own words, under the head of "Philanthropy" in *Walden*, are the amplest defence against this charge, to those who can appreciate them. In a deeper sense than we commonly think, charity begins at home. The man who, with any fidelity, obeys his own genius, serves men infinitely more by so doing, becoming an encouragement, a strengthener, a fountain of inspiration to them, than if he were to turn aside from his path and exhaust his energies in striving to meet their superficial needs. As a thing by the way, aside from our proper work, we may seek to remove external obstacles from the path of our neighbours, but no man can help them much who makes that his main business, instead of seeking evermore, with all his energies, to reach the loftiest point which his imagination sets before him, thus adding to the stock of true nobleness in the world.

But suppose all men should pursue Mr. Thoreau's course, it is asked triumphantly, as though, then, we should be sure to go back to barbarism. Let it be considered, in the first place, that no man could pursue his course who was a mere superficial imitator, any more than it would be a real imitation of Christ if all men were to make it their main business to go about preaching the Gospel to each other. Is it progress toward barbarism to simplify one's outward life for the sake of coming closer to Nature and to the realm of ideas? Is it civilization and refinement to be occupied evermore with adding to our material conveniences, comforts and luxuries, to make ourselves not so much living members as dead tools of society, in some bank, shop, office, pulpit or kitchen? If men were to follow Mr. Thoreau's steps, by being more obedient to their loftiest instincts, there would, indeed, be a falling off in the splendour of our houses, in the richness of our furniture and dress, in the luxury of our tables, but how poor are these things in comparison with the new grandeur and beauty which would appear in the souls of men. What fresh and inspiring conversation should we have, instead of the wearisome gossip which now meets us at every turn. Men toil on, wearing out body or soul, or both, that they may accumulate a needless amount of the externals of living; that they may win the regard of those no wiser than themselves; their natures become warped and hardened to their pursuits; they get fainter and fainter glimpses of the glory of the world, and, by and by, comes into their richly-adorned parlours some wise and beautiful soul, like the writer of these books, who, speaking from the fullness of his inward life, makes their luxuries appear vulgar, showing that, in a direct way, he has obtained the essence of that which his entertainers have been vainly seeking for at such a terrible expense.

It seems remarkable, that these books have received no more adequate notice in our Literary Journals. But the class of scholars are often as blind as others to any new elevation of soul. In *Putnam's Magazine*, Mr. Thoreau is spoken of as an oddity, as the Yankee Diogenes, as though the really ridiculous oddity were not in us of the "starched shirt-collar" rather than in this devotee of Nature and Thought. Some have praised the originality and profound sympathy with which he views natural objects. We might as well stop with praising Jesus for the happy use he has made of the lilies in the field. The fact of surpassing interest for us is the simple grandeur of Mr. Thoreau's position—a position open to us all, and of which this sympathy with Nature is but a single result. This is seen in the less descriptive, more purely thoughtful passages, such as that upon Friendship in the "Wednesday" of the *Week*, and in those upon "Solitude," "What I lived for," and "Higher Laws," in *Walden*, as well as in many others in both books. We do not believe that, in the whole course of literature, ancient and modern, so noble a discourse upon Friendship can be produced as that which Mr. Thoreau has given us. It points to a relation, to be sure, which, from the ordinary level of our lives, may seem remote and dreamy. But it is our thirst for, and glimpses of, such things which indicate the greatness of our nature, which give the purest charm and colouring to our lives. The striking peculiarity of Mr. Thoreau's attitude is, that while he is no religionist, and while he is eminently practical in regard to the material economies of life, he yet manifestly feels, through and through, that the loftiest dreams of the imagination are the solidest realities, and so the only foundation for us to build upon, while the affairs in which men are everywhere busying themselves so intensely are comparatively the merest froth and foam.

GEORGE ELIOT

[Review of *Walden*]†

In a volume called *Walden; or, Life in the Woods*, published last year, but quite interesting enough to make it worth while for us to break our rule by a retrospective notice—we have a bit of pure American life (not the 'go ahead' species, but its opposite pole), animated by that energetic, yet calm spirit of innovation, that practical as well as theoretic independence of formulæ, which is peculiar to some of the finer American minds. The writer tells us how he

† From *Westminster Review* 65 (January 1856): 302–3. Lengthy extracts from *Walden* have been omitted.

chose, for some years, to be a stoic of the woods; how he built his house, how he earned the necessaries of his simple life by cultivating a bit of ground. He tells his system of diet, his studies, his reflections, and his observations of natural phenomena. These last are not only made by a keen eye, but have their interest enhanced by passing through the medium of a deep poetic sensibility; and, indeed, we feel throughout the book the presence of a refined as well as a hardy mind. People—very wise in their own eyes—who would have every man's life ordered according to a particular pattern, and who are intolerant of every existence the utility of which is not palpable to them, may pooh-pooh Mr. Thoreau and this episode in his history, as unpractical and dreamy. Instead of contesting their opinion ourselves, we will let Mr. Thoreau speak for himself. There is plenty of sturdy sense mingled with his unworldliness.

* * *

[Review of *Excursions*]†

Mr. EMERSON's biographical sketch, devoted to the memory of his late friend, is appropriately placed as an introduction to this collection of his contributions to periodical literature,—probably the last relics that the world will receive of HENRY D. THOREAU. More by the breath of friendly opinion and applause, perhaps, than by his own writings, THOREAU is now widely known as the man who dared to "live his life" his own way, irrespective of any other law, a scorner of shams, the apostle of individuality in an age of association and compromise, a passionate lover and practicer of his theory, and consequently somewhat stern and severe in his isolation, but richly endowed with traits that endeared him to the few he admitted to intimacy. That which even the slightest tinge of affectation would make ridiculous, in THOREAU became noble and noteworthy, from the singleness of his aim and the directness with which he pursued it. Civilized man to him was nothing. Nature, all in all. "In society you will not find health, but in nature. Unless our feet at least stood in the midst of nature all our faces would be pale and livid. Society is always diseased, and the best is the most so; there is no scent in it so wholsome as that of the pines, nor any fragrance so penetrating and restorative as the life-everlasting in high pastures." So he wrote on his twenty-fifth year, and how firmly he exemplified his principles his biographer may tell, "He was a protestant a *l'outrance*,[1] and few lives contained so many renunciations.

† From *New York Times* (November 23, 1863): 2.
1. See n. 1, p. 395.

He was bred to no profession; he never married; he lived alone; he never went to church; he never voted; he refused to pay a tax to the State; he ate no flesh; he drank no wine, and though a naturalist he used neither trap nor gun." There is little chance of such a career being often repeated, and it must be confessed that good citizens are not manufactured after this type. A single Thoreau may occasionally be admirable as an asserter of truths too often overlooked and forgotten in the feverish complexity of our lives, but a nation of them would necessitate a return to the habits of his favorite Indians. The papers in this volume all have interest and everywhere display the familiarity with nature's workings that he had acquired by the reverential study of her mysteries. His peculiarities are less apparent in his writings than they seem to have been in personal association. He writes like a gentleman and a student familiar with the current train of literature illustrative of the natural sciences, as well as the common places of poetical allusion. The living man, it was, indeed, that annoyed him; in the world of books—the true spirit world—he could commune with the intellectual past unvexed by the presence of the personal. "The Natural History of Massachusetts," "The Succession of Forest Trees," "Wild Apples," are articles that perhaps no one but Thoreau could have written, stray gleanings of the vast amount of natural knowledge collected, not for transmission, and which died with its owner.

[Review of *Excursions*]†

Mr. Thoreau was a kind of Massachusett's Diogenes,[1] slightly sand-papered by some culture and by the influence of society, which he could no more avoid, though he wished to, than he could the aeration of his blood by breathing. He was a disagreeable man, and thought that his attempts to be a barbarian were wise. He had, however, a wonderful power of seeing natural phenomena, a mastery of good English for describing them, and a certain sharp small philosophy of life besides. Out of these elements are constructed the essays which form this book. They are noticeable and worth reading. Mr. Emerson's introduction overvalues Mr. Thoreau. And for this Mr. Emerson may be honored. He is well known to be generous of praise, giving whole and rounded commendations out of his genuine and great bounty to things and persons only partial or one-sided in desert.

---

† From the New York *Independent* (December 3, 1863): 2.
1. See n. 1, p. 384.

[Review of *Excursions*]†

"Excursions by Henry D. Thoreau" (Ticknor & Fields) is a very remarkable and delightful book. Mr. Thoreau was a scholar and naturalist living in Concord, Massachusetts, who believed in Concord, in the Indians, and in himself. He had doubts whether, upon the whole, the race had not deteriorated by civilization; and had a profound admiration for the red men as for those who knew the secrets and resources of nature much more intimately than any savant. His life and his books are an airy protest against science and civilization, while no man had made better use of the best results of each. His observation of the phenomena of nature was most thorough, sympathetic, and profound, and his descriptions are of the best in literature. Indeed, in what is called rural literature, he is unsurpassed for the union of shrewd insight, quaint, racy, and vigorous thought, and a delightful play of humor over all, shimmering, cool, and remote, like the aurora borealis. He had no love of moral precedents or religious traditions. The world of to-day he thought as good as Paradise, and God as near to Concord as to Eden. A fresh, sweet, sturdy, noble man. He lived known to a few only, but being dead he speaks to all of us. His "Excursions" is the most original book we have lately had, as well as the most valuable record of exact observation of nature.

[Review of *A Yankee in Canada, with Anti-Slavery and Reform Papers*]†

Thoreau was a keen observer of men and things, and possessed descriptive powers of no mean order. His notes and observations on Canada are highly characteristic. The most of the volume is made up of miscellaneous papers on "Anti-Slavery and Reform." Those on John Brown[1] and Thomas Carlyle[2] are the most important. Some of his views on civil and social questions were singular enough. His asceticism tinged his mind and made him morbid on many subjects.

---

† From *Harper's Weekly* (December 12, 1863): 787.
† From *The Eclectic Magazine* 67 (November 1866): 636.
1. John Brown (1800–1859), American abolitionist who advocated violent action to end slavery. Captured in his raid on the federal armory at Harpers Ferry, Virginia, Brown was hanged for treason on December 2, 1859 [*Editor*].
2. Thomas Carlyle (1795–1881), Scottish essayist, historian, translator of German literature and friend of Emerson. Thoreau's essay on Carlyle's works praises his deep humor, compassion, and literary style [*Editor*].

SIDNEY H. MORSE

[Review of A Yankee in Canada, with Anti-Slavery and Reform Papers]†

Thoreau's account of his trip into Canada and back is very interesting. But the papers of greater interest in this book, are "Civil Disobedience," "A Plea for Captain John Brown," "Thomas Carlyle and his Works," and "Life without Principle." His "Plea" for Captain Brown is a remarkable production. It was made under circumstances that proved him no unworthy compeer of the old hero himself. At that time, not a dozen courageous voices in this country said that Brown had in any sense done right. But one, to whom "civil disobedience" was a familiar thought, would naturally be among the first to detect amid the excitements of the hour, the cries of "treason," "insane," "misguided," &c., the truth of history.

RALPH WALDO EMERSON

Thoreau†

Henry D. Thoreau was the last male descendent of a French ancestor who came to this country from the isle of Guernsey. His character exhibited occasional traits drawn from this blood in singular combination with a very strong Saxon genius.

He was born in Concord, Massachusetts, on the 12th of July, 1817. He was graduated at Harvard College, in 1837, but without any literary distinction. An iconoclast in literature, he seldom thanked colleges for their service to him, holding them in small esteem, whilst yet his debt to them was important. After leaving the University, he joined his brother in teaching a private school, which he soon renounced. His father was a manufacturer of lead pencils, and Henry applied himself for a time to this craft, believing he could make a better pencil than was then in use. After completing his experiments, he exhibited his work to chemists and artists in Boston, and having obtained their certificates to its excellence and to its equality with the best London manufacture, he returned home contented. His friends congratulated him that he had now

† From *The Radical* 2 (April 1867): 512.
† Reprinted from Joel Myerson, "Emerson's 'Thoreau': A New Edition from Manuscript," *Studies in the American Renaissance, 1979,* ed. Joel Myerson (Boston: Hall, 1979): 35–55. *Walden* page numbers refer to this Norton Critical Edition.

opened his way to fortune. But he replied, that he should never make another pencil. "Why should I? I would not do again what I have done once." He resumed his endless walks, and miscellaneous studies, making every day some new acquaintance with Nature, though as yet never speaking of zoology or botany, since, though very studious of natural facts, he was incurious of technical and textual science.

At this time, a strong, healthy youth fresh from college, whilst all his companions were choosing their profession, or eager to begin some lucrative employment, it was inevitable that his thoughts should be exercised on the same question, and it required rare decision to refuse all the accustomed paths, and keep his solitary freedom at the cost of disappointing the natural expectations of his family and friends. All the more difficult that he had a perfect probity, was exact in securing his own independence, and in holding every man to the like duty. But Thoreau never faltered. He was a born protestant. He declined to give up his large ambition of knowledge and action for any narrow craft or profession, aiming at a much more comprehensive calling, the art of living well. If he slighted and defied the opinions of others, it was only that he was more intent to reconcile his practice with his own belief. Never idle or self-indulgent, he preferred when he wanted money, earning it by some piece of manual labor agreeable to him, as building a boat or a fence, planting, grafting, surveying, or other short work, to any long engagements. With his hardy habits and few wants, his skill in wood-craft, and his powerful arithmetic, he was very competent to live in any part of the world. It would cost him less time to supply his wants than another. He was therefore secure of his leisure.

A natural skill for mensuration, growing out of his mathematical knowledge, and his habit of ascertaining the measures and distances of objects which interested him, the size of trees, the depth and extent of ponds and rivers, the height of mountains and the airline distance of his favorite summits,—this, and his intimate knowledge of the territory about Concord, made him drift into the profession of land-surveyor. It had the advantage for him that it led him continually into new and secluded grounds, and helped his studies of nature. His accuracy and skill in this work were readily appreciated, and he found all the employment he wanted.

He could easily solve the problems of the surveyor, but he was daily beset with graver questions which he manfully confronted. He interrogated every custom, and wished to settle all his practice on an ideal foundation. He was a protestant à l'outrance[1] and few lives contain so many renunciations. He was bred to no profession; he

1. In the extreme [Editor].

never married; he lived alone; he never went to church; he never voted; he refused to pay a tax to the state; he ate no flesh, he drank no wine, he never knew the use of tobacco; and, though a naturalist, he used neither trap nor gun. He chose wisely, no doubt, for himself to be the bachelor of thought and nature. He had no talent for wealth, and knew how to be poor without the least hint of squalor or inelegance. Perhaps he fell into his way of living, without forecasting it much, but approved it with later wisdom. "I am often reminded," he wrote in his journal, "that, if I had bestowed on me the wealth of Crœsus, my aims must be still the same, and my means essentially the same." He had no temptation to fight against; no appetites, no passions, no taste for elegant trifles. A fine house, dress, the manners and talk of highly cultivated people were all thrown away on him. He much preferred a good Indian, and considered these refinements as impediments to conversation, wishing to meet his companion on the simplest terms. He declined invitations to dinner-parties, because there each was in every one's way, and he could not meet the individuals to any purpose. "They make their pride," he said, "in making their dinner cost much: I make my pride in making my dinner cost little." When asked at table, what dish he preferred, he answered, "the nearest." He did not like the taste of wine, and never had a vice in his life. He said, "I have a faint recollection of pleasure derived from smoking dried lily stems, before I was a man. I had commonly a supply of these. I have never smoked any thing more noxious."

He chose to be rich by making his wants few, and supplying them himself. In his travels, he used the railroad only to get over so much country as was unimportant to the present purpose, walking hundreds of miles, avoiding taverns, buying a lodging in farmers' and fishermen's houses, as cheaper, and more agreeable to him, and because there he could better find the men and the information he wanted.

There was somewhat military in his nature not to be subdued, always manly and able, but rarely tender, as if he did not feel himself except in opposition. He wanted a fallacy to expose, a blunder to pillory, I may say, required a little sense of victory, a roll of the drum, to call his powers into full exercise. It cost him nothing to say No; indeed he found it much easier than to say Yes. It seemed as if his first instinct on hearing a proposition was to controvert it, so impatient was he of the limitation of our daily thought. This habit of course is a little chilling to the social affections; and though the companion would in the end acquit him of any malice or untruth, yet it mars conversation. Hence no equal companion stood in affectionate relations with one so pure and guileless. "I love Henry," said one of his friends, "but I cannot like him: and as for taking his arm, I should as soon think of taking the arm of an elm-tree."

Yet hermit and stoic as he was, he was really fond of sympathy, and threw himself heartily and childlike into the company of young people whom he loved, and whom he delighted to entertain, as he only could, with the varied and endless anecdotes of his experiences by field and river. And he was always ready to lead a huckleberry party or a search for chestnuts or grapes. Talking one day of a public discourse, Henry remarked, that whatever succeeded with the audience, was bad. I said, "Who would not like to write something which all can read, like 'Robinson Crusoe'; and who does not see with regret that his page is not solid with a right materialistic treatment, which delights everybody." Henry objected, of course, and vaunted the better lectures which reached only a few persons. But, at supper, a young girl, understanding that he was to lecture at the Lyceum, sharply asked him, "whether his lecture would be a nice, interesting story such as she wished to hear, or whether it was one of those old philosophical things that she did not care about?" Henry turned to her, and bethought himself, and, I saw, was trying to believe that he had matter that might fit her and her brother, who were to sit up and go to the lecture, if it was a good one for them.

He was a speaker and actor of the truth,—born such,—and was ever running into dramatic situations from this cause. In any circumstance, it interested all bystanders to know what part Henry would take, and what he would say: and he did not disappoint expectation, but used an original judgment on each emergency. In 1845, he built himself a small framed house on the shores of Walden Pond, and lived there two years alone, a life of labor and study. This action was quite native and fit for him. No one who knew him would tax him with affectation. He was more unlike his neighbors in his thought, than in his action. As soon as he had exhausted the advantages of that solitude, he abandoned it. In 1847, not approving some uses to which the public expenditure was applied, he refused to pay his town-tax, and was put in jail. A friend paid the tax for him, and he was released. The like annoyance was threatened the next year. But, as his friends paid the tax, notwithstanding his protest, I believe he ceased to resist. No opposition or ridicule had any weight with him. He coldly and fully stated his opinion without affecting to believe that it was the opinion of the company. It was of no consequence if every one present held the opposite opinion. On one occasion he went to the University Library to procure some books. The Librarian refused to lend them. Mr. Thoreau repaired to the President, who stated to him the rules and usages which permitted the loan of books to resident graduates, to clergymen who were alumni, and to some others resident within a circle of ten miles' radius from the College. Mr. Thoreau explained to the President that the railroad had destroyed the old scale of distances,—that the library was useless, yes, and President and College useless, on the terms of his rules,—that the one benefit he owed to the College was its library,—that at this moment, not only his want of books was imperative, but he wanted a large number of books, and assured him that he Thoreau, and not the Librarian, was the proper custodian of these. In short, the President found the petitioner so formidable and the rules getting to look so ridiculous, that he ended by giving him a privilege which in his hands proved unlimited thereafter.

No truer American existed than Thoreau. His preference of his country and condition was genuine, and his aversation from English and European manners and tastes almost reached contempt. He listened impatiently to news or bon mots gleaned from London circles; and, though he tried to be civil, these anecdotes fatigued him. The men were all imitating each other, and on a small mould. Why can they not live as far apart as possible, and each be a man by himself? What he sought was the most energetic nature, and he wished to go to Oregon, not to London. "In every part of Great Britain," he wrote in his diary, "are discovered traces of the Romans, their funeral urns, their camps, their roads, their dwellings. But New England, at least, is not based on any Roman ruins. We have not to lay the foundations of our houses on the ashes of a former civilization."

But idealist as he was, standing for abolition of slavery, abolition of tariffs, almost for abolition of government, it is needless to say he found himself not only unrepresented in actual politics, but almost equally opposed to every class of reformers. Yet he paid the tribute of his uniform respect to the anti-slavery party. One man, whose personal acquaintance he had formed, he honored with exceptional regard. Before the first friendly word had been spoken for Captain John Brown, after the arrest, he sent notices to most houses in Concord, that he would speak in a public hall on the condition and character of John Brown,[2] on Sunday Evening, and invited all people to come. The Republican committee, the abolitionist committee, sent him word that it was premature and not advisable. He replied, "I did not send to you for advice but to announce that I am to speak." The hall was filled at an early hour by people of all parties and his earnest eulogy of the hero was heard by all respectfully, by many with a sympathy that surprised themselves.

---

2. "A Plea for Captain John Brown," delivered October 30, 1859. See n.1, p. 393 [*Editor*].

It was said of Plotinus, that he was ashamed of his body, and 'tis very likely he had good reason for it; that his body was a bad servant, and he had not skill in dealing with the material world, as happens often to men of abstract intellect. But Mr. Thoreau was equipped with a most adapted and serviceable body. He was of short stature, firmly built, of light complexion, with strong, serious blue eyes, and a grave aspect; his face covered in the late years with a becoming beard. His senses were acute, his frame well-knit and hardy, his hands strong and skilful in the use of tools. And there was a wonderful fitness of body and mind. He could pace sixteen rods more accurately than another man could measure them with rod and chain. He could find his path in the woods at night, he said, better by his feet than his eyes. He could estimate the measure of a tree very well by his eye; he could estimate the weight of a calf or a pig, like a dealer. From a box containing a bushel or more of loose pencils, he could take up with his hands fast enough just a dozen pencils at every grasp. He was a good swimmer, runner, skater, boatman, and would probably out-walk most countrymen in a day's journey. And the relation of body to mind was still finer than we have indicated. He said, he wanted every stride his legs made. The length of his walk uniformly made the length of his writing. If shut up in the house, he did not write at all.

He had a strong common sense, like that which Rose Flammock, the weaver's daughter, in Scott's romance, commends in her father, as resembling a yardstick, which, whilst it measures dowlas and diaper, can equally well measure tapestry and cloth of gold. He had always a new resource. When I was planting forest trees, and had procured half a peck of acorns, he said, that only a small portion of them would be sound, and proceeded to examine them, and select the sound ones. But finding this took time, he said, "I think, if you put them all into water, the good ones will sink," which experiment we tried with success. He could plan a garden, or a house, or a barn; would have been competent to lead a "Pacific Exploring Expedition"; could give judicious counsel in the gravest private or public affairs. He lived for the day, not cumbered and mortified by his memory. If he brought you yesterday a new proposition, he would bring you today another not less revolutionary. A very industrious man, and setting, like all highly organized men, a high value on his time, he seemed the only man of leisure in town, always ready for any excursion that promised well, or for conversation prolonged into late hours. His trenchant sense was never stopped by his rules of daily prudence, but was always up to the new occasion. He liked and used the simplest food, yet, when some one urged a vegetable diet, Thoreau thought all diets a very small matter; saying, that "the man who shoots the buffalo lives better than the man who boards at the Graham house." He said, "You can sleep near the railroad, and never be disturbed. Nature knows very well what sounds are worth attending to, and has made up her mind not to hear the railroad-whistle. But things respect the devout mind, and a mental ecstacy was never interrupted."

He noted what repeatedly befel him, that, after receiving from a distance a rare plant, he would presently find the same in his own haunts. And those pieces of luck which happen only to good players happened to him. One day walking with a stranger who inquired, where Indian arrowheads could be found, he replied, "Every where," and stooping forward, picked one on the instant from the ground. At Mount Washington, in Tuckerman's Ravine, Thoreau had a bad fall, and sprained his foot. As he was in the act of getting up from his fall, he saw for the first time, the leaves of the *Arnica mollis*.

His robust common sense, armed with stout hands, keen perceptions, and strong will, cannot yet account for the superiority which shone in his simple and hidden life. I must add the cardinal fact that there was an excellent wisdom in him, proper to a rare class of men, which showed him the material world as a means and symbol. This discovery, which sometimes yields to poets a certain casual and interrupted light serving for the ornament of their writing, was in him an unsleeping insight; and, whatever faults or obstructions of temperament might cloud it, he was not disobedient to the heavenly vision. In his youth, he said, one day, "The other world is all my art: my pencils will draw no other; my jack-knife will cut nothing else; I do not use it as a means." This was the muse and genius that ruled his opinions, conversation, studies, work, and course of life. This made him a searching judge of men. At first glance, he measured his companion, and, though insensible to some fine traits of culture, could very well report his weight and calibre. And this made the impression of genius which his conversation often gave.

He understood the matter in hand at a glance, and saw the limitations and poverty of those he talked with, so that nothing seemed concealed from such terrible eyes. I have repeatedly known young men of sensibility converted in a moment to the belief that this was the man they were in search of, the man of men, who could tell them all they should do. His own dealing with them was never affectionate, but superior, didactic; scorning their petty ways; very slowly conceding or not conceding at all the promise of his society at their houses or even at his own. "Would he not walk with them?"—He did not know. There was nothing so important to him as his walk; he had no walks to throw away on company. Visits were offered him from respectful parties, but he declined them. Admiring friends offered to carry him at their own cost to the Yellow

Stone River; to the West Indies; to South America. But though nothing could be more grave or considered than his refusals, they remind one in quite new relations of that fop Brummel's reply to the gentleman who offered him his carriage in a shower, "But where will *you* ride then?" And what accusing silences, and what searching and irresistible speeches battering down all defences, his companions can remember!

Mr. Thoreau dedicated his genius with such entire love to the fields, hills, and waters of his native town, that he made them known and interesting to all reading Americans, and to people over the sea. The river on whose banks he was born and died, he knew from its springs to its confluence with the Merrimack. He had made summer and winter observations on it for many years, and at every hour of the day and night. The result of the recent survey of the Water Commissioners appointed by the State of Massachusetts, he had reached by his private experiments, several years earlier. Every fact which occurs in the bed, on the banks, or in the air over it; the fishes, and their spawning and nests, their manners, their food; the shad-flies which fill the air on a certain evening once a year, and which are snapped at by the fishes so ravenously, that many of these die of repletion; the conical heaps of small stones on the river shallows, one of which heaps will sometimes overfill a cart,—these heaps the huge nests of small fishes; the birds which frequent the stream, heron, duck, sheldrake, loon, osprey; the snake, muskrat, otter, woodchuck, and fox, on the banks; the turtle, frog, hyla, and cricket, which make the banks vocal,—were all known to him, and, as it were, townsmen and fellow-creatures: so that he felt an absurdity or violence in any narrative of one of these by itself apart, and still more of its dimensions on an inch-rule, or in the exhibition of its skeleton, or the specimen of a squirrel or a bird in brandy. He liked to speak of the manners of the river, as itself a lawful creature, yet with exactness and always to an observed fact. As he knew the river, so the ponds in this region.

One of the weapons he used, more important than microscope or alcohol receiver, to other investigators, was a whim which grew on him by indulgence, yet appeared in gravest statement, namely, of extolling his own town and neighborhood as the most favored centre for natural observation. He remarked that the Flora of Massachusetts embraced almost all the important plants of America,—most of the oaks, most of the willows, the best pines, the ash, the maple, the beech, the nuts. He returned Kane's "Arctic Voyage" to a friend of whom he had borrowed it with the remark, that "most of the phenomena noted might be observed in Concord." He seemed a little envious of the Pole, for the coincident sunrise and sunset, or five minutes' day after six months. A splendid fact which Annursnuc[3] had never afforded him. He found red snow in one of his walks; and told me that he expected to find yet the *Victoria regia*[4] in Concord. He was the attorney of the indigenous plants, and owned to a preference of the weeds to the imported plants, as of the Indian to the civilized man: and noticed with pleasure that the willow bean-poles of his neighbor had grown more than his beans. "See these weeds," he said, "which have been hoed at by a million farmers all spring and summer, and yet have prevailed, and just now come out triumphant over all lanes, pastures, fields, and gardens, such is their vigor. We have insulted them with low names too, as pigweed, wormwood, chickweed, shad blossom." He says they have brave names too, ambrosia, stellaria, amelanchier, amaranth, etc.

I think his fancy for referring every thing to the meridian of Concord, did not grow out of any ignorance or depreciation of other longitudes or latitudes, but was rather a playful expression of his conviction of the indifferency of all places, and that the best place for each is where he stands. He expressed it once in this wise: "I think nothing is to be hoped from you, if this bit of mould under your feet is not sweeter to you to eat, than any other in this world, or in any world."

The other weapon with which he conquered all obstacles in science was patience. He knew how to sit immoveable, a part of the rock he rested on, until the bird, the reptile, the fish, which had retired from him, should come back, and resume its habits, nay, moved by curiosity should come to him and watch him.

It was a pleasure and a privilege to walk with him. He knew the country like a fox or a bird, and passed through it as freely by paths of his own. He knew every track in the snow, or on the ground, and what creature had taken this path before him. One must submit abjectly to such a guide, and the reward was great. Under his arm he carried an old music book to press plants; in his pocket, his diary and pencil, a spy-glass for birds, microscope, jack-knife, and twine. He wore straw hat, stout shoes, strong gray trowsers, to brave shrub-oaks and smilax, and to climb a tree for a hawk's or a squirrel's nest. He waded into the pool for the water-plants, and his strong legs were no insignificant part of his armour. On the day I speak of he looked for the menyanthes, detected it across the wide pool, and, on examination of the florets, decided that it had been in flower five days. He drew out of his breast-pocket his diary, and read the names of all the plants that should bloom on this day, whereof he kept account as a banker when

---

3. A hill in Concord [*Editor*].
4. South American water lily [*Editor*].

his notes fall due. The cypripedium not due till tomorrow. He thought, that, if waked up from a trance, in this swamp, he could tell by the plants what time of the year it was within two days. The redstart was flying about and presently the fine grosbeaks, whose brilliant scarlet makes the rash gazer wipe his eye, and whose fine clear note Thoreau compared to that of a tanager which has got rid of its hoarseness. Presently he heard a note which he called that of the night-warbler, a bird he had never identified, had been in search of twelve years, which always, when he saw it, was in the act of diving down into a tree or bush, and which it was vain to seek; the only bird that sings indifferently by night and by day. I told him he must beware of finding and booking it, lest life should have nothing more to show him. He said, "What you seek in vain for, half your life, one day you come full upon all the family at dinner. You seek it like a dream, and, as soon as you find it, you become its prey."

His interest in the flower or the bird lay very deep in his mind, was connected with Nature,—and the meaning of Nature was never attempted to be defined by him. He would not offer a memoir of his observations to the Natural History Society. "Why should I? To detach the description from its connections in my mind, would make it no longer true or valuable to me: and they do not wish what belongs to it." His power of observation seemed to indicate additional senses. He saw as with microscope, heard as with ear-trumpet, and his memory was a photographic register of all he saw and heard. And yet none knew better than he that it is not the fact that imports, but the impression or effect of the fact on your mind. Every fact lay in glory in his mind, a type of the order and beauty of the whole.

His determination on Natural History was organic. He confessed that he sometimes felt like a hound or a panther, and, if born among Indians, would have been a fell hunter. But, restrained by his Massachusetts culture, he played out the game in this mild form of botany and ichthyology. His intimacy with animals suggested what Thomas Fuller records of Butler the apiologist, that "either he had told the bees things or the bees had told him." Snakes coiled round his leg; the fishes swam into his hand, and he took them out of the water; he pulled the woodchuck out of its hole by the tail, and took the foxes under his protection from the hunters. Our naturalist had perfect magnanimity; he had no secrets: he would carry you to the heron's haunt, or even to his most prized botanical swamp;—possibly knowing that you could never find it again,—yet willing to take his risks.

No college ever offered him a diploma, or a professor's chair; no academy made him its corresponding secretary, its discoverer, or even its member. Whether[5] these learned bodies feared the satire of his presence. Yet so much knowledge of nature's secret and genius few others possessed, none in a more large and religious synthesis. For not a particle of respect had he to the opinions of any man or body of men, but homage solely to the truth itself. And as he discovered everywhere among doctors some leaning of courtesy, it discredited them. He grew to be revered and admired by his townsmen, who had at first known him only as an oddity. The farmers who employed him as a surveyor soon discovered his rare accuracy and skill, his knowledge of their lands, of trees, of birds, of Indian remains, and the like, which enabled him to tell every farmer more than he knew before of his own farm. So that he began to feel as if Mr. Thoreau had better rights in his land than he. They felt, too, the superiority of character which addressed all men with a native authority.

Indian relics abound in Concord, arrowheads, stone chisels, pestles, and fragments of pottery; and, on the river bank, large heaps of clam-shells and ashes mark spots which the savages frequented. These, and every circumstance touching the Indian, were important in his eyes. His visits to Maine were chiefly for love of the Indian. He had the satisfaction of seeing the manufacture of the bark-canoe, as well as of trying his hand in its management on the rapids. He was inquisitive about the making of the stone arrowhead, and, in his last days, charged a youth setting out for the Rocky Mountains, to find an Indian who could tell him that: "It was well worth a visit to California, to learn it." Occasionally, a small party of Penobscot, Indians would visit Concord, and pitch their tents for a few weeks in summer on the river bank. He failed not to make acquaintance with the best of them, though he well knew that asking questions of Indians is like catechizing beavers and rabbits. In his last visit to Maine, he had great satisfaction from Joseph Polis, an intelligent Indian of Oldtown, who was his guide for some weeks.

He was equally interested in every natural fact. The depth of his perception found likeness of law throughout nature, and, I know not any genius who so swiftly inferred universal law from the single fact. He was no pedant of a department. His eye was open to beauty, and his ear to music. He found these, not in rare conditions, but wheresoever he went. He thought the best of music was in single strains; and he found poetic suggestion in the humming of the telegraph wire.

His poetry might be bad or good; he no doubt wanted a lyric facil-

---

5. Among other revisions he made to "Thoreau" after Emerson's death, James Eliot Cabot changed this word to "Perhaps." See Myerson, "Emerson's Thoreau,'" 20–21, 72 [*Editor*].

ity, and technical skill; but he had the source of poetry in his spiritual perception. He was a good reader and critic, and his judgment on poetry was to the ground of it. He could not be deceived as to the presence or absence of the poetic element in any composition, and his thirst for this made him negligent and perhaps scornful of superficial graces. He would pass by many delicate rhythms, but he would have detected every live stanza or line in a volume, and knew very well where to find an equal charm in prose. He was so enamoured of the spiritual beauty, that he held all actual written poems in very light esteem in the comparison. He admired Æschylus and Pindar, but when some one was commending them, he said, that, "Æschylus and the Greeks, in describing Apollo and Orpheus, had given no song, or no good one. They ought not to have moved trees, but to have chaunted to the gods such a hymn as would have sung all their old ideas out of their heads, and new ones in." His own verses are often rude and defective. The gold does not yet run pure, is drossy and crude. The thyme and marjoram are not yet honey. But if he want lyric fineness, and technical merits, if he have not the poetic temperament, he never lacks the causal thought, showing that his genius was better than his talent. He knew the worth of the Imagination for the uplifting and consolation of human life, and liked to throw every thought into a symbol. The fact you tell is of no value, but only the impression. For this reason his presence was poetic, always piqued the curiosity to know more deeply the secrets of his mind. He had many reserves,—an unwillingness to exhibit to profane eyes what was still sacred in his own, and knew well how to throw a poetic veil over his experience. All readers of "Walden" will remember his mythical record of his disappointments:—

> "I long ago lost a hound, a bay horse, and a turtle-dove, and am still on their trail. Many are the travellers I have spoken concerning them, describing their tracks, and what calls they answered to. I have met one or two who had heard the hound, and the tramp of the horse, and even seen the dove disappear behind a cloud, and they seemed as anxious to recover them as if they had lost them themselves."(15)

His riddles were worth the reading, and I confide that, if at any time I do not understand the expression, it is yet just. Such was the wealth of his truth, that it was not worth his while to use words in vain.

His poem entitled "Sympathy" reveals the tenderness under that triple steel of stoicism, and the intellectual subtlety it could animate. His classic poem on "Smoke" suggests Simonides, but is better than any poem of Simonides. His biography is in his verses. His habitual thought makes all his poetry a hymn to the Cause of causes, the spirit which vivifies and controls his own.

> "I hearing get, who had but ears,
> And sight, who had but eyes before;
> I moments live, who lived but years,
> And truth discern, who knew but learning's lore."

And still more in these religious lines:—

> "Now chiefly is my natal hour,
> And only now my prime of life;
> I will not doubt the love untold,
> Which not my worth or want hath bought,
> Which wooed me young, and wooes me old,
> And to this evening hath me brought."

Whilst he used in his writings a certain petulance of remark in reference to churches or churchmen, he was a person of a rare, tender, and absolute religion, a person incapable of any profanation, by act or by thought. Of course, the same isolation which belonged to his original thinking and living detached him from the social religious forms. This is neither to be censured nor regretted. Aristotle long ago explained it, when he said, "One who surpasses his fellow citizens in virtue, is no longer a part of the city. Their law is not for him, since he is a law to himself."

Thoreau was sincerity itself, and might fortify the convictions of prophets in the ethical laws, by his holy living. It was an affirmative experience which refused to be set aside. A truth-speaker he, capable of the most deep and strict conversation; a physician to the wounds of any soul; a friend knowing not only the secret of friendship, but almost worshipped by those few persons who resorted to him as their confessor and prophet, and knew the deep value of his mind and great heart. He thought that without religion or devotion of some kind, nothing great was ever accomplished: and he thought that the bigoted sectarian had better bear this in mind.

His virtues of course sometimes ran into extremes. It was easy to trace to the inexorable demand on all for exact truth that austerity which made this willing hermit more solitary even than he wished. Himself of a perfect probity, he required not less of others. He had a disgust at crime, and no worldly success could cover it. He detected paltering as readily in dignified and prosperous persons as in beggars, and with equal scorn. Such dangerous frankness was in his dealing, that his admirers called him "that terrible Thoreau," as if he spoke, when silent, and was still present when he had departed. I think the severity of his ideal interfered to deprive him of a healthy sufficiency of human society.

The habit of a realist to find things the reverse of their appearance inclined him to put every statement in a paradox. A certain habit of antagonism defaced his earlier writings, a trick of rhetoric not quite outgrown in his later, of substituting for the obvious word and thought its diametrical opposite. He praised wild mountains and winter forests for their domestic air; in snow and ice, he would find sultriness; and commended the wilderness for resembling Rome and Paris. "It was so dry, that you might call it wet."

The tendency to magnify the moment, to read all the laws of nature in the one object or one combination under your eye, is of course comic to those who do not share the philosopher's perception of identity. To him there was no such thing as size. The pond was a small ocean; the Atlantic, a large Walden Pond. He referred every minute fact to cosmical laws. Though he meant to be just, he seemed haunted by a certain chronic assumption that the science of the day pretended completeness and he had just found out that the savans had neglected to discriminate a particular botanical variety, had failed to describe the seeds, or count the sepals. "That is to say," we replied, "the blockheads were not born in Concord, but who said they were? It was their unspeakable misfortune to be born in London, or Paris, or Rome; but, poor fellows, they did what they could, considering that they never saw Bateman Pond, or Nine-Acre-Corner, or Becky Stow's Swamp. Besides, what were you sent into the world for, but to add this observation?"

Had his genius been only contemplative, he had been fitted to his life, but with his energy and practical ability he seemed born for great enterprise and for command: and I so much regret the loss of his rare powers of action, that I cannot help counting it a fault in him that he had no ambition. Wanting this, instead of engineering for all America, he was the captain of a huckleberry party. Pounding beans is good to the end of pounding empires one of these days, but if, at the end of years, it is still only beans!—

But these foibles, real or apparent, were fast vanishing in the incessant growth of a spirit so robust and wise, and which effaced its defects with new triumphs. His study of nature was a perpetual ornament to him, and inspired his friends with curiosity to see the world through his eyes, and to hear his adventures. They possessed every kind of interest. He had many elegances of his own, whilst he scoffed at conventional elegance. Thus he could not bear to hear the sound of his own steps, the grit of gravel; and therefore never willingly walked in the road, but in the grass, on mountains, and in woods. His senses were acute, and he remarked that by night every dwelling-house gives out bad air, like a slaughter-house. He liked the pure fragrance of melilot. He honored certain plants with special regard, and over all the pond-lily,—then the gentian, and the *Mikania scandens*, and "Life Everlasting," and a bass tree which he visited every year when it bloomed in the middle of July. He

thought the scent a more oracular inquisition than the sight,—
more oracular and trustworthy. The scent, of course, reveals what is
concealed from the other senses. By it he detected earthiness. He
delighted in echoes, and said, they were almost the only kind of
kindred voices that he heard. He loved nature so well, was so happy
in her solitude, that he became very jealous of cities, and the sad
work which their refinements and artifices made with man and his
dwelling. The axe was always destroying his forest—"Thank God,"
he said, "they cannot cut down the clouds. All kinds of figures are
drawn on the blue ground, with this fibrous white paint."

I subjoin a few sentences taken from his unpublished manuscripts[7] not only as records of his thought and feeling, but for their
power of description and literary excellence.

"Some circumstantial evidence is very strong, as when you
find a trout in the milk."

"The chub is a soft fish, and tastes like boiled brown paper
salted."

"The youth gets together his materials to build a bridge to
the moon, or, perchance, a palace or temple on the earth, and,
at length, the middle-aged man concludes to build a woodshed
with them."

"The locust z---ing."

"Devil's-needles zig-zagging along the Nut-Meadow brook."

"Sugar is not so sweet to the palate, as sound to the healthy
ear."

"I put on some hemlock boughs, and the rich salt crackling
of their leaves was like mustard to the ear, the crackling of un-
countable regiments. Dead trees love the fire."

"The blue-bird carries the sky on his back."

"The tanager flies through the green foliage, as if it would
ignite the leaves."

"If I wish for a horse-hair for my compass-sight, I must go to
the stable; but the hair-bird with her sharp eyes goes to the
road."

"Immortal water, alive even to the superficies."

"Fire is the most tolerable third party."

"Nature made ferns for pure leaves, to show what she could
do in that line."

"No tree has so fair a bole, and so handsome an instep as
the beech."

"How did these beautiful rainbow tints get into the shell of
the freshwater clam, buried in the mud at the bottom of our
dark river?"

7. I.e., from Thoreau's Journal [Editor].

"Hard are the times when the infant's shoes are second-foot."

"We are strictly confined to our men to whom we give liberty."

"Nothing is so much to be feared as fear. Atheism may comparatively be popular with God himself."

"Of what significance the things you can forget? A little thought is sexton to all the world."

"How can we expect a harvest of thought, who have not had a seedtime of character?"

"Only he can be trusted with gifts, who can present a face of bronze to expectations."

"I ask to be melted. You can only ask of the metals that they be tender to the fire that melts them. To nought else can they be tender."

There is a flower known to botanists, one of the same genus with our summer plant called "Life Everlasting," a *Gnaphalium* like that, which grows on the most inaccessible cliffs of the Tyrolese mountains, where the chamois dare hardly venture, and which the hunter, tempted by its beauty, and by his love, (for it is immensely valued by the Swiss maidens,) climbs the cliffs to gather, and is sometimes found dead at the foot, with the flower in his hand. It is called by botanists the *Gnaphalium leontopodium,* but by the Swiss, *Edelweisse*, which signifies, *Noble Purity.* Thoreau seemed to me living in the hope to gather this plant, which belonged to him of right. The scale on which his studies proceeded was so large as to require longevity, and we were the less prepared for his sudden disappearance. The country knows not yet, or in the least part, how great a son it has lost. It seems an injury that he should leave in the midst his broken task, which none else can finish,—a kind of indignity to so noble a soul, that it should depart out of nature before yet he has been really shown to his peers for what he is. But he, at least, is content. His soul was made for the noblest society; he had in a short life exhausted the capabilities of this world; wherever there is knowledge, wherever there is virtue, wherever there is beauty, he will find a home.

JAMES RUSSELL LOWELL

Thoreau†

What contemporary, if he was in the fighting period of his life, (since Nature sets limits about her conscription for spiritual fields, as the state does in physical warfare), will ever forget what was somewhat vaguely called the "Transcendental Movement" of thirty years ago? Apparently set astir by Carlyle's[1] essays on the "Signs of the Times," and on "History," the final and more immediate impulse seemed to be given by "Sartor Resartus."

* * *

Scotch Presbyterianism as a motive of spiritual progress was dead; New England Puritanism was in like manner dead; in other words, Protestantism had made its fortune and no longer protested; but till Carlyle spoke out in the Old World and Emerson in the New, no one had dared to proclaim, *Le roi est mort: vive le roi!* The meaning of which proclamation was essentially this: the vital spirit has long since departed out of this form once so kingly, and the great seal has been in commission long enough; but meanwhile the soul of man, from which all power emanates and to which it reverts, still survives in undiminished royalty; God still survives, little as you gentlemen of the Commission seem to be aware of it,—nay, will possibly outlive the whole of you, incredible as it may appear. The truth is, that both Scotch Presbyterianism and New England Puritanism made their new avatar in Carlyle and Emerson, the heralds of their formal decease, and the tendency of the one toward Authority and of the other toward Independency might have been prophesied by whoever had studied history. The necessity was not so much in the men as in the principles they represented and the traditions which overruled them. The Puritanism of the past found its unwilling poet in Hawthorne, the rarest creative imagination of the century, the rarest in some ideal respects since Shakespeare; but the Puritanism that cannot die, the Puritanism that made New England what it is, and is destined to make America what it should be, found its voice in Emerson. Though holding himself aloof from all active partnership in movements of reform, he has been the sleeping partner who has supplied a great part of their capital.

The artistic range of Emerson is narrow, as every well-read critic must feel at once; and so is that of Æschylus, so is that of Dante,

---

† Written in 1865. From the Riverside Edition of *The Writings of James Russell Lowell* (Boston, 1890), vol. 1 *Literary Essays*, 361–81. *Walden* page numbers refer to this Norton Critical Edition.
1. Thomas Carlyle. See n. 2, p. 393.

so is that of Montaigne, so is that of Schiller, so is that of nearly every one except Shakespeare; but there is a gauge of height no less than of breadth, of individualty as well as of comprehensiveness, and, above all, there is the standard of genetic power, the test of the masculine as distinguished from the receptive minds. There are staminate plants in literature, that make no fine show of fruit, but without whose pollen, quintessence of fructifying gold, the garden had been barren. Emerson's mind is emphatically one of these, and there is no man to whom our æsthetic culture owes so much. The Puritan revolt had made us ecclesiastically and the Revolution politically independent, but we were still socially and intellectually moored to English thought, till Emerson cut the cable and gave us a chance at the dangers and the glories of blue water. No man young enough to have felt it can forget or cease to be grateful for the mental and moral *nudge* which he received from the writings of his high-minded and brave-spirited countryman.

* * *

Among the pistillate plants kindled to fruitage by the Emersonian pollen, Thoreau is thus far the most remarkable; and it is something eminently fitting that his posthumous works should be offered us by Emerson, for they are strawberries from his own garden. A singular mixture of varieties, indeed, there is:—alpine, some of them, with the flavor of rare mountain air; others wood, tasting of sunny road-side banks or shy openings in the forest; and not a few seedlings swollen hugely by culture, but lacking the fine natural aroma of the more modest kinds. Strange books these are of his, and interesting in many ways,—instructive chiefly as showing how considerable a crop may be raised on a comparatively narrow close of mind, and how much a man may make of his life if he will assiduously follow it, though perhaps never truly finding it at last.

I have just been renewing my recollection of Mr. Thoreau's writings, and have read through his six volumes in the order of their production.[2] I shall try to give an adequate report of their impression upon me both as critic and as mere reader. He seems to me to have been a man with so high a conceit of himself that he accepted without questioning, and insisted on our accepting, his defects and weaknesses of character as virtues and powers peculiar to himself. Was he indolent, he finds none of the activities which attract or employ the rest of mankind worthy of him. Was he wanting in the qualities that make success, it is success that is contemptible, and not himself that lacks persistency and purpose. Was he poor, money

---

2. *A Week on the Concord and Merrimack Rivers* (1849); *Walden; Or, Life in the Woods* (1854); *Excursions* (1863), with Emerson's essay "Thoreau" prefixed to the volume and titled "Biographical Sketch"; *The Maine Woods* (1864); *Cape Cod,* and *Letters to Various Persons* (1865) [*Editor*].

was an unmixed evil. Did his life seem a selfish one, he condemns doing good as one of the weakest of superstitions. To be of use was with him the most killing bait of the wily tempter Uselessness. He had no faculty of generalization from outside of himself, or at least no experience which would supply the material of such, and he makes his own whim the law, his own range the horizon of the universe. He condemns a world, the hollowness of whose satisfactions he had never had the means of testing, and we recognize Apemantus behind the mask of Timon. He had little active imagination; of the receptive he had much. His appreciation is of the highest quality; his critical power, from want of continuity of mind, very limited and inadequate. He somewhere cites a simile from Ossian, as an example of the superiority of the old poetry to the new, though, even were the historic evidence less convincing, the sentimental melancholy of those poems should be conclusive of their modernness. He had none of the artistic mastery which controls a great work to the serene balance of completeness, but exquisite mechanical skill in the shaping of sentences and paragraphs, or (more rarely) short bits of verse for the expression of a detached thought, sentiment, or image. His works give one the feeling of a sky full of stars,—something impressive and exhilarating certainly, something high overhead and freckled thickly with spots of isolated brightness; but whether these have any mutual relation with each other, or have any concern with our mundane matters, is for the most part matter of conjecture,—astrology as yet, and not astronomy.

It is curious, considering what Thoreau afterwards became, that he was not by nature an observer. He only saw the things he looked for, and was less poet than naturalist. Till he built his Walden shanty, he did not know that the hickory grew in Concord. Till he went to Maine, he had never seen phosphorescent wood, a phenomenon early familiar to most country boys. At forty he speaks of the seeding of the pine as a new discovery, though one should have thought that its gold-dust of blowing pollen might have earlier drawn his eye. Neither his attention nor his genius was of the spontaneous kind. He discovered nothing. He thought everything a discovery of his own, from moonlight to the planting of acorns and nuts by squirrels. This is a defect in his character, but one of his chief charms as a writer. Everything grows fresh under his hand. He delved in his mind and nature; he planted them with all manner of native and foreign seeds, and reaped assiduously. He was not merely solitary, he would be isolated, and succeeded at last in almost persuading himself that he was autochthonous. He valued everything in proportion as he fancied it to be exclusively his own. He complains in "Walden" that there is no one in Concord with whom he could talk of Oriental literature, though the man was liv-

ing within two miles of his hut who had introduced him to it. This
intellectual selfishness becomes sometimes almost painful in reading him. He lacked that generosity of "communication" which
Johnson admired in Burke. De Quincey tells us that Wordsworth
was impatient when any one else spoke of mountains, as if he had
a peculiar property in them. And we can readily understand why it
should be so: no one is satisfied with another's appreciation of his
mistress. But Thoreau seems to have prized a lofty way of thinking
(often we should be inclined to call it a remote one) not so much
because it was good in itself as because he wished few to share it
with him. It seems now and then as if he did not seek to lure others up "above our lower region of turmoil," but to leave his own
name cut on the mountain peak as the first climber. This itch of
originality infects his thought and style. To be misty is not to be
mystic. He turns commonplaces end for end, and fancies it makes
something new of them. As we walk down Park Street, our eye is
caught by Dr. Winship's dumb-bells, one of which bears an inscrip-
tion testifying that it is the heaviest ever put up at arm's length by
any athlete; and in reading Mr. Thoreau's books we cannot help
feeling as if he sometimes invited our attention to a particular
sophism or paradox as the biggest yet maintained by any single
writer. He seeks, at all risks, for perversity of thought, and revives
the age of *concetti* while he fancies himself going back to a pre-
classical nature. "A day," he says, "passed in the society of those
Greek sages, such as described in the Banquet of Xenophon, would
not be comparable with the dry wit of decayed cranberry-vines and
the fresh Attic salt of the mossbeds." It is not so much the True
that he loves as the Out-of-the-Way. As the Brazen Age shows itself
in other men by exaggeration of phrase, so in him by extravagance
of statement. He wishes always to trump your suit and to *ruff* when
you least expect it. Do you love Nature because she is beautiful? He
will find a better argument in her ugliness. Are you tired of the artificial man? He instantly dresses you up an ideal in a Penobscot Indian, and attributes to this creature of his otherwise-mindedness as
peculiarities things that are common to all woodsmen, white or red,
and this simply because he has not studied the pale-faced variety.

This notion of an absolute originality, as if one could have a
patent-right in it, is an absurdity. A man cannot escape in thought,
any more than he can in language, from the past and the present.
As no one ever invents a word, and yet language somehow grows by
general contribution and necessity, so it is with thought. Mr.
Thoreau seems to me to insist in public on going back to flint and
steel, when there is a match-box in his pocket which he knows very
well how to use at a pinch. Originality consists in power of digesting and assimilating thoughts, so that they become part of our life

and substance. Montaigne, for example, is one of the most original of authors, though he helped himself to ideas in every direction. But they turn to blood and coloring in his style, and give a freshness of complexion that is forever charming. In Thoreau much seems yet to be foreign and unassimilated, showing itself in symptoms of indigestion. A preacher-up of Nature, we now and then detect under the surly and stoic garb something of the sophist and the sentimentalizer. I am far from implying that this was conscious on his part. But it is much easier for a man to impose on himself when he measures only with himself. A greater familiarity with ordinary men would have done Thoreau good, by showing him how many fine qualities are common to the race. The radical vice of his theory of life was that he confounded physical with spiritual remoteness from men. A man is far enough withdrawn from his fellows if he keep himself clear of their weaknesses. He is not so truly withdrawn as exiled, if he refuse to share in their strength. "Solitude," says Cowley, "can be well fitted and set right but upon a very few persons. They must have enough knowledge of the world to see the vanity of it, and enough virtue to despise all vanity." It is morbid self-consciousness that pronounces the world of men empty and worthless before trying it, the instinctive evasion of one who is sensible of some innate weakness, and retorts the accusation of it before any has made it but himself. To a healthy mind, the world is a constant challenge of opportunity. Mr. Thoreau had not a healthy mind, or he would not have been so fond of prescribing. His whole life was a search for the doctor. The old mystics had a wiser sense of what the world was worth. They ordained a severe apprenticeship to law, and even ceremonial, in order to the gaining of freedom and mastery over these. Seven years of service for Rachel were to be rewarded at last with Leah. Seven other years of faithfulness with her were to win them at last the true bride of their souls. Active Life was with them the only path to the Contemplative.

Thoreau had no humor, and this implies that he was a sorry logician. Himself an artist in rhetoric, he confounds thought with style when he undertakes to speak of the latter. He was forever talking of getting away from the world, but he must be always near enough to it, nay, to the Concord corner of it, to feel the impression he makes there. He verifies the shrewd remark of Sainte-Beuve, "On touche encore à son temps et très-fort, même quand on le repousse."[3] This egotism of his is a Stylites pillar after all, a seclusion which keeps him in the public eye. The dignity of man is an excellent thing, but therefore to hold one's self too sacred and precious is the reverse of

---

3. "One is still in touch with one's times and very much so, even when one rejects them" [*Editor*].

excellent. There is something delightfully absurd in six volumes addressed to a world of such "vulgar fellows" as Thoreau affirmed his fellowmen to be. I once had a glimpse of a genuine solitary who spent his winters one hundred and fifty miles beyond all human communication, and there dwelt with his rifle as his only confidant. Compared with this, the shanty on Walden Pond has something the air, it must be confessed, of the Hermitage of La Chevrette.[4] I do not believe that the way to a true cosmopolitanism carries one into the woods or the society of musquashes. Perhaps the narrowest provincialism is that of Self; that of Kleinwinkel is nothing to it. The natural man, like the singing birds, comes out of the forest as inevitably as the natural bear and the wildcat stick there. To seek to be natural implies a consciousness that forbids all naturalness forever. It is as easy—and no easier—to be natural in a *salon* as in a swamp, if one do not aim at it, for what we call unnaturalness always has its spring in a man's thinking too much about himself. "It is impossible," said Turgot, "for a vulgar man to be simple."

I look upon a great deal of the modern sentimentalism about Nature as a mark of disease. It is one more symptom of the general liver-complaint. To a man of wholesome constitution the wilderness is well enough for a mood or a vacation, but not for a habit of life. Those who have most loudly advertised their passion for seclusion and their intimacy with nature, from Petrarch down, have been mostly sentimentalists, unreal men, misanthropes on the spindle side, solacing an uneasy suspicion of themselves by professing contempt for their kind. They make demands on the world in advance proportioned to their inward measure of their own merit, and are angry that the world pays only by the visible measure of performance. It is true of Rousseau, the modern founder of the sect, true of Saint Pierre, his intellectual child, and of Châteaubriand, his grandchild, the inventor, we might almost say, of the primitive forest, and who first was touched by the solemn falling of a tree from natural decay in the windless silence of the woods. It is a very shallow view that affirms trees and rocks to be healthy, and cannot see that men in communities are just as true to the laws of their organization and destiny; that can tolerate the puffin and the fox, but not the fool and the knave; that would shun politics because of its demagogues, and snuff up the stench of the obscene fungus. The divine life of Nature is more wonderful, more various, more sublime in man than in any other of her works, and the wisdom that is gained by commerce with men, as Montaigne and Shakespeare gained it,

---

4. A cottage occupied by Jean-Jacques Rousseau from April 1756 to December 1757 on the grounds of La Chevrette, the country estate of Madame d'Épinay, Rousseau's patron [*Editor*].

or with one's own soul among men, as Dante, is the most delightful, as it is the most precious, of all. In outward nature it is still
man that interests us, and we care far less for the things seen than
the way in which they are seen by poetic eyes like Wordsworth's or
Thoreau's, and the reflections they cast there. To hear the to-do
that is often made over the simple fact that a man sees the image of
himself in the outward world, one is reminded of a savage when he
for the first time catches a glimpse of himself in a looking-glass.
"Venerable child of Nature," we are tempted to say, "to whose science in the invention of the tobacco-pipe, to whose art in the tattooing of thine undegenerate hide not yet enslaved by tailors, we are
slowly striving to climb back, the miracle thou beholdst is sold in
my unhappy country for a shilling!" If matters go on as they have
done, and everybody must needs blab of all the favors that have
been done him by roadside and river-brink and woodland walk, as if
to kiss and tell were no longer treachery, it will be a positive refreshment to meet a man who is as superbly indifferent to Nature
as she is to him. By and by we shall have John Smith, of No.–12–
12th. Street, advertising that he is not the J. S. who saw a cow-lily
on Thursday last, as he never saw one in his life, would not see one
if he could, and is prepared to prove an alibi on the day in question.

Solitary communion with Nature does not seem to have been
sanitary or sweetening in its influence on Thoreau's character. On
the contrary, his letters show him more cynical as he grew older.
While he studied with respectful attention the minks and woodchucks, his neighbors, he looked with utter contempt on the august
drama of destiny of which his country was the scene, and on which
the curtain had already risen. He was converting us back to a state
of nature "so eloquently," as Voltaire said of Rousseau, "that he almost persuaded us to go on all fours," while the wiser fates were
making it possible for us to walk erect for the first time. Had
he conversed more with his fellows, his sympathies would have
widened with the assurance that his peculiar genius had more appreciation, and his writings a larger circle of readers, or at least a
warmer one, than he dreamed of. We have the highest testimony[5]
to the natural sweetness, sincerity, and nobleness of his temper,
and in his books an equally irrefragable one to the rare quality of
his mind. He was not a strong thinker, but a sensitive feeler. Yet his
mind strikes us as cold and wintry in its purity. A light snow has
fallen everywhere in which he seems to come on the track of the
shier sensations that would elsewhere leave no trace. We think
greater compression would have done more for his fame. A feeling
of sameness comes over us as we read so much. Trifles are recorded

5. Mr. Emerson, in his Biographical Sketch.

with an over-minute punctuality and conscientiousness of detail.
He registers the state of his personal thermometer thirteen times a
day. We cannot help thinking sometimes of the man who

> "Watches, starves, freezes, and sweats
> To learn but catechisms and alphabets
> Of unconcerning things, matters of fact,"

and sometimes of the saying of the Persian poet, that "when the
owl would boast, he boasts of catching mice at the edge of a hole."
We could readily part with some of his affectations. It was well
enough for Pythagoras to say, once for all, "When I was Euphorbus
at the siege of Troy"; not so well for Thoreau to travesty it into
"When I was a shepherd on the plains of Assyria." A naïve thing
said over again is anything but naïve. But with every exception,
there is no writing comparable with Thoreau's in kind, that is comparable with it in degree where it is best; where it disengages itself,
that is, from the tangled roots and dead leaves of a second-hand
Orientalism, and runs limpid and smooth and broadening as it
runs, a mirror for whatever is grand and lovely in both worlds.

George Sand says neatly, that "Art is not a study of positive reality," (*actuality* were the fitter word,) "but a seeking after ideal
truth." It would be doing very inadequate justice to Thoreau if we
left it to be inferred that this ideal element did not exist in him, and
that too in larger proportion, if less obtrusive, than his nature-
worship. He took nature as the mountain-path to an ideal world. If
the path wind a good deal, if he record too faithfully every trip over
a root, if he botanize somewhat wearisomely, he gives us now and
then superb outlooks from some jutting crag, and brings us out at
last into an illimitable ether, where the breathing is not difficult for
those who have any true touch of the climbing spirit. His shanty-
life was a mere impossibility, so far as his own conception of it
goes, as an entire independency of mankind. The tub of Diogenes[6]
had a sounder bottom. Thoreau's experiment actually presupposed
all that complicated civilization which it theoretically abjured. He
squatted on another man's land; he borrows an axe; his boards, his
nails, his bricks, his mortar, his books, his lamp, his fish-hooks, his
plough, his hoe, all turn state's evidence against him as an accomplice in the sin of that artificial civilization which rendered it possible that such a person as Henry D. Thoreau should exist at all.
Magnis tamen excidit ausis.[7] His aim was a noble and useful one, in
the direction of "plain living and high thinking." It was a practical

6. See n. 1, p. 384.
7. From Ovid, *Metamorphoses* 1.329, the last line of Phaeton's epitaph: "Here Phaeton
lies,/ Who drove his father's chariot: if he did not/ Hold it, at least he fell in splendid dar-
ing." For the story of Phaeton, see *Walden* 54 [*Editor*].

sermon on Emerson's text that "things are in the saddle and ride mankind," an attempt to solve Carlyle's problem (condensed from Johnson) of "lessening your denominator."[8] His whole life was a rebuke of the waste and aimlessness of our American luxury, which is an abject enslavement to tawdry upholstery. He had "fine translunary things" in him. His better style as a writer is in keeping with the simplicity and purity of his life. We have said that his range was narrow, but to be a master is to be a master. He had caught his English at its living source, among the poets and prose-writers of its best days; his literature was extensive and recondite; his quotations are always nuggets of the purest ore: there are sentences of his as perfect as anything in the language, and thoughts as clearly crystallized; his metaphors and images are always fresh from the soil; he had watched Nature like a detective who is to go upon the stand; as we read him, it seems as if all-out-of-doors had kept a diary and become its own Montaigne; we look at the landscape as in a Claude Lorraine glass; compared with his, all other books of similar aim, even White's "Selborne,"[9] seem dry as a country clergyman's meteorological journal in an old almanac. He belongs with Donne and Browne and Novalis; if not with the originally creative men, with the scarcely smaller class who are peculiar, and whose leaves shed their invisible thought-seed like ferns.

JOHN BURROUGHS

Another Word on Thoreau†

I

After Emerson, the name of no New England man of letters keeps greener and fresher than that of Thoreau. A severe censor of his countrymen, and with few elements of popularity, yet the quality of his thought, the sincerity of his life, and the nearness and perennial interest of his themes, as well as his rare powers of literary expression, win recruits from each generation of readers. He does not grow stale any more than Walden Pond itself grows stale. He is an

---

8. From Emerson's "Ode, Inscribed to W. H. Channing," lines 50–51; and Carlyle's *Sartor Resartus* 2.9: " 'the Fraction of Life can be increased in value not so much by increasing your Numerator as by lessening your Denominator' " [*Editor*].
9. See n. 1, p. 387.
† From the Riverby Edition of *The Writings of John Burroughs* (Boston and New York, 1922), vol. 23, *The Last Harvest*, pp. 103–71. *Walden* page numbers refer to this Norton Critical Edition.

obstinate fact there in New England life and literature, and at the end of his first centennial his fame is more alive than ever.

* * *

The most point-blank and authoritative criticism within my knowledge that Thoreau has received at the hands of his country-men came from the pen of Lowell about 1864, and was included in "My Study Windows." It has all the professional smartness and scholarly qualities which usually characterize Lowell's critical es-says. Thoreau was vulnerable, both as an observer and as a literary craftsman, and Lowell lets him off pretty easily—too easily—on both counts.

* * *

But though Lowell lets Thoreau off easily on these specific counts, he more than makes up by his sweeping criticism, on more general grounds, of his life and character. Here one feels that he overdoes the matter.

It is not true, in the sense which Lowell implies, that Thoreau's whole life was a search for the doctor. It was such a search in no other sense than that we are all in search of the doctor when we take a walk, or flee to the mountains or to the seashore, or seek to bring our minds and spirits in contact with "Nature's primal sani-ties." His search for the doctor turns out to be an escape from the conditions that make a doctor necessary. His wonderful activity, those long walks in all weathers, in all seasons, by night as well as by day, drenched by rain and chilled by frost, suggest a reckless kind of health. A doctor might wisely have cautioned him against such exposures. Nor was Thoreau a valetudinarian in his physical, moral, or intellectual fiber.

It is not true, as Lowell charges, that it was his indolence that stood in the way of his taking part in the industrial activities in which his friends and neighbors engaged, or that it was his lack of persistence and purpose that hindered him. It is not true that he was poor because he looked upon money as an unmixed evil. Thoreau's purpose was like adamant, and his industry in his own proper pursuits was tireless. He knew the true value of money, and he knew also that the best things in life are to be had without money and without price. When he had need of money, he earned it. He turned his hand to many things—land-surveying, lecturing, magazine-writing, growing white beans, doing odd jobs at carpen-tering, whitewashing, fence-building, plastering, and brick-laying.

Lowell's criticism amounts almost to a diatribe. He was naturally antagonistic to the Thoreau type of mind. Coming from a man near his own age, and a neighbor, Thoreau's criticism of life was an af-front to the smug respectability and scholarly attainments of the

class to which Lowell belonged. Thoreau went his own way, with an
air of defiance and contempt which, no doubt, his contemporaries
were more inclined to resent than we are at our distance. Shall this
man in his hut on the shores of Walden Pond assume to lay down
the law and the gospel to his elders and betters, and pass unre-
buked, no matter on what intimate terms he claims to be with the
gods of the woods and mountains? This seems to be Lowell's spirit.

"Thoreau's experiment," says Lowell, "actually presupposed all
that complicated civilization which it theoretically abjured. He
squatted on another man's land; he borrows an axe; his boards, his
nails, his bricks, his mortar, his books, his lamp, his fish-hooks, his
plough, his hoe, all turn state's evidence against him as an accomplice in the sin of that artificial civilization which rendered it possible that such a person as Henry D. Thoreau should exist at all."
Very clever, but what of it? Of course Thoreau was a product of the
civilization he decried. He was a product of his country and his
times. He was born in Concord and early came under the influence
of Emerson; he was a graduate of Harvard University and all his life
availed himself, more or less, of the accumulated benefits of state
and social organizations. When he took a train to Boston, or
dropped a letter in, or received one through, the post office, or read
a book, or visited a library, or looked in a newspaper, he was a
sharer in these benefits. He made no claims to living independently
of the rest of mankind. His only aim in his Walden experiment was
to reduce life to its lowest terms, to drive it into a corner, as he
said, and question and cross-question it, and see, if he could, what
it really meant. And he probably came as near cornering it there in
his hut on Walden Pond as any man ever did anywhere, certainly in
a way more pleasing to contemplate than did the old hermits in the
desert, or than did Diogenes in his tub, though Lowell says the tub
of the old Greek had a sounder bottom.

Lowell seemed to discredit Thoreau by attacking his philosophy
and pointing out the contradictions and inconsistencies of a man
who abjures the civilization of which he is the product, overlooking
the fact that man's theories and speculations may be very wide of
the truth as we view it, and yet his life be noble and inspiring. Now
Thoreau did not give us a philosophy, but a life. He gave us fresh
and beautiful literature, he gave us our first and probably only nature classic, he gave us an example of plain living and high thinking
that is always in season, and he took upon himself that kind of noble poverty that carries the suggestion of wealth of soul.

No matter how much Thoreau abjured our civilization, he certainly made good use of the weapons it gave him. No matter whose
lands he squatted on, or whose saw he borrowed, or to whom or
what he was indebted for the tools and utensils that made his life at

Walden possible,—these things were the mere accidents of his environment,—he left a record of his life and thoughts there which is a precious heritage to his countrymen. The best in his books ranks with the best in the literature of his times. One could wish that he had shown more tolerance for the things other men live for, but this must not make us overlook the value of the things he himself lived for, though with some of his readers his intolerance doubtless has this effect. We cannot all take to the woods and swamps as Thoreau did. He had a genius for that kind of a life; the most of us must stick to our farms and desks and shops and professions.

Thoreau retired to Walden for study and contemplation, and because, as he said, he had a little private business with himself. He found that by working about six weeks in the year he could meet all his living expenses, and then have all his winter and most of his summers free and clear for study. He found that to maintain one's self on this earth is not a hardship, but a pastime, if one will live simply and wisely. He said, "It is not necessary that a man should earn his living by the sweat of his brow unless he sweats easier than I do" (52). Was not his experiment worth while?

"Walden" is a wonderful and delightful piece of brag, but it is much more than that. It is literature; it is a Gospel of the Wild. It made a small Massachusetts pond famous, and the Mecca of many devout pilgrims.

Lowell says that Thoreau had no humor, but there are many pages in "Walden" that are steeped in a quiet but most delicious humor. His humor brings that inward smile which is the badge of art's felicity. His "Bean-Field" is full of it. I venture to say that never before had a hermit so much fun with a field of white beans.

Both by training and by temperament Lowell was disqualified from entering into Thoreau's character and aims. Lowell's passion for books and academic accomplishments was as strong as was Thoreau's passion for the wild and for the religion of Nature. When Lowell went to Nature for a theme, as in his "Good Word for Winter," his "My Garden Acquaintance," and the "Moosehead Journal," his use of it was mainly to unlock the treasures of his literary and scholarly attainments; he bedecked and bejeweled Nature with gems from all the literatures of the world. In the "Journal" we get more of the flavor of libraries than of the Maine woods and waters. No reader of Lowell can doubt that he was a nature-lover, nor can he doubt that he loved books and libraries more. In all his nature writings the poverty of the substance and the wealth of the treatment are striking. The final truth about Lowell's contributions is that his mind was essentially a prose mind, even when he writes poetry. Emerson said justly that his tone was always that of prose. What is his "Cathedral" but versified prose? Like so many cultivated men, he showed a talent for poetry, but not genius; as, on the other hand, one may say of Emerson that he showed more genius for poetry than talent, his inspiration surpassed his technical skill.

One is not surprised when he finds that John Brown was one of Thoreau's heroes; he was a sort of John Brown himself in another sphere; but one is surprised when one finds him so heartily approving of Walt Whitman and traveling to Brooklyn to look upon him and hear his voice. He recognized at once the tremendous significance of Whitman and the power of his poetry. He called him the greatest democrat which the world had yet seen. With all his asceticism and his idealism, he was not troubled at all with those things in Whitman that are a stumbling-block to so many persons. Evidently his long intercourse with Nature had prepared him for the primitive and elemental character of Whitman's work. No doubt also his familiarity with the great poems and sacred books of the East helped him. At any rate, in this respect, his endorsement of Whitman adds greatly to our conception of the mental and spiritual stature of Thoreau.

I can hold my criticism in the back of my head while I say with my forehead that all our other nature writers seem tame and insipid beside Thoreau. He was so much more than a mere student and observer of nature; and it is this surplusage which gives the extra weight and value to his nature writing. He was a critic of life, he was a literary force that made for plain living and high thinking. His nature lore was an aside; he gathered it as the meditative saunterer gathers a leaf, or a flower, or a shell on the beach, while he ponders on higher things. He had other business with the gods of the woods than taking an inventory of their wares. He was a dreamer, an idealist, a fervid ethical teacher, seeking inspiration in the fields and woods. The hound, the turtle-dove, and the bay horse which he said he had lost, and for whose trail he was constantly seeking, typified his interest in wild nature. The natural history in his books is quite secondary. The natural or supernatural history of his own thought absorbed him more than the exact facts about the wild life around him. He brings us a gospel more than he brings us a history. His science is only the handmaid of his ethics; his woodlore is the foil of his moral and intellectual teachings. His observations are frequently at fault, or wholly wide of the mark; but the flower or specimen that he brings you always "comes laden with a thought." There is a tang and a pungency to nearly everything he published; the personal quality which flavors it is like the formic acid which the bee infuses into the nectar he gets from the flower, and which makes it honey.

I feel that some such statement about Thoreau should precede or go along with any criticism of him as a writer or as an observer. He was, first and last, a moral force speaking in the terms of the literary naturalist.

* * *

II

Thoreau was not a great philosopher, he was not a great naturalist, he was not a great poet, but as a nature-writer and an original character he is unique in our literature. His philosophy begins and ends with himself, or is entirely subjective, and is frequently fantastic, and nearly always illogical. His poetry is of the oracular kind, and is only now and then worth attention. There are crudities in his writings that make the conscientious literary craftsman shudder; there are mistakes of observation that make the serious naturalist wonder; and there is often an expression of contempt for his fellow countrymen, and the rest of mankind, and their aims in life, that makes the judicious grieve. But at his best there is a gay symbolism, a felicity of description, and a freshness of observation that delight all readers.

* * *

Thoreau called himself a mystic, and a transcendentalist, and a natural philosopher to boot. But the least of these was the natural philosopher. He did not have the philosophic mind, nor the scientific mind; he did not inquire into the reason of things, nor the meaning of things; in fact, had no disinterested interest in the universe apart from himself. He was too personal and illogical for a philosopher. The scientific interpretation of things did not interest him at all. He was interested in things only so far as they related to Henry Thoreau. He interpreted Nature entirely in the light of his own idiosyncrasies.

Science goes its own way in spite of our likes and dislikes, but Thoreau's likes and dislikes determined everything for him. He was stoical, but not philosophical. His intellect had no free play outside his individual predilection. Truth as philosophers use the term, was not his quest but truth made in Concord.

* * *

An extremist he always was. Extreme views commended themselves to him because they were extreme. His aim in writing was usually "to make an extreme statement" (260). He left the middle ground to the school committees and trustees. He had in him the stuff of which martyrs and heroes are made. In John Brown he recognized a kindred soul. But his literary bent led him to take his own revolutionary impulses out in words. The closest he came to imitation of the hero of Harper's Ferry and to defying the Government was on one occasion when he refused to pay his poll-tax and thus got himself locked in jail overnight. It all seems a petty and ignoble ending of his fierce denunciation of politics and government, but it no doubt helped to satisfy his imagination, which so tyrannized over him throughout life. He could endure offenses against his heart and conscience and reason easier than against his imagination.

* * *

III

Thoreau's life was a search for the wild. He was the great disciple of the Gospel of Walking. He elevated walking into a religious exercise. One of his most significant and entertaining chapters is on "Walking." No other writer that I recall has set forth the Gospel of Walking so eloquently and so stimulatingly. Thoreau's religion and his philosophy are all in this chapter. It is his most mature, his most complete and comprehensive statement.

* * *

Wordsworth never knew the wild as we know it in this country— the pitilessly savage and rebellious; and, on the other hand, he never knew the wonderfully delicate and furtive and elusive nature that we know; but he knew the sylvan, the pastoral, the rustic-human, as we cannot know them. British birds have nothing plaintive in their songs; and British woods and fells but little that is disorderly and cruel in their expression, or violent in their contrasts.

Wordsworth gathered his finest poetic harvest from common nature and common humanity about him—the wayside birds and flowers and waterfalls, and the wayside people. Though he called himself a worshiper of Nature, it was Nature in her half-human moods that he adored—Nature that knows no extremes, and that has long been under the influence of man—a soft, humid, fertile, docile Nature, that suggests a domesticity as old and as permanent as that of cattle and sheep. His poetry reflects these features, reflects the high moral and historic significance of the European landscape, while the poetry of Emerson, and of Thoreau, is born of the wildness and elusiveness of our more capricious and unkempt Nature.

The walker has no axe to grind; he sniffs the air for new adventure; he loiters in old scenes, he gleans in old fields. He only seeks intimacy with Nature to surprise her preoccupied with her own affairs. He seeks her in the woods, the swamps, on the hills, along the streams, by night and by day, in season and out of season. He skims the fields and hillsides as the swallow skims the air, and what he gets is intangible to most persons. He sees much with his eyes, but he sees more with his heart and imagination. He bathes in Nature as in a sea. He is alert for the beauty that waves in the trees, that ripples in the grass and grain, that flows in the streams, that drifts in the clouds, that sparkles in the dew and rain. The hammer of the geologist, the notebook of the naturalist, the box of the herbalist, the net of the entomologist, are not for him. He drives no sharp bargains with Nature, he reads no sermons in stones, no books in running brooks, but he does see good in everything. The book he reads he reads through all his senses—through his eyes, his ears, his nose, and also through his feet and hands—and its pages are open everywhere; the rocks speak of more than geology to him, the birds of more than ornithology, the flowers of more than botany, the stars of more than astronomy, the wild creatures of more than zoölogy.

The average walker is out for exercise and the exhilarations of the road, he reaps health and strength; but Thoreau evidently impaired his health by his needless exposure and inadequate food. He was a Holy-Lander who falls and dies in the Holy Land. He ridiculed walking for exercise—taking a walk as the sick take medicine; the walk itself was to be the "enterprise and adventure of the day." And "you must walk like a camel, which is said to be the only beast which ruminates while walking" (263).

IV

Thoreau's friends and neighbors seem to have persuaded themselves that his natural-history lore was infallible, and, moreover, that he possessed some mysterious power over the wild creatures about him that other men did not possess. I recall how Emerson fairly bristled up when on one occasion while in conversation with him I told him I thought Thoreau in his trips to the Maine woods had confounded the hermit thrush with the wood thrush, as the latter was rarely or never found in Maine. As for Thoreau's influence over the wild creatures, Emerson voiced this superstition when he said, "Snakes coiled round his leg, the fishes swam into his hand, and he took them from the water; he pulled the woodchuck out of its hole by the tail, and took the foxes under his protection from the hunters." Of course Thoreau could do nothing with the wild creatures that you or I could not do under the same conditions.

* * *

V

Thoreau's faults as a writer are as obvious as his merits. Emerson hit upon one of them when he said, "The trick of his rhetoric is soon learned; it consists in substituting for the obvious word and thought, its diametrical antagonist." He praises wild mountains and winter forests for their domestic air, snow and ice for their warmth, and so on. (Yet Emerson in one of his poems makes frost burn and fire freeze.) One frequently comes upon such sentences as these: "If I were sadder, I should be happier"; "The longer I have forgotten you, the more I remember you." It may give a moment's pleasure when a writer takes two opposites and rubs their ears together in that way, but one may easily get too much of it. Words really mean nothing when used in such a manner. When Emerson told Channing that if he (Emerson) could write as well as he did, he would write a great deal better, one readily sees what he means. And when Thoreau says of one of his callers, "I like his looks and the sound of his silence," the contradiction pleases one. But when he tells his friend that hate is the substratum of his love for him, words seem to have lost their meaning. Now and then he is guilty of sheer bragging, as when he says, "I would not go around the corner to see the world blow up."

He often defies all our sense of fitness and proportion by the degree in which he magnifies the little and belittles the big. He says of the singing of a cricket which he heard under the border of some rock on the hillside one mid-May day, that it "makes the finest singing of birds outward and insignificant." "It is not so wildly melodious, but it is wiser and more mature than that of the wood thrush." His forced and meaningless analogies come out in such a comparison as this: "Most poems, like the fruits, are sweetest toward the blossom end." Which *is* the blossom end of a poem?

Thoreau advised one of his correspondents when he made garden to plant some Giant Regrets—they were good for sauce. It is certain that he himself planted some Giant Exaggerations and had a good yield. His exaggeration was deliberate. "Walden" is from first to last a most delightful sample of his talent. He belittles everything that goes on in the world outside his bean-field. Business, politics, institutions, governments, wars and rumors of wars, were not so much to him as the humming of a mosquito in his hut at Walden: "I am as much affected by the faint hum of a mosquito making its invisible and unimaginable tour through my apartment at earliest dawn, when I was sitting with door and windows open, as I could be by any trumpet that ever sang of fame. It was Homer's requiem; itself an Iliad and Odyssey in the air, singing its own wrath and wanderings. There was something cosmical about it" (63–4). One wonders what he would have made of a blow-fly buzzing on the pane.

He made Walden Pond famous because he made it the center of the universe and found life rich and full without many of the things that others deem necessary. There is a stream of pilgrims to Walden at all seasons, curious to see where so much came out of so little—

where a man had lived who preferred poverty to riches, and solitude to society, who boasted that he could do without the post office, the newspapers, the telegraph, and who had little use for the
railroad, though he thought mankind had become a little more
punctual since its invention.

Another conspicuous fault as a writer is his frequent use of false
analogies, or his comparison of things which have no ground of relationship, as when he says: "A day passed in the society of those
Greek sages, such as described in the Banquet of Xenophon, would
not be comparable with the dry wit of decayed cranberry-vines, and
the fresh Attic salt of the moss-beds." The word "wit" has no meaning when thus used. Or again where he says: "All great enterprises
are self-supporting. The poet, for instance, must sustain his body
by his poetry, as a steam planing-mill feeds its boilers with the shavings it makes." Was there ever a more inept and untruthful comparison? To find any ground of comparison between the two things he
compared, he must make his poet sustain his body by the scraps
and lines of his poem which he rejects, or else the steam planing-
mill consume its finished product.

"Let all things give way to the impulse of expression," he says,
and he assuredly practiced what he had preached.

* * *

VII

The craving for literary expression in Thoreau was strong and constant, but, as he confesses, he could not always select a theme. "I
am prepared not so much for contemplation as for forceful expression." No matter what the occasion, "forceful expression" was the
aim. No meditation, or thinking, but sallies of the mind. All his
paradoxes and false analogies and inconsistencies come from this
craving for a forceful expression. He apparently brought to bear all
the skill he possessed of this kind on all occasions. One must regard him, not as a great thinker, nor as a disinterested seeker after
the truth, but as a master in the art of vigorous and picturesque expression. To startle, to wake up, to communicate to his reader a little wholesome shock, is his aim. Not the novelty and freshness of
his subject-matter concerns him but the novelty and unhackneyed
character of his literary style. That throughout the years a man
should keep up the habit of walking, by night as well as by day, and
bring such constant intellectual pressure to bear upon everything
he saw, or heard, or felt, is remarkable. No evidence of relaxation,
or of abandonment to the mere pleasure of the light and air and of
green things growing, or of sauntering without thoughts of his Journal. He is as keyed up and strenuous in his commerce with the Ce-

lestial Empire as any tradesman in world goods that ever amassed a fortune. He sometimes wrote as he walked, and expanded and elaborated the same as in his study. On one occasion he dropped his pencil and could not find it, but he managed to complete the record. One night on his way to Conantum he speculates for nearly ten printed pages on the secret of being able to state a fact simply and adequately, or of making one's self the free organ of truth—a subtle and ingenious discussion with the habitual craving for forceful expression. In vain I try to put myself in the place of a man who goes forth into wild nature with malice prepense to give free swing to his passion for forcible expression. I suppose all nature-writers go forth on their walks or strolls to the fields and woods with minds open to all of Nature's genial influences and significant facts and incidents, but rarely, I think, with the strenuousness of Thoreau— grinding the grist as they go along.

* * *

XI

As a philosopher or expositor and interpreter of a principle, Thoreau is often simply grotesque. His passion for strong and striking figures usually gets the best of him. In discussing the relation that exists between the speaker or lecturer and his audience he says, "The lecturer will read best those parts of his lecture which are best heard," as if the reading did not precede the hearing! Then comes this grotesque analogy: "I saw some men unloading molasses-hogsheads from a truck at a depot the other day, rolling them up an inclined plane. The truckman stood behind and shoved, after putting a couple of ropes, one round each end of the hogshead, while two men standing in the depot steadily pulled at the ropes. The first man was the lecturer, the last was the audience." I suppose the hogshead stands for the big thoughts of the speaker which he cannot manage at all without the active coöperation of the audience. The truth is, people assemble in a lecture hall in a passive but expectant frame of mind. They are ready to be pleased or displeased. They are there like an instrument to be played upon by the orator. He may work his will with them. Without their sympathy his success will not be great, but the triumph of his art is to win their sympathy. Those who went to scoff when the Great Preacher spoke, remained to pray. No man could speak as eloquently to empty seats, or to a dummy audience, as to a hall filled with intelligent people, yet Thoreau's ropes and hogsheads and pulling and pushing truckmen absurdly misrepresent the true relation that exists between a speaker and his hearers. Of course a speaker finds it uphill work if his audience is not with him, but that it is not with him is usually his own fault.

Thoreau's merits as a man and a writer are so many and so great that I have not hesitated to make much of his defects. Indeed, I have with malice aforethought ransacked his works to find them. But after they are all charged up against him, the balance that remains on the credit side of the account is so great that they do not disturb us.

There has been but one Thoreau, and we should devoutly thank the gods of New England for the precious gift. Thoreau's work lives and will continue to live because, in the first place, the world loves a writer who can flout it and turn his back upon it and yet make good; and again because the books which he gave to the world have many and very high literary and ethical values. They are fresh, original, and stimulating. He drew a gospel out of the wild; he brought messages from the wood gods to men; he made a lonely pond in Massachusetts a fountain of the purest and most elevating thoughts, and, with his great neighbor Emerson, added new luster to a town over which the muse of our colonial history had long loved to dwell.

MODERN CRITICISM

Walden

F. O. MATTHIESSEN

Walden: Craftsmanship *vs.* Technique†

'You can't read any genuine history—as that of Herodotus or the
Venerable Bede—without perceiving that our interest depends not
on the subject but on the man,—on the manner in which he
treats the subject and the importance he gives it. A feeble writer
. . . must have what he thinks a great theme, which we are already
interested in through the accounts of others, but a genius—a
Shakespeare, for instance—would make the history of his parish
more interesting than another's history of the world.'
　　　　　　　　　　　　　　—THOREAU's *Journal* (March 1861)

It is apparent, in view of this last distinction of Coleridge's,[1] that
the real test of whether Thoreau mastered organic form can hardly
be made on the basis of accounting for the differences in body and
flavor between his portrayal of the natural world and Emerson's,
revelatory as these differences are. Nor can it be made by considering one of the rare occasions when his verse was redeemed by
virtue of his discipline in translating from the Greek Anthology. Nor
is it enough to reckon with the excellence of individual passages of
prose, since the frequent charge is that whereas Emerson was master of the sentence, Thoreau was master of the paragraph, but that
he was unable to go farther and attain 'the highest or structural
achievements of form in a whole book.' The only adequate way of
answering that is by considering the structure of *Walden* as a
whole, by asking to what extent it meets Coleridge's demand of
shaping, 'as it develops, itself from within.'

On one level *Walden* is the record of a personal experience, yet
even in making that remark we are aware that this book does not go
rightfully into the category of *Two Years Before the Mast* or *The Ore-*

---

†　From *American Renaissance* (Oxford: Oxford University Press, 1941), pp. 166–75. Copyright © 1941 by Oxford University Press, Inc. Reprinted by permission.
1. I.e., between imitation and mere copying. As Matthiessen explains, "Coleridge held that
the artist must not try to make a surface reproduction of nature's details, but 'must imitate that which is within the thing . . . for so only can he hope to produce any work truly
natural in the object and truly human in the effect' " [*Editor*].

gon Trail. Why it presents a richer accumulation than either of those vigorous pieces of contemporary history is explained by its process of composition. Although Thoreau said that the bulk of its pages were written during his two years of sojourn by the pond (1845–7), it was not ready for publication until seven years later, and ultimately included a distillation from his journals over the whole period from 1838. A similar process had helped to transform his week's boat trip with his brother from a private to a symbolical event, since the record was bathed in memory for a decade (1839–49) before it found its final shape in words. But the flow of the *Week* is as leisurely and discursive as the bends in the Concord river, and the casual pouring in of miscellaneous poems and essays that Thoreau had previously printed in *The Dial* tends to obscure the cyclical movement. Yet each day advances from dawn to the varied sounds of night, and Thoreau uses an effective device for putting a period to the whole by the shift of the final morning from lazy August to the first sharp forebodings of transforming frost.

The sequence of *Walden* is arranged a good deal more subtly, perhaps because its subject constituted a more central symbol for Thoreau's accruing knowledge of life. He remarked on how the pond itself was one of the earliest scenes in his recollection, dating from the occasion when he had been brought out there one day when he was four, and how thereafter 'that woodland vision for a long time made the drapery of my dreams.' By 1841 he had already announced, "I want to go soon and live away by the pond,' and when pressed by friends about what he would do when he got there, he had asked in turn if it would not be employment enough 'to watch the progress of the seasons'? In that same year he had said: 'I think I could write a poem to be called "Concord." For argument I should have the River, the Woods, the Ponds, the Hills, the Fields, the Swamps and Meadows, the Streets and Buildings, and the Villagers.' In his completed 'poem' these last elements had receded into the background. What had come squarely to the fore, and made the opening chapter by far the longest of all, was the desire to record an experiment in 'Economy' as an antidote to the 'lives of quiet desperation' that he saw the mass of men leading. This essay on how he solved his basic needs of food and shelter might stand by itself, but also carries naturally forward to the more poignant condensation of the same theme in 'Where I lived, and What I lived for,' which reaches its conclusion in the passage on wedging down to reality.

At this point the skill with which Thoreau evolved his composition begins to come into play. On the one hand, the treatment of his material might simply have followed the chronological outline; on the other, it might have drifted into being loosely topical. At first glance it may appear that the latter is what happened, that there is no real cogency in the order of the chapters. That would have been Lowell's complaint, that Thoreau 'had no artistic power such as controls a great work to the serene balance of completeness.'[2] But so far as the opposite can be proved by the effective arrangement of his entire material, the firmness with which Thoreau binds his successive links is worth examining. The student and observer that he has settled himself to be at the end of his second chapter leads easily into his discussion of 'Reading,' but that in turn gives way to his concern with the more fundamental language, which all things speak, in the chapter on 'Sounds.' Then, after he has passed from the tantivy of wild pigeons to the whistle of the locomotive, he reflects that once the cars have gone by and the restless world with them, he is more alone than ever. That starts the transition to the chapter on 'Solitude,' in which the source of his joy is to live by himself in the midst of nature with his senses unimpaired. The natural contrast is made in the next chapter on 'Visitors,' which he opens by saying how he believes he loves society as much as most, and is ready enough to fasten himself 'like a bloodsucker for the time to any full-blooded man' who comes his way. But after he has talked enthusiastically about the French woodchopper, and other welcome friends from the village, he remembers 'restless committed men,' the self-styled reformers who felt it their duty to give him advice. At that he breaks away with 'Meanwhile my beans . . . were impatient to be hoed'; and that opening carries him back to the earlier transition to the chapter on 'Sounds': 'I did not read books the first summer; I hoed beans.'

The effect of that repetition is to remind the reader of the time sequence that is knitting together all these chapters after the building of the cabin in the spring. From 'The Bean Field' as the sphere of his main occupation, he moves on, in 'The Village,' to his strolls for gossip, which, 'taken in homeopathic doses, was really as refreshing in its way as the rustle of leaves and the peeping of frogs.' Whether designedly or not, this chapter is the shortest in the book,

---

2. The don of Harvard was not entirely blind to the man of Concord. Even in his notorious essay on *Walden* in *My Study Windows* he perceived that Thoreau 'had caught his English at its living source, among the poets and prose-writers of its best days,' and compared him with Donne and Browne. When Lowell tried to dismiss Thoreau as a crank, he was really bothered, as Henry Canby has pointed out, by Thoreau's attack upon his own ideals of genteel living. How different from Emerson's is Lowell's tone when he says that while Thoreau 'studied with respectful attention the minks and woodchucks, his neighbors, he looked with utter contempt on the august drama of destiny of which his country was the scene, and on which the curtain had already risen.' As Mr. Canby had added: 'By destiny, Lowell clearly means the "manifest destiny" of the exploitation of the West, whose more sordid and unfortunate aspects Thoreau had prophesied two generations before their time of realization.' [For references to Lowell's essay, see pp. 412, 418, and 416 in this volume; *Editor*]

and yields to rambles even farther away from the community than
Walden, to 'The Ponds' and to fishing beyond 'Baker Farm.' As he
was returning through the woods with his catch, and glimpsed in
the near dark a woodchuck stealing across his path, then came the
moment when he 'felt a strange thrill of savage delight, and was
strongly tempted to seize and devour him raw.' And in the flash of
his realization of his double instinct towards the spiritual and the
wild, he has the starting point for the next two contrasting chapters,
'Higher Laws' and 'Brute Neighbors,' in considering both of which
he follows his rule of going far enough to please his imagination.

From here on the structure becomes cyclical, his poem of the
seasons or myth of the year. The accounts of his varied excursions
have brought him to the day when he felt that he could no longer
warm himself by the embers of the sun, which 'summer, like a departed hunter, had left.' Consequently, he set about finishing his
cabin by building a chimney, and called that act 'House-Warming.'
There follows a solid block of winter in the three chapters, 'Winter
Visitors,' 'Winter Animals,' and 'The Pond in Winter,' that order suggesting the way in which the radius of his experience contracted
then more and more to his immediate surroundings. However, the
last pages on the pond deal with the cutting of the ice, and end
with that sudden extraordinary expansion of his thought which an-
nihilates space and time.

The last movement is the advance to 'Spring.' The activity of the
ice company in opening its large tracts has hastened the break-up of
the rest of the pond; and, listening to its booming, he recalls that
one attraction that brought him to the woods was the opportunity
and leisure to watch this renewal of the world. He has long felt in
his observations that a day is an epitome of a year, and now he
knows that a year is likewise symbolical of a life; and so, in present-
ing his experience by the pond, he foreshortens and condenses the
twenty-six months to the interval from the beginning of one summer
to the next. In the melting season he feels more than ever the mood
of expanding promise, and he catches the reader up into this rich
forward course by one of his most successful kinesthetic images,
which serves to round out his cycle: 'And so the seasons went rolling
on into summer, as one rambles into higher and higher grass.' To
that he adds only the bare statement of when he left the woods, and
a 'Conclusion,' which explains that he did so for as good a reason as
he had gone there. He had other lives to live, and he knew now that
he could find for himself 'a solid bottom everywhere.' That discovery
gave him his final serene assurance that 'There is more day to dawn,'
and consequently he was not to be disturbed by the 'confused
tintinnabulum' that sometimes reached his midday repose. He recognized it for the noise of his contemporaries.

The construction of the book involved deliberate rearrangement of material. For instance, a single afternoon's return to the pond in the fall of 1852 was capable of furnishing details that were woven into half a dozen passages of the finished work, two of them separated by seventy pages. Nevertheless, since no invention was demanded, since all the material was a *donnée* of Thoreau's memory, my assertion that *Walden* does not belong with the simple records of experience may require more establishing. The chief clue to how it was transformed into something else lies in Thoreau's extension of his remark that he did not believe himself to be 'wholly involved in Nature.' He went on to say that in being aware of himself as a human entity, he was 'sensible of a certain doubleness' that made him both participant and spectator in any event. This ability to stand 'as remote from myself as from another' is the indispensable attribute of the dramatist. Thoreau makes you share in the excitement of his private scenes, for example, by the kind of generalized significance he can give to his purchase and demolishment of an old shanty for its boards:

> I was informed treacherously by a young Patrick that neighbor Seeley, an Irishman, in the intervals of the carting, transferred the still tolerable, straight, and drivable nails, staples, and spikes to his pocket, and then stood when I came back to pass the time of day, and look freshly up, unconcerned, with spring thoughts, at the devastation; there being a dearth of work, as he said. He was there to represent spectatordom, and help make this seemingly insignificant event one with the removal of the gods of Troy.

The demands he made of great books are significant of his owns intentions: 'They have no cause of their own to plead, but while they enlighten and sustain the reader his common sense will not refuse them.' Propaganda is not the source of the inner freedom they offer to the reader, for their relation to life is more inclusive than argument; or, as Thoreau described it, they are at once 'intimate' and 'universal.' He aimed unerringly to reconcile these two extremes in his own writing. His experience had been fundamental in that it had sprung from his determination to start from obedience to the rudimentary needs of a man who wanted to be free. Greenough[3] had seen how, in that sense, 'Obedience is worship,' for by discerning and following the functional patterns of daily behavior, you could discover the proportions of beauty that would express and complete them. It was Thoreau's conviction that by reducing

---

3. Horatio Greenough (1805–52), a sculptor and early proponent of the idea that architectural decoration should be functional. See Matthiessen, *American Renaissance*, 140–52 [*Editor*].

life to its primitive conditions, he had come to the roots from which healthy art must flower, whether in Thessaly or Concord. It was not just a figure of speech when he said that 'Olympus is but the outside of the earth everywhere.' The light touch of his detachment allows the comparison of his small things with great, and throughout the book enables him to possess the universe at home.

As a result *Walden* has spoken to men of widely differing convictions, who have in common only the intensity of their devotion to life. It became a bible for many of the leaders of the British labor movement after Morris. When the sound of a little fountain in a shop window in Fleet Street made him think suddenly of lake water, Yeats remembered also his boyhood enthusiasm for Thoreau. He did not leave London then and go and live on Innisfree. But out of his loneliness in the foreign city he did write the first of his poems that met with a wide response, and 'The Lake Isle'—despite its Pre-Raphaelite flavor—was reminiscent of *Walden* even to 'the small cabin' Yeats built and the 'bean rows' he planted in his imagination. *Walden* was also one of our books that bulked largest for Tolstoy when he addressed his brief message to America (1901) and urged us to rediscover the greatness of our writers of the fifties: 'And I should like to ask the American people why they do not pay more attention to these voices (hardly to be replaced by those of financial and industrial millionaires, or successful generals and admirals), and continue the good work in which they made such hopeful progress.' In 1904 Proust wrote to the Comtesse de Noailles: 'Lisez . . . les pages admirables de *Walden*. Il me semble qu'on les lise en soi-même tant elles sortent du fond de notre expérience intime.'[4]

In his full utilization of his immediate resources Thoreau was the kind of native craftsman whom Greenough recognized as the harbinger of power for our arts. Craftsmanship in this sense involves the mastery of traditional modes and skills; it has been thought of more often in connection with Indian baskets or Yankee tankards and hearth-tools than with the so-called fine arts. In fact, until fairly lately, despite Greenough's pioneering, it has hardly been consistently thought of in relation to American products of any kind. The march of our experience has been so dominantly expansive, from one rapid disequilibrium to the next, that we have neglected to see what Constance Rourke, among others, has now pointed out so effectively: that notwithstanding the inevitable restlessness of our long era of pioneering, at many stages within that process the strong counter-effort of the settlers was for communal

---

4. "Read the marvelous pages of *Walden*. It seems to me that one is reading them within oneself so much do they spring from the depths of one's intimate experience" [*Editor*].

security and permanence. From such islands of realization and ful-filment within the onrushing torrent have come the objects, the or-der and balance of which now, when we most need them, we can recognize as among the most valuable possessions of our continent. The conspicuous manifestation of these qualities, as Greenough al-ready knew, has been in architecture as the most social of forms, whether in the clipper, or on the New England green, or in the Shaker communities. But the artifacts of the cabinet maker, the potter and the founder, or whatever other utensils have been shaped patiently and devotedly for common service, are likewise a testimony of what Miss Rourke has called our classic art, recogniz-ing that this term 'has nothing to do with grandeur, that it cannot be copied or imported, but is the outgrowth of a special mode of life and feeling.'

Thoreau's deep obligation to such traditional ways has been ob-scured by our thinking of him only as the extreme protestant. It is now clear that his revolt was bound up with a determination to do all he could to prevent the dignity of common labor from being de-graded by the idle tastes of the rich. When he objected that 'the mason who finishes the cornice of the palace returns at night per-chance to a hut not so good as a wigwam,' he showed the identity of his social and aesthetic foundations. Although he did not use Gree-nough's terms, he was always requiring a functional relationship. What he responded to as beauty was the application of trained skill to the exigencies of existence. He made no arbitrary separation be-tween arts, and admired the Indian's woodcraft or the farmer's thorough care in building a barn on the same grounds that he ad-mired the workmanship of Homer.[5] The depth to which his ideals for fitness and beauty in writing were shaped, half unconsciously, by the modes of productive labor with which he was surrounded, or, in fact, by the work of his own hands in carpentry or pencil-making or gardening, can be read in his instinctive analogies. He knew that the only discipline for Channing's 'sublimo-slipshod style' would be to try to carve some truths as roundly and solidly as a stonecutter. He knew it was no good to write, 'unless you feel strong in the knees.' Or—a more unexpected example to find in him—he believed he had learned an important lesson in design from the fidelity with which the operative in the textile-factory had woven his piece of cloth.

The structural wholeness of *Walden* makes it stand as the firmest

5. Emerson also said, 'I like a man who likes to see a fine barn as well as a good tragedy.' And Whitman added, as his reaction to the union of work and culture, 'I know that pleasure filters in and oozes out of me at the opera, but I know too that subtly and un-accountably my mind is sweet and odorous within while I clean up my boots and grease the pair that I reserve for stormy weather."

product in our literature of such life-giving analogies between the processes of art and daily work. Moreover, Thoreau's very lack of invention brings him closer to the essential attributes of craftsmanship, if by that term we mean the strict, even spare, almost impersonal 'revelation of the object,' in contrast to the 'elaborated skill,' the combinations of more variegated resources that we describe as technique. This contrast of terms is still Miss Rourke's, in distinguishing between kinds of painting, but it can serve equally to demonstrate why Thoreau's book possesses such solidity in contrast, say, with *Hiawatha* or *Evangeline*. Longfellow was much the more obviously gifted in his available range of forms and subject matters. But his graceful derivations from his models—the versification and gentle tone of Goethe's *Hermann und Dorothea* for *Evangeline*, or the metre of the *Kalevala* for *Hiawatha*—were not brought into fusion with his native themes.[6] Any indigenous strength was lessened by the reader's always being conscious of the metrical dexterity as an ornamental exercise. It is certainly not to be argued that technical proficiency must result in such dilutions, but merely that, as Greenough saw, it was very hard for American artists of that day, who had no developed tradition of their own, not to be thus swamped by their contact with European influences. Their very aspiration for higher standards of art than those with which they were surrounded tended to make them think of form as a decorative refinement which could be imported.

The particular value of the organic principle for a provincial society thus comes into full relief. Thoreau's literal acceptance of Emerson's proposition that vital form 'is only discovered and executed by the artist, not arbitrarily composed by him,' impelled him to minute inspection of his own existence and of the intuitions that rose from it. Although this involved the restriction of his art to parochial limits, to the portrayal of man in terms only of the immediate nature that drew him out, his study of this interaction also brought him to fundamental human patterns unsuspected by Longfellow. Thoreau demonstrated what Emerson had merely observed, that the function of the artist in society is always to renew the primitive experience of the race, that he 'still goes back for materials and begins again on the most advanced stage.' Thoreau's scent for wildness ferreted beneath the merely conscious levels of cultivated man. It served him, in several pages of notes about a debauched muskrat hunter (1859), to uncover and unite once more the chief sources for his own art. He had found himself heartened

6. And as F. L. Pattee has said of *Hiawatha*, in *The Feminine Fifties* (1940): 'The only really Indian thing about the poem is the Indian summer haze that softens all its outlines, but even this atmosphere is Indian only in name: it was borrowed from German romantic poets.'

by the seemingly inexhaustible vitality of this battered character, 'not despairing of life, but keeping the same rank and savage hold on it that his predecessors have for so many generations, while so many are sick and despairing.' Thoreau went on, therefore, half-playfully to speculate what it was that made this man become excited, indeed inspired by the January freshet in the meadows:

> There are poets of all kinds and degrees, little known to each other. The Lake School is not the only or the principal one. They love various things. Some love beauty, and some love rum. Some go to Rome, and some go a-fishing, and are sent to the house of correction once a month . . . I meet these gods of the river and woods with sparkling faces (like Apollo's) late from the house of correction, it may be carrying whatever mystic and forbidden bottles or other vessels concealed, while the dull regular priests are steering their parish rafts in a prose mood. What care I to see galleries full of representatives of heathen gods, when I can see natural living ones by an infinitely superior artist, without perspective tube? If you read the Rig Veda, oldest of books, as it were, describing a very primitive people and condition of things, you hear in their prayers of a still older, more primitive and aboriginal race in their midst and round about, warring on them and seizing their flocks and herds, infesting their pastures. Thus is it in another sense in all communities, and hence the prisons and police.

The meandering course of Thoreau's reflections here should not obscure his full discovery that the uneradicated wildness of man is the anarchical basis both of all that is most dangerous and most valuable in him. That he could dig down to the roots of primitive poetry without going a mile from Concord accounts for his ability to create 'a true Homeric or Paphlagonian man' in the likeness of the French woodchopper. It also helps account for the fact that by following to its uncompromising conclusion his belief that great art can grow from the center of the simplest life, he was able to be universal. He had understood that in the act of expression a man's whole being, and his natural and social background as well, function organically together. He had mastered a definition of art akin to what Maritain has extracted from scholasticism: *Recta ratio factibilium*, the right ordering of the thing to be made, the right revelation of the material.

E. B. WHITE

Walden—1954†

In his journal for July 10–12, 1841, Thoreau wrote: "A slight sound at evening lifts me up by the ears, and makes life seem inexpressibly serene and grand. It may be in Uranus, or it may be in the shutter." The book into which he later managed to pack both Uranus and the shutter was published in 1854, and now, a hundred years having gone by, "Walden," its serenity and grandeur unimpaired, still lifts us up by the ears, still translates for us that language we are in danger of forgetting, "which all things and events speak without metaphor, which alone is copious and standard."

"Walden" is an oddity in American letters. It may very well be the oddest of our distinguished oddities. For many it is a great deal too odd, and for many it is a particular bore. I have not found it to be a well-liked book among my acquaintances, although usually spoken of with respect, and one literary critic for whom I have the highest regard can find no reason why anyone gives "Walden" a second thought. To admire the book is, in fact, something of an embarrassment, for the mass of men have an indistinct notion that its author was a sort of Nature Boy.

I think it is of some advantage to encounter the book at a period in one's life when the normal anxieties and enthusiasms and rebellions of youth closely resemble those of Thoreau in that spring of 1845 when he borrowed an axe, went out to the woods, and began to whack down some trees for timber. Received at such a juncture, the book is like an invitation to life's dance, assuring the troubled recipient that no matter what befalls him in the way of success or failure he will always be welcome at the party—that the music is played for him, too, if he will but listen and move his feet. In effect, that is what the book is—an invitation, unengraved; and it stirs one as a young girl is stirred by her first big party bid. Many think it a sermon; many set it down as an attempt to rearrange society; some think it an exercise in nature-loving; some find it a rather irritating collection of inspirational puffballs by an eccentric show-off. I think it none of these. It still seems to me the best youth's companion yet written by an American, for it carries a solemn warning against the loss of one's valuables, it advances a good argument for traveling light and trying new adventures, it rings with the power of positive adoration, it contains religious feelings without religious images, and it steadfastly refuses to record bad news. Even its pantheistic note is so pure as to be noncorrupting—pure as the flute-note blown across the pond on those faraway summer nights. If our colleges and universities were alert, they would present a cheap pocket edition of the book to every senior upon graduating, along with his sheepskin, or instead of it. Even if some senior were to take it literally and start felling trees, there could be worse mishaps: the axe is older than the Dictaphone and it is just as well for a young man to see what kind of chips he leaves before listening to the sound of his own voice. And even if some were to get no farther than the table of contents, they would learn how to name eighteen chapters by the use of only thirty-nine words and would see how sweet are the uses of brevity.

If Thoreau had merely left us an account of a man's life in the woods, or if he had simply retreated to the woods and there recorded his complaints about society, or even if he had contrived to include both records in one essay, "Walden" would probably not have lived a hundred years. As things turned out, Thoreau, very likely without knowing quite what he was up to, took man's relation to nature and man's dilemma in society and man's capacity for elevating his spirit and he beat all these matters together, in a wild free interval of self-justification and delight, and produced an original omelette from which people can draw nourishment in a hungry day. "Walden" is one of the first of the vitamin-enriched American dishes. If it were a little less good than it is, or even a little less queer, it would be an abominable book. Even as it is, it will continue to baffle and annoy the literal mind and all those who are unable to stomach its caprices and imbibe its theme. Certainly the plodding economist will continue to have rough going if he hopes to emerge from the book with a clear system of economic thought. Thoreau's assault on the Concord society of the mid-nineteenth century has the quality of a modern Western: he rides into the subject at top speed, shooting in all directions. Many of his shots ricochet and nick him on the rebound, and throughout the melee there is a horrendous cloud of inconsistencies and contradictions, and when the shooting dies down and the air clears, one is impressed chiefly by the courage of the rider and by how splendid it was that somebody should have ridden in there and raised all that ruckus.

When he went to the pond, Thoreau struck an attitude and did so deliberately, but his posturing was not to draw the attention of others to him but rather to draw his own attention more closely to himself. "I learned this at least by my experiment: that if one advances confidently in the direction of his dreams, and endeavors to live the life which he has imagined, he will meet with a success unexpected in common hours." The sentence has the power to resuscitate the youth drowning in his sea of doubt. I recall my exhilaration upon reading it, many years ago, in a time of hesitation and despair. It restored me to health. And now in 1954 when I salute Henry Thoreau on the hundredth birthday of his book, I am merely paying off an old score—or an installment on it.

In his journal for May 3–4, 1838—Boston to Portland—he wrote: "Midnight—head over the boat's side—between sleeping and waking—with glimpses of one or more lights in the vicinity of Cape Ann. Bright moonlight—the effect heightened by seasickness." The entry illuminates the man, as the moon the sea on that night in May. In Thoreau the natural scene was heightened, not depressed, by a disturbance of the stomach, and nausea met its match at last. There was a steadiness in at least one passenger if there was none in the boat. Such steadiness (which in some would be called intoxication) is at the heart of "Walden"—confidence, faith, the discipline of looking always at what is to be seen, undeviating gratitude for the life-everlasting that he found growing in his front yard. "There is nowhere recorded a simple and irrepressible satisfaction with the gift of life, any memorable praise of God." He worked to correct that deficiency. "Walden" is his acknowledgment of the gift of life. It is the testament of a man in a high state of indignation because (it seemed to him) so few ears heard the uninterrupted poem of creation, the morning wind that forever blows. If the man sometimes wrote as though all his readers were male, unmarried, and well-connected, it is because he gave his testimony during the callow years, and, for that matter, never really grew up. To reject the book because of the immaturity of the author and the bugs in the logic is to throw away a bottle of good wine because it contains a bit of the cork.

Thoreau said he required of every writer, first and last, a simple and sincere account of his own life. Having delivered himself of this chesty dictum, he proceeded to ignore it. In his books and even in his enormous journal, he withheld or disguised most of the facts from which an understanding of his life could be drawn. "Walden," subtitled "Life in the Woods," is not a simple and sincere account of a man's life, either in or out of the woods; it is an account of a man's journey into the mind, a toot on the trumpet to alert the neighbors. Thoreau was well aware that no one can alert his neighbors who is not wide awake himself, and he went to the woods (among other reasons) to make sure that he would stay awake during his broadcast. What actually took place during the years

1845–47 is largely unrecorded,[1] and the reader is excluded from
the private life of the author, who supplies almost no gossip about
himself, a great deal about his neighbors and about the universe.

As for me, I cannot in this short ramble give a simple and sincere
account of my own life, but I think Thoreau might find it instructive to know that this memorial essay is being written in a house
that, through no intent on my part, is the same size and shape of
his own domicile on the pond—about ten by fifteen, tight, plainly
finished, and at a little distance from my Concord. The house in
which I sit this morning was built to accommodate a boat, not a
man, but by long experience I have learned that in most respects it
shelters me better than the larger dwelling where my bed is, and
which, by design, is a manhouse not a boathouse. Here in the boathouse I am a wilder and, it would appear, a healthier man, by a safe
margin. I have a chair, a bench, a table, and I can walk into the water if I tire of the land. My house fronts a cove. Two fishermen have
just arrived to spot fish from the air—an osprey and a man in a
small yellow plane who works for the fish company. The man, I
have noticed, is less well equipped than the hawk, who can dive directly on his fish and carry it away, without telephoning. A mouse
and a squirrel share the house with me. The building is, in fact, a
multiple dwelling, a semidetached affair. It is because I am semidetached while here that I find it possible to transact this private
business with the fewest obstacles.

There is also a woodchuck here, living forty feet away under the
wharf. When the wind is right, he can smell my house; and when
the wind is contrary, I can smell his. We both use the wharf for
sunning, taking turns, each adjusting his schedule to the other's
convenience. Thoreau once ate a woodchuck. I think he felt he
owed it to his readers, and that it was little enough, considering the
indignities they were suffering at his hands and the dressing-down
they were taking. (Parts of "Walden" are pure scold.) Or perhaps he
ate the woodchuck because he believed every man should acquire
strict business habits and the woodchuck was destroying his market
beans. I do not know. Thoreau had a strong experimental streak in
him. It is probably no harder to eat a woodchuck than to construct
a sentence that lasts a hundred years. At any rate, Thoreau is the
only writer I know who prepared himself for his great ordeal by eating a woodchuck; also the only one who got a hangover from drinking too much water. (He was drunk the whole time, though he
seldom touched wine or coffee or tea.)

Here in this compact house where I would spend one day as de-

---

1. Although fragmentary, the Journal record of the Walden years is now available in *Journal 2: 1844–1848* (1984); for excerpts, see pp. 319–45 in this volume [*Editor*].

liberately as Nature if I were not being pressed by *The Yale Review*, and with a woodchuck (as yet uneaten) for neighbor, I can feel the companionship of the occupant of the pondside cabin in Walden woods, a mile from the village, near the Fitchburg right of way. Even my immediate business is no barrier between us: Thoreau occasionally batted out a magazine piece, but was always suspicious of any sort of purposeful work that cut into his time. A man, he said, should take care not to be thrown off the track by every nutshell and mosquito's wing that falls on the rails.

There has been much guessing as to why he went to the pond. To set it down to escapism is, of course, to misconstrue what happened. Henry went forth to battle when he took to the woods, and "Walden" is the report of a man torn by two powerful and opposing drives—the desire to enjoy the world (and not be derailed by a mosquito wing) and the urge to set the world straight. One cannot join these two successfully, but sometimes, in rare cases, something good or even great results from the attempt of the tormented spirit to reconcile them. Henry went forth to battle, and if he set the stage himself, if he fought on his own terms and with his own weapons, it was because it was his nature to do things differently from most men, and to act in a cocky fashion. If the pond and the woods seemed a more plausible site for a house than an in-town location, it was because a cowbell made for him a sweeter sound than a churchbell. "Walden," the book, makes the sound of a cowbell, more than a churchbell, and proves the point, although both sounds are in it, and both remarkably clear and sweet. He simply preferred his churchbell at a little distance.

I think one reason he went to the woods was a perfectly simple and commonplace one—and apparently he thought so, too. "At a certain season of our life," he wrote, "we are accustomed to consider every spot as the possible site of a house." There spoke the young man, a few years out of college, who had not yet broken away from home. He hadn't married, and he had found no job that measured up to his rigid standards of employment, and like any young man, or young animal, he felt uneasy and on the defensive until he had fixed himself a den. Most young men, of course, casting about for a site, are content merely to draw apart from their kinfolks. Thoreau, convinced that the greater part of what his neighbors called good was bad, withdrew from a great deal more than family: he pulled out of everything for a while, to serve everybody right for being so stuffy, and to try his own prejudices on the dog.

The house-hunting sentence above, which starts the Chapter called "Where I Lived, and What I Lived For," is followed by another passage that is worth quoting here because it so beautifully illustrates the offbeat prose that Thoreau was master of, a prose at once strictly disciplined and wildly abandoned. "I have surveyed the country on every side within a dozen miles of where I live," continued this delirious young man. "In imagination I have bought all the farms in succession, for all were to be bought, and I knew their price. I walked over each farmer's premises, tasted his wild apples, discoursed on husbandry with him, took his farm at his price, at any price, mortgaging it to him in my mind; even put a higher price on it—took everything but a deed of it—took his word for his deed, for I dearly love to talk—cultivated it, and him too to some extent, I trust, and withdrew when I had enjoyed it long enough, leaving him to carry it on." A copydesk man would get a double hernia trying to clean up that sentence for the management, but the sentence needs no fixing, for it perfectly captures the meaning of the writer and the quality of the ramble.

"Wherever I sat, there I might live, and the landscape radiated from me accordingly." Thoreau, the home-seeker, sitting on his hummock with the entire State of Massachusetts radiating from him, is to me the most humorous of the New England figures, and "Walden" the most humorous of the books, though its humor is almost continuously subsurface and there is nothing funny anywhere, except a few weak jokes and bad puns that rise to the surface like the perch in the pond that rose to the sound of the maestro's flute. Thoreau tended to write in sentences, a feat not every writer is capable of, and "Walden" is, rhetorically speaking, a collection of certified sentences, some of them, it would now appear, as indestructible as they are errant. The book is distilled from the vast journals, and this accounts for its intensity: he picked out bright particles that pleased his eye, whirled them in the kaleidoscope of his content, and produced the pattern that has endured— the color, the form, the light.

On this its hundredth birthday, Thoreau's "Walden" is pertinent and timely. In our uneasy season, when all men unconsciously seek a retreat from a world that has got almost completely out of hand, his house in the Concord woods is a haven. In our culture of gadgetry and the multiplicity of convenience, his cry "Simplicity, simplicity, simplicity!" has the insistence of a fire alarm. In the brooding atmosphere of war and the gathering radioactive storm, the innocence and serenity of his summer afternoons are enough to burst the remembering heart, and one gazes back upon that pleasing interlude—its confidence, its purity, its deliberateness—with awe and wonder, as one would look upon the face of a child asleep.

"This small lake was of most value as a neighbor in the intervals of a gentle rain-storm in August, when, both air and water being perfectly still, but the sky overcast, midafternoon had all the serenity of evening, and the wood-thrush sang around, and was heard from shore to shore." Now, in the perpetual overcast in which our days are spent, we hear with extra perception and deep gratitude that song, tying century to century.

I sometimes amuse myself by bringing Henry Thoreau back to life and showing him the sights. I escort him into a phone booth and let him dial Weather. "This is a delicious evening," the girl's voice says, "when the whole body is one sense, and imbibes delight through every pore." I show him the spot in the Pacific where an island used to be, before some magician made it vanish. "We know not where we are," I murmur. "The light which puts out our eyes is darkness to us. Only that day dawns to which we are awake." I thumb through the latest copy of "Vogue" with him. "Of two patterns which differ only by a few threads more or less of a particular color," I read, "the one will be sold readily, the other lie on the shelf, though it frequently happens that, after the lapse of a season, the latter becomes the most fashionable." Together we go outboarding on the Assabet, looking for what we've lost—a hound, a bay horse, a turtledove. I show him a distracted-farmer who is trying to repair a hay baler before the thunder shower breaks. "This farmer," I remark, "is endeavoring to solve the problem of a livelihood by a formula more complicated than the problem itself. To get his shoe strings he speculates in herds of cattle."

I take the celebrated author to Twenty-One for lunch, so the waiters may study his shoes. The proprietor welcomes us. "The gross feeder," remarks the proprietor, sweeping the room with his arm, "Is a man in the larva stage." After lunch we visit a classroom in one of those schools conducted by big corporations to teach their superannuated executives how to retire from business without serious injury to their health. (The shock to men's systems these days when relieved of the exacting routine of amassing wealth is very great and must be cushioned.) "It is not necessary," says the teacher to his pupils, "that a man should earn his living by the sweat of his brow, unless he sweats easier than I do. We are determined to be starved before we are hungry."

I turn on the radio and let Thoreau hear Winchell beat the red hand around the clock. "Time is but the stream I go a-fishing in," shouts Mr. Winchell, rattling his telegraph key. "Hardly a man takes a half hour's nap after dinner, but when he wakes he holds up his head and asks, 'What's the news?' If we read of one man robbed, or murdered, or killed by accident, or one house burned, or one vessel wrecked, or one steamboat blown up, or one cow run over on the Western Railroad, or one mad dog killed, or one lot of grasshoppers in the winter—we need never read of another. One is enough."

I doubt that Thoreau would be thrown off balance by the fantastic sights and sounds of the twentieth century. "The Concord nights," he once wrote, "are stranger than the Arabian nights." A four-engined air liner would merely serve to confirm his early views on travel. Everywhere he would observe, in new shapes and sizes, the old predicaments and follies of men—the desperation, the impedimenta, the meanness—along with the visible capacity for elevation of the mind and soul. "This curious world which we inhabit is more wonderful than it is convenient; more beautiful than it is useful; it is more to be admired and enjoyed than used," He would see that today ten thousand engineers are busy making sure that the world shall be convenient if they bust doing it, and others are determined to increase its usefulness even though its beauty is lost somewhere along the way.

At any rate, I'd like to stroll about the countryside in Thoreau's company for a day, observing the modern scene, inspecting today's snowstorm, pointing out the sights, and offering belated apologies for my sins. Thoreau is unique among writers in that those who admire him find him uncomfortable to live with—a regular hairshirt of a man. A little band of dedicated Thoreauvians would be a sorry sight indeed: fellows who hate compromise and have compromised, fellows who love wildness and have lived tamely, and at their side, censuring them and chiding them, the ghostly figure of this upright man, who long ago gave corroboration to impulses they perceived were right and issued warnings against the things they instinctively knew to be their enemies. I should hate to be called a Thoreauvian, yet I wince every time I walk into the barn I'm pushing before me, seventy-five feet by forty, and the author of "Walden" has served as my conscience through the long stretches of my trivial days.

Hairshirt or no, he is a better companion than most, and I would not swap him for a soberer or more reasonable friend even if I could. I can reread his famous invitation with undiminished excitement. The sad thing is that not more acceptances have been received, that so many decline for one reason or another, pleading some previous engagement or ill health. But the invitation stands. It will beckon as long as this remarkable book stays in print—which will be as long as there are August afternoons in the intervals of a gentle rainstorm, as long as there are ears to catch the faint sounds of the orchestra. I find it agreeable to sit here this morning, in a house of correct proportions, and hear across a century of time his flute, his frogs, and his seductive summons to the wildest revels of them all.

LEO MARX

[*Walden*'s Transcendental Pastoral Design]†

The incursion of the railroad in Sleepy Hollow, recorded by Hawthorne in 1844, typifies the moment of discovery. Recall the circumstances. On a fine summer morning the writer enters the woods and sits down to await "such little events as may happen." Writing in a pleasant if somewhat hackneyed literary idiom, he records sights and sounds. Then, extending his observations to nearby farms and pastures, and to the village in the distance, he sketches an ideal rural scheme. He locates himself at the center of an idyllic domain—a land of order, form, and harmony. Like Virgil's Arcadia or Prospero's "majestic vision" or Jefferson's republic of the middle landscape, this is a self-contained, static world, remote from history, where nature and art are in balance. It is as if the writer had set out to realize in his own person the felicity promised, since Shakespeare's time, by the myth of America as a new beginning.

In its simplest, archetypal form, the myth affirms that Europeans experience a regeneration in the New World. They become new, better, happier men—they are reborn. In most versions the regenerative power is located in the natural terrain: access to undefiled, bountiful, sublime Nature is what accounts for the virtue and special good fortune of Americans. It enables them to design a community in the image of a garden, an ideal fusion of nature with art. The landscape thus becomes the symbolic repository of value of all kinds—economic, political, aesthetic, religious. It has been suggested that the American myth of a new beginning may be a variant of the primal myth described by Joseph Campbell: "a separation from the world, a penetration to some source of power, and a life-enhancing return." Hawthorne's situation in Sleepy Hollow seems to figure a realization of the myth until, suddenly, the harsh whistle of the locomotive fills the air. Then discord replaces harmony and the tranquil mood vanishes. Although he later regains a measure of repose, a sense of loss colors the rest of his notes. His final observation is of some clouds that resemble the "shattered ruins of a dreamer's Utopia."[1]

---

† From *The Machine in the Garden: Technology and the Pastoral Ideal in America* (Oxford: Oxford University Press, 1964), pp. 227–29; 242–65. Copyright © 1964 by Oxford University Press, Inc. Reprinted by permission. *Walden* page numbers refer to this Norton Critical Edition.

1. Nathaniel Hawthorne, *The American Notebooks,* ed. Randall Stewart (New Haven: Yale University Press, 1932), 102–5. [On the myth of the New World, see] Philip Young,

In spite of the facile resolution and the bland, complaisant tone, there is unmistakable power latent in Hawthorne's casual composition. The sudden appearance of the machine in the garden is an arresting, endlessly evocative image. It causes the instantaneous clash of opposed states of mind: a strong urge to believe in the rural myth along with an awareness of industrialization as counterforce to the myth. Since 1844, this motif has served again and again to order literary experience. It appears everywhere in American writing. In some cases, to be sure, the "little event" is a fictive episode with only vague, incidental symbolic overtones. But in others it is a cardinal metaphor of contradiction, exfoliating, through associated images and ideas, into a design governing the meaning of entire works.

* * *

Soon after Emerson had set forth his program for Young Americans,[2] his young disciple Henry Thoreau put it to a test. He began his stay at Walden Pond in the spring of 1845, and the book he eventually wrote about it (*Walden* was not published until 1854) may be read as the report of an experiment in transcendental pastoralism. The organizing design is like that of many American fables: *Walden* begins with the hero's withdrawal from society in the direction of nature. The main portion of the book is given over to a yearlong trial of Emerson's prescription for achieving a new life. When Thoreau tells of his return to Concord, in the end, he seems to have satisfied himself about the efficacy of this method of redemption. It may be difficult to say exactly what is being claimed, but the triumphant tone of the concluding chapters leaves little doubt that he is announcing positive results. His most telling piece of evidence is *Walden*—the book itself. Recognizing the clarity, coherence, and power of the writing, we can only conclude—or so transcendental doctrine would have it—that the experiment has been a success. The vision of unity that had made the aesthetic order of *Walden* possible had in turn been made possible by the retreat to the pond. The pastoral impulse somehow had provided access to the order latent in the cosmos.

But the meaning of *Walden* is more complicated than this affirmation. Because Thoreau takes seriously what Emerson calls the "method of nature"—more seriously than the master himself—the

---

"Fallen from Time: The Mythic Rip Van Winkle," *The Kenyon Review* 22 (Autumn, 1960); 551; Frederick I. Carpenter surveys variants, " 'The American Myth': Paradise (To Be) Regained," *PMLA* 74 (1959), 599–606; R. W. B. Lewis, *The American Adam: Innocence, Tragedy, and Tradition in the Nineteenth Century* (Chicago: University of Chicago Press, 1955).

2. See Emerson, "The Young American," in *Nature, Addresses, and Lectures*, ed. Robert E. Spiller and Alfred R. Ferguson (Cambridge: Harvard University Press, 1971), 217–44, and Marx, *The Machine in the Garden*, 229–42 [*Editor*].

book has a strong contrapuntal theme. Assuming that natural facts properly perceived and accurately transcribed must yield the truth, Thoreau adopts the tone of a hard-headed empiricist. At the outset he makes it clear that he will tell exactly what happened. He claims to have a craving for reality (be it life or death), and he would have us believe him capable of reporting the negative evidence. Again and again he allows the facts to play against his desire, so that his prose at its best acquires a distinctly firm, cross-grained texture. Though the dominant tone is affirmative, the undertone is skeptical, and it qualifies the import of episode after episode. For this reason *Walden* belongs among the first in a long series of American books which, taken together, have had the effect of circumscribing the pastoral hope, much as Virgil circumscribes it in his eclogues. In form and feeling, indeed, Thoreau's book has much in common with the classic Virgilian mode.

Although the evidence is abundant, it is easy to miss the conventional aspect of *Walden*. In the second chapter Thoreau describes the site as an ideal pasture, a real place which he transforms into an unbounded, timeless landscape of the mind. And he identifies himself with Damodara (Krishna) in his rôle as shepherd, and with a shepherd in a Jacobean song:

> There was a shepherd that did live,
>   And held his thoughts as high
> As were the mounts whereon his flocks
>   Did hourly feed him by. (63)

Nevertheless, the serious affinity between *Walden* and the convention is disguised by certain peculiarities of American pastoralism, the most obvious being the literalness with which Thoreau approaches the ideal of the simple life. For centuries writers working in the mode had been playing with the theme, suggesting that men might enrich their contemplative experience by simplifying their housekeeping. (The shepherd's ability to reduce his material needs to a minimum had been one of his endearing traits.) Yet it generally had been assumed that the simple life was a poetic theme, not to be confused with the way poets did in fact live. In the main, writers who took the felicity of shepherds in green pastures as their subject had been careful to situate themselves near wealth and power. The effect of the American environment, however, was to break down common-sense distinctions between art and life. No one understood this more clearly than Henry Thoreau; skilled in the national art of disguising art, in *Walden* he succeeds in obscuring the traditional, literary character of the pastoral withdrawal. Instead of writing about it—or *merely* writing about it—he tries it. By telling his tale in the first person, he endows the mode with a credibility it had seldom, if ever, possessed. Because the "I" who addresses us in *Walden* is describing the way he had lived, taking pains to supply plenty of hard facts ("Yes, I did eat $8.74, all told. . . ." [44]), we scarcely notice that all the while he had been playing the shepherd's venerable rôle. He refuses to say whether the book is an explicit guide for living or an exercise in imaginative perception. We are invited to take it as either or both. Convinced that effective symbols can be derived only from natural facts, Thoreau had moved to the pond so that he might make a symbol of his life. If we miss the affinity with the Virgilian mode, then, it is partly because we are dealing with a distinctively American version of romantic pastoral.

No feature of *Walden* makes this truth more apparent than its topography. The seemingly realistic setting may not be a land of fantasy like Arcadia, yet neither is it Massachusetts. On inspection it proves to be another embodiment of the American moral geography—a native blend of myth and reality. The hut beside the pond stands at the center of a symbolic landscape in which the village of Concord appears on one side and a vast reach of unmodified nature on the other. As if no organized society existed to the west, the mysterious, untrammeled, primal world seems to begin at the village limits. As in most American fables, the wilderness is an indispensable feature of this terrain, and the hero's initial recoil from everyday life carries him to the verge of anarchic primitivism.[3] "We need the tonic of wildness," Thoreau explains, using the word "pasture" to encompass wild nature: "We need to witness our own limits transgressed, and some life pasturing freely where we never wander" (213). (The combined influence of geography and the romantic idea of nature—sublime Nature—gives rise to attitudes held by a long line of American literary heroes from Natty Bumppo to Ike McCaslin.) But Thoreau is not a primitivist. True, he implies that he would have no difficulty choosing between Concord and the wilderness. What really engages him, however, is the possibility of avoiding that choice. (Jefferson had taken the same position.) In *Walden*, accordingly, he keeps our attention focused upon the middle ground where he builds a house, raises beans, reads the *Iliad*, and searches the depths of the pond. Like the "navel of the earth" in the archaic myths studied by Mircea Eliade, the pond is the ab-

3. The difference between the typical American hero and the shepherd in traditional versions of pastoral is suggested by Renato Poggioli's account of that archetypal figure as one who "lives a sedentary life even in the open, since he prefers to linger in a grove's shade rather than to wander in the woods. He never confronts the true wild, and this is why he never becomes even a part-time hunter" [Renato Poggioli, "The Oaten Flute," *Library Bulletin*, XI (Spring, 1957), p. 152]. Given the circumstances of American life, our heroes do confront the true wild, and they often become hunters. But it is striking to notice how often they are impelled to restrict or even renounce their hunting. I am thinking of Natty Bumppo, Melville's Ishmael, Faulkner's Ike McCaslin, and Thoreau himself.

solute center—the *axis mundi*—of Thoreau's cosmos. If an alternative to the ways of Concord is to be found anywhere, it will be found on the shore of Walden Pond—near the mystic center.[4]

And it had best be found quickly. The drama of *Walden* is intensified by Thoreau's acute sense of having been born in the nick of time. Though the book resembles the classic pastoral in form and feeling, its facts and images are drawn from the circumstances of life in nineteenth-century America. By 1845, according to Thoreau, a depressing state of mind—he calls it "quiet desperation" (8)—has seized the people of Concord. The opening chapter, "Economy," is a diagnosis of this cultural malady. Resigned to a pointless, dull, routinized existence, Thoreau's fellow-townsmen perform the daily round without joy or anger or genuine exercise of will. As if their minds were mirrors, able only to reflect the external world, they are satisfied to cope with things as they are. In Emerson's language, they live wholly on the plane of the Understanding. Rather than design houses to fulfill the purpose of their lives, they accommodate their lives to the standard design of houses. Thoreau discovers the same pattern of acquiescence, a dehumanizing reversal of ends and means, in all of their behavior. He finds it in their pretentious furnishings, their uncomfortable clothing, their grim factories, the dispirited way they eat and farm the land and work from dawn to dusk. He locates it, above all, in their economy—a system within which they work endlessly, not to reach a goal of their own choosing but to satisfy the demands of the market mechanism. The moral, in short, is that here "men have become the tools of their tools" (29).

The omnipresence of tools, gadgets, instruments is symptomatic of the Concord way. Like Carlyle, Thoreau uses technological imagery to represent more than industrialization in the narrow, economic sense. It accompanies a mode of perception, an emergent system of meaning and value—a culture. In fact his overdrawn indictment of the Concord "economy" might have been written to document Carlyle's dark view of industrialism. Thoreau feels no simple-minded Luddite hostility toward the new inventions; they are, he says, "but improved means to an unimproved end. . . ." (39). What he is attacking is the popular illusion that improving the means is enough, that if the machinery of society is put in good order (as Carlyle had said) "all were well with us; the rest would care for itself!"[5] He is contending against a culture pervaded by this mechanistic outlook. It may well be conducive to material progress,

---

4. Mircea Eliade, *Cosmos and History, The Myth of the Eternal Return*, trans. William R. Trask, New York, 1959, pp. 16–17.
5. Thomas Carlyle, "Signs of the Times." In *Critical and Miscellaneous Essays* (New York: Belford, Clarke & Co., n.d.), 3.5–30.

but it also engenders deadly fatalism and despair. At the outset, then, Thoreau invokes the image of the machine to represent the whole tone and quality of Concord life or, to be more precise, anti-life:

> Actually, the laboring man has not leisure for a true integrity day by day; he cannot afford to sustain the manliest relations to men; his labor would be depreciated in the market. He has no time to be anything but a machine (7).

The clock, favorite "machine" of the Enlightenment, is a master machine in Thoreau's model of the capitalist economy. Its function is decisive because it links the industrial apparatus with consciousness. The laboring man becomes a machine in the sense that his life becomes more closely geared to an impersonal and seemingly autonomous system.[6] If the advent of power technology is alarming, it is because it occurs within this cultural context. When Thoreau depicts the machine as it functions within the Concord environment, accordingly, it is an instrument of oppression: "We do not ride upon the railroad; it rides upon us" (66). But later, when seen from the Walden perspective, the railroad's significance becomes quite different.

Thoreau's denunciation of the Concord "economy" prefigures the complex version of the Sleepy Hollow episode in the fourth chapter, "Sounds." The previous chapter is about "Reading," or what he calls the language of metaphor. Now he shifts to sounds, "the language which all things and events speak without metaphor, which alone is copious and standard" (78). The implication is that he is turning from the conventional language of art to the spontaneous language of nature. What concerns him is the hope of making the word one with the thing, the notion that the naked fact of sensation, if described with sufficient precision, can be made to yield its secret—its absolute meaning. This is another way of talking about the capacity of nature to "produce delight"—to supply value and meaning. It is the crux of transcendental pastoralism. Hence Thoreau begins with an account of magnificent summer days when, like Hawthorne at the Hollow, he does nothing but sit "rapt in a revery, amidst the pines and . . . sumachs, in undisturbed soli-

---

6. Thoreau's response to the mechanization of time reflects the heightened significance of the clock in the period of the "take-off" into full-scale industrialism. With the building of factories and railroads it became necessary, as never before, to provide the population with access to the exact time. This was made possible, in New England, by the transformation of the clockmaking industry. Before 1800 clocks had been relatively expensive luxury items made only by master craftsmen. Significantly enough, the industry was among the first to use machines and the principle of interchangeable part manufacture. By 1807, in Connecticut, Eli Terry had begun to produce wooden clocks in large numbers, and before he died in 1852 he was making between 10,000 and 12,000 clocks a year sold at $5.00 each.

tude and stillness" (79). These days, unlike days in Concord, are not "minced into hours and fretted by the ticking of a clock." Here is another pastoral interlude, a celebration of idleness and that sense of relaxed solidarity with the universe that presumably comes with close attention to the language of nature. For a moment Thoreau allows us to imagine that he has escaped the clock, the Concord definition of time and, indeed, the dominion of the machine. But then, without raising his voice, he reports the "rattle of railroad cars" in the woods.

At first the sound is scarcely audible. Thoreau casually mentions it at the end of a long sentence in which he describes a series of sights and sounds: hawks circling the clearing, a tantivy of wild pigeons, a mink stealing out of the marsh, the sedge bending under the weight of reed-birds, and then, as if belonging to the very tissue of nature: "and for the last half-hour I have heard the rattle of railroad cars, now dying away and then reviving like the beat of a partridge, conveying travellers from Boston to the country" (81). It would have been difficult to contrive a quieter entrance, which may seem curious in view of the fact that Thoreau then devotes nine long paragraphs to the subject. Besides, he insists upon the importance of the Fitchburg Railroad in the Walden scene; it "touches the pond" near his house, and since he usually goes to the village along its causeway, he says, "I . . . am, as it were, related to society by this link" (81).[7] And then, what may at first seem even more curious, he introduces the auditory image of the train a second time, and with a markedly different emphasis:

> The whistle of the locomotive penetrates my woods summer and winter, sounding like the scream of a hawk sailing over some farmer's yard, informing me that many restless city merchants are arriving within the circle of the town. . . .

Now the sound is more like a hawk than a partridge, and Thoreau playfully associates the hawk's rapacity with the train's distinctive mechanical cadence:

> All the Indian huckleberry hills are stripped, all the cranberry meadows are raked into the city. Up comes the cotton, down goes the woven cloth; up comes the silk, down goes the woollen; up come the books, but down goes the wit that writes them (81–2).

What are we to make of this double image of the railroad? First it is like a partridge, then a hawk; first it blends into the landscape

7. It is significant that Thoreau added this statement, with its obvious claim for the symbolic significance of the railroad, to the version of the episode he had published earlier in *Sartain's Union Magazine*, XI (1852), 66–8.

like the industrial images in the Inness painting,[8] but then, a moment later, it becomes the discordant machine of the Sleepy Hollow notes. What does the railroad signify here? On inspection the passage proves to be a sustained evocation of the ambiguous meaning of the machine and its relation to nature. Every significant image is yoked to an alternate:

> When I meet the engine with its train of cars moving off with planetary motion,—or, rather, like a comet . . .

Or the cloud of smoke

> . . . rising higher and higher, going to heaven while the cars are going to Boston, conceals the sun for a minute and casts my distant field into the shade. . . .

The point becomes explicit in a thought that Thoreau repeats like a refrain: "If all were as it seems, and men made the elements their servants for noble ends!" (82).

The image of the railroad on the shore of the pond figures an ambiguity at the heart of *Walden*. Man-made power, the machine with its fire, smoke, and thunder, is juxtaposed to the waters of Walden, remarkable for their depth and purity and a matchless, indescribable color—now light blue, now green, almost always pellucid. The iron horse moves across the surface of the earth; the pond invites the eye below the surface. The contrast embodies both the hope and the fear aroused by the impending climax of America's encounter with wild nature. As Thoreau describes the event, both responses are plausible, and there is no way of knowing which of them history is more likely to confirm. Earlier he had made plain the danger of technological progress, and here at the pond it again distracts his attention from other, presumably more important, concerns. Yet he is elated by the presence of this wonderful invention. In Concord, within the dominion of the mechanistic philosophy, the machine rode upon men, but when seen undistorted from Walden, the promise of the new power seems to offset the danger. Thoreau is delighted by the electric atmosphere of the depot and the cheerful valor of the snow-plow crews. He admires the punctuality, the urge toward precision and order, the confidence, serenity, and adventurousness of the men who operate this commercial enterprise:

> . . . when I hear the iron horse make the hills echo with his snort like thunder, shaking the earth with his feet, and breathing fire and smoke from his nostrils (what kind of winged horse or fiery dragon they will put into the new Mythology I

---

8. I.e., *The Lackawanna Valley* (1855) by George Inness. See Marx, *The Machine in the Garden*, 220–22 [*Editor*].

don't know), it seems as if the earth had got a race now worthy
to inhabit it. If all were as it seems, and men made the elements their servants for noble ends! (82)

If the interrupted idyll represents a crucial ambiguity, it also represents at least one certainty. The certainty is change itself—the
kind of accelerating change, or "progress," that Americans identify
with their new inventions, especially the railroad. For Thoreau, like
Melville's Ahab, this machine is the type and agent of an irre-
versible process: not mere scientific or technological development
in the narrow sense, but the implacable advance of history. "We
have constructed a fate," he writes, "an *Atropos*, that never turns
aside. (Let that be the name of your engine [83].)" The episode
demonstrates that the Walden site cannot provide a refuge, in any
literal sense, from the forces of change. Indeed, the presence of the
machine in the woods casts a shadow of doubt (the smoke of the
locomotive puts Thoreau's field in the shade) upon the Emersonian
hope of extracting an answer from nature. The doubt is implicit in
the elaborately contrived language used to compose this little
event. Recall that Thoreau had introduced the chapter on "Sounds"
as an effort to wrest an extra-literary meaning from natural facts;
his alleged aim had been to render sense perceptions with perfect
precision in "the language which all things and events speak without metaphor." What he actually had done, however, was quite the
reverse. To convey his response to the sound of the railroad he had
resorted to an unmistakably figurative, literary language. Few passages in *Walden* are more transparently contrived or artful; it is as if
the subject had compelled Thoreau to admit a debt to Art as great,
if not greater, than his debt to Nature.

The most telling qualification of Emersonian optimism, however,
comes in the deceptively plain-spoken conclusion to the episode.
Emerson had affirmed the political as well as the religious value of
the pastoral impulse. When he spoke in his public voice (as in "The
Young American") he interpreted the nation's movement toward
"nature" (signifying both a natural and a spiritual fact—both land
and landscape) as motion toward a new kind of technically advanced yet rural society. In effect he was reaffirming the Jeffersonian hope of embodying the pastoral dream in social institutions.
But Thoreau, abiding by his commitment to stand "right fronting
and face to face to a fact" (70), takes another hard look at the sight
of the machine in the American landscape:

> And hark! here comes the cattle-train bearing the cattle of
> a thousand hills, sheepcots, stables, and cow yards in the air,
> drovers with their sticks, and shepherd boys in the midst of
> their flocks, all but the mountain pastures, whirled along like

leaves blown from the mountains by the September gales. The air is filled with the bleating of calves and sheep, and the hustling of oxen, as if a pastoral valley were going by. . . . A carload of drovers, too, in the midst, on a level with their droves now, their vocation gone, but still clinging to their useless sticks as their badge of office. . . . So is your pastoral life whirled past and away. But the bell rings, and I must get off the track and let the cars go by;—

> What's the railroad to me?
> I never go to see
> Where it ends.
> It fills a few hollows,
> And makes banks for the swallows,
> It sets the sand a-blowing,
> And the blackberries a-growing.

but I cross it like a cart-path in the woods. I will not have my eyes put out and my ears spoiled by its smoke and steam and hissing (85–6).

Compared to popular, sentimental pastoralism, or to Emerson's well-turned evasions, there is a pleasing freshness about Thoreau's cool clarity. He says that the pastoral way of life—pastoralism in the literal, agrarian sense—is being whirled past and away. It is doomed. And he has no use for the illusion that the *Atropos* can be stopped. The first thing to do, then, the only sensible thing to do, is get off the track. Not that one need resign oneself, like the men of Concord, to the dominion of the mechanical philosophy. But how is the alternative to be defined? To answer the question had been the initial purpose of the Walden experiment; now its urgency is heightened by the incursion of history. If he is to find an answer, the writer's first duty is to protect his powers of perception. At this point Thoreau adopts a testy, tight-lipped, uncompromising tone: "I will not have my eyes put out and my ears spoiled by its smoke and steam and hissing."

The need for defense against the forces of history does not tempt Thoreau to a nostalgic embrace of the "pastoral life" that is being whirled away. Quite the contrary. In "The Bean-Field" he turns his wit against the popular American version of pastoral. The Walden experiment, as described in "Economy," had included a venture in commercial farming. In order to earn ten or twelve dollars by an "honest and agreeable method," he had planted two acres and a half, chiefly with beans. That is a lot of beans (he figures that the length of the rows, added together, was seven miles), and it meant a lot of work. Here, then, in "The Bean-Field" he turns to the "meaning of this so steady and self-respecting, this small Herculean labor. . . ." The chapter is a seriocomic effort to get at the lesson of agricultural experience. At the outset, recalling his first visit to the pond as a child, Thoreau invests the scene of his arduous labor with an appropriate bucolic ambience:

> And now to-night my flute has waked the echoes over that very water. . . . Almost the same johnswort springs from the same perennial root in this pasture, and even I have at length helped to clothe that fabulous landscape of my infant dreams, and one of the results of my presence and influence is seen in these bean leaves. . . . (107)

As he describes himself at work among his beans, Thoreau is the American husbandman. Like the central figure of the Jeffersonian idyll, his vocation has a moral and spiritual as well as economical significance. And his field bears a special relation to American circumstances. It produces beans which resemble neither English hay, with its synthetic quality (a result of precise, calculating, scientific methods), nor the rich and various crop produced spontaneously in the surrounding woods, pastures, and swamps. "Mine was, as it were, the connecting link between wild and cultivated fields; as some states are civilized, and others half-civilized, and others savage or barbarous, so my field was, though not in a bad sense, a half-cultivated field" (109). But Thoreau's husbandman cannot be characterized simply by his location in the middle landscape. Like Emerson's Young American, he blends Jeffersonian and romantic attitudes toward nature. When Thoreau describes the purpose of his bean-raising activity, accordingly, he falls into a comic idiom—a strange compound of practical, Yankee vernacular and transcendental philosophizing:

> It was a singular experience that long acquaintance which I cultivated with beans, what with planting, and hoeing, and harvesting, and threshing, and picking over and selling them,—the last was the hardest of all,—I might add eating, for I did taste. I was determined to know beans.

The better he had come to "know beans," the less seriously he had been able to take the rôle of noble husbandman. As the writer's account of that "singular experience" develops, he moves further and further from the reverential, solemn tone of popular pastoralism, until he finally adopts a mock-heroic attitude:

> I was determined to know beans. When they were growing, I used to hoe from five o'clock in the morning till noon, and commonly spent the rest of the day about other affairs. Consider the intimate and curious acquaintance one makes with various kinds of weeds—it will bear some iteration in the ac-

count, for there was no little iteration in the labor,—disturbing their delicate organizations so ruthlessly, and making such invidious distinctions with his hoe, levelling whole ranks of one species, and sedulously cultivating another. That's Roman wormwood,—that's pigweed,—that's sorrel,—that's pipergrass,—have at him, chop him up, turn his roots upward to the sun, don't let him have a fibre in the shade, if you do he'll turn himself t'other side up and be as green as a leek in two days. A long war, not with cranes, but with weeds, those Trojans who had sun and rain and dews on their side. Daily the beans saw me come to their rescue armed with a hoe, and thin the ranks of their enemies, filling up the trenches with weedy dead. Many a lusty crest-waving Hector, that towered a whole foot above his crowding comrades, fell before my weapon and rolled in the dust. (111)

In part Thoreau's irony can be attributed to the outcome of his bean venture. Although he does not call it a failure, the fact is clear enough. The cost of the operation was $14.72½ (he had hired a man to help with the plowing), the gross income $23.44, and the net profit $8.71½. This sum barely paid for the rest of his food, and to make ends meet he had hired himself out as a day laborer. In other words, the bean crop did not provide an adequate economic base for the life of an independent husbandman.[9] His own experience comports with what he observes of American farmers throughout the book. So far from representing a "pastoral life," a desirable alternative to the ways of Concord and the market economy, the typical farmer in *Walden* is narrow-minded and greedy. ***

The result of the venture in husbandry prefigures the result of the Walden experiment as a whole. Judged by a conventional (economic) standard, it is true, the enterprise had been a failure. But that judgment is irrelevant to Thoreau's purpose, as his dominant tone, the tone of success, plainly indicates. It is irrelevant because his aim had been to *know* beans: to get at the essential *meaning* of labor in the bean-field. And "meaning," as he conceives it, has nothing to do with the alleged virtue of the American husbandman or the merits of any institution or "way of life"; nor can it be located in the material or economic facts, where Concord, operating on the plane of the Understanding, locates meaning and value. Thoreau has quite another sort of meaning in view, as he admits when he says that he raised beans, not because he wanted beans to eat, "but, perchance, as some must work in fields if only for the sake of tropes and expression, to serve a parable-maker one day" (111).

9. For Thoreau's failure as a farmer, see Leo Stoller, "Thoreau's Doctrine of Simplicity," NEQ XXIX (Dec., 1956), 443–61.

This idea, which contains the gist of Thoreau's ultimate argument, also is implicit in the outcome of other episodes. It is implied
by his account of fishing at night—a tantalizing effort to get at the
"dull uncertain blundering purpose" (120) he detects at the end of
his line beneath the pond's opaque surface; and by that incomparable satire on the transcendental quest, the chase of the loon who
"laughed in derision" (160) at his efforts; and by his painstaking investigation of the pond's supposed "bottomlessness": ". . . I can assure my readers that Walden has a reasonably tight bottom at a not
unreasonable . . . depth" (192). In each case, as in "The Bean-
Field," the bare, empirical evidence proves inadequate to his purpose. Of themselves the facts do not, cannot, flower into truth;
they do not show forth a meaning, which is to say, the kind of
meaning the experiment had been designed to establish.[1] If the
promise of romantic pastoralism is to be fulfilled, nothing less than
an alternative to the Concord way will suffice. Although his tone
generally is confident, Thoreau cunningly keeps the issue in doubt
until the end. By cheerfully, enigmatically reiterating his failure to
extract an "answer"—a coherent world-view—from the facts, he
moves the drama toward a climax. Not until the penultimate chapter, "Spring," does he disclose a way of coping with the forces represented by the encroaching machine power.

At the same time, however, he carefully nurtures an awareness of
the railroad's presence in the Concord woods. (The account of the
interrupted idyll in "Sounds" is only the most dramatic of its many
appearances.) There is scarcely a chapter in which he does not
mention seeing or hearing the engine, or walking "over the long
causeway made for the railroad through the meadows. . . ." (179)
When the crew arrives to strip the ice from the pond, it is "with a
peculiar shriek from the locomotive" (198). And Thoreau takes special pains to impress us with the "cut" in the landscape made by the
embankment. He introduces the motif in the first chapter, after describing his initial visit to the Walden site:

> . . . I came out on to the railroad, on my way home, its yellow
> sandheap stretched away gleaming in the hazy atmosphere,
> and the rails shone in the spring sun . . . (31)

And he returns to it in "The Ponds":

> That devilish Iron Horse, whose ear-rending neigh is heard
> throughout the town, has muddied the Boiling Spring with his
> foot, and he it is that has browsed off all the woods on Walden

---

1. For Thoreau's attitude toward "fact" and "truth," see Perry Miller, "Thoreau in the Context of International Romanticism," *NEQ* XXXIV (June, 1961), 147–59 and Sherman
Paul, *The Shores of America, Thoreau's Inward Exploration* (Urbana: University of Illinois Press, 1958).

shore; that Trojan horse, with a thousand men in his belly, introduced by mercenary Greeks! Where is the country's champion, the Moore of Moore Hall, to meet him at the Deep Cut and thrust an avenging lance between the ribs of the bloated pest? (132)

The Deep Cut is a wound inflicted upon the land by man's meddling, aggressive, rational intellect, and it is not healed until the book's climax, the resurgence of life in "Spring." By that point the organizing design of *Walden* has been made to conform to the design of nature itself; like Spenser's arrangement of his eclogues in *The Shepheards Calendar*, the sequence of Thoreau's final chapters follows the sequence of months and seasons. This device affirms the possibility of redemption from time, the movement away from Concord time, defined by the clock, toward nature's time, the daily and seasonal life cycle. It is also the movement that redeems machine power. In the spring the ice, sand, and clay of the railroad causeway thaws. The wet stuff flows down the banks, assumes myriad forms, and arouses in Thoreau a delight approaching religious ecstasy. The event provides this parable-maker with his climactic trope: a visual image that figures the realization of the pastoral ideal in the age of machines.

* * *

Thoreau's study of the melting bank is a figurative restoration of the form and unity severed by the mechanized forces of history. Out of the ugly "cut" in the landscape he fashions an image of a new beginning. Order, form, and meaning are restored, but it is a blatantly, unequivocally figurative restoration. The whole force of the passage arises from its extravagantly metaphoric, poetic, literary character. At no point does Thoreau impute material reality to the notion of sand being transformed into, say, leopards' paws. It assumes a form that looks like leopards' paws, but the form exists only so far as it is perceived. The same may be said of his alternative to the Concord way. Shortly after the episode of the thawing sand, the account of the coming of spring reaches a moment of "seemingly instantaneous" change (209). A sudden influx of light fills his house; he looks out the window, and where the day before there had been cold gray ice there lies the calm transparent pond; he hears a robin singing in the distance and honking geese flying low over the woods. It is spring. Its coming, says Thoreau, is "like the creation of Cosmos out of Chaos and the realization of the Golden Age" (210).

This reaffirmation of the pastoral ideal is not at all like Emerson's prophecy, in "The Young American," of a time "when the whole land is a garden, and the people have grown up in the bowers of paradise." By comparison, the findings of the Walden experiment seem the work of a tough, unillusioned empiricist.[2] They are consistent with Thoreau's unsparing analysis of the Concord "economy" and with the knowledge that industrial progress is making nonsense of the popular notion of a "pastoral life." The melting of the bank and the coming of spring is only "like" a realization of the golden age. It is a poetic figure. In *Walden* Thoreau is clear, as Emerson seldom was, about the location of meaning and value. He is saying that it does not reside in the natural facts or in social institutions or in anything "out there," but in consciousness. It is a product of imaginative perception, of the analogy-perceiving, metaphor-making, mythopoeic power of the human mind. For Thoreau the realization of the golden age is, finally, a matter of private and, in fact, literary experience. Since it has nothing to do with the environment, with social institutions or material reality (any facts will melt if the heat of imaginative passion is sufficient), then the writer's physical location is of no great moment. At the end of the chapter on "Spring," accordingly, Thoreau suddenly drops the language of metaphor and reverts to a direct, matter-of-fact, referential idiom: "Thus was my first year's life in the woods completed; and the second year was similar to it. I finally left Walden September 6th, 1847" (214).

There is a world of meaning in the casual tone. If the book ended here, indeed, one might conclude that Thoreau, like Prospero at the end of *The Tempest*, was absolutely confident about his impending return to society. (Concord is the Milan of *Walden*.) But the book does not end with "Spring." Thoreau finds it necessary to add a didactic conclusion, as if he did not fully trust the power of metaphor after all. And he betrays his uneasiness, finally, in the arrogance with which he announces his disdain for the common life:

> I delight . . . not to live in this restless, nervous, bustling, trivial Nineteenth Century, but stand or sit thoughtfully while it goes by. What are men celebrating? They are all on a committee of arrangements, and hourly expect a speech from somebody. God is only the president of the day, and Webster is his orator. (221)

In the end Thoreau restores the pastoral hope to its traditional location. He removes it from history, where it is manifestly unrealizable, and relocates it in literature, which is to say, in his own consciousness, in his craft, in *Walden*.

---

2. In fairness to Emerson it should be said that by the late 1840s he, too, had become more skeptical about the compatibility of the pastoral ideal and industrial progress. His second visit to England in 1847 was in many ways a turning point in his intellectual development, and *English Traits* (1856) is one of our first and most penetrating studies of the new culture of industrialism. Ostensibly about England, the book manifestly was written with America's future economic development in view. Both the structure and the content of the book are governed by the machine-in-the-garden figure.

STANLEY CAVELL

[Captivity and Despair in *Walden* and "Civil Disobedience"]†

I have spoken of the sense of loss and of the vision of general despair which *Walden* depicts in its early pages, and of the crowing and trickery of the book as taking place over them or in the face of them. Despair and a sense of loss are not static conditions, but goads to our continuous labor: "That man who does not believe that each day contains an earlier, more sacred, and auroral hour than he has yet profaned, has despaired of life, and is pursuing a descending and darkening way" (64).

It is not merely the company of others that causes this. Going to Walden, for example, will not necessarily help you out, for there is no reason to think you will go there and live there any differently from the way you are going on now. "From the desperate city you go into the desperate country, and have to console yourself with the bravery of minks and muskrats" (9). "How to migrate thither" is the question. We are living "what is not life" (65), *pursuing* a descending and darkening way. And yet to realize his wish to live deliberately the writer went "*down* to the woods" (118). And downward is the direction he invites us in:

> Let us settle ourselves, and work and wedge our feet downward through the mud and slush of opinion, and prejudice, and tradition, and delusion, and appearance, that alluvion which covers the globe, through Paris and London, through New York and Boston and Concord, through church and state, through poetry and philosophy and religion, till we come to a hard bottom and rocks in place, which we can call *reality*, and say, This is, and no mistake; and then begin, having a *point d'appui*, below freshet and frost and fire, a place where you might found a wall or a state. . . . Be it life or death, we crave only reality. (70)

The path to a point of support and origin is not immediately attractive, but the hope in it, and the hope that we can take it, is exactly that we are *living* another way, pursuing death, desperate wherever we are; so that if we could go all the way, go *through* Paris and Lon-

---

† From *The Senses of Walden*, 70–93, 116–19. Copyright © 1981 by Stanley Cavell. Published by North Point Press and reprinted by permission. *Walden* and "Civil Disobedience" page numbers refer to this Norton Critical Edition.

don, *through* church and state, *through* poetry and philosophy and religion, we might despair of despair itself, rather than of life, and cast *that* off, and begin, and so reverse our direction.

He introduces his invitation to voyage as a matter of "settling ourselves." At the end:

> I love to weigh, to settle, to gravitate toward that which most strongly and rightfully attracts me . . . not suppose a case, but take the case that is; to travel the only path I can, and that on which no power can resist me. It affords me no satisfaction to commence to spring an arch before I have got a solid foundation. . . . There is a solid bottom everywhere. (221–22)

Settling has to do with weighing, then; and so does deliberating, pondering. To live deliberately would be to settle, to let ourselves clarify, and find our footing. And weighing is not just carrying weight, by your force of character and in your words; but lifting the thing that keeps you anchored, and sailing out. Then gravitation, in conjunction with what rightfully attracts you, might be in an upward as well as a downward direction—or what we call up and down would cease to signify. We crave only reality; but since "We know not where we are" (223) and only "esteem truth remote" (69)—that is, we cannot believe that it is under our feet—we despair of ourselves and let our despair dictate what we call reality: "When we consider what, to use the words of the catechism, is the chief end of man, and what are the true necessaries and means of life, it appears as if men had deliberately chosen the common mode of living because they preferred it to any other. Yet they honestly think there is no choice left" (9). The way we live is not necessary, in this "comparatively free country." The writer generally "[confines himself] to those who are said to be in *moderate* circumstances" (27), obviously implying that he thinks their case is extreme. It follows that this life has been chosen; that since we are living and pursuing it, we are choosing it. This does not appear to those leading it to be the case; they think they haven't the means to live any other way. "One young man of my acquaintance, who has inherited some acres, told me that he thought he should live as I did, *if he had the means*" (52). But the truth appears to the writer, as if in a vision, a vision of true necessities, that the necessaries of life *are* the means of life, the ways it is lived; therefore to say we haven't the means for a different way, in particular for a way which is to discover what the true necessaries and means of life in fact are, is irrational. It expresses the opinion that our current necessities are our final ones. We have defined our lives in front. What at first seems like a deliberate choice turns out to be a choice all right (they honestly think there is no choice *left*), but not a deliberate one, not one weighed and found good, but one taken without pondering, or lightly; they have never preferred it. And yet this is nothing less than a choice of one's life.

How does this come about? What keeps this nightmare from at least frightening us awake? It is a sort of disease of the imagination, both of the private imagination we may call religion and of the public imagination we may call politics. To settle, weigh, gravitate, he was saying, is a question of "taking the case that is," not "supposing a case." And earlier: "I am far from supposing that my case is a peculiar one; no doubt many of my readers would make a similar defense" (53). That is, from our own experience we draw or project our definitions of reality, as the empiricists taught us to do; only the experience we learn from, and know best, is our failure (cf. 68), the same old prospects are repeated back to us, by ourselves and by others. We were to be freed from superstition; instead the frozen hopes and fears which attached to rumored dictates of revelation have now attached themselves to the rumored dictates of experience. The writer calls us heathenish. (He calls himself that too because to an audience of heathens all devotions are heathenish; and because if what *they* do is called Christianity then he is a heathen—he lives outside the town.) Our education is sadly neglected; we have not learned in the moral life, as the scientists have in theirs, how to seek and press to the limits of experience; so we draw our limits well short of anything reason requires. The result is not that the reality this proposes to us, while confined, is at least safe. The result is a metaphysics of the imagination, of unexamined fantasy.

As I was desirous to recover the long lost bottom of Walden Pond, I surveyed it carefully, before the ice broke up, early in '46, with compass and chain and sounding line. There have been many stories told about the bottom, or rather no bottom of this pond, which certainly had no foundation for themselves. It is remarkable how long men will believe in the bottomlessness of a pond without taking the trouble to sound it. I have visited two such Bottomless Ponds in one walk in this neighborhood. Many have believed that Walden reached quite through to the other side of the globe. Some who have lain flat on the ice for a long time, looking down through the illusive medium, perchance with watery eyes into the bargain, and driven to hasty conclusions by the fear of catching cold in their breasts, have seen vast holes "into which a load of hay might be driven," if there were any body to drive it, the undoubted source of the Styx and entrance to the Internal Regions from these parts. Others have gone down from the village with a "fifty-six" and a wagon load of inch rope, but yet have failed to find any bottom; for while the "fifty-six" was resting by the way, they were paying out the rope in the vain attempt to fathom their truly immeasurable capacity for marvelousness. But I can assure my readers that Walden has a reasonably tight bottom at a not unreasonable, though at an unusual, depth. I fathomed it easily with a cod-line and a stone weighing about a pound and a half, and could tell accurately when the stone left the bottom, by having to pull so much harder before the water got underneath to help me. The greatest depth was exactly one hundred and two feet; to which may be added the five feet which it has risen since, making one hundred and seven. This is a remarkable depth for so small an area; yet not one inch of it can be spared by the imagination. What if all ponds were shallow? Would it not react on the minds of men? I am thankful that this pond was made deep and pure for a symbol. While men believe in the infinite some ponds will be thought to be bottomless. (191–92)

The human imagination is released by fact. Alone, left to its own devices, it will not recover reality, it will not form an edge. So a favorite trust of the Romantics has, along with what we know of experience, to be brought under instruction; the one kept from straining, the other from stifling itself to death. Both imagination and experience continue to require what the Renaissance had in mind, viz., that they be humanized. ("I brag for humanity," i.e., the humanity that is still to awaken, to have its renascence. And the writer praises science that humanizes knowledge, that "reports what those men already know practically or instinctively," as "a true *humanity*, or account of experience" [143], i.e., one of the humanities.) The Reformation, as in Luther and Milton, had meant to be a furthering of this too. It was not wholly ineffective: "Our manners have been corrupted by communication with the saints" (57). That is, false saintliness is hypocrisy, but true saintliness will seem to be bad manners to hypocrites.

The work of humanization is still to be done. While men believe in the infinite some ponds will be thought to be bottomless. So long as we will not take our beliefs all the way to genuine knowledge, to conviction, but keep letting ourselves be driven to more or less hasty conclusions, we will keep misplacing the infinite, and so grasp neither heaven nor earth. There is a solid bottom everywhere. But how are we going to weigh toward it, arrive at confident conclusions from which we can reverse direction, spring an arch, choose our lives, and go about our business?

Despair is not bottomless, merely endless; a hopelessness, or fear, of reaching bottom. It takes illusions for its object, from which, in turn, like all ill-educated experience, it is confirmed in what it already knew. So its conclusions too are somewhat hasty, its convictions do not truly convict us. This is a prophecy the writer hears from a cat with wings:

> Suddenly an unmistakable cat-owl from very near me, with the most harsh and tremendous voice I ever heard from any inhabitant of the woods, responded at regular intervals to the [loud honking of a] goose, as if determined to expose and disgrace this intruder from Hudson's Bay by exhibiting a greater compass and volume of voice in a native, and *boo-hoo* him out of Concord horizon. What do you mean by alarming the citadel at this time of night consecrated to me? Do you think I am ever caught napping at such an hour, and that I have not got lungs and a larynx as well as yourself? *Boo-hoo, boo-hoo, boo-hoo!* It was one of the most thrilling discords I ever heard. And yet, if you had a discriminating ear, there were in it the elements of a concord such as these plains never saw nor heard. (183)

If we find out what is foreign and what is native to us, we can find out what there really is to boo-hoo about, and then our quiet wailing will make way for something to crow about.

What has the writer's ear discriminated specifically? Evidently he has heard that all the elements of an apocalyptic concord, a new city of man, are present. We need nothing more and need do nothing new in order that our change of direction take place. This is expressed in the writer's sense that we are on the verge of something, perched; something is in the wind, Olympus is but the outside of earth everywhere; there is a solid bottom everywhere; the dumps and a budding ecstasy are equally possible from this spot, we need only turn around to find the track. "Nearest to all things is that power which fashions their being. *Next* to us the grandest laws are continually being executed" (94). Because we do not recognize the circumstances that encircle us, we do not allow them to "make our occasions"; instead of "looking another way" (69), we permit outlying and transient circumstances to distract us. The crisis is at hand, but we do not know how to grasp it; we do not know where or how to spend it, so we are desperate. But "it is a characteristic of wisdom not to do desperate things" (9). And "It is by a mathematical point only that we are wise, as the sailor or the fugitive slave keeps the polestar in his eye" (52). The day is at hand, and the effect of every vision is at hand—for example, of renaissance and reformation and revolution (we are to work our way through poetry and philosophy and church and state), which since the beginning of the modern age have been a "dinning in our ears" (219).

This is, no doubt, mystical to us. But the wretchedness and nervousness this writing creates[1] come from an equally undeniable, if intermittent, sense that the writer is being practical, and therefore that we are not. It is a sense that the mystery is of our own making; that it would require no more expenditure of spirit and body to let ourselves be free than it is costing us to keep ourselves pinioned and imprisoned within "opinion, and prejudice, and tradition, and delusion, and appearance." Our labors—the *way* we labor—are not responses to true need, but hectic efforts to keep ourselves from the knowledge of what is needful, from the promise of freedom, whose tidings we always call glad and whose bringer we always despise and then apotheosize (28), which is to say, kick upstairs. It is no excuse to us that few tidings really are glad, that for every real prophet there are legions of false ones speaking a vision of their own hearts, i.e., from what ails merely themselves. We are not excused from thinking it out for ourselves.

This writer's primary audience is neither the "degraded rich" nor the "degraded poor," but those who are in "*moderate* circumstances"; what we might call the *middle* class. We are not Chinese or Sandwich Islanders; nor are we *southern* slaves. "I sometimes wonder that we can be so frivolous, I may almost say, as to attend to the gross but somewhat foreign form of servitude called Negro Slavery, there are so many keen and subtle masters that enslave both north and south" (8). There is no mystery here; there is plain damnation. One mystery we make for ourselves is to say that Negro slavery is wholly foreign to us who are said to live in New England. South is for us merely a direction in which we look away from our own servitude. This is to recommend neither that we ought or ought not do something about Negro slavery; it is to ask why, if we will not attend to the matter, we attend to it—as if fascinated by something at once foreign and yet intimately familiar. We have not made the South foreign to us, we have not put it behind us, sloughed its slavery. We do not yet see our hand in it, any more than we see the connection between our making ourselves foreign to our government and the existence of roasting Mexicans and "strolling" Indians (16) (it was in the years immediately after Thoreau's graduation from Harvard that the eastern tribes were collected and, following Andrew Jackson's legislation, marched beyond the Mississippi); any more than we see the connection between what we call philanthropy and what we call poverty. We have yet "*to get our living together*" (52), to be whole, and to be one community. We are not settled, we have not clarified ourselves; our character,

---

1. An allusion to Emerson's response to the "old fault of unlimited contradiction" he found in Thoreau's writing: "It makes me nervous and wretched to read it." See *The Senses of Walden*, 11–12 [*Editor*].

and the character of the nation, is not (in another of his favorite words) transparent to itself (137).

> It is hard to have a southern overseer; it is worse to have a northern one; but worst of all when you are the slave-driver of yourself. Talk of a divinity in man! Look at the teamster on the highway, wending to market by day or night; does any divinity stir within him? His highest duty to fodder and water his horses! What is his destiny to him compared with the shipping interests? Does not he drive for Squire Make-a-stir: How god-like, how immortal, is he? See how he cowers and sneaks, how vaguely all the day he fears, not being immortal and divine, but the slave and prisoner of his own opinion of himself, a fame won by his own deeds. Public opinion is a weak tyrant compared with our own private opinion. What a man thinks of himself, that it is which determines, or rather indicates, his fate. Self-emancipation even in the West Indian provinces of the fancy and imagination,—what Wilberforce is there to bring that about? Think, also, of the ladies of the land weaving toilet cushions against the last day, not to betray too green an interest in their fates! As if you could kill time without injuring eternity. (8)

How did private opinion become a tyrant, a usurper, in service of interests not our own? Its power is such—not merely the magnitude of it, but the form of it—that we feel not merely helpless before it but without rights in the face of it. The drift of *Walden* is not that we should go off and be alone; the drift is that we *are* alone, *and* that we are never alone—not in the highest and not in the lowest sense. In the highest sense, we will know a good neighborhood when we can live there; and in the lowest, "Consider the girls in a factory—never alone, hardly in their dreams" (95). In such circumstances there is little point in suggesting that we assert ourselves, or take further steps; that merely asks the tyrant to tighten his hold. The quest of this book is for the recovery of the self, as from an illness: "The incessant anxiety and strain of some is a well-nigh incurable form of disease" (11).

Why should we explore ourselves when we already know our selves for cowards, sneaks, and slaves? "But men labor under a mistake" (7). Our labors are not callings, but neither are they misfortunes or accidents which have befallen us. In all, we take something for what it is not but, understandably enough, something it appears to be. That is the cause of our despair, but also cause for hope. We do not *know* that it is necessary for things to be as bad as they are; because we do not know why we labor as we do. We take one thing for another in every field of thought and in every mode of action. Religiously, our labors betoken penance, hence a belief in works without faith, hence blindness to faith; politically, our labors betoken a belief in fate, hence in a society whose necessities we have had no hand in determining, hence blindness to its origins; epistemologically, our labors betoken superstitions, commitments to uncertainties (11), refusals to know what we know. ("Man flows at once to God when the channel of purity is open" [149].)

The writer knows his readers will take the project of self-emancipation to be merely literary. But he also knows that this is because they take everything in a more or less literary way: everything is news to them, and it always comes from foreign parts, from some Gothic setting. "Shams and delusions are esteemed for soundest truths, while reality is fabulous" (68). We crave only reality, but we cannot stomach it; we do not believe in our lives; so we trade them for stories; their real history is more interesting than anything we now know.

How are we to become practical? How are we to "look another way," i.e., look in another way, with other eyes, in order to understand that it is harder to be "an overseer of the poor" (57) (i.e., of ourselves) than to let ourselves go? All our fields await emancipation—geography and places, literature and neighborhood, epistemology and eyes, anatomy and hands, metaphysics and cities. To locate ourselves in this maze, the first step is to see that we ourselves are its architects and hence are in a position to recollect the design. The first step in building our dwelling is to recognize that we have already built one.

Society remains as mysterious to us as we are to ourselves, or as God is. That we are the slave-drivers of ourselves has not come about "for private reasons, as [we] must believe" (11). It is an open realization of what we have made of the prophecy of democracy. It is what we have done with the success of Locke and the others in removing the divine right of kings and placing political authority in our consent to be governed together. That this has made life a little easier for some, in some respects, is a less important consequence than the fact that we now consent to social evil. What was to be a blessing we have made a curse. We do not see our hand in what happens, so we call certain events melancholy accidents when they are the inevitabilities of our projects (40), and we call other events necessities because we will not change our minds. The essential message of the idea of a social contract is that political institutions require justification, that they are absolutely without sanctity, that power over us is held on trust from us, that institutions have no authority other than the authority we lend them, that we are their architects, that they are therefore artifacts, that there are laws or ends, of nature or justice, in terms of which they are to be tested. They are experiments.

To learn that we have forgotten this is part of our education which is sadly neglected.

> We read that the traveler asked the boy if the swamp before him had a hard bottom. The boy replied that it had. But presently the traveler's horse sank in up to the girths, and he observed to the boy, "I thought you said that this bog had a hard bottom." "So it has," answered the latter, "but you have not got half way to it yet." So it is with the bogs and quick-sands of society; but he is an old boy that knows it. (222)

The bottom is our construction of it, our cursed consent to it, our obedience to it which we read as a muddle of accidents and necessities. The writer suggests this in saying that he "[desires] to speak impartially on this point, and as one not interested in the success or failure of the present economical and social arrangements" (41). Since "not interested in" evidently cannot mean that they have no interest for him, what does it mean? It means that he is one who is withdrawing his interest in it, placing his investment elsewhere. Or he "desires to speak" as if that were so, leaving it open whether it is the case. Not simply because he would make a fiction of his withdrawal, but because it is unclear how it is to be effected. This is in fact one of the standing mysteries of any theory of the social contract—how consent is shown, and therefore when and how its withdrawal can be shown.

It is, appropriately, in the chapter gently entitled "The Village" that the writer of *Walden* declares himself to be the author of "Civil Disobedience," the same man who had said that "I simply wish to refuse allegiance to the State, to withdraw and stand aloof from it effectually" (242). In that essay he describes himself as having felt, during his one night in jail, a kind of ecstasy of freedom. But that hardly constitutes "effectual" withdrawal from the state. He reprints a statement he said he put in writing to the effect that he did "not wish to be regarded as a member of any incorporated society which I have not joined." That seems to have disengaged him from the local church; and though he would "have signed off in detail from all the societies which [he] never signed on to . . . [he] did not know where to find a complete list" (238). The joke very quickly went sour. In particular, he could not name society or the government as such, because he knows he has somehow signed on. "How does it become a man to behave toward this American government today? I answer, that he cannot without disgrace be associated with it. I cannot for an instant recognize that political organization as *my* government which is the *slave's* government also" (230). Nevertheless, he recognizes that he *is* associated with it, that his withdrawal has not "dissolved the Union" between ourselves and the state (cf. 233), and hence that he is disgraced. Apparently, as things stand, one cannot but choose to serve the state; so he will "serve the state with [his conscience] also, and so necessarily resist it for the most part" (229). This is not a call to revolution, because that depends, as Locke had said, on supposing that your fellow citizens, in conscience, will also find that the time for it has come; and Thoreau recognizes that "almost all say that such is not the case now" (230).

Effective civil disobedience, according to Thoreau's essay, is an act that accomplishes three things: (1) it forces the state to recognize that you are against it, so that the state, as it were, attempts to withdraw your consent for you; (2) it enters an appeal to the people ". . . first and instantaneously, from them to the Maker of them, and, secondly, from them to themselves" (242), because the state has provided, in the given case, no other way of petition (234–35); (3) it identifies and educates those who have "voluntarily chosen to be an agent of the government" (235). ("How shall he ever know well what he is and does as an officer of the government, or as a man, until he is obliged to consider whether he shall treat me, his neighbor, for whom he has respect, as a neighbor and well-disposed man, or as a maniac and disturber of the peace, and see if he can get over this obstruction to his neighborliness without a ruder and more impetuous thought or speech corresponding with his action" [235].) One night in jail was not much in the way of such an action; in fact it lacked the second condition of such an act altogether, viz., the appeal to the people from themselves. But those who complain of the pettiness of that one night forget that the completion of the act was the writing of the essay which depicts it.

Even that is likely to be as ineffective as a quiet night in the Concord jail. First, because the state is "penitent to that degree that it [will hire] one to scourge it while it [sins], but not to that degree that it [will leave] off sinning for a moment" (233); second, because an appeal to the people will go unheard as long as they do not know who they are, and labor under a mistake, and cannot locate where they live and what they live for. Nothing less than *Walden* could carry that load of information. Like the *Leviathan*, and the *Second Treatise of Government*, and the *Discourse on the Origin of Inequality*—which we perhaps regard as more or less prescientific studies of existing societies—*Walden* is, among other things, a tract of political education, education for membership in the polis. It locates authority in the citizens and it identifies citizens—those with whom one is in membership—as "neighbors." What it shows is that education for citizenship is education for isolation. (In this sense, *Walden* is *Émile* grown up. The absence of Sophie only purifies the point.)

The writer of *Walden* keeps faith both with his vision of injustice in his early essay, and with his strategy in the face of it: he resists society by visibly withdrawing from it. "It is true, I might have resisted forcibly with more or less effect, might have run 'amok' against society; but I preferred that society should run 'amok' against me, it being the desperate party" (118). The writer's strategy, which enforces his position as neighbor, is to refuse society his voice, letting the desperate party run amok not merely eventually, but now, against his words, unable either to accept them or to leave them alone. And he reaffirms his earlier judgment that prisons are "the only [houses] in a slave State in which a free man can abide with honor" (236), by "caging" himself in the woods (61), keeping alive the fact and the imagination of injustice, and inhabiting "the more free and honorable ground" on which to be found by "the fugitive slave, and the Mexican prisoner on parole, and the Indian come to plead the wrongs of his race" (236)—all of whom make their appearance to him at Walden. He went there to "repeople the woods" (178); first, by being there; second, by imagining those who were there before; third, by anticipating those for whom he is preparing the ground, those who have come to these woods and must be renewed. And he demonstrates three captivities: that he is a prisoner of the state, as any man is whose government is native to him and is evil; that he is, like Saint Paul, a prisoner of Christ; and that we are held captive each by each and each by the others. These captivities show where we live and what we live for; and the source of strength, or the fulcrum, upon which we can change direction.

It is not the first time in our literature, and it will not be the last, in which society is viewed as a prison. As with Plato's cave, the path out is as arduous as the one the *Republic* requires of philosophers—and like the *Republic*, *Walden* is presided over by the sun, and begins with a stripping away of false necessities. Its opening visions of self-torture and of eternal labors and self-enslavement seem to me an enactment of the greatest opening line among our texts of social existence: "Man is born free, and everywhere he is in chains." What I take Rousseau to mean is that the *way* man is in bondage is comprehensible only of the creature who is, ontologically, free. Human societies, as we know them, could not exist except with each individual's choosing not to exercise freedom. To choose freedom would be to choose freedom for all (to make the will general); the alternative is that we choose partially, i.e., to further our privilege or party. The social contract is nowhere in existence, because we do not will it; therefore the undeniable bonds between us are secured by our obedience to agreements and compacts that are being made among ourselves as individuals acting privately and in secret, not among ourselves as citizens acting

openly on behalf of the polis. The logic of our position is that we
are conspirators. If this is false, it is paranoid; if it is not, we are
crazy. I mention this not to argue for it, or even to justify this reading of Rousseau, but only to suggest a degree of intimacy between
Rousseau's and Thoreau's understanding of society; and at the
same time to keep in mind the question of insanity to which the
writer of *Walden* recurs—or at any rate, the extremity and precari-
ousness of mood in which he writes.

I do not wish to impose a political theory upon the text of
Walden. On the contrary, if the guiding question of political theory
is "Why ought I to obey the state?" then Thoreau's response can be
said to reject the question and the subject. The state is not to be
obeyed but, at best, to be abided. It is not to be listened to, but
watched. Why ought I to abide the state? Because "it is a great evil
to make a stir about it." A government, however, is capable of
greater evil, "when its tyranny or its inefficiency are great and unendurable" (230). How do you know when this point has been
reached? Here the concept of conscience arises, upon which secular, or anyway empiricist philosophy has come to grief: what can
conscience be, other than some kind of feeling, of its essence private, a study for psychologists?—as though the "science," that is to
say knowledge, that the word "conscience" emphasizes can at most
register a lingering superstition. *Walden*, in its emphasis upon listening and answering, outlines an epistemology of conscience.

The opening visions of captivity and despair in *Walden* are traced
full length in the language of the first chapter, the longest, which
establishes the underlying vocabulary of the book as a whole.
"Economy" turns into a nightmare maze of terms about money and
possessions and work, each turning toward and joining the others.
No summary of this chapter will capture the number of economic
terms the writer sets in motion in it. There is profit and loss,
rich and poor, cost and expense, borrow and pay, owe and own,
business, commerce, enterprises, ventures, affairs, capital, price,
amount, improvement, bargain, employment, inheritance, bankruptcy, work, trade, labor, idle, spend, waste, allowance, fortune,
gain, earn, afford, possession, change, settling, living, interest,
prospects, means, terms. But the mere listing of individual words
gives no idea of the powers of affinity among them and their radia-
tion into the remainder of language. They are all ordinary words
that we may use, apparently literally, in evaluating any of our investments of feeling, or expenses of spirit, or turns of fortune.
There is just enough description, in this chapter, of various enterprises we think of as the habitual and specific subjects of econom-
ics, to make unnoticeable the spillage of these words over our lives

as a whole. It is a brutal mocking of our sense of values, by forcing a finger of the vocabulary of the New Testament (hence of our understanding of it) down our throats. For that is the obvious origin or locus of the use of economic imagery to express, and correct, spiritual confusion: what shall it profit a man; the wages of sin; the parable of talents; laying up treasures; rendering unto Caesar; charity. What we call the Protestant Ethic, the use of worldly loss and gain to symbolize heavenly standing, appears in *Walden* as some last suffocation of the soul. America and its Christianity have become perfect, dreamlike literalizations or parodies of themselves.

The network or medium of economic terms serves the writer as an imitation of the horizon and strength both of our assessments of our position and of our connections with one another; in particular of our eternal activity in these assessments and connections, and of our blindness to them, to the fact that they are ours. The state of our society and the state of our minds are stamped upon one another. This was Plato's metaphysical assumption in picturing justice and its decline; it was the secret of Rousseau's epistemology. To let light into this structure of terms, to show that our facts and ideas of economy are uneconomical, that they do not meet but avoid true need, that they are as unjust and impoverishing within each soul as they are throughout the soul's society, *Walden* cuts into the structure of economic terms at two major points, or in two major ways: (1) it attacks its show of practicality by dramatizing the mysteriousness of ownership, and (2) it slips its control of several key terms.

I do not claim that Locke is the only or even the actual representative of the mystery of ownership that *Walden* encounters. But the *Second Treatise* is as formative of the conscience, or the unconsciousness, of political economy as any other work, and its preoccupations are coded into *Walden*. When we read that "the cost of a thing is the amount of what I will call life which is required to be exchanged for it" (24), it is inevitable that we should think of the so-called labor theory of value. The mysticism of what society thinks practical shows up nakedly in what anybody recognizes as the foolishness of Locke's justifications of ownership, in particular his idea that what originally entitles you to a thing is your having "mixed your labor" with it, and that what entitles you to more than you need is your "improvement" of the possession, your not wasting it. "Economy is a subject which admits of being treated with levity, but it cannot so be disposed of" (23). The writer might at that point have had in mind Locke's argument that an individual's accumulation of vastly more money than he can spend is not a case of waste because money is metal and hence can be kept in heaps without being spoiled. The mysteries *Walden* goes into about buying and selling all the farms in his neighborhood, and

about annually carrying off the landscape (59), suggest that nobody really knows how it happens that anyone owns anything at
all, or why it is that, as Locke puts it, though the earth was given
to us in common, it is now so uncommonly divided and held. This
is not to say that any of our institutions might not be practically
justified (the writer of *Walden* describes and accepts a perfectly
practical justification for the institution of money: that it is more
convenient than barter). But in fact if you look at what we do under our pleas of economy, you see that no merely practical motives
could inspire these labors.

Political economy is the modern form of theodicy, and our labors
are our religious mysteries. This is an explicit meaning the writer
gives, toward the end of "Economy," to his having spoken at its beginning of our "outward condition." He recounts an Indian custom
described in Bartram, in which members of a community cleanse
their houses and, having provided themselves with new clothes and
utensils and furniture, throw the old together on a common heap,
"consume it with fire," fast, and declare a "general amnesty" (50).
They are beginning again.

> The Mexicans also practiced a similar purification . . . in the
> belief that it was time for the world to come to an end . . .
>   . . . I have scarcely heard of a truer sacrament, that is, as the
> dictionary defines it, "outward and visible sign of an inward
> and spiritual grace." (50)

So our labors, our outward condition, which he more than once describes as something to which we are "religiously devoted," are our
sacraments, and the inward state they signal ("our very lives are our
disgrace") is our secret belief that the world has already come to an
end for us. Such actions are inspired, but not, as the writer says he
believes in the case of the Mexicans, "directly from Heaven." We labor under a mistake. What will save us from ourselves is nothing
less than salvation.

The second major strategy I said *Walden* uses to cut into the circling of economic terms is to win back from it possession of our
words. This requires replacing them into a reconceived human existence. That it requires a literary redemption of language altogether has been a theme of my remarks from the beginning; and I
have hoped to show that it simultaneously requires a redemption of
the lives we live by them, religiously or politically conceived, inner
and outer. Our words have for us the meaning we give to them. As
our lives stand, the meaning we give them is rebuked by the meaning they have in our language—the meaning, say, that writers live
on, the meaning we also, in moments, know they have but which
mostly remains a mystery to us. Thoreau is doing with our ordinary

assertions what Wittgenstein does with our more patently philosophical assertions—bringing them back to a context in which they are alive. It is the appeal from ordinary language to itself; a rebuke of our lives by what we may know of them, if we will. The writer has secrets to tell which can only be told to strangers. The secrets are not his, and they are not the confidences of others. They are secrets because few are anxious to know them; all but one or two wish to remain foreign. Only those who recognize themselves as strangers can be told them, because those who think themselves familiars will think they have already heard what the writer is saying. They will not understand his speaking in confidence.

The literary redemption of language is at the same time a philosophical redemption; the establishment of American literature undertaken in *Walden* requires not only the writing of a scripture and an epic, but a work of philosophy. The general reason is as before: *Walden* proposes new mysteries because we have already mystified ourselves; it requires new literary invention because we have already made our lives fabulous; it requires theology because we are theologized. We have already philosophized our lives almost beyond comprehension. The more famous perception of this is assumed in Marx's eleventh slogan concerning Feuerbach: "Philosophers have only interpreted the world in various ways; the point, however, is to change it." The changes required have to be directed to the fact that it is not only philosophers who have interpreted the world, but all men; that all men labor under a mistake—call it a false consciousness; and that those who learn true labor are going to be able to do something about this because they are the inheritors of philosophy, in a position to put philosophy's brags and hopes for humanity, its humanism, into practice. Why this is or is not going to happen now, and where, and how, are other matters. Who knows what our lives will be when we have shaken off the stupor of history, slipped the drag of time?

* * *

Leaving *Walden*, like leaving Walden, is as hard, is perhaps the same, as entering it. I have implied that the time of crisis depicted in this book is not alone a private one, and not wholly cosmic. It is simultaneously a crisis in the nation's life. And the nation too must die down to the root if it is to continue to recognize and neighbor itself. This is to be expected of a people whose groping for expression produced a literature by producing prophecy. They have had the strength to warn themselves. The hero of the book—as is typical of his procedures—enacts this fact as well as writes it, depicts it in his actions as well as his sentences. Of course the central action of building his house is the general prophecy: the nation, and the nation's people, have yet to be well made. And that the day is at hand for it to depart from its present constructions is amply shown in its hero's beginning and ending his tale with departures from Walden.

Two other of his actions specifically declare the sense of leaving or relinquishing as our present business. On the morning the writer went to dismantle the shanty he had bought as materials for his dwelling, and cart them to his new site, his labors were watched by one neighbor Seeley, who was taking the opportunity, as the writer was "treacherously informed," to steal what good nails, staples, and spikes the shanty yielded. "He was there to represent spectatordom, and help make this seemingly insignificant event one with the removal of the gods of Troy" (33). Again, a classical myth shields a myth closer to home:

> Son of man, thou dwellest in the midst of a rebellious house, which have eyes to see, and see not; they have ears to hear, and hear not; for they are a rebellious house.
>   Therefore, thou son of man, prepare thee stuff for removing, and remove by day in their sight; and thou shalt remove from thy place to another place in their sight: it may be they will consider, though they be a rebellious house. (Ezekiel 12:2–3)

The next step, if they do not consider, will be to go forth as into captivity. The writer's next step, accordingly, will be to return to civilization. The present constitution of our lives cannot go on. "This people must cease to hold slaves . . . though it cost them their existence as a people" (231). I do not quite wish to claim that Thoreau anticipated the Civil War; and yet the *Bhagavad Gita* is present in Walden—in name, and in moments of doctrine and structure. Its doctrine of "unattachment," so far as I am able to make that out, is recorded in *Walden*'s concept of interestedness. (This is, to my mind, one of Thoreau's best strokes. It suggests why "disinterestedness" has never really stabilized itself as a word meaning a state of impartial or unselfish interest, but keeps veering toward meaning the divestment of interest altogether, uninterestedness, ennui. Interestedness is already a state—perhaps the basic state—of relatedness to something beyond the self, the capacity for concern, for implication. It may be thought of as the self's capacity to mediate, to stand, between itself and the world.) Like *Walden*, the *Bhagavad Gita* is a scripture in eighteen parts; it begins with its hero in despair at the action before him; and it ends with his understanding and achieving of resolution, in particular his understanding of the doctrine (in which the image of the field and the knower of the field is central) that the way of knowledge and the way of work are one and the same, which permits him to take up the action it is his to perform and lead his army against an army of his kindred.

The second leaving, or relinquishment, is this:

> Now the trunks of trees on the bottom, and the old log canoe, and the dark surrounding woods, are gone, and the villagers, who scarcely know where it lies, instead of going to the pond to bathe or drink, are thinking to bring its water, which should be as sacred as the Ganges at least, to the village in a pipe, to wash their dishes with!—to earn their Walden by the turning of a cock or drawing of a plug! That devilish Iron Horse, whose ear-rending neigh is heard throughout the town, has muddied the Boiling Spring with his foot, and he it is that has browsed off all the woods on Walden shore. . . .

> . . . Though the woodchoppers have laid bare first this shore and then that, and the Irish have built their sties by it, and the railroad has infringed on its border, and the icemen have skimmed it once, it is itself unchanged, the same water which my youthful eyes fell on; all the change is in me. . . . It struck me again to-night, as if I had not seen it almost daily for more than twenty years,— Why, here is Walden, the same woodland lake that I discovered so many years ago; where a forest was cut down last winter another is springing up by its shore as lustily as ever; the same thought is welling up to its surface that was then; it is the same liquid joy and happiness to itself and its Maker, ay, and it *may* be to me. It is the work of a brave man surely, in whom there was no guile! He rounded this water with his hand, deepened and clarified it in his thought, and in his will bequeathed it to Concord. I see by its face that it is visited by the same reflection; and I can almost say, Walden, is it you? (132)

Walden was always gone, from the beginning of the words of *Walden*. (Our nostalgia is as dull as our confidence and anticipation.) The first man and woman are no longer there; our first relation to the world is no longer secured by the world. To allow the world to change, and to learn change from it, to permit it strangers, are conditions of knowing it now. This is why its knowledge is a heroic enterprise. The hero departs from his hut and goes into an unknown wood from whose mysteries he wins a boon that he brings back to his neighbors. The boon of Walden is *Walden*. Its writer cups it in his hand, sees his reflection in it, and holds it out to us. It is his promise, in anticipation of his going, and the nation's, and Walden's. He is bequeathing it to us in his will, the place of the book and the book of the place. He leaves us in one another's keeping.

BARBARA JOHNSON

A Hound, a Bay Horse, and a Turtle Dove: Obscurity in *Walden*†

The experience of reading Thoreau's *Walden* is often a disconcerting one. The very discrepancy between the laconic, concrete chapter titles and the long, convoluted sentences of the text alerts the reader to a process of level-shifting that delights and baffles—indeed, that delights because it baffles. Consider, for example, the following passage:

> I sometimes despair of getting any thing quite simple and honest done in this world by the help of men. They would have to be passed through a powerful press first, to squeeze their old notions out of them, so that they would not soon get upon their legs again; and then there would be some one in the company with a maggot in his head, hatched from an egg deposited there nobody knows when, for not even fire kills these things, and you would have lost your labor. Nevertheless, we will not forget that some Egyptian wheat was handed down to us by a mummy. (21)

It is difficult to read this passage without doing a double take. The logical seriousness of the style of "Nevertheless, we will not forget . . ." in no way prepares the reader for the sudden appearance of wheat in a mummy. The passage shifts with unruffled rapidity from abstract generalization to dead figure ("squeeze their old notions out of them") to a soon-to-reawaken figure hidden in a cliché ("maggot in the head") to mininarrative ("deposited there nobody knows when") to folk wisdom ("Not even fire kills these things") to counterclaim ("Nevertheless, we will not forget . . ."). By the time one reaches the mummy, one no longer knows what the figure stands for, whether it, like the mummy, is dead or alive, or even where the boundaries of the analogy (if it *is* an analogy) lie.

It is paradoxical that a writer who constantly exhorts us to "Simplify, simplify" should also be the author of some of the most complex and difficult paragraphs in the English language. What is it about this seemingly simple account of life in the woods that so often bewilders the reader, making him, in Emerson's words, "nervous and wretched to read it"?

† From *A World of Difference* (Baltimore: Johns Hopkins University Press, 1987), pp. 49–56. Reprinted by permission of Johns Hopkins University Press. *Walden* page numbers refer to this Norton Critical Edition.

In an article entitled "*Walden*'s False Bottoms," Walter Benn Michaels amply demonstrates the book's capacity to engender nervousness as he details the long history of readers' attempts to cope with *Walden*'s obscurity, first by attributing it to Thoreau's alleged "want of continuity of mind" (James Russell Lowell), then by subsuming it under the larger patterns of *Walden*'s literary unity (Matthiessen, Anderson), then by considering it as a challenge to the reader's ability to read figuratively (Cavell, Buell). Walter Benn Michaels ends his own account of the undecidability of *Walden*'s contradictions by saying, "It's heads I win, tails you lose. No wonder the game makes us nervous."[1]

The passage through which I would like to gain access to one of the principal difficulties of *Walden*'s game is precisely a passage about losing. It is one of the most often-discussed passages in the book, a fact that is in itself interesting and instructive. The passage stands as an isolated paragraph, seemingly unrelated to what precedes or follows:

> I long ago lost a hound, a bay horse, and a turtle-dove, and am still on their trail. Many are the travellers I have spoken concerning them, describing their tracks and what calls they answered to. I have met one or two who had heard the hound, and the tramp of the horse, and even seen the dove disappear behind a cloud, and they seemed as anxious to recover them as if they had lost them themselves. (15)

It should come as no surprise that the hound, the bay horse, and the turtle dove are almost universally seen as symbols by Thoreau's readers. The questions asked of this passage are generally, What do the three animals symbolize? and Where did the symbols come from? The answers to these questions are many and varied: for T. M. Raysor, the animals represent the "gentle boy" Edmund Sewall, Thoreau's dead brother John, and the woman to whom he unsuccessfully proposed marriage, Ellen Sewall; for Francis H. Allen, the symbols represent "the vague desires and aspirations of man's spiritual nature"; for John Burroughs, they stand for the "fine effluence" that for Thoreau constitutes "the ultimate expression of the fruit of any created thing." Others have seen in the symbols "a mythical record of [Thoreau's] disappointments" (Emerson), a "quest . . . for an absolutely satisfactory condition of friendship" (Mark Van Doren), the "wildness that keeps man in touch with nature, intellectual stimulus, and purification of spirit" (Frank Davidson), and a "lost Eden" (Alfred Kazin). Sources for Thoreau's symbols are said to be found in such diverse texts as Voltaire's *Zadig*

1. Walter Benn Michaels, "*Walden*'s False Bottoms," *Glyph* 1; *Johns Hopkins Textual Studies* (Baltimore: Johns Hopkins University Press, 1977), pp. 132–49.

(Edith Peairs), the "Chinese Four Books" that Thoreau edited for *The Dial*, an old English ballad, an Irish folk tale, and a poem by Emerson.[2]

The sense shared by all readers that the hound, the bay horse and the turtle dove *are* symbols, but that what they symbolize is unclear, is made explicit in the following remarks by Stanley Cavell:

> I have no new proposal to offer about the literary or biographical sources of those symbols. But the very obviousness of the fact that they are symbols, and function within a little myth, seems to me to tell us what we need to know. The writer comes to us from a sense of loss; the myth does not contain more than symbols because it is no set of desired things he has lost, but a connection with things, the track of desire itself.[3]

The notion that what is at stake here is not any set of lost *things* but rather the very fact of *loss* seems to find confirmation in the replies that Thoreau himself gave on two different occasions to the question of the passage's meaning. In a letter to B. B. Wiley, dated April 26, 1857, he writes:

> How shall we account for our pursuits if they are original? We get the language with which to describe our various lives out of a common mint. If others have their losses, which they are busy repairing, so have I *mine*, & their hound & horse may *perhaps* be the symbols of some of them. But also I have lost, or am in danger of losing, a far finer & more etherial treasure, which commonly no loss of which they are conscious will symbolize—this I answer hastily & with some hesitation, according as I now understand my own words. (*Annotated Walden*, 157–58)

And on another occasion, as the *Variorum* tells it:

> Miss Ellen Watson, in "Thoreau Visits Plymouth" . . . , reports that when Thoreau visited Plymouth, Mass., a year or two after the publication of *Walden*, he met there "Uncle Ed" Watson who asked him what he meant when he said he lost "a hound, a horse, and a dove." Thoreau replied, "Well, Sir, I suppose we have all our losses." "That's a pretty way to answer a fellow," replied Uncle Ed. (270)

2. For detailed bibliographical information on these and other readings of the passage, see *The Annotated Walden*, ed. Philip Van Doren Stern (New York: Clarkson N. Potter, 1970), pp. 157–58, and *The Variorum Walden*, ed. Walter Harding (New York: Twayne, 1962), pp. 270–72.
3. Stanley Cavell, *The Senses of Walden* (San Francisco: North Point, 1981), p. 51. [A portion of Cavell's book, dealing further with loss and despair, is reprinted in this volume, pp. 465–81 *Editor*].

Most readers have shared Uncle Ed's disappointment at this answer that seems no answer at all. The editors of the *Annotated* and *Variorum Waldens* both conclude their surveys of the literature on the subject in a similar way:

> In conclusion, however, it should be pointed out that there is no unanimity on interpretation of these symbols and the individual critic is left free to interpret as he wishes. (*Variorum*, 272)

> Since there is no clear explanation, each reader will have to supply his own. (*Annotated Walden*, 158)

In attempting to fill these enigmatic symbols with interpretive content, most readers have assumed that the hound, the bay horse, and the turtle dove were figurative containers or concrete vehicles into which some deeper, higher, or more abstract meanings could be made to fit. This is what the business of interpreting symbols is all about. In cases like the present, where there exists no unanimity or clarity about the symbols' meanings, readers tend to believe *not* that there is something inadequate about the way they are asking the question, but that each individual becomes "free" to settle on an answer for himself.

Before going back to attempt a different type of analysis of this passage, I would like first to quote in its entirety the paragraph that immediately precedes the hound-horse-dove passage in the text:

> In any weather, at any hour of the day or night, I have been anxious to improve the nick of time, and notch it on my stick too; to stand on the meeting of two eternities, the past and future, which is precisely the present moment; to toe that line. You will pardon some obscurities, for there are more secrets in my trade than in most men's, and yet not voluntarily kept, but inseparable from its very nature. I would gladly tell all that I know about it, and never paint "No Admittance" on my gate.
>
> I long ago lost a hound, a bay horse, and a turtle-dove, and am still on their trail. Many are the travellers I have spoken concerning them, describing their tracks and what calls they answered to. I have met one or two who had heard the hound, and the tramp of the horse, and even seen the dove disappear behind a cloud, and they seemed as anxious to recover them as if they had lost them themselves. (14–15)

There appears at first sight to be no relation between these two paragraphs. Yet the very abruptness of the transition, the very discrepancy of rhetorical modes, may perhaps indicate that the first paragraph consists of a set of instructions about how to read the second. It is surely no accident that one of the most enigmatic passages in *Walden* should be placed immediately after the sentence "You will pardon some obscurities." If the secret identities of the hound, the horse, and the dove are never to be revealed, it is not, says Thoreau, that they are being *voluntarily* withheld. Such secrets are simply inseparable from the nature of my trade—that is, writing. "I would gladly tell all that I know about it, and never paint 'No Admittance' on my gate." But all I *know* about it is not all there *is* about it. You are not being forcibly or gently kept away from a knowledge I possess. The gate is wide open, and that is why the path is so obscure. The sign "obscurity" is pointing directly at the symbols, making the sentence read, "I long ago lost an X, a Y, and a Z," and you are supposed to recognize them not as obscure symbols, but as symbols standing for the obscure, the lost, the irretrievable.

But yet, we insist, your X, Y, and Z are so *particular*—so houndlike, so horselike, so birdlike. If they merely symbolize the lost objects as such, why do we hear the baying of the hound and the tramp of the horse? Why do those fellow travellers give us such precise reports?

Ah, but you see, Thoreau might answer, the symbols *are* symbols, after all. What is lost is always intensely particular. Yet it is known only in that it is lost—lost in one of the two eternities between which we clumsily try to toe the line.

To follow the trail of what is lost is possible only, it seems, if the loss is maintained in a state of transference from traveller to traveller, so that each takes up the pursuit as if the loss were his own. Loss, then, ultimately belongs to an other; the losses we treat as our own are perhaps losses of which we never had conscious knowledge ourselves. "If others have their losses, which they are busy repairing, so have I *mine*, & their hound & horse may *perhaps* be the symbols of some of them. But also I have lost, or am in danger of losing, a far finer & more etherial treasure, which commonly no loss *of which they are conscious* will symbolize."

Walden's great achievement is to wake us up to our own lost losses, to make us participate in the transindividual movement of loss in its infinite particularity, urging us passionately to follow the tracks of we know not quite what, as if we had lost it, or were in danger of losing it, ourselves.

In order to communicate the irreducibly particular yet ultimately unreadable nature of loss, Thoreau has chosen to use three symbols that clearly *are* symbols but that do not really symbolize anything outside themselves. They are figures for which no literal, proper term can be substituted. They are, in other words, catachreses—"figures of abuse," figurative substitutes for a literal term that does not exist. Like the "legs" and "arms" of our favorite recliner,

Thoreau's hound, horse, and dove belong to a world of homely figurative richness, yet the impersonal literality they seem to pre-
suppose is nowhere to be found. The structure of catachretic
symbolism is thus the very structure of transference and loss.
Through it Thoreau makes us see that every lost object is always, in
a sense, a catachresis, a figurative substitute for nothing that ever
could be literal.

It could be said that Nature itself is for Thoreau a catachretic
symbol that enables him to displace his discourse without filling in
its symbolic tenor. But in order to analyze a more particular aspect
of the way in which Thoreau's catachretic rhetoric creates obscurity in *Walden*, let us first look at a more traditional and semantically "full" use of nature imagery: the *analogies* drawn between
natural objects and human predicaments.

I begin with a somewhat atypically explicit analogy:

> One day . . . I saw a striped snake run into the water, and he
> lay on the bottom, apparently without inconvenience, as long
> as I staid there, or more than a quarter of an hour; perhaps be-
> cause he had not yet fairly come out of the torpid state. It ap-
> peared to me that for a like reason men remain in their present
> low and primitive condition; but if they should feel the influ-
> ence of the spring of springs arousing them, they would of ne-
> cessity rise to a higher and more ethereal life. (31–32)

No rhetorical strategy could be more classical than this weaving of
analogy between the natural and the human worlds. It is the mark
of the moralist, the evangelist, the satirist, and the lyric poet, all of
which Thoreau indeed is. From the New Testament to Aesop and
Swedenborg, the natural world has been a source of figures of the
preoccupations and foibles of man. As Emerson puts it in his own
essay on Nature:

> The memorable words of history and the proverbs of nations
> consist usually of a natural fact, selected as a picture or para-
> ble of a moral truth. Thus; A rolling stone gathers no moss; A
> bird in hand is worth two in the bush; A cripple in the right
> way will beat a racer in the wrong; Make hay while the sun
> shines; 'Tis hard to carry a full cup even; Vinegar is the son of
> wine; The last ounce broke the camel's back; Long-lived trees
> make roots first;—and the like. In their primary sense these
> are trivial facts, but we repeat them for the value of their ana-
> logical import. What is true of proverbs, is true of all fables,
> parables, and allegories.[4]

4. Ralph Waldo Emerson, *Selected Prose and Poetry* (New York: Holt, Rinehart, and Winston, 1964), p. 20.

Yet although Thoreau draws on many centuries of analogical writing, there is a subtle difference in his rhetorical use of nature, and it is the specificity of that difference that I would like to attempt to identify in conclusion. The difference begins to become perceptible in the following examples:

> Why has man rooted himself thus firmly in the earth, but that he may rise in the same proportion into the heavens above?—for the nobler plants are valued for the fruit they bear at last in the air and light, far from the ground, and are not treated like the humbler esculents, which, though they may be biennials, are cultivated only till they have perfected their root, and often cut down at top for this purpose, so that most would not know them in their flowering season. (14)

> We don garment after garment, as if we grew like exogenous plants by addition without. Our outside and often thin and fanciful clothes are our epidermis or false skin, which partakes not of our life, and may be stripped off here and there without fatal injury; our thicker garments, constantly worn, are our cellular integument, or cortex; but our shirts are our liber or true bark, which cannot be removed without girdling and so destroying the man. (20)

In both these examples, what begins as a fairly routine analogy tends, in the course of its elaboration, to get wildly out of hand. The fascination with the vehicle as an object of attention in its own right totally eclipses the original anthropomorphic tenor. Words like "esculents," "biennials," "cortex," and "liber" pull away from their subordinate, figurative status and begin giving information about themselves, sidetracking the reader away from the original thrust of the analogy. In the first example, what begins as an opposition between nobler and humbler men and plants collapses as it is revealed that the humbler plants are humble only because they are never *allowed* to flower. In the second example, the hierarchy of integuments ends by privileging not the skin but the shirt as that part of a man that cannot be removed without destroying him. In an effort to show that man is confused about where his inside ends and his outside begins, Thoreau resorts to a logic of tree growth which entirely takes over as the exogenous striptease procedes.

It is perhaps in the "Bean-field" chapter that the rhetorical rivalries between the literal and the figurative, the tenor and the vehicle, become most explicit. On the one hand, Thoreau writes, "I was determined to know beans," and goes on to detail the hours of hoeing and harvesting, listing the names of weeds and predators, and accounting for outgo and income down to the last half penny. And on the other, he admits that "some must work in fields if only for the sake of tropes and expression, to serve a parable-maker one day" (111). He speaks of sowing the seeds of sincerity, truth, simplicity, faith, and innocence, asking, "Why concern ourselves so much about our beans for seed, and not be concerned at all about a new generation of men?" (113).

The perverse complexity of *Walden*'s rhetoric is intimately related to the fact that it is never possible to be sure what the rhetorical status of any given image is. And this is because what Thoreau has done in moving to Walden Pond is to move *himself*, literally, into the world of his own figurative language. The literal woods, pond, and bean field still assume the same classical rhetorical guises in which they have always appeared, but they are suddenly readable in addition as the nonfigurative ground of a naturalist's account of life in the woods. The ground has shifted, but the figures are still figures. When is it that we decide that Thoreau never lost that hound, that horse, and that dove? It is because we can never be absolutely sure, that we find ourselves forever on their trail.

Walden is obscure, therefore, to the extent that Thoreau has *literally* crossed over into the very parable he is writing, where *reality itself* has become a catachresis, both ground and figure at once, and where, he tells us, "if you stand right fronting and face to face to a fact, you will see the sun glimmer on both its surfaces, as if it were a cimeter, and feel its sweet edge dividing you through the heart and marrow" (70).

ROBERT SATTELMEYER

The Remaking of *Walden*†

By late 1848 and early 1849 the literary component of the "private business" that Henry Thoreau had gone to Walden Pond to transact seemed finally about to begin yielding a return on his investment. Since he had left his cabin in September 1847, after a stay of just over two years, Thoreau had been working alternately on two books that he had begun there. The first was *A Week on the Concord and Merrimack Rivers*, a compendium of his early works and a tribute to his late brother John woven into the narrative of a boating and hiking expedition they had taken in 1839. Like its successor, *A Week* was the product of a long gestation—almost ten years elapsed

---

† From *Writing the American Classics*, ed. James Barbour and Tom Quirk (Chapel Hill: University of North Carolina Press, 1990), pp. 53–78. Copyright © 1990 University of North Carolina Press. Reprinted by permission. *Walden* page numbers refer to this Norton Critical Edition.

between the experience on which it was based and the publication of the book. The second, called *Walden, or Life in the Woods*, treated his experiment at the pond and contained as a counterpoint an ambitiously conceived indictment of American and particularly New England materialist values. Now, some eighteen months later, *A Week* was finally finished and *Walden*, Thoreau thought, was also close to completion. He approached publishers with this two-book package, and after W. D. Ticknor offered to publish *Walden* but required him to underwrite the printing of *A Week* at a cost of $450, Thoreau finally arranged with James Munroe to publish *A Week* and to follow it up with *Walden*. He would still have to guarantee the cost of producing *A Week*, but Munroe at least did not require payment in advance, offering to let Thoreau repay the costs from the sales of the book.[1]

* * *

But "literary contracts are little binding," as he had prophetically written in the first draft of *Walden* (a remark he later canceled), and a number of circumstances were even then developing that would subvert his plans to publish *Walden* on the heels of *A Week*. His literary fortunes, his friendships, his domestic relations, his characteristic pursuits, and even his notion of his proper literary métier were to be transformed during the next year; and the book that he thought of as nearing completion would undergo an even more startling metamorphosis over the next five years, doubling in size, radically changing its structure, and shifting in subtle but profound ways the themes of its earliest versions before it finally saw print in the summer of 1854. The transformation, though dramatic, was natural and inevitable, for the book was an expression of the life, Thoreau's attempt to fulfill his own first requirement of a writer and render a simple and sincere account of himself. This task, as he knew, paradoxically rendered him liable to the charge of obscurity, for it was his real and not merely his actual life that he must attempt to represent. As his relations changed over the years, as his reflections on his life at the pond deepened, as his interest in nature became at once more passionate and more professional, and as his sense of his literary vocation developed in response to early disappointments, the book evolved along with the author until it became less a simple history of his life at Walden alternating with a critique of contemporary culture, and more the sum of his histories simultaneously present in a text at once fabular, mythic, scientific, and even scriptural in its dimensions.

1. See Linck C. Johnson, "Historical Introduction." In Henry D. Thoreau, *A Week on the Concord and Merrimack Rivers*, ed., Carl F. Hovde, William L. Howarth, and Elizabeth Hall Witherell (Princeton: Princeton University Press, 1980), 469–470.

* * *

In 1850, then, Thoreau had a manuscript of *Walden* that only inchoately reflected what he had learned at the pond, that did not embody the new directions his life was taking, and that was in any event probably unsalable. So he ceased thinking of the manuscript as finished, or nearly so. Perhaps he was temporarily soured on book publishing after his experience with *A Week*, but probably he was also awaiting such developments as his new modes of life and writing would bring. He did not let the book lie fallow, for he drafted into the journal passages of reflection on his life in the woods that were clearly intended for the manuscript and that were eventually added in later revisions.[2] But apparently he did not begin to revise the manuscript as a whole until sometime in 1852. Then he began energetically to work on *Walden* again, adding new material and revising previous drafts in four distinguishable stages, not counting his final fair copy for the printer, between 1852 and 1854.[3] Thus, although there are seven identifiable manuscript drafts (or, more precisely, partial drafts) of *Walden*, ranging from 1846 to 1854, its composition mainly took place in two phases. The first stage includes the first draft written at Walden in 1846–47, along with the second and third drafts that were written nearly together in 1848–49 and that primarily polish material in the first draft. The second stage consists of the four successive partial drafts written between 1852 and the book's publication in 1854.

* * *

Although there are doubtless subtle stages of growth that could be traced through virtually every year between 1845, when Thoreau began to write entries in the journal that were clearly designed for some literary work based on his life at the pond, and 1854, when the book was finally published, the most dramatic story involves the remaking of the book that took place during the second phase of composition between 1852 and 1854. Thoreau's conception of the work greatly enlarged and matured during these years, and if some of the portions that were added during this phase conflict with assertions made in the earlier versions, it is a mark of Thoreau's maturity as a writer and a thinker that he allowed such inconsistencies to stand. Much of the richness of the book ultimately derives, I be-

---

2. Henry D. Thoreau, *Journal 3: 1848–1851*, ed. Robert Sattelmeyer, Mark R. Patterson, and William Rossi (Princeton: Princeton University Press, 1990), "Historical Introduction," 483–84.
3. See J. Lyndon Shanley, *The Making of Walden* (Chicago: University of Chicago Press, 1957), 30–32; Ronald A. Clapper, "The Development of *Walden*: A Genetic Text," Ph. D. dissertation, University of California, Los Angeles, 1967, 31–32; see also Stephen Adams and Donald A. Ross, *Revising Mythologies: The Composition of Thoreau's Major Works* (Charlottesville: University Press of Virginia, 1988), 162–192, which appeared while this essay was in press.

lieve, from Thoreau's incorporation of reflections from the intervening years that are allowed to stand alongside accounts of his life
that he actually wrote at the pond, so that *Walden* is at once both
retrospective and dramatic. It embodies a summing but not a summing up of experience. I do not believe this effect was the result of
a conscious design on Thoreau's part, but rather that it came about
with a certain organic inevitability from the writer's steadfast application to his task during a period of artistic and intellectual growth.

At the same time, of course, Thoreau was highly self-conscious
about the process of revision, and *Walden*, moreover, like so many
other American books, calls attention to itself as a deliberately
composed text. It begins with an allusion (itself added in a late revision) to the very process of composition that I have been discussing: "When I wrote the following pages, or rather the bulk of
them, I lived alone, in the woods." This seemingly straightforward
reference to the immediate contextual circumstances of the book
introduces us immediately by means of a characteristic wordplay to
the writer's awareness of the difference between his immediate and
his later, mediated vision: only the "bulk" or gross proportions of
the book may be said to have been composed at the pond.

The greatest difference between the 1846–49 versions and the
1852–54 versions is that the second half of the book is much more
extensively developed in the later versions. Shanley summarized
the difference between the first draft and the published version as
follows:

> It [the first draft] represents various parts of *Walden* very un-
> evenly. It contains approximately 70 per cent of the first half—
> "Economy" through "The Bean Field"; a little less than 30 per
> cent of "The Village" through "Higher Laws" [chapters 8–11],
> and none of "Conclusion." Likewise, the second and third ver-
> sions, written in 1848–49, consist essentially of a recopying
> with some revision of the first two-thirds of the first draft, car-
> rying the story only through the material of the sixth chapter,
> "Visitors."[4]

Obviously these early versions were composed with a lecture audience in mind, and they may in fact have been used by Thoreau as
his lecture manuscript itself—a large mass of material that was not
divided into chapters but that could easily be broken up to suit the
number and length of his speaking engagements. The fact that a
greater proportion of this early material survives in the finished
form of the first half of the book than in the second half means
that the early chapters of *Walden* are much more closely tied to

---

4. Shanley, 94; see also Clapper, 30.

Thoreau's original design and purposes than the later chapters. These, in turn, he wrote for the most part with a book in mind, and they tend more than the first chapters to reflect his interests and concerns during the 1850s.

In reading the book, then, one responds to and follows not only the temporal structure of the Walden experience (the two years of Thoreau's life compressed into a single annual cycle from one spring to the next) but also and perhaps more subliminally the larger development of the narrator over the course of a decade of spiritual and intellectual growth. The effect is not one of "before" and "after," or of two different accounts of the growth of a mind such as one finds in the early and late versions of Wordsworth's *Prelude*, but rather of an earlier self subsumed but still present, as it were, within the later. Nevertheless some of the principal differences between the earlier and later versions of *Walden*, and to some extent the first and second halves of the book, may be described.

The early chapters, particularly "Economy" and "Where I Lived, and What I Lived For," betray their lineage as lecture material in a number of ways, the most obvious of which is their rhetorically high profile: they are more satiric, hyperbolic, confrontational, and full of invective than the later chapters. "I should not presume to talk so much about myself and my affairs as I shall in this lecture," the first version of *Walden* begins, "if very particular and personal inquiries had not been made concerning my mode of life." Beginning with this sardonic acknowledgment of those who had minded his business for him, Thoreau launches a counterattack against the "mean and sneaking lives" his contemporaries lived.[5] And, as he makes clear in an early journal draft of this lecture from the winter of 1845–46, he was particularly concerned to say something about his audience's "outward condition or circumstances in this world."[6] *Walden* was thus at first quite narrowly and parochially conceived: it was not until the post-1852 revisions that the phrase "Addressed to My Townsmen" was dropped from Thoreau's working title. The account of his own life in this version serves as an example that contrasts with the misapplication of force in most lives, but it is not a story whose deeper implications are fathomed. In fact, in the first draft his account of himself ends quite lamely—"Thus was my first year's life in the woods completed"—for clearly Thoreau did not yet realize what the experience signified for himself, however much he was aware of its exemplary potential for his contemporaries.[7]

The early versions and early chapters are also more outer-

5. Shanley, 105, 108.
6. Henry D. Thoreau, *Journal 2: 1842–1848*, ed. Robert Sattelmeyer (Princeton: Princeton University Press. 1984), 187.
7. Shanley, 208.

directed because they were largely conceived and executed during the height of Thoreau's interest in reform during the mid- to late 1840s. He had composed a lecture on reform and reformers during this period, written about reformers in *A Week*, and of course written "Resistance to Civil Government" in response to his night in jail in 1845. The 1840s were a millennial decade generally, and reform movements, ranging in seriousness from abolitionism to Sylvester Graham's advocacy of male chastity and a high-fiber diet, were pandemic in American culture. Within Transcendentalism itself there was a lively debate over reform, and the movement had spawned experimental communities at Brook Farm and Fruitlands. Responding to this climate, Thoreau conceived of his life at Walden at first as a kind of experimental community of one that could serve as a counterexample not only to the unawakened among his townspeople but also to the false reforms and reformers of his age. His earliest journal entries at Walden during the summer of 1845 blend accounts of his life with a critique of contemporary values and culture, and the first draft already contains an indictment of foolish philanthropy and false reforms.[8] Although he continued to be interested in the problem of reforming and reformers and would add much to this section of "Economy" through the various versions, by the early 1850s Thoreau's concern with social and political issues, like that of the nation at large, was increasingly focused on slavery, its extension, and the enforcement of the Fugitive Slave Law. These issues did not lend themselves to treatment in his manuscript in progress, and they would not culminate for him until the addresses he would deliver on John Brown after the Harper's Ferry raid in 1859. He would develop the book as a whole along quite different lines, be less insistent upon addressing the outward condition of humanity, and come to regard his experience at Walden less as an example to misguided reformers and more as a personal quest involving doubt and uncertainty as well as discovery.

The clearest indication of this change may be seen in the character of the narrator and his rhetoric in the second half of the book, the portion that was mostly written after 1852. From "The Ponds" on, the book is more introspective, meditative, and descriptive and contains relatively few passages of sustained satire. When there is a brief return to the themes of "Economy," as in the account of the Irishman John Field and his family in "Baker Farm," Thoreau's criticism is muted by sympathy, and the family is presented in such homely detail and with such particularity that, like their chickens, they become too humanized to roast well. Beginning with its namesake chapter, the pond itself becomes a major character, and

8. Shanley, 133–137.

Thoreau appears to have been pacified by its waters. In contrast to his stance in the early chapters, like Ishmael in *Moby-Dick* he no longer seems to have a maddened hand and splintered heart turned against the wolfish world; like Ishmael, too, he turns instead to a journey in which meditation and water are wedded and which has as its aim the discovery of the ungraspable phantom of life—even if he has to be content with less exotic surroundings and pursuits: traveling a good deal in Concord, having for a soothing savage Alek Therien the woodchopper, and fishing for pouts on Walden Pond.

The major mark of the book's altered conception in the post-1852 expansions is the extent to which Thoreau developed and amplified the seasonal cycle that undergirds the structure of *Walden*. Shanley describes, for example, the changes made in this aspect of the book during the fifth version, written during late 1852 and early 1853:

> The greatest growth in Thoreau's conception of *Walden* resulted, however, from his seeing how he might fill out his account of the progress of the seasons and describe the changes they had brought in his daily affairs and thoughts; by doing so, he would express more adequately the richness and the completeness of his experience. He had to develop particularly the fall and part of the winter. He did so by greatly enlarging "Brute Neighbors," by developing "House-Warming" for the first time, and by completing "Winter Visitors"; he also made significant though smaller additions to "Winter Animals" and "The Pond in Winter." There was so much new material in version V that Thoreau was not able simply to insert it in previous copy as he had done with most of the new material in IV. He had to make fresh copy of practically all of "The Ponds," "Higher Laws," "Brute Neighbors," "House-Warming," "Former Inhabitants; and Winter Visitors," and "The Pond in Winter."[9]

The cumulative effect of these additions was to alter the focus of the book radically. In the early versions the critique of American culture dominated ("Economy" and "Where I Lived, and What I Lived For" still make up nearly a third of the finished book, and represented an even larger proportion in the early drafts), in which the story of Thoreau's own life served, as we have already seen, as a counterpoint. The cyclical pattern of the year was relatively unimportant. Now, however, with the annual cycle developed and amplified, there exists for the first time a "story" with a kind of plot: the journey or quest of the narrator passing through various changes marked by the progress of the season and advancing toward some

9. Shanley, 67.

kind of self-knowledge. The book begins to acquire mythic and archetypal dimensions and, in the relative deemphasis of social criticism attendant upon the expansion of these other elements, becomes less topical and more universal in its reference.

Doubtless the addition of material about fall, winter, and the second spring contributes to verisimilitude and to a felt sense of the passage of a year. There is a satisfying structural coherence about this pattern as realized in the finished book, a kind of harmonic or tonic closure felt in arriving once more at spring. At the same time, however, this is a relatively simple, unsophisticated, and not particularly novel structure. The same pattern may be said to inform the *Farmer's Almanac*. Nor is the discovery of the seasonal cycle itself what is most important. Critics have occasionally pointed to a journal entry for 18 April 1852, in which Thoreau announces "For the first time I perceive this spring that the year is a circle," as marking such an insight and signaling a new design for *Walden* (*J*, 3:438).[1] But surely Richard Lebeaux is correct to point out that "more likely, he was indicating that this was the first time *this spring* that he had seen the year is a circle."[2] For a naturalist to observe for the first time at age thirty-five that the year is a circle is equivalent to a hydrologist's discovering that water runs downhill. As Robert D. Richardson, Jr., has recently observed, with several decades of critical explication of the seasonal structure in mind, "We have made too much of the seasonal structure of *Walden*, too easily assuming that the book's message is to accept the seasonal cycle of nature as final wisdom. Such a view, essentially objective, conservative, and tragic, is not at last what Thoreau wanted or taught."[3]

Thoreau developed the seasonal emphasis of *Walden* not because it was the logical structure for his book but because he was interested in the seasons of his own life and because he came to believe, as he put it in the fall of 1857, "These regular phenomena of the seasons get at last to be—they were *at first* of course—simply and plainly phenomena or phases of my life. The seasons and all their changes are in me." He concluded this entry by remarking "The perfect correspondence of Nature to man, so that he is at home in her!" (*J*, 10:127).[4] The remaking of *Walden* in large part involves an effort to tell the truth of the first proposition by following out the

---

1. *The Journal of Henry D. Thoreau*, ed. Bradford Torrey and Francis H. Allen (Boston: Houghton Mifflin, 1949), 3:438. Subsequent references to this edition are cited parenthetically in the text.

2. Richard Lebeaux, *Thoreau's Seasons* (Amherst: University of Massachusetts Press, 1984), 159.

3. Robert D. Richardson, Jr., *Thoreau: A Life of the Mind* (Berkeley and Los Angeles: University of California Press, 1986), 310.

4. The importance of this passage is pointed out by Lebeaux, 293; I am also indebted in the following passages on the seasons of *Walden* to Lebeaux's discussion of the issue in chapter 5, "Second Spring," 151–197.

artistic implications of the second—the "perfect correspondence" by which nature's seasons express our own.

It was the need to probe the meaning of his Walden experience, to come to terms with the great event in his life, and by writing to relive and recapture that experience, rather than discovering that the year is a circle, that stimulated Thoreau to begin expanding his manuscript in 1852. In January—the tenth anniversary of his brother John's death and very close to the time he began working on the manuscript again—he asked himself in the journal:

> But why I changed? why I left the woods? I do not think that I can tell. I have often wished myself back. I do not know any better how I ever came to go there. Perhaps it is none of my business, even if it is yours. . . . I must say that I do not know what made me leave the pond. I left it as unaccountably as I went to it. To speak sincerely, I went there because I had got ready to go; I left it for the same reason. (*J*, 3:214, 216)[5]

Two days later, on 24 January, he admonished himself to take up his pen in the service of fathoming such mysteries at the same time that he lamented his own inability to recapture the glorious past:

> If thou art a writer, write as if the time were short, for it is indeed short at the longest. Improve each occasion when thy soul is reached. Drain the cup of inspiration to its last dregs. Fear no intemperance in that, for the years will come when otherwise thou wilt regret opportunities unimproved. The spring will not last forever. These fertile and expanding seasons of thy life, when the rain reaches thy root, when thy vigor shoots, when thy flower is budding, shall be fewer and farther between. Again I say, remember thy Creator in the days of thy youth. . . . Why did I not use my eyes when I stood on Pisgah? Now I hear those strains but seldom. My rhythmical mood does not endure. I cannot draw from it and return to it in my thoughts as to a well all the evening or the morning. I cannot dip my pen in it. I cannot work the vein, it is so fine and volatile. Ah, sweet, ineffable reminiscences! (*J*, 3:221–22)

This despondency, a recurring nightmare of the Romantics, who most feared that they might cease to feel, was only temporary, but it points toward the complex of emotions that led Thoreau to reconceive *Walden*. Uncertainty about his motives for going to and leaving the pond dogged him, and he felt that he must answer those questions for himself through his writing, even though he temporarily doubted his ability to work the vein. He must create an account of his former experience that would satisfy the demands of

5. See Journal selections, p. 361 [*Editor*]

imagination and memory, rather like the speaker of Frost's "The Road Not Taken," who really knows that there was no perceptible difference between the two paths at the time but also knows that he must invent a story that will account for the distance he has traveled and also link himself with his own past: "I shall be telling this with a sigh / Somewhere ages and ages hence."

So the new work on *Walden* primarily expanded the later sections of the book that describe autumn, winter, and the second spring, a seasonal epoch in which mature affirmation comes only after a long probation and after having faced doubt, anxiety, and even evil in both the self and nature. At the same time, it needs to be kept in mind that much of this pattern is implicit, as Thoreau tends to editorialize less and to write less explicitly about himself in these sections, depending more on the "perfect correspondence" between man and nature to endow his descriptions of natural phenomena with human significance.

Something of an exception to this pattern of implicitness, and an exception that may serve by its expository nature as a convenient example of the altered tone of Thoreau's thinking, is the chapter "Higher Laws," most of which was added, apparently, during the fourth through the seventh versions. It had started out as a treatise on fishing and hunting, leading to a discussion of diet and advocating vegetarianism on both economic and philosophical grounds. In this respect it was consistent with the emphasis on reform and the subject matter of the early versions. Until the sixth version, in fact, it carried the title "Animal Food."[6] But the original tension in the chapter—Thoreau's genuine ambivalence about hunting and especially fishing—is eventually cast into the shade in later versions by a more serious conflict between "animal" and "spiritual": "We are conscious of an animal in us, which awakens in proportion as our higher nature slumbers" (149). This conflict most dramatically expressed itself for Thoreau over the issues of what he termed chastity and sensuality. Whatever the efficient cause of this concern, he was troubled by his own inability to master this side of his nature. He cannot speak of these topics, he fears, without betraying his own impurity. In the fifth version he canceled an even more revealing sentence: "I do not know how it is with other men, but I find it very difficult to be chaste."[7] These fears, obviously arising out of personal experience of some kind, lead to the pronouncement that "Nature is hard to be overcome, but she must be overcome" (150), a statement that seems hopelessly in conflict with the narrator's stance toward nature elsewhere.

This assertion may be reconcilable with Thoreau's attitude to-

6. Clapper, "The Development of *Walden*," 566.
7. Clapper, "The Development of *Walden*," 588.

ward nature in other passages, but the tension is really central to the completed book, I think, and a sign of maturity on Thoreau's part, a recognition that nature and the human self in which it is reflected have depths heretofore unplumbed but needing to be faced. Thoreau's apprehensions about purity and chastity, while they may appear only quaint or priggish to a twentieth-century audience, represent an acknowledgement by him of a part of his nature more basic (and base) than he had previously seen. Something of this recognition carried over and expressed itself in his revisions of other portions of *Walden*, in the course of which he was able to develop this line of thought in more positive ways.

The realization that his own as well as external nature possessed such subterranean dimensions could be exhilarating as well as disquieting. It carried Thoreau some distance toward a theory of the unconscious and led him to speculate on the extent to which intellectual and creative activity was dependent upon functions of the mind that lay below the threshold of conscious thought. Characteristically, he expressed his insight in terms of a correspondence between man and nature, in a journal entry in 1851, just before beginning his major reworking of *Walden*. Having read the botanist Asa Gray's description of how a plant grows upward toward the light and simultaneously downward, he observed:

> So the mind develops from the first in two opposite directions: upwards to expand in the light and air; and downwards avoiding the light to form the root. One half is aerial, the other subterranean. The mind is not well balanced and firmly planted, like the oak, which has not as much root as branch, whose roots like those of the white pine are slight and near the surface. One half of the mind's development must still be root,—in the embryonic state, in the womb of nature, more unborn than at first. For each successive new idea or bud, a new rootlet in the earth. The growing man penetrates yet deeper by his roots into the womb of things. The infant is comparatively near the surface, just covered from the light; but the man sends down a tap-root to the centre of things. (*J*, 2:203)

The most dramatic application of this perspective in *Walden* is Thoreau's radical revision and amplification of the climactic sand foliage passages in "Spring" during the last versions, where this "truly *grotesque*" (that is, coming from underground) vegetation manifests the generative and creative forces of nature, however visceral or excremental its appearance (205). Thoreau had reached an earlier stage of understanding the beneficial potential of such threatening and disturbing natural forces on his first trip to the Maine wilderness in 1846, when he came in contact on Mount Katahdin with a kind of nature that threatened to extinguish rather than heighten consciousness and when he had also faced the fact that here "one could no longer accuse institutions and society, but must front the true source of evil" (that is, the self).[8] This knowledge in turn had already led him to express in the first draft of *Walden*, composed the following year, a theory of the necessity of wild nature to the human psyche that incorporated the essentially ungraspable nature of nature as a positive fact: "At the same time that we are in earnest to explore and learn all things, we require that all things be mysterious and unexplorable, that land and sea be infinitely wild, unsurveyed and unfathomed by us because unfathomable. We can never have enough of Nature" (213).[9]

Paradoxically, that we can never have enough of nature and that nature must also be overcome are but different expressions of the same fact, the complexity of our own nature that grows upward and downward at the same time. There is a womb of nature and an answering womb—dark, unconscious, and powerful—in the mind. Ultimately Thoreau renders nature more complexly in the later versions of *Walden* because he sees human nature more complexly, starting with his own. Accounts of natural phenomena convey little of what Thoreau termed in *A Week* "the mealy-mouthed enthusiasm of the lover of Nature." To the fourth version, for example, he added the account of the battle of the ants to "Brute Neighbors," unflinchingly observing—even under a microscope—the "internecine war" in nature that was going on underfoot. And the owls in "Sounds," which in the first versions stood rather conventionally and melodramatically for the "fallen souls that once in human shape night-walked the earth," come to suggest by the fourth version "a vast and undeveloped nature which men have not recognized. They represent the stark twilight and unsatisfied thoughts which all have." As one might almost predict, the last phrase originally read "which I have."[1]

The expansion of the fall and winter chapters of the manuscript during the second stage of composition thus created a strong counterpoint to and eventual transformation of the dominant spring imagery of *Walden*. The new proportions suggest, of course, that Thoreau became increasingly concerned with his own awakening and less obsessed with waking up his neighbors. They also suggest, at the level of seasonal change in the narrator, that the second spring is of a different order of magnitude than and not merely a repetition of the first, and comes as a result of his having sent down his "tap-root into the centre of things." By doing so, he succeeds

8. Thoreau, "Ktaadn, and the Maine Woods." In *The Maine Woods*, ed. Joseph J. Moldenhauer (Princeton: Princeton University Press, 1972), 16.
9. Shanley, 207.
1. Clapper, 361–364.

himself, the self that like an infant was "comparatively near the surface" in understanding the phenomena of his own life.

The second spring is a kind of second growth intimately related
and akin to the second growth of autumn itself, a time when fruits
mature and seeds ripen. Thoreau had not earned the affirmations
of the "Conclusion" (the last chapter to be written) until he had
achieved the mature growth depicted in "The Ponds" through
"Spring." This phase of *Walden*, in which autumnal imagery
abounds, points toward the predominantly autumnal atmosphere of
Thoreau's later essays: the close of "Walking," say, or the whole of
"Wild Apples" and "Autumnal Tints." He had arrived at an autumnal phase in his own life, in which the fruit of his earlier experiences at Walden had matured, experiences that enjoy a kind of
second spring in his imaginative recreation of them in the book.
The questions he had begun his revision by asking ("But why I left
the woods?") he could now answer: "I left the woods for as good a
reason as I went there. . . . " (217). Thoreau largely effaced from
the final text the fact that this affirmation arose out of a profound
experience of self-doubt and even disgust (such as we glimpse in
"Higher Laws"), but it is evident in the manuscript, in which the
following aside to the passage just quoted is preserved:

> If the reader think that I am vainglorious, and set myself above
> others, I assure him that I could tell a pitiful story respecting
> myself as well as him if my spirits held out, could encourage
> him with a sufficient list of failures, and flow humbly as the
> gutters. I think worse of myself than he is likely to think of me,
> and better too, being better acquainted with the man. Finally, I
> will tell him this secret, if he will not abuse my confidence—I
> put the best face on the matter.[2]

Nevertheless the fable of *Walden*, he thought, expressing his mature vision (and contained in miniature in the story of the Artist of
Kouroo in the "Conclusion"), had a lasting quality that would make
up for early disappointments and self-doubts. He believed himself
to be, in the best and most nearly literal sense of the term, a late-
bloomer, and he confided as much to his journal in April 1854,
while reading proof for *Walden*:

> Some poets mature early and die young. Their fruits have a de-
> licious flavor like strawberries, but do not keep till fall or win-
> ter. Others are slower in coming to their growth. Their fruits
> may be less delicious, but are a more lasting food and are so
> hardened by the sun of summer and the coolness of autumn
> that they keep sound over winter. The first are June-eatings,

2. Clapper, 854.

early but soon withering; the last are russets, which last till June again. (*J*, 6:190–91)[3]

Besides the emphasis on the seasons and the corresponding story of individual growth, the most important major change between the early and later versions of *Walden* lies in the more learned and scientific cast of the later additions and revisions. The maturity of the final version is not a matter of age and self-knowledge alone, but of knowledge of the world. It takes the form of a theory of nature, which, as Emerson had said in his first book, *Nature*, was the aim of all science. In the finished version of *Walden* Thoreau is a scientist; not a scientist in precisely the sense we assume the term to mean today, but a scientist nevertheless, one who believed that the results of his investigations into nature expressed actual and not merely "poetic" truth. "Spring"—and especially the climactic account of thawing sand and clay in the railroad cut—contains not only the apogee of Thoreau's personal growth and rebirth but also the conclusion of his scientific investigation of the laws that underlie natural phenomena. The fact that these two investigations culminate together does not mean that one is a "symbol" of the other but rather that, for Thoreau, there really was a "perfect correspondence of Nature to man" that it was his mission to describe.

Thoreau's development as a natural scientist during the years of *Walden*'s second growth was coincident, however, with his more general development as a reader and thinker. He had always possessed something of a scholarly cast of mind, and since college he had kept a series of commonplace books in which he recorded passages from his reading. But like his journal-keeping, after 1850 this note-taking became more detailed and regular, and over the years his store of learning found its way into the *Walden* manusript in hundreds of quotations from and allusions to his reading.[4] These additions were spread throughout the manuscript, so that the consistently high level of allusiveness becomes a persistent textural and even thematic element of the entire book, deepening its level of reference, mitigating the parochial nature of its subject matter, and extending its appeal, by implication, to a much broader audience than the "my townsmen" of the original subtitle.

***In *Walden* these allusions work as part of the retrospective urge of the book that complements the immediacy of the material actually composed at the pond; they constitute a "re-search" impulse that broadens the implications of particular episodes and connects the activities described to the wider human community both past and present.

---

3. See Journal selections, p. 375 [*Editor*].
4. See Sattelmeyer, *Thoreau's Reading* (Princeton: Princeton University Press, 1988), 75–77.

In this context Thoreau's scientific expansions to *Walden* are a subset of these pervasive amplifications drawn from reading and observation. On a more fundamental level, however, the more scientific cast of the revised book, with its emphasis on the careful and detailed description of such central phenomena as the pond itself, the habits of various animals—now identified by genus and species as well as popular name—the Walden ice, and above all the thawing sand and clay of the railroad embankment, reflects Thoreau's commitment to natural history studies (along with writing, of course) as his principal life's work. Until quite recently at any rate, it has been the custom to derogate Thoreau's abilities as a scientist, as though his unfitness in this field were a necessary precondition to taking him seriously as an artist. But whatever the actual merits of his scientific work, it is clear that he regarded his studies seriously, and equally clear that he had a good grasp of contemporary theoretical controversies in the natural sciences during the years before Darwin's *Origin of Species* (1859) signaled the triumph of a paradigm that has held sway ever since.[5] Certainly he was not doing "normal" science from a post-Darwinian perspective; he was, however, operating according to scientific traditions and theoretical orientations quite viable in his own day, and it is from this perspective that his natural history studies in *Walden* (as well as his post-*Walden* essays in this field) are best understood.

Basic to Thoreau's methodology as a naturalist is an emphasis on perception and the centrality of the observer, features which today of course tend to relegate natural history to the status of "soft" science if it is considered a scientific discipline at all. He inherited this emphasis from Goethe, who was the founding father, so to speak, of the German school of *Naturphilosophie* from which Thoreau drew much of his theoretical orientation and whose most distinguished practitioner in America was Louis Agassiz. For Thoreau the perceiving consciousness was not a "personality" that distorted the accuracy of observation but a necessary component of the equation by which phenomena could be understood and rendered meaningful. In order to write "The Ponds," for instance, one of the key chapters of *Walden*, he worked for several years observing Walden under different conditions, making excursions for that specific purpose and writing up his observations in the journal for eventual incorporation into the book. The portrait that eventually emerged emphasized the purity of the pond and the myriad ways that any natural fact, carefully and accurately perceived, dissolves

---

5. See Sattelmeyer, 78–92; also John Hildebidle, *Thoreau, A Naturalist's Liberty* (Cambridge: Harvard University Press, 1984); William L. Howarth, *The Book of Concord* (New York: Viking Press, 1982), 190–211; and William Rossi, " 'Laboratory of the Artist': Henry Thoreau's Literary and Scientific Use of the Journal, 1848–1854," Ph.D. dissertation. University of Minnesota, 1986, especially 151–201.

the difference between perceiver and perceived: "A lake is the land-scape's most beautiful and expressive feature. It is earth's eye; look-ing into which the beholder measures the depth of his own nature" (128). This statement is not finally a geologic anthropomorphism, or even a literary conceit, but an expression of the belief that the study of nature is ultimately the study of the self, for it is only after many years of observation that this relationship suggests itself (this particular passage first appeared in the sixth version).

Thoreau's descriptions of the ponds are largely about the process of perception itself, emphasizing that what we see when we look at a body of water is its surface and a boundary where two elements meet. The results of observation here depend upon the position of the observer relative to the object observed—a kind of perceptual relativity that points out (as relativity theory in physics also does) the illusory nature of absolute measurement. Walden is "a perfect forest mirror" that registers all change and all life on its surface, above its surface, and even below its surface, while at the same time continually changing color itself depending on conditions both known and unknown. The picture of the pond is a series of partial perceptions, each stressing the vantage point of the per-ceiver as a major component. In the four paragraphs that constitute the central description of Walden Pond itself, for example, we find the following markers of place: "You may see from a boat," "I have in my mind's eye," "Standing on the smooth sandy beach," "When you invert your head," "From a hilltop," and "on such a height as this, overlooking the pond" (128–29).

The final perspective in this section, a paragraph that first ap-pears in the fifth version, takes us in imagination to a still higher vantage point and demonstrates concretely how the seen proves the unseen:

> A field of water betrays the spirit that is in the air. It is con-tinually receiving new life and motion from above. It is inter-mediate in its nature between land and sky. On land only the grass and trees wave, but the water itself is rippled by the wind. I see where the breeze dashes across it by the streaks or flakes of light. We shall, perhaps, look down thus on the sur-face of air at length, and mark where a still subtler spirit sweeps over it. (129–30)

Characteristically, Thoreau begins by emphasizing a key word—"field"—that operates, like nature itself, at several levels simultane-ously, suggesting a range of meanings from the most obvious (an open expanse) to progressively more complex suggestions of the re-lation between the observer and what is observed: a field as that which is bounded (field of vision); a field as the subject of study or calling (as in his "half-cultivated field" in "The Bean Field"); and as a space upon which something is drawn or projected. The surface of the pond is more interesting and significant for the meaning it may transmit than for any significance which may be said to reside in it intrinsically. Both nature and the language with which the poet describes it are, as Emerson said in "The Poet," vehicular and transitive.

If "The Ponds" stresses methodology and the importance of the observer, "Spring" emphasizes results. The famous passages describing the sand foliage that effloresces on the railroad cut—sure evidence of a spring that "precedes the green and flowery spring"—announce the discovery of a law in nature, a discovery that coincides with Thoreau's own second spring. His perception, rightly trained and furnished once more with several years' careful study of the phenomenon, is able to anticipate spring and discern the operation of fundamental principles of generation and creativity in nature, while at the same time discovering the operation of the same power in himself. It needs to be stressed that the thawing sandbank is not intended by Thoreau as a figurative equivalent of his own awakening but rather as evidence of the operation of a law that animates both nature and man.

Like the descriptions of the ponds, Thoreau's account of the sand foliage was the product of several years of observation and evolution in his thought. In the first version the phenomenon elicits only a brief mention as one of the signs of spring:

> As I go back and forth over the rail-road through the deep cut I have seen where the clayey sand *like lava* had flowed down when it thawed and as it streamed it assumed the forms of vegetation, of vines and stout pulpy leaves—unaccountably interesting and beautiful—as if its course were so to speak a diagonal between fluids & solids—and it were hesitating whether to stream in to a river, or into vegetation—for vegetation too is such a stream as a river, only of a slower current.[6]

By the final version this account had grown to more than 1,500 words, and what was at first "unaccountably interesting and beautiful" came eventually to illustrate no less than "the principle of all the operations of Nature," the underlying ur-phenomenon of the leaf, which metamorphoses from the lowest and presumably inorganic forms of matter upward to higher life forms until "the very globe continually transcends and translates itself, and becomes winged in its orbit" (206).[7] Thoreau was composing material for

6. Shanley, 204.
7. For Journal passages indicating Thoreau's successive study of this phenomenon, see pp. 345–47; 355–56; 371; and 374–75 [*Editor*].

this section in the journal right up until *Walden* went to press. He added the climactic phrase "There is nothing inorganic," as well as the longer passage quoted below, in an entry for 5 February 1854. This conclusion is less a private testimony of faith than a challenge to prevailing scientific paradigms:

> The earth is not a mere fragment of dead history, stratum upon stratum like the leaves of a book, to be studied by geologists and antiquaries chiefly, but living poetry like the leaves of a tree, which precede flowers and fruit,—not a fossil earth, but a living earth; compared with whose great central life all animal and vegetable life is merely parasitic. (207)

Here, translating and metamorphosing the figure of the leaf, he contrasts his discovery of the creative force working through nature to both the older eighteenth-century argument from design, which discovered evidence of creation at some former date, and the developing orthodoxy of positivist science, which sees all nature ultimately as matter capable of being broken down and analyzed. To say that the earth is "living poetry" is not merely to make a figure of speech but to express a conviction that the same power that animates the poet's creativity works through and animates nature as well. Thoreau did not think of himself as making a statement that was poetically true only. One of his key revisions in this section of "Spring" was to alter his conception of the agency behind this power. In an early version he had felt himself to be standing "in the studio of an artist" when witnessing this phenomenon, but in the final version he stands "in the *laboratory* of the Artist who made the world and me" (emphasis added).[8] This fusion of the perspective of the scientist and the artist reflects Thoreau's stubborn resistance to the notion of there being two truths—one imaginative and one scientific—and likewise reflects the extent to which the climactic insights of *Walden* owe their origin to his own absorption in the natural sciences during the book's second growth.

Walden ultimately invalidates the apology Thoreau once offered for his attempt to fuse life and art—"My life has been the poem I would have writ / But I could not both live and utter it." His response to changes in himself as well as in his outward circumstances during the 1850s, along with his newfound commitments to the journal and his natural history studies, helped him to deepen and enrich the story of his life at the pond far beyond its expression in the book he wanted to publish in 1849. At the same time, the formal elements of *Walden*—its architectonics, its style, the relation of its parts to the whole—ought not to be considered as fixed

8. *Walden* 205; see Rossi, 200.

or final in the version that Thoreau published in 1854. Its form no less than its content was dictated by his life, and had he delayed publishing it still further the book would doubtless have continued to evolve along with him. His revisions were not directed toward filling out or realizing a design that he kept before him but toward incorporating stages of growth within the design that already existed. *Walden* is, in this respect, an archetypal Romantic text, like *Leaves of Grass*, that developed as its author developed and that preserves experience while continually reinterpreting it.

* * *

H. DANIEL PECK

The Worlding of Walden†

"Why do precisely these objects which we behold make a world?" Thoreau asks in "Brute Neighbors," chapter 12 of *Walden*. This is the central question that *Walden* seeks to answer and to which *Walden* itself is an answer. The word "precisely" reveals the assumption underlying the question, with its clear implication that the world as we know it corresponds exactly to our needs and expectations. "Why has man," Thoreau continues, "*just* these species of animals for his neighbors; as if nothing but a mouse could have filled this crevice?" (153; emphasis added). The world we know through perception is a "fitting" world, a world of balance and symmetry. In the terms of our discussion of the Journal, it is a category filled to its exact limits and no more, "a world with full and fair proportions" (220), as Thoreau calls the staff made by the artist of Kouroo.

The brief descriptions of Thoreau's "brute neighbors" that follow these questions are, he seems to say, as full an answer as anyone will ever need: the "mice which haunted my house"; the phoebe that "built in my shed"; the robin that found protection in the pine next to the hut; the partridge that led her brood past the windows; the otter and raccoon that lived nearby; the woodcock probing for worms; the turtledoves that sat over the spring; the red squirrel "coursing down the nearest bough" (153–55).

The simple, enumerative quality of this passage (it resembles both in form and intention one of the Journal's lists) makes clear that

---

† From *Thoreau's Morning Work: Memory and Perception in A Week on the Concord and Merrimack Rivers, the Journal, and Walden* (New Haven: Yale University Press, 1990), pp. 117–32. Copyright © 1990. Reprinted by permission of Yale University Press. *Walden* page numbers refer to this Norton Critical Edition.

these "neighbors" are constituents of a world already organized and prepared by nature for human perception, and that perception, in fact, has very little work to do: "You only need sit still long enough in some attractive spot in the woods that *all* its inhabitants may exhibit themselves to you by turns" (155; emphasis added). Walden is that axial point from which, by simply watching and waiting, one may "behold" the full kaleidoscope of nature's phenomena.

This is the centralized perspective that was announced earlier in the chapter "Where I Lived, and What I Lived For": "Wherever I sat, there I might live, and the landscape radiated from me accordingly" (58). Everything that enters this radius, by definition, belongs to a proximate world, a world of "the nearest bough." Like the red squirrel, all the creatures perceived from this perspective are "familiar" (155) to Thoreau; they are already familiarized, prepared for the imagination by their placement within the world of Walden.

But immediately following this brisk enumeration of the animals and birds in Thoreau's peaceable kingdom, the chapter takes an abrupt turn: "I was witness to events of a less peaceful character" (155). And, indeed, the description of the ant-war that follows shows us a rapacious natural world sharply at odds with that of the turtledove and the phoebe. But what it also shows us is a different mode of apprehension, a different way of "beholding." So often discussed is this famous set piece that I need not recount here the pitched battle of the ants or the brilliant play of metaphor with which it is narrated. For the purpose of this discussion, the most important element of the piece is a Thoreauvian gesture having nothing to do with the battle as such: "I took up the chip on which the three [ants] I have particularly described were struggling, carried it into my house, and placed it under a tumbler on my window-sill, in order to see the issue. Holding a microscope to the first-mentioned red ant, I saw that, though he was assiduously gnawing at the near fore-leg of his enemy . . . his own breast was all torn away" (156).

Mere watchful waiting is insufficient to view these brute neighbors (the oxymoron making itself felt in this context). Their size, as well as the complexity of their movements, requires that they be scrutinized under a microscope. For all the self-conscious literary allusiveness of the piece, its dominant spirit is that of the observer-scientist, and the microscope itself is a figure for this analytical mode of apprehension. The naturalist's view of nature makes itself felt often in the Journal, but in *Walden* it is generally subordinated to other, more "aesthetic" modes of apprehension. This is one reason, apart from its hyperbolic and burnished prose, why the ant-war passage sometimes seems out of place, rather like some of the more intrusive digressions in *A Week*.

As different as the ant-war is from the scene that precedes it, however, these passages share one important trait: both the simple beholding of the one and the intense scrutiny of the other are the acts of a subject-viewer totally in control of his perceptions. But now, following Thoreau's description of the ant-war, we find ourselves in the realm of the fortuitous: "Once I was surprised to see a cat walking along the stony shore of the pond, for they rarely wander so far from home"; "Once, when berrying, I met with a cat with young kittens in the woods, quite wild, and they all, like their mother, had their backs up and were fiercely spitting at me" (158).

These instances of the unexpected and the "wild" are followed by the description of a mysterious " 'winged cat,' " whose presence in the town of Lincoln several years before the Walden experiment was reported to Thoreau by Mrs. Gilian Baker, who had taken it in. Everything about this creature is elusive: when Thoreau goes to see it, it has "gone a-hunting in the woods, as was her wont," and he is "not sure whether it was a male or female." This winged cat, never actually observed by Thoreau, finally becomes a local legend: "Some thought it was part flying-squirrel or some other wild animal, which is not impossible, for, according to naturalists, prolific hybrids have been produced by the union of the marten and domestic cat" (158). But, in the end, no naturalist will ever have the opportunity to examine this strange animal, whose hybrid nature symbolizes its essential mystery and unclassifiability.[1]

The surprising cats described in this passage prepare us for the wildest of Walden's creatures, the loon.[2] Though its appearance is predictable ("the loon . . . came, as usual" [158]), the announcement of its arrival—"his wild laughter"—signals how unpredictable its actions are. Now the "surprise" caused by the cats is replaced by astonishment, wonder, and disorientation. The sense of the fortuitous increases: "As I was paddling along the north shore one very calm October afternoon, . . . suddenly one [loon], sailing out from the shore toward the middle a few rods in front of me, set up his wild laugh and betrayed himself."

The calm is broken and the chase is on, but Thoreau's pursuit is

---

1. Thoreau secures a set of the creature's "wings," but he does not report having studied them, and their import in the passage is to intensify rather than diminish the mystery.
2. As Charles R. Anderson, considering the loon passage as a reworking of an Algonquin myth, points out, Thoreau gives the loon a wildness "entirely missing from the Indian legends" and gave even greater emphasis to this quality in the first version of "Brute Neighbors" (*The Magic Circle of Walden* [New York: Holt, Rinehart, and Winston, 1968], 196–97). This great passage, as well as the passage that begins "Why do these objects which we behold make a world?", are late additions to *Walden*—both indebted to Thoreau's rich discoveries of perception in the early 1850s. See Shanley, *The Making of Walden*, 72–73, and Adams and Ross, *Revising Mythologies*, 169–70. [Full bibliographical information for works cited only by author and title in this excerpt may be found in the Selected Bibliography—*Editor*.]

repeatedly interrupted, his expectations defeated at every "turn": "He dived again, but I miscalculated the direction he would take" (159); "again and again, when I was straining my eyes over the surface one way, I would suddenly be startled by his unearthly laugh behind me." The loon's laugh, as well as its "long-drawn unearthly howl," are the sounds of the uncanny: "the wildest sound that is ever heard here" (160). In contrast to the winged cat, here is a creature that never can be domesticated.

The loon's "demoniac laughter" is mocking; unlike the gentle creatures that surround the hut, but the loon insists upon its separateness from its observer. Thoreau's failed pursuit of the loon dramatizes this creature's refusal to be contained (familiarized) within the Edenic vision of Walden sketched earlier in the chapter, or to be brought under the naturalist's microscope, as in the ant-war passage. It exists in a realm beyond the proximate world of Thoreau's hut. (Here is a creature at home in all dimensions, in water and sky, in the depths and heights of Walden.) The entire scene emphasizes the independence of object from subject: "While he was thinking one thing in his brain, I was endeavoring to divine his thought in mine." Unlike the ants, which Thoreau picks up and takes indoors to examine, his "adversary" (159) the loon escapes him, "disappearing far away on the tumultuous surface" (160).

But if the loon insists upon its separateness from Thoreau, scenically they are one. Hunter and hunted (it is a visual hunt) merge into a single ambience, a dance between subject and object: "It was a pretty game, played on the smooth surface of the pond, a man against a loon" (159). The "against" of the final phrase may remind us of the antagonism of the ant-war, but surely Thoreau also intends the word in a pictorial sense: a man *set against* the background of a loon and both set against the background of Walden, which is the stage on which their drama unfolds.

To a greater degree than any of the preceding sections of "Brute Neighbors," the loon passage invites us to picture Thoreau himself within the scene, so that the scene—in its totality—becomes the object of the reader's eye. ("[C]an we separate the man," Emerson asks in *Nature*, "from the living picture?"[3]) Thoreau is too busy pursuing the loon to really behold it; it is we who do the beholding, and as we do so a world comes into being.

The diving and plunging of the loon, as well as Thoreau's pursuit, are part of a lovely dance between the self and nature, in something of the sense that Suzanne Langer intends when she says that "dance creates a world of powers" and shows us "a display of inter-

3. *The Collected Works of Ralph Waldo Emerson*, ed. Alfred R. Ferguson et al. (Cambridge, Mass.: Harvard University Press, 1971-), 1:15.

acting forces."[4] Around these images of power and force, the dance
merges with the hunt. Thoreau is a "hunter" of the loon, not in the
sense of predation, but in the sense described by José Ortega y Gasset in his *Meditations on Hunting:* "All means of pursuit and capture which the hunter employs, correspond to countermeasures of
evasion that the prey employs," dramatizing "a relationship in
which two systems of instincts confront each other."[5]

Not only is the loon a symbol of Thoreau's own spiritual deep-
diving, as most critics have viewed it. It also is a pure dramatization, or "immanence," of the relation between man and loon—a
relation founded more on difference than on similarity. Without
difference, without otherness, there could be no dance. The relationship that Thoreau describes as "a man against a loon" should
thus also be understood as an encounter, in which the loon
emerges "over against" the spatial "background" of the Pond. These
are the terms Martin Buber employs to describe the encounter between "I" and "Thou," in which the greatest intimacy (in Thoreau's
terms, "correspondence") results from the full "emergence" of
"Thou."[6] For Thoreau to "divine [the loon's] thought in mine" is ultimately to make this encounter, and, in doing so, to discover the
"wildness" that resides within himself.

This great passage, then, introduces still another form of beholding that characterizes *Walden* at some of its most powerful and lyric
moments. To behold in this way is to emphasize the "holding," not
in the sense of possession, but in the sense of a vibrant, organic
world brought into being and "held" steadily before us. Unlike the
scene of watchful waiting depicted earlier in "Brute Neighbors,"
the loon passage emphasizes the self as a creator (a dancer and
hunter, in this sense as well) in the world beheld.

This thought returns us, of course, to the artist of Kouroo, whose
own "world of full and fair proportions" was "made" in exactly this
way: "When the finishing stroke was put to his work, it suddenly *expanded* before the eyes of the *astonished* artist into the fairest of all
the creations of Brahma" (220; emphases added). The creation of
this staff ("a new system") brings a world into being and sustains it
through imagination. We may also be reminded of the mythical creation of Walden itself, "the work of a brave man . . . [who] rounded
this water with his hand" (132).

4. Suzanne Langer, *Problems of Art: Ten Philosophical Lectures* (New York: Charles Scribner's Sons, 1957), 10.
5. José Ortega y Gasset, *Meditations on Hunting,* trans. Howard B. Wescott (New York:
   Charles Scribner's Sons, 1972), 87.
6. The relevant passage from Buber follows: "The *Thou* appears, to be sure, in space, but
   in the exclusive situation of what is over against it, where everything else can be only the
   background out of which it emerges, not its boundary and measured limit" (*I and Thou,*
   2d ed., trans. Ronald G. Smith [New York: Charles Scribner's Sons, 1958], 30).

The loon passage implicitly revises Thoreau's earlier answer to the question "Why do precisely these objects which we behold make a world?" The fullest answer to this question is that objects do not, by themselves, make a world; worlds are "made" by the interaction—the "dance"—of the creative self and the world. This is the same answer that the Journal, through its continuous play of association, gives over and over again through the long course of its development.

But "Brute Neighbors" concludes with a return to the mode of apprehension with which it began, that of watchful waiting: "For hours, in fall days, I watched the ducks cunningly tack and veer and hold the middle of the pond. . . . When compelled to rise they would sometimes circle round and round and over the pond at a considerable height" (160). The ducks' veering and circling suggest the loon's movements, but here the perceiver remains stationary, contemplative, a viewer rather than an actor in the scene. But this final scene is not merely a "frame" for the great loon passage, a way of highlighting its drama. Rather, its placement reminds us that contemplation is, as much as the "dance," a way of involving oneself in nature. Both watchful waiting from a stationary, centralized perspective, as well as the joyful dance of creation, are avenues to "correspondence," and *Walden* is characterized by a movement back and forth between these modes. In this, it closely resembles Whitman's "Song of Myself," which validates both "loafing" and "[s]peeding through space" as means to fulfillment. Like Whitman, Thoreau is "[b]oth in and out of the game" (secs. I, 5, 33, 4).

Thus, the chapter "Brute Neighbors" may be understood as pivotal; it presents in anecdotal form the two most important modes of apprehension characterizing *Walden* as a whole. On the one hand, its scenes of watchful waiting recall the "serenity" (133) of "The Ponds," where we found Thoreau "floating over [Walden's] surface as the zephyr willed, having paddled my boat to the *middle*, and lying on my back across the seats, in a summer forenoon, dreaming awake" (131; emphasis added). This is the perspective of centralized solitude whose aesthetic and spiritual advantages were asserted earlier in the same chapter. "The forest has never so good a setting, nor is so distinctly beautiful, as when seen from the middle of a small lake" (128).

On the other hand, the loon passage of "Brute Neighbors" anticipates the climatic chapter "Spring," with its dramatization of a flowing, "living" earth and of a beholder intimately involved in nature's processes. In that chapter, Thoreau's "alert[ness] for the first signs of spring" (203), like his anticipation of the loon's initial appearance, signals a participatory role. (As Ortega says, "[t]he hunter is the alert man" whose alertness takes him to "an authentic 'outside,' " to the condition of being "*within* the countryside.")[7] And like the unpredictable loon or the "surprising" cats, the "sand foliage" is remarkable because of "its springing into existence thus *suddenly*" (205; emphasis added). As much as the loon, the sand foliage suggests transformation to Thoreau: "The very globe continually transcends and translates itself, and becomes winged in its orbit" (206). Finally, "Spring" follows the loon passage in its rendering of a world "made" through creation and still in the process of being created: "I am affected as if in a peculiar sense I stood in the laboratory of the Artist [the phrase conjoins science and art] who made the world and me,—had come to where he was still at work, sporting on this bank, and with excess of energy strewing his fresh designs about" (205).

But the distinction between the contemplative and creative modes of apprehension, as they are depicted in *Walden*, can be overdrawn. The contemplative mode involves its own form of engagement with the natural world. Reverie, as Bachelard reminds us, is an active process; it is what Whitman called inviting the soul. In his philosophical meditation, *The Inward Morning* (a phrase taken from Thoreau), Henry Bugbee describes this process: "The present in question seems to expand itself extensively into temporal and spatial distances. And it is as if one's perception of everything distinct were engaged in alignment with a center from which one moves to greet each thing knowingly."[8]

This is the expansive spirit in which Thoreau greets Walden's forest creatures from the axial perspective of his hut, "knowing" each of them in turn as they enter his arc of perception. Though one may remain stationary while experiencing it, familiarization is an act of extending perception—a fact Thoreau acknowledges more fully in "Winter Animals," the chapter that is the counterpart to "Brute Neighbors." In "Winter Animals," the whole environment of the Pond is made proximate: "Walden . . . was my yard." Here we witness the process (now more difficult, but also more transparent, because of the starkness of the winter landscape) through which Thoreau perceives, and thus incorporates, the rabbits, squirrels, jays, chickadees, titmice, and sparrows into the world of his "yard." Even the mysterious hooting owl becomes "quite familiar to me at last" (183), the final phrase confirming that familiarization is an active process.

7. Ibid., 150, 141, 142. For a consideration of "alertness (as) a way of being in the world" in Thoreau's work, especially as this relates to English romantic poets such as Wordsworth, see Frederick Garber, "Thoreau's Ladder of Alertness," *Thoreau Quarterly* 14 (Summer/Fall 1982): 118.
8. Henry G. Bugbee, Jr., *The Inward Morning: A Philosophical Exploration in Journal Form* (State College, Pa.: Bald Eagle Press, 1958), 52.

Similarly, the experience of "floating over [Walden's] surface as the zephyr willed" is hardly unengaged. Thoreau, after all, deliberately "paddled [his] boat to the middle" in order to gain a perspective of centrality and serenity. And the reverie with which he is rewarded is described by the powerful oxymoron, "dreaming *awake*" (131; emphasis added). Such wakeful dreaming is what Bugbee calls a "bathing in fluent reality."[9]

Conversely, the drama of the self's engagement in nature that we witness in the loon passage and in "Spring" involves a form of contemplation—a wonderment before the processes of the world: "And so the seasons went rolling on into summer, as one rambles into higher and higher grass." The loon itself becomes an object of contemplation at the conclusion of "Spring," where it joins the phoebe and other gentler birds in a vision of nature's interrelatedness (214). In the end, the contemplative and creative modes of apprehension reflect one another, are part of the same essential activity, and serve a single purpose: they "enact the 'worlding' of the world."

This phrase comes from an essay by Richard Pevear, who uses it in a discussion of the poetry of George Oppen. Pevear places Oppen's work in contrast to the "solipsism of so much of contemporary writing" and understands it as an antidote to the "worldlessness" of the postwar period.[1] It was, of course, a nineteenth-century version of worldlessness—the condition of "quiet desperation" (8)—that sent Thoreau to the Pond to recover *his* world, and *Walden* may be considered the "poem" he wrote toward his recovery. He was, as many have observed, prescient in understanding how the technology and coercive social structures emerging in his time could alienate people from nature and turn them into machines.[2] One of his reasons for going to Walden, like many another utopian of his day, was to recover the very ground of being, to "world" the world in this quite literal sense.

Thoreau, of course, had his own "solipsism" to overcome: the alienation that results from philosophical idealism, in its privileging of consciousness and subjectivity. Idealism challenged his vividly experienced sense of a vital, organic earth, and at Walden he put it to the test of his experiment in living. By refusing to be un-worlded, he establishes his relevance for out time, especially in his demonstration that perception can bridge the chasm between spirituality

9. Ibid.
1. Richard Pevear, "Poetry and Worldlessness," *Hudson Review* 29 (Summer 1976): 318, 315, 319.
2. The most comprehensive treatment of Thoreau's relevance to twentieth-century political and social issues is to be found in Michael Meyer, *Several More Lives to Live: Thoreau's Political Reputation in America* (Westport, Conn.: Greenwood Press, 1977).

and sensory experience. *Walden* is remarkable in its anticipation of the phenomenological position of twentieth-century philosophers such as Maurice Merleau-Ponty: that "immanence and transcedence [meet] in perception."[3]

But Thoreau's relation to contemporary thought should not be overstated. The worlding enacted by *Walden* does not attempt to redress so profound a condition of "worldlessness" as described by Pevear and other commentators upon postwar alienation. Thoreau did not feel as radically dispossessed of the world as many men and women of the late twentieth century. He did not have to confront the concentration camps, the bomb, and modern totalitarianism—the conditions of "terror" that, according to Isaac Rosenfeld, created "an age of enormity" in which individuals are dwarfed before the massive, often incomprehensible, movements of vast nation-states. And one may add to this list of terrors the ecological destruction of our time, which Thoreau only partially foresaw. These are the conditions in which a writer like Oppen, through a poetry of immanence, strives to bring the very world back into being. We may also think of Charles Olson, who struggles in his *Maximus Poems* to "construct" "an actual earth of value."[4]

For Thoreau, it was not necessary to assert the "actuality" of the world or to "construct" it in quite the sense that Olson intends; his earth of value remained in place, at hand, in the very midst of civilization. That his experiment takes place only "a mile from any neighbor" (5) testifies to his confidence in nature's powers of renewal and its accessibility. The problem was not to bring being out of nothingness, but to demonstrate that all the various "worlds" we might inhabit were supported by one world—nature: "There is a solid bottom everywhere" (222). *Walden*'s morning work is to remind Thoreau and his neighbors of nature's proximity and importance: "alert and healthy natures *remember* that the sun rose clear" (9; emphasis added). The "restless, nervous, bustling, trivial Nineteenth Century" (221) had obscured, rather than obliterated, nature's centrality to human life, and what was needed was a reorientation, or repositioning, of the self toward the world.

This repositioning occurs steadily throughout the early chapters of *Walden*, and its realization is confirmed in the chapter "The Village," in which Thoreau's almost anthropological analysis of Concord's human structures (115–16) shows how psychologically

---

3. Maurice Merleau-Ponty, "The Primacy of Perception and Its Philosophical Consequences," trans. James M. Edie, in Merleau-Ponty's *The Primacy of Perception and Other Essays on Phenomenological Psychology, the Philosophy of Art, History, and Politics*, ed. James M. Edie (Evanston, Ill.: Northwestern University Press, 1964), 16.
4. Isaac Rosenfeld, "The Meaning of Terror," in *An Age of Enormity: Life and Writing in the Forties and Fifties*, ed. Theodore Solotaroff (Cleveland: World Publishing Co., 1962) 206–9; Olson, *The Maximus Poems*, 584.

distanced from civilization he has become. At this point, he has achieved for himself the state of being he recommends to "pilgrims" in the earlier chapter "Visitors"—to "really [have] left the village behind" (106). His sentient, "dreaming" return to "my snug harbor in the woods" (117) confirms the full relocation of his perspective and prepares us for the "worlding" that occurs so magnificently in the subsequent chapter "The Ponds."[5]

The point is that, given the proper perspective, the world would "world" itself. Changeless and perennial, like Walden Pond, the world would appear to grow by assuming its true proportions, if we adopted the right mode of apprehension. At Walden, a world gradually comes into being and enlarges as the doors of perception are cleansed through the discipline of solitude. This is the process that occurs in "The Ponds" and, with the different emphasis I have indicated, in the climactic chapter "Spring." In both cases, the "little world" of Walden becomes big, which is to say, as big as it really is: "The universe is wider than our views of it" (214).

In stressing Walden's expansiveness, I intend to revise somewhat the traditional notion of the Pond as a microcosm. Certainly its various images as " 'God's Drop' " (133), as "crystal" (135), and as "earth's eye" (128) suggest a concentrated or condensed (symbolic) representation of the cosmos. But if, from one point of view, Walden gathers the cosmos, from another point of view, it opens into it; "earth's eye" looks out, and, to the extent that we can align our own vision with that of Walden (itself a cosmos), we may gain a "broad margin" (79) for our lives.[6]

The worlding of Walden is more than anything else a process of dilation, which culminates in the final chapter's images of exploration (214–16), expansion, and "*Extra vagance*" (218). We can track the essential movement of *Walden* by shifting our view from the modest hut whose construction is meticulously described in the first chapter, "Economy," to the "cavernous house" (164) of which Thoreau dreams in "House-Warming." This dreamhouse is a place for dwelling, in the most profound and satisfying sense of this word, and serves as an analogue for the capacious sense of habitation that the world of Walden, as cosmos, offers to Thoreau.

But it is important to remember that this grand house could not

---

5. That not everyone has the capacity to reposition himself in this way, even given the opportunity, is demonstrated in "Higher Laws" by the case of John Farmer (151).

6. Cf. "A Winter Walk," where Thoreau writes: "In summer it [the Pond] is the earth's liquid eye; a mirror in the breast of nature" (*The Writings of Henry David Thoreau* [Boston: Houghton Mifflin, 1906], 5:174); and *Journal 1: 1837–1842*, ed. Elizabeth Hall Witherell et al. (Princeton: Princeton University Press, 1981), 198, from which this ("Winter Walk") passage derives. See also Emerson in *Nature*: "The ruin or the blank, that we see when we look at nature, is in our own eye. The axis of vision is not coincident with the axis of things, and so they appear not transparent but opake" (*Collected Works*, 1: 43).

have taken imaginative form in *Walden* without Thoreau's having first rendered the building of his hut. Among the many ways in which "Economy" prepares us for the book's subsequent developments, this is the most important. As Martin Heidegger writes, "We attain to dwelling . . . only by means of building." He reminds us that "[t]he Old English and High German word for building, *buan*, means to dwell," "to stay in a place," and that this experience earns for us a sense of "peace" which, in turn, is freeing. Dwelling, which begins with building and the cultivation of the "near," ultimately leads to dwelling "on the earth" and "under the sky."[7]

Thoreau's description of Walden Pond supports this formulation, for immediately after exclaiming, "How peaceful the phenomena of the lake!" (129), he shows how "[it] is intermediate between land and sky" (130)—a link to the heavens. And whether or not you attain "*Extra vagance*," we should remember, "depends on how you are yarded" (218)—depends, that is, on the fact of your *being* yarded.[8] The process of familiarization by which Walden becomes "my yard" is the necessary preparation for the expansion of spirit and perception celebrated in the "Conclusion."

This observation suggests the way in which Walden is both a closely circumscribed setting and also one of vast, unlimited extension. On the one hand, the Pond is "stoned . . . and fringed . . . with pine woods" (91), and its "horizon [is] bounded by woods" (96). But such boundaries are not, according to Heidegger, necessarily restrictive: "A boundary is not that at which something stops but, as the Greeks recognized, the boundary is that from which something *begins its presencing*."[9] And such presencing—what we have called worlding—changes our relation to space. As Thoreau writes in describing the transformation that has occurred for him at Walden, "Both place and time were changed, and I dwelt nearer to those

---

7. Martin Heidegger, "Building Dwelling Thinking," in *Poetry, Language, Thought*, trans. Albert Hofstadter (New York: Harper, Row, 1971), 145, 146, 149. Cf. Burbick, who writes: "[U]nlike Heidegger, Thoreau has an empirical need to assert a particular geographical site, which leads him to a pragmatic consideration of space" (*Thoreau's Alternative History*, 61). But as my discussion indicates, Heidegger's notion of dwelling implicitly contains—indeed necessitates—"a particular geographical site." And, in any case, Thoreau's relation to Walden is "pragmatic" only in part.

8. Cf. Lewis H. Miller, Jr., who argues that "Thoreau's most effective writing relies on a paradoxical tension arising from his secure awareness of limits," and that the artistic success of *Walden* depends on its being "a world bounded for the sake of boundlessness." Miller's counterpoint is *The Maine Woods*, where, he says, Thoreau "confronts a limitless wilderness which defies precise measurement and exact determination of boundaries, [and, as a result,] the elasticity of his imagination atrophies and his writing suffers" ("The Artist as Surveyor in *Walden* and *The Maine Woods*, ESQ 21 [2d quarter 1975]: 76, 77). See also Schneider, who writes, "After exploring the extremes of his world, [Thoreau] felt that it was crucial to return always to a balanced middle position" ("Reflections in Walden Pond," 68).

9. Heidegger, "Building Dwelling Thinking," 154.

parts of the universe and to those eras in history which had most attracted me. Where I lived was as far off as many a region viewed nightly by astronomers" (63).[1]

At Walden, the "interval" between the near and the far (between, for example, the proximate world of Thoreau's hut and the more distant world inhabited by the loon) disappears: "[S]pace as interval," Heidegger writes, becomes "space as pure extension."[2] And when space becomes extension, everything is proximate; we are at home in the universe: "Why should I feel lonely? is not our planet in the Milky Way?" (93).

When Thoreau recalls, in "The Bean-Field," the Pond as "that fabulous landscape of my infant dreams" (107), he is calling forth the capacious and primary vision of childhood in which, according to Wordsworth, we saw the world as it really is. But the oneiric terms with which Thoreau evokes his childhood vision of Walden show the difficulty of sustaining this vision in adulthood ("civilization").[3] For him, art is the vehicle through which it may be preserved and reexperienced.[4] We have seen how *Walden* makes a world, how it enacts that process; now we are in a position to see how it attempts to secure the world thus made. Like the mature Journal, it does so by drawing the boundaries of the perceptual category that its phenomena define and fill; it "pictures" the world, specifically by enlarging it. This is the sense in which Walden is "a world of *full* and fair proportions" (emphasis added), a world filled almost to overflowing but ultimately held steadily in place by "the equilibrium of the whole lake" (126)—by the totality of Thoreau's aesthetic vision.

Thoreau's confidence in his ability to create such a picture of the world is stated in "Where I Lived, and What I Lived For": "it is . . . glorious to carve and paint the very atmosphere and medium through which we look, which morally we can do" (65). When "carved" and "painted," Thoreau's picture of Walden will, he fervently hopes, overcome the "corrosion of time" (73)—exactly the

1. In this chapter, "Where I Lived, and What I Lived For," Thoreau says that in actuality Walden is "somewhat higher than" the village of Concord, but that in imagination it becomes for him "a tarn high up on the side of a mountain, its bottom far above the surface of other lakes" (62). "Where I Lived"—the space that the location called Walden opens to imagination—is a place *extended*.
2. Ibid., 156. What Heidegger calls "space as *extensio*" (155) might, from a mythological perspective such as that of Mircea Eliade, be called "sacred." For a compelling reading of *Walden* from this perspective, see David E. Whisnant, "The Sacred and the Profane in *Walden*," *Centennial Review* 14 (Summer 1970): 267–83.
3. There are several examples in *Walden* of Thoreau's own failure to do so. His accidental discovery, in "House-Warming," of the groundnut—the "fabulous fruit" of his youth—prompts this reaction: "I had begun to doubt if I had ever dug and eaten [it] in childhood, as I had told, and had not dreamed it" (161).
4. Cf. Emerson in *Nature*: "A work of art is an abstract or epitome of the world" (*Collected Works*, 1:16).

purpose of books as he states it in "Reading." That is, the book called *Walden* will preserve the world of which Walden is "made." His hope for this book is that, like the Artist of Kouroo's staff, it will be "a perfect work [in which] time does not enter" (219).

But, of course, time does enter *Walden*. In "Sounds," Thoreau is "reminded of the lapse of time" (79) by the railroad, according to whose whistle the farmers "set their clocks" (83). Even the idyll of "The Ponds" is interrupted by the "ear-rending neigh" of the "devil-ish Iron Horse" (132), with all the implications of destructive temporality that this sound conveys. But the force of the book, its desideratum, is exactly that of the Artist of Kouroo: to reveal that "the former lapse of time had been an illusion" (220). From beginning to end, the illusory nature of time and change is what *Walden* seeks to prove. And the great chapter "Spring," with its affirmation of the smoothly running axle of the universe, the circle of time in which all change is contained ("[a]nd so the seasons went rolling on" [214]), shows how much *Walden* shares the spatial vision of the mature Journal.[5]

But, in its desire to bring time under control, *Walden* also exhibits its relation to *A Week*. Its method, however, is different from that of the earlier work, a difference signaled by the pun, "My days were not days of the week" (79). As I pointed out in discussing Thoreau's first book, its voyaging in time is essentially linear—encountering time's discrete manifestations as the voyagers touch different points along the shores of the Concord and the Merrimack rivers. The voyaging of *Walden*, by contrast, is that of "great-*circle* sailing" (215; emphasis added), a voyaging circumscribed by the boundaries of a pond but spiraling outward to the Milky Way.

In one of Thoreau's several mythological renderings of Walden's origins, he speculates in this way: "in some other geological period it may have flowed [in the Concord River], and by a little digging, which God forbid, it can be made to flow thither again" (133). If, in *A Week*, Thoreau addressed the problem of time by entering its stream, in *Walden* he chooses a body of water cut away, isolated and protected, from that stream, "without any visible inlet or outlet" (121). This Pond, as Thoreau puns, is *"Walled-in"* (126).[6]

It is in the nature of *Walden* as a pastoral that the river of time runs dangerously near and that the Pond's integrity is vulnerable to

---

5. The Pond, Thoreau writes in "Spring," measures "the *absolute* progress of the season" (201; emphasis added), replacing the railroad as timekeeper. The image of the great wheel of the seasons is implicit everywhere in this chapter, as, for example, in the pun I have italicized in the following passage: "As every season seems best to us *in its turn*, so the coming in of spring is like the creation of Cosmos out of Chaos, and the realization of the Golden Age" (210).

6. An analogue is the Hollowell farm, "half a mile from the nearest neighbor, and separated from the highway by a broad field[,] . . . protected . . . by its fogs from frosts." (60).

the erosion ("digging") of time. Walden, of course, is even more immediately vulnerable to that aggressive tributary of "progress," the railroad, which "has infringed on its border" (132). Pastorals are always defined by what they exclude and by the tensions or "interruptions" they exhibit in the act of excluding. What ultimately preserves pastorals like *Walden* from their contingent dangers is not only their spatial isolation—the boundaries they maintain—but also the language in which they are rendered.

In "The Pond in Winter," pieces of Walden's ice are "carried off" (199) in the railroad cars, after they have been cut and stacked by a small army of workers. But this apparently destructive activity, accompanied by "a peculiar shriek from the locomotive" (198), leaves the Pond intact. Walden, according to Thoreau, remains uninjured for three reasons: only a small portion of the ten thousand tons of stacked ice is actually removed and "[t]hus the pond recovered the greater part" (199); the cutting itself was brief, lasting only sixteen days, and left Walden the same "pure sea-green" (200) vision of solitude it had always been; and finally, the ice that was removed has "mingled with the sacred water of the Ganges," thus allowing Thoreau symbolically to "meet the servant of the Brahmin," whose bucket "grate[s] together in the same well" (200–1) with his.

In our own age of vast ecological destruction, the first two reasons are not very compelling. A more efficient ice-cutting industry might well have hauled away a larger portion of the Pond; and the brief harvest of 1846–47 might in another year have greatly extended itself, if the activity had proved profitable. Thoreau, of course, knew this; in other writings, he demonstrates his certain knowledge that the natural world could be permanently damaged by industrial and technological forces. But it is in the nature of *Walden*, as a pastoral, largely to diminish this threat, or, rather, to overcome it through the power of rhetoric.[7] This is why Thoreau's final reason for Walden's preservation, so purely fanciful, is also the most compelling. The water—and world—of Walden is convincingly preserved in this chapter through an act of imagination.

* * *

7. I do not mean this quite in the same sense as Leo Marx does when he says that in *Walden*, Thoreau "removes [the pastoral hope] from history, where it is manifestly unrealizable, and relocates it in literature [its traditional location]" (*The Machine in the Garden: Technology and the Pastoral Ideal in America* [New York: Oxford University Press, 1964], 265 [reprinted in this volume, p. 464]). In *Walden*, Thoreau is never so definitive as this, never completely removes his pastoral vision from history. This vision is "literary," to be sure, but literary rather in the same sense that Paul and Percival Goodman's alternative models of community are—imaginable, in some sense even realizable, human worlds. See their *Communitas: Means of Livelihood and Ways of Life* (New York: Random House, 1947), esp. chap. 1. Thoreau's pastoral is, we may say, creative and visionary in its exploration ("visioning") of the possibilities of the future, both for the self and, by implication, for society.

LAURA DASSOW WALLS

Walden as Feminist Manifesto†

Of all the canonical nineteenth-century American texts, the case could be made for *Walden* as the most paradigmatically masculine. Thoreau opens it by trumpeting his achievements in those manly pioneer activities: escaping from civilization, clearing the woods, building his house with his own two hands, plowing and planting the ground. He neither needs nor desires a frontier wife, but declares his male self-sufficiency. This book will be, he proclaims, by and about the "first person," his own self and thus, through narrative craft, the fashioning of selfhood within the freedom of nature and against the constraining world of "civilized life" (5).

These dichotomies invoke the familiar Emersonian distinction between the "ME" and the "NOT ME", according to which the self is defined as everything which is *not* "Nature," not "NOT ME."[1] In Emerson, of course, that other which is Nature is "she," all that he reclaims as his "beautiful mother," which his teachings will enable us to commodify, spiritualize, and finally to transcend.[2] In Thoreau, too, Nature is gendered feminine against an omnipresent male narrator and his universe of "*man*kind." The assumptions seem firmly in place: the masculine, active self against that feminine and acted-upon other, Nature.

The presence of such gender-specific language, combined with *Walden*'s opening insistence on self-sufficiency, have suggested to some that a woman reading Thoreau should find herself radically excluded. That is, she must read the self-fashioning of *Walden* either against *her* own self, by identifying with the male narrator, or against the literary establishment which has declared the universality, even the scriptural status, of Thoreau's text.[3] This particular line of analysis has a logical coherence that appeals to me, even as I am troubled by its relentless consistency. For while I respect their sensitivity to

† From *ISLE: Interdisciplinary Studies in Literature and Environment* 1.1 (Spring 1993): 137–44. Reprinted by permission. Authorial footnotes have been condensed and in some cases omitted by the editor; "Walking" and *Walden* page numbers refer to this Norton Critical Edition.

1. Ralph Waldo Emerson, *Nature* in *Emerson's Prose and Poetry*, edited by Joel Porte and Saundra Morris (New York: Norton, 2001), 28.
2. Ibid., 38.
3. See Judith Fetterley, *The Resisting Reader; A Feminist Approach to American Fiction* (Bloomington: Indiana University Press, 1978), and Irene C. Goldman, "Feminism, Deconstruction, and the Universal: A Case Study on *Walden*" in *Conversations: Contemporary Critical Theory and the Teaching of Literature*, edited by Charles Moran and Elizabeth F. Penfield (Urbana, Ill.: National Council of Teachers of English, 1990), 129.

the pain Thoreau is said to inflict on female students, I am never-theless pained myself by the violence such an interpretation does to my own experience. As a naive 16-year-old, I found in *Walden*, back in 1971, permission not to be dominated by the dictates of fashion or of domesticity, and a guide who suggested to me how I might fashion my self in my own manner. In other words, I had no trouble locating myself in Thoreau's text, hence I am reluctant now to disal-low a reading that was then enormously "empowering."

There are at least three ways in which *Walden* and Thoreau's writing more generally encourage the kind of feminist reading I un-wittingly gave it so many years ago. First, the beginning of *Walden* elaborately strips away the artifacts of social existence in order to show their very artifactuality. As he strips away things, the social structures they bolster fall away too. By refusing to own or be owned by things, the narrator eliminates not only the bulk of men's foolish labor but the very structures that govern "women's work." "Housekeeping" becomes, not the women's chore, but a necessary and beautiful aspect of the economy of living: "Before we can adorn our houses with beautiful objects the walls must be stripped, and our lives must be stripped, and beautiful housekeeping and beautiful living be laid for a foundation . . ." (29). So to the well-intentioned lady who offered him a doormat: upon seeing that it would take room in the house and time to shake out, Thoreau de-clines; "It is best to avoid the beginnings of evil" (49).

This may be just a humorous anecdote, yet Thoreau is exact on the ways in which the master creates the slave. For example, society may seem to gain in establishing the hierarchy by which a man breaks and boards an animal to do work; but "are we certain that what is one man's gain is not another's loss, and that the stable-boy has equal cause with his master to be satisfied?" (42). Men are, he suggests to the woman reader, too much in the habit of creating work for women to do, and work of the wrong kind. Our houses are "cluttered and defiled" with our furniture,

> . . . and a good housewife would sweep out the greater part
> into the dust hole, and not leave her morning's work undone.
> Morning work! By the blushes of Aurora and the music of
> Memnon, what should be man's *morning work* in this world? I
> had three pieces of limestone on my desk, but I was terrified to
> find that they required to be dusted daily, when the furniture
> of my mind was all undusted still, and I threw them out the
> window in disgust. (28)

An alert housekeeper might notice, in this passage, the solution Thoreau does *not* offer: to keep the limestone and hire or marry the woman who will dust it.

Does tossing the limestone out free women, or free men *from* women? The answer seems to depend on whether one assumes housekeeping as woman's main identity. In a recent testimonial to her own reading of *Walden*, Alice de Montigny recounts how as an abandoned working mother caring for two young children she first identified with the cast-offs: "The trusted one had unquestionably thrown his daughters and me out the window as if we were three dusty pieces of limestone. I cried myself to sleep." But awakening hours later, she returned to the passage with a very different interpretation: "For the first time in my life I was affording myself a major personal choice: I could surrender to ennui, burying myself forever in domestic busy-work, or I could secure a little free time to toss those limestones and face the vulnerability of new frontiers in friendship"—including her new "friendship" with Henry David Thoreau.[4]

Thus while his conventional reiteration of masculine pronouns may make us wince today, Thoreau's underlying philosophy turns the basis for gender conventions into rubble. The house that follows the minimal dictates of nature will have nothing to gather dust, eliminating "domestic busy-work." Later in *Walden* Thoreau dreams of his ideal house, a single "cavernous" hall in which everything is within view and to hand, a shelter "containing all the essentials of a house, and nothing for housekeeping"(164). In such a house, the binary division between social and natural has given way altogether, and men and women will be equally free.

Free to do what? To learn, for one thing: to be students together, in a form of village-based cooperative education. "It is time that we had uncommon schools, that we did not leave off our education when we begin to be men and women. It is time that villages were universities . . ." (77). Men alone, of course, were allowed into higher education, but Thoreau's reform reimagines both the hierarchical structure of university education, and the gender exclusion that cemented the hierarchy. His own students were both girls and boys, and he was most at ease with those of his Walden visitors, "Girls and boys and young women" who "seemed glad to be in the woods. They looked in the pond and at the flowers, and improved their time." In this they were quite unlike the men of business, ministers, "doctors, lawyers, and uneasy housekeepers," young men and the old, infirm and timid "of whatever age or sex" who thought only of dangers (105–6). His catalogue of uneasy male visitors indicates how delinquent *he* was. Neither doctor, lawyer, minister nor man of business himself, he behaved more like the child or young woman.

4. Alice de Montigny, "I Discover Thoreau," *The Thoreau Society Bulletin* 198 (Winter 1992): 5.

Second, then, the breakdown of social artifacts proposed in *Walden*, such that Thoreau assumes the dual role of house builder and housekeeper, creates a gender fluidity which is born out both in his own social position and in his Journal. Against the social constraints on actual men and women (including those which demanded that he, as the son, leave home to make his fortune while his sisters were allowed to stay—a prospect which reduced him to tears,)[5] Thoreau sought in his Journal to define feminine and masculine principles in nature:

> I cannot imagine a woman no older than I. The feminine is the mother of the masculine.
> . . . The oracular nature of woman still in some sense broods over the masculine. Man's wisdom compared with womans [sic] fertile & dewy instinct (affection) is like the lightning which issues from the bosom of the cloud—except that at last man becomes woman & woman man[.][6]

The gender blending of the last statement, in which boundaries dissolve and each becomes the other, typifies Thoreau's language for that ultimate feminine other, Nature. While the cold and inquiring scientist is clearly "he," the poet's intense "warm" sympathy with nature slides into identification with "her," until the poet's own gender is ambivalent. Thoreau's stance, finally, is to flow between both male and female ideals:

> I love Nature partly *because* she is not man, but a retreat from him. None of his institutions control or pervade her . . . . He is constraint, she is freedom to me. He makes me wish for another world. She makes me content with this. None of the joys she supplies is subject to his rules and definitions. What he touches he taints.[7]

In this symphony of "he" and "she," Thoreau is either and both, finding his own existence in the very play of their relationship across his grudging acceptance of constraint and his desire for freedom. As he concludes, "There are two worlds, the post-office and nature. I know them both."[8]

Against these meditations in his irritation, even fury, at the failures of actual women, who instead of exemplifying the female

5. Walter Harding, ed., *Thoreau as Seen by His Contemporaries* (1960 rep.; New York: Dover, 1989), 45.
6. Henry D. Thoreau, *Journal*, John C. Broderick, general editor. 3 vol. (Princeton: Princeton University Press, 1981–), 3: 44. Hereafter, Princeton *Journal*.
7. Henry David Thoreau, *The Journal of Henry David Thoreau*, ed. Bradford Torrey and Francis H. Allen. 14 vols. (1906; rep. New York: Dover Publications, 1962), 4: 445. Hereafter, 1906 *Journal*.
8. Ibid., 4: 446.

principle of freedom seemed to be the enforcers of privilege, conventionality, and stultifying, even mindless, conformity. He rages absurdly at the woman who would "elicit the miracle of a seat where none is" solely on the basis of her gender,[9] at the ladies who weave "toilet cushions against the last day" (8), at the "tailoress" who, slave to Fashion (also a "she"), tells him "gravely" that "They do not make them so now" (20), at "Mrs. S—"whose lecture aroused Thoreau's interest but who turned out to be "a woman in the too common sense after all," demanding courtesy instead of sense and argument: "The championess of woman's rights still asks you to be a ladies man."[1] Women as they matured became the fussy arbiters of diet, fashion, proper behavior, clean sheets, the perilous household ritual of dinner. Thoreau's disappointment made his reaction doubly bitter, bordering on misogyny. Women's actual behavior seemed a perversion, whether they dominated him into submission or, by acting submissive and "feminine," maneuvered him into the male role of dominance. Both patterns evoked in him the anger of a frustrated social idealist who, crossed by gender conventions, suddenly found his own fluent gender identity rigidified into a source of conflict.

Third, in Thoreau's gender construction the female is prior and gives rise to, is "mother to," the male. More generally, the feminine is the condition for the existence of the masculine, even as Nature—"the wild"—becomes the ground and condition for culture. In *Walden*, Thoreau takes up the differences between woods and village, body and spirit, nature and culture, and by putting them into play shows how each term finally inhabits or becomes the other. Yet the fundamental and enabling presence is a natural, unconstructed other that grounds and makes possible the construction of a civil self within a society, even as it also promises the dissolution of that self in the decreation of chaos. This presence is ultimately "the feminine," a term which is both natural, Nature herself, and cultural, the basic differentiation of society into gendered halves. So the feminine becomes the condition of possibility for culture, as it rests on nature, and culture's virtues—courage, justice, freedom—as they too are finally feminine.[2]

The absence of "the feminine" from *Walden* is an illusion of surface. It is massively present as the "scandalous" term that slides across and disrupts the division between nature and culture on which *Walden* is founded, the very division Thoreau is attempting to challenge. While he is deconstructing his own society down to

9. Princeton *Journal*, 1: 246–7.
1. 1906 *Journal*, 3: 168.
2. Princeton *Journal*, 1: 206.

its very seams, he retains this one massive contradiction. Yet what engages me here is less the satisfaction of poststructuralist theory than the fact that Thoreau himself provides both the original insight and the terminology with which I can express it. For I suspect that Thoreau understood the rupture at the heart of *Walden*, since he went on to write about it in the essay "Walking, or the Wild." Already in the "Spring" chapter of *Walden*, the "Chaos" of winter generated the emergent "Cosmos" of spring (210), and almost immediately, Cosmos generated Chaos, the exuberant destruction of "myriads" in a violent rain of "flesh and blood" (213). In "Walking," the two are portrayed as the two interacting and imbricated paired powers of nature, the fertile muck of decay, creation and decreation, each generated out of the other. In naming the generative, self-organizing chaos of Nature "the wild," Thoreau allows for a conception of Nature not as Emerson's beautiful and vulnerable matron, but as the harridan who growled at him on Ktaadn, "Why seek me where I have not called you and then complain that I am not your genial mother".[3] In "Walking" she is personified as "this vast, savage, howling mother of ours, Nature, lying all around, with such beauty, and such affection for her children, as the leopard . . ." (281).

In this image of Nature as leopard mother, Thoreau figures generation and predation in one, our genial mother with talons. The sinister edge even to his celebration of nature as the principle of "freedom" is suggested in the continuation of the passage quoted above:

> [Nature] is a place beyond the jurisdiction of human governments. Pile up your books, the records of sadness, your saws and your laws. Nature is glad outside, and her merry worms within will ere long topple them down. There is a prairie beyond your laws. Nature is a prairie for outlaws.[4]

Lawful man and outlaw nature: this feminine principle which grounds and undoes our world is finally redemptive. Indeed, it offers *the* promise of redemption to our otherwise dry, sterile, and inbred civilizations: "In Wildness is the preservation of the World" (273). By dissociating himself from a determinative "law" or *logos* as the cohering center, Thoreau devised an alternative, decentered, and relational world constructed on the ethic of interaction rather than dominance, knowledge not through control but through "sympathy" and the intimacy of sensual contact, action not alone but through the cooperation of the community's individ-

3. Ibid., 2: 340.
4. 1906 *Journal*, 4: 446.

ual members. In Thoreau's writing the social gender hierarchy, the dominance of female by male, has in a sense exploded from within. The latent contradiction exposed by twentieth-century feminist argument generated in Thoreau an alternative ideal of social organization and even, in the years after *Walden*, an experimental approach to a *non*-objectivist science that bears comparison with the feminist science advocated today by Evelyn Fox Keller and Sandra Harding.[5]

These, in summary, are my conclusions, which I want to think are available to anyone who reads beyond the culture-bound rhetoric of gender limitation. In them, and in Thoreau, I at least have found and continue to find tremendous liberating potential, and I suspect I am not the first woman to find in *Walden* a feminist manifesto. And, if I may continue the politics of the personal in my own career as a teacher and critic, I sincerely hope not to be the last.

LAWRENCE BUELL

Thoreau and the Natural Environment†

Thoreau is today considered the first major interpreter of nature in American literary history, and the first American environmentalist saint. This position did not come easily to him, however. Until almost a half-century after his death, he remained a rather obscure figure; and during his life and career—our main interest here—Thoreau had to struggle to arrive at the deep understanding of nature for which he is remembered today. He started adult life from a less advantageous position than we sometimes realize, as a village businessman's son of classical education rather than as someone versed in nature through systematic botanical study, agriculture, or more than a very ordinary sort of experiential contact with it. Unlike William Bartram, Thoreau had no man of science for a father; unlike Thomas Jefferson, he had no agrarian roots. His first intellectual promptings to study and write about nature were from books, school, and literary mentors like Ralph Waldo Emerson. Though he celebrated wildness, his was not the wildness of the

---

5. Evelyn Fox Keller, *Reflections on Gender and Science* (New Haven: Yale University Press, 1985); Sandra Harding, *The Science Question in Feminism* (Ithaca: Cornell University Press, 1986).

† From *The Cambridge Companion to Henry David Thoreau*, ed. Joel Myerson, 171–93. Copyright © 1995 Cambridge University Press. Reprinted by permission. Authorial footnotes have been condensed and in some cases omitted by the editor; *Walden* page numbers refer to this Norton Critical Edition.

moose but of the imported, cultivated escapee from the orchard that he celebrated in his late essay, "Wild Apples."[1] Thoreau's career in pursuit of nature thus became one of fitful, irregular, experimental, although increasingly purposeful, self-education in reading landscape and pondering the significance of what he found there.

Thoreau is often thought of as Emerson's earthy opposite. But it would be truer to imagine him as moving gradually, partially, and self-conflictedly beyond the program Emerson outlined in *Nature* (1836), which sacralized nature as man's mystic counterpart, arguing (in "Language") that physical nature could be decoded as a spiritually coherent sign-system. Emerson's theory of "correspondence," derived chiefly from the Swedish mystic Emanuel Swedenborg, validated the authority of the inspired creative imagination as the means by which nature's meanings were to be read. The idea that natural phenomena had spiritual as well as material significance had a life-long appeal to Thoreau, although he increasingly took an empirical and "scientific" approach to nature after 1850; indeed, a strong undertone of his growing commitment to exact observation and to keeping tabs on contemporary scientific thought was a lingering testiness at what he took to be its pedantry and formalism. (Emerson himself was, ironically, less critical of science and technology, although far less knowledgeable.)[2] Hence Thoreau's famous explanation for his refusal to give a full answer to the Association for the Advancement of Science's query as to what kind of scientist he was ("I am a mystic, a transcendentalist, and a natural philosopher to boot," he told his *Journal*.)[3] Yet Thoreau became increasingly interested in defining nature's structure, both spiritual and material, for its own sake, as against how nature might subserve humanity, which was Emerson's primary consideration. In order to attend as closely to nature as he did late in life, Thoreau had to overcome not only the limits of his classical education and his

---

1. "The wild apple," as Steven Fink observes, "is the European who, like himself or the backwoodsman, has reattached himself and adapted to the natural environment" (*Prophet in the Marketplace: Thoreau's Development as a Professional Writer* [Princeton: Princeton University Press, 1992], 278); and p. 637 in this volume [*Editor*].

2. On Emerson's theory of correspondence, see especially Sherman Paul, *Emerson's Angle of Vision* (Cambridge: Harvard University Press, 1952). On the Emerson-Thoreau relation, the most detailed study is Joel Porte, *Emerson and Thoreau: Transcendentalists in Conflict* (Middletown, Conn.: Wesleyan University Press, 1966), which, however, overstates the contrasts between the two. For a more balanced view see Robert D. Richardson, Jr., *Henry Thoreau: A Life of the Mind* (Berkeley: University of California Press, 1986). On Thoreau and science, the classic article is Nina Baym, "Thoreau's View of Science," *Journal of the History of Ideas* 26 (1965): 221–34; but see also Walter Harding, "*Walden*'s Man of Science," *Virginia Quarterly Review* 57 (1981): 45–61; and several essays on "Thoreau as Scientist," in *Thoreau's World and Ours*, ed. Edmund A. Schofield and Robert C. Baron (Golden, Colo.: North American Press, 1993), pp. 39–73.

3. Henry David Thoreau, *The Journal of Henry David Thoreau*, edited by Bradford Torrey and Francis H. Allen. 14 vols. (1906; rpt. New York: Dover Publications, 1962), 5:4. Hereafter cited in text as *J*.

early Transcendentalist idealism, but also of an intense preoccupation with himself, his moods, his identity, his vocation, his relation to other people. This narcissism he surmounted by defining as an essential part of his individuality the intensity of his interest in and caring for physical nature itself.

One of the reasons that *Walden* is Thoreau's greatest book is that the transitional struggles of a lifetime are pulled into it so fully and complexly. In this essay I shall concentrate on it especially, not only because it is Thoreau's most enduring work, but because it embeds much of the history of his relationship with nature, as it unfolded from his apprentice years to his intellectual maturity. This we can see especially well if we think of *Walden* not just as a finished product but also as a work in process, a work that took almost a decade of accumulation and revision to complete: the decade that happened to be the most crucial period of Thoreau's inner life.

To show the promise of this approach, let us start our examination with some passages from "The Ponds." Here we can see Thoreau, as he reworked and expanded his material from the few simple descriptive paragraphs of his first draft (1846–7), beginning to convert himself from romantic poet to natural historian and environmentalist.

In a previous chapter, the speaker nostalgically remembers having been first taken to the pond at the age of four, so that it became "one of the oldest scenes stamped on my memory" (107). In "The Ponds," however, early childhood reminiscence seems to produce pain. "When I first paddled a boat on Walden, it was completely surrounded by thick and lofty pine and oak woods" (131). "But since I left those shores," he goes on, "the woodchoppers have still further laid them waste, and now for many a year there will be no more rambling through the aisles of the woods, with occasional vistas through which you see the water. My Muse may be excused if she is silent henceforth. How can you expect the birds to sing when their groves are cut down?" (132). This is an arresting sequence for several reasons. First, obviously, because the outburst against woodchoppers abruptly halts the sort of nostalgic fantasy that was indulged earlier. But arresting too because of what it excludes. We are told that the choppers have *still further* laid waste the trees; yet no previous depredations have been mentioned. Perhaps the idyllic mood was so compelling that Thoreau could not bear to discuss them, or (more likely, I think) Thoreau presumed that his nineteenth-century audience—which in the first instance he imagined as his inquisitive Concord neighbors—would take it for granted that the groves of their youth had been steadily thinned. For such was indeed the case; the percentage of woodland in the town of Concord had been steadily declining during Thoreau's life-

time, reaching an all-time low of little more than 10 percent almost
at the moment Thoreau penned this sentence.

Even more noteworthy is the transience of the speaker's protest.
It does proceed for another paragraph, chiefly devoted to complaints about the "devilish Iron Horse" that has "muddied the Boiling Spring with his foot." The speaker looks for a "champion" that
will meet the engine at "the Deep Cut and thrust an avenging lance
between the ribs of the bloated pest." But this pugnacity dissipates
as the next paragraph assures us that "Nevertheless, of all the characters I have known, perhaps Walden wears best, and best preserves its purity." A little later on, we are further reassured by the
fancy that the railroad workers are somehow refreshed by Walden
as the train whisks by: "the engineer does not forget at night, or his
nature does not, that he has beheld this vision of serenity and purity once at least during the day" (132–33). Walden has been transformed back into a pristine sanctuary again.

This sequence dramatizes several important things about Thoreau's naturism. First, it shows that "thinking like a mountain" did
not come any more naturally to him than it did to Aldo Leopold, in
the famous essay of that title (from *Sand County Almanac*) in
which the father of modern environmental ethics confesses his
slow awakening to the importance of predators in an ecosystem.[4]
Thoreau first wrote *Walden* without even mentioning the history of
the abuses suffered by the Concord landscape, even though he was
well aware of them. (For example, the Concord and Fitchburg Railroad, laid along the west end of Walden Pond the year before
Thoreau moved there, was a significant cause of regional deforestation, for creating roadways and for fuel.) Nor was Thoreau unaware
that forest conservation was already a public issue. In the first section of *Report on the Trees and Shrubs Growing Naturally in the
Forests of Massachusetts* (1846), which Thoreau read soon after
publication and consulted frequently thereafter, George B. Emerson had warned that "the axe has made, and is making, wanton and
terrible havoc. The cunning foresight of the Yankee seems to desert
him when he takes the axe in hand."[5] Yet even in the finished version of "The Ponds," produced amid recurring Journal complaints
at the philistine obtuseness of some of the profit-minded clients for
whom he worked as surveyor, Thoreau did not sound the preservationist note loudly. Why? Probably not because he feared readers

---

4. Aldo Leopold, *A Sand County Almanac* (New York: Oxford University Press, 1949),
   pp. 130–33.
5. G. B. Emerson, *Report* (Boston: Dutton and Wentworth, 1846), p. 2. For the history of
   Concord's woods, see Gordon G. Whitney and William C. Davis, "From Primitive Woods
   to Cultivated Woodlots: Thoreau and the Forest History of Concord, Massachusetts,"
   Journal of Forest History 30 (April 1986): 70–81.

would disapprove but because his desire to imagine Walden as an unspoiled place overrode his fears about its vulnerability. You cannot argue simultaneously that sylvan utopia can be found within the town limits and that the locale is being devastated at an appalling rate; and the vision of a pristine nature close by appealed irresistibly to Thoreau for personal as well as rhetorical reasons. It was emotionally important to him to believe in Walden as a sanctuary, and it was all the easier for him to do so in the face of contrary evidence given the power that the myth of nature's exhaustlessness continued to hold over many of the astutest minds of his day.

Even if Thoreau had stressed Concord's environmental degradation, he might not have opposed it primarily for nature's sake. In the passages we have reviewed, the denuding of Walden is lamented mainly on grounds of personal taste, as a blow to "My Muse," as ruining the solace of Thoreau's pondside rambles.

Yet the dominance of such aesthetic motives does not imply ethical anaesthesia. As Leopold was later to observe, the cultivation of a noncomplacent bonding to nature at the aesthetic level is one of the paths to environmental concern; so we should not minimize the potential impact of the challenge the speaker throws out at the chapter's end, when he declares of the ponds, "How much more beautiful than our lives, how much more transparent than our characters, are they! . . . Nature has no human inhabitant who appreciates her. . . . She flourishes most alone, far from the towns where they reside. Talk of heaven! ye disgrace earth" (137). The rhetoric here teeters between the old-fashioned jeremiad's familiar call to spiritual purification and a more pointedly environmental protectionist eviction of humanity fallen from nature. Either way, spiritual renewal is tied more concretely to nature appreciation than in (say) Emerson, who certainly would never have thought of calling Walden a "character." Finally, Thoreau's pleasing dramatization of the nurturing bond to nature, not only for the nostalgic speaker but even for the inattentive brakeman and engineer, is more likely to reinforce in attentive readers a sense of the rightness of an unsullied nature than to reinforce complacency in the railroad system as an unmixed good.

Because Thoreau, when redrafting *Walden*, added much more to the second half of the book than to the first, it is not strange that the sorts of alterations we have been considering reflect the changing ratio of homocentrism to ecocentrism as the book as a whole unfolds. In "Economy," Walden figures chiefly as a good site for an enterprise. Nature is hardly yet present except as a theater for the speaker to exercise his cabin-craft in. Thoreau proceeds for fully one-ninth of the book before providing the merest glimpse of the pond. "Economy" 's message of simplification is certainly consistent

with an environmentalist perspective, as it is for James Fenimore
Cooper's Leatherstocking, but Thoreau does not as yet advocate it
on this ground. Not until the later chapter on "Higher Laws" does
Thoreau restate his philosophy of abstemiousness as anything like
an environmental ethic, questioning the killing and eating of animals and fish. This slow expansion of the sense of moral accounta-
bility toward nonhuman creatures is symptomatic. As *Walden*
unfolds, the mock-serious discourse of enterprise, implicit in which
is the notion of the speaker as the self-creator of his environment,
gives way to a more ruminative prose in which the speaker appears
to be finding himself within his environment. The prose begins to
turn significantly in this direction as it moves from the heroic clas-
sicism of "Reading," with its pedagogical didactics, to "Sounds,"
where the "language" of "all things and events" impresses itself
upon the contemplative. Thoreau's own language helps us to put
this directional movement of *Walden* in perspective. Earnest struggle partially gives way to receptivity, self-absorption to extrospec-
tion. Thoreau's language helps us to chart this movement. His
favorite pronoun, "I," appears in the two opening chapters an average of 6.6 times per page; in the next six (through "The Village"),
5.5 times per page; in the next five ("The Ponds" through "House-
Warming"—the last chapter in which the speaker modifies his
environment, through plastering), 5.2; in the final five ("Former
Inhabitants" through "Conclusion"), 3.6. Roughly inverse to this is
his usage of the following cluster: "Walden," "pond(s)," and the various nominal and adjectival forms of "wild": once every 1.8 pages
for the first two chapters, 1.1 times per page during the next six
(through "Village"), 2.3 times per page during the rest of the book.[6]
   These are crude indices. For a more complex understanding of
Thoreau's ecocentric revision process, let us go back to the micro-
level and examine the use of one small telltale framing device. During the first pondside vignette in "Economy," the speaker devotes a
sentence to remembering that "on the 1st of April it rained and
melted the ice, and in the early part of the day, which was very
foggy, I heard a stray goose groping about over the pond and cackling as if lost, or like the spirit of the fog" (32). An emblematic fowl,
forsooth: suggesting both the spirit of nature and the uncertain
spirit of the speaker, who has already chronicled his losses in symbolic form (hound, bay horse, turtle-dove). The sentence uses the
logic of correspondence delicately, evoking it but not depending on
it for dogma—true to the uneasy tone of the image. In "Spring," to
help draw the year into a symbolic circle Thoreau makes this image

6. Tabulations derived from Darlene A. Ogden and Clifton Keller, *"Walden": A Concor-
dance* (New York: Garland, 1985).

return: "some solitary goose in the foggy mornings, seeking its companion, and still peopling the woods with the sound of a larger life than they could sustain." This is actually the second of a two-part series of anecdotes, pursued through several paragraphs, the first of which begins: ". . . I was startled by the *honking* of geese flying low over the woods, like weary travelers getting in late from southern lakes, and indulging at last in unrestrained complaint and mutual consolation. Standing at my door, I could hear the rush of their wings; when, driving toward my house, they suddenly spied my light, and with hushed clamor wheeled and settled in the pond. So I came in, and shut the door, and passed my first spring night in the woods" (210). Thoreau continues by describing the behavior of the "large and tumultuous" flock (he counts them: twenty-nine) the next morning as they disport on the pond, then fly off toward Canada, "trusting to break their fast in muddier pools." Then, after brief mention of a duck flock, comes the solitary goose passage. This sequence is significant in several ways. First, as a formal opening and closing device. Second, as confirmation of the move to a textured and "extrospective" rendering of the natural world, whose particularity is now so cogent that the exact number of the large flock must be reported. One wonders if Thoreau might have been trying to answer Emerson's challenge in "Literary Ethics" to "go into the forest" and describe the undescribed: "The honking of the wild geese flying by night; the thin note of the companionable titmouse in the winter day; the fall of swarms of flies in autumn, from combats high in the air . . . the turpentine exuding from the tree;— and indeed any vegetation, any animation, any and all, are alike unattempted."[7] Third, as a recognition of the delicacy of the complementary project to which *Walden* is committed, namely to turn nature to human uses: nature as a barometer and stimulus to *my* spiritual development. True, the geese are personified; they seem to participate in a logic of natural symbols: geese returning equals spring which equals (we soon find, to no surprise) spiritual renewal. Yet here they are more literalized: when they arrive, the speaker goes indoors so as not to scare them. Though they feel like projections of human desire ("peopling the woods with the sound of a larger life than they could sustain"), the difference between their realm and his is underscored. There is no quick emblematic fix as there was in "Economy" ("like the spirit of the fog"). The correspondence framework remains implicit, but it is complicated by the facticity of the waterfowl and the speaker's respect for their interests. This respect is what begins to modulate Thoreau's romantic

---

7. Ralph Waldo Emerson, "Literary Ethics," *Nature, Addresses, and Lectures*, ed. Robert E. Spiller and Alfred R. Ferguson (Cambridge: Harvard University Press, 1971), p. 106.

enthusiasm toward something like environmental awareness in the modern sense.

But the passage complicates the case I have been building as to the correlation between *Walden*'s unfolding and the biographical unfolding of Thoreau's own environmental consciousness. For these developments do not quite synchronize. It happens, for example, that the earliest surviving Journal entry that Thoreau used in *Walden* (from March 1840, five years before the experience itself: still another comment on wild geese, by the way) was not inserted into the text until the *final* extant manuscript version (1853)[8]. Again, both geese anecdotes just discussed come from the 1846 Journal, the time of the original Walden experience (*PJ* 2:214, 192–3), and the language used in *Walden* is very close to the original Journal language. On the other hand, although both anecdotes appear as early as the book's first draft (1846–7), it was not until the latest extant manuscript versions that the material became fully elaborated. In version E (1852–3), Thoreau first devised the sentence about shutting his door and passing his first spring night in the woods; and not until version F (1853) did he repeat the stray goose image in "Spring"—before that, it appeared only in "Economy" in phrasing much less faithful to the Journal record than the late addition to "Spring."[9] In his revision, furthermore, Thoreau used the stray goose image at the head of a descriptive paragraph drawing upon his increasingly extensive seasonal observations since 1850, listing sundry other spring signs like pigeons, martins, frogs, tortoises. This strengthens the naturalistic dimension of the image. So Thoreau revised *both* to accentuate schematic design (the circle of the year, the goose as a motif) *and* naturalistic detail more scrupulously respectful of nature's otherness and more "realistic" from the standpoint of the documentary record; and this revision did not simply entail drawing on the more mature findings of the post-Walden years when Thoreau became increasingly the practicing naturalist, but also upon the writings of his "Transcendentalist period."

So Thoreau's biography, the composition of *Walden*, and the "plot" of the published version do not correlate neatly. He began and ended his career fascinated by the vision of the natural realm as correspondent to the human estate. He could not get past the Emersonian axiom that "Nature must be viewed humanly to be viewed at all" (*J* 4:163). No matter how devoted his naturalism became, he continued to want to organize his observations into intel-

---

8. Henry D. Thoreau, *Journal*, John C. Broderick, general editor. 3 vol. (Princeton: Princeton University Press, 1981–), 1:119. Hereafter cited in text as *PJ*.
9. Ronald Earl Clapper, "The Development of *Walden*: A Genetic Text," Ph.D. diss., University of California, Los Angeles, 1967, pp. 827, 831–32.

lectual, moral, and aesthetic patterns. This at times whetted his appetite for natural history (for instance, his hypothesis of the succession of forest trees, generalizing from some of his observations about the dispersion of seeds) and at other times it reinforced him in the roles of mystic and aesthete, ransacking the local terrain for picturesque views (despite complaining about the bookishness of William Gilpin and other theorists on the subject) and subjecting landscape configurations to symbolic interpretation, like the elaborate conceit about the moral significance of the intersection of lines of greatest length, breadth, and depth, which he half-playfully, half-solemnly infers from his survey of Walden Pond.[1] In the revision of *Walden*, therefore, Thoreau sometimes even seems to move "backward" from his later "naturalist" stage to his earlier "poet" stage, as when he takes his initial (1846–7) straightforward vignette of observing a striped snake arising from its torpid state and turns it into a symbol of regeneration in version C.[2] Yet, overall, Thoreau's revisions show an irregular movement toward discovery, retrieval, and respect for the realm of physical nature whose substantial reality must be honored in the face of the desire to appropriate it for one's own uses.

Indeed, *Walden* reflects Thoreau's pursuit not of one or two but of a cluster of distinct approaches to nature, none of which was wholly original or unique to him. All may be found widely pursued throughout American writing, sometimes indebted to his example. Some of these environmental "projects" were part of the text's original intent, indeed of the original Walden experiment itself. Some developed later, between the two major bursts of compositional activity: 1846–7 and 1852–3. In order to understand fully what nature meant to Thoreau, we need to examine seven of these projects in turn, in the expectation of arriving at an overall picture that is shifting and pluriform, not tidily coherent or reducible to one or two sweeping statements.

One of Thoreau's earliest dreams as a writer and a follower of nature was the pastoral project of recovering for a time, both in experience and in his writing, the feel of a pristine simplicity such as he associated with pre-Columbian America or, more typically, with ancient Greece; in Thoreau's schoolbook version of the Greeks, they symbolize the morning of the human race. (He reminded himself in

---

1. The best extended studies in print of Thoreau's natural history interests are John Hildebidle, *Thoreau: A Naturalist's Liberty* (Cambridge: Harvard University Press, 1983) and William Howarth's biography, *The Book of Concord: Thoreau's Life as a Writer* (New York: Viking, 1982). For Thoreauvian landscape aesthetics, see especially H. Daniel Peck, *Thoreau's Morning Work: Memory and Perception in "A Week on the Concord and Merrimack Rivers," the Journal, and "Walden"* (New Haven: Yale University Press, 1990).
2. Clapper, "The Development of *Walden*," p. 158n.

1840 that "The Greeks were boys in the sunshine . . .—the Romans were men in the field—the Persians women in the house—the Egyptians old men in the dark" [*PJ* 1:154].) Walden, both the experience and the book, was a pastoral return in two symbolic senses as well as in the literal: a "psychocultural" return, in the spirit of romantic sentimentalism defined by Schiller, to the Homeric world;[3] and a psychobiographical return driven by Wordsworthian reminiscences of former times spent more fully within nature, glimpses of which Thoreau allows us in the boyhood boating memories noted earlier. This nostalgia for youth later became intensified by nostalgia for life at Walden, kept alive by hundreds of additional returns, in body and in recollection, that Thoreau made to the site and in re-examining details of the experiment. So the 1846–7 parable of the author's long-lost hound, bay horse, and turtle-dove, (15) came to apply as much to the Walden experience itself as to the past before the experience.[4] There is an exact, though buried, parallel between the vague sadness of that passage in "Economy" and the passage in "Conclusion" (added in 1853) that asserts that "I left the woods for as good a reason as I went there" (217), which in the 1852 Journal version reads "I left it as unaccountably as I went to it" (*PJ* 4:276).[5]

Pastoralism may lead as easily to a bogus as to an actual ruralism. Thoreau was fully aware of the reductions of pastoral art ("the pasture as seen from the hall window" [*PJ* 1:488]), but he was not above yielding to their blandishments, especially during that first excited summer.

One key sign of this in Thoreau's work that presaged (and, through his influence, helped to shape) the whole course of American literary naturism was the opening up of a split between pastoral and agrarian sensibility that did not originally exist. As Leo Marx has shown, Crèvecoeur and the Virginia planters domesticated the Greco-Roman pastoral ideal in a specifically agrarian context,[6] as did Jefferson's Yankee federalist counterpart, Timothy Dwight. Thoreau, however, satirized ordinary farming as part and parcel of the soul-

3. The network of classical pastoral and epic allusions developed in *Walden* was strongly present in the first summer's Journal kept there. See Ethel Seybold, *Thoreau: The Quest and the Classics* (New Haven: Yale University Press, 1951), pp. 48–63. For the romanticist idealization of ancient Greece as (comparatively) a state of nature, see Friedrich von Schiller, *Naive and Sentimental Poetry and On the Sublime*, trans. and ed. Julius A. Elias (New York: Ungar, 1966), pp. 102–6.
4. Stanley Cavell, *The Senses of "Walden"* (1973; rpt. San Francisco: North Point Press, 1981), pp. 51–52 and passim, is particularly sensitive on the general issue of temporal multilayering, as is Barbara Johnson, "A Hound, a Bay Horse, and a Turtle Dove: Obscurity in *Walden*," *A World of Difference* (Baltimore: Johns Hopkins University Press, 1987), pp. 49–56. See selections by Cavell and Johnson in this volume [*Editor*].
5. See Journal selections, p. 361 [*Editor*].
6. Leo Marx, *The Machine in the Garden: Technology and the Pastoral Ideal in America* (New York: Oxford University Press, 1964), pp. 73–144.

withering false economy of the work ethic, against which he set his own ethos of contemplative play, which approached farming in a willfully poetic fashion: "Shall I not rejoice also at the abundance of the weeds whose seeds are the granary of the birds?" (115)

* * *

Without denying an element of class-based hauteur to Thoreau's intricate allusiveness, his pastoralism was much more a utopian dissent from the economic system than Jefferson's, which was an outright idealization of what he would like to have kept as the status quo. The prominence of stolid agriculturalists among the establishment in Thoreau's district provoked him to a mode of pastoralism condescending to actual farmers. This then became the American literary naturist mainstream, with some partial exceptions like Robert Frost (who is not much of an exception, once one starts noticing the distinctions he draws between self and neighbors in poems like "Mending Wall") and a few clear exceptions like Wendell Berry. In the tradition of Thoreau's not talking much about his social life while at *Walden*, American literary naturists generally underrepresent community. The segmentation of "nature" from "civilization," "country" from "town," already endemic to pastoral, gets even more accentuated.[7]

* * *

A third project of which the same could be said was Thoreau's experiment in frugality. In principle, any habitat might do for this, for economic and moral self-regulation were the keys to its success. In practice, Christian, classical, and romantic precedent all dictated that the best kind of place to conduct such an experiment was rural and the right mode of production was preindustrial and homespun. Hence, Thoreau's droll critique in "The Bean-Field" of the contemporary movement to mechanize and intensify agriculture. Though Thoreau was more interested in the harvest of the spirit than in the hard-earned wisdom he mock-seriously imparts about how to grow beans, it is not wrong to call him "an articulate champion of the preservation of the values of subsistence farming," as environmental historian Carolyn Merchant does. For Thoreau's allegiances, when it came to choosing between options, were all against upscale commercialized farming and on the side of what is now called "sustainable" agriculture: a small-scale, produce-for-needs-rather-than-gain style of husbandry that observed the rhythms he found in the Roman agriculturalists, whose works he read with increasing seriousness in the latter stages of Walden's composition—Cato's *De Re Rustica* (he called it "my 'Cultivator' "

---

7. Peter Fritzell, *Nature Writing and America: Essays upon a Cultural Type* (Ames: Iowa State University Press, 1990), pp. 153–71, stresses this point strongly.

[60]), for example.[8] Turning from that book to present-day Concord, Thoreau was pleased to imagine that "the farmer's was pretty much the same routine then as now." "And Cato but repeated the maxims of a remote antiquity" (*PJ* 4:31). This was wishful thinking, as Thoreau himself knew (cf. *J* 6:108, for instance), but it illustrates his need to resupply a georgic dimension to his pastoral and ascetic commitments.

* * *

A fourth project, Thoreau's interest in natural history, also came to maturity during the years of composing *Walden* rather than during the experiment itself. During the last dozen years of his life, Thoreau made himself into what we would now call a field biologist of considerable skill: in botany especially, but also in zoology, ornithology, entomology, and ichthyology.[9] The most elaborate of his several aspirations in this line was the plan of devising a comprehensive account of the unfolding of the seasons as physical *and* mental events.[1] The first version of *Walden* does not deal with seasonal change as such until the last tenth of the manuscript. Although Thoreau insisted in that first draft that "I am on the alert for the first signs of spring,"[2] he did not begin a detailed recording of seasonal flora and fauna until 1851, reaching a plateau of minute sophistication in 1852 ("my year of observation" [*J* 4: 174]), when he made an extraordinarily careful effort to chart seasonal changes through mid-May (*J* 4:65). By the summer of 1851, Thoreau had begun thinking seriously of this as a major literary venture: "A Book of the seasons—each page of which should be written in its own season & out of doors or in its own locality whatever it be" (*PJ* 3:253). About this same time, Thoreau becomes irrepressibly eager to identify first appearances of this flower or that bird, to discover foretastes or afterthoughts of one season in another, to identify microseasons—the season of leafing, the season

---

8. Carolyn Merchant, *Ecological Revolutions: Nature, Gender, and Science in New England* (Chapel Hill: University of North Carolina Press, 1989), p. 256. For Thoreau's interest in the Roman agriculturalists, see Richardson, *Henry Thoreau*, pp. 248–52. For Thoreau's bean-farming in the context of Concord's agricultural history, see Robert A. Gross, "The Great Bean-Field Hoax: Agriculture and Society in Thoreau's Concord," *Virginia Quarterly Review* 60 (1984): 361–81.

9. Scholarship on Thoreau's natural history interests conclusively establishes three points about Thoreau's prowess and commitment as a naturalist, quite apart from the more ulterior and metaphysical/aesthetic motives that regulated his interest in the "scientific" study of nature. First, that his interest in various branches of natural history became increasingly serious and systematic during the 1850s. Second, that Thoreau's skills as an observer of phenomena were remarkably good, especially in botany. Third, that Thoreau achieved several historic firsts as a naturalist: he was the first to study a body of water systematically, the first to discover the principle of forest succession.

1. See especially Leo Stoller," A Note on Thoreau's Place in Phenology," *Isis* 47 (1956): 172–81, and Peck, *Thoreau's Morning Work*, pp. 47–48.

2. J. Lyndon Shanley, *The Making of "Walden," with the Text of the First Version* (Chicago: University of Chicago Press, 1957), p. 202.

of fogs, the season of fires—and indeed to think of each day as its own possible season sign-system: comprehensive, evanescent, ductile. The final version of *Walden* reflects Thoreau's growing phenlogical interest by structuring its last major section ("House-Warming" through "Spring") as a seasonal chronicle.

Thoreau's phenological investigations moved his thought toward the kind of multisided inquiry into nature's internal connections that Ernst Haeckel baptized in 1866 as "ecology."[3] Thoreau's late-life studies of plant succession and seed dispersal were a further, more scientifically sophisticated stage.[4] What motivated Thoreau, as he sought to arrange his data, was not the desire for empirical knowledge alone but also the desire for patterns of significance. In this we see the legacy of the old Emersonian correspondence project continuing to affect Thoreau's work even as he became increasingly committed to the scientific study of nature. At all stages of his life, Thoreau had an overriding penchant for conceiving of nature, as H. Daniel Peck puts it, in terms of "frameworks of cognition" that appealed to him for their aesthetic power as much as for their empirical and epistemological solidity. Peck cites Thoreau's preference for finding in seasonal data essential phenomenological designs ("What 'makes' November is not its placement in the year's chronology, but its interrelated properties") and his interest in seeing the visual elements of the Concord environment as coherent arrangements, which Peck rightly says puts Thoreau in the company of landscape aestheticians like Gilpin and John Ruskin, despite his complaints about their bookishness.[5]

This interest in landscape aesthetics can be thought of as a fifth project in itself. Limited though Thoreau's formal knowledge of fine art was, throughout his adult life he liked to see land as landscape, as scene: to relish the elements of composition, self-containment, light, color, texture.

* * *

I have not tried to make an *exhaustive* inventory of Thoreau's range of motives and analytical equipment in approaching nature. A complete survey could take an entire book—and has. Even at that, there is bound to be endless dispute over the priority of one motive or another. Enough has been said to make a couple of complicated fundamental points very clear. First, that the motives that thrust Thoreau toward nature were multiple and shifting, convergent but

---

3. For Haeckel's significance, see Anna Bramwell, *Ecology in the 20th Century: A History* (New Haven: Yale University Press, 1989), pp. 39–63.

4. "The Dispersion of Seeds" has been published, together with several of Thoreau's other late natural history manuscripts, in *Faith in a Seed* (Washington, D.C.: Island Press Shearwater Books, 1993).

5 Peck, *Thoreau's Morning Work*, pp. 83, 95, 81.

also at times conflicting. The growing empiricism of his natural history project, for instance, was partially at odds with his pastoral and correspondence projects but was both fueled and regulated by these more long-standing and more poetic interests. And second, the patchwork of convergent and dissonant motives just described, interacting with another dimension of his thought, which I shall get to in a moment, produced both a certain astigmatism and a wondrous acuity of environmental vision: segmentation, disproportion, blurring of focus. One of *Walden*'s more frustrating charms is that it so easily loses the reader in the landscape of the text. The presentation of the Concord environment is deliberately off-center: town cultural geography from the margin. It tells us more than we want to know about some of Thoreau's favorite spots but leaves us with a fragmentary impression of the surroundings compared to what one would find in a more conventional report of traveling in Concord, like Timothy Dwight's.[6] Though *Walden* supplies one or two sketchy panoramas of Thoreau's neighborhood, for the most part it is unclear where anything is located in relation to anything else. Where is the bean-field in relation to the pond? Where are the various ponds in relation to each other? Are the cellar holes of the "former inhabitants" scattered throughout the woods or clustered together? Where is Concord's single grove of "sizeable" beeches to be found? Just how sequestered from the public roads is Thoreau's cabin? All that the noninitiate can bring into focus, if it occurs to him or her to think about such matters, is that Thoreau lives a mile from any neighbor and a mile or so from town on the wooded shore of the pond.

Thoreau's eccentricity as a local guide reflected, in part, his continuing commitment to a subjective, aesthetic vision, in part his practice as a naturalist segmenting the landscape into discrete micro-locales, and in part a final, seventh environmental project, which might loosely be called "political." By terming it "political" (in quotation marks), I mean to suggest Thoreau's interest in provoking social reflection and change rather than participation in the political process as such. This dimension of Thoreau's sensibility is notoriously hard to pin down, for Thoreau's turn toward nature was partly an accomodation to and partly a dissent from nineteenth-century norms of thinking. Insofar as *Walden* caters to romantic armchair fantasies of returning to nature, it can be said to do nothing more than pretend to challenge the status quo. But insofar as Thoreau must be read as seriously proposing the conversion of such fantasies into an actual life-style, *Walden* is almost violently anticonventional. From one standpoint, Thoreau stands accused of

---

6. See my discussion of "Lococentrism from Dwight to Thoreau," *New England Literary Culture* (Cambridge: Cambridge University Press, 1986), pp. 323–25.

retreating into privatism, into quietism, after an initial diatribe that appears to attack the forces of capitalism and consumerism head-on. From another standpoint, however, that "retreat" is wholly consistent with Thoreau's initial antisocial thrust: it is as if the author, at some rather early point assuming that the reader (as opposed to the general public) is with him, completes the process of conversion, to which the reader was somewhat disposed anyhow, by immersing him or her so completely in the life according to nature that the reader will be incapable of re-entering civilized life again on the same terms as before.[7] Thoreau's refusal to organize the Walden landscape tidily for his reader may be one sign of his intent to get us irretrievably lost in it.

Thoreau's politics of nature was further complicated by his deepening commitment to nature's interest against the human interest. His frequent insistence that he preferred the companionship of trees and animals was undoubtedly sincere, even if not the whole story. This quickened his search for secluded pockets of wildness that he could savor as unappreciated, unfrequented jewels of the Concord region. From here it was but a short step, in principle, to a self-conscious environmentalist politics: a defense of nature against the human invader. But this step, as we saw when discussing "The Ponds," did not come as readily to Thoreau as a late twentieth-century reader, living in the post–Rachel Carson age of environmental apocalypse, might expect of so environmentally sensitive a person. Thoreau had preservationist leanings before he wrote *Walden*; but his most forthright statements came near the end of his life and were never published. Even at that, he was nowhere near writing an extended treatise on environmental degradation like that of Vermonter polymath George Perkins Marsh, whose *Man and Nature* (1864) was Anglo-America's first major work of environmental history and the first major conservationist manifesto.[8] Thoreau would have seconded Marsh's indictment of man's degradation of nature, though he would probably have disputed that the remedy for human engineering's errors was better

7. Leo Marx thoughtfully appraises this duality from a standpoint slightly, but importantly, different from my own: "As he settles into his life at the pond . . . the problems of ordinary people recede from his consciousness," thereby "dissipating the radical social awareness" generated "at the outset. Considered as a single structure of feeling," however, "Thoreau's masterwork may be described as superbly effective in transmuting incipiently radical impulses into a celebration of what Emerson calls 'the infinitude of the private man' " ("Henry Thoreau: The Two Thoreaus," *The Pilot and the Passenger* [New York: Oxford University Press, 1988], p. 98).

8. Thoreau could not have been aware of Marsh's environmental researches, nor was Marsh more than idly interested in Thoreau, if that. I have found no substantive references to Thoreau in the Marsh papers at the University of Vermont. As Roderick Nash notes in *Wilderness and the American Mind*, 3rd ed. (New Haven: Yale University Press, 1982), pp. 104–5, Marsh's approach to environmental issues was by and large utilitarian, not romantic.

human engineering. But the magnum opus Thoreau was drafting at the time Marsh was at work on his was an ecological *summa*, not a book of public policy. As we see from "The Succession of Forest Trees," the one tip of the iceberg to be published during Thoreau's lifetime, this work would have chided the public more for failures of observation and knowledge than for crimes against the land.[9] The circumstances of that lecture-essay's production dramatize Thoreau's political in-betweenness: it was an expository discourse addressed nominally to farmers attending the annual county fair, or "cattle show," and aimed beyond that to announce to the scientific community the discovery of the principle of forest succession, which is Thoreau's main claim to fame as a pioneer of ecological science.[1] Thoreau speaks, as always, in a somewhat oppositional voice, as someone who knows he's considered a crank and is proud of it, as someone looking down on his audience from the height of superior wisdom about seed dispersion ("surely, men love darkness rather than light");[2] but the underlying aim of the address is less to disorder the status quo than to strengthen it, and by implication prove the author's value to society, by contributing useful new information to farmers and naturalists. Thoreau chided his audience on its ignorance of natural systems but did not advocate the radical reorganization of town property into parklands, an idea he broaches in the peroration of the unfinished "Huckleberries." The ecological and environmentalist aspects of Thoreau's thought were symbiotic, but the first matured before the second had time to.[3]

This was predictable. Thoreau felt society's threat to him more

---

9. For a discussion of the relation of "Succession" (*Excursions* [Boston: Ticknor & Fields, 1863], pp. 135–60) to the ambitious unfinished project, "The Dispersion of Seeds," of which it was a part, see Howarth, *The Book of Concord*, pp. 192–99, and Robert D. Richardson, Jr.'s "Introduction" to *Faith in a Seed*, pp. 3–17.
1. The most widely available discussion of Thoreau's overall contribution to modern ecological thought is Donald Worster's discussion of "Thoreau's Romantic Ecology," *Nature's Economy: The Roots of Ecology* (Garden City, N.Y.: Doubleday, 1979), pp. 57–111. Worster paints in broad brushstrokes and accords Thoreau a prominence that is truer to his retrospective canonization than to the facts of the history of ecological theory. For correctives by historians of science, see Frank Egerton, "The History of Ecology: Achievements and Opportunities, Part One," *Journal of the History of Biology* 16 (1983): 259–60; and Hunter Dupree, "Thoreau as Scientist: American Science in the 1850s," *Thoreau's World and Ours*, ed. Schofield and Baron, pp. 42–47. In addition, see two bibliographical articles both entitled "Thoreau in the Current Scientific Literature" by Robin S. McDowell, *Thoreau Society Bulletin*, no. 143 (1978): 2, and no. 172 (1985): 3–4, calling attention to the frequency of Thoreau citations in the *Science Citation Index*. My check of more recent volumes of the *SCI* bears out McDowell's claim that "real" contemporary scientists take Thoreau seriously.
2. Thoreau, "The Succession of Forest Trees," *Excursions*, p. 160.
3. For Thoreau in the context of the history of environmentalism, see (for example) Worster, *Nature's Economy*; Nash, *Wilderness and the American Mind*, pp. 84–96; and Max Oehlschlaeger, *The Idea of Wilderness* (New Haven: Yale University Press, 1991), pp. 133–71. This subject has been more sketchily explored than the subject of Thoreau's scientific credentials, perhaps because environmentalism in America as an organized movement did not begin until the end of the nineteenth century.

keenly than he felt humanity's threat to nature, so it was not surprising that the process of first immersing himself in and then studying nature was more absorbing to him than the cause of defending the environment against its human attackers. Indeed, one could go further than this and say that Thoreau's ability to package nature usefully (as in "Forest Trees") or in an aesthetically pleasing way (as in "Autumnal Tints") served as a more stable bridge between himself and elements of the larger society (local agriculturalists, urban and suburban readers) than did his more explicitly political discourses like "Resistance to Civil Government" or "Slavery in Massachusetts." Even in the Northeast, natural history topics were more widely palatable lyceum fare than abolitionist credos.[4]

So Thoreau was not John Muir. Yet Thoreau leads to Muir; indeed, Thoreau became one of Muir's heroes. For both, a deeply personal love and reverence for the nonhuman led in time to a fiercely protective feeling for nature that later generations have rightly seized upon as a basis for a more enlightened environmental ethic and policy. For both, aesthetics was continuous with environmentalism.

---

4. For Thoreau's natural history writing as a strategy of audience and marketplace accommodation, see especially Fink, *Prophet in the Marketplace*.

"Civil Disobedience" and "Slavery in Massachusetts"

RICHARD DRINNON

Thoreau's Politics of the Upright Man†

"In imagination I hie me to Greece as to an enchanted ground," Thoreau declared in his *Journal* and then proved himself as good as his word in his lecture on "The Rights & Duties of the Individual in relation to Government." There was not a major figure in the classical background of anarchism whom Thoreau did not draw upon in some way. Though he may have been unaware of Zeno's strictures against Plato's omnicompetent state, he assuredly honored the Stoic for his individualism, his use of paradox, perhaps his belief in transcendent universal laws, certainly his serenity—"play high, play low," Thoreau observed with delight, "rain, sleet, or snow—it's all the same with the Stoic." He read Ovid with pleasure, used a quotation from the *Metamorphoses* as an epigraph for his *Week on the Concord and Merrimack Rivers*, and must have been well aware of Ovid's nostalgia for a time when there was no state and "everyone of his own will kept faith and did the right." But he found the most dramatic presentation of libertarian views in the *Antigone* of Sophocles. In this great drama of rebellion the central conflict was between the spirited Antigone and her uncle Creon, a not unkind man who had just ascended the throne of Thebes. Corrupted a little already by his power, blinded more than a little by bureaucratic definitions of right and wrong and advancing specious reasons of state as justification for his actions, Creon forbade the burial of the dead traitor Polynices. Driven by love for her slain brother and more by her awareness of the unambiguous commands of the gods to bury the dead, Antigone defied Creon's order. When she was brought before the king, she proudly avowed her defiance:

† From *The Massachusetts Review* 4.1 (Autumn 1962): 126–38. Copyright © 1963, The Massachusetts Review, Inc. *Walden* page numbers refer to this Norton Critical Edition.

For it was not Zeus who proclaimed these to me, not Justice
who dwells with the gods below; it was not they who established these laws among men. Nor did I think that your procla-
mations were so strong, as, being a mortal, to be able to
transcend the unwritten and immovable laws of the gods. For
not something now and yesterday, but forever these live, and
no one knows from what time they appeared. I was not about
to pay the penalty of violating these to the gods, fearing the
presumption of any man.

In his lecture on the individual and the state, which became the essay printed first as "Resistance to Civil Government" and later
under the famous title "Civil Disobedience," Thoreau echoed
Antigone's magnificent lines in his admission that "it costs me less
in every sense to incur the penalty of disobedience to the State
than it would to obey" and in his declaration that "they only can
force me who obey a higher law than I." Like Sophocles' heroine,
Thoreau made quite clear his rejection of the Periclean argument
of Creon that the highest responsibility of the individual must be to
the state and his rejection of the later Platonic assumption of a
pleasing harmony between the laws of man and the laws of the
gods. The kernel of Thoreau's politics was his belief in a natural or
higher law; for the formulation of his essay on this subject, his in-
debtedness to the Greek tragedian was considerable.

Yet no single work provided Thoreau with his key concept.[1] In his
day the doctrine of a fundamental law still covered Massachusetts
like a ground fog. It had survived the classical period, had become
the eternal law of Aquinas, the anti-papal fundamental law of
Wycliffe, and, through Calvin, Milton, and Locke, had flowed
across the Atlantic to furnish the colonists with their indispensable
"Word of God." The more secular emphasis of the eighteenth century on the "unalienable Rights" possessed by every individual in a
state of nature made little difference in end result—little difference
at least in doctrine, for all along men had thought it natural for a
higher law to be the basis for legislation. In nineteenth-century
Massachusetts the existence of a fundamental, higher law was accepted by radicals such as Alcott and Garrison, by liberals such as
William Ellery Channing, and by conservatives such as Justice
Joseph Story. These older countrymen of Thoreau were joined by

---

1. Thanks to the careful researches of Ethel Seybold, *Thoreau: The Quest and the Classics*
(New Haven: Yale University Press, 1951), 16, 17, 24, 66, 75, we know that Thoreau
read the *Antigone* at Harvard and probably twice thereafter, once at the time he was
working up his lecture on the dangers of civil disobedience and once in the 1850s. Unfortunately Miss Seybold overstates her case by making the *Antigone* "probably responsible for one whole section of Thoreau's thought and public expression. From it must have
come his concept of the divine law as superior to the civil law, of human right as greater
than legal right."

Emerson, whose essay on "Politics," published five years before "Civil Disobedience," had a more direct influence on the young rebel. To be sure, Emerson approached the crass Toryism of Chancellor Kent in discussing "higher law" by attaching it to the power of property. But Emerson was usually much better—at his worst he could sound like an early incarnation of Bruce Barton—than his lines on wealth and property would suggest; most of "Politics" was on the higher ground of a radical Jeffersonianism:

> Hence the less government we have the better—the fewer laws and the less confided power. The antidote to this abuse of formal government is the influence of private character, the growth of the Individual . . . the appearance of the wise man; of whom the existing government is, it must be owned, but a shabby imitation. . . . To educate the wise man the State exists, and with the appearance of the wise man the State expires. The appearance of character makes the State unnecessary. The wise man is the State.[2]

Emerson even averred that "good men must not obey the law too well."

The similarity of Emerson's point of view and even his language to Thoreau's must be clear to anyone who has carefully read "Civil Disobedience." Living where he did when he did, Thoreau could hardly have escaped the doctrine of a higher law. It was hardly fortuitous that *all* the most notable American individualist anarchists—Josiah Warren, Ezra Heywood, William B. Greene, Joshua K. Ingalls, Stephen Pearl Andrews, Lysander Spooner, and Benjamin Tucker—came from Thoreau's home state of Massachusetts and were his contemporaries. Tying the development of American anarchism to native traditions and conditions, Tucker uttered only a little white exaggeration when he claimed that he and his fellow anarchists were "simply unterrified Jeffersonian democrats."[3]

Thus the doctrine of higher law, as Benjamin Wright once remarked, logically leads to philosophical anarchism. True, but this truth can be misleading without the warning note that the logic has to be followed out to the end. Half-way covenants can lead to something very different. John Cotton, for instance, believed in a higher law, yet came down on the side of authority and the Massachusetts establishment; Roger Williams believed no less in a higher law, yet came down on the side of freedom and the individual. Like all ideas, that of a higher law could become a weapon in the hands

2. *The Complete Essays* (New York: Modern Library, 1940), 431.
3. Quoted in Rudolf Rocker, *Pioneers of American Freedom* (Los Angeles: Rocker Publications Committee, 1949), 150. A more recent and helpful study of early American anarchism is James J. Martin, *Men against the State* (DeKalb, Illinois: Adrian Allen Associates, 1953).

of groups and institutions. For Thomas Aquinas *lex aeterna* meant the supremacy of the church, for Thomas Hobbes the "Law of Nature" meant the supremacy of the state. For Jefferson and Paine, natural law meant revolution and the establishment of a counter state. But for Thoreau it meant no supremacy of church over state or vice versa, or of one state over another, or of one group over another. It meant rather the logical last step of *individual action*. Belief in higher law *plus* practice of individual direct action *equal* anarchism. "I must conclude that Conscience, if that be the name of it," wrote Thoreau in the *Week*, "was not given us for no purpose, or for a hindrance." From Antigone to Bronson Alcott, Thoreau, and Benjamin Tucker, the individuals who acted on the imperatives of their consciences, "cost what it may," were anarchists.[4]

2.

So much for the main sources and the master pillars of Thoreau's political position. I have argued that in those crucial matters in which expediency was not applicable, it added up to anarchism. But the question of whether this made him a workaday anarchist lands us in the middle of a tangle. Was Thoreau really an individualist, an anarchist, or both, or neither? Emma Goldman defined anarchism as "the philosophy of a new social order based on liberty unrestricted by man-made law" and once spent an evening in Concord vainly trying to persuade Franklin Sanborn that under this definition Thoreau was an anarchist. Joseph Wood Krutch doubts that Thoreau felt a direct responsibility for any social order, old or new, and stresses his "defiant individualism."[5] Sherman Paul, on the other hand, laments that "one of the most persistent errors concerning Thoreau that has never been sufficiently dispelled is that Thoreau was an anarchial individualist."[6] Still, "Thoreau was not an anarchist but an individualist," argues John Haynes Holmes.[7] The tangle becomes impassable with Paul's additional observation that Thoreau "was not objecting to government but to what we now call the State."

---

4. In 1875, Tucker followed Thoreau's example and refused to pay the poll tax of the town of Princeton, Massachusetts; he was imprisoned in Worcester a short while for his refusal—see Martin, *Men against the State*, pp. 203–04. It had almost become a habit in the area. Three years before Thoreau spent his night in jail, Alcott was arrested for not paying his poll tax. Thoreau was probably influenced by his example and by the civil disobedience agitation of William Lloyd Garrison and his followers—see Wendell Glick, " 'Civil Disobedience': Thoreau's Attack upon Relativism," *Western Humanities Review*, VII (Winter 1952–53), 35–42.
5. Krutch, *Henry David Thoreau* (New York: William Sloane, 1948), 133–35.
6. Paul, *The Shores of America: Thoreau's Inward Exploration* (Urbana: University of Illinois Press, 1958), 75–80, 377. Paul emphasizes Thoreau's willingness to have "governmental interference for the general welfare."
7. Holmes, "Thoreau's 'Civil Disobedience,' " *Christian Century*, LXVI (January–June 1949), 787–89.

There are two main reasons for this muddle. Thoreau was himself partially responsible. His sly satire, his liking for wide margins for his writing, and his fondness for paradox provided ammunition for widely divergent interpretations of "Civil Disobedience." Thus, governments being but expedients, he looks forward to a day when men will be prepared for the motto: "That government is best which governs not at all" (227). The reader proceeds through some lines highly critical of the American government, only to be brought up sharp, in the third paragraph, by the sweet reasonableness of the author: "But, to speak practically and as a citizen, unlike those who call themselves no-government men, I ask for, not at once no government, but *at once* a better government" (228). Those who discount Thoreau's radicalism snap up this sentence which seems clear on the face of it: Do not think me an extremist like the Garrisonians and anarchists, he seems to be saying, but think of me as one who moderately desires a better government now. But is this all he wants? Might he not favor, a *little later*, no government? Shattered by this doubt, the reader is thrown forward into another bitter attack on the American government and on the generic state. It becomes increasingly clear that critics who have tried to put together a governmentalist from Thoreau's writings on politics have humorlessly missed the point. He does indeed say that he will take what he can from the state, but he also twits himself a little for inconsistency: "In fact, I quietly declare war with the State, after my fashion, though I will still make what use and get what advantage of her I can, as is usual in such cases" (242). Compare Thoreau's wry position here with that of Alex Comfort, the English anarchist, written a hundred years later: "We do not refuse to drive on the left hand side of the road or to subscribe to national health insurance. The sphere of our disobedience is limited to the sphere in which society exceeds its powers and its usefulness. . . .[8] But let us back up a bit. What was the nature of the "better government" he wanted at once? Obviously it was one that would stay strictly in its place and ungrow—progressively cease to exist. What was the "best government" he could imagine? He has already told us and the essay as a whole supports his declaration: a government "which governs not at all."

But the main obstacle to any clear cut identification of Thoreau's politics has been the uncertain shifting borders of anarchism, liberalism, and socialism in the nineteenth century and after. No series of definitions has succeeded in decisively marking out their fron-

---

8. Quoted by Nicolas Walter, "Disobedience and the New Pacifism," *Anarchy*, No. 14 (April 1962), 113. It is worth noting that Walter thinks "Thoreau wasn't an anarchist," though he believes that "the implications of his action and his essay are purely anarchist. . . ."

tiers. Stephen Pearl Andrews, for instance, the erudite contemporary of Thoreau, conceived of himself as at one and the same time a believer in the socialism of Charles Fourier and the anarchism of Josiah Warren. The intermingling of socialism and anarchism is further illustrated by Mikhail Bakunin, the founder of communist-anarchism, who thought of himself as a socialist and fought Marx for the control of the First International. Even Marx has been called an ultimate anarchist, in the sense that he presumably favored anarchism after the state withered away. But perhaps the closest analogue to Thoreau was William Morris. Working closely with Peter Kropotkin for a number of years, Morris rejected the parliamentarians and joined forces with the libertarians in the Socialist League of the 1880's—the League was eventually taken over completely by anarchists!—and wrote *News from Nowhere* which was anarchist in tone and sentiment. Yet his explanation of why he refused to call himself an anarchist was obviously confused and showed that he was rejecting individualist anarchism and not Kropotkin's communist anarchism.[9]

A somewhat comparable confusion mars a recent attempt to analyze Thoreau's position. He was not "an anarchical individualist," argues Paul, because he went to Walden not "for himself alone but to serve mankind." It would be easy to quote passages from *Walden* which seem to call this contention into question. One example: "What good I do, in the common sense of that word, must be aside from my main path, and for the most part wholly unintended." Another: "While my townsmen and women are devoted in so many ways to the good of their fellows, I trust that one at least may be spared to other and less humane pursuits" (53). Yet this would be to read Thoreau literally. Unquestionably, as he informed us in "Civil Disobedience," he was "as desirous of being a good neighbor as I am of being a bad subject" (241). The distinction was crucial. Though he served the state by declaring war on it, in his own way, he served society for a lifetime by trying to understand and explain Concord to itself. The manageable unit of society—unlike the vast abstraction in Washington or even Boston—was drawn to the human scale of Concord and other villages. If men lived simply and as neighbors, informal patterns of voluntary agreement would be established, there would be no need for police and military protection, since "thieving and robbery would be unknown" (118), and there would be freedom and leisure to turn to the things that matter. Thoreau's community consciousness was the essential, di-

9. George Woodcock and Ivan Avakumovic, *The Anarchist Prince* (London: T. V. Boardman, 1950), 216–19. Thoreau's great influence on the English left dates back to this period when many were filled with idealism and with admiration for the "sublime doctrine" of anarchism.

alectical *other* of his individuality. Consider the following from
Walden:

> It is time that villages were universities, and their elder inhab-
> itants the fellows of universities, with leisure . . . to pursue lib-
> eral studies the rest of their lives. Shall the world be confined
> to one Paris or one Oxford forever? Cannot students be
> boarded here and get a liberal education under the skies of
> Concord? . . . Why should our life be in any respect provincial?
> If we will read newspapers, why not skip the gossip of Boston
> and take the best newspaper in the world at once? . . . As the
> nobleman of cultivated taste surrounds himself with whatever
> conduces to his culture—genius—learning—wit—books—
> paintings—statuary—music—philosophical instruments and
> the like; so let the village do. . . . To act collectively is accord-
> ing to the spirit of our institutions. . . . Instead of noblemen,
> let us have noble villages of men. (77–8)[1]

One nobleman who also agitated for noble villages was the anarchist Kropotkin. He could have agreed completely with Thoreau's
preoccupation with his locality and his readiness to act collectively
"in the spirit of our institutions." In *Mutual Aid* (1902), Kropotkin
celebrated the vital growth of society in the ancient Greek and medieval cities; he sadly outlined the consequences of the rise of cen-
tralization when the state "took possession, in the interest of
minorities, of all the judicial, economical, and administrative
functions which the village community already had exercised in the
interest of all." Like Thoreau, Kropotkin advocated that the community's power be restored and that local individuality and creativity be left free to develop. The closeness of their views—though
Kropotkin must have thought Thoreau too much an individualist
like Ibsen!—points up the mistake of Sherman Paul and others in
equating the "anti-social" with the "anarchical." Society and the
state, as Thoreau and Kropotkin were very much aware, should not
be confused or identified.

The definition of Emma Goldman quoted above will have to do
for our purposes, then, though we must keep in mind its approximate nature and the greased-pole slipperiness of the political theory from which Thoreau's views are so often confidently said to
have differed. Under this definition Thoreau was always an anar-

---

1. By all means see Lewis Mumford's fine discussion of Thoreau in his chapter on "Renewal of the Landscape," in *The Brown Decades* (New York: Dover Publications, 1955),
   64–72. Mumford credits Thoreau with the achievement of helping "to acclimate the
   mind of highly sensitive and civilized men to the natural possibilities of the environment" and gives him a major place in the history of regional planning in America. The
   influence of Thoreau on Paul Goodman, who describes himself as a "community anarchist," is apparent to anyone who has read his and his brother Percival's *Communitas*
   (Chicago: University of Chicago Press, 1947).

chist in matters of conscience, an ultimate anarchist for a time "when men are prepared for it," and in the meanwhile an anarchical decentralist. But enough of this attempt to stuff the poet and mystic in one political slot. Actually Thoreau's writings may yet help to explode all our conventional political categories.

3.

"We scarcely know whether to call him the last of an older race of men, or the first of one that is to come," admitted an English critic in *The Times Literary Supplement* for 12 July 1917. "He had the toughness, the stoicism, the unspoilt senses of an Indian, combined with the self-consciousness, the exacting discontent, the susceptibility of the most modern. At times he seems to reach beyond our human powers in what he perceives upon the horizon of humanity." With remarkable insight, the writer had perceived Thoreau's perplexing doubleness and had even touched the edge of his higher, profoundly exciting unity.

Of Thoreau's "unspoilt senses of an Indian" and his passion for the primitive there can be no question. "There is in my nature, methinks," he declared in the *Week*, "a singular yearning toward all wildness." To the end he was convinced that "life consists with wildness" (274). But this conviction did not rest on a sentimental-romantic view of our "rude forefathers." The crude relics of the North American tribes, their improvident carelessness even in the woods, and their "coarse and imperfect use" of nature repelled him. His unpleasant experience of a moose-hunt in Maine led to the reflection: "No wonder that their race is so soon exterminated. I already, and for weeks afterwards, felt my nature the coarser for this part of my woodland experience, and was reminded that our life should be lived as tenderly and daintily as one would pluck a flower."[2] Yet Thoreau never gave up his conviction that, standing so close, Indians had a particularly intimate and vital relationship with nature. "We talk of civilizing the Indian," he wrote in the *Week*, "but that is not the name for his improvement. By the wary independence and aloofness of his dim forest life he preserves his intercourse with his native gods, and is admitted from time to time to a rare and peculiar society with nature. He had glances of starry recognition to which our saloons are strangers."

By way of contrast, "the white man comes, pale as the dawn, with a load of thought, with a slumbering intelligence as a fire raked up, knowing well what he knows, not guessing but calculat-

2. Quoted in Albert Keiser, *The Indian in American Literature* (New York: Oxford University Press, 1933), 227.

ing; strong in community, yielding obedience to authority; of experienced race; of wonderful, wonderful common sense; dull but capable, slow but persevering, severe but just, of little humor but
genuine; a laboring man, despising game and sport; building a
house that endures, a framed house. He buys the Indian's moccasins and baskets, then buys his hunting-grounds, and at length
forgets where he is buried and plows up his bones."[3] In this list of
the bourgeois virtues, the keen, far-reaching social criticism of
"Life Without Principle"—first entitled "Higher Law"—and indeed
of *Walden* itself is anticipated. Calculating for the main chance,
this obedient white man had cut his way through thousands of Indians in order to rush to the gold diggings in California, "reflect
the greatest disgrace on mankind," and "live by luck, and so get
the means of commanding the labor of others less lucky, without
contributing any value to society! And that is called enterprise! I
know of no more startling development of the immortality of trade.
. . . The hog that gets his living by rooting, stirring up the soil so,
would be ashamed of such company."[4] In this powerful essay on
"Life Without Principle," he concluded that "there is nothing, not
even crime, more opposed to poetry, to philosophy, ay, to life itself,
than this incessant business." An economist of importance, as the
first chapter of *Walden* may yet prove to a skeptical world, Thoreau
saw clearly that the accumulation of wealth really leads to the
cheapening of life, to the substitution for man of the less-than-hog-
like creature who calculates and lays up money and even fails to
root up the soil in the process. "What is called politics," he wrote in
"Life Without Principle," "is comparatively something so superficial
and unhuman, that practically I have never fairly recognized that it
concerns me at all." The war against Mexico, the scramble for territory and power, and other debauches in nationalism were, he
trusted, a different manifest destiny from his own. In his letter to
Parker Pillsbury on the eve of the fighting at Fort Sumter, he reported that he did "not so much regret the present condition of
things in this country (provided I regret it at all) as I do that I ever
heard of it. I know one or 2 who have this year, for the first time,
read a president's message; but they do not see that this implies
a fall in themselves, rather than a rise in the president. Blessed
were the days before you read a president's message. Blessed are
the young for they do not read the president's message."[5] Yet,

---

3. *Works*, 1, 52–53; see also 55.
4. "Life without Principle."
5. His reference to "manifest destiny" appeared in his letter to H. G. O. Blake, 27 February
   1853; his letter to Pillsbury was dated 10 April 1861—*The Correspondence of Henry
   David Thoreau*, eds. Walter Harding and Carl Bode (New York: New York University
   Press, 1958), 296, 611.

despite all these devastating shafts aimed at the institutions reared up by the "pale as dawn" white man, Thoreau honored learning as much or more than any man in America. Far from advocating a return to some preliterate bliss, he advocated, in his chapter on "Reading" in *Walden*, a study of "the oldest and the best" books, whose "authors are a natural and irresistible aristocracy in every society, and, more than kings or emperors, exert an influence on mankind" (73).

Thus Thoreau's doubleness, of which he was well aware: "I find an instinct in me conducting to a mystic spiritual life, and also another to a primitive savage life" (143). It was one of his great achievements to go beyond the polarities of "Civilization and Barbarism"—alternatively attractive poles which drew most of Thoreau's contemporaries helplessly back and forth like metal particles—to come close to a creative fusion: "We go eastward to realize history and study the works of art and literature, retracing the steps of the race," he wrote in the serene summary of his walks. "We go westward as into the future, with a spirit of enterprise and adventure" (269). Thoreau wanted the best for his countrymen from both nature and civilization, past and present. He perceived clearly the meaning of America. It was an opportunity for new beginnings: "The Atlantic is a Lethean stream, in our passage over which we have had an opportunity to forget the Old World and its institutions. If we do not succeed this time, there is perhaps one more chance for the race left before it arrives on the banks of the Styx; and that is in the Lethe of the Pacific, which is three times as wide" (269). Had he lived with unflagging powers for another decade or so, he might have used his laboriously accumulated notebooks of "Extracts relating to the Indians" to show why the aborigines enjoyed "a rare and peculiar society with nature." It is indisputable that his interest in classical mythology, ancient societies, and contemporary tribes was an anthropological concern for the enduring features of life in groups. His interest in savages was much like that of Claude Lévi-Strauss and might have been expressed in the latter's words: "The study of these savages does not reveal a Utopian state in Nature; nor does it make us aware of a perfect society hidden deep in the forests. It helps us to construct a theoretical model of society which corresponds to none that can be observed in reality, but will help us to disentangle 'what in the present nature of Man is original, and what is artificial.' "[6] Thoreau's theoretical model, which came from all his efforts to drive life into a corner and get its measurements, made it clear that the efforts of his neighbors to live for the superfluous made

6. Lévi-Strauss, "Tristes Tropiques," *Encounter*, XC (April 1961), 40.

their lives superfluous. Through careful inspection of his model, he was able to see, years before Lenin, that at bottom the state is a club. To cooperate with it, especially in matters of importance, is to deny life, for the state, like a standing army, is organized power and at the disposal of hate. "You must get your living by loving," confidently declared this supposedly narrow village eccentric. Clearly, he aspired to create for his countrymen a "new heaven and a new earth," just as each of Greece's sons had done for her. The look of this new heaven is suggested by a passage in the *Week*. On Saturday, after he and John had made the long pull from Ball's Hill to Carlisle Bridge, they saw "men haying far off in the meadow, their heads waving like the grass which they cut. In the distance the wind seemed to bend all alike. As the night stole over, such a freshness was wafted across the meadow that every blade of grass seemed to teem with life."

To this feeling of the correspondence of man to nature, "so that he is at home in her," Thoreau added poetic intuitions of an individualism to come. With his common sense, he realized that the notorious common sense of his countrymen was insane. The important questions were buried under daily rounds of trivia. Living was constantly deferred. No joyful exuberance was allowed to slip by prudence. Thoreau could have joined William Blake in his belief that "Prudence is a rich, ugly old maid, courted by Incapacity." The incapacity was partly the result of a split between the head and the heart, thought and feeling, and the absurd belief that the intellect alone enables man to meet life. In his final summing up, in the essay "Walking," he warned that the most we can hope to achieve is "Sympathy with Intelligence . . . a discovery that there are more things in heaven and earth than are dreamed of in our philosophy" (283). But his neighbors not only had an overfaith in abstract reasoning and in the general efficacy of the intellect; they also distrusted the body. William Blake could thrust through the prudishness of his time to rediscover the body; hemmed in by the moral sentimentalism of his family, by Emersonian etherealness, and his own confirmed virginity, Thoreau had more difficulty. His embarrassing admission—"what the essential difference between man and woman is, that they should be thus attracted to one another, no one has satisfactorily answered"—is indeed, as Krutch points out, "a real howler."[7] Nevertheless, he took a sensuous delight in his body, claiming in the *Week* that "we need pray for no higher heaven than the pure senses can furnish, a purely sensuous life. Our present senses are but rudiments of what they are destined to become." Here is a body mysticism which placed Thoreau in the tradition of

7. Krutch, *Thoreau*, 207.

Jacob Boehme and William Blake. It presupposed, Norman Brown observes, that "the consciousness strong enough to endure full life would be no longer Apollonian but Dionysian—consciousness which does not observe the limit, but overflows; consciousness which *does not negate any more*."[8] Shocked by phallic forms in nature, the stiff-backed Thoreau yet remarked that he worshipped most constantly at the shrine of Pan—Pan, the upright man of the Arcadian fertility cult, famous for his Dionysiac revels with the mountain nymphs![9] The vision of individuals with spiritual development and the simple animal strength to affirm their bodies was one of the important contributions of this paradoxical celibate. It was a vision sensed and acted upon, in their own ways, by Isadora Duncan and Emma Goldman and Randolph Bourne and Frank Lloyd Wright. It exerts its appeal to the poetic libertarian strain in radicalism, to men as diverse as e. e. cummings, Karl Shapiro, Henry Miller, Paul Goodman, Kenneth Patchen, Herbert Read, the late Albert Camus and Nicolas Berdyaev. A recent, rather extravagant form is perhaps Allen Ginsberg's notion of "Socialist-Co-op Anarchism." In any form it is revolutionary.

"One thing about Thoreau keeps him very near to me," Walt Whitman remarked. "I refer to his lawlessness—his dissent—his going his absolute own road let hell blaze all it chooses."[1] Thousands of young people know exactly what Whitman meant. A few perhaps can see that Thoreau's death was his greatest achievement, for it showed that his philosophy had taught him how to die—and therefore how to live. Some can appreciate and understand his two years at Walden Pond. But many are ready, like the young Indian lawyer in South Africa in 1907, to be impressed that Thoreau "taught nothing he was not prepared to practice in himself."[2] Like Gandhi, they are ready to draw on Thoreau's "Civil Disobedience" for "a new way" of handling political conflict. Thoreau thereby made another major contribution to radical politics, for anarchism and socialism have traditionally been strong on ends and weak or worse on means. It is true that Thoreau was himself unclear about violence, as his splendid tribute to John Brown and his occasional callow observations on war show—"it is a pity," he wrote a correspondent in 1855, "that we seem to require a war from time to time to assure us that there is any manhood still left in man."[3] Yet he

8. Brown, *Life against Death* (Middletown, Conn.: Wesleyan University Press, 1959), 308–11.
9. *Works*, 1, 65. I should not place any great reliance on this passage, which apparently was valued in part for its shock value, if it stood alone. It does not.
1. Quoted by Walter Harding, *A Thoreau Handbook* (New York: New York University Press, 1959), 201.
2. Quoted by George Hendrick, "The Influence of Thoreau's 'Civil Disobedience' on Gandhi's *Satyagraha*," *New England Quarterly*, XXIX (1956), 464.
3. Letter to Thomas Cholmondeley, 7 February 1855—see *Correspondence of Thoreau*, 371.

went farther than most in thinking his way through this problem.
More importantly, like Antigone he left us the powerful, burning,
irresistible appeal of has example. It is as timely as the banner
"Unjust Law Exists" which marched beside Camus' "Neither Vic-
tims Nor Executioners" in the recent Washington youth demon-
strations. It is as timely as Bertrand Russell's sit-down in Trafalgar
Square. It may even help us survive the disease called modern
history.

BARRY WOOD

Thoreau's Narrative Art in "Civil Disobedience"†

The enormous influence of "Civil Disobedience," not only on
thinkers like Tolstoy and Gandhi but also on the British Labor
Movement and American life generally, is well known. Combined
with a few other Thoreau essays—"Slavery in Massachusetts," "A
Plea for Captain John Brown," and perhaps the "Economy" chapter
of *Walden*—it has inspired commentary so extensive that a recent
book appeared devoted solely to "Thoreau's political reputation in
America."[1] Yet the single-minded emphasis in commentary on "Civil
Disobedience" to the political rather than the artistic suggests a vir-
tual blind spot even among the most sensitive critics, while at the
same time revealing more about the shifting political attitudes in
our time than Thoreau's. The fact is that Thoreau's reputation (in
other areas too, not simply political) is out of all proportion to the
ideas he sets forth, or even to the experiences upon which these
ideas are hung. He was not the first to live in a cabin by a pond
near Concord, nor the first to travel in New Hampshire, Cape Cod,
or the Maine Woods, nor even the first to climb Wachusett, Saddle-
back, or Ktaadn. Before Thoreau withheld his poll tax Bronson Alcott had done the same.[2] Even the ideas of "Civil Disobedience"
had important forerunners: Emerson's "Politics" and Paley's *Moral
and Political Philosophy* for instance.[3] What accounts for Thoreau's
influence, lies elsewhere—in the artistic power of his work and the
sense of drama running through all his writings. In the major works
this sense of drama approaches what Hyman calls "a vast rebirth

† From *Philological Quarterly* 60 (1981): 106–15. Reprinted by permission. *Walden* and
  "Civil Disobedience" page numbers refer to this Norton Critical Edition.
1. Michael Meyer, *Several More Lives to Live: Thoreau's Political Reputation in America*
   (Westport, Conn.: Greenwood Press, 1977).
2. See John C. Broderick, "Thoreau, Alcott, and the Poll Tax," *SP*, 53 (1956), 612–26.
3. See Raymond Adams, "Thoreau's Sources for 'Resistance to Civil Government,'" *SP*, 42
   (1945), 640–53.

ritual,"[4] but everywhere we find the use of a sustained narrative thread which leads the reader forward in anticipation of discovery. The speaking "I" is always present, as Thoreau himself notes with no apologies on the first page of *Walden*, and this leads to a mode of writing which demonstrates discovery, the achievement of perspective, the awakening of vision, and spiritual renewal. Whatever ideas appear are enfolded in a story, so much so that the narrative structure is often the key to the ideas.

If the narrative elements of Thoreau's writings have not been stressed, neither have they been missed. The relations between the works and specific events, excursions, or sojourns in Thoreau's life are well known. But these facts are often passed over as a biographical element less interesting than the presumed "message" being developed. Such an omission ignores what the narrative ordering of the work actually *accomplishes* in the unfolding and development of the ideas. In the case of "Civil Disobedience" it has not yet been shown how narrative order operates as a synthesizing device for the reconciliation of the two realms of experience—the real and the transcendent. I imagine that Thoreau is more generally linked with Emerson than Melville among writers of his time, but some perspective is gained by comparing him with both. Emerson typically engineered his transcendental philosophy through symbolism by using Nature as a "vehicle of thought" or a "symbol of spirit"; that is, he demonstrated that man lives simultaneously in two worlds which are joined in moments of "exhilaration" or, at times of creativity, when the scholar becomes Man Thinking or the poet becomes a "liberating god." Melville accomplished the same linkage of two worlds through his voyages during which his Tajis and Ishmaels find themselves literally travelling across the boundary from the real world into the transcendental. Symbol in Emerson and narrative in Melville both have a synthesizing capacity.[5] Thoreau stands, as it were, midway: we find in him the same duality of worlds and we find him using both symbolism and narrative journeys to give a single account a double reference.

In "Civil Disobedience" there appear to be two rather different centers of interest. One derives from the political ideas set forth about which so much has been written. The other focuses on the

---

4. In Sherman Paul, ed., *Thoreau: A Collection of Critical Essays* (Englewood Cliffs, N.J.: Prentice-Hall, Inc., 1962), 28.
5. My slightly exaggerated emphasis here is not intended to deny Melville's extensive use of symbolism which permeates his works. However, the narrative dimension of romances like *Mardi or Moby Dick* (only partially offset by what Frye describes as the "anatomy" strand of prose fiction) is in marked contrast to Emerson's generically different prose strategies. The only Emerson essay which is arguably structured as a narrative is "Experience" with its personified "lords of life" and persistent images of travelling, generally westward.

story of Thoreau's night in jail, probably July 23 or 24, 1846. Reference to this story is made obliquely in *A Week*,[6] but the version occurring later, in *Walden*, provides a fuller account:

> One afternoon, near the end of the first summer, when I went to the village to get a shoe from the cobbler's, I was seized and put into jail, because, as I have elsewhere related, I did not pay a tax to, or recognize the authority of, the state which buys and sells men, women, and children, like cattle at the door of its senate-house. I had gone down to the woods for other purposes. But, wherever a man goes, men will pursue and paw him with their dirty institutions, and, if they can, constrain him to belong to their desperate odd-fellow society. It is true, I might have resisted forcibly with more or less effect, might have run "amok" against society; but I preferred that society should run "amok" against me, it being the desperate party. However, I was released the next day, obtained my mended shoe, and returned to the woods in season to get my dinner of huckleberries on Fair-Haven Hill. (118)

In "Civil Disobedience" this rather undramatic event is given considerable narrative scope, especially in the central paragraphs which are properly separated and set in reduced type in authoritative editions.[7] This narrative effectively divides the essay into three parts. There is, in the two flanking sections, an important tonal difference, suggesting that the central narrative is operating as a bridge between the two sections of philosophical argument.[8]

Thoreau says of his night in jail that "it was like travelling into a far country, such as I had never expected to behold, to lie there for one night. . . . It was to see my native village in the light of the middle ages, and our Concord [River] was turned into a Rhine stream, and visions of knights and castles passed before me" (240). This vision of "a far country" and "a long journey," with imagery from Europe and the middle ages, is completed, as in the *Walden* account, by Thoreau's retreat from the village and ascent of "one of our highest hills, two miles off" (241). Embedded in this account is a series of contrasts: most obviously, the village world of Concord

---

6. Henry David Thoreau, *A Week on the Concord and Merrimack Rivers* (Boston: Houghton Mifflin, 1906), 135–36.

7. Lane, "Civil Disobedience": A Bibliographical Note," *PBSA*, 63 (1969), 295–96.

8. For an alternate approach to the narrative see Thomas R. Carper, "The Whole History of Thoreau's 'My Prisons,' " *Emerson Society Quarterly*, no. 50 (1968), 35–38. Carper too finds that "the political significance of the document is a side issue" and stresses its status as "an artistic statement, of antagonisms and needs [in Thoreau] which could be declared in no other way" (35). Carper does not isolate the section in reduced type completely but includes the long paragraph preceding it ("I have paid no poll-tax . . . pitied it"); his emphasis, however, falls on the friendship which develops between Thoreau and his cell-mate, "for here is a relationship such as would characterize the perfect and glorious state of which Thoreau has dreamed" (36).

and the natural world beyond it where the narrative begins and ends; the darkness of the night spent in jail and the sunlight of the days preceding and following it; the "medieval" quality of the Concord scene and the immediacy and spontaneity of the huckleberrying party moving up the high hill. The narrative movement—from the natural world into the village and back to the natural—sets forth in dramatic terms the dialectical progress of the larger essay: contrasts in the narrative suggest the contrasting views of the State set forth in the first and third sections; and the movement through the narrative middle, like Thoreau's own movement through the night in the Concord jail, provides a "before" and "after" polarity basic to the political idea of the essay. What *is* is seen against what *could be*. Indeed, if the transcendentalist is understood as attempting to see *this* world in terms of *another*, the *real* as against the *ideal*, then the narrative center of "Civil Disobedience" can be seen as a powerful rhetorical strategy for linking the two views of the State. The narrative journey from one view to another, from one realm to another, makes possible a synthesis of the two in a higher third.

That Thoreau is operating within a polar view of things is everywhere apparent; it is part of his transcendentalist heritage. In the first part of the essay his criticism of "standing government" links the ruling mechanism in America with "tradition . . . endeavoring to transmit itself unimpaired to posterity"; this is contrasted with the "vitality and force of a single living man" (227). Here again is the Emersonian dilemma posed in the opening lines of *Nature*—the "retrospective" quality of American life with men desperately in need of their own "original relation to the universe"—recast in political terms. Repeatedly this dichotomy is observed: government is opposed by "character"; legislators with their tariff restrictions are contrasted with the "bounce" of a trade and commerce made of India rubber (a good example of what Bowling calls "social criticism as poetry"); government by "majority" is opposed by government by "conscience"; law is contrasted with "right"; machines are balanced by "men"; and the persistence of slavery in "a nation which has undertaken to be the refuge of liberty" is cited as grounds for "honest men to rebel and revolutionize" (228–30). In Thoreau's view, the ideal possibilities of democracy are not realized because of "the opponents to a reform . . . who are more interested in commerce and agriculture than they are in humanity" (231).

As Thoreau describes it, American life is full of contradictions and American policy is inconsistent with its stated values. Moreover, no *political* solution can eliminate these problems. At best a democratic society resorts to the vote—an artificial procedure for deciding who shall have their say by reducing right to might. The divisive tensions of society are thus left unresolved, precisely because "voting *for the right is doing* nothing for it" (232). Doing *something* means, for Thoreau, resolving the polarities through action which carries dichotomies to a new level where they can be synthesized in a higher unity. "Action from principle, the perception and the performance of right,—changes things and relations; it is essentially revolutionary" (233). *Revolutionary*: the word is perfectly chosen, for it suggests that real action transfers political contradictions from the social world of stalemate to the cyclical, organic world of new creation. Here natural law, or what Thoreau terms "higher law" (239), functions to resolve contradictions. Exactly this kind of organic resolution appears in Thoreau's final remarks before he describes his night in jail:

> I perceive that, when an acorn and a chestnut fall side by side, the one does not remain inert to make way for the other, but both obey their own laws, and spring and grow and flourish as best they can, till one, perchance, overshadows and destroys the other. If a plant cannot live according to its nature, it dies; and so a man. (239)

The first long section of "Civil Disobedience" thus describes in symptomatic terms the basic problems of American political life, and sets a course for their solution. Tensions and polarities, Thoreau feels, may be overcome by "action from principle"; and the notion of *action* thus leads directly into Thoreau's account of his own actions. His narrative, then, is clearly the beginning of a process which will lead from the problematic politics described to the idealized vision at the end of the essay. Thoreau's action, of course, was that of not paying his poll-tax, an act of resistance to civil government.

What the central narrative accomplishes is a transformation of the basic political dichotomies into a more dramatic form. The true nature of these dichotomies is rooted out, for Thoreau's actions force the State to make clear its generally unstated view of the truly self-reliant man. As Thoreau details his night in jail it becomes clear that physical incarceration is, short of capital punishment, the closest thing to death that the State can manage. Thoreau sees that the State's answer to opposition is tantamount to murder, as his imagery reveals. Thus, while he is literally put *in* jail, figuratively he is put well *below* the realm of ordinary society in a place of wood, stone, and iron where he says the window gratings "strained the light" (238).[9] The night spent in the dark cell, described as a

---

9. For a description of the rather "formidable" Concord jail where Thoreau spent the night see Walter Harding, *The Days of Henry Thoreau: A Biography* (New York: Alfred A. Knopf, 1970), 202–03.

journey into a far country, parallels Dante's night spent in a dark wood in Canto I of *The Inferno* which was figuratively *his* journey into the far country of hell. Thoreau's night, like Dante's, is followed by an emergence at dawn and a renewed vision of the world. The night in prison is thus cast as a kind of mythic descent: Thoreau's remarks about the shedding and flowing of blood through the Mexican war—"I see this blood flowing now" (236)— recall Dante's imagery of Phlegethon; and the view from his cell, leading him to "a closer view of my native town. I was fairly inside of it" (240), suggests a descent into the belly of Leviathan so prominent in medieval mythology and iconography. Here indeed is Piers Plowman's harrowing of hell transferred to New England soil. Thoreau's descent, symbolically cast as a journey into death and hell, gives rise to a vision of his native town and the Concord River as locked in a kind of hellish death[1]—ossified in a Massachusetts version of the middle ages, yet as unsubstantial as the old world "Rhine stream" into which it seems to turns as he looks on. This vision of death is followed by a symbolic rebirth at dawn when Thoreau is released from prison.[2] Not only does he experience "a change" in his vision (241) but he comes out of the darkness of his cell to ascend a hill, paralleling again Dante's ascent of Mount Purgatory in his climb toward the final haven of the *Paradiso*. That the hill Thoreau climbs is not only "one of our highest" but also named Fair-Haven completes the pattern of spiritual rebirth.

The narrative center of "Civil Disobedience," then, is more than a piece of biography thrown in the midst of a primarily political essay. It is instead the key to the dual vision of the essay. The entire section of the essay preceding the narrative middle is an expansion of that night's vision of death. From this very low level, symbolically entombed, the individual is bound to experience life in the State as a series of contradictions whose precise meaning is death for the

1. That Thoreau's imagery of the present State of Massachusetts as a kind of hell is intentional is verified by his account in *A Week* where he writes: "As for Massachusetts, that huge she Briareus, Argus, and Colchian Dragon conjoined, set to watch the Heifer of the Constitution and the Golden Fleece, we would not warrant our respect for her, like some compositions, to preserve its qualities through all weathers" (135). This application of underworld and hellish imagery to the State was not unique to Thoreau. Note, for instance, the sentence in "Civil Disobedience"—"Some are petitioning the State to dissolve the Union, to disregard the requisitions of the President" (233)—a reference to the Abolitionist William Lloyd Garrison who later (July 4, 1854) ceremonially burned a copy of the Constitution, denouncing it as "a covenant with death and an agreement with hell." Thoreau was present on this occasion, where he read his "Slavery in Massachusetts."

2. In discussing the motifs of baptism, rebirth, renewal in Thoreau's works, R. W. B. Lewis, *The American Adam: Innocence, Tragedy, and Tradition in the Nineteenth Century* (Chicago: University of Chicago Press, 1955), remarks on the "reverence of his [Thoreau's] age for children" typical of the Romantics, and Thoreau's attempt at "recapturing the outlook of children," a Jungian "impulse to return to the womb" (26); the Concord jail cell, like the pond in *Walden*, thus functions symbolically to provide a psychological basis for the death-rebirth archetype evident in the imagery of the account.

moral and spiritual man. The journey through death followed by emergence and ascent effects a narrative synthesis: political contradictions are metaphorically carried up Fair-Haven Hill from which point a new perspective is gained, leading to the resolution of these contradictions in a "higher" view.

The third part of "Civil Disobedience," like the first, may be seen as an expansion of the central narrative, this time of his changed vision from Fair-Haven Hill. In place of the polarized world of the present (and past) America, Thoreau sets forth the "really free and enlightened State" he imagines for the future (246): a fusion of the individual and the State into mutual service. Here the individual will not be powerless, dominated by the "overwhelming brute force" of millions (242); instead the State will come to "recognize the individual as a higher and independent power, from which all its own power and authority are derived" (246). Thoreau's vision here parallels Emerson's reconciliation of "society" and "solitude" whereby the greatest individual self-reliance derives from the fullest assimilation of society by the individual soul and the ideal society is constructed from completely self-reliant men. Thus, if "the last improvement possible in government"—considered without reference to the individual—is democracy with its domination of the man by the majority, "is it not possible to take a step further towards recognizing and organizing the rights of man?" (246). This "step further" is metaphorically a step upwards:

> Seen from a lower point of view, the Constitution, with all its faults, is very good . . . but seen from a point of view a little higher, they [this State and this American government] are what I have described them; seen from a higher still, and the highest, who shall say what they are, or that they are worth looking at or thinking of at all? (243)

Significantly, the essay rises and ends on a note of heavenly vision: "a still more perfect and glorious State, which also I have imagined, but not yet anywhere seen" (246).

If we approach "Civil Disobedience" primarily as a political essay as thousands of readers have done, the two flanking views of the State inevitably receive a horizontal reading, the second functioning as a solution to problems presented in the first. Some dozens of commentators who find Thoreau politically naive or his strategies for reform unclear have obviously assumed this kind of structure. The central narrative suggests, however, something akin to renewed vision or imaginative rebirth for which a programmatic reading is inadequate. In the upward passage from night to day, bondage to freedom, Concord jail to Fair-Haven Hill, Thoreau builds a vertical narrative order which transcends political categories—which moves from the realm of understanding to the realm of imagination. We are reminded of a relevant remark about this in *Walden*: "When one man has reduced a fact of the imagination to be a fact to his understanding, I foresee that all men will at length establish their lives on that basis" (11).

What Thoreau displays is a typically romantic perspective: a desire for a genuine metamorphosis in which the existing State is to die and an ideal state born in its place. From this standpoint, however, the ideal does not simply succeed or replace the real but is rather synthesized from it, as blossoming new life is synthesized from the materials of death. Thoreau's transcendental picture of the perfect State evolves from his death-vision of the present state and is in fact impossible without that death-vision. The narrative center of "Civil Disobedience" is therefore the vehicle for an imaginative synthesis, providing a mythic layering to his entry into and emergence from jail at dawn such that the reconciliation of opposites in this passage is a version of heroic triumph. Those commentators who have noted the considerable differences between the idealized account Thoreau gives and the event as reported by others are exactly right: it is precisely this displacement of the real event to the level of heroic narrative that validates the idealized vision of the essay. This is the essence of the artistry of "Civil Disobedience" and it is integral to interpretation.[3]

This reading of the essay as narrative emphasizes its obvious similarities with Thoreau's other writings, especially *Walden*. Thoreau's passage from Concord jail to Fair-Haven Hill had already occurred in less dramatic form the previous summer (1845) with his move to Walden Pond, and his changed vision of Concord in the essay underlines the focus in the later book on renewal and rebirth. Like "Civil Disobedience," with its discussion of the contradictions in the existing State, *Walden* begins with a long discussion of economic contradictions—the development of industry that leads to waste, the abundance of things that crushes human freedom, the poverty of wealth, the institutional life of civilization

3. This emphasis on the centrality of the narrative carries an interesting corollary. Many commentators on narrative (Scholes and Kellogg, Sheldon Sacks, Tzetvan Todorov) have argued that narrative begins with some kind of disequilibrium and ends when this disequilibrium has been removed. If we reflect on the first section of "Civil Disobedience," the real State Thoreau describes suggests a condition of disequilibrium, typified perhaps by the uneasy balance of majority rule. Indeed, we could stress Thoreau's perspective, in which case his *vision* of the present State suggests a psychological disequilibrium felt as he contemplates it. The story moves him from this disequilibrium (his vision of "death") to an equilibrium in which he is psychologically reborn through a new vision of the whole, integrated, idealized State. "Civil Disobedience" thus constitutes a study in identity development; see Richard Lebeaux, *Young Man Thoreau* (New York: Harper and Row, 1977) for a study of Thoreau's identity development based on Erik Erikson's paradigm outlined in *Childhood and Society* (rev. 1963) and illustrated in *Young Man Luther* (1958).

that submerges the self-reliant soul. Like the essay with its vision at dawn, *Walden* is full of morning visions, culminating in the re-birth ritual of spring. Such images of metamorphosis in *Walden* as the bank of thawing clay on late winter morning or the resurrection of a "beautiful bug" from an old apple-wood table enhance and val-idate the archetype of death and rebirth at the center of the "Civil Disobedience" narrative.

In Thoreau's major excursions and books, it appears that he de-signed his art around a series of journeys which thus became pas-sages from the real to the transcendent—symbolized in the fron-tier regions west of Concord ("Walking"), the upper reaches of the Merrimack (*A Week*), the heights of mountains ("A Walk to Wachusett"), the primitive depths of the forest (*The Maine Woods*), or the tranquil waters of the pond (*Walden*). "I went to the woods," he wrote in *Walden*, "because I wished to live deliberately" (65). In "Civil Disobedience" we discover a similar passage, perhaps the only one that Thoreau did not deliberately plan: a walk to the cob-bler's store to get a shoe interrupted, redirected, stalled for a dozen hours by a night in jail, then resumed the next morning. It is not surprising that the artistic account took on the shape of all the other passages in his works with their ascending movements toward morning, spring, hills, mountains, and the sun.

EVAN CARTON

The Price of Privilege:
"Civil Disobedience" at 150†

One hundred and fifty years ago, in a revolutionary season, Henry David Thoreau lectured at the Concord Lyceum on "The Rights and Duties of the Individual in Relation to Government." The philoso-pher and reformer Bronson Alcott, who came out on that January evening to hear his friend, reported that the mixed crowd of local working people and Boston intellectuals gave Thoreau "an attentive audience." Some months later, Thoreau's lecture was published un-der the title "Resistance to Civil Government," but we—like its ear-lier twentieth-century readers, Mahatma Gandhi and Martin Luther King Jr.—have come to know it as "Civil Disobedience."

For many Americans today, the phrase and the essay "Civil Dis-obedience" evoke another, somewhat less distant, revolutionary season: not 1848 but 1968, and the "years of hope, days of rage," as

† From *The American Scholar* 67.4 (Autumn 1998): 105–12. Reprinted by permission.

Todd Gitlin has called them, that 1968 symbolized and culminated. More than any other piece of American writing, "Civil Disobedience" inspired and authorized the civil rights movement, the Vietnam War protest movement, and the student unrest of the sixties. Teach-ins, debates, and symposia were devoted to the politics of conscience that Thoreau had invented, and between 1967 and 1972, theologians, historians, political philosophers, legal theorists, think tank savants, and Supreme Court justices published more than a dozen books with the phrase "civil disobedience" in their titles. Thirty years ago, readers of Thoreau's great essay—whether they were activists or scholars, and whether they felt permitted or provoked by it—understood "Civil Disobedience" to be about the privilege and the pricelessness of personal conscience. Today, my college students understand it differently, and maybe better. For them, and for me, "Civil Disobedience" is about the price of class and national privilege.

"What is perhaps most remarkable about Thoreau," wrote Archibald MacLeish on the album jacket of his 1968 recorded reading of "Civil Disobedience," "is his relation to us in the middle decades of the Twentieth Century." That relation, according to MacLeish, is one of camaraderie in moral struggle and of the shared discovery "that the essential freedom is freedom to dissent." MacLeish's Thoreau is the archetypical morally autonomous romantic, a man with whom "we" naturally identify. (MacLeish took for granted a consensus among subject, writer, and reader.) This is the same Thoreau whom Yale University chaplain and antiwar activist William Sloane Coffin Jr. championed during a 1972 debate on the question: "Civil Disobedience: Aid or Hindrance to Justice?" Thoreau, Gandhi, and King are "heroes to us today," Coffin remarked, "because they represent those individual consciences of the world which, as opposed to the mass mind, best represent the universal conscience of mankind."

A generation ago, "Civil Disobedience" was taken to license a conscientious minority that, however embattled, conceived itself to be freely and securely "opposed" to the errors of the mass mind and the crimes of the mass society. Thousands of readers found justification for holding antiestablishment beliefs ("Any man more right than his neighbors constitutes a majority of one") and, even more crucially, for flouting laws in order to redress social injustices:

> If the injustice is part of the necessary friction of the machine of government, let it go, let it go; perchance it will wear smooth;—certainly the machine will wear out. If the injustice has a spring, or a pulley, or a rope, or a crank, exclusively for itself, then perhaps you may consider whether the remedy will

not be worse than the evil; but if it is of such a nature that it requires you to be the agent of injustice to another, then, I say, break the law. Let your life be a counter-friction to stop the machine.

Even unsympathetic readers like Coffin's interlocutor Morris Leibman, who assailed the notion that "these deliverances [of individual conscience] are sufficient of themselves . . . to override all other rules or obligations," reinforced the era's common premise: that the modern Thoreauvian was someone who, on personal moral grounds, chose to reject and override the established terms of the social contract rather than someone whose sense of inescapable implication by that contract obliged him to act on social grounds.

Mario Savio's 1964 bullhorn oration, which inaugurated the free-speech sit-in at Berkeley's Sproul Hall and marked the emergence of radical student activism on campuses across America, exemplified this sixties reading, in which a morally enlightened and unimplicated individual resists an objectified governmental or institutional force. Savio called explicitly for "civil disobedience" and proceeded to define and defend such action in a close paraphrase of Thoreau: "There's a time when the operation of the machine becomes so odious, makes you so sick at heart, that you can't take part. And you've got to put your bodies upon the gears and upon the wheels, upon the levers, upon all the apparatus, and you've got to make it stop."

In precisely this spirit, throughout the later years of the decade, middle-class students conscientiously assailed the machine of the U.S. Selective Service System in blithe innocence or denial of the fact that they—having been one of them, I should say we—were the machine's principal beneficiaries, that our adult representatives had built it and managed it in order to save people like us from going to Vietnam. The reading of Thoreau's essay that would have taught us to see our privilege and its price was unavailable to most of us then. To many young people today, it is irresistible.

"Civil Disobedience" narrates and reflects on Thoreau's one-night incarceration in Middlesex County Jail in July of 1846 for refusing to pay a $1.50 Massachusetts poll tax. The apparently random circumstances of his apprehension—he was arrested as he walked into Concord center from his cabin in the woods near Walden Pond to retrieve a shoe that he had left at the shoemaker's to be resoled—are actually germane to a contemporary understanding of the essay. For notwithstanding its mythic image as a private haven within a state of nature, Thoreau's cabin actually sat within the Concord town limits on land owned by Ralph Waldo Emerson. And, indeed, in the developing commercial society of Thoreau's time (not to mention our fully developed one), even the man who proposed to march to the beat of his own inner drummer depended on others for the shoe leather that allowed him to march at all.

More primary, I am suggesting, than the principle of personal conscience in "Civil Disobedience" is Thoreau's unflinching recognition of human interdependency and his acceptance of its moral and political entailments for the citizens of a democracy. Thoreau does not withhold his tax simply to register his private conscientious objection to the Mexican War and the expansion of slavery. His action is based on the premise that his taxpaying citizenship in a democracy that countenances slaveholding and forcibly subdues its weaker neighbor makes him a slaveholder and an imperialist, whatever sentiments he may cherish or whatever votes he may have cast to the contrary. "If a thousand men were not to pay their tax-bills this year," he writes, "that would not be a violent and bloody measure, as it would be to pay them."

Thoreau's image of taxpaying, a routine form of civil obedience, as "a violent and bloody measure" conveys the key rhetorical motif and political tactic of "Civil Disobedience": the refusal of the moral buffer that citizens of complex modern societies enjoy by virtue of the characteristically distant, mediated, and indirect relationships between their political or economic actions and those actions' ultimate effects. In other words, one's tax or one's consumer dollar does not simply disappear into the coffers of a faraway government or a spectral corporation; it funds acts that may be immoral, and the funder must therefore acknowledge his role as an accomplice. The essay's central episode—Thoreau's confrontation with his neighbor, the taxgatherer—both exemplifies the practice of civil disobedience and explains why Thoreau sees it as a necessary component not only of democratic politics but of a fully human life:

> I meet this American government, or its representative, the State government, directly, and face to face, once a year, no more, in the person of its tax-gatherer. . . . My civil neighbor, the tax-gatherer, is the very man I have to deal with,—for it is, after all, with men and not with parchment that I quarrel,— and he has voluntarily chosen to be an agent of the government. How shall he ever know well what he is and does as an officer of the government, or as a man, until he is obliged to consider whether he shall treat me, his neighbor, for whom he has respect, as a neighbor and well-disposed man, or as a maniac and disturber of the peace . . .

More than a refusal to contribute monetarily to the Mexican War and to the national accommodation of slavery, Thoreau's act is an effort to dramatize and to redress the attenuation of "face to face" relations between citizen and government and between person and person, neighbor and neighbor. When citizens of a democracy meet their government face to face, Thoreau radically suggests, they are obliged to recognize that its face is their own. In this encounter, the founding figure of American political speech—"government of the people, by the people, and for the people"—must be either embodied or abandoned. That is the burden that Thoreau understands both his neighbor and himself to carry. By "what he is and does," the taxpayer, no less than the taxgatherer, constitutes the government and thus bears personal responsibility for whatever it is and does in his name.

Thoreau knows what some of my students instantly and painfully intuit: that this burden is overwhelming. Qualifying it slightly, he remarks: "It is not a man's duty, as a matter of course, to devote himself to the eradication of any, even the most enormous wrong; he may still properly have other concerns to engage him." But, he continues, deliberately using another corporeal image of unbuffered social relations, "If I devote myself to other pursuits and contemplations, I must first see, at least, that I do not pursue them sitting upon another man's shoulders."

Perhaps the most profound and prophetic insight of "Civil Disobedience" is contained in this apparently unremarkable sentence. What Thoreau perceives is not only that it is possible to be "sitting upon another man's shoulders" without knowing it, but that in an increasingly interdependent and stratified society, such a position becomes the norm for many and comes to seem acceptable, even inevitable, to most. This simultaneously private and public state of being, Thoreau further perceives, cripples both the liberal ideal of social justice and the conservative ideal of self-reliance and responsibility. If I devote myself to my private pursuits and contemplations while unknowingly sitting on another's shoulders, I am not only the blithe oppressor of someone else; I lack the autonomy that I imagine myself to possess and, in truth, do not even know who I am. This is Thoreau's point in the passage that directly follows and illustrates his shoulder-sitter metaphor:

> See what gross inconsistency is tolerated. I have heard some of my townsmen say, "I should like to have them order me out to help put down an insurrection of the slaves, or to march to Mexico;—see if I would go;" and yet these very men have each, directly by their allegiance, and so indirectly, at least, by their money, furnished a substitute. . . . Thus, under the name of order and civil government, we are all made at last to pay homage to and support our own meanness. After the first blush of sin, comes its indifference; and from immoral it becomes, as it were, unmoral, and not quite unnecessary to that life which we have made.

The University of Texas undergraduates who read American literature with me are generally intelligent, middle-class, well inten-
tioned, moderately—yet compassionately—conservative, and for
the most part unafflicted by the premature cynicism and jadedness
that may hang more heavily over America's coastal adolescents than
over their inland peers. While these students, as a group, are capable of critically challenging the ideas and attitudes of the authors
we study, they are, by temperament, more inclined to sympathy, appreciation, the search for common ground, and even the acceptance of instruction and influence. But, with increasing regularity,
vehemence, and manifest discomfort in recent years, they have dis-
liked "Civil Disobedience."

They often can't quite say why. Of course, they share Thoreau's
moral opposition to slavery and expansionist warfare, yet they feel
repugnance toward his essay and toward him. "I don't know. He's
just such a jerk," they say. "He thinks you can just live in your own
little dream world." "He's lazy." "Anyone could rationalize anything
that way." "He only cared about himself." "He lived off of other
people, too." "It's not his argument, it's his tone—the essay's so
self-righteous." Yet I invariably hear in their tone, when they say
these things, more confusion and hurt than frank indignation. Of
all the sociologically powerful and troubling works—many of them
long neglected or relatively new—that now find a place in the
American literary canon and on the undergraduate syllabus, "Civil
Disobedience" is the one that causes them the most pain.

What accounts for this response? At first it surprised me; I assumed, perhaps naïvely, that "Civil Disobedience" was one of those
works young people would always be drawn to because it confirmed
their own struggles for identity and moral direction. But I now
think that it brings them—brings us, materially and educationally
advantaged Americans, peacefully attending to our own pursuits
and contemplations—face to face with what we already know but
rarely acknowledge: that the price we pay today for this seemingly
modest privilege is heavy and growing heavier.

The United States, one hundred and fifty years after Thoreau delivered his lecture at the Concord Lyceum, is not enslaving a sixth
of its population or pursuing a war of imperial aggression. In some
respects, reading "Civil Disobedience" would be less difficult for
my students and me if it were. For, were we the immediate beneficiaries of such conditions, our own social positions and options
would at least be clearer. "If I have unjustly wrested a plank from a
drowning man," Thoreau writes, metaphorically depicting a democratic populace that willingly profited from the theft of black labor
and Mexican land, "I must restore it to him though I drown myself
. . . [For] he that would save his life, in such a case, shall lose it."

Our case in 1998 is not so stark. But we who possess the resources and the craft to navigate the waters of contemporary American life with some degree of success cannot help seeing many flailing beside our rudders.

The defining national event in the lives of this generation of students is economic stratification—the widening divide between the roughly 20 percent of Americans for whom the last two decades have brought growing shares of opportunity and wealth and the 80 percent whose stagnating or declining standard of living has been coupled with rising financial insecurity and psychological stress. My students—most of them members of or plausible aspirants to the 20 percent—are particularly aware that their prospects in life correlate more closely with competitive educational achievement than ever before. Moreover, they have seen this competition begin in childhood, under increasingly unequal circumstances, as private schools and the better-funded public schools (often effectively privatized through corporate sponsorship and direct parental gifts) afford the advantaged early access to advanced educational technologies, years of practice on preparatory aptitude and achievement tests, and trained advisers and editors to oversee the composition of college application essays.

If college students suspect that a "winner take all" principle may be at work in the educational process through which they are passing, they see that principle even more plainly in the business and professional world into which they hope to pass. That world, as contemporary students encounter it, is governed by an inverse and ever more polar relationship between opportunity's scale and opportunity's availability—a relationship exemplified by the familiar conjunction of record stock prices and executive salaries with corporate downsizing and the expatriation of production. It is a world that one must train for not only technically but, more than at any time in the last half century, psychologically.

"Civil Disobedience" exposes and undoes the psychological training that in one way or another we have all internalized. It dissolves the buffer between us and the host of distant sins that, in Thoreau's stunningly precise formulation, "from immoral [have become], as it were, unmoral, and not quite unnecessary to that life which we have made." When we "just do it" in our Nikes, my students hear Thoreau whispering: Are you in fact doing it on the shoulders of the Indonesian (or now, because of a recent rise in the price of Indonesian labor, Vietnamese) sweatshop workers who make those Nikes for pennies an hour? When we enjoy scientific pursuits and contemplations in our university's new Jim Bob Moffett Building, Thoreau challenges: Are you sitting on the shoulders of the South Asian islanders whose home Moffett's Freeport Mining Company has been literally grinding to powder while extracting from it billions of dollars worth of minerals? Who among us, peacefully pursuing our private lives, would choose to listen to a constant barrage of such discomfiting questions?

Even if we postmodern shoulder sitters clearly discerned all those who bore our weight and firmly resolved to get down, it would be hard—far harder than it was for Thoreau—to know how to begin. So I don't blame my students for resisting "Civil Disobedience." In fact, since I believe in the educational value of critical counterstatement, and since it would be hypocritical, as well as cruel, to assume a stance of unqualified advocacy when I teach this essay, I encourage them to sharpen their terms of resistance to it. Thoreau is an anarchist, some students come to argue, whereas democratic government depends upon respect for the principles of majority rule and due procedural change. He is an egotist, others claim, a person who falsely holds his own moral understanding to be universal and absolute, whereas in fact morality is variable and relative. He is an isolate, a third group points out, assuming the moral luxury of someone without family or ambition (and with a benefactor who let him build a squatter's cabin on his land) to wash his hands of a society in which he has no practical investment. He is a fraud, cries a fourth contingent, dressing up a pleasant breezy night in a comfortable whitewashed room with a picturesque view of the village (and chocolate milk for breakfast) as a martyrdom to conscience.

All of these objections are reasonable. Yet while they may aptly criticize Thoreau's position, none seem effectively to parry his emotional and ethical thrust. If many of my students are wounded by their reading of Thoreau, as—despite their defenses—I believe they are, it is not so much a wound that his words deliver as one that they expose. This wound is the price of privilege. It is a price paid in various currencies by all of us for whom life, liberty, and the pursuit of happiness remain inalienable rights and reasonable expectations. It is paid in nameless, low-frequency fear; in deepening political cynicism; in the curious mixture of adulation and contempt that our society heaps on celebrities, its symbols of unfettered yet undeserved personal privilege; in our resigned familiarity with the cardboard messages of the damaged and deprived Americans who daily stand at highway intersections and with the saga of deprivation and damage serialized on the nightly news.

This is the tax that Thoreau collects, even from the students who resist him—civil young people insufficiently inured to "the necessary friction," as Thoreau puts it, of a social engine that seems theirs to ride but not to steer. That such young people incur this soul tax in reading "Civil Disobedience" may be regarded, to paraphrase MacLeish, as what is bleakest about Thoreau's relation to us in the last decade of the twentieth century. Yet it may also be seen as what is most hopeful. For it testifies to the unlikely currency—the expenditures of the sixties notwithstanding—of F. O. Matthiessen's 1941 declaration on Thoreau: "His vitality as a revolutionary is still unexhausted."

ROBERT A. GROSS

Quiet War with the State:
Henry David Thoreau and Civil Disobedience†

Few political protests have achieved so little in their time and gained so much subsequent renown as Henry David Thoreau's gesture of "civil disobedience" against the Mexican War, now approaching its 160th anniversary in July 2006. A year into his sojourn at Walden Pond, on the outskirts of Concord, Massachusetts, and several months after the start of hostilities, so the familiar story goes, Thoreau took the radical step of refusing to pay his taxes in order to protest the war. For that act of conscience, he was taken by the town constable and locked up in the local jail, where he spent the night, only to be released the next day after someone, probably his aunt, paid the tax on his behalf. Thoreau then returned to Walden woods to continue the experiment of independent living in nature that he would ultimately transform into a literary classic. *Walden*, published in 1854, established his enduring reputation as a writer. The political protest made him equally famous. In 1849, Thoreau published an account of his anti-war action in an obscure publication with the unlikely name *Aesthetic Papers*. Originally called "Resistance to Civil Government," the essay has become known worldwide as "Civil Disobedience," the title it was given in an 1866 collection of Thoreau's writings issued four years after his death. Offering a principled justification for conscientious refusal to comply with immoral laws, "Civil Disobedience" has entered our political lexicon and made its mark on history through its influence on twentieth-century movements for nonviolent, democratic change, from Mahatma Gandhi's campaign for Indian independence to Martin Luther King's leadership of the civil rights cause in the United States. Russian anarchists, members of

† From *The Yale Review* 93.4 (2005): 1–17. Reprinted by permission. The original version of this essay was delivered as the inaugural lecture for the Henry David Thoreau Chair in Multidisciplinary Studies at the National Autonomous University of Mexico on June 7, 2004.

the Danish resistance in World War II, early opponents of South African apartheid have all claimed Thoreau as an inspiration. Appropriately, in Mexico he has been heralded as a key source for the nonviolent challenge of native peoples to federal and state laws on indigenous rights and culture. "The ghost of Henry D. Thoreau walks proudly through the indigenous regions of Mexico," declared Luis Hernández Navarro in *La Jornada* on 4 September 2001. "His example has spread to all corners."

Yet, for all the acclaim it has won, Thoreau's act of civil disobedience was utterly irrelevant to the course of events in Mexico starting with the annexation of Texas by the United States in December 1844 and culminating in the Treaty of Guadalupe Hidalgo in February 1848. Although it occurred not long after the conflict had begun and well before the dramatic victories by U.S. forces at Monterrey and Veracruz, and although it took place in New England, the heart of American opposition to the Polk administration's aggressive policy, Thoreau's anti-war gesture came and went without any public impact. The local newspaper, the Concord *Freeman*, said nothing about the arrest, nor did anybody in the Boston press, not even the militant abolitionist periodical *The Liberator*, whose editor William Lloyd Garrison was quick to condemn the war as one "of aggression, of invasion, of conquest, and rapine—marked by ruffianism, perfidy, and every other feature of national depravity." Thoreau provided no public explanation of his action until late January 1848, when he came before his neighbors at the Concord Lyceum and delivered a lecture on "The Rights and Duties of the Individual in Relation to Government." By then, the war had wound down, and peace lay at hand. The Treaty of Guadalupe Hidalgo was already a year old by the time the lecture finally appeared in print. No one can accuse Thoreau of seeking publicity.

Surprisingly, once he did get around to explaining himself, Thoreau had hardly anything to say about the very event—the war between the United States and Mexico—that triggered his "Resistance to Civil Government." Opponents of "Mr. Polk's War" regularly denounced the administration for starting the conflict and then lying about its cause; newly elected Whig congressman Abraham Lincoln demanded to know the exact "spot" where Mexican troops had invaded U.S. territory and spilled "American blood on American soil." Thoreau eschewed such concerns. He took it for granted that top officials had gotten the nation into an illegal and undemocratic war. The conflict was "the work of comparatively a few individuals using the standing government as their tool; for, in the outset, the people would not have consented to this measure." Let others worry, too, about the corrupting effects of the war on

American character. To Ralph Waldo Emerson, the Transcendentalist sage, Anglo-Saxon civilization, with its irrepressible "race-drive," was destined to spread across the continent. Far better to await the inevitable triumph of American culture than to prevail by violence and risk contamination by an alien people he deemed "degraded and corrupt." Thoreau, the erstwhile disciple of Emerson, avoided all such speculation about causes and consequences. He kept his focus on the essential design of the war: to expand the empire of slavery. "When a sixth of the population of a nation which has undertaken to be the refuge of liberty are slaves, and a whole country is unjustly overrun and conquered by a foreign army, and subjected to military law," he thundered, "I think that it is not too soon for honest men to rebel and revolutionize." This was the common sentiment among New England abolitionists, and Thoreau never deviated from that line.

If the anti-war protest was belated, it was also something of an afterthought. Thoreau had actually stopped paying his taxes sometime in 1842 or 1843, while Texas was still an independent republic and war with Mexico was not on the horizon. He did so without fanfare, withdrawing his support for a state he considered hostile to individual freedom. This action expressed a militant spirit of anarchism stirring among radical abolitionists in the Boston area, who denied the right of any institution—church, state, or family—to coerce the individual. Prominent among them was Thoreau's Concord neighbor, the Transcendentalist Bronson Alcott, who joined in founding the New England Non-Resistance Society in 1839. The group was dedicated to the principle of "gospel love"; taking the Sermon on the Mount as their guide, they renounced every exercise of force and violence, whether imposed by government or committed by private persons. "I look upon the Non-Resistance Society as an assertion of the right of self-government," Alcott proclaimed. "Why should I employ a church to write my creed or a state to govern me? Why not write my own creed? Why not govern myself?" In this spirit, Alcott also stopped paying his local taxes, for which he was briefly arrested in 1843, only to be released within a few hours after a fellow townsman intent on avoiding a public scandal picked up the debt. The episode was a dress rehearsal for Thoreau's act of tax resistance, and Alcott may well have been his model. But Thoreau never embraced the cause of Non-Resistance; in fact, he argued against it in a debate at the Concord Lyceum, with Alcott on the opposing side. Far from turning the other cheek, he was prepared to defy authority, when necessary, and to court confrontation. And so it was that when Samuel Staples, the town constable, finally caught up with Thoreau in the summer of 1846 and demanded payment of four years' back taxes, the young radical provoked a crisis. Staples, an occasional hunting companion of Thoreau's, offered to lend him the money, if that was the problem. But Thoreau refused. The constable then warned his recalcitrant friend that he was risking arrest. "As well now as any time, Sam," was the reply. Had Staples been more attentive to his duties and dunned the delinquent taxpayer sooner, Thoreau might have gone to jail in 1844 or 1845—before the war with Mexico had even begun.

Even the tax he refused to pay had nothing to do with slavery or the war. It was a local poll tax, assessed annually on all males over age sixteen in every Massachusetts township, in order to pay the costs of town, county, and state government. In the 1840s, the charge was usually $1.50, two or three days' wages for a common laborer—the amount levied on Thoreau, which local tax records from early 1842 show him as paying. It took some tortuous reasoning to connect this ancient tax, dating back to the Puritans, to the support of the federal government or to the financing of an "unrighteous and unjust" war. The Polk administration paid for its volunteer troops in Mexico by raising tariffs on imported goods. For this reason, Ralph Waldo Emerson was baffled by his young friend's vehicle of protest. "Refusing payment of the state tax does not reach the evil so nearly as many other methods within your reach," Emerson reflected in his private journal. "The [Massachusetts] state tax does not pay the Mexican War. Your coat, your sugar, your Latin & French & German book, your watch does." If Thoreau really meant to deprive the government of funds to fight the war, he should refrain from buying these goods.

It is hardly surprising that, apart from a few intimates and a couple of casual onlookers, nobody bothered to remark on Thoreau's brief confrontation with the law. For in July 1846, he was an unmarried, twenty-nine-year-old Harvard graduate who had yet to realize the great hopes of family and friends. Since finishing college in 1837, he had taught school, worked as a private tutor, helped out in his father's pencil business, and been a handyman in Emerson's household. None of these efforts did much to advance his worldly prospects. Nor had he made significant progress in his ambitions as a writer. Though he proudly claimed "letters" as his "profession," he had published little. A short obituary in the local newspaper, a report to Garrison's *Liberator* on the abolitionist Wendell Phillip's speech at the Concord Lyceum, a few essays on classical and Oriental writers in the Transcendentalist journal *The Dial*, edited by his mentor Emerson: that was the corpus of Thoreau's publications down through 1846. The sojourn at Walden was meant to change all that. It constituted a writer's retreat, where Thoreau could cultivate prose along with his beans, and it proved spectacularly productive, yielding one book, *A Week on the Concord and Merrimack Rivers*, published in 1849, the first draft of another, *Walden*, and several articles and lectures. Thoreau had to take time away from his writing desk to get arrested. But to the outside world, he seemed an eccentric ne'er-do-well living idly in the woods. On the town's tax rolls, he was merely one among many landless laborers, obliged to others for their daily bread.

Living "alone, in the woods, a mile from any neighbor," enjoying solitude in nature, and absorbed in his writing, Thoreau might well have ignored the drumbeat of war. Walden offered a refuge from all the expectations and pressures limiting his creativity. "I dwelt nearer to those parts of the universe and to those eras in history which had most attracted me," he recalled. "Where I lived was as far off as many a region viewed nightly by astronomers." Thoreau liked to feign indifference to current events, and he dismissed the value of the daily press. "I am sure that I never read any memorable news in a newspaper." "Read not the Times," he advised. "Read the Eternities." But he was incapable of following his own counsel. His hometown paper, the *Concord Freeman*, was enthusiastic about Texas annexation, and when war came, it called on readers to rally around the troops. The voice of the local Democratic Party, the *Freeman*, allowed no room for dissent. The opposition Whigs decried the war but approved funds for its support, lest they be accused of betraying American soldiers in harm's way. Then as now, critics of the war were charged with undermining military morale. In Concord, opinion was closely divided, with voters favoring the Democrats by narrow margins. Sam Staples may well have gained from arresting Thoreau; in 1847, the Democratic constable won easy election as the town's representative to the state legislature. In this pro-war setting, Thoreau surely despaired of his neighbors.

But what to do? For the abolitionist Garrison, the answer was simple: "at every sacrifice," he counseled readers of the *Liberator* ". . . refuse enlistment, contribution, aid and countenance to the war." Thoreau's sisters Helen and Sophia embraced that stance. Active abolitionists since the mid-1830s, they pledged to resist the war in a collective statement signed by some 290 fellow radicals and printed in the *Liberator* early in June 1846. Would their brother join them? Although he had stopped paying taxes after 1842, Thoreau did not refuse all public duties. As late as 1844, he turned out for the annual militia muster on the town common. But while living in the woods, he stayed away, preferring the bean field to the training field. If this was an anti-war protest, Thoreau never called attention to it, and no authority ever called him to account. (The penalty for non-attendance was a fine, another tax he could have refused to pay.) In contrast to his sisters, solitary action was

Thoreau's way. He found inspiration in the idealistic figure of Wendell Phillips, the elite Boston lawyer turned abolitionist orator, who spoke out against Texas annexation before the Concord lyceum in March 1845. So moved was Thoreau by the absolute integrity of the speaker, whose every utterance was delivered "earnestly . . . wisely and bravely, without counsel or consent of any," that he sent a fulsome report to the *Liberator*. In Thoreau's eyes, Phillips was "an eloquent speaker and a righteous man."

Yet, Thoreau had withdrawn into the woods "to transact some private business" and not to engage in public protest. What, then, provoked him into action? The answer, it appears, was a powerful anti-war speech by Ralph Waldo Emerson on the Fourth of July 1846. Lamenting the "inaction and apathy" of Massachusetts citizens who opposed the war but did nothing to stop it, Emerson indicted the motives of the rich and respectable. Pusillanimous Whig merchants and bankers, fearful of alienating Southern customers, put profit over principle; other citizens were loath to set aside propriety in forthright defense of morality. "People are respecters, not of essential, but of external law, decorum, routine, and official forms." The only hope lay in the example of the abolitionists, "this fervent, self-denying school of love and action," ready to be martyrs to a holy cause. Printed in *The National Anti-Slavery Standard* on 16 July 1846, this address spoke to Thoreau's mood. Answering Emerson's call, Thoreau overcame his inclinations and made a stand for conscience. Ironically, his mentor disapproved, calling the act of tax refusal "mean and skulking and in bad taste." In Emerson's judgment, tax resistance by abolitionists, "hot headed partialists" obsessed with "a few specialized grievances," was appropriate. Not so when it was committed by his disciple Thoreau, whose focus should rest on broader concerns. "Your true quarrel," Emerson opined, "is with the state of Man."

Coincidence and purpose thus combined to spur Thoreau into radical action. The "hermit of Walden" seized on his chance encounter with Sam Staples to provoke a confrontation that would dramatize his hostility to a state committing crimes against humanity. No matter that the poll tax was ill-suited to his end. Staple's demand for back taxes afforded a pretext for Thoreau to make a symbolic protest against a national government he could do nothing to change. His real target was his neighbors, whose political convictions he might affect through his example of self-sacrifice for the sake of conscience. To be sure, Thoreau was still a radical anarchist, for whom governmental coercion, and not just the war against Mexico, remained the fundamental issue. Shortly after leaving jail, Thoreau remarked, "The only highwayman I ever met was the state itself— When I have refused to pay the tax which is demanded for that protection I did not want, itself has robbed me— When I have asserted the freedom it declared it has imprisoned me." But he kept those opinions to his journal. In any case, his aunt took the wind out of his sails by paying the overdue taxes, and he was obliged to return to Walden, having failed to influence even his old friend Staples, who, for all his congeniality, readily turned himself into an instrument of the state. "The jailor or constable as a mere man and neighbor . . . may be a right worthy man with a thought in the brain of him—," Thoreau lamented, "but as the officer & tool of the state, he has no more understanding or heart than his prison key or his staff." Consequently, Thoreau bided his time and postponed a public explanation of his protest until after he completed his sojourn in the woods and returned to civilization.

The result was worth the wait. Thoreau transformed his symbolic gesture of opposition to the war into a personal declaration of independence. Rejecting the claims of the state, he upheld the sovereignty of the individual, the "higher and independent power" from which government properly derives "all its own power and authority." Thoreau wrapped himself in the mantle of the men who had made "the Revolution of '75," the Minutemen of Concord who had faced off against invading British Regulars at the Old North Bridge on 19 April 1775 and sparked the war for American independence. "Resistance to Civil Government" reenacted that moment and reaffirmed its guiding principle: "the right of revolution; that is, the right to refuse allegiance to and to resist the government, when its tyranny or its inefficiency are great and unendurable." This was the original Revolution of Thomas Jefferson and Thomas Paine. Faced with an unjust demand from the ruling powers, Thoreau determined "to refuse allegiance to the State, to withdraw and stand aloof from it effectually." Though he took up no arms, he was engaged, like his revolutionary forebears, in active resistance to oppression: "I quietly declare war with the State, after my fashion."

Yet Thoreau took the revolutionary tradition and turned it to individualistic purposes the founders of the Republic would have abhorred. "I love mankind," he quipped after his arrest. "I hate the institutions of their fathers." True to his word, he invoked his version of 1776 to repudiate the legacy of the revolutionary generation. He was equally scornful of the contemporary scene, finding fault with virtually everything around him. In his damning judgment, the characteristic institutions of the United States in the mid-nineteenth century betrayed the authentic spirit of the Revolution. Not surprisingly, this sweeping attack on American society did not go down well with conventional patriots. After "Resistance to Civil Government" was published in 1849, one Boston newspaper dismissed it as "crazy," while the Boston *Courier* likened Thoreau to the European revolutionaries of 1848. The editors offered "an earnest prayer that he may become a better subject, in time." If not, let him "take a trip to France, and preach his doctrine" of resistance to the "Red Republicans." Few others deigned to comment. The essay would have to wait until the twentieth century to find an appreciative audience. Even so, "Civil Disobedience" stands for a radical individualistic strain of American thought that flourished among Transcendentalists and abolitionists in the three decades before the Civil War and occupies a critical place in our intellectual heritage from that time—Thoreau's disdain for inherited ideas and traditions notwithstanding.

What so aroused Thoreau's fury? When the liberal French aristocrat Alexis de Tocqueville visited the United States in 1831, he set out to identify the key practices and institutions at the heart of the Republic. Two realms stood out in his view. The first was politics, the forum of popular self-government, of which the United States was the exemplar in the Western world of the time. Democracy in America, Tocqueville discovered, was founded on the active engagement of citizens in the affairs of government at all levels. "The people are . . . the real directing power; and although the form of government is representative, it is evident that the opinions, the prejudices, the interests, and even the passions of the people are hindered by no permanent obstacles from exercising a perpetual influence on the daily conduct of affairs." Complementing the political arena and extending the power of the people was the second sphere, the voluntary association, which enlisted private individuals in a host of organizations formed for mutual benefit. "Americans of all ages, all conditions, and all dispositions constantly form associations," Tocqueville observed. "The most democratic society on the face of the earth is that in which men have, in our time, carried to the highest perfection the art of pursuing in common the object of their common desires and have applied this new science to the greatest number of purposes." Tocqueville took the measure of these twin institutions, warning against the potential "tyranny of the majority," worrying about the leveling effects of too much equality, and balancing his criticism with praise for Americans' love of liberty and independence.

Henry David Thoreau, who came of age in the 1820s and 1830s, looked at the same society as had Tocqueville—or more precisely, his little corner of New England—and identified the same characteristic institutions. But far more than the skeptical Frenchman, the Yankee was appalled by what he saw, and in "Civil Disobedience," he gives vent to that disgust. Consider his reactions to the mass democratic politics of the Jacksonian age, with its fierce party competition and its panoply of techniques—caucuses, conventions, newspapers, speeches, parades, barbecues—designed to stir the enthusiasm of the people and bring out their votes. This was a system contrived by and large for white men only; in the 1830s and 1840s, it came to embrace the vast majority of them, even as it excluded blacks in most states (though not in Thoreau's Concord, where a handful of African Americans did cast their ballots). But it was not the racism of American politics that disturbed Thoreau. Rather, he concentrated his scorn on the politicians of his day, whose cheap words and petty quarrels he deemed irrelevant to the serious business of life. "I hear of a convention to be held at Baltimore, or elsewhere, for the selection of a candidate for the Presidency, made up chiefly of editors, and men who are politicians by profession; but I think, what is it to any independent, intelligent, and respectable man what decision they may come to . . . ?" His opinion of the U.S. Congress was no higher. "If we were left solely to the wordy wit of legislators in Congress for our guidance, uncorrected by the seasonable experience and the effectual complaints of the people, America would not long retain her rank among the nations." That judgment surely resonates with many U.S. citizens today.

Behind these witty sentiments lay a radical disaffection from popular democracy as it was practiced even in the small towns of New England in the 1840s. Thoreau spurned the ordinary exercises of political action by his contemporaries. In the late 1830s, as he was reaching adulthood, the reform impulse surged, inspiring thousands of ordinary citizens—women as well as men—to join in mass petitions to their state legislatures and to Congress. The people called on their representatives to ban the sale of hard liquor, to prohibit the delivery of mail on the Sabbath, to stop the forcible removal of the Cherokee Indians from Georgia, and to take vigorous steps to stem the expansion of slavery. The Thoreau family threw themselves into campaigns on behalf of the dispossessed, as did the Emersons. Hardly a petition against slavery circulated in Concord without attracting the signatures of Henry's parents, his aunts, his older brother, his two sisters. For a while, he lined up alongside them; in 1837, twenty-year-old "D. H. Thoreau"—he had not yet demanded to be known as "Henry David"—joined with 127 other men, including his father and brother John, to oppose the annexation of Texas. He also signed petitions calling on Congress to end slavery and the slave trade in the District of Columbia and to bar the admission of Florida into the Union as a slave state. But after 1840, his name drops off the lists. He remained silent even in 1845, when a new campaign was mounted to oppose the annexation of Texas—a drive led by his aunts among Concord's women and supported by his sisters and father. For all his hatred of slavery, Thoreau was determined to go it alone. "It is not my business," he told readers, "to be petitioning the governor or the legislature any more than it is theirs to petition me; and, if they should not hear my petition, what should I do then?"

Vote them out of office, his contemporaries would have said, but Thoreau wasn't listening. In common with Garrison and other radical abolitionists, he declined to participate in a political system fatally flawed by its reliance on force and its compromise with slavery. But Thoreau had further objections. "All voting is a sort of gaming, like chequers or backgammon," he maintained, "with a slight moral tinge to it, a playing with right and wrong, with moral questions; and betting naturally accompanies it." How could anyone leave moral choices to chance? Right or wrong is not simply a matter of opinion, to be inscribed on paper ballots and counted up to produce a decision. "Even voting *for the right* is *doing* nothing for it. It is only expressing to men feebly your desire that it should prevail." Not that American politics ever allowed a true choice. In the Jacksonian party system, as Thoreau saw it, voting was reduced to a symbolic decision among alternatives carefully circumscribed by political "demagogues" from the start. Many historians of the period would agree. Yet, even if elections did provide clear-cut options on moral questions, Thoreau could not abide the principle of majority rule. In American politics, decisions are made according to mathematical rule: whoever gets one vote more than his or her rivals wins. To Thoreau, this quantitative logic was anathema. Rather than wait until they achieve "a majority of one," men of conscience should trust to their convictions. "I think that it is enough if they have God on their side . . . any man more right than his neighbors, constitutes a majority of one already."

For the vices of American life, moral reformers prescribed a host of remedies, but in Thoreau's unsparing view, they were part of the problem, *not* the solution. In *Walden*, he painted a scathing picture of the "philanthropist," who projects his personal distress onto society at large, then organizes a reform group to relieve it. "If any thing ail a man, so that he does not perform his functions . . . he forthwith sets about reforming—the world." But the characteristic vehicle of reform, the benevolent association, operated on flawed premises. The temperance society solicited pledges to abstain from drinking; the Bible and tract societies collected money to distribute pious works to the poor; the anti-slavery society gathered up signatures on petitions. Every one had its exclusive cause, pursued with unflagging zeal. "There are a thousand hacking at the branches of evil to one who is striking at the root." The sorry results of this "partial" strategy were evident in the ineffectiveness of abolitionists in challenging the war against Mexico. Thoreau repeated Emerson's complaint: the anti-slavery forces were all talk and no action. The Garrisonians boldly announce "no union with slaveholders," but instead of busying themselves with useless petitions to break up the Union, "why do they not dissolve it themselves—the union between themselves and the State,—and refuse to pay their quota into its treasury?"

The new mass society taking shape in the 1840s was built on numbers. "Men are become of no account," Emerson warned in the "American Scholar" address of 1837. "Men in history, men in the world of to-day are bugs, are spawn, and are called 'the mass' and the 'herd.' " Construed as units in the mass, individuals served as raw materials for the large-scale enterprises of the era: the textile mills, the slave plantations, the political parties, the benevolent empire. Aggregating numbers—votes, signatures, dollars—to achieve specialized ends: this was the operating principle Thoreau detected in America at mid-century, and in "Resistance to Civil Government" he refused its quantitative mentality. "Our statistics are at fault. The population has been returned too large. How many *men* are there to a square thousand miles in this country? Hardly one."

If Thoreau was impatient with reformers, he had no sympathy with conservatives, particularly the Whig politicians and voters whose opposition to the war was entirely rhetorical. "There are thousands who are *in opinion* opposed to slavery and to the war," he observed, "who yet in effect do nothing to put an end to them. . . . They hesitate, and they regret, and sometimes they petition; but they do nothing in earnest and with effect." Some feared to act out of misguided loyalty to the American government, to which they paid unthinking allegiance out of habit. "This American government,—what is it but a tradition, though a recent one, endeavoring to transmit itself unimpaired to posterity, but each instant losing some of its integrity?" Others closely calculated their self-interest, judging public policies by their pocketbooks. Such were the "hundred thousand merchants and farmers" in Massachusetts "who are more interested in commerce and agriculture than they are in humanity, and are not prepared to do justice to the slave and to Mexico, *cost what it may*." In Massachusetts senator Daniel Webster, the perpetual contender for the Whig presidential nomination, they found the perfect spokesman, who put a towering intellect into the service of vested interests. Webster followed the rule of "policy and expediency"; he approached all questions with a utilitarian calculus, carefully weighing the costs and benefits of decisions even on matters of principle. Known as "the Defender of the Constitution," the cautious lawyer and statesman was devoted to "the men of '87," who had gathered in Philadelphia back in 1787 and drawn up the compact for national government. If the framers of the Constitution had made an immoral bargain with slaveholders to secure their ends, so be it. The senator from Massachusetts would never question their decisions; his mission was to uphold existing institutions. But for Thoreau, the real Founding Fathers were the brave men of 1775, who had met the Redcoats at the North Bridge and launched a revolution.

For all his admiration for the "Revolution of '75," Thoreau had actually strayed far from the Minutemen and their world. The New England colonists who took up arms against the British on the famous day of 19 April 1775 were defending a communal society whose ideals were antithetical to Thoreau's. They fought to preserve ancient institutions laid down by the Puritan fathers, those "worthy Ancestors" who had taken refuge from English tyranny in "the American Wilderness" and built a self-governing way of life around town, church, militia, schools, and family. This corporate community was made up of ranks and orders, all knit together in a well-ordered hierarchy. Just as the earth "has Mountains and Plains, Hills and Vallies," New Englanders believed, so "there are the Distinctions of Superiours and Inferiours, Rulers and Ruled, publick and private Orders of Men." In this patriarchal society, sons and daughters were expected to follow faithfully in their fathers' and mothers' paths, with one generation succeeding another on the land. The dominant ideal was to "live thickly" amid kin and neighbors, who gathered in the meetinghouse each Sabbath to worship together under a minister supported by their taxes. That blueprint for community was never fully realized, certainly not in Concord, which over the two centuries since its founding in 1635 had felt the force of dynamic social changes and developed into a more diverse and fluid place. Even so, the intellectual heritage of the Puritans, though attenuated, persisted into Thoreau's time. "Who could live alone and independent?" the Reverend Ezra Ripley, Concord's minister for six decades, from 1778 to 1841, once asked his congregation. "Who but some disgusted hermit or half crazy enthusiast will say to society, I have no need of thee; I am under no obligation to my fellow-men?"

The Reverend Ripley, the step-grandfather of Ralph Waldo Emerson, never anticipated the Transcendentalists and their world. The infant he baptized as "David Henry Thoreau," raised under his preaching, "signed off" from Ripley's church once he came of age. "Know all men by these presents," he declared with a flourish, "that I, Henry Thoreau, do not wish to be regarded as a member of any incorporated society which I have not joined." The young man prized his independence from nearly all institutions, as he boldly asserted in "Resistance to Civil Government." "I am not responsible for the successful working of the machinery of society. I am not the son of the engineer." Indeed, he recommended his self-sufficient way of life at Walden as the best means of preserving individual integrity. How could the man of wealth exercise moral independence? "The rich man . . . is always sold to the institution which makes him rich. Absolutely speaking, the more money, the less virtue." To the eighteenth-century statesmen who created the American republic, the possession of property was the bulwark of civic responsibility. Thoreau up-ended that equation. In his outlook, the fewer goods, the greater independence. "You must hire or squat somewhere, and raise but a small crop, and eat that soon. You must live within yourself, and depend upon yourself . . . and not have many affairs."

What obligation, then, did he have to society? "Every man in a republic," insisted the prominent Philadelphia revolutionary Benjamin Rush in 1787, "is public property. His time and talents—his youth—his manhood—his old age—nay more, life, all belong to his country." Nothing could be farther from Thoreau's thinking. Even as he went to jail to protest slavery and the war, he denied any responsibility to do so. "It is not a man's duty, as a matter of course, to devote himself to the eradication of any, even the most enormous wrong; he may still properly have other concerns to engage him." Civil disobedience had a different justification. Thoreau asserted a principle of negative obligation: he would *not*, directly or indirectly, be complicitous in injustice to others, even if called on by the state to do so. "If I devote myself to other pursuits and contemplations, I must first see, at least, that I do not pursue them sitting upon another man's shoulders." This was the extent of social responsibility: in Thoreau's moral imagination, each individual was a sovereign self, free and independent—and respectful of the boundaries between itself and others.

Yet that line was not so firm after all. In "Resistance to Civil Government," Thoreau undercut his principle of negative obligation with an affirmation of positive duty. "Under a government which imprisons any unjustly, the true place for a just man is also a prison." Here Thoreau's rhetoric goes beyond the moral calculation he had urged as a rule: Are you sitting on somebody else's shoulders? He opens a way for the expression of social solidarity. When the man of conscience is true to his principles and refuses to be "the agent of injustice to another," he will find himself in a select society of heroic souls, whose bodies may be confined behind bars but whose spirits are free. Such individuals constitute a "wise minority" in society and should be cherished. "Heroes, patriots, martyrs, reformers in the great sense, and *men*," they "serve the

State with their consciences also, and so necessarily resist it for the most part; and [so] they are commonly treated by it as enemies." In sacrificing for the right, they become as selfless servants of the common good as any eighteenth-century republican. It is time to recognize their virtue. "Why does [the government] always crucify Christ, and excommunicate Copernicus and Luther, and pronounce Washington and Franklin rebels?" In refusing to pay his taxes and going to jail for the night, Thoreau was joining that exalted company. And he did it all for the sake of his neighbors.

And so, it turns out that Thoreau's quixotic act of civil disobedience—refusing a tax that had no bearing on the war and offering no explanation for his protest until the war was at an end—ultimately led him back to the community he so often upbraided. In the desire to sacrifice himself for principle and the common good, in imagining himself as Christ crucified, he was a faithful son of the Puritans and a loyal keeper of the "revolution of '75." The terms of his dissent were set by the world he had inherited: the interdependent community of Concord and New England. Thoreau was locked into opposition with a culture to which he was tightly bound. "I first saw the light in the quiet village of Concord, of Revolutionary memory," he once wrote in an autobiographical sketch for his Harvard classmates. "I shall ever pride myself upon the place of my birth—may she never have cause to be ashamed of her sons. If I forget thee, O Concord, let my right hand forget her cunning."

And what lessons are there for the rest of us, who live well beyond Thoreau's Concord in the fragile, interdependent global society of the twenty-first century? They lie in the unexpected fusion of seemingly antithetical strands in "Resistance to Civil Government": the strident libertarian voice rejecting all coercive institutions, the strenuous moralist intent on serving society through an act of conscience. In our time, many Americans have inherited Thoreau's disdain for politics, his distaste for money-making as an end in itself, his insistence on the individual as the basic unit of the social order. What is missing these days is the appreciation of the many threads that bind us all. In his life, Thoreau discovered time and again that action from principle was imperative to avoid "sitting upon another man's shoulders." "Action from principle,—the perception and performance of right,—changes things and relations [he wrote in "Resistance to Civil Government"]; it is essentially revolutionary, and does not consist wholly with anything which was. It not only divides states and churches, it divides families; aye, it divides the *individual*, separating the diabolical in him from the divine." Paradoxically, such action, the foundation of civil disobedience, also connects the individual more closely to others. To fulfill this ethic would surely be as fully a revolutionary act today as it was in Thoreau's time.

ALBERT J. VON FRANK

Fourth of July†

> What, to the American slave, is your 4th of July? I answer; a day that reveals to him, more than all other days in the year, the gross injustice and cruelty to which he is the constant victim.
> Frederick Douglass[1]

At home in Concord during the Burns trial,[2] Thoreau was busy loafing at his ease, quite literally "observing a spear of summer grass," as his journals tell us. He was also observing the riot of the cankerworms in the black cherry trees and in a general sort of way supervising the "revolution of the seasons." He could not spare the time to come to Boston, preferring instead "to be present at the birth of shadow" in the first expansion of young leaves. He very much blamed "such a time as this" for dragging his attention away to the poisonous vulgarity of the newspapers, but he read them and took the measure of the Burns case from Boston's proslavery sheets as well as from the *Liberator* and the *Commonwealth*. On the day of the rendition, he took his mother and sister on a boat ride along the Assabet to Annursnack.[3]

On the next day arrived two Worcester friends, H. G. O. Blake and Theo Brown, who had undoubtedly come from Boston. That weekend, indoors and out, they talked about justice and heroism, themes that kept them coming back to the name of their mutual friend Higginson.[4] For Thoreau, it was an occasion to find fault with fame:

> In some cases fame is perpetually false and unjust. Or rather I should say that she *never* recognizes the simple heroism of an action, but only as connected with its apparent consequence.

† From *The Trials of Anthony Burns: Freedom and Slavery in Emerson's Boston* (Cambridge: Harvard University Press, 1998), pp. 276–85. Copyright © 1998 Harvard University Press. Reprinted by permission. Authorial footnotes have been condensed and in some cases omitted by the editor; *Walden* and "Slavery in Massachusetts" page numbers refer to this Norton Critical Edition.
1. Frederick Douglass, *The Frederick Douglass Papers*, John W. Blasingame. 5 vols. (New Haven: Yale University Press, 1979–92), 2: 192.
2. See n. 2, p. 247 [*Editor*].
3. Henry David Thoreau, *The Journal of Henry David Thoreau*, Bradford Torrey and Francis H. Allen. 14 vols. (New York: Dover Publications, 1962), 6: 303–4, 314, 323.
4. Thomas Wentworth Higginson; see n. 2, p. 247 [*Editor*].

It praises the interested energy of the Boston Tea Party, but will be comparatively silent about the more bloody and disinterestedly heroic attack on the Boston Court-House, simply because the latter was unsuccessful. Fame is not just. It never finely or discriminately praises, but coarsely hurrahs. The truest acts of heroism never reach her ear, are never published by her trumpet.

In fact until June 10, when he was arrested, Higginson was the reverse of famous, his secret close-guarded by friends and kept from the ears of the police. Thereafter it was evident that he, unlike his more obscure co-defendants, would be the focus of useful publicity in a political trial. At this point Lucy Stone suggested that, for fame's sake and for the sake of the cause, it would be best altogether if the minister were convicted and hanged.[5]

Thoreau had his own reasons for thinking about fame at this time. Since March he had been reading and revising galley proofs for *Walden*, expecting publication in June, recalling all the while the failure of his first book just five years before. No, fame was never just, never discriminating: people were "so occupied with the factitious cares and superfluously coarse labors of life that its finer fruits cannot be plucked by them" (7). Concerned about the reception of *Walden*, he had nevertheless learned to curb his longing for general approval and to expect little or nothing in the way of commendation. Besides, there was nothing heroic—comparatively speaking—about publishing a book. He would put that work aside, delaying its appearance until August, and speak out on the Burns matter.

Thoreau's speaking fell somewhat accidentally into a struggle over ideological ownership of the Fourth of July. On June 4, when Thoreau in his journal compared Higginson's heroism to that of the mock-Indians of the Revolution, Higginson, in his *Massachusetts in Mourning*, was calling for the cancellation of Fourth of July ceremonies in Worcester. It would be a mockery, he felt, to rejoice much at this time in the nation's freedom. Four days later, the Boston Vigilance Committee[6] called on all the towns of the Commonwealth to imitate "the worthy example of the City of Providence" and omit the usual celebrations. Then,

> As if to glory in their shame, and wantonly to outrage heaven and earth, the City Authorities of Boston,—*fresh from the kid-*

---

5. Ibid., 325, 328; Mary Thacher Higginson, *Thomas Wentworth Higginson: The Story of His Life* (1914; rpt. Port Washington, N.Y.: Kennikat Press, n.d.), 147; Stone quoted in Tilden G. Edelstein, *Strange Enthusiasm: A Life of Thomas Wentworth Higginson* (New Haven: Yale University Press, 1968), 171. [Lucy Stone (1818–93), suffragist, abolitionist, and advocate of gender equality—*Editor*].

6. Like those in other northern towns, the Boston Vigilance Committee sought to protect the city's African-American populations from southern "kidnappers" [*Editor*].

napping of Anthony Burns,—have made the most extensive
preparations to celebrate the Fourth of July with all the pomp
and circumstance of a hollow, man-stealing patriotism, ending
with a costly display of fireworks in the evening, in which such
bitter mockeries as *"America is free,"* and *"statutes of Liberty
and Justice,"* (!!) are to be emblazoned in fiery forms, for the
admiration of a people in vassalage to Southern slave-hunters
and slave-drivers!

In response—or simultaneously—the Massachusetts Anti-Slavery
Society called for a counterdemonstration, "A Grand Mass Meeting
of the Friends of Freedom," to assemble at a picnic ground in
Framingham to hear such speakers as Garrison, Phillips, Charles
Remond, Stephen S. Foster,[7] and Lucy Stone. While certain newspapers condemned the abolitionists for trenching on the national
jubilee and for "getting up funeral processions and parading about
the coffins and chains," others were determined to

Raise no starry banner—tears of shame its brightness dims!
On its silken folds, blood-written, see the names of BURNS and
      SIMMS![8]
Did it wave above the "Acorn" as the guardian of the sea?
When it floated o'er the "Morris," did it set the captive free?

Or yet to

                    Tear down the flaunting lie!
                        Half-mast the starry flag!
                    Insult no sunny sky
                        With this polluted rag!
                    Destroy it, ye who can!
                        Deep sink it in the waves!
                    It bears a fellow-man
                        To groan with fellow-slaves.[9]

Such forthright clamor over symbols, with its suggestion of a displacement of antagonism, reminds us that the clamor over Burns
had truly and all along been a fight of the same sort: all of it seems
to confess in its rhetoric that there is something at the center that
cannot be directly got at or contended with and so is practically ab-

---

7. William Lloyd Garrison (1805–1879), abolitionist leader, founder of American Anti-
   Slavery Society in 1833, and newspaper, *The Liberator*; Wendell Phillips (1811–1884),
   wealthy Boston abolitionist, labor reformer, and orator; Charles Lenox Remond
   (1810–1873), African-American orator and abolitionist leader; Stephen Simmons Foster
   (1809–1881), prosperous farmer, conscientious objector, and abolitionist [*Editor*].
8. Thomas Sims. See n. 5, p. 248 [*Editor*].
9. *Liberator*, June 16, 23, 1854; "Not with Idle Boasts of Freedom," written by "Carrie" for
   the Framingham gathering, in *Liberator*, July 7, 1854; "The Flaunting Lie," by Charles
   G. Halpine, published anonymously as "Hail to the Stars and Stripes" in the New York
   Tribune, June 13, 1854.

sent. From this comes the impression that all the respondents individually, all whose attention had been drawn by Anthony Burns and his difficulty, had more or less "missed the point" and got angry, by default, with something nearby. We can make out, in a rough way, what it is that prevents a particular individual from responding pertinently and so becoming, as we may say, heroic and famous. In looking at the event retrospectively, which is to say with some illusory sense of having seen the whole of it, what we in fact see most are the limitations of the actor's approach—how that is fatally delimited by a culture that makes this person a Democrat or a Freesoiler and that one religious or careful of his reputation, makes this one concerned about labor and that one about law, and how their approach makes their action small and partial. Granting that history is the sum of these contingent disappointments and granting that history is eminently worthwhile on that confession, still no narrative can be assembled that fails altogether to suggest the standard by which we know and judge these actions (as we surely do) as partial. Irresistibly we look for the one who least "misses the point," the hero for whom the center is not empty or who succeeds, somehow, in plausibly filling it.

At Framingham, Thoreau came closer than anyone else to naming that center, closer than anyone to defining the quality of displacement and deference in the rhetoric of all the others.

When Independence Day arrived, however, time was short, and there were many who wished to address the meeting. Besides the featured speakers, the crowd heard from a number of others who, like Thoreau, had come forward too late for publicity. Sojourner Truth and Abby Kelley Foster spoke that day, as did John C. Cluer, a Court House rioter, and Moncure Conway,[1] giving his first antislavery speech. None but the main speakers, however, got much attention in the press afterward, and of these Garrison may be said to have stolen the show by recourse to spectacle. He first read the Declaration of Independence, then discussed the contrasting principles embodied in the Fugitive Slave Law, Edward G. Loring's decision, and Benjamin R. Curtis' charge to the grand jury defining the treason of Parker[2] and Phillips. Finally, to give the source of all this latter-day corruption, he read the proslavery clauses in the Constitution. He thereupon burned all these documents (except the Declaration) one after the other, saying after the last, "So per-

1. Sojourner Truth (c. 1799–1883), African-American abolitionist and womens' rights advocate; Abigail Kelley Foster (1810–1887) radical abolitionist leader and women's rights advocate; Moncure Daniel Conway (1832–1907), transcendentalist, Unitarian minister, and writer [Editor].
2. Benjamin Robbins Curtis (1809–1874), associate justice of the U.S. Supreme Court; Theodore Parker (1810–1860), transcendentalist, Unitarian minister, and anti-slavery activist. Loring's decision, see n. 6, p. 248 [Editor].

ish all compromises with tyranny. 'And let all the people say *Amen!'* "
Which, of course, with only a smattering of protest, they did.[3]

Phillips, who would shortly be arrested, said to the crowd at
Framingham:

> When [the work of this summer] is done, I will be proud of the
> old Bay State. I used to be proud of her. Time was when I took
> on my lips the name of the old Commonwealth with a glow of
> conscious pride that gave depth to the tones of my voice, and
> an added pulse to the heart. I was proud of her; but my pride
> all vanished when I saw that old Indian on her banner [the flag
> of Massachusetts] go floating down State Street with the Slave
> Brigade, with Ben Hallett and the U.S. Marshal and a chained
> slave beneath him. I have lost all pride in Massachusetts till
> she redeems herself from that second day of June. Let us roll
> up a petition, a hundred thousand strong, for the removal of
> Judge Loring.[4]

Recalling that day of pastoral exhortation, Austin Bearse, captain
of the *Moby-Dick* and doorman for the BVC,[5] said, "They kindled
Liberty's altar flames till the bush glowed with her divine presence."
Moncure Conway recalled: "That day I distinctly recognized that
the antislavery cause was a religion." It was altogether a very satisfactory affair.[6]

That Thoreau's speech went so largely unnoticed may be owing to
the fact that he gave a much shorter version than was afterward
published. However that may be, Garrison noticed it, asked for the
manuscript, and printed the complete text in the *Liberator* on
July 21. Horace Greeley noticed it there and copied it into the New
York *Tribune* on August 2 with an admiring headnote that acknowledged its peculiar authenticity:

> The lower-law journals so often make ado about the speeches
> in Congress of those whom they designate champions of the
> Higher Law, that we shall enlighten and edify them, undoubt-
> edly, by the report we publish this morning of a genuine
> Higher Law speech—that of Henry D. Thoreau at the late cel-
> ebration of our National Anniversary in Framingham, Mass.,

---

3. *Liberator*, July 7, 1854. The burning of the documents had been suggested to Garrison
   by Henry C. Wright; see *Liberator*, June 30, 1854.
4. Phillips, quoted in Austin Bearse, *Reminiscences of Fugitive-Slave Days in Boston*
   (Boston: Warren Richardson, 1880), 13.
5. Boston Vigilance Committee. See n. 6, p. 587.
6. Ibid.; Daniel Moncure Conway, *Autobiography: Memories and Experiences*. 2 vols.
   (Boston: Houghton Mifflin, 1904), 1: 185; see also *Liberator*, July 14 and 28, 1854; *National Anti-Slavery Standard*, June 17 and August 12, 1854; Dorothy Sterling, *Ahead of
   Her Time: Abby Kelley and the Politics of Anti-Slavery* (New York: W.W. Norton, 1991),
   293–94.

where Wm. Lloyd Garrison burned a copy of the Federal Constitution. No one can read this speech without realizing that the claims of Messrs. Sumner, Seward and Chase[7] to be recognized as Higher-Law champions are of very questionable validity. Mr. Thoreau is the Simon-Pure article.

There are many points of similarity between "Slavery in Massachusetts" and other contemporary statements. As many another outraged onlooker had done, Thoreau attacked the commissioner, the governor, the mayor, the military, and the newspapers; but although he did all this very wittily and memorably, the distinctive significance of the address (and what entitles it to Greeley's encomium) is the self-consistent point of view from which the judgments come. At the most basic level, there is in it none of the struggle and perplexity apparent, for example, in Gannett's sermon of conversion, for the simple reason that there is no conversion: the address draws as much on journal material from the Sims rendition of 1851 as from entries inspired by Burns. Nor for that matter is it anywhere at odds with "Resistance to Civil Government." Unlike many—perhaps most—of the commentators on the Burns case, Thoreau is not arguing with himself, though it may be, as some have suggested, that he now understands his position a little better than he had.[8]

Such fundamental consistency is important because Thoreau's main topic and allegation is that the point of view adopted by others is quite ordinarily compromised, sometimes comically, more often tragically. And every compromise he identifies is caused by the individual's ceding some of his autonomy and liberty to the state or to the institutions of the public culture. Men suppose, for example, that voting helps: "The fate of the country," he said, as though in response to Phillips, "does not depend on how you vote at the polls—the worst man is as strong as the best at that game; it does not depend on what kind of paper you drop into the ballot-box once a year, but on what kind of man you drop from your chamber into the street every morning" (256). Men suppose that they can untangle the present dilemma by tracing the history of the Constitution: "The question is not whether you or your grandfather, seventy years ago, did not enter into an agreement to serve the devil, and that service is not accordingly now due; but whether you will not now, for once and at last, serve God,—in spite of your own past recre-

7. Salmon Portland Chase (1808–1873), U.S. Senator from Ohio; William Henry Seward (1801–1872), U.S. Senator from New York; Charles Sumner (1811–1874), U.S. Senator from Massachusetts; all staunchly opposed the Fugitive Slave Law [Editor].

8. See Robert C. Albrecht, "Conflict and Resolution: 'Slavery in Massachusetts,'" ESQ: A Journal of the American Renaissance 19 (1973): 179–88, for a fine general reading of the speech and pp. 179, 184–86 for a more particular discussion of Thoreau's use of the Sims material.

ancy, or that of your ancestor,—by obeying that eternal and only just CONSTITUTION, which He, and not any Jefferson or Adams, has written in your being" (255).

In general, Thoreau believes that the besetting mistake, even among ardent reformers, is that the higher law is taken for a sort of court of appeals—a part of the public sphere to bring sin to—rather than occupied as a home and dwelling place.

Since 1850, when Seward introduced the term into the senatorial debate over the Compromise measures, abolitionists had appropriated "the higher law" in an increasingly routine way to endorse the righteousness of opposing slavery. In this they were abetted by a class of men who supposed that the currency of "higher law" doctrine would (even more than "natural law" doctrine) help to promote their theological or evangelical goals. The tendency in both cases was to arrive at an instrumental application of the concept. Nominally it was an ultimate form of constitution; practically it was a means to a particular end, as can readily be seen from the restricted contexts in which the term comes up. But the notion (without the name) had been a central defining element in Emerson's aggressively noninstrumental thought—and in Thoreau's—for decades before Seward spoke. In the thought of the Transcendentalists, as in that of philosophical idealists generally, the concept of a law higher than any that space and time could show had been extensively explored, not as a tool for blocking the Compromise of 1850, but in the broadest possible sense of freeing slaves or (what is the same thing) producing a free point of view.

There is an implication in this that no point of view can be truly free that is also predominantly instrumental—that if freedom is wanted for a particular person, group, or purpose, the point of view that wants it is mortgaged to the prospect as well as to the means of bringing it about. Garrison is perhaps an instance of this ironic sort of slavery, a point that was not lost on his detractors then or now, or on those, like Hawthorne, who satirized reformers for seeming, in their monomania, too much like the blind leading the blind. Sumner is perhaps in his own way another instance. Yet no one criticized this sort of self-immolating commitment to a purpose more than Emerson, who valued "sphericity" over excessive development in one direction, who supposed that one was freer (not more enthralled) the higher the law one obeyed, and who supposed that we were the rightful inheritors of the *whole* universe, culpable only when we retreated, voluntarily, into a corner.

Yet Higginson attacking the Court House was a hero to Thoreau, as in a year or so the militant John Brown[9] would also become. The

9. See n. 1, p. 393 [*Editor*].

point about these men, from Thoreau's perspective, is that they did not wait to gather majorities, but responded as free men answerable to a conscience that could not abide the presence of evil. Had they consulted the practicalities a bit more, they might not have acted at all. In both cases failure—as Thoreau shrewdly noted— was precisely the indicator of the hero's contempt for instrumentality and of the peremptory quality of the call of the higher law. Failure is *often* more heroic than success and more useful to the human race for putting it in mind of the value of having the higher law for a motive and for demeaning the cheap and partial efficacy of a reliance on tactics, policies, and confederates.

"They who have been bred in the school of politics," Thoreau announced, "fail now and always to face the facts." Instrumentalists, Freesoilers, tacticians, anti-Nebraska men, lovers of policy, those who would reform the outsides of things, men whose revolution was not permanent but occasional, "put off the day of settlement indefinitely, and meanwhile the debt accumulates." The slave does not need the "half measures and make-shifts" of the politicians; what he needs is freedom and an end to scheming and deferring (247).[1]

In a very special way, Thoreau stood before the Framingham crowd to represent the very freedom that the slave was denied, the freedom that, in Thoreau's view, Massachusetts had not protected and defended because, when all was said and done, the state had not thought to value it. The state did not value freedom or personal liberty because, having so rarely seen these qualities exemplified, it did not understand them. (Thoreau had a book in press that would wake his neighbors up and acquaint them with a life of "extravagant" freedom [218].)

"Slavery in Massachusetts" was not to be the response, once more, of a slave to a slave case, but a report issued from free soil about conditions there. The judgments would not sound like the heading of a petition, but would have the quality of prophecy and doom. To be free is to be unimplicated, which in turn is the best and perhaps the only perspective from which one can see that in the present case servile behavior has been passing itself off as authority. Being free means, furthermore, speaking with olympian disdain of that masquerade. In the best-remembered passage from the speech, Thoreau said:

> Massachusetts sat waiting Mr. Loring's decision, as if it could in any way affect her own criminality. Her crime, the most conspicuous and fatal crime of all, was permitting him to be

---

1. Here and in the first three paragraphs of the speech, Thoreau refers elliptically to the Concord meeting on June 22, so that his slighting references to "politicians" must be taken to include Emerson.

the umpire in such a case. It was really the trial of Massachusetts. Every moment that she hesitated to set this man free, every moment that she now hesitates to atone for her crime, she is convicted. The Commissioner on her case is God; not Edward G. God, but simple God. (251)

The Transcendentalists' stock-in-trade was to startle their readers with an altered point of view. Their business was to see things differently and to persuade us that the difference was finally that between our slavery and their freedom, our customary allegiance to a lower law and theirs to a higher. Readers who liked their work found it instructive, liberating, revolutionary. Here Thoreau puts Edward G. Loring in his place, not by offering an opinion of his actions, but by seeing him as a pathetic substitute God, whose ridiculousness was supported by a population all too eager to vest him with powers not his own. The law becomes a system whereby people, having ceded questions of right and wrong to petty officials, are thrust into the position of merely hoping that right will prevail—a situation that does not, in Thoreau's view, accord with the original relation of free men to the moral world.

Thoreau's idea is that slavery, or unfreedom, subverts and reverses everything (hence the prevailing tone of irony in all his published work). Just as Hildreth[2] had found that slavery was "illegal" because it was philosophically inconsistent with basic legal principles and therefore unregulatable by anything resembling law, so in Thoreau's writings we recognize regimes of freedom by their ironic or antithetical relation to regimes of slavery. "The law will never make men free," he says; "it is men who have got to make the law free. They are the lovers of law and order, who observe the law when the government breaks it" (252). This makes sense and is to be distinguished from anarchy only on the assumption that the higher law is inscribed in the conscience of those free men who independently regulate their conduct by it. Freedom then means the ability to sustain allegiance to the highest law and to resist the inverting forces of compromise.

The address concludes with a call to action: "We have used up all our inherited freedom," he said, alluding to what makes the Fourth of July, for most Americans, a mainly commemorative ritual. "If we would save our lives, we must fight for them." He is very explicit about the life that has been lost: "I feel that my investment in life here is worth many per cent less since Massachusetts last deliberately sent back an innocent man, Anthony Burns, to slavery. I dwelt before, perhaps, in the illusion that my life passed somewhere *be-*

2. Richard Hildreth (1807–1865), historian, novelist, and lawyer; author of *Despotism in America* (1840, 1854) on the consequences and legal basis of slavery [*Editor*].

tween heaven and hell, but now I cannot persuade myself that I do not dwell *wholly within* hell" (258).

> I walk toward one of our ponds; but what signifies the beauty of nature when men are base? We walk to lakes to see our serenity reflected in them; when we are not serene, we go not to them. Who can be serene in a country where both the rulers and the ruled are without principle? The remembrance of my country spoils my walk. My thoughts are murder to the State, and involuntarily go plotting against her (258–59).

He wants the serenity, the remembered country, and voluntary control over his thoughts restored. For all his self-reliant individualism, he cannot claim in the best of mortal times to have lived wholly within heaven on any strength of private rectitude. The moral condition of society matters, as this case tells him, for to the extent that unprincipled behavior announces itself in others, he finds himself drawn out, implicated, and unfree. The failure in one man to honor freedom, it turns out, is the whole source of slavery in another—and Thoreau will not make that mistake himself. He is here this Fourth of July to publish freedom and make it famous.

He ends his address, as he was to end *Walden*, with a hopeful turn to the rebirth of nature in spring—what he had been devotedly studying in his eccentric freedom during the trial. He mentions a white water lily he had recently seen, an emblem of purity in which he found a reassuring pledge that the "integrity and genius" of nature were yet "unimpaired," and that "there is virtue even in man, too, who is fitted to perceive and love it." Thoreau presents himself not as one who, like so many of the others, can feel free only while contentiously demanding it, but as one for whom it is a permanent value, routine and domestic—as one who can speak from it as well as for it. The lily—or nature—is a standard that puts mean actions to shame and "suggests what kind of laws have prevailed longest and widest, and still prevail." To know such a standard is immediately to know "how inconsistent your deeds are with it" (259). The larger, higher, and more independent that standard is which you use, the more free you are of inferior and compromising points of reference and the less likely, in the end, to crucify Anthony Burns.

"Walking" and "Wild Apples"

WILLIAM ROSSI

"The Limits of an Afternoon Walk": Coleridgean Polarity in Thoreau's "Walking"†

For a work widely regarded as Thoreau's "central essay, . . . as *Walden* is [his] central book," and 'the touchstone of Thoreau's imaginative life," "Walking" remains poorly understood as a literary composition.[1] Partly no doubt because of the abstract nature of the essay, partly because of its apparently rambling, disjointed form, critical attention has tended to focus on Thoreau's conceptions of the West, and especially on "the Wild" and the importance of "wildness" in his thought and writings. One effect of this focus has been to mark "Walking" as Thoreau's position paper on the need to preserve wild lands (stridently affirmed in the slogan "In Wildness is the preservation of the World"), shifting attention away from the essay's problematic form and obscuring its rhetorical dimension.

Of those who have pursued the essay's structural complexity, only James McIntosh and Frederick Garber have been even modestly satisfied with it.[2] For McIntosh, the central feature of Thoreau's experimental excursion is a process by which the speaker's initial intransigence "becomes surreptitiously more tolerant and inclusive, and his voice becomes quieter until it attains a final exalted serenity" in the essay's celebrated sunset coda, evidence that the Wild is progressively transformed into the Good, "and nature into spirit".[2] Similarly, while analyzing deftly the way Thoreau "turns the static contrast of the urbane and the unexplored into an interplay of . . . opposed but complementary movements toward the wildness in the

† From *ESQ: A Journal of the American Renaissance* 33 (1987): 94–109. Reprinted by permission. Authorial footnotes have been condensed and in some cases omitted by the editor; "Walking" and *Walden* page numbers refer to this Norton Critical Edition.
1. Robert D. Richardson, Jr., *Henry Thoreau: A Life of the Mind* (Berkeley: University of California Press, 1986), p. 224; Joel Porte, "Henry Thoreau and the Reverend Poluphloisboios Thalassa," in *The Chief Glory of Every People*, ed. Matthew J. Bruccoli (Carbondale: Southern Illinois University Press, 1973), p. 194.
2. James McIntosh, *Thoreau as Romantic Naturalist: His Shifting Stance toward Nature* (Ithaca: Cornell University Press, 1974), pp. 287–88.

West and the savage in the self," Garber too reads the speaker's excursion as a successfully "redemptive" one: an "unremitting forward movement into the wild centers of man and nature" that yields "an increase in the content of the mind."[3]

These are good Emersonian readings. Regarding the world the speaker saunters into as an "*other me*," which eventually (as Emerson says) the active soul "disposes of . . . within the circuit of its expanding life," these critics would have their speaker affirm with the author of "The American Scholar," "So much only of life as I know by experience, so much of the wilderness have I vanquished and planted, or so far have I extended my being, my dominion."[4] But if "Walking" is Thoreau's most emphatic formulation of the Wild as indomitably, radically Other, how can the speaker so easily dispose of it within the circuit of his expanding life? Garber correctly identifies this central conflict in Thoreau's work as a whole with the "basic tensions" inherent in his "twin desires—one for radical wildness and another for reclamation." But because he reads "Walking" as celebrating redemptive reclamation, Garber must judge it "finally, insufficient" and look elsewhere in Thoreau's writings for a truer encounter with radical wildness.[5]

Evidence of Thoreau's profound interest in Coleridgean polarity, recently identified by Robert Sattelmeyer and Richard Hocks, illuminates without simply resolving precisely this basic tension in his writings, and particularly in "Walking." In extracts Thoreau made in late 1848 or early 1849 from Coleridge's posthumously published *Hints towards a More Comprehensive Theory of Life*, Coleridge adapts Schelling's *Naturphilosophie* to argue that polarity, the "most general law" of "the principle of individuation," is the spiritual law operative in the organization and evolution of nature (organic and inorganic) and of humankind. At the present moment, "Man and Nature" stand "at the apex of the living pyramid": he has "the whole world in counterpoint to him," yet, as a "compendium of Nature," he contains "an entire world in himself." But as the "form of polarity . . . has accompanied the law of individuation up its whole ascent" from metals to man, so further individuation is inevitably a polar process. "As the height, so the depth. The intensities must be at once opposite and equal."[6]

3. Frederick Garber, *Thoreau's Redemptive Imagination* (New York: New York University Press, 1977), pp. 63, 11.
4. Ralph Waldo Emerson, *The Collected Works of Ralph Waldo Emerson*, ed. Alfred R. Ferguson et al. (Cambridge: Harvard University Press, 1971–83), 1: 59.
5. Garber, 45, 38.
6. Sattelmeyer and Hocks, "Thoreau and Coleridge's *Theory of Life*," *Studies in the American Renaissance* (Charlottesville: University Press of Virginia, 1985), p. 271. A facsimile of the extracts is printed in *Thoreau's Literary Notebook*, ed. Kenneth Walter Cameron (Hartford, Conn.: Transcendental Books, 1964), pp. 359–62.

As Thoreau worked on versions of what would become "Walking" during the next seven or eight years following his reading of the *Theory of Life*, he continued to read and recommend Coleridge. To B. B. Wiley, an admirer who in April 1857 had requested a copy of the "Walking" lecture (when Thoreau was in the midst of revising it), and who had found Coleridge's Trinitarianism repugnant, Thoreau urged, "I think you must read Coleridge again & further— skipping all his theology—i.e. if you value precise definitions & a discriminating use of language."[7]

There can be little doubt that, as Sattelmeyer and Hocks suggest, Coleridge's natural philosophy and particularly his "precise" and "discriminating" explication of the dynamics of polarity affected Thoreau deeply, catalyzing his interest in nature and scientific explanation, and thereby influencing the shape of his career after *Walden*. To judge by "Walking," polarity also provided a hermeneutic for comprehending a central fact of consciousness. This is the notorious fact of spiritual life Emerson once stigmatized as "the worst feature" of "double consciousness": the apparently impermeable membrane, or mutually exclusive relation, between ideal moments of higher knowledge and the ordinary "actual" awareness into which those moments are all but immemorially absorbed. As Emerson had noted, "the two lives, of the understanding and the soul, which we lead, really show very little relation to each other, never meet and measure each other: one prevails now, all buzz and din; and the other prevails then, all infinitude and paradise; and with the progress of life, the two discover no greater disposition to reconcile themselves."[8] Coleridgean polarity afforded Thoreau a compelling principle which could adequately account for, without explaining away or simply resolving, this central problem of self-culture and its bearing on the Wild. The result is a view of "Walking" as a much less simply affirmative essay than has been recognized, as well as one possessing greater and more complex structural and rhetorical coherence.

Before turning to the essay, though, I should emphasize that if we approach Coleridgean polarity too abstractly and if we expect the "opposites" we will be concerned with ultimately to be "reconciled," then we misconceive the fundamentally concrete and dynamic nature of the polar relation, and will miss as well the way it pervades "Walking" like a "power," to use Coleridge's term. If (according to one of the formulations Thoreau extracted) "in the identity of the two counter-powers Life *sub*sists" and "in their strife, it

7. *The Correspondence of Henry David Thoreau*, ed. Walter Harding and Carl Bode (New York: New York University Press, 1958), pp. 475, 478.
8. Emerson, 1: 213–14.

*con*sists," then "reconciliation" of the sort usually meant would result in stasis and "death" (unless simultaneously it gave rise to a new dynamic). However it may have been for other writers, as Thoreau learned it from Coleridge, "polarity" amounted to more than the abstract belief that "things are dual and have two realities without which they cannot be adequately comprehended," though this is the common usage now.[9]

Such a definition, for instance, does not help us apprehend the tensive and "wild" quality of Thoreau's hard saying in "Walking," that "What we call knowledge is often our positive ignorance; ignorance our negative knowledge" (282). Yet we cannot understand what he means by "fertility" as a quality of knowledge until we do apprehend it. Rather, the distinguishing feature of polarity as a mode of thought is that it permits us not merely to conceive two opposite poles but to imagine simultaneously the productive relation between them—what Coleridge called their "living and generative interpenetration."

* * *

I

At the beginning of the essay's second section (on the West), the impulse to "go in search of the springs of life" (263) is explicitly associated with the phenomenon of magnetic attraction. Those, presumably, who have "a genius . . . for sauntering" (260) are particularly sensitive to this "subtle magnetism in Nature," which, the speaker believes, "if we unconsciously yield to it, will direct us aright" (267).

> When I go out of the house for a walk, uncertain as yet whither I will bend my steps, and submit myself to my instinct to decide for me, I find, strange and whimsical as it may seem, that I finally and inevitably settle southwest, toward some particular wood or meadow or deserted pasture or hill in that direction. My needle is slow to settle . . . but it always settles between west and south-southwest. The future lies that way to me, and the earth seems more unexhausted and richer on that side. . . . I turn round and round irresolute sometimes for a quarter of an hour, until I decide, for a thousandth time, that I will walk into the southwest or west. Eastward I go only by force; but westward I go free. (268)

While modern critics have been led by Thoreau's conceit to investigate the significance of his affinity for the westerly direction (partic-

---

9. Robert M. Greenberg, "Shooting the Gulf: Emerson's Sense of Experience," *ESQ*, 31 (1985): 216.

ularly in connection with the American westward movement), many nineteenth-century readers would have been alerted to the operation of a deeper principle, since for them the metaphor still called up the mystery of a force that repels equally as it attracts. As Thomas Mc-Farland has shown, not only did the doctrine of polarity dominate German *Naturphilosophie* (the scientific tradition within which Thoreau initially worked)[1] but the magnetism metaphor, "made popular by eighteenth-century empirical investigations of electrical laws," had wide currency among romantic writers generally.[2]

That Thoreau's conceit serves not merely to express the speaker's unconscious attraction to the Wild but also to intimate a formative principle underlying the whole excursion is suggested by the series of binary oppositions that form the topical structure of the essay. Beginning with the explicit avowal that even the standpoint from which his thoughts are uttered is diametrically opposed to the view his audience takes for granted, (260) the speaker addresses successively the topics of walking versus sitting indoors, West versus East, the New versus the Old World, the Wild versus the civilized, and, most pointedly, "useful ignorance" versus "useful knowledge," before this high ground of discourse gives way unexpectedly to "crisis" and to questions of "Gentle breeze, that wanderest unseen, . . . Why hast thou left my ear so soon?" (284). These pairs of opposites are not conceived as mutually exclusive logical opposites, but dynamically, as polar ones. The speaker thus associates the West with the westering energy of his contemporaries and then defines it in dynamic contrast with a kind of mental *movement* to the East: that direction in which "we go . . . to realize history and study the works of art and literature, retracing the steps of the race" (269). As he expresses the relation epigrammatically, "*Ex Oriente lux; ex Occidente* FRUX. From the East light; from the West fruit."(271)[3] Simi-

---

1. As Sattelmeyer and Hocks note, "this tradition had its most condensed exposition" in the *Theory of Life* (p. 283). Louis Agassiz, of course, whose work Thoreau knew, also had his early training in this tradition. See Edward Lurie, *Louis Agassiz: A Life in Science* (Chicago: University of Chicago Press, 1960), pp. 59–63, 83–84, 283–84. In addition to absorbing *Naturphilosophie* from Coleridge and his reading of Goethe, Thoreau would have discussed its progress in contemporary British biology with Emerson, who mentions meeting its exponents in letters home to Lydian in 1848, and who pursued it in his reading upon his return; see *The Letters of Ralph Waldo Emerson*, ed. Ralph L. Rusk (New York: Columbia University Press, 1939), IV, 41–42, 55, and *The Journals and Miscellaneous Notebooks of Ralph Waldo Emerson*, ed. William Gilman et al. (Belknap of Harvard University Press, 1960–82) XI, 93, 153, 199–200; XIII, 113.

2. McFarland, *Romanticism and the Forms of Ruin: Wordsworth, Coleridge, and Modalities of Fragmentation* (Princeton: Princeton University Press, 1981), pp. 297, 313.

3. Compare Thoreau's epigram with the "compass of nature," an idea Coleridge borrowed from Henrik Steffens (a follower of Schelling) in which East—West comprises the axis of becoming, and North—South that of being. See Trevor H. Levere, *Poetry Realized in Nature: Samuel Taylor Coleridge and Early Nineteenth-Century Science* (Cambridge: Cambridge University Press, 1981), pp. 114–19; and H. J. Jackson, " 'Turning and turning': Coleridge on Our Knowledge of the External World," *PMLA*, 101 (1986): 848–56.

larly, in the preceding section, the walker himself is defined not exclusively but relatively, as one who is more successful than his
neighbors at overcoming a resistance to obey the sauntering impulse. He avoids the destructive tension that by early afternoon
makes them schizophrenic—and makes him wonder that its accumulation does not produce "a general explosion heard up and down
the street"—by transforming it, homeopathically, into a healthy desire to "go in search of the springs of life" (262, 260).

But the most important polar relation among the essay's topics,
one which is paradigmatic for the others, is that between the "civilized" and "the Wild." Its polar quality is immediately apparent
from the fact that, as Thoreau conceives its relation to the civilized,
the Wild is at once deeply attractive and deeply repulsive. While
"cities import it at any price" and "men plow and sail for it," at its
most potent (as the speaker desires) it is "a wildness whose glance
no civilization can endure"; something no civilization, *as* civilization, can endure is yet that on which it depends for its life, a truth
he finds expressed in mythology as well as in his own experience:

> The story of Romulus and Remus being suckled by a wolf is
> not a meaningless fable. The founders of every state which has
> risen to eminence have drawn their nourishment and vigor
> from a similar wild source. It was because the children of the
> Empire were not suckled by the wolf that they were conquered
> and displaced by the children of the northern forests who
> were. (273)

If this were the conventional romantic, primitivist argument it is
sometimes taken to be, the relation between these states of being
would be construed as dichotomous rather than polar. That is, one
half of the dichotomy ("Nature" or "the Wild") would be advanced
as the genuine article needed to replace the "artificial" one. But,
while it is less vigorous, "the civilized" is hardly less real. Indeed, by
his wit, learned allusions, and digressions into etymology, not to
mention his self-conscious use of the excursion form, the speaker
knowingly embodies "culture"[4]—precisely why he yearns to embody
the Wild. Because he is aware that, in Coleridge's language, "the
intensities must be at once opposite and equal," he has taken a self-
acknowledged "extreme" stance on behalf of "Nature" as against
"the champions of civilization" (260) in the effort to reacquaint his
audience with the Wild, with a pole of their being from which they
are unwittingly alienated. Yet, appropriately, the Wild is evidenced
less in examples of pure nature—actually the essay contains little

---

4. Richard A. Hocks, "Thoreau, Coleridge, and Barfield: Reflections on the Imagination
and the Law of Polarity," *Centennial Review* 17 (1973): 178–82.

nature description compared to earlier and later natural history essays—than in the very products of civilization itself: its history, its
mythology, the act of knowledge by which (from the Transcendentalist perspective) it most perceptibly advances, even the activities
of its domestic animals. It is not a contradiction in "Walking,"
therefore, but a fact of its polar structure and mode of thought that
the farther the walker moves out, in his ideal walk, *into* nature, the
more (and more deeply) his thinking engages culture.

Again, the essay is no conventional pastoral, attempting to reconcile opposing systems of urban and rural values, though this is well
documented as a common mid-century conceptual strategy, one
that by the mid-1850's had even become "a firmly established principle of American suburban planning." The speaker of "Walking" is
no conciliator. Rather than a reconciliation attained by eliminating
the "less desirable aspects" of city and country life, as planners
were suggesting,[5] he achieves an imaginative, if fleeting, sense of
harmony between city and country by fronting, yet "reverencing,"
the *independence* of each, living in the tension that sustains them.
To borrow McFarland's succinct formulation, he realizes imaginatively that both the civilized and the wild are "necessary to a unity
that exists only by their opposition".[6]

It is significant, then, that in the narrative and in his illustrations
of his experience, the walker's relation to the Wild is consistently
imaged in terms of a spatial opposition in which a deeper identity
(or "sympathy") also exists. Although the Wild is figured a few times
as a source underneath or deeper inside ordinary experience—
"every tree sends its fibres forth in search of the Wild"; the Wild is
"the strength, the marrow of Nature" (273, 276)—much more frequently it is imaged in pointed contrast to that experience. While
the impetus that constitutes the primary narrative thrust of the essay is toward the Wild, it is "a glance which no civilization can endure." Or, again, a sense of internal/external conflict yet "sympathy"
is suggested by the narrator's affirmation that "my spirits infallibly
rise in proportion to the outward dreariness" of the Wild (275). And
in his most emphatic, and punning, illustration of a fronting relation to the Wild, the speaker humorously assaults his audience's
sense of middle-class propriety by preferring a swamp to the customary front yard, acknowledging as he does ("though you may
think me perverse") their instinctive repugnance:

5. John Archer, "Country and City in the American Romantic Suburb," *Journal of the Soci-
    ety of Architectural Historians*, 42 (1983): 140, 155. Kenneth V. Egan, Jr., argues in
    "Thoreau's Pastoral Vision in 'Walking,'" *American Transcendental Quarterly*, 57 (1985):
    21–30, that Thoreau's essay shares controlling themes, metaphors, and structure with
    the Western pastoral tradition.
6. McFarland, 322.

> I derive more of my subsistence from the swamps which sur-
> round my native town than from the cultivated gardens in the
> village . . . Why not put my house, my parlor, behind this plot,
> instead of behind that meagre assemblage of curiosities, that
> poor apology for a Nature and Art, which I call my front-yard?
> (275)

The rich though slippery significance of the Wild for Thoreau is
thus conveyed more through a representation of its dynamic, polar
relation to civilization and to the walker's civilized imagination,
than by any definition of it as abstract and absolute.

Finally, because the Wild and the civilized are polar opposites,
their interaction is productive. In terms of the historical, or evolu-
tionary, argument that operates in the essay as a panoramic backdrop for the individual walker,[7] this circumstance entails a view of
polar forces in history. Thus, in a sentence that imitates the fruitful
impulse it describes, "From this western impulse coming in contact
with the barrier of the Atlantic *sprang* the commerce and enterprise
of modern times" (270, my emphasis). For the individual consciousness, the relation is productive of insight to the extent that
the poles' simultaneous independence and interpenetration can
be imaginatively cognized, or re-cognized. Hence, the "fertility"
Thoreau associates with the Wild is the generative *potential* it embodies not in itself but for an interacting consciousness.

The most dramatic instances of moments of productive interaction occur at the culmination of the essay's "Knowledge" section
and in the "crisis" of the Spaulding farm episode that follows.
These we will examine more closely below. But a good illustration is
provided by a similar kind of "event" recorded in the Journal in late
October 1850, at the time Thoreau was beginning to define and explore the Wild dimension of his experience. When, in what appears
to be an early version of the Spaulding farm episode, Thoreau asks,
"What is the beauty of this Landscape but a certain fertility in
me,"[8] he is not describing a subjective or narcissistic "imposing" of
the self on nature. The "beauty" of the landscape is not simply
"me," but rather an unanalyzable whole produced by the coincidence of "landscape" and "me": the manifestation to consciousness
of underlying unity or relation. The dynamic sense of that rela-

---

7. The essay's racialist historical argument is that the evolution of white, Western, civilized
   consciousness has been accompanied (in polar fashion) by a devolution, or gradual ex-
   tinction, of its wild vitality or spiritual depth, a situation symbolized for Thoreau by the
   destruction of forest land. Hence the slogan, "In wildness is the preservation of the
   world." For Thoreau's impact as "philosopher of wildness" on land preservation, see
   Roderick Nash, *Wilderness and the American Mind*, 3rd ed. (New Haven: Yale University
   Press, 1982), pp. 84–95.
8. *The Journal of Henry David Thoreau*, ed. Bradford Torrey and Francis H. Allen (1906;
   rpt. New York: AMS Press, 1968), II, 77.

tion—in which the invigoration of human power and consciousness is felt as the renewed experience of its source—is represented as a sense of simultaneous independence from and identity with the spectacle. In this way Thoreau images both the mutual independence and the interdependence of self and nature, while at the same time he suggests the inexhaustible potential of perception.

II

The polar thinking that informs Thoreau's presentation of his topics in "Walking" is also figured in the structure of the walker's narrative. Here, as he had in the earlier essays, "A Walk to Wachusett" and "A Winter Walk," Thoreau exploits the excursion form as the "fundamental metaphor for his mode of discovery."[9] But now, as its title suggests, the vehicle is not any particular walk the speaker has taken but the *activity* itself, Thoreau's metaphor for the polar process of discovery or spiritual growth that the generalized narrative enacts.

"Walking" thereby represents Thoreau's alternative version of the Transcendentalist doctrine of self-culture popularized by Emerson. Tracing Emerson's development of this concept from its Unitarian sources to his mature thought, David Robinson has detailed how Emerson "remained faithful to the ends of the idea . . . as the Unitarians preached it," but differed from them as to the kind of "discipline" necessary to achieve those ends. According to Robinson, "the best illustration of the subtle difference in the nature of discipline they propose" is the way Emerson and his Unitarian mentors employ contrasting metaphors of wilderness and garden in describing the soul's proper growth. While for the Unitarians, "Discipline was the method that channeled the growth of the soul into the preconceived harmony" of a planned garden, discipline for the early Emerson was "man's constant effort to exercise his potential fully."[1]

In his desire to substitute a swamp for a manicured front yard, and to be "assured that I am growing apace and rankly" (283), Thoreau's difference from the Unitarians is obvious and emphatic. Yet he differs from Emerson as well. Besides suggesting the possibilities of unhindered growth, for Thoreau wilderness also, and above all, suggests "fertility" and all we have seen it implies. Indeed, in his negative emphasis on the too-conscious desire to realize one's potential, Thoreau appears to be countervailing a general oversubscription to Emerson's principles and message. As he remarks in

---

9. Sherman Paul, *The Shores of America; Thoreau's Inward Exploration* (Urbana: University of Illinois Press, 1958), p. 413.
1. Robinson, *Apostle of Culture: Emerson as Preacher and Lecturer* (Philadelphia: University of Pennsylvania Press, 1982), p. 122.

Walden, "Do not seek so anxiously to be developed, to subject your-self to many influences to be played on; it is all dissipation." (221) The fullest statement of this position, one contrary to the early Emersonian injunction to vanquish and plant the wilderness of mind and so extend "my being, my dominion," occurs in "Walking."

> I would not have every man nor every part of a man cultivated, any more than I would have every acre of earth cultivated: part will be tillage, but the greater part will be meadow and forest, not only serving an immediate use, but preparing a mould against a distant future, by the annual decay of the vegetation which it supports. (282)

Opposing conventional exhortations concerning the potential culti-vation of the whole mind—and the whole continent—the speaker advocates a kind of ecology of mind (to borrow Gregory Bateson's title), or Transcendental ecology, a vital relation between certain "fertile" (or creative) activities of mind and the productivity of adja-cent "cultivated" ground. But this vitality is maintained not, prima-rily, by any conscious "development" so much as by a kind of natural forgetting, even mental rot: the preparation of "a mould against a distant future, by the annual decay of the vegetation which it supports."

Obviously, the results or fruit of this kind of ecological law can-not be possessed but rather emerge from a transaction of con-sciousness, which the active soul must intuitively discover how to make and remake. Accordingly, although (ideally speaking) his des-tination and route are always, when successful, the same, the walker can be neither certain nor complacent. Always there is a tension, a hesitation or uncertainty, about which way to walk: al-though daily he decides "for a thousandth time" on the same direc-tion, each day he is "irresolute" at the start. And the same novel yet almost familiar sense infuses as well the "limits of an afternoon walk" or a life's. As he states early in the essay,

> My vicinity affords many good walks; and though for so many years I have walked almost every day, and sometimes for sev-eral days together, I have not yet exhausted them. An ab-solutely new prospect is a great happiness, and I can still get this any afternoon. . . . There is in fact a sort of harmony dis-coverable between the capabilities of the landscape within a circle of ten miles' radius, or the limits of an afternoon walk, and the threescore years and ten of human life. It will never become quite familiar to you. (264)

It is in this dynamic sense, then, that "the day" needs perpetually to be "redeemed" (262). The speaker's quest for the Wild is therefore not, as Garber claims, "ultimately . . . a drive toward the creative center of being"[2], because within this shifting predominance of energies there is no absolutely definable center. An active sense of creatively seeing anew the landscape—and, correlatively, the self—is not achieved at some point during the quest (whenever "the center" is reached), but is a quality of the questing activity itself. It is the "spirit" of the walk; and the activity of that spirit, or "power," in both its coming to fullness and its abrupt ebbing, is what the narrative as a whole expresses.

The invitation to walk comes at the end of the essay's first section, as the prophetic speaker, afoot with his vision, intones somewhat ominously, "Let us improve our opportunities [to walk], then, before the evil days come" (267). As Melville used it in *Pierre* (though with a diabolically different result), and as Thoreau's audience might well have apprehended, the compass metaphor, which then initiates the walk, is a clear indication that we are accompanying the saunterer on an ideal journey, a walk "perfectly symbolical of the path which we love to travel in the interior and ideal world" (268). Accordingly, as the excursion expands toward the ideal Wild pole to which the walker is attracted, suggestions of the actual Concord landscape (such as the Marlborough road) fade or metamorphose into a landscape of thought, and his instinctive sense of direction merges with a more universal impulse. In a scale of nature and mind reminiscent of Coleridge's *Theory of Life*, the same power that manifests outwardly in the magnetic attraction exhibited by the compass needle and inwardly in the promptings of the narrator's genius and "prevailing tendency of my countrymen" reappears in birds and quadrupeds as "the migratory instinct," and in the ancient mythology of "the race" and activities of Western discoverers as the dream of "the Great West" (269).

At the beginning of the next (the Wild) section, this ideal West itself becomes "but another name for the Wild" (273), and the psychic terrain exhibits even fewer geographical markers than did the preceding section. By the speaker's primary allusions, too—no longer European explorers and naturalists, but Gordon-Cumming on the "Hottentots," Darwin on the Fuegians, "Hindoos," Homer, and Confucius—it is clear that the walk now purportedly exists entirely on the ideal or universal plane. Passing then into the section on knowledge and "ignorance," and thus from Wild being to Wild knowing, the ideal walk moves toward its climax and moment of greatest expansion. In a statement recalling Coleridge's insistence that "the intensities must be at once opposite and equal," the speaker now proposes a new society for which he believes "there is equal need."

2. Garber, 45.

> We have heard of a Society for the Diffusion of Useful Knowledge. It is said that knowledge is power, and the like. Methinks there is equal need of a Society for the Diffusion of Useful Ignorance, what we will call Beautiful Knowledge, a knowledge useful in a higher sense: for what is most of our boasted so-called knowledge but a conceit that we know something, which robs us of the advantage of our actual ignorance? What we call knowledge is often our positive ignorance; ignorance our negative knowledge. (282)

As he had earlier so perversely flaunted his desire for a wild, fronting relation to nature as to prefer swamps to front yards, so here the speaker humorously inverts his audience's "civilized" assumptions by proposing (originally, on the platform of the Lyceum itself) a "Society for the Diffusion of Useful Ignorance." But, again, the wit and perversity are purposeful. Reconceiving ignorance in dynamic relation to its opposite, not simply as the absence of knowledge, but as a state of potential (or "negative") knowledge, he forces the reader momentarily to contemplate side-by-side two conditions of mind habitually considered as mutually exclusive. If the very syntax of this cryptic aphorism images polar interaction, so the interpenetration of the two conceptions engenders a concrete sense, however fleeting, of the reader's own "fertility."

The dramatic version of such a moment of insight occurs subsequently for the walker as well. Following almost immediately upon his aphoristic formulation, he attempts a definition of "beautiful knowledge" that appropriately recalls his earlier figure for the revelation of "genius" as "a light . . . like the lightning's flash, which perchance shatters the temple of knowledge itself" (277).

> I do not know that this higher knowledge amounts to anything more definite than a novel and grand surprise on a sudden revelation of the insufficiency of all that we called Knowledge before,—a discovery that there are more things in heaven and earth than are dreamed of in our philosophy. (283)

"Knowledge" is regarded here not as an object that might reduce to "power" but as a transient sense of epistemological fertility, a sense that our knowledge is not only something we have and wield, Baconian fashion, but something we are. Emerson's characterization of "the first fruit of a new knowledge" as "a new curiosity" and Thoreau's as a fertile sense of one's potential, relative to what one actually knows, are similar. In addition, for Thoreau this moment is not unequivocally one of unalloyed expansion or "progress evermore," as Emerson thought,[3] but equally one of contraction: the discovery of "the insufficiency of all we called Knowledge before."

---

3. Quoted in Robinson, 114.

Thus, the heart of this moment of expansion—and the peak of the essay's narrative trajectory—is the "revelation" of a definition couched almost entirely in the negative, an antidefinition, really. The transient moment of self-knowing witnesses the deconstruction of what that self had called its "Knowledge." For what the self knows in this moment is neither its knowledge, nor—nakedly—itself, but the underlying fertile (or creative) process that constitutes its most vital being: the awareness simultaneously of a growth of self and a decay that makes further growth possible. In this light, the statement following the antidefinition—that "a successful life knows no law"—has itself, inevitably perhaps, a certain doubleness about it, for it is at once factual and ironic. "Obey the law which reveals," Thoreau had written in his Journal while drafting his first lecture on the Wild.[4] Yet, *that* law cannot be "known" in the usual (or "useful") sense of the word, but only grasped by imagination and, in "a successful life," lived.

The fall, from this point, is precipitous. Although, with Emerson, Thoreau held that "Ideal is not opposed to Real, but to Actual, for the Ideal is the Real," such an ideal walk has "never yet been taken by us through this actual world." Consequently, the sense of "crisis" that prevails in the next section is a direct result of the walker's experience of the fertile yet repellent truth, which closes the section on knowledge, the product of confrontation with "a glance which no civilization can endure." As in the descent from Katahdin, the "crisis" section of the essay (and particularly the Spaulding farm episode) functions as the delayed, reflective climax Thoreau frequently liked to employ in his excursions. The sentences that begin this "crisis," therefore, suggest that the walker has been returned, abruptly, to that actual world, and that a contracting process is well under way.

> It is remarkable how few events or crises there are in our histories, how little exercised we have been in our minds, how few experiences we have had. I would fain be assured that I am growing apace and rankly, though my very growth disturb this dull equanimity,—though it be with struggle through long, dark, muggy nights or seasons of gloom. (283)

Technically, a "crisis" is a turning point, one that may portend alike the improvement or the decline of the patient. In "Walking," the equivocal sense of the word is fully operative. While semantically it suggests a high point, the indication of a better state, the tone not only of this but of all subsequent paragraphs—the need to be *assured* "that I am growing apace and rankly" in the face of

---

4. *The Journal of Henry David Thoreau*, II, 171.

"this dull equanimity"—suggests the downward slide of postecstatic experience.[5]

Most interesting, however, and illustrative once again of the co-presence and shifting predominance of energies in "Walking," is the fact that this new tone indicates the presence of a voice altogether different from the prophetic voice that has dominated the essay from its emphatic opening. As prophet, the "Walker" had opposed his heroic life to the flabby existence of his sedentary townspeople, half-mockingly professing to be "astonished at their powers of endurance, to say nothing of their moral insensibility, . . . who confine themselves to shops and offices the whole day for weeks and months, aye, and years almost together" (262). This is the voice that asserts, "we should go forth on the shortest walk . . . in the spirit of undying adventure" (261) and that "shudders for these comparatively degenerate days of my native village" (276). Only guardedly and indirectly in sections preceding the "crisis" does the walker admit his actual likeness to his neighbors, as when he remarks that "sometimes" he does not get outdoors until "the eleventh hour, . . . too late to redeem the day" (262), or confesses that he "sometimes . . . cannot shake off the village" and himself experiences a kind of schizophrenia or "doubleness" in the woods: "What business have I in the woods, if I am thinking of something out of the woods? I suspect myself, and cannot help a shudder . . . for this may sometimes happen" (264). But in these earlier sections of the essay, he affects to "know very well" that although some of his neighbors "can remember and have described to me some walks which they took ten years ago, in which they were so blessed as to lose themselves for half an hour in the woods," they have "confined themselves to the highway ever since, whatever pretensions they may make to belong to this select class" of Walkers (261).

Reversing this oppositional stance, the speaker now emphasizes his identity with his audience. By means of plural pronouns particularly, he admits to sharing the "dull equanimity" of those whom he had earlier scorned. It is as if we no longer accompanied "the Walker" who can gnomically discourse on a Wild he seems able to inhabit at will, but a "walker" whose experience is more discontinuous, more "actual":

5. John Broderick long ago demonstrated a recurrent pattern of departure and return in Thoreau's prose in "The Movement of Thoreau's Prose," *American Literature*, 33 (1961): 133–42, a description Garber has refined and identified as "a basic cadence in Thoreau's thought," one that represents "the working rhythm of the mind at the edge of experience" (p. 139). For a comprehensive analysis of Thoreau's use of the romantic excursion genre, see Lawrence Buell, *Literary Transcendentalism: Style and Vision in the American Renaissance* (Ithaca: Cornell University Press, 1973), pp. 188–207.

> When, at rare intervals, some thought visits one, as perchance
> he is walking on a railroad, then, indeed the cars go by without
> his hearing them. But soon, by some inexorable law, our life
> goes by and the cars return. (283-84)

One measure of how the confidence and certainty of the
prophetic voice have been reversed is the ironic status, now, of his
earlier assertion that "Eastward I go only by force; but westward I
go free" (268). Often quoted by those who equate Thoreau too simply with this voice, the epigram indeed expresses vigorously the
consciousness of a walker on the way to the Wild. But that is only
one pole of the doubleness "Walking" explores. And just as the ultimate encounter with the Wild was foreseen the moment the walker
hit the inspired direction that would carry him to the top of his
stride, so the moment is now in sight when he will turn eastward,
back to town. Nor, ironically, is it quite his own "force" that initiates his return, but that of the "inexorable law." In this way the
structure of the excursion itself seems to imitate that law; and
Thoreau thereby suggests that while ideal experience must be distinguished from "actual," it rarely occurs disentangled—that is to
say, cannot be divided—from it.

This distinguishable yet double sense of being—the sense that
"with regard to Nature, I live a sort of border life, on the confines
of a world into which I make occasional and transient forays only"
(284)—is dramatized in the episode on Spaulding's farm, which follows. Here the walker imaginatively realizes, if he only briefly sustains, an awareness of the intermingling of both states, a moment
of double vision when "the walker in the familiar fields which
stretch around my native town sometimes finds himself in another
land than is described in their owners' deeds" (284). And just as he
had represented his relation to the Wild chiefly in terms of spatial
opposition, so a felt sense of polarity operates here, visually, where
the vision of an "ancient and altogether admirable and shining family" is generated by "the setting sun lighting up the opposite side of
a stately pine wood."

> I saw their park, their pleasure-ground, beyond through the
> wood, in Spaulding's cranberry-meadow. The pines furnished
> them with gables as they grew. Their house was not obvious to
> vision; the trees grew through it. I do not know whether I
> heard the sounds of a suppressed hilarity or not. They seemed
> to recline on the sunbeams. . . . The farmer's cart path, which
> leads directly through their hall, does not in the least put them
> out, as the muddy bottom of a pool is sometimes seen through
> the reflected skies. They never heard of Spaulding, and do not
> know that he is their neighbor,—notwithstanding I heard him

whistle as he drove his team through the house. Nothing can equal the serenity of their lives. (284–85)

Like "the muddy bottom of a pool . . . seen through reflected skies," both the actual white pine wood and cranberry meadow and the visionary house are kept in focus here. As in the journal passage discussed above, the actual and ideal intermingle, yet remain distinct. The "ancient and altogether admirable and shining family" both depends upon the imaginative participation of the perceiver's (and the reader's) consciousness and seems to enjoy an independent existence without.

Although the leisurely and lyrical description makes the vision seem timeless, by the inexorable law, of course, it cannot last:

> But I find it difficult to remember them. They fade irrevocably out of my mind even now while I speak, and endeavor to recall them and recollect myself. It is only after a long and serious effort to recollect my best thoughts that I become again aware of their cohabitancy. (285)

The family's "cohabitancy" (and the plural possessive makes the equation of the family with "my best thoughts" nicely ambiguous) suggests that the ideal world is immanent and dependent for its realization upon the individual mind participating in it. Equally important, the dramatization brings out how that experience inevitably falls short of fulfillment—even while just as inevitably it carries in its fading the promise of potential fulfillment. One result of the return to a sense of the limitations of actual experience is thus the correlative sense of *potential* that contact with the ideal has produced. Only now it is as if the memory itself were fertile. Like the forest land Thoreau would not have cultivated (nor "every man, nor every part of a man"), the inevitable fading of such an experience prepares "a mould . . . by the annual decay of the vegetation which it supports." Still, the fact of decay and death pervades the remainder of the essay, as the speaker walks the fine line between hope and melancholy. As he had intuited earlier, within the climactic moment, "with respect to knowledge we are all children of the mist" (283); so now, well on the other side of that moment, "our winged thoughts" seem sadly domesticated, "turned to poultry" (285). Correspondingly, the essay itself fragments in the paragraphs immediately following the Spaulding farm episode into separate, apparently discontinuous musings.

The understated complexity of the essay's conclusion, much less confident than that of *Walden*, is rooted in the delicate relation Thoreau evokes between this inevitable state of fading and death and the sense of potential arising out of it: as, in the closing image of an autumnal sunset, there lingers at once the memory and the promise of fruition. Here not only do all the essay's themes and motifs reappear, as Garber has observed,[6] but so does the polar structure by which Thoreau expresses their relation to experience. Again, the scene is represented as an evanescent product momentarily coalescing in the midst of a "field" of opposite and interpenetrating qualities. Walking home through a meadow at the end of a day "last November," the "softest, brightest morning sunlight fell on the dry grass and on the stems of the trees in the opposite horizon . . . while our shadows stretched long over the meadow eastward." What cheers the walker most is the thought that "this was not a solitary phenomenon" but "would happen forever and ever." This assurance of the possibility of recurrent illumination not only for the walker, but—as the walker's companion now reappears and the essay circles back toward society—for all walkers, is now seen to embrace fully the audience as well:

> So we saunter toward the Holy Land, till one day the sun shall shine more brightly than ever he has done, shall perchance shine into our minds and hearts, and light up our whole lives with a great awakening light, as warm and serene and golden as on a bankside in autumn. (287)

"Thus, in the identity of the two counterpowers, life *sub*sists; in their strife it *con*sists; and in their reconciliation it at once dies and is born again into a new form, either falling back into the life of the whole, or starting anew in the process of individuation." This proposition, which Thoreau copied from Coleridge's *Theory of Life*, underpins perhaps his most intricate, certainly his most experimental, literary excursion. The form it takes is especially successful in the way it represents, at the center of self-culture, an ineluctable and disturbing tension between the double sense of "actual" limitation and ideal promise, the very tension in which the walker's life "*con*sists." This is why, despite the speaker's assurance of recurrent illumination and the faithful lyricism of the final scene, there hovers over it a sense of melancholy resignation and even death. Ultimately, though, on the polar model, the lyricism and faith are justified. For, just as at the heart of its utmost "expansion" the walker discovers his consciousness of the Wild already contracting, so now, in "falling back into the life of the whole" there is already, again, the sense that he is "starting anew in the process of individuation."

6. Garber, 217–22.

NEILL MATHESON

Thoreau's *Gramática Parda:*
Conjugating Race and Nature†

> These are wild animals (beasts) What constitutes the difference
> between a wild beast & a tame one? How much more human the
> one than the other!—Growling scratching roaring—with whatever
> beauty & gracefulness still untameable this Royal Bengal tiger or
> this leopard. They have the character & the importance of another
> order of men.
>
> Thoreau, *Journal* (June 26, 1851)[1]

> [The African Hall of the American Museum of Natural History] is
> not a random world . . . but the moment of origin where nature
> and culture, private and public, profane and sacred meet—a mo-
> ment of incarnation in the encounter of man and animal.
>
> Donna Haraway, *Primate Visions*[2]

Thoreau's essay "Walking" proposes a movement beyond the nation
and its politics, beyond the law, into a "nature" imagined as primordial, prior to "civilized" culture. The idea of walking becomes a
metaphor for metaphor itself, the passage across boundaries, beyond proper limits or distinctions, but it is also a metaphor for the
end of metaphor, the impossible unmediated encounter with the
real and the wild. The essay repeatedly asserts the fundamental
separateness of the natural and the political, in order to promise a
departure from politics: the "political world" has "its place merely,
and does not occupy all space"; one can easily walk beyond the
"narrow field" of "politics," the "most alarming" of all man's "affairs," into wild nature (265).[3] Nevertheless, "Walking" implies a
more fundamental politicization of the very concept of nature in its
plural meanings, both human and nonhuman, than this gesture of
separation might suggest. What it calls for is not a flight into
nature, a pure escape from culture, but rather a new ecology, a
healthier culture regrounded through a return to origins, to the

---

† From *Arizona Quarterly* 57.4 (Winter 2001): 1–43. Reprinted by permission. Authorial
footnotes have been condensed and in some cases omitted by the editor; "Walking" and
Walden page numbers refer to this Norton Critical Edition.
1. Henry D. Thoreau, *Journal*, John C. Broderick, Robert Sattelmeyer, and Elizabeth Hall
Witherell, general editors. 5 vols. (Princeton: Princeton University Press, 1981–),
3:276–77. Hereafter cited in text.
2. Donna Haraway, *Primate Visions: Gender, Race, and Nature in the World of Modern Science* (New York: Routledge, 1989), 29.
3. Critical appraisals of "Walking" have often implicitly replicated this division between the
natural and the political by assimilating the essay to Thoreau's nature-writing, putatively
distinct from his political writings.

moment of first emergence of culture from nature. In "Walking," Thoreau imagines the revitalization of civilized man through a return to intimate, feral contact with wild nature.[4] This revitalization is necessary because white European American men are in danger of becoming "dissipated," corrupted by materialism and by idleness and sensuality, traits associated for Thoreau with a culture alienated from nature, located symbolically in the "degeneracy" of the village (265).[5] Thoreau's vision of regeneration is utopian, in that its fulfillment demands not only a reframing of the relationship between the human and nonhuman nature, but a radical rethinking of existing social, political, and economic arrangements—in short, of civilization itself as he sees it. Yet his evocation of "another order of men" occurs in the subjunctive, not as a proposal of specific reforms, but as an expression of desire for something that can only be imagined in terms of alterity and futurity.

Wildness is the principal name the essay gives for the difference and otherness it invokes, but this set of ideas takes on racial meaning as well. If "Walking" sets out to reimagine the relationship between nature and culture, racial difference plays a more essential role in this project than its seemingly peripheral status would imply. I want to follow the tracks of Thoreau's engagement with race in the essay, leading into its margins, and beyond them; his *Journal* in the early 1850s displays a persistent interest in speculating about the filiations of race with culture and wildness, and placing it in dialogue with "Walking" opens the essay's sometimes oblique comments into various broader contexts. Thoreau's racial imagination as revealed by "Walking" and the *Journal* is strongly influenced by his reading of travel literature, natural history, and racial science, particularly in his adoption of a rhetoric of primitivism that understands non-white races as still united with nature, prior to the break that leads to culture and civilization. Yet Thoreau's notions of race are also original and idiosyncratic in antebellum America, not so much in his positive valuation of the wild man's fusion with nature (a version of romantic primitivism or "savagism"), but in his intimation that race is mu-

---

4. My thinking about these issues has been influenced by Haraway. For her, the encounter with African animals staged within the space of the Museum of Natural History aims to revitalize American manhood through the "hygiene of nature" (*Primate Visions*, 30). Her discussion of the Museum and its creators resonates with my characterization of Thoreau, but there are also crucial differences: Thoreau likewise is concerned with preserving masculinity from a version of the threat of decadence; for him, though, unlike the protectors of white racial purity Haraway describes, white European American culture is itself pathological (white skin color becomes the most prominent bodily sign of this pathology, as I will discuss below), and needs to be re-envisioned.

5. The injurious effects of this degenerate social state are physiological as well as moral. Thoreau's concern about dissipation as a loss of male vitality implies significant affinities with the male purity movement, exemplified by such writers as Sylvester Graham and John Todd, whose 1830s anti-masturbation tracts expressed profound anxieties about male sexuality.

table, transformable, taking shape in response to "environmental" factors such as climate, and more fundamentally in relation to nature itself. "Walking" implicitly offers an environmental theory of race, but also a racialized version of environmentalism; in this sense, I argue, the ecocritical Thoreau is also the racial Thoreau. Through a renegotiation of man's relation to nature, Thoreau would imagine a new racial identity that is no longer simply "white." Yet his positioning of racial otherness on the side of nature prevents him from seeing non-white identities as similarly capable of being reimagined; finally, the racial transformation the essay hints at seems only to involve white men. My account of these issues in "Walking" thus differs from recent critical analyses of Thoreau's environmentalism, such as Lawrence Buell's important study of Thoreau's "environmental imagination," by arguing that Thoreau's vision of a new ecology cannot be separated from his conflicted engagement with multiple ideologies of race.[6] The utopian project sketched out in "Walking" calls for a rethinking of racial identities as a key part of its aim of social transformation (and a significant source of its exhilaration), yet in the end Thoreau's ideas about race limit as well as enable the conception of a new ecology that would profoundly reimagine the human in relation to nature.

The urgency of Thoreau's desire to depart from the "political world" becomes more legible in the context of political developments during the early 1850s, when "Walking" first appeared as a lecture, much of it drawn from *Journal* passages written in the same years (he continued to revise and expand the lecture throughout the decade, and it was published in 1862, shortly after his death).[7] His resistance to the national politics of expansion and slavery was sharpened and focused by the new Fugitive Slave Law, particularly after it was successfully enforced in Boston in early April 1851. When Thoreau delivered "Walking" (then entitled "The Wild") for the first time a week or two later, he announced his sense of an imperative to address the law explicitly. Yet, though he altered the lecture's opening for this purpose, the gesture that results seems curiously to sidestep the issue even while acknowledging it: "I feel that I owe my audience an apology for speaking to them tonight on any other subject than the Fugitive Slave Law on which every man is bound to express a distinct opinion,—but I had

---

6. Buell does suggest that Thoreau's environmentalism points toward the need for a larger social transformation, though he does not speculate about its relation to Thoreau's thinking about race. Lawrence Buell, *The Environmental Imagination: Thoreau, Nature Writing, and the Formation of American Culture* (Cambridge: Harvard University Press, 1995).

7. See William Rossi, "The Journal, Self-Culture, and the Genesis of 'Walking'" *Thoreau Quarterly* 16 (1984): 137–55 for an account of the relationship between the essay and the Journal.

prepared myself to speak a word now for Nature—for absolute freedom & wildness, as contrasted with a freedom and culture simply civil—to regard man as an inhabitant, or a part and parcel of nature—rather than a member of society."[8] Thoreau's apology proceeds with hardly a pause into the opening words of the lecture (which would remain very much the same in the published essay: "I wish to speak a word for Nature, for absolute freedom and wildness . . ." [260]), as if the argument that follows can substitute in some way for direct political expression on the topic of slavery, offering the promise of "absolute freedom" in place of the struggle for a merely "civil" freedom. The first public expression of the lecture that would become "Walking" occurs then as a displacement of what Thoreau understood to be the urgent political crisis precipitated by the Fugitive Slave Law. Instead, he would "speak a word" for a "Nature" disjunct from the political evils of which the law is synecdochic, a nature where, as he claims near the end of the essay, "no fugitive slave laws are passed" (286). The politics of despair and compromise that Thoreau associates with the Fugitive Slave Law is a silent backdrop for the essay's attempt to imagine a life outside the law ("a successful life knows no law" [283]), to think "man" in different terms, "as an inhabitant . . . of Nature." This project recalls Thoreau's "experiment" in *Walden*, but it also suggests the efforts of nineteenth-century travel literature and anthropology to delineate man in nature, the savage or wild man.

Though he rarely traveled beyond New England himself, Thoreau was a voracious consumer of travel writing, reading hundreds of works in the genre over his lifetime. In the early 1850s *Journal*, passages that would go into "Walking" appear alongside, and are often drawn from, extensive notes on the reading of assorted works of travel literature. "Walking" itself is a form of meta-travel writing, a more reflexive and literary meditation on various modes and tropes of travel, as its very title suggests. Robert Sattelmeyer interprets Thoreau's interest in travel writing as "a means of giving his own microcosmic focus on Concord and New England a global resonance." [9] This global register provided more than a cosmopolitan backdrop for Thoreau's writings, though; it entangled them in a network of ideologically motivated narratives of the rela-

---

8. From the manuscript of "The Wild," quoted in Walter Harding, *The Days of Henry Thoreau: A Biography* (Princeton: Princeton University Press, 1992), 315. Harding also provides an account of this sequence of events.

9. Robert Sattelmeyer, *Thoreau's Reading: A Study in Intellectual History with Bibliographical Catalogue* (Princeton: Princeton University Press, 1988), 48. Sattelmeyer refers to John Aldrich Christie's listing of "nearly two hundred" works of travel literature read by Thoreau, and adds that Christie's inventory could have "included many others" (47–48). Buell also discusses the importance of travel writing in shaping Thoreau's own mode of "environmental prose" (416–19).

tions of nations and peoples. Mary Louise Pratt argues that the "planetary consciousness" produced by travel writing was implicated from the start in the ideological work of constructing the world according to European imperialist interests.[1] Natural history, emerging in the mid-eighteenth century in close contact with travel writing, was an especially powerful discourse for generating a new global consciousness, ordering the natural world—plants, animals, and even humans—according to a classificatory system and empirical method that originated in Europe, but was aimed at comprehending the entire world. Among the most spectacular features of the reports of explorers were their accounts of non-European peoples; travel writing and anthropology converged in the invention, depiction, and classification of "primitive" man.

Thoreau was fascinated by the productive intersection of travel, natural history, and anthropology. "Walking" as much as any of Thoreau's works manifests a global consciousness informed by these discourses. If it situates itself at times within Concord and its environs, it is saturated with references drawn from travel all over the world; the essay's motto might be: Think (and read) globally, Walk locally. While Buell stresses the importance in Thoreau's work of a "realist" mode of representation rooted in a commitment to the observation of nature on a local level, I contend that for Thoreau it is only through the tropes of a global literary consciousness that a new ecology can be imagined. Thoreau's aim of imagining "another order of men" beyond the politics of nation and empire is complicated by his appropriations and interpolations from discourses of travel and natural history that are themselves frequently racist, nationalist, and imperialist. Though he claims that walking carries the individual walker beyond the limits of nation and politics, maintaining that the nature he walks out into belongs only nominally to national space ("You may name it America, but it is not America" [265]), the work of a good portion of the essay is to invoke geographic boundaries and relations, in order to position "America" and "the West" within a more global mapping of the migrations of cultures and peoples. "Walking" retells the story of the founding of the New World, legitimated by the ideology of America as "nature's nation," but it also hints at a more surprising counter-narrative, which brings New World nature into contact with other, imaginary geographies, particularly with images and signs drawn from travel writing about the exploration of Africa.

---

1. Mary Louise Pratt, *Imperial Eyes: Travel Writing and Transculturation* (New York: Routledge, 1992), 24–37. Pratt asserts that "travel and exploration writing produced 'the rest of the world' for European readerships" (5), making sense of the non-European world by bringing it within European systems of knowledge, thus participating in the intellectual work of empire.

In the first half of the essay, Thoreau situates his exploration of the meaning of walking within the context of the westward migration of European peoples, claiming that the inclination towards the west that he observes in his own walks parallels "the general movement of the race" (269), from the "exhausted" soil and culture of Europe to the unspoiled land and unlimited promise of the New World. America is the destination, the destined nation, the "future" for European "man," who needs the revitalizing influence of a culture more firmly rooted in nature.

* * *

This section of "Walking" is concerned with mapping patterns of (European) migration, positing a natural force, an "impulse" or "magnetism" impelling both race and individual westward. The virtue of the West, and therefore apparently of America, is that of nature itself, as the essay's most frequently quoted environmentalist slogan announces: "The West of which I speak is but another name for the Wild; and what I have been preparing to say is, that in Wildness is the preservation of the World" (273). This motto then is not just an environmentalist statement of the intrinsic value of wildness, but also an assertion of nationalist ideology, in which "The West" is synonymous with "the Wild," and America is grounded in nature. Thoreau's argument for wildness is also an argument for the superiority of American nature *and* culture.

African Beasts and American Manhood

> What does Africa,—what does the West stand for?
> *Walden* (215)

The essay's privileging of an America legitimated by association with nature leads to a discussion of comparative natural history, in which Thoreau cites an assortment of naturalists and explorers who praise the superiority of New World plants, animals, and landscapes in comparison to their European counterparts. Thoreau asks rhetorically, "Where on the globe can there be found an area of equal extent with that occupied by the bulk of our States, so fertile and so rich and varied in its productions, and at the same time so habitable by the European, as this is?" (270). Nature is more beautiful and varied, both larger and wilder in America, yet its superiority is also asserted in terms of its habitability for Europeans; America's attractiveness is legible only in relation to Europe, as a sequel that surpasses the original. Natural history here is a stage for nationalist ideology, so broadly argued that at times it seems self-conscious, even parodic. Illustrating the potential instrumentality of natural history for empire, the New World's fitness for European "man" is revealed to the scientist's eye by the very order of nature, as Thoreau's quotation from the geographer Arnold Henry Guyot proclaims: "As the plant is made for the animal, as the vegetable world is made for the animal world, America is made for the man of the Old World . . ." (270). The garden of American nature has been waiting for the European, the only animal that can fill the vacant niche at the top of the food chain. Indeed, the habitability of the New World is evidenced by the relative absence of dangerous predators that might threaten or rival man: one of the virtues of American nature is "that in this country there are no, or at most very few, *Africanae bestiae*, African beasts, as the Romans called them, and that in this respect also it is peculiarly fitted for the habitation of man" (271). Unlike the "city of Singapore," whose "inhabitants are annually carried off by tigers," "the traveler can lie down in the woods at night almost anywhere in North America without fear of wild beasts." The "fact" of a gentle, habitable New World nature, indicated by the relative absence of dangerous animals in America, was the material and ideological product of European colonization and expansion, which generated the "natural" signifier that legitimated it; the absence of native predators was the result of European colonization, not its precondition. Further extending the rhetorical strategy of emptying the New World to accommodate colonization, this discussion omits any mention of Native Americans, as if American nature were uninhabited before the European. Yet the domestication of American nature as eminently habitable for Europeans threatens to erode the very difference that constituted its superiority in relation to Europe, making Thoreau's claim about the absence of wild beasts rather equivocal. His use of the Latin phrase *"Africanae bestiae,"* immediately following a Latin quotation from Linnaeus, seems a playful instance of this equivocation, condensing a strange set of global relations: it employs the prestigious European language of natural history to invoke African beasts, in effect taming them with a mock-scientific designation, in order to pay tribute to a "peculiarly" American habitability. The essay's hyperbolic expression of the ideology of European expansion into the New World exposes conflicting imperatives: American nature must be like Europe, in order to be hospitable to European man, but it must also be sharply different, in order to have the potent wildness necessary to bring about his revitalization. The claim that there are no dangerous "African" animals in America also indicates a deficiency in New World nature, then. Given his privileging of "absolute freedom and wildness" in the essay, the very lack of the "fear of wild beasts" suggests that American nature is safer, more domesticated and European, than the equation of the West with the Wild implies.

Yet there are in fact African beasts, and African people, in "Walking," and by extension in Thoreau's imagining of New World nature. Africa and its natural history supply him with some especially critical metaphors, employed at key moments in the essay. So for example he imagines a wildness inimical to civilization in terms of savage African appetites, the devouring of African antelopes: "Give me a wildness whose glance no civilization can endure,—as if we lived on the marrow of koodoos devoured raw" (273). This central formulation obliquely personifies wildness as the hostile glance of the wild man, irrecoverable for culture; it stages an encounter seemingly beyond culture, beyond metaphor, even though so evidently mediated by the sensational trope of the African savage. Perhaps most surprising, through the subjunctive promise of its simile, "we" are identified (proleptically) not with "civilization," but with wildness; Thoreau imagines us as one day wielding such a glance ourselves. This wild figure is set up by the reporting of a piece of crude ethnographic detail, drawn from Thoreau's reading of an African travel narrative (written by the "hunter" Roualeyn George Gordon-Cumming): "The Hottentots eagerly devour the marrow of the koodoo and other antelopes raw, as a matter of course." A European description of the behavior of an African people serves as the source of the figurative language that Thoreau uses to represent wildness, the alleged customs of the "Hottentots" providing him with a lurid image of wildness. This invocation of the African as a figure of savagery is characteristic of the way Africa and Africans were constructed in the European American imagination, a construction greatly shaped by travel literature.[2] His description of "Hottentots" appropriates the racist rhetoric of much travel writing, employing a trope of savagery that is a well-worn and highly derogatory racist caricature, but inverting its valuation, so that it becomes the very emblem of the celebration of wildness. Thoreau simultaneously encourages and forecloses an identification with this figure of the savage African, representing it as civilization's absolute other, but appropriating its wildness to envision a new community of which "we" are a part.

Michael Taussig suggests that both the destructive and healing power imputed to wildness by the European imagination might de-

2. Patrick Brantlinger and Jean and John Comaroff describe the contours of the European construction of the savage, bestial African, and the contributing role of travel literature in shaping it. "Hottentots" was a denigrating European name for an indigenous South African people, thus a term that itself implies the colonialist perspective of European travel-writing. [Patrick Brantlinger, "Victorians and Africans: The Genealogy of the Myth of the Dark Continent," *"Race," Writing, and Difference*, ed. Henry Louis Gates, *Critical Inquiry* 12 (1985): 166–203; Jean Comaroff, and John Comaroff. *Of Revelation and Revolution: Christianity, Colonialism, and Consciousness in South Africa* (Chicago: University of Chicago Press, 1991).]

rive from the threat it poses to "the symbolic function itself": wildness breaks open the totalizing "unity of the symbol," introducing "slippage" "between signifier and signified."[3] Wildness likewise functions as a disruption of conventional symbolic meanings in "Walking," defamiliarizing and destabilizing a chain of invested identifying signs—"American," "civilized," "white." Thoreau claims that wildness is disorienting to common sense itself as constituted in European American culture: "The wildest dreams of wild men, even, are not the less true, though they may not recommend themselves to the sense which is most common among Englishmen and Americans to-day" (278). But this wildness is always mediated by Western culture, seen through the eyes of the European (or European American). If Thoreau embraces its disruptive potential, its value comes from its supplementary relation to white American culture, as the spur that impels society towards radical transformation. Wildness is threatening to civilized man, but also potentially salutary, a restorative tonic (figured as the "infusion of hemlock spruce or arbor-vitae in our tea" that brings strength [273], or the uncultivated meadow or swamp, containing "the strength, the marrow, of Nature," essential to "man's health" (276). Its agency is dangerous but potent: "Some forms of disease, even, may prophesy forms of health" (278). Wildness is recuperated for cultural work through the very marking of its difference, though that difference is necessary for its efficacy. Yet if the encounter with the wild seems staged as a moment in the consolidation or expansion of social order, for Thoreau it is not for the purpose of propping up the status quo, but rather of wrenching us free, opening up the possibility of a new "order of men."

"Africa" here is a locus for such wildness, an imaginary space onto which Thoreau projects a life in which "man" and nature are not yet irrevocably separated by an alienating culture. This imagined primordial scene gives rise to a series of figurative exchanges between the human and the animal, which are not contained within the European stereotype of the African as bestial, animalistic. Thoreau moves from imagining the eating of antelopes to the wish that "man" might be like an antelope:

3. Michael Taussig, *Shamanism, Colonialism, and the Wild Man: A Study in Terror and Healing* (Chicago: University of Chicago Press, 1987), 210. Though Taussig emphasizes the disruptive character of wildness, he acknowledges that it is "incessantly recruited by the needs of order (and indeed, this is one of anthropology's most enduring tasks and contributions to social order)." Yet if wildness is constantly recuperated "so that it can serve order as a counterimage," it must "retain its difference" to fulfill this purpose; Taussig suggests that this "paradox" is highly volatile, and that in the end wildness falls "on the side of chaos" (220). It is important to underscore that this paradoxical and disruptive wildness is a construction generated by European culture, projected onto an imagined space beyond culture (and typically onto "primitive" peoples), where it can perform the work of being order's shadow.

> The African hunter Cumming tells us that the skin of the
> eland, as well as that of most other antelopes just killed, emits
> the most delicious perfume of trees and grass. I would have
> every man so much like a wild antelope, so much a part and
> parcel of nature, that his very person should thus sweetly ad-
> vertise our senses of his presence, and remind us of those
> parts of nature which he most haunts. (273–74)

The eland's skin bears the trace of a more intimate relationship
with nature, an immersion that can be apprehended only when the
animal is "just killed." A kind of animal proxy, the African antelope's
death and entry into the discourse of travel enables the vision of a
re-immersion in nature that would restore American "man" to
health, reintroducing him into his proper natural habitat. Africa
functions as a compensatory rhetorical resource in Thoreau's account of New World nature. The ideology of America as "nature's
nation," of the West as the Wild, fails to conceal a lack in the American relation to nature, creating the need for a wilder African nature as supplement.

   If America is to Europe as nature to culture, wildness to civilization, it stands in an inverse relation to Africa. African zoology
supplies the trope used to evoke a connection to nature lost by
Americans in another of the essay's central figures:

> Here is the vast, howling mother of ours, Nature, lying all
> around, with such beauty, and such affection for her children,
> as the leopard; and yet we are so early weaned from her breast
> to society, to that culture which is exclusively an interaction of
> man on man,—a sort of breeding in and in, which produces at
> most a merely English nobility, a civilization destined to have a
> speedy limit. (281)

In this figuring of nature as leopard mother, the dangerous and alluring wildness associated with African animals earlier in the essay
is combined with fierce maternal love, a mother both nurturing and
feral. Alienation from nature is constructed as premature separation from the mother, into a decadent "culture" characterized by
"breeding in and in," an "interaction of man on man" no longer restrained and legitimated by nature. The *Journal* version of the sentences that immediately follow this passage makes the sexual
undercurrent in its imaging of decadence more explicit (the last
sentence below was left out of "Walking"): "In society—in the
best institutions of men—I remark a certain precocity—When we
should be growing children—we are already little men. Infants as
we are we make haste to be weaned from our great mother's breast
& cultivate our parts by intercourse with one another" (3:191). Social life involves an unchaste precocity, an impulsive rush into

"intercourse" with each other. Social life is sexual life here, as Thoreau imagines it; his phrasing seems to conflate precocious intellectual and sexual development, since "parts" can refer both to abilities or talents and to genitalia. Instead of a "true culture" still rooted in nature, we occupy an alienated, degenerate culture in which we only "cultivate our parts" with each other.

In the imaginary geography sketched out by this passage and others in "Walking," America is situated uneasily between Africa and Europe, the child caught in a perilous family romance: the cultural pathology of the American relation to nature begins with a premature break from a primordial union with the mother, a maternal nature fleetingly but suggestively imagined as African; estrangement from this nature leads to an inbred, decadent, doomed European culture ("a merely English nobility, a civilization destined to have a speedy limit"). Earlier in the essay Thoreau appropriates the myth of Romulus and Remus to imagine the founding of Western civilization in relation to a wild animal mother: "The story of Romulus and Remus being suckled by a wolf is not a meaningless fable. The founders of every state which has risen to eminence have drawn their nourishment and vigor from a similar wild source" (273). The decadent culture of the "Empire" (Roman, British) failed because its later children "were not suckled by the wolf," unlike "the children of the northern forests" who "conquered and displaced" them. In the *Journal*, Thoreau makes it clear that this fable should be the nationalist story of America's founding: "America is the she wolf to day and the children of exhausted Europe exposed on her uninhabited & savage shores are the Romulus & Remus who having derived new life & vigor from her breast have founded a new Rome in the west" (3:186). This sentence is not included in "Walking," though, and the indigenous "she wolf" that nurtures American culture is replaced by the African leopard from whose breast we were weaned too soon; a native wildness imagined as the ground for American culture is displaced, made foreign. In "Walking," African natural history helps to tell the story of a pathological American family romance, featuring the troubled relationship between nature and culture.

Though seemingly incidental, African signs have a certain prominence in the essay, playing a crucial role in the signifying economy of some of its central passages. Thoreau's allusions to African people and wildlife, but also to a wide range of other non-Western, "exotic" places and cultures, furnish tropes for representing an American cultural crisis.

* * *

Thoreau and the Menagerie

> No visitor to a merely physical Africa could see these animals.
> This is a spiritual vision made possible only by their death and lit-
> eral re-presentation. Only then could the essence of their lives be
> present. Only then could the hygiene of nature cure the sick vi-
> sion of civilized man.
>
> Donna Haraway[4]

Thoreau's record in the *Journal* of his visit to a menagerie in
1851 provides an important intertext for the unexpected appearance of signs of African natural history in "Walking," opening up a
quite different context for an encounter with African animals. His
reflections on this experience, which he returned to intermittently
in the *Journal* over the next year or so, enter into the essay only elliptically, but they help to illuminate not only his interest in
leopards and other African animals, but also his imagining of the
interrelationship between these creatures and man. He first describes the exhibit in an entry from late June, 1851:

> Visited a menagerie this afternoon I am always surprised to
> see the same spots & stripes on wild beasts from Africa & asia.
> & also from South America—on the Brazilian tiger and the
> African Leopard, and their general similarity. All these wild
> animals—Lions tigers—chetas—Leopards &c Have one hue
> tawny & commonly spotted or striped— What you may call
> the pard color. A color & marking which I had not associated
> with America.

In the menagerie's collection of wild animals from all over the
world, the large cats are most prominent to Thoreau's eye, and
what he sees in them is a profound (though external) similarity. In
spite of their diverse regional origins, they share "the same sports &
stripes," and their fur has the same "tawny" hue, "the pard color."
This family resemblance, "their general similarity," is located on the
surface, in the color of skin or hide, though it may be visible only to
an especially discerning gaze, one able to perceive fundamental
unity in spite of apparent difference. In addition to his perception
of a common identity shared by these "beasts," Thoreau is struck by
their wildness:

> These are wild animals (beasts) What constitutes the differ-
> ence between a wild beast & a tame one? How much more
> human the one than the other!— Growling scratching roaring—
> with whatever beauty & gracefulness still untameable this
> Royal Bengal tiger or this leopard. They have the character &

4. *Primate Visions*, 30.

the importance of another order of men. The majestic lion—
the King of beasts—he must retain his title. (3:276–77)

In this symbolic intersection of animal and man, it is the wild
beasts that are "much more human"; their "untameable" wildness
suggests sovereignty, a "title" in oneself that Thoreau would claim
for the individual person. The difference between the animal and
the human seems to get displaced onto "the difference between a
wild beast & a tame one," making it possible to imagine new affinities between beast and man. Thoreau recognizes in them a "color &
marking" which he had not previously "associated with America,"
but finding them in a menagerie in Massachusetts prompts him to
think about the meaning they might hold for white European
American men. If the wild animals seem more human to him than
the tame, it is because they are proxies for a human potentiality as
yet unrealized: they point to the utopian possibility of "another order of men," apart from the existing social order found in Europe or
America.

The spectacle of the menagerie becomes an invested site for
Thoreau's imagining of the human place in the natural order, making it possible, through an animal surrogate, "to regard man as an
inhabitant . . . of nature" ("Walking" 260). His subsequent references to the menagerie enact various exchanges and crossings between man and animal. These passages imply that the wildness of
animals might provide glimpses of an elusive but prized human
wildness. In a *Journal* entry that would appear much altered in
"Walking," he likens the "cries" of the menagerie's animals to
"wildest strains" of "the finest music," translated into nature
(3:342–43); in "Walking," it is the "wildness" in "a strain of music"
that reminds him of the "cries emitted by wild beasts" (279). As the
"Walking" passage continues, Thoreau turns again from wild animals to imagining a better mode of human social interaction: "Give
me for my friends and neighbors wild men, not tame ones. The
wildness of the savage is but a faint symbol of the awful ferity with
which good men and lovers meet." In a later *Journal* passage it is
not the wildness but the theatricality of the menagerie's animals,
the apparent awareness of being on display, that forms an imagined
point of contact between the animal and the human: Thoreau
compares a roadside animal attraction to "the circus & menagerie
combined," and remarks of the animals, "so human they were—
exhibiting themselves" (4:40–41).

* * *

In the menagerie species go astray. It is thus the site of a disorienting vision as well as a unifying one, as if it represents a conceptual
wildness in spite of its vulgar domestications. As much tropological

as zoological, the menagerie's wildness suggests the violence of figuration itself, disordering the classificatory discourse of natural history. It forms a crucial backdrop for "Walking," in which Thoreau would reimagine white European American men in relation to wildness and alterity.

Dismantling Whiteness: Skin Color and the Environment

Can the Ethiopian change his skin, or the leopard his spots?

Jeremiah

* * *

In its imagining of American manhood restored through intimate contact with (African) wildness, "Walking" likewise suggests that one might find a new image of the self in the spectacle of alterity. Through a series of oblique reflections on skin color and race, the essay casts the racial identity of man in nature as mutable, impressionable, capable of being remade anew. This rethinking of race begins with a strong version of racial environmentalism, including a renewed assertion of the importance of climate: "For I believe that climate does thus react on man" (271). Invoking the incomparable promise of American nature projected by travelers and naturalists, Thoreau asks, "Will not man grow to greater perfection intellectually as well as physically under these influences?" The migration of Europeans to the New World exposes them to new environmental influences, resulting in a new man (as Crevecoeur claimed), though the changes envisioned by Thoreau are generally less tangible and more metaphorical than the physiological alterations theorized by some earlier environmentalists ("I trust that we shall be more imaginative, that our thoughts will be clearer, fresher, and more ethereal, as our sky,—our understanding more comprehensive and broader, like our plains,—our intellect generally on a grander scale, like our thunder and lightning . . ." [271–72]). He does speculate about the physical effects of the sun's rays, however, and tanned skin becomes one of the essay's principal metaphors for exposure to the natural environment. The implications of the essay's version of environmental determinism are most interesting in its allusions to skin color, which bring European American identity into relation with other cultures and peoples.

He first introduces the thematics of skin in terms of the thicker skin, tanned and calloused, created by a life outdoors. Exposure to the natural environment, to the "sun and wind," alters skin and by extension character, causing "a thicker cuticle to grow over some of the finer qualities of our nature . . . as severe manual labor robs the hands of some of their delicacy of touch"; "staying in the house, on the other hand, may produce a softness and smoothness, not to say thinness of skin, accompanied by an increased sensibility to certain impressions" (263). Though he concedes that it may be "a nice matter to proportion rightly the thick and thin skin," Thoreau clearly privileges skin that bears the mark of exposure to the elements, which he equates with experience itself. Skin is the impressionable outer surface of the embodied self, an index of man's proximity to nature (figured by the eland skins smelling of the "trees and grass" that synecdochize the antelopes' habitat). But skin registers more than exposure to climate or contact with nature in the essay; it is also marked by the social meanings of gender, class, and race. The passage concludes with a more resonant statement of the social legibility of thick and thin skin: "The callous palms of the laborer are conversant with finer tissues of self-respect and heroism, whose touch thrills the heart, than the languid fingers of idleness. That is mere sentimentality that lies abed by day and thinks itself white, far from the tan and callus of experience." The rough skin of the implicitly male laborer is valued over the idle domesticity of a sentimental middle-class culture strongly coded as feminine. (A page earlier Thoreau complains that women "are confined to the house still more than men," and implies that they are likely to spend their days reclining [262], apparently overlooking for the moment the existence of domestic work.) Self-love is divided between heroic "self-respect" and "mere sentimentality," between good and bad forms of auto-eroticism; the masculine palms of the laborer have touched finer, thrilling tissues, in contrast to the luxurious but enervating narcissistic pleasures of "the languid fingers of idleness." The soft skin of this womanly hand images the decadence of a feminized culture estranged from nature, a version of the society whose members have weaned themselves prematurely from nature in order to "cultivate" their "parts" with each other. White skin is the very sign of this estrangement. Whiteness is the accomplishment of a social elite that stays indoors and "thinks itself white," marking itself off from the laborer's tanned skin as well as racialized skin color. Thoreau's formulation suggests that whiteness is something constructed or achieved, as much a product of the work of thinking as of a life indoors; it is a self-identification that confers a privileged status with respect to race and class stratification, and that is made possible by a repudiation of non-white identities, and beyond them of nature itself.

Thoreau's project of reimagining man in relation to nature in the essay requires undoing this white self-identification, exposing whiteness to the (darkening) light of day. In an 1852 *Journal* entry, Thoreau recounts seeing boys swimming, remarking that their skin is "the not often seen flesh color" (5:90). The "flesh color" of their naked bodies, like the unifying "pard color" seen in the previous year's trip to the menagerie, seems to undermine sharp distinctions between types. He declares that "as yet we have not man in nature," because men are "forbidden to expose their bodies under the severest penalties," and then describes the actual color of the boys' skin: "A pale pink which the sun would soon tan. White men! There are no white men to contrast with the red & the black—they are of such colors as the weaver gives them." The revelation of this passage, reiterated in "Walking," is that "man in nature" is not white. Here the environmentalist assertion of the mutability of skin color as racial marker gives way to the more radical evacuation of whiteness as a category with respect to nature. "White" skin does not exist in nature: it is soon tanned by the sun, but it disappears even more quickly under the pressure of empirical observation, which reveals a range of skin colors in its place; whiteness can be maintained as an identity only by covering up the skin with clothing, that is, removing man from nature. Rather than simply legitimating the status quo, typically the purpose of appeals to nature as the ground of race, Thoreau's aim here is to destabilize the opposition between whiteness and other racial categories, revealing its asymmetry. Yet the liberating prospect of re-envisioning whiteness is made possible by the assumption that it is *the* socially constructed position; the very mobility granted here to the identity formerly known as white does not seem to extend to "the red & the black," which remain fixed in nature. Thoreau's attempt to imagine a new man in nature seems to imply a movement with respect to race that is in one direction only.

The wish that "white men" might be transformed through contact with wild nature relies on the implicit elision of any categorical difference between tanned skin and racially marked skin color, as if both represent stages in man's alteration through exposure to the modifying effects of the natural environment. Thoreau returns to these ideas in a passage in "Walking" that invokes travelers' reports of encounters with other races:

> A tanned skin is something more than respectable, and perhaps olive is a fitter color than white for a man,—a denizen of the woods. "The pale white man!" I do not wonder the African pitied him. Darwin the naturalist says, "A white man bathing by the side of a Tahitian was like a plant bleached by the gardener's art, compared with a fine, dark green one, growing vigorously in the open fields." (274)

White skin is the product of an artificial culture and cultivation, of the "gardener's art," in contrast to olive, the badge of a masculinity imagined as inhabiting nature (in the *Journal* version of this passage, "olive or red" are the "fittest" colors for man in nature [3:84], making it clearer that Thoreau is envisioning a range of non-white racial identities). The passage inverts traditional moral and aesthetic hierarchies of skin color, though it does so by affirming the fundamental association of whiteness with culture, non-white skin color with nature. Non-white skin is aligned with vigorous health, the result of a salutary immersion in nature, embodied in the Tahitian in Charles Darwin's botanical simile; the white man, at odds with nature, appears bloodless and sickly, and so becomes the object of African pity.

* * *

"Walking" critiques a white middle-class American social world exhibiting signs of a kind of cultural pathology, inhabited by men who are increasingly effete, dissipated, degraded by their relation to commerce, and shut off from the restorative power of wild nature; Thoreau speaks of "these comparatively degenerate days of my native village" (276). Against this perceived decadence, "Walking" calls for a new ecology, a new grammar of man's relation to the natural world, which would be the foundation for a revitalized American culture. Implying that this ecology cannot be found in white European American society, Thoreau envisions the possibility of a hybrid knowledge emerging through an encounter with darkness and wildness. Near the end of the essay, shortly after his figuring of nature as leopard, he gestures towards such a knowledge, in a punning formulation that gathers together a number of strands developed earlier:

> There are other letters for the child to learn than those which Cadmus invented. The Spaniards have a good term to express this wild and dusky knowledge,—*Gramática parda*, tawny grammar,—a kind of motherwit derived from that same leopard to which I have referred. (282)

The Spanish idiom *gramática parda* implies an alternative, nonstandard mode of knowledge, something like slyness, cunning, or savvy, but it suggests other meanings as well. *Parda* means dark, as "dusky" suggests. Thoreau privileges this dark knowledge in opposition to metaphors of enlightenment ("there may be an excess even of informing light" [281]), marking it off from conventional rationality (it is a "higher knowledge," which may not amount to "anything more definite" than a "revelation of the insufficiency of all that we called Knowledge before" [283]). It becomes clear in this passage that what the essay is calling for is a new epistemic as well as social order: a way of seeing and knowing, a relation to the world that would bring culture back into alignment with nature. *Parda* is derived from "leopard," an etymological pun that affiliates this grammar with the essay's central figure for nature and wildness. As "motherwit," it would restore the maternal relation lost through having been "so early weaned" from the leopard mother into culture. Thoreau's visit to the menagerie, with its revelation of the "tawny" "pard color" of the leopards and other wild cats, inspiring the idea of "another order of men," is surely in the background of this conception of a wilder grammar; here too an animal figure enables a new vision of the human.

Various commentators—most famously Gary Snyder in his environmentalist essay "Tawny Grammar"—have focused on this moment as the essay's central formulation of Thoreau's demand for a new ecology, ethos, or mode of expression.[5] Yet its potential racial implications have been overlooked; Thoreau's use of the phrase *gramática parda* implies a rethinking of human nature that has embedded racial significance. *Pardo* can refer to such pard colors as brown or dun, and more specifically to dark or brown skin color, and so by extension to people of mixed race ancestry. This potential racial meaning is preserved in Thoreau's translation. The word "tawny" comes from the same root as "tan," and thus connects with the essay's thematic of tanned skin as the sign of man's alteration through exposure to the natural environment, an idea that I contend is conflated with racially marked skin color through the suggestion of racial environmentalism. "Tawny" in fact was often used to describe non-white skin color, especially the coloration of Native Americans (Thoreau refers in his *Journal* to "the real tawny Indian face."[6] As a noun, it had been a racial epithet since the colonial era. *Pardo/a* was similarly substantivized. According to Mary Louise Pratt, the term *pardo* was used in Spanish America as a more general designation than *mulatto* or *mestizo*, loosely describing a range of non-white racial groupings, roughly comparable to the English word "colored."[7] *Pardo* seems to imply a hybrid identity, neither "white" nor "black," the bane of the polygenesist scientists, for whom hybrids threatened to blur the distinction between putative species. Thoreau's sly pun suggests that a new knowledge and culture, the grammar for a healthier relation between the human and the natural, can only be found by renouncing an artificial whiteness marked off from other class and race identities, in order to return to a nature imagined as non-white, made up of an unpredictable and unclassifiable range of colors, "such colors as the weaver gives them."

5. Gary Snyder, "Tawny Grammar," in *The Practice of the Wild* (San Francisco: North Point Press, 1990), 48–77. Snyder quotes this passage of "Walking" in order to speculate about a "grammar . . . of culture and civilization itself" that might enable "society" to "stay on better terms with nature" (76).
6. Henry David Thoreau, *The Journal of Henry David Thoreau*, 14 vols., ed. Bradford Torrey and Francis H. Allen (New York: Dover Publications, 1962), 8:390.
7. Pratt, *Imperial Eyes*, 239 n. 4.

"Walking" calls for a darkening of white American culture, re-grounding it in wild nature. The essay demands a new ecology in the fullest sense, entailing a radical transformation of social and political relations, of the human itself. I argue that this utopian project is thoroughly caught up in, and even enabled by, Thoreau's thinking about race, informed by his reading of travel literature and natural history, among other contemporary cultural discourses. The attempt to imagine a new man, no longer white, may also be a response, both idiosyncratic and culturally embedded, to an untenable national politics exemplified by the Fugitive Slave Law, and more generally to a perceived cultural pathology associated with the exclusionary construction of whiteness as an identity. This wish to alter or displace white identity through an encounter with racial otherness supplements the essay's investment in the aim of legitimating and naturalizing the European American as native to North America, part of the natural order itself. Both "Walking" and the *Journal* attest to the fleeting but recurrent vision of a new "order of men," seen for a moment in the alterity of animal proxies, African wildness, or racial difference. This vision is fundamentally limited in its scope, however: it seems to be a vision of transformation solely for white men, in which women emerge from the gendered universal "man" only to be linked symbolically with the deadening domestic culture that needs rehabilitation. Moreover, it implies no corresponding new conception of non-white peoples and cultures, except insofar as the nature and wildness with which they remain associated are themselves revalued.

The new social order imagined by "Walking" is as tenuous and indefinite as the perception at the essay's end of an "ancient and altogether admirable and shining family" living in the woods beyond the town, whose "house was not obvious to vision." This family never enters into the decadent society of the village, living somehow outside existing social, economic, and political relations ("They are of no politics. There was no noise of labor"), and they elude representation: "I find it difficult to remember them. They fade irrevocably out of my mind even now while I speak, and endeavor to recall them and recollect myself. . . . If it were not for such families as this, I think I should move out of Concord"(285). "Walking" insists that the vision of a new man, reunited with wild nature, is equally impossible, unsustainable, and necessary.

STEVEN FINK

The Language of Prophecy:
Thoreau's "Wild Apples"†

Henry Thoreau's transcendentalist assumptions about the role of the writer created in him a deep-seated ambivalence about his relation to the public: the chief American advocate of withdrawal from institutional authority found himself caught between the urge for independence from the community and the simultaneous need to engage its attention. His desire for philosophical, moral, and literary self-sufficiency was rooted not in misanthropy but in his desire to assume the role of American prophet (a desire shared by most of the other New England transcendentalists as well). This ambition demanded that the seer emerge from the isolation of his private vision to become the public bard or "sayer." Whether as a Jeremiah rebuking the sins and backslidings of the populance or as a Moses catching sight of a new life in the new land, the American prophet had to come down from the mountaintop to impart his vision to the people.

For Thoreau, the act of writing (and of publishing) was the descent necessary to the fulfillment of his prophetic role. Despite his protestations to the contrary, he was hardly indifferent to the public's response to his work. In a voice that derived its authority from spiritual withdrawal, the prophet and reformer directly exhorted a readership that alone could gratify his ambitions as a writer. Thoreau's mixed feelings about the proper relationship between author and audience led to a similar ambivalence in his ideas about the form of prophetic discourse itself. Thoreau's development as a writer, in fact, can be traced through his efforts to find a mode of discourse that was both faithful to his private vision and intelligible to the community.

* * *

Throughout his career, Thoreau assumed a fundamental correspondence between the actual and the ideal—between "facts" and "truths"—and throughout *A Week* his narrative method was to use natural facts as a springboard for extended passages of abstract moral philosophizing. After *A Week*, however, Thoreau gradually altered his narrative strategy: he became increasingly guarded about explicitly voicing those abstract truths and began to rely more heav-

† From *The New England Quarterly* 59 (1986): 212–30. Reprinted by permission. Authorial footnotes have been condensed and in some cases omitted by the editor; "Wild Apples" page numbers refer to this Norton Critical Edition.

ily on his careful descriptions of natural facts alone to carry the burden of the ideal. As his explicit commentary decreased and the symbolic density of his language increased, Thoreau of course ran a greater risk of having the "hasty" reader miss his point, but he decreased the risk of offending that reader.[1] Furthermore, he came to recognize the need for an element of dissimulation. He tried to make readers think his works appealed to their own values, as in the opening chapter of *Walden* in which he ironically uses the language of capitalist business ventures, thereby engaging the materialist and utilitarian interests of the public while the larger purpose of the chapter (and the book) is to undermine those very interests.

The perfection of such strategies is achieved in "Wild Apples," a late essay that concedes the power of an unenlightened audience to thwart the prophet's mission without, however, abandoning that mission. The apparent modesty of "Wild Apples" is a calculated and richly subversive rhetorical stance. The essay deserves careful study if for no other reason than to dispel the impression that Thoreau's last years were ones of failure and decay, for what seems at first a slight, whimsical piece is actually a highly crafted personal autobiography, a national biography, and an American jeremiad.

"Wild Apples" was first presented as a lecture in February 1860. Shortly before his death, Thoreau sent a somewhat revised version to the *Atlantic Monthly*, where it was published in November 1862. Walter Harding characterizes the piece as Thoreau's "most successful 'familiar essay,' a delightful blending of wit and wisdom, filled with whimsical humor and facetious catalogs of imaginary species of fruit."[2] Indeed, from the beginning "Wild Apples" has been appreciated as one of Thoreau's better nature essays—careful and precise though never strictly scientific. Yet the deliberate reader will soon discover that the essay's informative and entertaining observations also carry a finely wrought symbolic significance.

The complexity of Thoreau's rhetorical task is signaled in the opening section of the essay, "The History of the Apple Tree." "It is remarkable," he begins, "how closely the history of the apple tree is connected with that of man" (288). He goes on to cite evidence of prehistoric links between man and the apple tree and then to catalogue allusions to the apple in the ancient literature of the Hebrews, Greeks, Romans, and Scandinavians. Thoreau's catalogue, a conventional introduction for a familiar essay easily recognized by

---

1. The author alludes to Thoreau's distinction in *A Week* between two types of readers: "It is the characteristic of great poems that they will yield of their sense in due proportions to the hasty and the deliberate reader. To the practical they will be common sense, and to the wise wisdom." Henry D. Thoreau, *A Week on the Concord and Merrimack Rivers*, ed. Carl F. Hovde (Princeton, N.J.: Princeton University Press, 1980), p. 147 [*Editor*].
2. Walter Harding, *The Days of Henry Thoreau* (New York: Knopf, 1965), p. 436.

a nineteenth-century audience, itself has a somewhat complex rhetorical function. On the one hand, it provides an opportunity for the author to display his erudition and to dignify his choice of topics by aligning it (and himself) with some established tradition. Yet these claims for the subject's importance must, in turn, be made somewhat facetiously; thus the author displays his cleverness and sets the appropriate tone for the familiar essay: the topic is, he implies, relatively trivial but worthy of the reader's casual attention in a moment of leisure, for it will prove to be both entertaining and informative.

In "Wild Apples," however, Thoreau goes beyond this convention and suggests that the history of the apple tree is a metaphor for the history of man himself. In a *Journal* entry of 15 February 1860 (just after his Lyceum readings of "Wild Apples"), Thoreau alluded to the technique used to achieve his purpose:

> As in the expression of moral truths we admire any closeness to the physical fact which in all language is the symbol of the spiritual, so, finally, when natural objects are described, it is an advantage if words derived originally from nature, it is true, but which have been turned (*tropes*) from their primary signification to a moral sense, are used, i.e., if the object is personified.[3]

Thoreau's subject, the study of the apple, is a familiar one—both as literal object and as symbol—so it serves him well as a vehicle through which he can appeal to his twofold audience of hasty and deliberate readers.

As he traces the history of the apple tree, then, Thoreau is both providing a discussion of natural history and preparing the reader for a discussion of human destiny—implicitly conflating the two:

> Pliny, adopting the distinction of Theophrastus, says, "Of trees there are some which are altogether wild (*sylvestres*), some more civilized (*urbaniores*)." Theophrastus includes the apple among the last; and, indeed, it is in this sense the most civilized of all trees. It is as harmless as a dove, as beautiful as a rose, and as valuable as flocks and herds. It has been longer cultivated than any other, and so is more humanized; and who knows but, like the dog, it will at length be no longer traceable to its wild original? It migrates with man, like the dog and horse and cow: first, perchance, from Greece to Italy, thence to England, thence to America; and our Western emigrant is still marching steadily toward the setting sun with the seeds of

---

3. *The Journal of Henry D. Thoreau*, 14 vols. (Boston: Houghton, Mifflin, 1906), 13: 145. Unless otherwise noted, subsequent references to the *Journal* are to this edition and will be cited parenthetically in the text.

the apple in his pocket, or perhaps a few young trees strapped to his load. (289–90)

Like the apple, man's western migration contains his fate. Thoreau exploits the conventional myth of the progress of civilization from Greece to the New World and goes on to justify the "manifest destiny" of the western migration by cataloguing the beneficial effects of the introduction of the apple to America upon indigenous insects, birds, quadrupeds, and even Indians. At the same time, Thoreau subtly inverts the conventional understanding of the "progress" of civilization: he implies the danger of a kind of diminishment in losing the traces of our "wild original." And by portraying the apple as enhancing the environment because it has adapted to it, Thoreau introduces one of the central themes of the essay: his preference for the wild to the cultivated apple and, symbolically, his belief that man himself will fulfill his destiny not by exploiting the American landscape but by allowing it to naturalize him.

Thoreau goes on to provide his readers with detailed, lively descriptions of the apple tree's flower and fruit and a quite specific calendar of the stages of the apple's growth. The information, both entertaining and practical, also serves Thoreau's prophetic impulse. He writes of the apple tree generally, "The flowers of the apple are perhaps the most beautiful of any tree's, so copious and so delicious to both sight and scent," and he notes how, walking through an orchard, "you pass through a little region possessed by the fragrance of ripe apples, and thus enjoy them without price, and without robbing anybody" (290, 291). The fragrance of apples thus evoked appeals to "common sense," but the fragrance is also a symbol of the spiritual qualities inherent in all creation. Thus the orchard becomes the prelapsarian Garden and the apple a symbol, not of man's Fall, but of the possibility of renewed innocence.[4] In order to transform America into the Garden, Thoreau insists, we must cultivate what he called the "uncommon senses" so that we may perceive the paradise around us; in other words, we must acknowledge uses of nature higher than mere commodity in order to recover that place in which we may enjoy the fruit "without price and without robbing anybody." Making his point more explicit, Thoreau adds, "There is thus about all natural products a certain volatile and ethereal quality which represents their highest value, and which cannot be vulgarized, or bought and sold" (291). Significantly, Thoreau's discussion of the "ethereal" qualities of apples

---

4. On Thoreau's use of the Genesis story of the Fall in "Wild Apples," see Kevin P. Van Anglen, "A Paradise Regained: Thoreau's *Wild Apples* and the Myth of the American Adam," *ESQ* 27 (1981): 28–37; and Robert Sattelmeyer's introduction to Thoreau's *Natural History Essays* (Salt Lake City: Peregrine Smith, 1980).

falls under his treatment of the cultivated rather than the wild apple, for Thoreau wants to stress that the true value of even the most marketable apple is not measured in such directly utilitarian terms.

When Thoreau turns from the cultivated to the wild apple, he focuses his analogy between man and apple:

> Most fruits which we prize and use depend entirely on our care. Corn and grain, potatoes, peaches, melons, etc., depend altogether on our planting; but the apple emulates man's independence and enterprise. It is not simply carried, as I have said, but, like him, to some extent, it has migrated to this New World, and is even, here and there, making its way amid the aboriginal trees. (295)

On the level of the entertaining familiar essay, "man" is the subordinate component in the man-apple analogy: he is introduced for the sake of illustration, to enliven what might otherwise be a rather dry, purely scientific topic. For the "prophetic" moral essay, however, the wild apple is subordinate. Having been "turned," as Thoreau said, "from their primary signification to a moral sense," wild apples are only the apparent and not the actual subject of this discourse. As Thoreau noted in a *Journal* entry for 23 February 1860, "A fact stated barely is dry. It must be the vehicle of some humanity in order to interest us. . . . Ultimately the moral is all in all, and we do not mind it if inferior truth is sacrificed to superior" (*Journal*, 13:160). Thoreau risks little here as he celebrates the adaptation and naturalization of the apple in the New World; yet the "deliberate" reader will recognize that Thoreau's theme in "Wild Apples" is the same one he had stated so explicitly in *A Week*:

> Men nowhere, east or west, live yet a *natural* life, round which the vine clings, and which the elm willingly shadows. Man would desecrate it by his touch, and so the beauty of the world remains veiled to him. He needs not only to be spiritualized, but *naturalized*, on the soil of the earth.[5]

In a brief digression on the indigenous crab apple, Thoreau begins to develop his apple tree symbolism with greater precision:

> Nevertheless, *our* wild apple is wild only like myself, perchance, who belong not to the aboriginal race here, but have strayed into the woods from the cultivated stock. Wilder still . . . there grows elsewhere in this country a native and aboriginal crab-apple, *Malus coronaria*, "whose nature has not yet been modified by cultivation." (295)

---

5. Henry D. Thoreau, *A Week on the Concord and Merrimack Rivers,* ed. Carl F. Hovde (Princeton, N.J.: Princeton University Press, 1980), p. 379.

Thoreau describes the native habitat, size, flower, and fruit of the indigenous apple, and he briefly narrates his own first sighting of the tree on his 1861 trip to Minnesota (material he added to the essay just prior to its publication). Then he makes his transition from the discussion of the crab apple to his next section on the wild apple by remarking of the crab, "But though these are indigenous, like the Indians, I doubt whether they are any hardier than those backwoodsmen among the apple trees, which, though descended from cultivated stocks, plant themselves in distant fields and forests, where the soil is favorable to them" (296). With this sentence, Thoreau fully establishes his metaphorical equation: the "cultivated stock" is the European settler in the civilized communities of the east; the wild apple is the European who, like himself or the backwoodsman, has reattached himself and adapted to the natural environment; and the indigenous crab apple is the native American Indian.

Looking back, then, we find that Thoreau's comments on the aboriginal tree are simultaneously applicable to the aboriginal American. He quotes from his authority Michaux, for example, that "if, on being cultivated, it does not yield new and palatable varieties, it will at least be celebrated for the beauty of its flowers, and for the sweetness of its perfume" (295). Thoreau seems to have found Michaux's observations interesting not only for their literal meaning but because they captured his feelings about the Indian as well. Thoreau felt that the Indian probably could not and, in fact, should not be civilized, or "cultivated"; that his integrity and worth should be respected even though his age had passed; that the study of the Indian was essential to the inheritors of the New World even though he would not play a leading role in the destiny of America.[6] In a *Journal* entry for February 1859, Thoreau had criticized the historians' neglect of the Indian and proclaimed, "But even the indigenous animals are inexhaustibly interesting to us. How much more, then, the indigenous man of America!" (*Journal*, 11:437).

Thoreau's special interest was in the wild apple derived from cultivated stocks—in the white man who had learned to live independently in the New World—and so he turns to the wild apple saying, "These are the ones whose story we have to tell" (296). In the sec-

6. Thoreau's attitude toward the Indians was ambivalent and complex and changed over the course of his life. In an early *Journal* entry, for example, he wrote, "They seem to me a distinct and equally respectable people, . . . and not to be inoculated with the twilight civilization of the white man." In 1858 he wrote, "Everybody notices that the Indian retains his habits wonderfully,—is still the same man that the discoverers found. The fact is, the history of the white man is the history of improvement, that of the red man a history of fixed habits and stagnation." (See *Journal*, 1:445; 10:251–52.) Yet much of Thoreau's energies in his later career were devoted to the study of the American Indian and aboriginal races generally.

tion headed "How the Wild Apple Grows," Thoreau's levels of signification multiply and his language becomes increasingly dense.
Thoreau's detailed account, based on careful observation of the actual growth of wild apple trees over a period of several years, is also
an exemplary lesson in self-reliance and, on another level still, a private record of his own experience. "I know of no trees," he writes,
"which have more difficulties to contend with, and which more sturdily resist their foes." Their chief foe, aside from "drought and other
accidents," is the cow, "a fellow-emigrant from the old country," who
browses on their shoots (296). The story of the wild apple's heroic
triumph over the cattle is not only an example of Thoreau's nature
writing at its finest but the story of his own triumph over his "fellow-
emigrants." As early as his 1838 lecture on "Society," and frequently
thereafter, Thoreau had characterized the mass of men as "cattle,"[7]
and the alert reader begins to suspect here that there is a sharper
edge to Thoreau's essay than was at first apparent. As the wild apple
is cut back by the cattle year after year, "it does not despair" but
grows "more stout and scrubby, until it forms, not a tree as yet, but
a little pyramidal, stiff, twiggy mass, almost as solid and impenetrable as a rock. . . . No wonder they are prompted to grow thorns at
last, to defend themselves against such foes" (297).

> The cows continue to browse them thus for twenty years or
> more, keeping them down and compelling them to spread, un-
> til at last they are so broad that they become their own fence,
> when some interior shoot, which their foes cannot reach, darts
> upward with joy: for it has not forgotten its high calling, and
> bears its own peculiar fruit in triumph. (297–98)

Here is Thoreau's declaration of his own endurance and of the
means that have enabled him to proclaim victory at last. For twenty
years Thoreau himself had been "browsed" by superficial readers
and kept down by a society of cattle who did not realize he had a
richer fruit to bear. He, too, had been forced to surround his "interior shoot"—his private inspiration and ambition—with a protective
and increasingly thorny fence of material both to satisfy and to fend
off browsers. But, like the wild apple, Thoreau did not forget his
high calling. The anecdote continues:

> Such are the tactics by which it finally defeats its bovine foes.
> Now, if you have watched the progress of a particular shrub,
> you will see that it is no longer a simple pyramid or cone, but
> that out of its apex there rises a sprig or two, growing more
> lustily perchance than an orchard-tree, since the plant now de-

---

7. "One goes to a cattleshow expecting to find many men and women assembled, and be-
   holds only working oxen and neat cattle" (*Journal, Volume I, 1837–1844*, ed. John C.
   Broderick et al. [Princeton: Princeton University Press, 1981], p. 36). See also, e.g.,
   Journal 2: 453 (3 September 1851) and 14: 306 (3 January 1861).

votes the whole of its repressed energy to these upright parts.
In a short time these become a small tree, an inverted pyramid
resting on the apex of the other, so that the whole has now the
form of a vast hour-glass. The spreading bottom, having served
its purpose, finally disappears, and the generous tree permits
the now harmless cows to come in and stand in its shade.
(298)

The reading public, Thoreau's "bovine foes," have shaped his
own "wild" American self and the expression of that self in his writing. In typical Thoreauvian fashion, he has converted hardship and
failure into the source of his ultimate triumph: the twenty years of
browsing, which kept his growth scrubby and stunted and which
seemed to force him to naturalize himself and adapt to the native
soil (literally, on the shores of Walden Pond), were the source of
the independence and endurance that permit a second growth that
surpasses that of the "orchard-tree"—the genteel writers who satisfy cultivated tastes. In his triumph, the cows become harmless
and the tree generous.

The anecdote represents the perfection of Thoreau's mature style
and exemplifies the very tactics by which he outwits his "foes."
Thoreau is careful up to this point not to insist too heavily on the
symbolic import of the anecdote, which, on a strictly literal level,
remains both informative and entertaining—the two qualities the
general public demands. The autobiographical dimension of this
section of the essay is always fully embedded in the straightforward, though carefully selected, nature description. But because
the wild apple has further significance as an exemplary (as opposed
to private) emblem of self-reliance, endurance, and native strength,
Thoreau gradually brings this public level of symbolic meaning into
higher relief. "Through what hardships it may attain to bear a sweet
fruit! . . . Who knows but this chance wild fruit . . . may be the
choicest of all its kind, and foreign potentates shall hear of it, and
royal societies seek to propagate it" (298–299). On the autobiographical level, Thoreau is expressing his private hope that his own
fruits—his writings—may one day be sought after as the choicest of
their kind; but his desire is generalized and made exemplary:

> What a lesson to man! So are human beings, referred to the
> highest standard, the celestial fruit which they suggest and as-
> pire to bear, browsed on by fate; and only the most persistent
> and strongest genius defends itself and prevails. . . . Poets and
> philosophers and statesmen thus spring up in the country pas-
> tures, and outlast the hosts of unoriginal men. (299)

Thoreau's account thus satisfies both the "hasty and the deliberate reader," yielding both common sense and wisdom. Further, in
the published essay, Thoreau is careful to temper the merely per-

sonal references and to maintain a genial tone that emphasizes the literal or, as in this case, a socially acceptable moral that tends to enhance his identification with his audience. Yet in the original *Journal* entry from which this anecdote was drawn, Thoreau's personal identification with the fate of the wild apple is clearer, as is his contempt for his "cultivated" contemporaries. There, Thoreau immediately made the analogy between the wild apple and "the rude, neglected genius from amid the country hills" in whom he clearly sees himself. His personal frustration, resentment, and hope are clear in his description of the wild apple tree/man, who

> grows broad and strong, and scraggy and thorny, hopelessly stunted, you would say, and not like a sleek orchard tree all whose forces are husbanded *and the precious early years not lost*, and when at first, within this rind and hedge, the man shoots up, you see the thorny scrub of his youth about him, and he walks like an hour-glass, aspiring above, it is true, *but held down and impeded by the rubbish of old difficulties overcome*, and you seem to see his sands running out. But at length, thanks to his rude culture, he attains to his full stature, and every vestige of the thorny hedge which clung to his youth disappears, and he bears golden crops of Porters or Baldwins, *whose fame will spread* through all orchards for generations to come, while *that thrifty orchard tree which was his competitor will, perchance, have long since ceased to bear its engrafted fruit and decayed.* (*Journal*, 11:269–70, 31 October 1858; emphasis mine)

This passage needed to undergo several important transformations before Thoreau could present it to the public, the most important of which was suppressing the personal bias and the tone of frustration and anger that it brought on. For it is obvious that Thoreau resents the loss of his "precious early years," while the cultivated orchard trees—those urbane writers who were his contemporaries and whom he explicitly characterizes here as his "competitors"—flourished. More than a hint of malice is betrayed in his strangely violent concluding image of their death and decay. The "competition" was, of course, for fame, and Thoreau's identification with the wild apple implies his belief that *his* victory would be over the long run, that his true audience would be the "generations to come." With this evidence of his submerged bitterness, it is all the more telling that Thoreau chose to face his readers with apparent benevolence rather than open scorn.

While Thoreau revised his material in order to achieve a lighter, more generous tone, he was also willing to manipulate and, to some extent, misrepresent the natural facts in order to make the material conform to his symbolic construct. Thoreau, who had begun recording his annual observations of local wild apple trees as early as 1850 (though without any clear sense of their metaphorical significance), noted in his 1853 entries that the apple scrubs were "first planted by the cows, then browsed by them and kept down stubborn and thorny for years. . . . You see the cow-dung everywhere now with a hundred little trees springing up in it. Thus the cows create their own shade and food" (*Journal*, 5:179–80). It was not until his *Journal* entries of 1857 that Thoreau fully grasped the particular symbolic application of his observations, and he then discovered that the actual symbiotic relation between cattle and wild apples did not suit his purpose. The cattle, the "browsers," needed to be more clearly represented as the enemy; the wild apple, as his image of both personal and exemplary self-sufficiency, needed to appear more independent and more "generous." In his studies of seeds in general and of "The Succession of Forest Trees" in particular, Thoreau naturally found it essential to point out the importance of birds and animals in transporting seeds. Here, however, it was just as important to minimize that relationship. As Thoreau noted in a *Journal* entry cited earlier, "Ultimately, the moral is all in all, and we do not mind if inferior truth is sacrificed to superior."

In the essay the superior truth would presumably be the exemplary character represented by the wild apple, but his willingness to shape his material to his needs also allowed Thoreau to have a private joke at the expense of the "browsers," his superficial readers. In a *Journal* entry for 1853, Thoreau had complained that his contemporaries hired him as a surveyor but not as a lecturer: "All the while that they use only your humbler faculties, your higher unemployed faculties, like an invisible cimetar, are cutting them in twain. Woe be to the generation that lets any higher faculty in its midst go unemployed! That is to deny God and know him not, and he, accordingly, will know not of them" (*Journal*, 6:21–22).[8] Acknowledging two distinct classes of readers, Thoreau manipulated the language of "Wild Apples" in such a way that he was able to inflict private attacks, intended to cut "like an invisible cimetar," on the conventional readers who remained unable to perceive the prophet in their midst.

This multilayered prose is sustained, then, with varying degrees of intensity, throughout the essay. In describing "The Fruit and Its Flavor," Thoreau advises the reader of the best times to pick the wild apples and defends their "more racy and wild American flavors" (300). He suggest that they are best eaten out-of-doors, where the eater partakes of the environment that nourished them—and, implicitly, is himself naturalized too—but adds, "Of course no fla-

8. See Journal selections, pp. 370–71 [*Editor*].

vors are thrown away; they are intended for the taste that is up to
them. Some apples have two distinct flavors, and perhaps one half
of them must be eaten in the house, the other outdoors" (302). The
observation is candid, no flight of fancy—Thoreau even quotes a
letter of 1782 to the Boston Academy to verify his assertion—but it
is also a comment on his own writing and his readers, the eaters
of his fruit. Thoreau's essay can accommodate whatever taste is
up to it—either the hasty, practical reader or the deliberate, wise
reader—and there are flavors for both. He adds, however, "So there
is one *thought* for the field, another for the house. I would have my
thoughts, like wild apples, to be food for walkers, and will not warrant them to be palatable if tasted in the house" (303).

Thoreau's section on "The Last Gleaning" is a wonderfully written account of searching for the last of the windfall late in the year.
Full of fine, detailed, close observations, it represents Thoreau's nature writing at its best. Since Thoreau has made the analogy clear
between the wild apples and his "thoughts," however, we read this
section simultaneously on a literal and a symbolic level, for it is a
wry lesson on how to find not only those apples but those *thoughts*
that "lie concealed" in "lurking places," "where they are covered by
leaves [punning here, as he had on "browsers"], safe from cows
which may have smelled them out" (306).

In the final section of the essay, on "The 'Frozen-Thawed' Apple,"
Thoreau writes,

> Those which a month ago were sour, crabbed, and quite un-
> palatable to the civilized taste, such at least as were frozen
> while sound, let a warmer sun come to thaw them,—for they
> are extremely sensitive to its rays,—are found to be filled with
> a rich sweet cider. (307)

Here we have literal observation, exemplary symbol, and personal
symbol. Like the anecdote at the conclusion of *Walden* about the
"beautiful bug" which emerged from an apple-tree table after sixty
years "to enjoy its perfect summer at last," this is a fable of metamorphosis. It is a millennial vision of the triumph of the self-reliant
and principled individual who endures to create a new world, and it
is a symbol of Thoreau's faith in the ripening of his own works under the genial rays of future time.

But unlike *Walden*, "Wild Apples" concludes not in the opti-
mistic tone of the visionary but in the castigating tone of the biblical jeremiad. The commercial failures of his most ambitious works
had not entirely dispelled Thoreau's faith, but they had displaced
it from his own to future generations. He issues a final warning:
"The era of the Wild Apple will soon be past. It is a fruit which will
probably become extinct in New England" (308). At first his tone

is nostalgic, a lament for lost pleasures and opportunities. Thoreau
fears that the wild apple, which in its very toughness and durabil-
ity represented the fruits of democracy, available to even the humblest, will be replaced by the cultivated apple available only in the
marketplace. "Now that they have grafted trees, and pay a price for
them, they collect them into a plat by their houses, and fence
them in,—and the end of it all will be that we shall be compelled
to look for our apples in a barrel" (308). As the wild apple disappears, so does the naturalized man in whom Thoreau has placed
his hopes for America. As he noted in a *Journal* entry for 26 November 1860.

> Do not think that the fruits of New England are mean and in-
> significant, while those of some foreign land are noble and
> memorable. Our own, whatever they may be, are far more im-
> portant to us than any others can be. They educate us, and fit
> us to live in New England. Better for us is the wild strawberry
> than the pineapple, the wild apple than the orange, the hazel-
> nut or pignut than the cocoanut or almond, and not on ac-
> count of their flavor merely, but the part they play in our
> education. (*Journal*, 14:274)[9]

Thoreau ends his essay with a stark vision cautiously expressed
not in his own words but in those of the Book of Joel:

> The vine is dried up, and the fig tree languishes; the pome-
> granate tree, the palm tree also, and the apple tree, even all
> the trees of the field, are withered: because joy is withered
> away from the sons of men. (309)

The passage is especially striking when we recognize it as the alternative to his description, earlier in the essay, of the triumphant wild
apple: "when some interior shoot, which its foes cannot reach,
darts upward with joy: for it has not forgotten its high calling, and
bears its own peculiar fruit in triumph."

In one of the most recent commentaries on Thoreau and his
work, Richard Bridgman sees in the quotations that conclude "Wild
Apples" another symptom of the "dark Thoreau" whose "imagination ever returned to . . . the dismal . . . . Hence Thoreau chose to
conclude this sunnily realistic essay with a series of diatribes from
the prophet Joel. . . . The apocalyptic violence of these quotations
in context is astonishing. Their presence is explicable only by referring to Thoreau's constitutional pessimism."[1] Yet there are other ex-

---

9. This paragraph serves as part of Thoreau's introduction to his late "Wild Fruits" project
   (from which he culled "Wild Apples"), according to Bradley Dean's reconstruction of the
   manuscript. See Henry David Thoreau, *Wild Fruits*, ed. Bradley P. Dean (W. W. Norton,
   2000), p. 5 [*Editor*].
1. Richard Bridgman, *Dark Thoreau* (Lincoln: University of Nebraska Press, 1982), p. 279.

planations, more consistent with the skillful and deliberate crafting of this complex essay. Even for the reader who has regarded "Wild Apples" as a "sunnily realistic" familiar essay and nothing more, Thoreau's conclusion would seem neither inexplicable nor astonishing; rather, it would be regarded as another instance of the witty mock seriousness and hyperbole that Thoreau has provided throughout the essay, as an ironic elevation into the prophet's rage of the genteel essayist's civilized nostalgia for the passing of a simpler, rustic era. As such, the closing neatly rounds out the essay by complementing the opening catalogue of classical and scriptural allusions to the fruit. In this respect, it is of utmost importance that the diatribe not come from the author's own mouth, for the quotation allows the "hasty" reader to regard the closing as no more than a final example of the author's erudition and wit. Still, the essay does end on a disconcerting dying fall, and the "deliberate" reader will recognize that the prophecy is indeed genuine and applicable. Bridgman is indeed correct to note a deep-seated pessimism in the passage but not when he implies that a pessimism crippling and uncontrollable mars an otherwise pleasant essay. Rather, that pessimism is the culmination of the genuinely prophetic vein running throughout the essay, a thorny, protective pessimism aimed at Thoreau's own audience but that he controls and uses to create his art and triumph at last.

Even though his lecture versions of "Wild Apples" in February 1860 were apparently quite successful,[2] Thoreau nevertheless complained in the pages of his *Journal* the following week,

> Always you have to contend with the stupidity of men. It is like a stiff soil, a hard-pan. If you go deeper than usual, you are sure to meet with a pan made harder even by the superficial cultivation. The stupid you have always with you. Men are more obedient at first to words than ideas. They mind names more than things. Read to them a lecture on "Education," naming that subject, and they will think that they have heard something important, but call it "Transcendentalism," and they will think it moonshine. Or halve your lecture, and put a psalm at the beginning and a prayer at the end of it and read it from a pulpit, and they will pronounce it good without thinking. (*Journal*, 13:145)

Assessing his audience thus harshly, Thoreau had devised a literary strategy sufficient to his purposes. He had never given up his desire for acclaim in the literary marketplace, but it had usually eluded

---

2. Thoreau first read "Wild Apples" at the Concord Lyceum on 8 February 1860, at what proved to be his final appearance there. Contemporary reports suggest it was highly successful. One auditor considered it "the best lecture of the season" and noted that "at its close there was long and continued applause." Thoreau successfully repeated the lecture the following week in Bedford (Harding, *Days of Henry Thoreau*, p. 436).

him; nor had he ever lost the conviction of his calling to be a prophet to America. At the end of his career, he achieved a degree of success in both areas by having learned how to appeal to two audiences. Thoreau's late essays, including "Wild Apples," did find a measure of popular success both as lectures and in print in the *Atlantic Monthly*. It was largely because of these (and the posthumously published travel books on Maine and Cape Cod) that Thoreau's reputation as a nature writer was kept alive after his death. Thoreau was not without his small following of "deliberate" readers during his lifetime, but for the most part this audience—those responsive to his embedded prophetic vision—emerged slowly in the years after his death. Early and repeated failures had driven Thoreau to regard posterity as his ultimate audience even as he did his best to win over the popular audience of his day. Ultimately, it was this dual effort that provided the impetus for his finest art.

LANCE NEWMAN

[Capitalism and Community in *Walden* and *Wild Fruits*]†

Thoreau is extravagant, even self-consciously defiant, when he claims in *Walden* to feel more at home at the Pond than in Concord:

> Yet I experienced sometimes that the most sweet and tender, the most innocent and encouraging society may be found in any natural object, even for the poor misanthrope and most melancholy man. There can be no very black melancholy to him who lives in the midst of nature and has his senses still. There was never yet such a storm but it was Aeolian music to a healthy and innocent ear. Nothing can tightly compel a simple and brave man to a vulgar sadness. While I enjoy the friendship of the seasons I trust that nothing can make life a burden to me. (91–2)

This is more than a simple claim to be comfortable in woods where his neighbors felt uneasy. The invidiousness of the distinction between nature and society becomes so strong that Thoreau transplants the few desiderata remaining in Concord, cultivating them in the woods instead:

---

† From *Our Common Dwelling: Henry Thoreau, Transcendentalism, and the Class Politics of Nature*. (New York: Palgrave Macmillan, 2005), pp. 133–41, 171–72, 177–83. Copyright © 2005 Lance Newman. Reprinted by permission. Authorial footnotes have been condensed and in some cases omitted by the editor; page numbers of *Walden* and the essays on Thoreau by Emerson and Lowell refer to this Norton Critical Edition.

I have never felt lonesome, or in the least oppressed by a sense of solitude, but once, and that was a few weeks after I came to the woods, when, for an hour, I doubted if the near neighborhood of man was not essential to a serene and healthy life. To be alone was something unpleasant. But I was at the same time conscious of a slight insanity in my mood, and seemed to foresee my recovery. In the midst of a gentle rain while these thoughts prevailed, I was suddenly sensible of such sweet and beneficent society in Nature, in the very pattering of the drops, and in every sight and sound around my house, an infinite and unaccountable friendliness all at once like an atmosphere sustaining me, as made the fancied advantages of human neighborhood insignificant, and I have never thought of them since. Every little pine needle expanded and swelled with sympathy and befriended me. I was so distinctly made aware of the presence of something kindred to me, even in scenes which we are accustomed to call wild and dreary, and also that the nearest of blood to me and humanest was not a person nor a villager, that I thought no place could ever be strange to me again. (92)

Gentle, sweet, beneficent, friendly, sustaining, sympathetic, kindred, nearest of blood, humanest: this rising catalogue paints a community all the more tightly bound the larger it grows, with nature occupying the far end of every social bond. It is not just that Thoreau feels strongly about rural landscapes. The sharp negative remains firmly in place: such feelings are not possible in the company of other people.

Reversals like this seemed perverse to many of Thoreau's early readers, For instance, Emerson records, in his Journal for August 1843, his feelings about the early excursion essay, "A Winter Walk," which rehearses many of the distinctive rhetorical strategies on which *Walden* depends:

H. D. T. sends me a paper with the old fault of unlimited contradiction. . . . He praises wild mountains & winter forests for their domestic air; villagers & wood choppers for their urbanity; and the wilderness for resembling Rome & Paris. With the constant inclination to dispraise cities & civilization, he can yet find no way to honour woods & woodmen except by paralleling them with towns and townsmen.

Emerson's frustration measures the degree to which his *protégé* was writing against the grain.[1] The most familiar contemporary idiom for description of forested hills such as those around Walden Pond

---

1. Ralph Waldo Emerson, *The Journals and Miscellaneous Notebooks of Ralph Waldo Emerson*, ed. William H. Gilman, Ralph H. Orth, et al., 16 vols. (Cambridge: Harvard University Press, 1960–82), 9:9–10.

focused exactly on their forbidding emptiness, on the awful sublimity of endless repetition. Such a landscape was read as a field of conquest, of struggle for the establishment of civilization within and against an encompassing, and potentially engulfing, nature. By describing a comfortable community in nature and opposing it to the alienated life of Concord, Thoreau was appropriating and modifying an alternative tradition. The pastoral valorized a middle or picturesque landscape in opposition to the deprivations of both the city and the wilderness. His strongest modification of the pastoral, then, is to erase the bonds between humans that had been its central focus and claim membership in a community of nature.[2]

Thoreau's sense of kinship with raindrops and pine needles has been central focus of the ecocritical reassessment of his work. His writing records, it is argued, the lived experience of ecocentric consciousness compelling an ethical stance toward nature. His sympathy with the nonhuman is said to mark him as ahead of his time, as recognizing the moral standing of beings now included, by the more environmentally advanced, in a concentrically expanding ecological republic. He is said to have practiced, a hundred years early, what Aldo Leopold later formalized when he argued that the social contract should include "soils, waters, plants, and animals" and that "a thing is right when it tends to preserve the integrity, stability, and beauty of the biotic community. It is wrong when it tends otherwise." This is a powerful reading of Thoreau's significance. But how do we respond to the cynical response to Thoreau's professed love of nature that has been common for so long? James Russell Lowell, for instance, makes this famous postmortem assessment:

> Thoreau's experiment actually presupposed all that complicated civilization which it theoretically abjured. He squatted on another man's land; he borrows an axe; his boards, his nails, his bricks, his mortar, his books, his lamp, his fish-hooks, his plough, his hoe, all turn state's evidence against him as an accomplice in the sin of that artificial civilization which rendered it possible that such a person as Henry D. Thoreau should exist at all. (417)

Although we can simply dismiss this as cynical chatter and move on, we would do well to assess seriously Lowell's implied claim: that perfection of the kind Thoreau sought is only possible under tightly controlled conditions, that moral absolutism is based on an erasure of the social context within which alone such choices be-

2. The two best accounts of the cultural politics of the pastoral remain Leo Marx, *The Machine in the Garden: Technology and the Pastoral Ideal in America* (New York: Oxford University Press, 1964) and Raymond Williams, *The Country and the City* (New York: Oxford University Press, 1973).

come meaningful. Michael Gilmore updates Lowell's claim, reading *Walden*'s density and opacity as a rhetorical strategy meant to render the book uncommodifiable by a developing literary market that Thoreau saw as impure. Thoreau voices a "profound hostility to the process of exchange" along with a "conviction that literature can change the world," but "the aesthetic strategies he adopts to accomplish political objectives involve him in a series of withdrawals from history; in each case the ahistorical maneuver disables the political. . . ." Chief among these maneuvers is the hypostatization of nature into an unchanging transcendental reality. Gilmore goes on to argue that *Walden* is a "defeated text" since Thoreau's retreat into the transcendental is the outcome of "a crisis of confidence in the likelihood of civic reform and the idea of writing as a means of instigating it."[3]

But when Thoreau declared independence from a degraded historical republic and allegiance to an alternative natural community, he hoped that his retreat would end in a decisive advance. The simple problem/solution structure of *Walden* attests to Thoreau's immersion in the main currents of thought in New England: "Economy" delivers its harsh critique of Concord, where "the mass of men live lives of quiet desperation" (8), then the rest of the book builds gradually to the redemptive climax of "Spring" and "Conclusion." And since Emerson remarked in his eulogy that Thoreau was in himself "a practical answer to the theories of the socialists," it has been common to observe that in moving to Walden Pond, Thoreau established an experimental community of one, analogous in its impulse to the collective venture at Brook Farm. But the observation usually stopped there, largely because of Thoreau's proverbial hostility to reformers, recorded in the numerous jabs at urban philanthropists for their unctuousness and punctilio, and in one seemingly conclusive passage from his Journal for March 1841: "As for these communities—I think I had rather keep a batchelor's hall in hell than go to board in heaven.— Dost think thy virtue will be boarded with you? It will never live on the interest of your money, depend upon it.[4]

Thoreau's disagreements were more thoughtful than such an easy jab indicates. Sterling Delano recently discovered, at long last, documentary evidence that Thoreau visited Brook Farm. He went there on December 3, 1843 and not long afterward Farm resident George P. Bradford wrote at letter to Emerson, inquiring worriedly

3. Aldo Leopold, *A Sand County Almanac* (New York: Oxford University Press, 1949), 224–25. Michael T. Gilmore, *American Romanticism and the Marketplace* (Chicago: University of Chicago Press, 1985), 35, 49.
4. Henry D. Thoreau, *Journal*, John C. Broderick, Robert Sattelmeyer, and Elizabeth Hall Witherell, general editors, 6 vols. (Princeton University Press, 1981–), 1:277.

after Thoreau and expressing regret at having allowed a man with such delicate health to depart in an omnibus during a snowstorm. Bradford also remarks, tantalizingly, "We are quite indebted to Henry for his brave defense of his thought which gained him much favor in the eyes of some of the friends here who are of the like faith." Bradford's letter confirms what has long been suspected—that Thoreau was more than simply aware of the goings on at Brook Farm. He saw himself as engaged in a vitally important conversation with the utopian socialists there. In February 1847, Thoreau lectured at the Concord Lyceum on the Walden experiment. Emerson's account of that evening in a letter to Fuller makes clear not only the intended audience of Thoreau's performance, but also the quite genial tone of the relationship: "Mrs. Ripley & other members of the opposition came down the other night to hear Henry's Account of his housekeeping at Walden Pond . . . and were charmed with the witty wisdom which ran through it all." We often spend our best energies differentiating ourselves from those to whom we are closest. The fact is that Thoreau and the Brook Farmers were far closer in their thinking about society and the meaning of leaving it than it has been common to admit. And *Walden*, both the book and the retreat, was an attempt to answer the socialists by putting into practice Emersonian ideas about the pedagogy of nature, cultural leaders, and national revival.[5]

Walden follows the logic of Association[6] by articulating a moral critique of capitalist social relations that is rooted in a tentatively materialist analysis of economic relationships. The book's first sentence frames its concerns: "When I wrote the following pages, or rather the bulk of them, I lived alone, in the woods, a mile from any neighbor, in a house which I had built myself, on the shore of Walden Pond, in Concord, Massachusetts, and earned my living by the labor of my hands only" (5). Rhetorically, the emphasis here is on the last phrase. The cabin is located in an intermediate space, just a short walk into the woods, and the pond is firmly contained in the township. Moreover, the string of miscellaneous descriptors that locate the cabin also foreground the definite assertion about who built it, an assertion that is repeated in the alliterative final phrase. *Walden* is not a book that is mainly about the woods. It is about earning a living there. And its accounts of aesthetic experience of nature mainly demonstrate what gets lost—along with read-

---

5. Sterling Delano, "Thoreau's Visit to Brook Farm," *Thoreau Society Bulletin*, 220/221 (Fall 1997–Spring 1998): 1–2. Ralph Waldo Emerson, letter to Margaret Fuller, February 28, 1847, in *The Letters of Ralph Waldo Emerson*, ed. Ralph L. Rusk and Eleanor M. Tilton, vol. 3 (New York: Columbia University Press, 1939), 3:377–378.
6. Communitarian principle developed from the principles of the French social philosopher Charles Fourier (1772–1837), and practiced at the utopian socialist community of Brook Farm [*Editor*].

ing, introspection, spirituality—when work dominates our lives. The book's introduction, the pages that precede its systematic discussion of the four basic necessities of life, "Food, Shelter, Clothing, and Fuel," mount an analysis of the process whereby these forms of ideal experience have been cheapened. (11)[7]

"Economy" begins by announcing as its topic its audience's "outward condition or circumstances in this world, in this town, what it is, whether it is necessary that it be as bad as it is, whether it cannot be improved as well as not." From this starting point, Thoreau describes the effects of capitalist property relations, labor relations, and competition on the lives of individual workers and farmers. One on hand, there are those small farmers "whose misfortune it is to have inherited farms, houses, barns, cattle, and farming tools; for these are more easily required than got rid of" (6). On the other, there are those who "are poor . . . and have come to this page to spend borrowed or stolen time, robbing your creditors of an hour" (7–8). Both face the trap of debt and to escape it must "persuade your neighbor to let you make his shoes, or his hat, or his coat, or his carriage, or import his groceries for him . . ." (8). Thoreau performs a delicate balancing act here, giving clear attention to the hard material reality of economic relationships between individuals, but then showing that these relationships have moral and social content that gets forgotten. The things that get done for money are the kinds of basic human tasks that carry individual lives forward and bind communities together, and they are demeaned, as human interactions, by their intrication in a cash economy. Thoreau generalizes from his observations on the "outward condition" of his readers to an overall assessment of the effect of capitalist social relations on the character of human aesthetic and spiritual experience. Not only do most people work so much that their inner lives are emptied out, but also the moral character of individual human lives is compromised specifically because they occur within a constraining web of competitive economic relationships, a market: "the laboring man has not leisure for a true integrity day by day; he cannot afford to sustain the manliest relations to men; his labor would be depreciated in the market" (7).[8]

Much of the rest of "Economy," after this first framing section, sets out to document various forms of moral debility that are produced when basic human needs are transformed by competitive

7. Leonard Neufeldt, *The Economist: Henry Thoreau and Enterprise* (New York: Oxford University Press, 1989) shows that *Walden* parodies the conventions structuring contemporary guidebooks for young men that propose to show them the path to material and social success. Bob Pepperman Taylor, *America's Bachelor Uncle: Thoreau and the American Polity* (Lawrence: University of Kansas Press, 1996), 75–97 provides a concise summary of Thoreau's economic argument in *Walden*.

8. The best summary analysis of *Walden's* critique of capitalist social relations is Gilmore, *American Romanticism*, 35–51.

social relations. Thoreau deplores luxury as an accretion, a kind of plaque that comes with civilization, and focuses especially on the competitive acquisition and ostentatious display of luxury goods as a display of social and economic power: "It is an interesting question how far men would retain their relative rank if they were divested of their clothes. Could you, in such a case, tell surely of any company of civilized men, which belonged to the most respected class" (19)? Thoreau describes how this kind of competition for cultural power entraps people so that they become "slave-drivers" of themselves. And he observes that this process is set in motion by the ruling class: "It is the luxurious and dissipated who set the fashions which the her so diligently follow" (28). Thus, it is specifically in the context of class societies that most "of the luxuries, and many of the so called comforts of life [become] positive hinderances to the elevation of mankind" (13). Fine clothes, for instance, are hindrances not only because the hard labor required to get them prevents plucking life's finer fruits. But also, they require participation in an economic system based on exploitation, a "factory system" in which "the condition of the operatives is becoming every day more like that of the English" of Manchester and Birmingham. After all, in this degraded society, "the principal object is, not that mankind may be well and honestly clad, but, unquestionably that the corporations may be enriched" (21). In other words, material structures at the level of whole social orders entangle people in moral relationships that must be taken seriously.

Thoreau recognizes most clearly that moral experience is rooted in materiality when he states that people "are so occupied with the factitious cares and superfluously coarse labors of life that its finer fruits cannot be plucked by them." But this crucial sentence also reveals his conviction that "most men even in this comparatively free country" become entangled in capitalist economic relations "through mere ignorance and mistake" (7). After making such a clear assessment of the moral effects of material social relations, Thoreau adopts a cavalierly voluntarist position about how to respond. He is startling confident. He is astonished that people "honestly think there is no choice left" (9), after all, "what a man thinks of himself, that it is which determines, or rather indicates, his fate" (8). And he sets out to demonstrate just this possibility by renouncing all forms of luxury, choosing not to spend his time "in earning rich carpets or other fine furniture, or delicate cookery, or a house in the Grecian or the Gothic style" (51). Moreover, because he acknowledges that the basic necessities must be secured before it is possible "to entertain the true problems of life with freedom" (11–12), he determines to secure them by his own labor outside the nexus of material social relationships.

Thoreau carries this anticapitalist polemic through to the end, but he hints at a consciousness that his experiment has failed. Individual withdrawal from the market into the world of ideal beans turns out not to be as easy as it might seem, for "wherever a man goes, men will pursue and paw him with their dirty institutions" (118). Thoreau reveals this anxiety quite clearly at the end of "Economy": "When formerly I was looking about to see what I could do for a living . . . I thought often and seriously of picking huckleberries." Like hoeing beans, berry picking would have been an attempt to negotiate an individual solution to a social crisis, and Thoreau acknowledges as much: "But I have since learned that trade curses everything it handles; and though you trade in messages from heaven, the whole curse of trade attaches to the business" (51). An individual solution, in other words, is incommensurate with the problem as he has laid it out—unless his individual actions can be made to seem a necessary prelude to a broader social transformation.

In these last pages of "Economy," Thoreau acknowledges that his experiment "is very selfish," but he defiantly, even petulantly, satirizes his socialist neighbors: "a large house is not proportionally more expensive than a small one, since one roof may cover, one cellar underlie, and one wall separate several apartments." Still he insists that he prefers to live alone since "it will commonly be cheaper to build the whole yourself than to convince another of the advantage of the common wall; and when you have done this, the common partition, to be much cheaper, must be a thin one, and that other may prove a bad neighbor, and also not keep his side in repair." He goes on to accuse the [Brook] Farmers of hypocrisy, claiming that "what so saddens the reformer is not his sympathy with his fellows in distress, but, though he be the holiest son of God, is his private ail. Let this be righted, let the spring come to him, the morning rise over his couch, and he will forsake his generous companions without apology." And he concludes by offering this characteristic advice: "If, then, we would indeed restore mankind by truly Indian, botanic, magnetic, or natural means, let us first be as simple and well as Nature ourselves, dispel the clouds that hang over our own brows, and take up a little life into our pores. Do not stay to be an overseer of the poor, but endeavor to become one of the worthies of the world."

As if to demonstrate the power of his ideas, Thoreau enacts restoration by natural means in "The Ponds," *Walden*'s central chapter, which dramatizes the scholarly narrative of natural instruction, with its new geography of nature versus society. But it also reveals the existence of a critical fault-line built into that geography. The chapter opens with a four-paragraph proem in which its controlling themes are established in two emblematic excursions.

The first is a westward ramble, a release from "human society and gossip." This ramble delivers a compressed reminder of the full-blown analysis of Concord that Thoreau carries out in the book's first chapter, "Economy":

> [Huckleberries] do not yield their true flavor to the purchaser of them, nor to him who raises them for the market. . . . It is a vulgar error to suppose that you have tasted huckleberries who never plucked them. A huckleberry never reaches Boston; they have not been known there since they grew on her three hills. . . . The ambrosial and essential part of the fruit is lost with the bloom which is rubbed off in the market cart, and they become mere provender.

What is lost when natural objects are incorporated into commercial transactions is a cluster of desiderata: spontaneity, organicism, authenticity, individuality, "the tonic of wildness"—all these are "rubbed off" by commodification and what should be a meal for the spirit becomes "mere provender" (119).

If the right way to get hold of huckleberries is to gather them yourself, the same goes for fish, the object of the second excursion in Thoreau's proem. It turns out there is far more to harvesting food in the wild than the pleasure of outwitting the market. Doing so, one is returned, sometimes sharply, to transcendental truths:

> These [midnights spent fishing] were very memorable and valuable to me,—anchored in forty feet of water, and twenty or thirty rods from the shore, surrounded sometimes by thousands of small perch and shiners, dimpling the surface with their tails in the moonlight, and communicating by a long flaxen line with mysterious nocturnal fishes which had their dwelling forty feet below. . . . At length you slowly raise, pulling hand over hand, some horned pour squeaking and squirming to the upper air. It was very queer, especially in dark nights, when your thoughts had wandered to vast and cosmogonal themes in other spheres, to feel this faint jerk which came to interrupt your dreams and link you to Nature again. It seemed as if I might next cast my line upward into the air, as well as downward into this element which was scarcely more dense. Thus I caught two fishes as it were with one hook. (120–21)

Thoreau, in this tableau, plays a representative scholarly seeker of (self-) knowledge. He floats alone above nature's glittering surface. He is initially distracted by thousands of bright, but insignificant phenomena of the kind immediately accessible to empirical observation, or "understanding." But he is quickly hailed by deeper noumena, which reveal themselves to him by direct intuition. The truths apprehended by intuition operating on nature are the higher laws that form the basis of Transcendentalist ontology. These laws explain the connections between apparently unrelated things. Water and air, for instance, a liquid and a gas, are both fluids and thus behave alike. Just so, and crucially, the natural and the supernatural worlds are structured by cognate laws. Thoreau's punch line—two fishes, one hook—is a distillation of the doctrine of correspondence. Sherman Paul remarks that for "those who see the creation as broken in half, correspondence is a way of joining the spiritual and natural halves" for natural phenomena, if properly apprehended, indicate the working of the divine laws according to which creation was and remains structured.[9]

Thoreau's proem, then, like *Walden* as a whole, takes the form of a problem and solution. There is Concord with its deadening commercial order. Then there is Walden Pond, offering restorative contact with the ideal.

* * *

Thoreau spent his final winter putting his literary affairs in order. At the beginning of April 1862, a month before he died, he sent his last essay, "Wild Apples," to the *Atlantic Monthly*. He had excerpted the essay from a longer book-length manuscript, which he left wrapped in a large sheet of paper. On this wrapper, he had written a title, *Wild Fruits*. This manuscript passed through several collections for the next century and a half and has only recently been published.[1] On its surface, the book is a botanical guide to the wild plants of New England. But it moves far beyond the work of cataloguing and identifying. "Most of us are still related to our native fields as the navigator to undiscovered islands in the sea. We can any afternoon discover a new fruit there which will surprise us by its beauty and sweetness".[2] These are the book's first sentences. Most of us, it turns out, are related to Thoreau's writings in the same way. To read *Wild Fruits* is to be surprised by a beauty and sweetness we do not at all associate with the antagonistic hermit of *Walden*. The manuscript is incomplete, fragmentary, and sometimes self-contradictory, so any reading of it necessarily amounts to a speculative construction of a possible book. Even so, *Wild Fruits* clearly confirms the trajectory of Thoreau's traverse from idealism and individualism to materialism and communalism. It is a guide-

9. Sherman Paul, *Emerson's Angle of Vision* (Cambridge: Harvard University Press, 1952), 3–4. For an account of how this central idea structured the whole of Transcendentalist millennialism, see Catherine L. Albanese, *Corresponding Motion: Transcendental Religion and the New America* (Philadelphia: Temple University Press, 1977).
1. Henry David Thoreau, *Wild Fruits*, Bradley P. Dean (New York: W.W. Norton, 2000). For an account of the provenance of the "Wild Fruits" manuscript, see 285–86, 287 n. See William Howarth, *The Literary Manuscripts of Henry David Thoreau* (Columbus: Ohio State University Press, 1974), 322–26, for a physical description of the manuscripts.
2. *Wild Fruits*, 3.

book, yes, but it is also a visionary portrait of a devotional life on the land. It not only envisions an organic community as an alternative to capitalism, it works to convoke such a community by modeling rituals of natural communion.[3]

* * *

Wild Fruits envisions a potential alternative to capitalist ecosocial relations. It recounts a body of natural knowledge and experience of which the implied subject is an organic community living "a simple and wholesome" life on the land, "gathering health and happiness and inspiration" in the woods of New England. And more than envisioning such a utopian community, the text attempts as well to convoke it, to call it into existence by encouraging the ritual harvest and consumption of wild fruits. For Thoreau, gathering berries is an activity for a sacramental party, a collective aesthetic experience. In the entry for "Viburnum Nudum," he writes, "September 3. Now is the season for these comparatively rare but beautiful wild berries which are not food for man. . . . Now is the time for *Beautiful* Berrying, for which children have no vacation. They should have a vacation for their imaginations as much as for their bodies." Like gathering beautiful berries, eating wild apples demands a communal subject: "You cannot read at the same time, as when you are eating an apple. It is a social employment." Moreover, Thoreau's community of fruit pickers and eaters takes its identity and character from its particular environment: "The tropical fruits are for those who dwell in the tropics. . . . It is not the orange of Cuba but rather the checkerberry of the neighboring pasture that most delights the eye and the palate of the New England child." Not only is this community rooted in a specific place, its annual experience is tuned to the cycle of the year: "Our diet, like that of the birds, must answer to the season."[4]

As utopian and apparently whimsical as this vision is, Thoreau recognizes that wild fruits can only take on the meaning he ascribes to them within an entirely new kind of society. Investing wild fruits with such rich meanings is a matter of artifice, of deliberately envisioning an alternative to the course of historical development he has described. This way of thinking is implied, for instance, in his description of the wild apple as "wild only like myself, perchance, who belong not to the aboriginal race here, but have strayed into the woods from the cultivated stock."[5] Convoking such a community is a matter, then, of deliberately straying into the woods, of

3. The late natural history essays, "Autumnal Tints," "Wild Apples," and "Huckleberries," excerpted from the "Wild Fruits" manuscript, have only begun to receive serious critical attention in the past few decades.
4. *Wild Fruits*, 121, 219, 3, 107.
5. Ibid., 79. Compare "Wild Apples," p. 295 in this volume [*Editor*].

rewilding society, of collectively reviving lapsed ways of living on
the land that were characteristic of native and agrarian cultures:

> It would be well if we accepted these gifts [of wild apples] with
> more joy and gratitude, and did not think it enough simply to
> put a fresh load of compost about the tree. Some old English
> customs are suggestive at least. I find them described chiefly in
> Brand's *Popular Antiquities*. It appears that "on Christmas eve
> the farmers and their men in Devonshire take a large bowl of
> cider, with a toast in it, and carrying it in state to the orchard,
> they salute the apple trees with much ceremony, in order to
> make them bear well the next season."[6]

Consciously reinhabiting such lost lifeways can, for Thoreau, transform human relations with the land. Thus, after describing the experience of preparing and eating acorns for the first time, Thoreau
concludes, "now that I have discovered the palatableness of this
neglected nut, life has acquired a new sweetness for me, and I am
related to the first men. . . . Nature seems the more friendly to me."
Likewise, Thoreau reports with obvious pleasure on the new urban
ritual of eating roasted chestnuts: "I have seen more chestnuts on
the streets of New York than anywhere else this year—large and
plump ones roasting in the street, and popping on the steps of
banks and exchanges. Was surprised to see that the citizens made
as much of the nuts of the wild wood as the squirrels. Not only the
country boys—all New York goes a-nutting."[7] Throughout the text,
the suffix, "a-," designates the ritual activities that bind together
Thoreau's imagined community: a-strawberrying, a-huckleberrying,
a-nutting. Thoreau did more than write about berrying as a ritual of
communion; his Journal, along with the journals and correspondence of such friends as Louisa May Alcott and Ellen Emerson, are
full of accounts of berrying and nutting excursions to the Concord
woods. These group excursions, these huckleberry parties, "took
place every year" and Thoreau "was the acknowledged town leader,"
organizing in material reality what he envisions in *Wild Fruits*.[8]

Given the social forces that Thoreau saw as responsible for alienation from nature, it is not perhaps surprising that he saw eating
wild fruits as a democratic activity. He not only celebrates the way
that "all New York goes a-nutting" so that there are "chestnuts for
cabmen and newsboys", but he also ridicules, in antielitist terms,
what he represents as overly cultivated fruits. Pears, for instance,
"are a more aristocratic fruit than apples." He describes the extra-

---

6. Ibid., 76. Compare "Wild Apples," p. 292–93 in this volume [*Editor*].
7. Ibid., 182, 213.
8. I am indebted to Sandy Petrulionis for pointing out the connection between Thoreau's
   imagined and actual berrying parties.

ordinary care that is taken to bring them to market, wrapped in tissue for wealthy customers. "Yet they have neither the beauty nor the fragrance of apples. Their excellence is in their flavor, which speaks to a grosser sense. They are *glout-morceaux*. Hence, while children dream of apples, ex-judges realize pears." Hyper-cultivated fruits are for hyper-cultivated members of the ruling classes: "They are named after emperors, kings, queens, dukes, and duchesses. I fear I shall have to wait till we get to pears with American names, which a republican can swallow. The next French Revolution will correct all that.[9] By contrast, with the overrefined pear that vitiates tastes and appetites, wild fruits invigorate the democratic consumer: "It takes a savage or a wild taste to appreciate a wild fruit. What a healthy out-of-door appetite it takes to relish the apple of life, the apple of the world then!"[1] Now, renewed vigor is not just a matter of individual well-being, though health was of course a matter of grave concern for Thoreau; renewal is also a communal, even a political concern. It is no rhetorical accident that he defiantly celebrates the eating of chestnuts "on the steps of banks and exchanges." These institutions operate as synecdoches for the profit-driven social order that produces the debilitating alienation from nature he hopes wild fruits will cure. More generally, the democratic community of wild fruit eaters will be fortified to bear the general malaise of modernity: "We require just so much acid as the cranberries afford in the spring. . . . They cut the winter's phlegm, and now you can swallow another year of this world without other sauce."[2]

* * *

For some readers, the sweetest discovery in *Wild Fruits* will come in an untitled section that makes up the last the six pages of the book. Leo Stoller combined this passage with material from several entries into an essay that was published in 1970 as a small book titled *Huckleberries*.[3] But it is in *Wild Fruits* that this material has been restored to its original textual environment, where it comes as a culminating peroration. The passage, which appears to be a draft of material for a lecture, is an explicit argument in support of col-

9. *Wild Fruits*, 127.
1. Ibid., 87. Compare "Wild Apples," p. 303 in this volume [*Editor*].
2. For a discussion of Thoreau's developing conception of knowledge production as a democratic and communal project, see Laura Dassow Walls, *Seeing New Worlds: Henry David Thoreau and Nineteenth-Century Natural Science* (Madison: University of Wisconsin Press, 1995), 142–44.
3. Henry David Thoreau, *Huckleberries*, Leo Stoller, ed. (Iowa City: Windhover Press of the University of Iowa, 1970), 166–202. Stoller's version of "Huckleberries" has been reprinted in three Thoreau collections: Henry David Thoreau, *The Natural History Essay*, ed. Robert Sattelmeyer (Salt Lake City: Peregrine Smith, 1980); Henry David Thoreau, *Collected Essays and Poems*, ed. Elizabeth Witherell (New York: The Library of America, 2001); Henry D. Thoreau, *Wild Apples and Other Natural History Essays*, ed. William Rossi (Athens: University of Georgia Press, 2002).

lective action to preserve large tracts of land as wilderness. Its first paragraph contains a precise abstract of its overall argument. Thoreau begins with a lament: "How little we insist on truly grand and beautiful natural features. There may be the most beautiful landscapes in the world within a dozen miles of us, for aught we know—for their inhabitants do not value nor perceive them, and so have not made them known to others. . . ." The problem is identified as one of recognizing the importance of wilderness, but more than that, Thoreau implies that people have been blinded by something quite specific: "if a grain of gold were picked up there or a pearl found in a fresh-water clam, the whole state would resound with the news." So far, this is a consolidating restatement of themes that have been developing throughout *Wild Fruits*.

But now Thoreau introduces a new thought: "Thousands annually seek the White Mountains to be refreshed by their wild and primitive beauty, but when the country was discovered a similar kind of beauty prevailed all over it—and much of this might have been preserved for our present refreshment if a little foresight and taste had been used." He is proposing explicitly here, what he has elsewhere in his work only hinted at: conscious decision-making by the community to preserve wild land. Next Thoreau describes a "noble oak wood" at the town of Boxboro: "Let it stand fifty years longer and men will make pilgrimages to it from all parts of the country". Nevertheless, "it is likely to be cut off within a few years for ship-timber . . ." Arguing that the "rising generation" should have an opportunity to learn what an oak or a pine is by observing the "best specimens," he argues that "it would be wise for the state to purchase and preserve a few such forests. If the people of Massachusetts are ready to found a professorship of Natural History, do they not see the importance of preserving some portions of Nature herself unimpaired?"[4]

* * *

Wild Fruits, then, offers a second answer to the question framed by the "Economy" chapter of *Walden*. Where *Walden* offers an idealist and organic individualist solution to that problem, *Wild Fruits* offers a process—utopian to be sure, but significant nevertheless— for transforming ideas into motivating collective experiences and therefore into material forces for change. There is a moment in which *Walden* hints at this future: Thoreau describes a transformative epiphany in which he merges his "intelligence with the earth." This is a significant departure from the disembodied consciousness, the "transparent eyeball" of Emersonian orthodoxy. More and more, Thoreau saw understanding as a moment of active integration with

4. *Wild Fruits*, 233, 235.

the world, rather than one of contemplative separation or abstraction. And more and more, Nature was the material world of Concord *and* the Walden woods rather than an ideal category—the Emersonian "Not Me."[5]

On January 24, 1856, Thoreau meditated in his Journal on elms, the species that is the subject of the first entry in *Wild Fruits*. "I find that into my idea of the village has entered more of the elm than of the human being" for most people do not have "a tithe of the dignity, the true nobleness and comprehensiveness of view" that the elms do. This pessimistic assessment may seem to cut against his hopes for collective transformation of ecosocial relations, but it soon becomes clear that he has only certain human beings in mind. Elms "are free-soilers" for they "send their roots into many a conservative's Kansas and Carolina, who does not suspect such underground railroads." Not only are Thoreau's elms antislavery activists, but like the ecosocial historian of *Wild Fruits* and the community he hoped to call together, they took "a firmer hold on the earth that they may rise higher into the heavens."[6] Perhaps, Thoreau remembered this vision of the abolitionist elms of Concord on the day he drafted several pages *Wild Fruits* on the reverse sides of broadsheets he had printed to announce a memorial service for John Brown.[7] And perhaps it was with a sense of the social and political importance of serious play that Thoreau inhabited the office of "captain of a huckleberry party." (407)

5. Ralph Waldo Emerson, *Nature* in *Emerson's Prose and Poetry*, ed. Joel Porte and Saundra Morris (New York: W. W. Norton, 2001), 29, 28.
6. Henry David Thoreau, *The Journal of Henry David Thoreau*, ed. Bradford Torrey and Francis H. Allen. 14 vols. (New York: Dover Publications, 1962), 8:139–40.
7. William Howarth, *The Book of Concord: Thoreau's Life as a Writer* (New York: Viking Press, 1982), 181.

Henry D. Thoreau: A Chronology

1817   Born David Henry Thoreau on July 12 in Concord, Massachusetts, the third child (after Helen, b. 1812, and John Jr., 1815) of John Thoreau and Cynthia Dunbar.

1818   Family moves to Chelmsford, Massachusetts; Sophia born here in 1819.

1821   Family moves to Boston, Massachusetts.

1823   Family returns to Concord, Massachusetts, where John Thoreau establishes a pencil-making business.

1833   John and Cynthia send David Henry, as the more scholarly boy, to Harvard College, although he nearly fails entrance examinations.

1834   To help finance his schooling, Henry and his father travel to New York City to sell their pencils to stores.

1835   Takes thirteen-week leave of absence to earn money teaching school in Canton, Massachusetts; studies German with Unitarian minister and Transcendentalist Orestes Brownson.

1837   In the spring, reads *Nature*, published the year before by Ralph Waldo Emerson, who had moved to Concord from Boston with his wife, Lydia Jackson, in 1835. Becomes a regular member of Emerson's "Transcendental Club." Graduates from Harvard, nineteenth in a class of forty-seven, and begins teaching position at Center School in Concord only to resign a few weeks later after being reprimanded for not using corporal punishment. About this time he changes his name to Henry David. In October begins keeping a journal, probably prompted by Emerson.

1838   In April delivers his first lecture before the Concord Lyceum, on "Society." Unsuccessful at finding another teaching position, he opens a private school with his brother, John, in September, taking over the Concord Academy.

1839   In late August the Thoreau brothers make a two-week journey by boat, stage, and foot to the sources of the Merrimack River and the summit of Mount Washington in New Hampshire's White Mountains.

1840   Publishes his first essay, on "Aulus Persius Flaccus," the Roman poet, and his first poem, "Sympathy," in the Transcendentalist periodical, *The Dial*; in July, he proposes marriage to Ellen Sewell, who rejects him four months later.

1841   The Thoreau brothers' school closes; Henry is invited to live at Emerson's for one year (later extended to two) in exchange for house and garden work.

1842   On January 11, John Thoreau dies of tetanus; two weeks later Emerson loses his five-year-old son, Waldo, to scarlatina. Henry assists Emerson in editing *The Dial*, where he publishes his first natural history piece, "The Natural History of Massachusetts." In July helps welcome newlyweds Nathaniel and Sophia Hawthorne by plowing and planting their garden.

1843   Contributes the literary excursion "A Walk to Wachusett" to the *Boston Miscellany* and his review of a utopian tract, "Paradise (To Be) Regained," to the *United States Magazine and Democratic Review*. In May moves to Staten Island, New York, where he tutors the son of Emerson's brother, William, and scouts the literary market. Disappointed and homesick, returns to Concord seven months later.

1844   Success of the family pencil business, aided by Henry's improvements in grinding graphite and mixing lead, enables the family to build their own house on the southwest edge of Concord. In April, Henry and Edward Hoar accidentally set fire to woods near Fair Haven Bay while cooking fish in a pine stump, burning over three hundred acres.

1845   In March, begins clearing pines for a hut on land Emerson purchased the previous fall along the shore of Walden Pond, moving in on July 4, Independence Day. Writes a lengthy essay on the works of Thomas Carlyle; completes the first draft of *A Week on the Concord and Merrimack Rivers*, a memorial of the brothers' 1839 excursion; and begins drafting material in his journal for a second book, on life at Walden.

1846   In February, lectures on "The Writings and Style of Thomas Carlyle" at the Concord Lyceum; in July, while on an errand to the cobbler's, is arrested and jailed for nonpayment of poll taxes, but the next day, after an anonymous family member pays the tax, he is released, though "mad as the devil." On West Indies Emancipation Day (August 1) hosts the Concord Women's Anti-Slavery Society celebration and picnic at Walden. In late August, takes a two-week trip by steamer, buggy, boat, and foot, into the

Maine woods with five other men, where he climbs Mount Katahdin.

1847   Ostensibly in response to his neighbors' queries about life at Walden, Thoreau lectures two or three times in Lincoln and Concord on "A History of Myself." "Thomas Carlyle and His Works" appears as the lead article in *Graham's Magazine*. He collects fish and other local natural history specimens for Harvard professor Louis Agassiz. Leaves Walden Pond on September 6 to stay with Lidian and the children while Emerson is on lecture tour in England.

1848   Lectures at the Concord Lyceum twice on "The Relation of the Individual to the State" and also on his excursion to Katahdin. Travels to Gloucester and Salem, Massachusetts, to deliver sections of the "Economy" chapter of a second book manuscript he is polishing while negotiating with prospective publishers about *A Week*. "Ktaadn and the Maine Woods" appears in *Sartain's Union Magazine of Literature and Art* in five installments. Having circulated handbills advertising his services as a land surveyor, he begins surveying professionally in November.

1849   During winter and spring, he continues to lecture from *Walden* manuscript in Concord, Lincoln, Salem, Worcester, and in Portland, Maine; "Resistance to Civil Government" is published in *Aesthetic Papers* in May, as is *A Week on the Concord and Merrimack Rivers* by James Munroe & Co., with Thoreau underwriting the cost of production. Older sister, Helen, dies of consumption on June 14. After making an excursion to Cape Cod with Ellery Channing in October, he begins the first of eleven "Indian notebooks," compiling information on the history, anthropology, and ethnobotany of native people. By this time reviews of *A Week* indicate its likely commercial failure.

1850   During this year Thoreau settles into the practice of regular journal writing in the morning and often evening, and walking in the afternoon. With its natural history observations and other contents carefully indexed and volumes sequentially numbered, the Journal becomes an open-ended imaginative work in its own right. He lectures in Concord, South Danvers, and Newburyport, Massachusetts, on "An Excursion to Cape Cod," and makes another trip to Cape Cod in late June. Soon after returning, is dispatched by Emerson to recover the physical and literary remains of Margaret Fuller, who drowned in a shipwreck off Fire Island with her son and husband. In September, takes a railroad and steamer excursion to Montreal with Channing. In

December, is elected a corresponding member of the Boston Society of Natural History.

1851 Lectures in Clinton, Massachusetts, and Portland, Maine, on the Cape Cod excursion and, in Medford, Massachusetts, on "Economy," reading from the now-shelved *Walden* manuscript. In April develops a new lecture on "Walking, or the Wild," given in Concord and Worcester, and, by December, another on the Canada excursion, delivered in Lincoln. When Thomas Sims, a fugitive slave from Georgia, is arrested in Boston and returned, Thoreau fumes in his Journal against the Fugitive Slave Law, expecting to speak against it in Concord. In October puts another fugitive slave on the train to Canada. During late spring and summer he experiments with walking by moonlight, recording these and other local excursions in the Journal.

1852 Probably in January begins substantially revising the *Walden* manuscript. Besides two lectures on the Canada excursion, one on "The Wild," and a separate talk on "Walking," he lectures four times from his *Walden* material and publishes two excerpts, "The Iron Horse" and "Poet Buying a Farm," in *Sartain's Union Magazine*.

1853 Three of five installments of "An Excursion to Canada" appear in *Putnam's Monthly Magazine* before Thoreau withdraws the last two because of editorial liberties taken with his "heresies." In September returns to the Maine woods accompanied by his cousin, George Thatcher, and guided by Penobscot lumberman, Joe Aitteon, a trip described in a lecture he delivers before the Concord Lyceum in December. In October receives remaining 706 copies of *A Week* (out of one thousand printed) from his publisher, figuring that the book had cost him $290, a debt still not quite repaid. Comments in his journal that "I have now a library of nearly nine hundred volumes, over seven hundred of which I wrote myself."

1854 On July 4, speaks at the Massachusetts Anti-Slavery Society counterdemonstration in Framingham, organized to pro-test the arrest and return to Virginia of escaped slave Anthony Burns. His address, "Slavery in Massachusetts," is published three week later in *The Liberator*, then reprinted in the *New-York Daily Tribune*. *Walden* is published on August 9 by Ticknor & Fields. In the fall and early winter, he lectures on "Moonlight" in Plymouth, "The Wild" in Philadelphia, and "What Shall It Profit?"—an early version of the essay "Life Without Principle"—in New Bedford and Nantucket, Massachusetts, and Providence, Rhode Island.

1855   During January and February, lectures on "What Shall It Profit?" in Worcester and Concord. Makes a third trip to Cape Cod for two weeks in July with Ellery Channing; three installments of the Cape Cod excursion appear this summer in *Putnam's Monthly* before the magazine discontinues the series.

1856   In April, begins to investigate the succession of forest trees. In November, delivers a series of three lectures in Perth Amboy, New Jersey, while surveying two hundred acres on the shore of Raritan Bay. Along with Bronson Alcott, travels to Brooklyn to visit Walt Whitman, whom he judges "the greatest democrat the world has seen," one who "has spoken more truth than any American or modern that I know." In December, delivers "Walking, or the Wild" in Amherst, New Hampshire.

1857   In February, lectures twice on "Walking, or the Wild," at Fitchburg and Worcester, Massachusetts; meets radical abolitionist Captain John Brown in Concord. In June, makes a ten-day excursion to Cape Cod, his fourth, and the next month a third trip to the Maine woods, this time in the company of Penobscot guide Joe Polis.

1858   In January and February, he delivers two lectures on Maine woods; "Chesuncook" runs in summer issues of the *Atlantic Monthly*; makes a seventeen-day botanizing trip to the White Mountains with Edward Hoar.

1859   On February 3, his father, John Thoreau, dies, age seventy-one. He delivers a new lecture on "Autumnal Tints" four times, in Concord, Worcester, and Lynn, Massachusetts. In October, begins writing *Wild Fruits*. Two weeks after John Brown's arrest on October 18 at Harpers Ferry, Virginia, he speaks on "The Character and Actions of Capt. John Brown," repeating it a few days later in Boston and Worcester. On December 2, the day of Brown's execution, reads "The Martyrdom of John Brown" in Concord.

1860   In February, lectures twice on "Wild Apples," in Concord and Bedford. "A Plea for Captain John Brown" is published in *Echoes of Harper's Ferry*, edited by James Redpath, and on July 4 he reads "The Last Days of John Brown" at Brown's gravesite in North Elba, New York. In September, he reads "The Succession of Forest Trees," part of *The Dispersion of Seeds*, at a local agricultural fair, after which the address is printed in the *New-York Weekly Tribune*. Contracts a severe cold in late November or early December, that will lead to his death, either from exposure to Bronson Alcott's or while counting tree rings on Fair Haven Hill.

Rapidly develops bronchitis but travels to Waterbury, Connecticut, to deliver "Autumnal Tints" on December 11, his last lecture.

1861   Confined to house by illness through February. In May, he travels to Minnesota with Horace Mann Jr. in hopes of recovering his health. Makes a steamer excursion three hundred miles up the Minnesota River to the Lower Sioux Agency; returns to Concord on July 9, his condition unimproved and probably worse from travel.

1862   In February, with Sophia's help, begins preparing for posthumous publication of essays in Ticknor & Fields's *Atlantic Monthly* ("Walking," "Autumnal Tints," "Wild Apples," and "Life Without Principle") as well as for the reprinting of *Walden* and reissuing of *A Week*. Dies May 6 in Concord, age forty-four.

Selected Bibliography

• Indicates works excerpted in this volume.

The definitive catalogue of Thoreau's manuscripts is William L. Howarth, *The Literary Manuscripts of Henry David Thoreau* (Columbus: Ohio State University Press, 1974). For studies of Thoreau's reception, see headnote to Reviews and Posthumous Assessments, pp. 379–80. Especially useful bibliographies of criticism published since 1941 are: *A Bibliography of the Thoreau Society Bulletin Bibliographies, 1941–1969*, edited by Walter Harding (Troy, N.Y.: Whitston, 1971); Lewis Leary, "Henry David Thoreau" in *Eight American Authors*, revised edition, ed. James Woodress (New York: Norton, 1971), 129–71; Walter Harding and Michael Meyer, *The New Thoreau Handbook* (New York: New York University Press, 1980); and Michael Meyer, "Henry David Thoreau" in *The Transcendentalists: A Review of Research and Criticism*, ed. Joel Myerson (New York: Modern Language Association of America, 1984), 260–85.

The Thoreau bibliography can be updated by consulting the *MLA International Bibliography* (New York: Modern Language Association of American, 1964–), published annually, and "Additions to the Thoreau Bibliography" in *The Thoreau Society Bulletin* (1941–), published quarterly. Authoritative reviews of current scholarship and criticism on Emerson, Thoreau, Fuller, and Transcendentalism may be found in *American Literary Scholarship: An Annual* (Durham: Duke University Press, 1971–).

The following reference works are highly recommended: *Encyclopedia of Transcendentalism* (New York: Greenwood, 1996) and *The American Renaissance in New England*, second series (Detroit: Gale Group, 2000), both edited by Wesley T. Mott; *Henry David Thoreau: A Documentary Volume*, edited by Richard J. Schneider (Detroit: Gale, 2004); and *American History through Literature, 1820–1870*, edited by Janet Gabler-Hover and Robert Sattelmeyer (Detroit: Charles Scribner's Sons, 2006).

The homepage of The Thoreau Society [*www.thoreausociety.org*], the oldest and one of the largest author societies in the United States, contains information on Thoreau-related activities and resources as well as on membership. The website of The Writings of Henry D. Thoreau [*www.library.ucsb.edu/thoreau/writings main.html*], a scholarly edition producing accurate texts of Thoreau's complete works, provides information about manuscripts, textual editing, and biography as well as online journal transcripts, an updated bibliography, and links to related sites.

Literary Historical, Cultural, and Environmental Contexts

Abrams, Robert E. *Landscape and Ideology in American Renaissance Literature: Topographies of Skepticism*. Cambridge: Cambridge University Press, 2004.
Baker, Anne. *Heartless Immensity: Literature, Culture, and Geography in Antebellum America*. Ann Arbor: University of Michigan Press, 2006.
Bellin, Joshua David. *The Demon of the Continent: Indians and the Shaping of American Literature*. Philadelphia: University of Pennsylvania Press, 2001.
Bellis, Peter J. *Writing Revolution: Aesthetics and Politics in Hawthorne, Whitman and Thoreau*. Athens: University of Georgia Press, 2003.
Bennett, Michael. *Democratic Discourses: The Radical Abolition Movement and Antebellum American Literature*. New Brunswick, N.J.: Rutgers University Press, 2005.
Botkin, Daniel B. *No Man's Garden: Thoreau and a New Vision for Civilization and Nature*. Washington, DC: Island Press, 2001.

Bromell, Nicholas K. *By the Sweat of the Brow: Literature and Labor in Antebellum America*. Chicago: University of Chicago Press, 1993.

Buell, Lawrence. *Literary Transcendentalism: Style and Vision in the American Renaissance*. Ithaca, N.Y.: Cornell University Press, 1973.

———. *New England Literary Culture: From Revolution through Renaissance*. New York: Cambridge University Press, 1986.

Capper, Charles, and Conrad Edick Wright, eds. *Transient and Permanent: The Transcendentalist Movement and Its Contexts*. Boston: Massachusetts Historical Society, 1999.

Donahue, Brian. *The Great Meadow: Farmers and the Land in Colonial Concord*. New Haven, Conn.: Yale University Press, 2004.

Foster, David R. *Thoreau's Country: Journey through a Transformed Landscape*. Cambridge, Mass.: Harvard University Press, 1999.

Fresonke, Kris. *West of Emerson: the Design of Manifest Destiny*. Berkeley: University of California Press, 2003.

Gatta, John. *Making Nature Sacred: Literature, Religion and Environment in America from the Puritans to the Present*. New York: Oxford University Press, 2004.

Gilmore, Michael T. *American Romanticism and the Marketplace*. Chicago: University of Chicago Press, 1985.

Gleason, William A. *The Leisure Ethic: Work and Play in American Literature, 1840–1940*. Stanford, Calif.: Stanford University Press, 1999.

Gura, Philip F. *The Wisdom of Words: Language, Theology, and Literature in the New England Renaissance*. Middletown: Wesleyan University Press, 1981.

Jehlen, Myra. *American Incarnation: The Individual, the Nation, and the Continent*. Cambridge, Mass.: Harvard University Press, 1986.

Lee, Maurice S. *Slavery, Philosophy, and American Literature, 1830–1860*. New York: Cambridge University Press, 2005.

• Marx, Leo. *The Machine in the Garden: Technology and the Pastoral Ideal in America*. New York: Oxford University Press, 1964.

• Mattheissen, F. O. *American Renaissance: Art and Expression in the Age of Emerson and Whitman*. New York: Oxford University Press, 1941.

McDowell, Deborah E. and Arnold Rampersad, eds. *Slavery and the Literary Imagination*. Baltimore: Johns Hopkins University Press, 1989.

Packer, Barbara. "The Transcendentalists." *The Cambridge History of American Literature, Volume 2, 1820–1865*. Ed. Sacvan Bercovitch. New York: Cambridge University Press, 1995. 329–604.

Petroski, Henry. *The Pencil: A History of Design and Circumstance*. New York: Knopf, 1990.

Petrulionis, Sandra Harbert. *To Set This World Right: The Antislavery Movement in Thoreau's Concord*. Ithaca, N.Y.: Cornell University Press, 2006.

Pease, Donald. *Visionary Compacts: American Renaissance Writings in Cultural Context*. Madison: University of Wisconsin Press, 1987.

Porte, Joel. *Consciousness and Culture: Emerson and Thoreau Reviewed*. New Haven: Yale University Press, 2004.

Reynolds, David S. *Beneath the American Renaissance: The Subversive Imagination in the Age of Emerson and Melville*. New York: Knopf, 1988.

Reynolds, Larry J. *European Revolutions and the American Literary Renaissance*. New Haven, Conn.: Yale University Press, 1988.

Ryden, Kent C. *Landscape with Figures: Nature and Culture in New England*. Iowa City: University of Iowa Press, 2001.

Scholnick, Robert J., ed. *American Literature and Science*. Lexington: University Press of Kentucky, 1992.

von Frank, Albert C. *The Sacred Game: Provincialism and Frontier Consciousness in American Literature*. Cambridge: Cambridge University Press, 1985.

West, Michael. *Transcendental Wordplay: America's Romantic Punsters and the Search for a Language of Nature*. Athens: Ohio University Press, 2000.

Weisbuch, Robert. *Atlantic Double-Cross: American Literature and British Influence in the Age of Emerson*. Chicago: University of Chicago Press, 1986.

Wilson, Eric. *Romantic Turbulence: Chaos, Ecology, and American Space*. New York: St. Martin's Press, 2000.

Thoreau: Biographical Studies

Bridgman, Richard. *Dark Thoreau*. Lincoln: University of Nebraska Press, 1982.

Harding, Walter. *The Days of Henry Thoreau*. New York: Knopf, 1965.

Howarth, William L. *The Book of Concord: Thoreau's Life as a Writer*. New York: Viking, 1982.

Paul, Sherman. *The Shores of America: Thoreau's Inward Exploration*. Urbana: University of Illinois, 1958.

Richardson, Robert D., Jr. *Henry Thoreau: A Life of the Mind*. Berkeley: University of California Press, 1986.

Sattelmeyer, Robert. *Thoreau's Reading: A Study in Intellectual History with Bibliographical Catalogue*. Princeton, N.J.: Princeton University Press, 1988.

Schneider, Richard J. *Henry David Thoreau*. Boston: Twayne, 1987.

Smith, Harmon. *My Friend, My Friend: The Story of Thoreau's Relationship with Emerson*. Amherst: University of Massachusetts Press, 1999.

Thoreau: Collections

Cain, William E., ed. *A Historical Guide to Henry David Thoreau*. New York: Oxford University Press, 2000.

• Myerson, Joel, ed. *The Cambridge Companion to Henry David Thoreau*. New York: Cambridge University Press, 1995.

———. *Critical Essays on Thoreau's Walden*. Boston: Hall, 1988.

Petrulionis Sandra Harbert and Laura Dassow Walls, eds. *More Day to Dawn: Thoreau's Walden for a New Century*. Amherst: University of Massachusetts Press, 2006.

Sayre, Robert F., ed. *New Essays on Walden*. New York: Cambridge University Press, 1992.

Schneider, Richard J., ed. *Approaches to Teaching Thoreau's Walden and Other Works*. New York: Modern Language Association, 1996.

———. *Thoreau's Sense of Place: Essays in American Environmental Writing*. Iowa City: University of Iowa Press, 2000.

———. "Walden the Place and Walden the Book." Special issue, *The Concord Saunterer* 12/13 (2004/2005).

Schofield, Edmund A., and Robert C. Baron, eds. *Thoreau's World and Ours: A Natural Legacy*. Golden, Colo.: North American Press, 1993.

Thoreau: Critical Studies

General

Adams, Stephen, and Donald A. Ross. *Revising Mythologies: The Composition of Thoreau's Major Works*. Charlottesville: University Press of Virginia, 1988.

Bennett, Jane. *Thoreau's Nature: Ethics, Politics, and the Wild*. Thousand Oaks, Calif.: Sage, 1994.

Burbick, Joan. *Thoreau's Alternative History: Changing Perspectives on Nature, Culture, and Language*. Philadelphia: University of Pennsylvania Press, 1987.

Fink, Steven. *Prophet in the Marketplace: Thoreau's Development as a Professional Writer*. Princeton, N.J.: Princeton University Press, 1991.

Garber, Frederick. *Thoreau's Fable of Inscribing*. Princeton, N.J.: Princeton University Press, 1991.

Golemba, Henry. *Thoreau's Wild Rhetoric*. New York: New York University Press, 1990.

Guthrie, James R. *Above Time: Emerson's and Thoreau's Temporal Revolutions*. Columbia: University of Missouri Press, 2001.

Hodder, Alan D. *Thoreau's Ecstatic Witness*. New Haven, Conn.: Yale University Press, 2001.

Howarth, William. *Walking with Thoreau: A Literary Guide to the Mountains of New England* Boston: Beacon Press, 2001.

McIntosh, James. *Thoreau as Romantic Naturalist: His Shifting Stance toward Nature*. Ithaca, N.Y.: Cornell University Press, 1974.

Milder, Robert. *Reimagining Thoreau*. New York: Cambridge University Press, 1995.

Neufeldt, Leonard. *The Economist: Henry Thoreau and Enterprise*. New York: Oxford University Press, 1989.

Robinson, David. *Natural Life: Thoreau's Worldly Transcendentalism*. Ithaca, N.Y.: Cornell University Press, 2004.

Sayre, Robert F. *Thoreau and the American Indians*. Princeton, N.J.: Princeton University Press, 1977.

Scharnhorst, Gary. *Henry David Thoreau: A Case Study in Canonizataion*. Columbia, S.C. Camden House, 1993.

Tauber, Alfred I. *Henry David Thoreau and the Moral Agency of Knowing*. Berkeley: University of California Press, 2001.

Ecocriticism

Branch, Michael P., ed. *Reading the Roots: American Nature Writing Before Walden*. Athens: University of Georgia Press, 2004.

• Buell, Lawrence. *The Environmental Imagination: Thoreau, Nature Writing, and the Formation of American Culture*. Cambridge, Mass.: Harvard University Press, 1995.

Fritzell, Peter A. *Nature Writing and America: Essays upon a Cultural Type*. Ames: Iowa State University Press, 1990.

Mazel, David. *American Literary Environmentalism*. Athens: University of Georgia Press, 2000.

McGregor, Robert Kuhn. *A Wider View of the Universe: Henry Thoreau's Study of Nature*. Urbana: University of Illinois Press, 1997.

McKusick, James C. *Green Writing: Romanticism and Ecology*. New York: St. Martin's Press, 2000.

McMurry, Andrew. *Environmental Renaissance: Emerson, Thoreau, and the Systems of Nature*. Athens: University of Georgia Press, 2003.

Morton, Timothy. *Ecology without Nature: Rethinking Environmental Aesthetics*. Cambridge, Mass.: Harvard University Press, 2007.

• Newman, Lance. *Our Common Dwelling: Henry Thoreau, Transcendentalism, and the Class Politics of Nature*. New York: Palgrave Macmillan, 2005.

O'Grady, John P. *Pilgrims to the Wild: Everett Ruess, Henry David Thoreau, John Muir, Clarence King, Mary Austin*. Salt Lake City: University of Utah Press, 1993.

Phillips, Dana. *The Truth of Ecology: Nature, Culture, and Literature in America*. New York: Oxford University Press, 2003.

Slovic, Scott. *Seeking Awareness in American Nature Writing: Henry Thoreau, Annie Dillard, Edward Abbey, Wendell Berry, and Barry Lopez*. Salt Lake City: University of Utah Press, 1992.

Sweeting, Adam. *Beneath the Second Sun: A Cultural History of Indian Summer*. Hanover: University Press of New England, 2003.

Walls, Laura Dassow. *Seeing New Worlds: Henry David Thoreau and Nineteenth-Century Natural Science*. Madison: University of Wisconsin Press, 1995.

Westling, Louise H. *The Green Breast of the New World: Landscape, Gender, and American Fiction*. Athens: University of Georgia Press, 1996.

"Civil Disobedience" and "Slavery in Massachusetts"

Abbott, Philip. "Henry David Thoreau, the State of Nature, and the Redemption of Liberalism." *Journal of Politics* 47 (1985): 183–208.

Albrecht, Robert C. "Conflict and Resolution: 'Slavery in Massachusetts.'" *ESQ: A Journal of the American Renaissance* 19 (1973): 179–88.

Buranelli, Vincent. "The Case against Thoreau." *Ethics* 67 (1957): 257–68.

• Carton, Evan. "The Price of Privilege: 'Civil Disobedience' at 150." *The American Scholar* 67.4 (1998): 105–12.

• Drinnon, Richard. "Thoreau's Politics of the Upright Man." *Massachusetts Review* 4 (1962): 126–35.

Duban, James. "Conscience and Consciousness: The Liberal Christian Context of Thoreau's Political Ethics." *New England Quarterly* 60 (1987): 208–22.

Glick, Wendell. "Civil Disobedience: Thoreau's Attack upon Relativism." *Western Humanities Review* 7 (1952): 35–42.

• Gross, Robert A. "Quiet War with the State: Henry Thoreau and Civil Disobedience." *The Yale Review* 93 (2005): 1–17.

Herr, William A. "A More Perfect State: Thoreau's Concept of Civil Government." *Massachusetts Review* 16 (1975): 470–87.

Meyer, Michael. *Several More Lives to Live: Thoreau's Political Reputation in America.* Westport: Greenwood Press, 1977.

Simon, Myron. "Thoreau and Anarchism." *Michigan Quarterly Review* 23 (1984): 360–84.

Petrulionis, Sandra Harbert. "Editorial Savoir Faire: Thoreau Transforms His Journal into 'Slavery in Massachusetts.' " *Resources for American Literary Study* 25.2 (1999): 206–31.

Rosenblum, Nancy L. "The Inhibitions of Democracy on Romantic Political Thought: Thoreau's Democratic Individualism." *The Lessons of Romanticism: A Critical Companion.* Ed. Thomas Pfau and Robert F. Gleckner. Durham: Duke University Press, 1998. 55–75.

• von Frank, Albert J. *The Trials of Anthony Burns: Freedom and Slavery in Emerson's Boston.* Cambridge, Mass.: Harvard University Press, 1998.

• Wood, Barry. "Thoreau's Narrative Art in 'Civil Disobedience.' " *Philological Quarterly* 60 (1981): 106–15.

Walden and the Journal

Anderson, Charles R. *The Magic Circle of Walden.* New York: Holt, Rinehart, and Winston, 1968.

Bickman, Martin. *Walden: Volatile Truths.* New York: Twayne, 1992.

Blakemore, Peter. "Reading Home: Thoreau, Literature, and the Phenomenon of Inhabitation." *Thoreau's Sense of Place.* 115–32.

Cafaro, Philip. *Thoreau's Living Ethics: Walden and the Pursuit of Virtue.* Athens: University of Georgia Press, 2004.

Cameron, Sharon. *Writing Nature: Henry Thoreau's Journal.* New York: Oxford University Press, 1985.

• Cavell, Stanley. *The Senses of Walden.* Expanded ed. San Francisco: North Point Press, 1981.

Gross, Robert A. "Culture and Cultivation: Agriculture and Society in Thoreau's Concord." *Journal of American History* 69 (1982): 42–61.

Howarth, William. " 'Where I Lived': The Environs of *Walden.*" *Approaches to Teaching Walden and Other Works.* 56–62.

• Johnson, Barbara. *A World of Difference.* Baltimore: Johns Hopkins University Press, 1987.

Johnson, William C., Jr. *What Thoreau Said: Walden and the Unsayable.* Moscow: University of Idaho Press, 1994.

Long, Larry. "The Bible and the Composition of *Walden.*" *Studies in the American Renaissance* (1979): 309–41.

Maynard, W. Barksdale. *Walden: A Cultural History.* Oxford: Oxford University Press, 2003.

Michaels, Walter Benn. "*Walden*'s False Bottoms." *Glyph* 1 (1977): 132–49.

Miller, Perry. "Thoreau in the Context of International Romanticism." *New England Quarterly* 24 (1961): 147–59.

Neufeldt, Leonard N. and Mark A. Smith, "Going to Walden Woods: Walden, *Walden*, and American Pastoralism." *Arizona Quarterly* 55.2 (1999): 57–86.

Otterberg, Henrik. *Hound, Bay Horse, and Turtle-Dove: Obscurity and Authority in Thoreau's Walden.* Gothenburg, Sweden: Gothenburg University Press, 2005.

• Peck, H. Daniel. *Thoreau's Morning Work: Memory and Perception in A Week on the Concord and Merrimack Rivers, the Journal and Walden.* New Haven, Conn.: Yale University Press, 1990.

Sattelmeyer, Robert. "Depopulation, Deforestation, and the Actual Walden Pond." *Thoreau's Sense of Place.* 235–43.

• ———. "The Remaking of *Walden.*" *Writing the American Classics.* Ed. James Barbour and Tom Quirk. Chapel Hill: University of North Carolina Press, 1990. 53–78.

Schneider, Richard J. "Reflections in Walden Pond: Thoreau's Optics." *ESQ: A Journal of the American Renaissance* 21 (1975): 65–75.

———. "Thoreau and Nineteenth-Century Landscape Painting." *ESQ: A Journal of the American Renaissance* 31 (1985): 67–88.

Schulz, Dieter. "Thoreau's House." *Values in American Society.* Ed. Tibor Frank. Budapest, Hungary: Eötvös Loránd University, 1995. 29–39.

Shanley, J. Lyndon, *The Making of Walden, with the Text of the First Version.* Chicago: University of Chicago Press, 1957.

- Walls, Laura Dassow. "Walden as Feminist Manifesto." *ISLE: Interdisciplinary Studies in Literature and Environment* 1.1 (1993): 137–44.

  Warner, Michael. "Walden's Erotic Economy." *Comparative American Identities: Race, Sex, and Nationality in the Modern Text.* Ed. Hortense J. Spillers. New York: Routledge, 1991. 157–74.

"Walking" and "Wild Apples"

Berger, Michael Benjamin. *Thoreau's Late Career and 'The Dispersion of Seeds': The Saunterer's Synoptic Vision.* Rochester, N.Y.: Camden House, 2000.

- Fink, Steven. "The Language of Prophecy: Thoreau's 'Wild Apples.' " *New England Quarterly* 59.2 (1986): 212–30.

  Grusin, Richard. "Thoreau's Extravagant Economy of Nature." *American Literary History* 5 (1993): 30–50.

  Hildebidle, John. *Thoreau, a Naturalist's Liberty.* Cambridge, Mass.: Harvard University Press, 1984.

  Hoag, Ronald Wesley. "Thoreau's Later Natural History Essays." *Cambridge Companion to Henry David Thoreau.* 152–70.

- Matheson, Neill. "Thoreau's *Gramática Parda*: Conjugating Race and Nature." *Arizona Quarterly* 57.4 (2001): 1–43.

  Moldenhauer, Joseph J. "Thoreau, Hawthorne, and the 'Seven-Mile Panorama.' " *ESQ: A Journal of the American Renaissance* 44 (1998): 227–74.

  Nabhan, Gary Paul. "Learning the Language of Fields and Forests." *Faith in a Seed: The Dispersion of Seeds and Other Late Natural History Writings.* By Henry D. Thoreau. Ed. Bradley P. Dean. Washington, D.C.: Island Press, 1993. xi–xviii.

  Robinson, David. "Thoreau's 'Walking' and the Ecological Imperative." *Approaches to Teaching Walden and Other Works.* 169–74.

- Rossi, William. " 'The Limits of an Afternoon Walk': Coleridgean Polarity in Thoreau's 'Walking.' " *ESQ: A Journal of the American Renaissance* 33 (1987): 94–109.

  Schneider, Richard J. " 'Climate Does Thus React on Man': Wildness and Geographic Determinism in Thoreau's 'Walking.' " *Thoreau's Sense of Place.* 44–60.

  Van Anglen, Kevin P. "A Paradise Regained: Thoreau's "Wild Apples" and the Myth of the American Adam." *ESQ: A Journal of the American Renaissance* 27 (1981): 28–37.